T0311569

Panel Data Econometrics

Panel Data Econometrics

Empirical Applications

Edited By

Mike Tsionas

ACADEMIC PRESS

An imprint of Elsevier

Academic Press is an imprint of Elsevier
125 London Wall, London EC2Y 5AS, United Kingdom
525 B Street, Suite 1650, San Diego, CA 92101, United States
50 Hampshire Street, 5th Floor, Cambridge, MA 02139, United States
The Boulevard, Langford Lane, Kidlington, Oxford OX5 1GB, United Kingdom

Notices
Knowledge and best practice in this field are constantly changing. As new research and experience
broaden our understanding, changes in research methods, professional practices, or medical
treatment may become necessary.

Practitioners and researchers must always rely on their own experience and knowledge in
evaluating and using any information, methods, compounds, or experiments described herein.
In using such information or methods they should be mindful of their own safety and the safety
of others, including parties for whom they have a professional responsibility.

To the fullest extent of the law, neither the Publisher nor the authors, contributors, or editors,
assume any liability for any injury and/or damage to persons or property as a matter of
products liability, negligence or otherwise, or from any use or operation of any methods,
products, instructions, or ideas contained in the material herein.

Library of Congress Cataloging-in-Publication Data
A catalog record for this book is available from the Library of Congress

British Library Cataloguing-in-Publication Data
A catalogue record for this book is available from the British Library

ISBN 978-0-12-815859-3

For information on all Academic Press publications
visit our website at https://www.elsevier.com/books-and-journals

Publisher: Candice Janco
Acquisition Editor: Scott Bentley
Editorial Project Manager: Susan Ikeda
Production Project Manager: Maria Bernard
Cover Designer: Miles Hitchen

Typeset by SPi Global, India

Working together
to grow libraries in
developing countries

www.elsevier.com • www.bookaid.org

Contents

18.   Panel Data in Transportation Research   583

Rico Merkert and Corinne Mulley

19.   Panel Data in Banking: Research Issues and Data Peculiarities   609

David Humphrey

22. The Income-Health Gradient: Evidence From Self-Reported Health and Biomarkers in Understanding Society

*Apostolos Davillas, Andrew M. Jones and
Michaela Benzeval*

23. Application in Banking: Securitization and Global Banking

*Andrada Bilan, Hans Degryse, Kuchulain O'Flynn and
Steven Ongena*

Contributors

Numbers in paraentheses indicate the pages on which the authors' contrbutions begin.

Paul D. Allison (547), University of Pennsylvania, Philadelphia, PA, United States

Sofia Anyfantaki (865), Athens University of Economics and Business; Bank of Greece, Athens, Greece

Scott E. Atkinson (495), Department of Economics, University of Georgia, Athens, GA, United States

Michaela Benzeval (709), Institute for Social and Economic Research, University of Essex, Colchester, United Kingdom

Keshab Bhattarai (665), University of Hull Busines School, Hull, United Kingdom

Andrada Bilan (743), University of Zurich and Swiss Finance Institute, Zürich, Switzerland

Apostolos Davillas (709), Institute for Social and Economic Research, University of Essex, Colchester, United Kingdom

Jan de Dreu (839), BBVA, Global Debt Advisory, Ciudad BBVa, Madrid, Spain

Hans Degryse (743), KU Leuven, Leuven, Belgium; CEPR, Washington, DC, United States

Dong Ding (405), Department of Economics, Rice University, Houston, TX, United States

Kyriakos Drivas (771), Department of International & European Economic Studies, Athens University of Economics and Business, Athens, Greece

Claire Economidou (771), Department of Economics, University of Piraeus, Piraeus, Greece

Almas Heshmati (885, 931), Department of Economics, Sogang University, Seoul, South Korea

David Humphrey (609), Florida State University, Tallahassee, FL, United States

Vasso Ioannidou (839), Accounting and Finance Department, Lancaster University Management School, Lancaster, United Kingdom

Geraint Johnes (467), Lancaster University Management School, Lancaster University, Lancaster, United Kingdom

Jill Johnes (467), Huddersfield Business School, University of Huddersfield, Huddersfield, United Kingdom

Andrew M. Jones (709), Department of Economics and Related Studies, University of York, York, United Kingdom; Centre for Health Economics, Monash University, Clayton, VIC, Australia

Sarantis Kalyvitis (865), Athens University of Economics and Business, Athens, Greece

Margarita Katsimi (865), Athens University of Economics and Business, Athens, Greece CESifo, Munich, Germany

Nam Seok Kim (885), Department of Economics, Maxwell School of Citizenship and Public Affairs, Syracuse University, Syracuse, NY, United States

Konstantinos N. Konstantakis (953), National Technical University of Athens, Athens, Greece

Georgia Kosmopoulou (521), University of Oklahoma, Norman, OK, United States

Esfandiar Maasoumi (931), Department of Economics, Emory University, Atlanta, GA, United States

E.C. Mamatzakis (801), University of Sussex Business School, University of Sussex, Brighton, United Kingdom

Rico Merkert (583), The University of Sydney Business School, NSW, Sydney, Australia

Panayotis G. Michaelides (953), National Technical University of Athens, Athens, Greece

Enrique Moral-Benito (547), Bank of Spain, Madrid, Spain

Corinne Mulley (583), The University of Sydney Business School, NSW, Sydney, Australia

Daniel Nedelescu (521), University of Oklahoma, Norman, OK, United States

Kuchulain O'Flynn (743), University of Zurich and Swiss Finance Institute, Zürich, Switzerland

Steven Ongena (743), University of Zurich and Swiss Finance Institute, Zürich, Switzerland; KU Leuven, Leuven, Belgium; CEPR, Washington, DC, United States

Fletcher Rehbein (521), University of Oklahoma, Norman, OK, United States

Robin C. Sickles (405), Department of Economics, Rice University, Houston, TX, United States

Christoph Siebenbrunner (639), University of Oxford, Mathematical Institute; Institute for New Economic Thinking, Oxford, United Kingdom

Michael Sigmund (639), Oesterreichische Nationalbank (OeNB), Vienna, Austria

C. Staikouras (801), School of Business Administration, Athens University of Economics and Business, Athens, Greece

Biwei Su (931), Department of Economics, Sogang University, Seoul, South Korea

Eirini Thomaidou (865), Athens University of Economics and Business, Athens, Greece

Mike G. Tsionas (771,801,953), Department of Economics, Lancaster University Management School, Lancaster, United Kingdom

Richard Williams (547), University of Notre Dame, Notre Dame, IN, United States

General Introduction

Panel data always have been at the center of econometric research and have been used extensively in applied economic research to refute a variety of hypotheses. The chapters in these two volumes represent, to a large extent, much of what has been accomplished in the profession during the last few years. Naturally, this is a selective presentation and many important topics have been left out because of space limitations. The books cited at the end of this Introduction, however, are well known and provide more details about specific topics. The coverage extends from fixed and random effect formulations to nonlinear models and cointegration. Such themes have been instrumental in the development of modern theoretical and applied econometrics.

Panel data are used quite often in applications, as we see in Volume 2 of this book. The range of applications is vast, extending from industrial organization and labor economics to growth, development, health, banking, and the measurement of productivity. Although panel data provide more degrees of freedom, their proper use is challenging. The modeling of heterogeneity cannot be exhausted to fixed and random effect formulations, and slope heterogeneity has to be considered. Dynamic formulations are highly desirable, but they are challenging both because of estimation issues and because unit roots and cointegration cannot be ignored. Moreover, causality issues figure prominently, although they seem to have received less attention relative to time-series econometrics. Relative to time-series or cross-sections, the development of specification tests for panel data seems to have been slower than usual.

The chapters in these two volumes show the great potential of panel data for both theoretical and applied research. There are more opportunities as more problems arise, particularly when practitioners and economic theorists get together to discuss the empirical refutation of their theories or conjectures. In my view, opportunities are likely to arise from three different areas: the interaction of econometrics with game theory and industrial organization; the prominence of both nonparametric and Bayesian techniques in econometrics; and structural models that explain heterogeneity beyond the familiar paradigm of fixed/random effects.

1. Detailed Presentation

In Chapter 1, Stephen Hall provides background material about econometric methods that is useful in making this volume self-contained.

In Chapter 2, Jeffrey M. Wooldridge and Wei Lin study testing and estimation in panel data models with two potential sources of endogeneity: that because of correlation of covariates with time-constant, unobserved heterogeneity and that because of correlation of covariates with time-varying idiosyncratic errors. In the linear case, they show that two control function approaches allow us to test exogeneity with respect to the idiosyncratic errors while being silent on exogeneity with respect to heterogeneity. The linear case suggests a general approach for nonlinear models. The authors consider two leading cases of nonlinear models: an exponential conditional mean function for nonnegative responses and a probit conditional mean function for binary or fractional responses. In the former case, they exploit the full robustness of the fixed effects Poisson quasi-MLE; for the probit case, they propose correlated random effects.

In Chapter 3, William H. Greene and Qiushi Zhang point out that the panel data linear regression model has been studied exhaustively in a vast body of literature that originates with Nerlove (1966) and spans the entire range of empirical research in economics. This chapter describes the application of panel data methods to some nonlinear models such as binary choice and nonlinear regression, where the treatment has been more limited. Some of the methodology of linear panel data modeling can be carried over directly to nonlinear cases, while other aspects must be reconsidered. The ubiquitous fixed effects linear model is the most prominent case of this latter point. Familiar general issues, including dealing with unobserved heterogeneity, fixed and random effects, initial conditions, and dynamic models, are examined. Practical considerations, such as incidental parameters, latent class and random parameters models, robust covariance matrix estimation, attrition, and maximum simulated likelihood estimation, are considered. The authors review several practical specifications that have been developed around a variety of specific nonlinear models, including binary and ordered choice, models for counts, nonlinear regressions, stochastic frontier, and multinomial choice models.

In Chapter 4, Jeffrey S. Racine and Christopher F. Parmeter provide a survey of nonparametric methods for estimation and inference in a panel data setting. Methods surveyed include profile likelihood, kernel smoothers, and series and sieve estimators. The practical application of nonparametric panel-based techniques is less prevalent than nonparametric density and regression techniques. The material covered in this chapter will prove useful and facilitate their adoption by practitioners.

In Chapter 5, Kien Tran and Levent Kutlu provide a recent development in panel stochastic frontier models that allows for heterogeneity, endogeneity, or both. Specifically, consistent estimation of the models' parameters as well as observation-specific technical inefficiency is discussed.

In Chapter 6, Stefanos Dimitrakopoulos and Michalis Kolossiatis discuss how Bayesian techniques can be used to estimate the Poisson model, a well-known panel count data model, with exponential conditional mean. In particular, they focus on the implementation of Markov Chain Monte Carlo methods to various specifications of this model that allow for dynamics, latent heterogeneity and/or serial error correlation. The latent heterogeneity distribution is assigned a nonparametric structure, which is based on the Dirichlet process prior. The initial conditions problem also is addressed. For each resulting model specification, they provide the associated inferential algorithm for conducting posterior simulation. Relevant computer codes are posted as an online supplement.

In Chapter 7, Chih-Hwa Kao and Fa Wang review and explain the techniques used in Hahn and Newey (2004) and Fernandez-Val and Weidner (2016) to derive the limit distribution of the fixed effects estimator of semiparametric panels when the time dimension tends to infinity jointly with the cross-section dimension. The techniques of these two papers are representative and understanding their working mechanism is a good starting point. Under a unified framework, this paper explicitly points out the difficulties in extending from models with fixed dimensional parameter space to panels with individual effects and from panel with individual effects to panel with both individual and time effects, and how Hahn and Newey (2004) and Fernandez-Val and Weidner (2016) solve them.

In Chapter 8, Bo Honore and Ekaterini Kyriazidou study the identification of multivariate dynamic panel data logit models with unobserved fixed effects. They show that in the pure VAR(1) case (without exogenous covariates) the parameters are identified with as few as four waves of observations and can be estimated consistently at rate square-root-n with an asymptotic normal distribution. Furthermore, they show that the identification strategy of Honore and Kyriazidou (2000) carries over in the multivariate logit case when exogenous variables are included in the model. The authors also present an extension of the bivariate simultaneous logit model of Schmidt and Strauss (1975) to the panel case, allowing for contemporaneous cross-equation dependence both in static and dynamic frameworks. The results of this chapter are of particular interest for short panels, that is, for small T.

In Chapter 9, Subal Kumbhakar and Christopher F. Parmeter notice that, in the last 5 years, we have seen a marked increase in panel data methods that can handle unobserved heterogeneity, persistent inefficiency, and time-varying inefficiency. Although this advancement has opened up the range of questions and topics for applied researchers, practitioners, and regulators, there are various estimation proposals for these models and, to date, no comprehensive discussion about how these estimators work or compare to one another. This chapter lays out in detail the various estimators and how they can be applied. Several recent applications of these methods are discussed, drawing connections from the econometric framework to real applications.

In Chapter 10, Peter Pedroni discusses the challenges that shape panel cointegration techniques, with an emphasis on the challenge of maintaining the robustness of cointegration methods when temporal dependencies interact with both cross-sectional heterogeneities and dependencies. It also discusses some of the open challenges that lie ahead, including the challenge of generalizing to nonlinear and time varying cointegrating relationships. The chapter is written in a nontechnical style that is intended to make the information accessible to non-specialists, with an emphasis on conveying the underlying concepts and intuition.

In Chapter 11, by P.A.V.B. Swamy, Peter von zur Muehlen, Jatinder S. Mehta, and I-Lok Chang show that estimators of the coefficients of econometric models are inconsistent if their coefficients and error terms are not unique. They present models having unique coefficients and error terms, with specific applicability to the analyses of panel data sets. They show that the coefficient on an included nonconstant regressor of a model with unique coefficients and error term is the sum of bias-free and omitted-regressor bias components. This sum, when multiplied by the negative ratio of the measurement error to the observed regressor, provides a measurement-error bias component of the coefficient. This result is important because one needs the bias-free component of the coefficient on the regressor to measure the causal effect of an included nonconstant regressor of a model on its dependent variable.

In Chapter 12, Arne Heggingsen and Geraldine Henningsen give practical guidelines for the analysis of panel data with the statistical software R. They start by suggesting procedures for exploring and rearranging panel data sets and for preparing them for further analyses. A large part of this chapter demonstrates the application of various traditional panel data estimators that frequently are used in scientific and applied analyses. They also explain the estimation of several modern panel data models such as panel time series models and dynamic panel data models. Finally, this chapter shows how to use statistical tests to test critical hypotheses under different assumptions and how the results of these tests can be used to select the panel data estimator that is most suitable for a specific empirical panel data analysis.

In Chapter 13, Robin Sickles and Dong Ding empirically assess the impact of capital regulations on capital adequacy ratios, portfolio risk levels and cost efficiency for banks in the United States. Using a large panel data of US banks from 2001 to 2016, they first estimate the model using two-step generalized method of moments (GMM) estimators. After obtaining residuals from the regressions, they propose a method to construct the network based on clustering of these residuals. The residuals capture the unobserved heterogeneity that goes beyond systematic factors and banks' business decisions that affect its level of capital, risk, and cost efficiency, and thus represent unobserved network heterogeneity across banks. They then reestimate the model in a spatial error framework. The comparisons of Fixed Effects, GMM Fixed Effect models with spatial fixed effects models provide clear evidence of the existence of unobserved spatial effects in the interbank network. The authors find a stricter capital requirement causes banks to reduce investments in risk-weighted assets, but at the same time, increase holdings of nonperforming loans, suggesting the unintended effects of higher capital requirements on credit risks. They also find the amount of capital buffers has an important impact on banks' management practices even when regulatory capital requirements are not binding.

   In Chapter 14, Gerraint Johnes and Jill Johnes survey applications of panel data methods in the economics of education. They focus first on studies that have applied a difference-in-difference approach (using both individual and organization level data). Then they explore the way in which panel data can be used to disentangle age and cohort effects in the context of investigating the impact of education on subsequent earnings. The survey next examines the role of panel data in assessing education peer effects and intergenerational socioeconomic mobility. The review ends by looking at adaptations of methods to assess efficiency in a panel data context, and dynamic discrete choice models and their importance in the context of evaluating the likely effects of policy interventions. The survey is intended to highlight studies that are representative of the main areas in which the literature has been developed, rather than to be encyclopedic.

   In Chapter 15, corresponding author Scott Atkinson analyzes panel data studies of the most widely examined energy consumption industries—electric power, railroads, and airlines. For electric power, the choices between utility level versus plant-level data, cross-sectional versus panel data, and pooled-data analysis versus fixed-effects (FE) estimation generally makes little difference. A consensus also exists across estimates of cost, profit, and distance functions, the systems including these functions. Generally, studies reject homogeneous functional forms and find nearly constant returns to scale (RTS) for the largest firms. Residual productivity growth declines over time to small, positive levels, and substantial economies of vertical integration exist. Cost saving can accrue from a competitive generating sector. Controversy remains regarding the Averch-Johnson effect and the relative efficiency of publicly owned versus privately owned utilities. Railroads exhibit increasing RTS, substantial inefficiencies, and low productivity growth. Airlines operate close to constant RTS and enjoy modest productivity growth. Substantial inefficiencies decrease with deregulation. A valuable alternative to FE estimation is a control function approach to model unobserved productivity.

   In Chapter 16, Georgia Kosmopoulou, Daniel Nedelescu, and Fletcher Rehbein survey commonly used methods and provide some representative examples in the auction literature in an effort to highlight the value of panel data techniques in the analysis of experimental data obtained in the laboratory.

   In Chapter 17, Paul D. Allison, Richard Williams, and Enrique Moral-Benito point out that panel data make it possible both to control for unobserved confounders and to allow for lagged, reciprocal causation. Trying to do both at the same time, however, leads to serious estimation difficulties. In the econometric literature, these problems have been solved by using lagged instrumental variables together with the generalized method of moments (GMM). In this chapter, the authors show that the same problems can be solved by maximum likelihood estimation implemented with standard software packages for structural equation modeling (SEM). Monte Carlo simulations show that the ML-SEM method is less biased and more efficient than the GMM method under a wide range of conditions. ML-SEM also makes it possible to test and relax many of the constraints that typically are embodied in dynamic panel models.

In Chapter 18, Rico Merkert and Corinne Mulley notice that panel data have been widely used for analyzing both the demand and supply sides of transport operations. Obtaining true panels at the international level, however, appears to be difficult for various reasons. For the demand side, their peer review of the transport literature has demonstrated that pseudo panel data can be treated as if it is true panel data. For the supply side, this approach results in many studies using unbalanced panels instead. In terms of methods, they find that the DEA approach overcomes the problems of conflicting KPIs when considering overall cost efficiency while providing a robust tool for implementing change through the understanding of the key determinants of efficiency. Their case study about determinants of urban and regional train operator efficiency has evidenced, that the spatial context matters for the sample composition of DEA panel analysis in transport and that separating the panel into context specific subsamples can produce more robust results.

In Chapter 19, David Humphrey outlines the problems encountered when using banking panel data. Workarounds and solutions to these problems are noted. Although many of these problems occur when selecting and obtaining a panel data set, others are specific to the topics investigated, such as bank scale and scope economies, technical change, frontier efficiency, competition, and productivity. Illustrative results from published studies on these topics also are reported.

In Chapter 20, Christoph Siebenbrunner and Michael Sigmund point out that financial contagion describes the cascading effects that an initially idiosyncratic shock to a small part of a financial system can have on the entire system. They use two types of quantile panel estimators to imply that if certain bank-specific drivers used by leading regulatory authorities are good predictors of such extreme events, where small shocks to some part of the system can cause the collapse of the entire system. Comparing the results of the quantile estimation to a standard fixed-effects estimator they conclude that quantile estimators are better suited for describing the distribution of systemic contagion losses. Comparing the results to the aforementioned regulations, they find several recommendations for improvement.

In Chapter 21, Keshab Bhattarai reviews applications of panel data models. The process of substitution of labor by capital as discussed in Karabarbounis and Neiman (2014) and Picketty (2014) has increased the capital share, causing a reduction in labor share of about 10% magnitude. They also studied the impacts of trade and aid on economic growth. Fixed and random effect estimates show that investment rather than aid was a factor contributing to growth. Exports tied to aid are always harmful for growth of recipient countries. Although the evidence is mixed for the individual economies, there appear to be trade-offs between unemployment and inflation in the panel of Organisation for Economic Co-operation and Development (OECD) countries as shown by the random and fixed effect models in which the Hausman test is in favor of random effect model. A simple VAR model with two lags on inflation and unemployment shows persistence of inflation and unemployment rates among the OECD economies. The ratio of investment to GDP (gross domestic product) is a significant determinant of growth rates across OECD countries, and FDI contributes positively to growth. Regression results are robust on the grounds of stationarity and cointegration criteria. Threshold panel models developed by Hansen (1997) and Caner and Hansen (2004) show how to study regime changes occurring in the real world.

In Chapter 22, Andrew Jones, Apostolos Davillas, and Michaela Benzeval add to the literature about the income-health gradient by exploring the association of short-term and long-term income with a wide set of self-reported health measures and objective nurse-administered and blood-based biomarkers, as well as employing estimation techniques that allow for analysis beyond the mean. The income-health gradients are greater in magnitude in cases of long-run rather than cross-sectional income measures. Unconditional quantile regressions reveal that the differences between the long-run and the short-run income gradients are more evident toward the right tails of the distributions, where both higher risk of illnesses and steeper income gradients are observed.

In Chapter 23, Steve Ongena, Andrada Bilan, Hans Degryse, and Kuchulain O'Flynn review the data, econometric techniques, and estimates with respect to two recent and salient developments in the banking industry, i.e., securitization and globalization. The traditional banking market has become wider in its business models, through securitization, and in its geographical dispersion, through global operations. Both developments have brought new challenges for the understanding of basic questions in banking. Questions such as what determines credit flows or what are the channels of transmission for monetary policy recently have been addressed through this new optic. This review establishes that access to micro data has enabled researchers to arrive at increasingly better identified and more reliable estimates.

In Chapter 24, Claire Economidou, Kyriakos Drivas, and Mike Tsionas develop a methodology for stochastic frontier models of count data allowing for technological and inefficiency induced heterogeneity in the data and endogenous regressors. They derive the corresponding log-likelihood function and conditional mean of inefficiency to estimate technology regime-specific inefficiency. They apply our proposed methodology for the states in the United States to assess efficiency and growth patterns in producing new knowledge in the United States. The findings support the existence of two distinct innovation classes with different implications for their members' innovation growth.

In Chapter 25, Emmanuel Mamatzakis and Mike Tsionas propose a novel approach to identify life satisfaction and thereby happiness within a latent variables model for British Household Panel Survey longitudinal data. By doing so, they overcome issues related to the measurement of happiness. To observe happiness, they employ a Bayesian inference procedure organized around

Sequential Monte Carlo (SMC)/particle filtering techniques. Happiness efficiency captures individuals' optimal happiness to be achieved should they use their resource endowment efficiently. In addition, they propose to take into account individual-specific characteristics by estimating happiness efficiency models with individual-specific thresholds to happiness. This is the first study that departs from restrictions that happiness efficiency, and thereby inefficiency, would be time-invariant. Key to happiness is to have certain personality traits; being agreeable and being an extrovert assist efforts to enhance happiness efficiency. On the other hand, being neurotic would impair happiness efficiency.

In Chapter 26, Vasso Ioannidou and Jan de Dreu study how the introduction of an explicit deposit insurance scheme in Bolivia in 2001 affected depositors' incentives to monitor and discipline their banks for risk-taking. They find that after the introduction of the explicit deposit insurance scheme, the sensitivity of deposit interest rates and volumes to bank risk is reduced significantly, consistent with a reduction in depositor discipline. This effect operates mainly though large depositors—the class of depositors who were sensitive to their banks' risk in the first place. The authors also find that the larger the decrease in depositor discipline is, the larger the insurance coverage rate is. Deposit interest rates and volumes become almost completely insensitive to bank risk when the insurance coverage is higher than 60%. The results provide support for deposit insurance schemes with explicit deposit insurance limits per depositor.

In Chapter 27, Sarantis Kalyvitis, Sofia Anyfantaki, Margarita Katsimi, and Eirini Thomaidou review the growing empirical literature that explores the determinants of export prices at the firm level. They first present evidence from empirical studies that link firm export pricing to destination characteristics (gravity-type models). The main implications of channels that can generate price differentiation, such as quality customization, variable markups, and exchange rate pass-through, and financial frictions then are explored. A newly compiled panel data set from Greek exporting firms is used to present evidence from regressions with export price as the dependent variable and show how the main economic hypotheses derived in theoretical models are nested in empirical specifications.

In Chapter 28, Almas Hermati and Nam Seok Kim investigate the relationship between economic growth and democracy by estimating a nation's production function specified as static and dynamic models using panel data. In estimating the production function, they use a single time trend, multiple time trends, and the general index formulations to the translog production function to capture time effects representing technological changes of unknown forms. In addition to the unknown forms, implementing the technology shifters model enabled this study to find possible known channels between economic growth and democracy. Empirical results based on a panel data of 144 countries observed from 1980 to 2014 show that democracy had a robust positive impact on economic growth. Credit guarantee is one of the most significant positive links between economic growth and democracy. In order to check the robustness of these results, a dynamic model constructed with a flexible adjustment speed and a target level of GDP also is tested.

In Chapter 29, Almas Hesmati, Esfandiar Maasoumi, and Biwei Su examine the evolution of well-being (household income) of Chinese households over time, and its determinants. They study (stochastic) dominance relations based on Chinese Household Nutrition Survey (CHNS) data. They reveal a profile of general mobility/inequality and relative welfare in China over time and among population subgroups. The authors report that from 2000 to 2009, welfare has improved steadily along with Chinese economic development and growth. Pairwise comparison of subgroups reveals that there is no uniform ranking by household type, gender of household head, or age cohort. Married group and nonchild rearing group second order dominate single/divorced group and child rearing group. Inequality in subgroups with different educational levels and household sizes suggests groups with higher education and smaller household size tend to be better off than their counterparts. Longitudinal data allow estimation of permanent incomes, which smooth out short-term fluctuations. Treating the data as a time series of cross sections also avoids imposition of constant partial effects over time and across groups. This is appropriate given the observed heterogeneity in this population. Individual/group specific components are allowed and subsumed in conditional dominance rankings, rather than identified by panel data estimation methods.

In Chapter 30, Mike G. Tsionas, Konstantinos N. Konstantakis, and Panayotis G. Michaelides present a production function, which is based on a family of semi-parametric artificial neural networks that are rich in parameters, in order to impose all the properties that modern production theory dictates. Based on this approach, this specification is a universal approximator to any arbitrary production function. All measures of interest, such as elasticities of substitution, technical efficiency, returns to scale, and total factor productivity, also are derived easily. Authors illustrate our proposed specification using data for sectors of the US economy. The proposed specification performs very well and the US economy is characterized by approximately constant RTS and moderate TFP, a finding that is consistent with previous empirical work.

General References

Baltagi, B.H., 2001. Econometric analysis of panel data, second ed. John Wiley & Sons.
Cameron, A.C., Trivedi, P.K., 2010. Microeconometrics using Stata, Rev. ed. Stata Press Publ.
Greene, W.H., 2012. Econometric analysis, seventh ed. Prentice Hall, Upper Saddle River, NJ. 740 p.
Hsiao, C., 2002. Analysis of panel data, second ed. Cambridge University Press.
Wooldridge, J.M., 2010. Econometric analysis of cross section and panel data, second ed. MIT Press, Cambridge, MA.

Chapter 13

Capital Regulation, Efficiency, and Risk Taking: A Spatial Panel Analysis of US Banks

Dong Ding and Robin C. Sickles
Department of Economics, Rice University, Houston, TX, United States

Chapter Outline

1 Introduction

Since the process of bank deregulation started in the 1970s, the supervision of banks has relied mainly on the minimum capital requirement. The Basel Accord has emerged as an attempt to create an international regulatory standard about how much capital banks should maintain to protect against different types of risks. The financial crisis of 2007–09 revealed that, despite numerous refinements and revisions during the last two decades, the existing regulatory frameworks are still inadequate for preventing banks from taking excessive risks. The crisis also highlighted the importance of the interdependence and spillover effects within the financial networks.

To prevent future crises, economists and policymakers must understand the dynamics of the intertwined banking systems and the underlying drivers of banks' risk-taking to better assess risks and adjust regulations. Theoretical predictions about whether more stringent capital regulation curtails or promotes

Panel Data Econometrics. https://doi.org/10.1016/B978-0-12-815859-3.00013-5

banks' risk-taking behavior are ambiguous. It is ultimately an empirical question how banks behave in the light of capital regulation. This chapter seeks to investigate the drivers of banks' risk-taking in the United States and to test how banks respond to an increase in capital requirements.

Many empirical studies test whether increases in capital requirements force banks to increase or decrease risks (Aggarwal & Jacques, 2001; Barth, Caprio, & Levine, 2004; Camara, Lepetit, & Tarazi, 2013; Demirguc-Kunt & Detragiache, 2011; Jacques & Nigro, 1997; Lindquist, 2004; Rime, 2001; Shrieves & Dahl, 1992; Stolz, Heid, & Porath, 2003). For example, Shrieves and Dahl (1992) and Jacques and Nigro (1997) suggest that capital regulations have been effective in increasing capital ratios and reducing asset risks for banks with relatively low capital levels. They also find that changes in risk and capital levels are positively related, indicating that banks that have increased their capital levels over time also have increased their risk appetite. Other studies, such as Stolz et al. (2003) and Van Roy (2005), however, report a negative effect of capital on the levels of risk taken by banks. Overall, both theoretical and empirical studies are not conclusive as to whether more stringent capital requirements reduce banks' risk-taking.

A different strand of literature provides evidence that efficiency is also a relevant determinant of bank risk. In particular, Hughes, Lang, Mester, Moon, et al. (1995) link risk-taking and banking operational efficiency together and argue that higher loan quality is associated with greater inefficiencies. Kwan and Eisenbeis (1997) link bank risk, capitalization, and measured inefficiencies in a simultaneous equation framework. Their study confirms the belief that these three variables are jointly determined. Additional studies about capital, risk, and efficiency are conducted by Williams (2004), Altunbas, Carbo, Gardener, and Molyneux (2007), Fiordelisi, Marques-Ibanez, and Molyneux (2011), Deelchand and Padgett (2009), and Tan and Floros (2013).[1] Taken together, these two strands of the empirical literature about banking business practices imply that bank capital, risk, and efficiency are all related.

The third strand of literature deals with applying spatial econometrics to model banking linkages and the transmission of shocks in the financial system. Although spatial dependence has been studied extensively in a wide range of social fields, such as regional and urban economics, environmental sciences, and geographical epidemiology, it is not yet very popular in financial applications, although there are some applications in empirical finance. For example, Fernandez (2011) tests for spatial dependency by formulating a spatial version of the capital asset pricing model (S-CAPM). Craig and Von Peter (2014) find significant spillover effects between German banks' probabilities of distress and the financial profiles of connected peers through a spatial probit model. Other studies such as Asgharian, Hess, and Liu (2013), Arnold, Stahlberg,

---

1. See Table A.2 for a concise summary of the recent empirical studies on capital, risk and efficiency.

and Wied (2013), and Weng and Gong (2016) analyze spatial dependencies in stock markets. The empirical literature, however, appears to be silent about examining the effects of financial regulation on risks while taking spatial dependence into account. Banks' behaviors are likely to be inherently spatial. Ignoring these spatial correlations would lead to model misspecification, and consequently, biased parameter estimates.

In this chapter, we combine these different strands of literature. Using a large sample of US banking data from 2001 to 2016, we empirically assess the impact of capital regulation on capital adequacy ratios, portfolio risk levels, and efficiency of banks in the United States under spatial frameworks. The sampling period includes banks that report their balance sheet data according to both the original Basel I Accord and the Basel II revisions (effective from 2007 in the United States), and up to the most available date on 2016-Q3. More precisely, this chapter addresses the following questions: To what extent are banks' risk-taking behaviors and cost efficiency sensitive to capital regulation? How do capital buffers affect a bank's capital ratios, the level of risk it is willing to take on, and its cost efficiency? How does the result change by taking into account spatial interactions among observed banks?

This chapter makes several contributions to the discussion about bank capital, risk, and efficiency and has important policy implications. First, this analysis provides an empirical investigation linking capital regulation on bank risk-taking, capital buffer, and bank efficiency in a spatial setting. The introduction of spatial dependence allows us to determine the importance of network externalities after controlling for bank specific effects and macroeconomic factors.

Second, this chapter proposes a new approach for creating a spatial weights matrix. The key challenge in investigating spatial effects among banks is in defining the network, or in other words, constructing the spatial weights matrix. Spatial weights matrix usually is constructed in terms of the geographical distance between neighbors. In financial markets, however, it is not necessarily the case, given that most transactions are performed electronically. We propose a method to construct a spatial weights matrix based on clustering of residuals from regressions. The residuals aim to capture the unobserved heterogeneity that goes beyond systematic factors and banks' own idiosyncratic characteristics and can be interpreted as a representation of unobserved network heterogeneity.

Third, this study employs a significantly larger and more recent data set than previous studies that used data only up to 2010. In addition, because Basel III maintains many of the defining features of the previous accords, this study will shed light on how a more risk-sensitive capital regulation (i.e., Basel III) could influence banks' behaviors in the United States after the financial crisis.

The rest of the chapter is organized as follows. Section 2 lays out the regulatory background of this study. Section 3 explains the model. Section 4 outlines the estimation methodology and addresses several econometric issues. Section 5 describes the data. Section 6 presents and discusses the empirical findings and Section 7 presents conclusions.

2 Regulatory Background

The purpose of the Basel Committee on Banking Supervision is two-fold: to provide greater supervision of the international banking sector and to promote competition among banks internationally by having them comply with the same regulatory standards (Jablecki et al., 2009). All three Basel Accords are informal treaties, and members of the Basel Committee are not required to adapt their rules as national laws. For example, the United States adopted Basel II standards only for its 20 largest banking organizations in 2007. Regardless, the accords have led to greater universality in global capital requirements, even in countries that are not on the Basel Committee.

Basel I, implemented in 1988, was designed to promote capital adequacy among banks internationally by promoting an acceptable ratio of capital to total risk-weighted assets. Specifically, Basel I required the ratio between regulatory capital and the sum of risk-weighted assets to be greater than 8%. This has become an international standard, with more than 100 countries adopting the Basel I framework. The first Basel Accord divided bank capital into two tiers to guarantee that banks hold enough capital to handle economic downturns. Tier 1 capital, the more important of the two, consists largely of shareholder's equity. Tier 2 consists of items such as subordinated debt securities and reserves. The primary weakness of Basel I was that capital requirements were associated only with credit risk and did not include operational or market risk. Additionally, risk weights assigned to assets are fixed within asset categories, creating incentives for banks to engage in regulatory capital arbitrage. For example, all commercial loans were assigned the same risk weight category (100%) regardless of the inherent creditworthiness of the borrowers, which tended to reduce the average quality of bank loan portfolios.

Basel II was published in June 2004 and was introduced to combat regulatory arbitrage and improve bank risk management systems. The Basel II Accord was much more complex and risk-sensitive than Basel I and placed greater emphasis on banks' own assessment of risk. Basel II was structured in three pillars: Pillar 1 defined the minimum capital requirements; pillar 2 was related to the supervisory review process; and pillar 3 established the disclosure requirements about the financial condition and solvency of institutions. Basel II made several prominent changes to Basel I, primarily in regard to how risk-weighted assets were to be calculated. In addition to credit risk, Basel II extended the risk coverage to include a capital charge for market and operational risk. The total risk-weighted assets (RWA_T) was calculated as follows:

$$RWA_T = RWA_C + 12.5(OR_C + MR_C)$$

where RWA_C denotes the risk-weighted assets for credit risk. MR_C is the market risk capital charge, and OR_C is the operational risk capital charge.

Basel II also allowed banks to use internal risk models to determine the appropriate risk weights of their own assets after approved by regulators.

Additionally, Basel II calculated the risk of assets held in trading accounts using a Value at Risk approach, which takes into account estimates of potential losses based on historical data.

In the aftermath of the financial crisis of 2007–2009, the Basel Committee revised its capital adequacy guidelines, which became Basel III (BCBS, 2011). The primary additions to Basel II were higher capital ratios for both Tier 1 and Tier 2 capital, the introduction of liquidity requirement, and the incorporation of a leverage ratio to shield banks from miscalculations in risk weightings and higher risk weightings of trading assets. As shown in Table 1, although the minimum regulatory capital ratio remained at 8%, the components constituting the total regulatory capital had to meet certain new criteria. A capital conservation buffer of 2.5% was introduced to encourage banks to build up capital buffers during normal times. Liquidity risk also received much attention in Basel III. A liquidity coverage ratio (LCR) and a net stable funding ratio (NSFR) were implemented in 2015 and have became a minimum standard applicable to all internationally active banks on a consolidated basis on January 1, 2018 (BIS, 2018). Midway through the Basel III consultative process, the United States enacted the Dodd-Frank Wall Street Reform and Consumer Protection Act (Dodd-Frank Act) in 2010. The Dodd-Frank Act is generally consistent with Basel III but further addressed systemic risk by identifying a set of institutions

TABLE 1 Evolution of Minimum Capital Requirements From Basel I to Basel III

	Basel I	Basel II 2013	Basel III						
			2014	2015	2016	2017	2018	2019
Common equity Tier 1 ratio (%)		3.5	4	4.5	4.5	4.5	4.5	4.5
Capital conservation buffer (%)					0.625	1.25	1.875	2.5
Min Tier 1 capital (%)	4	4	4.5	5.5	6	6	6	6
Min total capital (%)	8	8	8	8	8	8	8	8
Liquidity coverage ratio (%)				60	70	80	90	100

Source: Bank for International Settlements, http://www.bis.org/bcbs/basel3.htm.

as systemically important financial institutions (SIFIs). The Dodd-Frank Act placed more stringent capital requirements for these SIFIs and required them to undertake periodic stress tests (DFAST) to ensure these institutions are well capitalized in aggregate stress scenarios.

In spite of these changes, critics remain skeptical that the same issues that plagued Basel II regarding incorrect risk weights, as well as ease of circumvention are still prominent in Basel III. It is believed that regulatory capital requirements should be sufficiently attuned to the riskiness of bank assets. Vallascas and Hagendorff (2013), however, find a low-risk sensitivity of capital requirements that enable banks to build up capital buffers by under-reporting their portfolio risk. Because the risk-weighting methodology remained essentially unchanged in Basel III, banks still will have the incentive to game the system by obtaining securities that might prove disastrous unexpectedly (Lall, 2012).

3 Hypotheses and Models

3.1 The Relationships Among Capital, Risk, and Efficiency: Theoretical Hypotheses

The prevalence of a minimum capital requirement is based primarily on the assumption that banks are prone to engage in moral hazard behavior. The moral hazard hypothesis is the classical problem of excessive risk-taking when another party is bearing part of the risk and cannot easily charge for that risk. Because of asymmetric information and a fixed-rate deposit insurance scheme, the theory of moral hazard predicts that banks with low levels of capital have incentives to increase risk-taking in order to exploit the value of their deposit insurance (Kane, 1995). The moral hazard problem is particularly relevant when banks have high leverage and large assets. According to the too-big-to-fail argument, large banks, knowing that they are so systemically important and interconnected that their failure would be disastrous to the economy, might count on a public bailout in case of financial distress. Therefore, they have incentives to take excessive risks and exploit the implicit government guarantee. In addition, the moral hazard hypothesis predicts that inefficiency is related positively to risks because inefficient banks are more likely to extract larger deposit insurance subsidies from the FDIC to offset part of their operating inefficiencies (Kwan & Eisenbeis, 1996). This suggests the following hypothesis.

Hypothesis 1. There exists a negative relationship between capital/efficiency and risk, because banks with higher leverage and lower efficiency have incentives to take higher risks to exploit existing flat deposit insurance schemes.

With regard to the relationship between cost efficiency and risks, Berger and DeYoung (1997) outline and test the bad luck, bad management, and skimping hypotheses using Granger causality test. Under the bad luck hypothesis, external exogenous events lead to increases in problem loans for the banks. The increases in risk incur additional costs and managerial efforts. Therefore, cost efficiency is expected to fall after the increase in problem loans. Under the bad management hypothesis, managers fail to control costs, which results in low cost efficiency, and they perform poorly at loan underwriting and monitoring. These underwriting and monitoring problems eventually lead to high numbers of nonperforming loans as borrowers fall behind in their loan repayments. Therefore, the bad management hypothesis implies that lower cost efficiency leads to an increase in problem loans. The skimping hypothesis, however, implies a positive Granger-causation from measured efficiency to problem loans. Under the skimping hypothesis, banks skimp on the resources devoted to underwriting and monitoring loans, reducing operating costs and increasing cost efficiency in the short run. In the long run, however, nonperforming loans increase as poorly monitored borrowers fall behind in loan repayments.

Milne and Whalley (2001) develop a continuous-time dynamic option pricing model that explains the incentives of banks to hold their capital buffers above the regulatory required minimum. The capital buffer theory states that adjustments in capital and risk depend on banks' capital buffers. It predicts that, after an increase in the regulatory capital requirement (the same impact as a direct reduction in the capital buffer), capital and risk initially are related negatively as long as capital buffers are low, and after a period of adjustment when banks have rebuilt their capital buffers to some extent, capital and risk become positively related. This leads to the following hypothesis.

Hypothesis 2. The coordination of capital and risk adjustments depends on the amount of capital buffer that a bank holds. Well-capitalized banks adjust their buffer capital and risk positively while banks with a low capital buffer try to rebuild an appropriate capital buffer by raising capital and simultaneously lowering risk.

3.2   Empirical Model

Taken together, these studies and the models on which they are based imply that bank capital, risk, and efficiency are determined simultaneously and can be expressed in general terms as follows:

$$RISK_{i,t} = f\left(Cap_{i,t}, Eff_{i,t}, X_{it}\right)$$
$$Cap_{i,t} = f\left(Risk_{i,t}, Eff_{i,t}, X_{it}\right) \qquad (1)$$
$$Eff_{i,t} = f\left(Cap_{i,t}, Risk_{i,t}, X_{it}\right)$$

where X_{it} are bank-specific variables.

Following Shrieves and Dahl (1992), we use a partial adjustment model to examine the relationship between changes in capital and changes in risk. Shrieves and Dahl (1992) point out that capital and risk decisions are made simultaneously and are interrelated. In the model, observed changes in bank capital ratios and risk levels are decomposed into two parts: a discretionary adjustment and an exogenously determined random shock such that:

$$\Delta CAP_{i,t} = \Delta^d CAP_{i,t} + \epsilon_{i,t}$$
$$\Delta RISK_{i,t} = \Delta^d CAP_{i,t} + \mu_{i,t}$$

(2)

where $\Delta CAP_{i,t}$ and $\Delta RISK_{i,t}$ are observed changes in capital and risk, respectively, for bank i in period t. $\Delta^d CAP_{i,t}$ and $\Delta^d RISK_{i,t}$ represent the discretionary adjustments in capital and risk. $\epsilon_{i,t}$ and $\mu_{i,t}$ are the exogenous random shocks. Banks aim to achieve optimal capital and risk levels, but banks might not be able to achieve their desired levels quickly. Therefore, banks can adjust capital and risk levels only partially toward the target levels. The discretionary adjustment in capital and risk is modeled in the partial adjustment framework:

$$\Delta^d CAP_{i,t} = \alpha \left(CAP_{i,t}^* - CAP_{i,t-1} \right)$$
$$\Delta^d RISK_{i,t} = \beta \left(RISK_{i,t}^* - RISK_{i,t-1} \right)$$

(3)

where α and β are speed of adjustment; $CAP_{i,t}^*$ and $RISK_{i,t}^*$ are optimal level of capital and risk; and $CAP_{i,t-1}$, and $RISK_{i,t-1}$ are the actual levels of capital and risk in the previous period.

Substituting Eq. (3) into Eq. (2), and accounting for the simultaneity of capital and risk decisions, the changes in capital and risk can be written as:

$$\Delta CAP_{i,t} = \alpha \left(CAP_{i,t}^* - CAP_{i,t-1} \right) + \gamma \Delta RISK_{i,t} + \epsilon_{i,t}$$
$$\Delta RISK_{i,t} = \beta \left(RISK_{i,t}^* - RISK_{i,t-1} \right) + \phi \Delta CAP_{i,t} + \mu_{i,t}$$

(4)

Eq. (4) shows the observed changes in capital and risk are a function of the target capital and risk levels, the lagged capital and risk levels, and any random shocks. Examples of exogenous shocks to the bank that could influence capital or risk levels include changes in regulatory capital standards or macroeconomic conditions.

3.2.1 Network Model

Shocks that affect banks' decisions are likely to spill over to other banks, creating systemic effect. Following Denbee, Julliard, Li, and Yuan (2017), we model the network effect on banks' capital and risk-holding decisions as a shock propagation mechanism in which banks' decisions depend upon how the individual bank's shock propagates to its direct and indirect neighbors.

We decompose banks' decisions into a function of observables and an error term that captures the spatial spillover generated by the network:

$$Y_{it} = \underbrace{\alpha_i}_{\text{fixed effect}} + \underbrace{\sum_{m=1}^{M} \beta_m X_{it}}_{\substack{\text{effect of observable} \\ \text{bank characteristics}}} + \underbrace{\sum_{p=1}^{P} \gamma_p Macro_t}_{\substack{\text{impact of systematic} \\ \text{risk factors}}} + u_{it} \qquad (5)$$

$$u_{it} = \underbrace{\lambda \sum_{j=1}^{N} w_{ij} u_{jt}}_{\text{shock propagation}} + \epsilon_{it} \qquad (6)$$

where Y_{it} are banks' capital and risk holding decisions, λ is a spatial autoregressive parameter, and w_{ij} are the network weights. The network component u_{it} is thus modeled as a residual term.[2] The vector of shocks to all banks at time t can be rewritten in matrix form as:

$$u_t = (I_N - \lambda W) - 1\epsilon_t \equiv M(\lambda, W)\epsilon_t$$

and expanding the inverse matrix as a power series yields:

$$M(\lambda, W) = I + \lambda W + \lambda^2 W^2 + \lambda^3 W^3 + \cdots \qquad (7)$$

$$= \sum_{k=0}^{\infty} \lambda^k W^k \qquad (8)$$

where λ also can be interpreted as network multiplier effect. We need $|\lambda| < 1$ for stability. The matrix $M(\lambda, W)$ measures all direct and indirect effects of a shock to bank i on bank j.

The network impulse-response function of banks' capital and risk holdings, to a one standard deviation shock σ_i to a given bank i is given by:

$$IRF_i(\lambda, \sigma_i) \equiv \frac{\partial Y_t}{\partial \epsilon_{i,t}} = 1' M(\lambda, W)_i \sigma_i$$

The average network multiplier resulting from a unit shock equally spread across the n banks can be expressed as:

$$1' M(\lambda, W) 1 \frac{1}{n} = \frac{1}{1 - \lambda}$$

A positive λ indicates an amplification effect that a shock to any bank would be amplified by the banking network system. A negative λ, however, indicates a dampening effect on shock transmission.

---

2. There also might be a more general spatial autoregressive structure that the network effect is modeled in the dependent or independent variables. This study, however, focuses on spillovers in how shocks of one bank propagate to other banks, which is best represented by the spatial error model.

3.2.2 Measures of Capital and Risk

Given the regulatory capital requirements associated with Basel I, II, and III, capital ratios are measured in three ways: Tier 1 risk-based ratio, total risk-based ratio, and Tier 1 leverage ratio. Tier 1 risk-based capital ratio is the proportion of core capital to risk-weighted assets in which core capital basically consists of common stock and disclosed reserves or retained earnings. Tier 2 capital includes revaluation reserves, hybrid capital instruments, and subordinated term debt, general loan-loss reserves, and undisclosed reserves. Total risk-based ratio is the percentage of Tier 1 and Tier 2 capital of risk-weighted assets. Tier 1 leverage ratio is the ratio of Tier 1 capital to total assets. The higher the ratio is, the higher the capital adequacy.

The literature suggests a number of alternatives for measuring bank risk. The most popular measures of bank risk are the ratio of risk-weighted assets to total assets (RWA) and the ratio of non-performing loans to total loans (NPL). The ratio of risk-weighted assets is the regulatory measure of bank portfolio risk and was used by Shrieves and Dahl (1992), Jacques and Nigro (1997), Rime (2001), Aggarwal and Jacques (2001), Stolz et al. (2003) and many others. The standardized approach to calculating risk-weighted assets involves multiplying the amount of an asset or exposure by the standardized risk weight associated with that type of asset or exposure. Typically, a high proportion of RWA indicates a higher share of riskier assets. Since its inception, risk-weighting methodology has been criticized because it can be manipulated (for example, via securitization), NPL, therefore, is used as a complementary risk measure as it might contain information on risk differences between banks not caught by RWA. Nonperforming loans is measured by loans past-due 90 days or more and nonaccrual loans and reflect the ex-post outcome of lending decisions. Higher values of the NPL ratio indicate that banks ex-ante took higher lending risks and, as a result, have accumulated ex-post higher bad loans.

3.2.3 Variables Affecting Changes in Capital, Risk and Efficiency

The target capital ratio and risk level are not observable and typically depend on some set of observable bank-specific variables, as we do in our analysis. Loan loss provisions ($LLPs$) as a percentage of assets are included as a proxy for asset quality. A higher level of $LLPs$ indicates an expectation of more trouble in the banks' portfolios and a resulting greater need for capital, and therefore might capture ex-ante credit risk or expected losses. The loan-to-deposit ratio (LTD) is used commonly to assess a bank's liquidity. If the ratio is too high, the bank might not have enough liquidity to cover any unforeseen fund requirements; conversely, if the ratio is too low, the bank might not be earning as much as it otherwise earns. Size likely will affect a bank's capital ratios, efficiency, and level of portfolio risk, because larger banks are inclined to have larger investment opportunity sets and are granted easier access to capital markets. For these reasons, they have been found to hold fewer capital ratios than their smaller counterparts (Aggarwal & Jacques, 2001). We include the natural log of total assets as the proxy for bank size. Bank profitability is expected to have a positive effect on bank capital if the bank prefers to increase capital through retained earnings. An indicator of profitability is measured by return on assets (*ROA*) and return on equity (*ROE*).

Macroeconomic shocks, such as a recession and falling housing prices, also can affect capital ratios and portfolios of banks. To capture the effect of common macroeconomic shocks that might have affected capital, efficiency, and risk during the period of study, the annual growth rate of real US GDP and Case-Shiller Home Price Index are included as controls. Crisis is a dummy variable that takes the value of 1 if the year is 2007, 2008, or 2009.

The regulatory pressure variable describes the behavior of banks close to or below the regulatory minimum capital requirements. Capital buffer theory predicts that an institution approaching the regulatory minimum capital ratio might have incentives to boost capital and reduce risk to avoid the regulatory cost triggered by a violation of the capital requirement. We compute the capital buffer as the difference between the total risk-weighted capital ratio and the regulatory minimum of 8%. Consistent with previous work, we use a dummy variable *REG* to signify the degree of regulatory pressure that a bank is under. Because most banks hold a positive capital buffer, we use the 10th percentile of the capital buffer over all observations as the cutoff point. The dummy *REG* is set equal to 1 if the bank's capital buffer is less than the cutoff value, and zero otherwise. To test the previous predictions, we interact the dummy *REG* with variables of interest. For example, in order to capture differences in the speeds of adjustment of low and high buffer banks, we interact *REG* with the lagged dependent variables Cap_{t-1} and $Risk_{t-1}$. To assess differences in short-term adjustments of capital and risk that depend on the degree of capitalization, we interact the dummy *REG* with $\Delta Risk$ and ΔCap in the capital and risk equations, respectively. A summary of variables description is presented in Table C.2 in the Appendix.

Given the discussion above, Eq. (1) can be written as:

$$
\begin{aligned}
\Delta Risk_{i,t} = {} & \alpha_0 + \alpha_1 \Delta Cap_{i,t} + \alpha_2 Eff_{i,t} + \alpha_3 RISK_{i,t-1} + \alpha_4 X_{i,t} + \alpha_5 \Delta Macro_t \\
& + \alpha_6 REG_{i,t} \times \Delta Cap_{i,t} + \alpha_7 REG_{i,t} \times Risk_{i,t-1} + v_{i,t} \\
\Delta Cap_{i,t} = {} & \gamma_0 + \gamma_1 \Delta Risk_{i,t} + \gamma_2 Eff_{i,t} + \gamma_3 Cap_{i,t-1} + \gamma_4 X_{i,t} + \gamma_5 \Delta Macro_t \qquad (9) \\
& + \gamma_6 REG_{i,t} \times \Delta Risk_{i,t} + \gamma_7 REG_{i,t} \times Cap_{i,t-1} + u_{i,t} \\
Eff_{i,t} = {} & \sigma_0 + \sigma_1 \Delta Risk_{i,t} + \sigma_2 \Delta Cap_{i,t} + \sigma_3 X_{i,t} + \sigma_4 \Delta Macro_t + w_{i,t}
\end{aligned}
$$

3.2.4 Measures of Cost Efficiency

Consistent with conventional bank efficiency studies, we use stochastic frontier analysis (SFA) to estimate efficiency for each bank. SFA, proposed by Aigner, Lovell, and Schmidt (1977) and Meeusen and Van den Broeck (1977), often is referred to as a composed error model where one part represents statistical noise with symmetric distribution and the other part represents inefficiency. See Appendix A for a more detailed description of stochastic frontier models. Cost efficiency is the most widely used efficiency criterion in the literature, and measures the distance of a banks cost relative to the cost of the best practice bank when both banks produce the same output under the same conditions. A bank's production function uses labor and physical capital to attract deposits. The deposits are used to fund loans and other earning assets. Inputs and outputs are specified according to the intermediation model Sealey and Lindley (1977).

Following Altunbas et al. (2007), we specify a cost frontier model with two-output, three-input, and a translog specification of the cost function:

$$
\begin{aligned}
\ln TC = \beta_0 + \gamma t + 0.5\gamma t^2 \\
+ \sum_{h=1}^{3} (\alpha_h + \theta_h t) \ln w_h + \sum_{j=1}^{2} (\beta_j + c_h t) \ln y_j \\
+ 0.5 \left(\sum_{j=1}^{2} \sum_{k=1}^{2} \beta_{jk} \ln y_j \ln y_k + \sum_{h=1}^{3} \sum_{m=1}^{3} \lambda_{hm} \ln w_h \ln w_m \right) \\
+ \sum_{i=1}^{2} \sum_{m=1}^{3} \rho_{im} \ln y_i \ln w_m - u + v
\end{aligned}
\tag{10}
$$

where TC represents the total cost, y are outputs, w are input prices, and t is a time trend to account for technological change, using both linear and quadratic terms. Inputs are borrowed funds, labor, and capital. Outputs are securities and loans. The inclusion of a quadratic time trend and a time interaction with outputs and input prices enables the measurement of time-dependent effects in costs, such as the pure technical change and nonneutral technological shifts of the cost frontier. The term v is a random error that incorporates both measurement error and luck. The term u is a firm effect representing the bank's technical inefficiency level, measuring the distance of an individual bank to the efficient cost frontier. A description of input and output variables are shown in Table C.1 in the Appendix.

4 Estimation

4.1 Endogenity

The system of Eq. (9) suffers from endogeneity of variables that will make OLS estimators inconsistent. The instrumental variable (IV)—generalized method of moments (GMM) estimator is suited to deal with endogeneity issues by means of appropriate instruments. Arellano and Bond (1991) suggest a GMM estimator that uses lagged levels of endogenous variables as instruments for equations in first differences. Blundell and Bond (1998) find that the lagged levels might become poor instruments for first-differenced variables, especially if the variables are highly persistent. Their modification of the estimator includes lagged levels and lagged differences. Therefore, we use the two-step efficient GMM procedure and the instruments (in lags and difference form) as suggested by Blundell and Bond (1998). These GMM types of instruments for endogenous capital and risk variables also are used in Stolz et al. (2003), Fiordelisi et al. (2011), and De-Ramon, Francis, and Harris (2016). To avoid the proliferation of the instrument set, we follow Roodman (2009)'s advice to collapse the instrument matrix so that there are not unique instruments for each time period as in Arellano and Bond (1991), and the number of lags is up to two.

To verify that the instruments are statistically valid, we use Hansen's J-test (for GMM estimator) and Sargan's test (for 2SLS estimator) of overidentifying restrictions. The null hypothesis is that the instruments are valid instruments, i.e., uncorrelated with the error term, and that the excluded instruments are correctly excluded from the estimated equation. A failure to reject the null should be expected in the GMM regression. To evaluate the strength of instruments, we look at Cragg-Donald Wald F statistic and compare it to Stock and Yogo (2002) critical values for testing weakness of instruments. To reject the null of weak instruments, the Cragg-Donald F statistic must exceed the tabulated critical values.

4.2   Spatial Correlation

In order to estimate the network model described in Section 3.2.1, we need to map the observed adjustment in capital and risk as well as efficiency levels into two components: the common factors and the unobserved network ones. To do this, we employ a fixed effect spatial error model (SEM). The model takes the form:

$$y_{it} = X'_{it}\beta + e_{it}$$
$$e_{it} = e_i + \phi_t + u_{it}$$

where e_i denotes the vector of individual effects, ϕ_t is a time period effect to capture common shocks, and u_{it} is the remainder disturbances independent of e_i. The term u_{it} follows the first-order autoregressive error dependence model:

$$u_{it} = \lambda \sum_{j=1}^{N} w_{ij} u_{jt} + \epsilon_{it}$$
$$\epsilon \sim N(0, \sigma^2 I_N)$$

where W is the matrix of known spatial weights and λ is the spatial autoregressive coefficient. Or, in matrix notation

$$Y = X\beta + \mathbf{u},$$
$$\mathbf{u} = \lambda W \mathbf{u} + \epsilon$$

As with autocorrelation in time series, a failure to account for spatial error correlation when $\lambda \neq 0$ would cause a misspecification of the error covariance structure and therefore compromise interval estimates and tests of the importance of various regulatory interventions.

Therefore, we further decompose the error term in Eq. (9) to capture the spatial dependence generated by the network:

$$\Delta RISK_{i,t} = \alpha_0 + \alpha_1 \Delta Cap_{i,t} + \alpha_2 Eff_{i,t} + \alpha_3 RISK_{i,t-1} + \alpha_4 X_{i,t} + \alpha_5 \Delta Macro_t$$
$$+ \alpha_6 REG_{i,t} \times \Delta Cap_{i,t} + \alpha_7 REG_{i,t} \times Risk_{i,t-1} + v_{i,t}$$

$$\Delta Cap_{i,t} = \gamma_0 + \gamma_1 \Delta Risk_{i,t} + \gamma_2 Eff_{i,t} + \gamma_3 Cap_{i,t-1} + \gamma_4 X_{i,t} + \gamma_5 \Delta Macro_t$$
$$+ \gamma_6 REG_{i,t} \times \Delta Risk_{i,t} + \gamma_7 REG_{i,t} \times Cap_{i,t-1} + u_{i,t}$$

$$Eff_{i,t} = \sigma_0 + \sigma_1 \Delta Risk_{i,t} + \sigma_2 \Delta Cap_{i,t} + \sigma_3 X_{i,t} + \sigma_4 \Delta Macro_t + w_{i,t}$$

$$u_{it} (\text{or } v_{it} \text{ and } w_{it}) = \lambda \sum_{j=1}^{N} w_{ij} u_{jt} + \epsilon_{it}$$

$$(11)$$

This error term in the system of equations describes the process of bank i, which is the residual of individual bank i's risk-taking behavior/capital adjustment/level of efficiency in the network that is not because of bank-specific characteristics or systematic factors. The weights matrix, w_{ij}, is assumed to be constant over time. If there is no spatial correlation between the errors for connected banks, i and j, the spatial error parameter λ will be 0, and the model reduces to the standard nonspatial model in which the individual observations are independent of one another. If $\lambda \neq 0$, then we have a pattern of spatial dependence between the errors for connected banks. This could reflect other kinds of misspecifications in the systematic component of the model, in particular, omitted variables that are spatially clustered. Typically, we expect to see a positive spatial correlation, implying the clustering of similar units, i.e., the errors for observation i tend to vary systematically in size with the errors for its nearby observations, j. The previous discussion suggests the following hypothesis.

Hypothesis 3. There exists unobserved spatial dependence among banks such that any shocks on bank i will have an impact on bank j, and the size of impact depends on the (economic) distance between them (i.e., $\lambda > 0$).

As outlined in the Appendix B, we can estimate the parameters of the fixed-effect spatial error model using a quasimaximum likelihood (QML) approach.

Prior to fitting a spatial regression model to the data, we can test for the presence of spatial dependence using Moran's test to the residuals from an OLS regression. In general, Moran's statistic is given by:

$$M = \frac{N}{\sum_i \sum_j w_{ij}} \frac{\sum_i \sum_j wij(X_i - \overline{X})(X_j - \overline{X})}{\sum_i (X_i - \overline{X})^2}$$

where N is the number of spatial units indexed by i and j, X is the variable of interest, $\overline{X}$ is the mean of X, and w_{ij} is the (i, j)-element of the spatial weights matrix.

4.2.1 Spatial Weights Matrix and Financial Network

The choice of the spatial weights matrix is of crucial importance to estimate the spatial model. Commonly employed methods to assign weights include contiguity, k-nearest neighbor, distance decay, and nonspatial definitions. In the Euclidean distance case, distance is measured in terms of the inverse, or proximity, so that the weight attached to a distant bank is smaller than one that is near. In the common boundary and nearest neighbor cases, each element w_{ij} is a binary indicator of whether banks i and j share a common market boundary or are nearest neighbors, respectively. Different from commonly estimated spatial models, we do not consider physical distance in constructing the weighting matrix in this study because the interlinkages in the banking sector usually go beyond the geographical boundaries. In particular, geographical proximity can facilitate financial integration, but it is not a necessary condition for such an integration to hold, given that most transactions now are performed electronically. Therefore, the challenge is how to construct a structure of the economic distance between banks and define the channel for cross-sectional spillovers.

In this section, we describe several approaches to identify banking networks. In banking literature, several ways are considered to construct networks building on the economic concept of intermediation. For example, some authors use bilateral exposure positions based on balance sheet data (e.g., asset, liabilities, deposit, and loans) to construct the interbank networks (see Craig & Von Peter, 2014; Craig, Koetter, and Kruger, 2014; Upper & Worms, 2004). Furfine (2003) and Bech and Atalay (2010) use interbank payment flows to quantify the bilateral federal funds exposures in the US federal funds market. Fig. 1 illustrates the evolution in the international financial networks, showing the trend of increasing scale and interconnectivity.

In addition to bilateral exposures, Fernandez (2011) uses correlation between key financial indicators in the CAPM framework to construct weighting matrices. The metric distance between bank i and j is specified as:

$$d_{ij} = \sqrt{2(1 - \rho_{ij})}$$

where ρ is Spearman's correlation coefficient between a specific financial indicator (e.g. market-to-book ratio and market cap relative to bank size) associated with banks i and j.

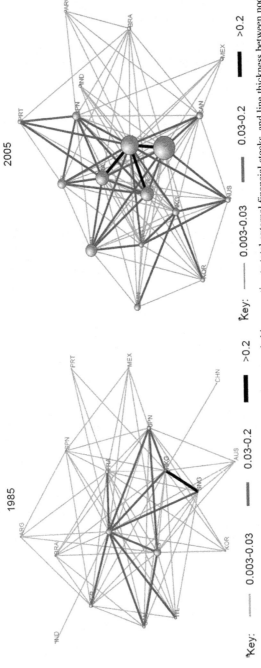

FIG. 1 The global financial network in 1985 and 2005. The nodes are scaled in proportion to total external financial stocks, and line thickness between nodes is proportional to bilateral external financial stocks relative to GDP. ((*Figure taken from Haldane, A. (2009). Rethinking the financial network, april 2009. Speech delivered at the Financial Student Association, Amsterdam.*))

Estimated interbank network

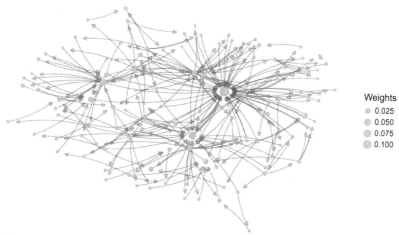

FIG. 2   Estimated interbank network based on assets, capital buffer, and liabilities. Note: Weight is a function of assets, capital buffer, and liabilities.

We construct the network based on clustering of residuals. The key idea is to first estimate Eq. (9) using two-step GMM regression and obtain the residuals $\hat{u}_{it}$ from the regressions. The residuals capture the unobserved heterogeneity that goes beyond systematic factors and banks' own idiosyncratic characteristics and therefore might be a representation of unobserved network heterogeneity across banks. Based on the residuals $\hat{u}_{it}$, we construct data-driven correlation networks through different clustering methods. Here we consider k-nearest-neighbor and hierarchical clustering methods. These different clusters might be a way to represent the latent markets that the bank operates. For example, Fig. 2 represents one of the outputs of the framework in terms of network visualization, and it is a visualization of the estimated network based on assets, capital buffer and liabilities. Fig. 3 is a network visualization of the top 10 banks in the United States by asset size in 2007 and 2015. Node size is proportional to total asset size of the bank.

K-nearest-neighbor classifier is one of the most commonly used cluster methods that usually is based on the Euclidean distance between observations. Alternatively, we can implement a hierarchical clustering approach. We implement Ward's hierarchical clustering procedure, and an example of the clustering output is displayed as a dendrogram in Fig. 4.

Now let's define the weights matrix. Let W be the k-dimensional square matrix representing a network composed of k banks. Each entry w_{ij} represents the possible connection between banks i and j. The spatial weights matrix is then defined as:

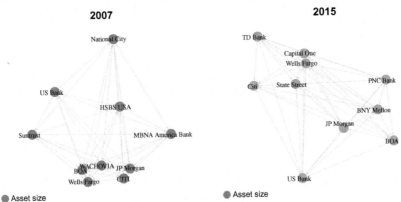

FIG. 3 Network visualization of the top 10 banks in the United States by asset size in 2007 and 2015. Node size is proportional to total asset size of the bank. Note: Wachovia was acquired by Wells Fargo in 2008. MBNA America Bank (renamed to FIA Card Services) was acquired by BOA in 2014. National City Bank was closed in 2009.

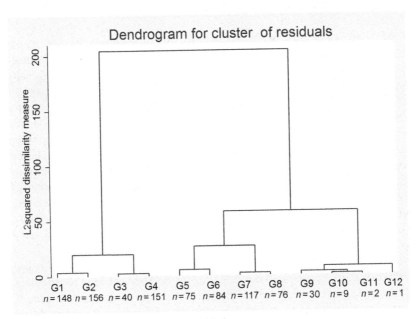

FIG. 4 Dendrogram plots of the cluster of residuals.

$$W_{ij} = \begin{cases} 1, & \text{if } j \in G_i \\ 0, & \text{otherwise} \end{cases}$$

where G_i denotes the group of i. An example of the binary weights matrix is as follows:

$$W = \begin{bmatrix} 0 & 1 & 0 & 1 \\ 1 & 0 & 1 & 0 \\ 0 & 1 & 0 & 1 \\ 1 & 0 & 1 & 0 \end{bmatrix}$$

where the diagonal contains only null elements (each bank is not its own neighbor), and the network is symmetric. According to Elhorst (2003), W is row-normalized such that the elements of each row sum to unity. Therefore, the spatial weights matrix W is a row-normalized binary contiguity matrix, with elements $w_{ij} = 1$, if two spatial units are in the same group and zero otherwise.

The spatial weights matrix, W, should satisfy certain regularity conditions:

Assumption A1 The diagonal elements of W are set to zero, because no spatial unit can be viewed as its own neighbor.

Assumption A2 The matrices $(I_N - \lambda W)^{-1}$ are nonsingular, where I_N represents the identity matrix of order N.

Assumption A3 (a) The row and column sums of the matrices W, and $(I_N - \lambda W)^{-1}$ before W is row-normalized should be uniformly bounded in absolute value as N goes to infinity (Kelejian & Prucha, 1998), or

Assumption A3 (b) The row and column sums of W before W is row-normalized should not diverge to infinity at a rate equal to or faster than the rate of the sample size N (Lee, 2004).

4.2.2 Estimation and Testing When the Weights Matrix Is Misspecified

Proper specification of the weighting matrix in the spatial error model is a rather daunting task for econometricians. The specification of the spatial weights matrix W requires a prior knowledge of the spatial correlation between units, and W needs to be exogenous to the model. Therefore, the right choice of a spatial weights matrix is crucial to identify the correct model. To address this issue, in this section, we include a discussion about the estimation and testing when the weights matrix is misspecified and propose a method to test for the misspecification of the weight matrix and ways of refinement.

Work by Qu and Lee (2015) and Liu and Prucha (2018) focuses on issues related to our objectives. Qu and Lee (2015) tackle the issue of an endogenous spatial weights matrix by exploring the model structure of spatial weights in a cross-sectional setting. They overcome the endogeneity problem using control function methods and propose three estimation methods: two-stage instrumental variable (2SIV) method, quasimaximum likelihood estimation (QMLE) approach, and generalized method of moments (GMM).

Liu and Prucha (2018) introduce a robust testing procedure by generalizing the widely used Moran (1950) I test for dependence in spatial networks. The problem in using the Moran I and available LM tests for spatial models is that we often are unsure about how to specify the weight matrix employed by the test and therefore need to adopt a sequential testing procedure based on different specifications of the weight matrix. Motivated by this problem, Liu and Prucha (2018) propose a single test statistic by incorporating information from multiple weight matrices. In this sense, the test statistic combines a set of Moran I tests into a single test. By its construction, the generalized Moran I test could be useful for detecting network-generated dependence in a wide range of situations, including those in which the weights matrix representing the network is misspecified and/or endogenous.

We propose an alternative approach to test for misspecification of the weighting matrix by using a two-step method based on the use of general factor-type structures introduced in Kneip, Sickles, and Song (2012) and Bai (2009).

Consider the following spatial error model:

$$Y_{it} = X_{it}\beta + u_{it} \tag{12}$$

$$u_{it} = \lambda \sum_{j=1}^{N} w_{ij} u_{jt} + \varepsilon_{it}^* \tag{13}$$

$$\varepsilon_{it}^* = \eta_{it} + v_{it} \tag{14}$$

where $\eta_{it} = \omega_i + \varpi_t$ and where $\Omega_{N \times N}$ is a sparse matrix of terms that pick up any possible misspecified spatial correlations not addressed by the specification of the weighting matrix W. The assumption about the measurement error in W is crucial. Suppose the true W is a banded matrix. Then, by definition, any algorithm determining the cluster structure of the data will fail to a certain extent. It will determine, say K clusters—i.e., K diagonal blocks—where the true W is not block-diagonal. In our model, we wish to first test for the presence of spatial effects left over after the estimation of the system with $\omega_i = 0$ and then respecify the covariance structure to address any leftover spatial correlations that might still exist because of the original misspecification using the standard approaches we outlined. The extent to which a simple clustering estimator fails—in case that the true W is not block-diagonal—depends on standard issues for clusters and to what extent the decay within blocks is misspecified by the assumed W in comparison with the true weighting matrix. A question is how to compare inadequate estimators in such a test that will depend on the distance (the measurement error) between the true and the identified W. There may be points that are outside of any cluster but correlated with others (undertreatment) and others that are inside the identified W and are truly independent (overtreatment). The outcome will depend on the variance-covariance of the overtreated and undertreated observations with the rest of the units. To do this, we again turn to the Kneip et al. (2012) estimator.

Kneip et al. (2012) (KSS) estimator can be used in the model setting we are considering by framing the misspecified weighting matrix in the error term above as:

$$Y_{it} + X_{it}\beta + \lambda \sum_{j=1}^{N} w_{ij} u_{jt} + \eta_{it} + v_{it} \tag{15}$$

The effects η_{it} are assumed to be affected by a set of underlying factors and are formulated by linear combinations of some basic functions:

$$\eta_{it} = \sum_{r=1}^{L} \delta_{ir} g_r(t) \tag{16}$$

For identifiability, it is assumed that $\sum_i^n \eta_{it} = 0,\ \ t = 1, \ldots, T$. The intercept α_t can be eliminated by transforming the model to the centered form,

$$y_{it} - \bar{y}_t = (X_{it} - \bar{X}_t)'\sum_{r=1}^{L} \delta_{ir} g_r(t) + v_{it} + \bar{v}_t \tag{17}$$

where $\bar{y}_t = \frac{1}{n}\sum_i y_{it}, \bar{X}_t = \frac{1}{n}\sum_i X_{it}$ and $\bar{v}_i = \frac{1}{n} v_{it}$. Denote $\tilde{y}_{it} = y_{it} - \bar{y}_t$ and $\tilde{X}_{it} = X_{it} - \bar{X}_t$, we return to the model setting

$$\tilde{y}_{it} = \tilde{X}_{it}'\beta + \sum_{r=1}^{L} \delta_{ir} g_r(t) + \tilde{v}_{it} \tag{18}$$

We can see that the individual effects η_{it} are assumed to be determined by a number of underlying factors, which are represented by a set of basis functions $(g_1(t), \ldots, g_L(t))$. Denote $\mathcal{L} \equiv span\{g_1, \ldots g_L\}$ to be the space of the underlying factors. A problem is that the set of basis functions is not unique, and therefore a normalization is needed for the estimation problem to be well defined. KSS used the following normalization.

(a) $\frac{1}{n}\sum_{i=1}^{n} \delta_{i1}^2 \geq \frac{1}{n}\sum_{i=1}^{n} \delta_{i2}^2 \geq \cdots \geq \frac{1}{n}\sum_{i=1}^{n} \delta_{iL}^2 \geq 0$

(b) $\frac{1}{n}\sum_{i=1}^{n} \delta_{ir} = 0$ and $\frac{1}{n}\sum_{i=1}^{n} \delta_{ir}\delta_{is} = 0$ for all $r, s \in 1, \ldots, L, r \neq s$.

(c) $\frac{1}{T}\sum_{t=1}^{T} g_r(t)^2 = 1$ and $\frac{1}{T}\sum_{t=1}^{T} g_r(t)g_s(t) = 0$ for all $r, s \in 1, \ldots, L, r \neq s$.

Provided that $n > L$, $T > L$, conditions (a)–(c) do not impose any restrictions, and they introduce a suitable normalization, which ensures identifiability of the components up to sign changes (instead of δ_{it}, g_r, we can use $-\delta_{ir}$, $-g_r$). Note that (a)–(c) lead to orthogonal vectors g_r as well as empirically uncorrelated coefficients δ_i. Bai (2003) uses expectations in (a) and (b), which leads to another standardization and different basis functions, which are determined from the eigenvectors of the (conditional) covariance matrix. Additionally, the KSS method uses cross-validation to determine the dimension of the underlying factor space, and then applies spline theory to obtain the estimates of basis functions.

The two-step version of the weighting matrix estimator proceeds as follows. First, estimate the original model with the possibly misspecified weighting matrix, assuming that the misspecified portion of the weighing matrix is orthogonal to the spatial weights and the other regressors. Next, construct the residuals from this regression and use them to estimate the factor structure of the $\eta'_{it}s$. We then can decompose the estimated factors into cross-section and time effects ($\eta_{it} + \omega_i + \varpi_t$) and use the estimated $\omega'_i s$ to test for the presence of misspecified spatial effects. If the testing results (possibly using the generalized new Moran test of Liu and Prucha (2018)) suggest that spatial errors are still present we can use the estimated $\omega'_i s$ to further refine our models of the weighting matrix using the methods we have deployed.

4.3   Correction for Selection Bias

An additional issue when estimating Eq. (11) arises when observations are missing in the spatial model. This can occur for several different reasons, but in the banking study, it occurs because banks are either merged or they are dissolved. Often the reasons for the banks no longer having autonomy or leaving the industry are not because of criteria that are easily modeled by econometricians. As discussed in Almanidis, Qian, and Sickles (2014), one approach to deal with this issue is to express the data for a bank on a pro-forma basis that goes back in time to account for mergers, that is, all past balance sheet and income observations of nonsurviving banks are added to the surviving banks. This approach is adopted by the Federal Reserve in estimating risk measurement models, such as the Charge-off at Risk Model (Frye & Pelz, 2008). This option is preferable when a large bank acquires a much smaller bank. An alternative is to use a balanced panel by deleting banks that attrite from the sample. This is the traditional approach that is applied by many existing studies in the banking literature. However, there is a potential for substantial selection bias arising from the correlation of the error terms in the selection and capital/risk/efficiency equations. In order to use the available spatial econometrics toolbox that applies to balanced panel only and account for selection bias, we apply a Heckman (1979) type 2-step correction.

The first step of the Heckman type estimation is dealt with by using a probit regression of all banks in the full sample, with the stay/exit dummy as a function of a set of bank-specific and market characteristics variables:

$$\Pr(S = 1 \,|\, Z) = \Phi(Z\gamma)$$

where $S = 1$ if the bank stays in the market and $S = 0$ otherwise, Z is a vector of explanatory variables, γ is a vector of unknown parameters, and Φ is the cumulative distribution function of the standard normal distribution. From these estimates, the nonselection hazard, what Heckman (1979) referred to as the inverse Mills ratio, m_i for each observation i is computed as

$$m_i = \frac{\phi(Z'\hat{\gamma})}{\Phi(Z'\hat{\gamma})}$$

where ϕ denotes the standard normal density function. The inverse Mills ratio (*invmills*) or m_{it}, then is added to the regression specified by Eq. (1) on a subsample of balanced panels excluding banks that exit the market. This is the second step of the procedure and a significant coefficient of *invmills* indicates the existence of sample selection bias.

5 Data

All bank-level data are constructed from the Consolidated Report of Condition and Income (referred to as the quarterly Call Reports) provided by the Federal Deposit Insurance Corporation (FDIC). The sample includes all banks in the Call Report covering the period from 2001:Q1 to 2016:Q3. Complete data of period 2001–2010 are available from the website of the Federal Reserve Bank of Chicago,[3] and data after 2011 are available from the FFIEC Central Data Repository's Public Data Distribution site (PDD).[4] We also collected data about US Gross Domestic Product (GDP) and Case-Shiller Home Price Index from Federal Reserve Bank of St. Louis. We filter the sample as follows. First, we drop missing data for key variables in the model. The variables computed from the Call Reports frequently have a few extreme outliers, most likely because of reporting errors or small denominators, so we drop the lowest and highest 1% of the observations for key variables. We also dropped banks with negative and zero total assets, deposits, and loans. Finally, we eliminate very small banks (total assets less than $25 million) and banks observed in only one year, which could introduce bias. We end up with unbalanced panel data about 8055 distinct banks, yielding 330,970 bank-quarter observations over the whole sample period. To do spatial analysis using spatial econometrics toolbox that applies to the balanced panel only, we keep banks that existed for all periods, leading to a balanced panel data of 889 banks, yielding 55,118 bank-quarter observations over the whole sample period.

Table 2 presents a descriptive summary of key variables in the full sample (panel A) and compares the sample mean for three periods: pre-crisis, crisis, and post-crisis (panel B). All variables are averaged by banks from 2001 to 2016. Fig. 5 shows the time series plots of bank risks, capital ratios, assets, profits, liquidity, and average capital and interest costs for the average bank from 2001 to 2016.

In general, the majority of banks in the sample have been well capitalized throughout the sample period. The average bank has exceeded the minimum required capital ratio by a comfortable margin. In our sample, the mean capital

---

3. https://www.chicagofed.org/banking/financial-institution-reports/commercial-bank-data.
4. https://cdr.ffiec.gov/public/PWS/DownloadBulkData.aspx.

TABLE 2 Summary Statistics of the Portfolios of US Banks

Panel A: Descriptive Statistics of Key Variables for the Full Sample Period

	Mean	Std. Dev.	Min	Max
Stochastic frontier arguments				
Cost of physical capital	0.20	0.21	0.02	1.97
Cost of labor	35.05	18.46	8.33	102.43
Cost of borrowed funds	0.01	0.01	0.00	0.04
Total securities ($million)	51.19	74.95	0.41	770
Total loans ($million)	160.17	212.36	7.61	1726
Total cost ($million)	6.30	8.94	0.25	167
Regression arguments				
Assets ($million)	239.4	301.6	9.6	3540
Equity ($million)	24.6	32.5	0.7	577
Deposit ($million)	196.0	240.2	7.5	2666
Net income ($million)	1.3	2.9	−261.6	109
Return on assets (%)	0.54	0.64	−27.48	9.16
Return on equity (%)	5.32	6.56	−304.34	83.21
Risk weighted assets (%)	68.05	11.80	36.43	95.78
NPL ratio (%)	2.73	2.73	0.00	51.27
Loan loss provision (%)	0.24	0.54	−20.92	44.54
Tier1 capital ratio (%)	15.30	5.38	7.23	43.09
Risk-based capital ratio (%)	16.43	5.37	9.91	43.48
Tier1 leverage ratio (%)	10.02	2.46	6.08	20.64
Capital buffer (%)	8.43	5.37	1.91	35.48

Panel B: Sample Mean of Key Variables During Pre-crisis, Crisis and Post-Crisis Period

	Pre-crisis	Crisis	Post-crisis
	2001q1–2007q2	*2007q3–2009q4*	*2010q1–2016q3*
Stochastic frontier arguments			
Cost of physical capital	0.201	0.192	0.192

TABLE 2 Summary Statistics of the Portfolios of US Banks—cont'd

Panel B: Sample Mean of Key Variables During Pre-crisis, Crisis and Post-Crisis Period

	Pre-crisis	Crisis	Post-crisis
	2001q1–2007q2	2007q3–2009q4	2010q1–2016q3
Cost of labor	30.365	35.505	40.053
Cost of borrowed funds	0.014	0.016	0.004
Total securities ($million)	42.819	46.613	62.849
Total loans ($million)	128.651	171.229	189.787
Total Cost ($million)	5.747	7.702	6.205
Regression arguments			
Assets ($million)	192.100	244.572	289.565
Equity ($million)	18.815	24.544	31.085
Net income ($million)	1.342	0.899	1.451
Deposit ($million)	155.824	196.543	240.498
Return on assets (%)	0.652	0.404	0.477
Return on equity (%)	6.720	3.989	4.440
Risk weighted assets (%)	68.244	71.086	66.302
NPL ratio (%)	2.216	3.328	2.994
Loan loss provision (%)	0.193	0.356	0.246
Loan-deposit ratio (%)	78.125	81.887	74.809
	14.882	14.573	16.125

Continued

TABLE 2 Summary Statistics of the Portfolios of US Banks—cont'd

Panel B: Sample Mean of Key Variables During Pre-crisis, Crisis and Post-Crisis Period

	Pre-crisis	Crisis	Post-crisis
	2001q1–2007q2	2007q3–2009q4	2010q1–2016q3
Tier1 capital ratio (%)			
Risk-based capital ratio (%)	16.015	15.674	17.276
Tier1 leverage ratio (%)	9.752	9.955	10.354
Capital buffer (%)	8.015	7.674	9.276

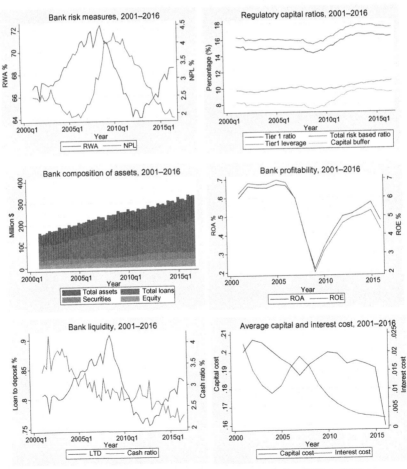

FIG. 5 Time series plots of key variables for the pooled sample from 2001 to 2016.

buffer above capital requirements is 8.43%. The average Tier 1 capital ratio is 15.26%, and the average risk-based capital ratio is 16.43% from 2001 to 2016. The findings show that banks tend to hold considerable buffer capital.

Comparing average bank portfolios during the pre-crisis, crisis, and post-crisis periods, it is evident that an average bank was hit hard by the financial turmoil. The average *ROE/ROA* dropped from its highest level (7%/0.7%) in 2005 to its lowest (2%/0.2%) in 2009. The time trend of capital ratios shows a steady movement until a drop in 2008 and then picked up after 2010. The time series plots of two measures of bank risks show a similar trend. Liquidity is measured by cash ratio and *LTD*. The average *LTD* ratio increased steadily until the financial crisis hit and reached the peak of almost 100% in 2009, then fell precipitously until 2012, and have been rising again. The high *LTD* during crisis period suggests insufficient liquidity to cover any unforeseen risks. This sharp drop in *LTD* since 2010 could be attributed to the tightened credit management by banks after the financial crisis, the contraction in lending demand because of the sluggishness of the economy, and the measures undertaken by the government to curb excessive lending.

6 Results

We conduct two main analyses to study the effect of capital regulation on bank capital, risk, and efficiency. In the first analysis, we use a full sample of the unbalanced panel by employing two-step GMM fixed-effects estimation and the results are analyzed in Section 6.2. In the second analysis, we exacted the residuals from the GMM FE regressions in the first analysis and use those to construct the weighting matrices using a balanced panel. We re-estimate the simultaneous equations using spatial FE, FE, and GMM FE respectively. The results are analyzed in Section 6.3. Capital ratios are measured by Tier 1 risk-based ratio. We also did additional tests that used two other measures of capital ratios, and none of these causes material changes to the results reported in the tables.

6.1 Estimation of Cost Efficiency

We estimate cost efficiency specifications in Eq. (10) using Battese and Coelli (1992)'s method. Parameter estimates are reported in Table D.1 in the Appendix. Estimates of the firm-specific inefficiencies, $E[u_i \,|\, \epsilon_i]$, were computed using the Jondrow et al. method. Table D.1 shows average cost inefficiency at US banks to be about 0.508 and mean cost efficiency to be 0.619. That is, given its particular output level and mix, on average, the minimum cost is about 61.9% of the actual cost. Alternatively, if a bank were to use its inputs as efficiently as possible, it could reduce its production cost by roughly 50.8%.

Table 3 presents the level of cost efficiency for the entire sample and for different ownership and size classes from 2001 to 2016. Cooperative banks have

TABLE 3 Cost Efficiency Scores by Size and Type of Banks Over Years

	Commercial Banks	Cooperative Banks	Savings Banks	Large Banks	Small Banks	Full Sample
2001	0.667	0.740	0.642	0.581	0.668	0.667
2002	0.661	0.734	0.636	0.575	0.662	0.661
2003	0.653	0.729	0.625	0.558	0.655	0.653
2004	0.646	0.718	0.616	0.549	0.648	0.645
2005	0.638	0.712	0.607	0.539	0.640	0.638
2006	0.630	0.703	0.598	0.527	0.633	0.630
2007	0.624	0.684	0.588	0.513	0.626	0.623
2008	0.620	0.680	0.584	0.504	0.623	0.619
2009	0.615	0.671	0.576	0.492	0.619	0.614
2010	0.608	0.665	0.567	0.479	0.612	0.606
2011	0.600	0.651	0.556	0.465	0.604	0.599
2012	0.597	0.650	0.547	0.469	0.601	0.595
2013	0.588	0.648	0.542	0.469	0.592	0.587
2014	0.578	0.646	0.529	0.459	0.583	0.576
2015	0.569	0.642	0.515	0.451	0.574	0.567
2016	0.564	0.639	0.508	0.455	0.569	0.561

Notes: Large banks are banks with assets greater than $1 billion, and small banks are banks with assets less than $1 billion.

higher costs efficiency than commercial and savings banks. The results are in line with findings by Altunbas, Carbo Valverde, and Molyneux (2003), who showed that cooperative banks have higher cost efficiency than commercial banks. Also, smaller banks are more cost-efficient than the larger banks during all periods.

6.2 GMM Results for the Full Sample

6.2.1 Relationships Between Changes in Capital, Risk and Efficiency

Table D.2 shows the GMM fixed-effects estimates of risk, capital, and efficiency equation for the full sample using two different measures of risk. Fixed effects are used to account for the possible bank-specific effects and provide consistent estimates. The Hansen statistics also are presented. The nonsignificance of the Hansen J-statistics indicates that the null hypothesis of valid instruments cannot be rejected for each model, confirming the validity of the instruments used.

The empirical results show that there is a strong positive two-way relationship between changes in *NPL* and changes in capital. This means banks' *NPL* holdings increase when capital increases and vice versa. This finding is consistent with Shrieves and Dahl (1992), suggesting the unintended effects of higher capital requirements on credit risk. When risk is measured by risk-weighted assets, however, the relationships become negative, contrary to the findings by Shrieves and Dahl (1992) but consistent with Jacques and Nigro (1997). This together suggests that when capital ratio increases, banks reduce ex-ante investments in risk-weighted assets but, at the same time, can have ex-post higher non-performing loans. The different signs on *NPL* and *RWA* raise concern whether risk-weighted assets are a credible measure of risk. It might be the case that banks optimize their capital by under-reporting *RWA* in an attempt to minimize regulatory burdens. Banks have two ways to boost their capital adequacy ratios: by increasing the amount of regulatory capital held or by decreasing risk-weighted assets. Therefore, if banks capital adequacy ratios fall, banks can reduce risk-weighted assets immediately to increase the capital ratio to meet the regulatory requirement. Nonperforming loans, however, will stay on the balance sheets and increase over time because of compounded unpaid interests. The high nonperforming loans can erode a bank's financial health despite having lower rates of risk-weighted assets.

The results show a positive relationship between efficiency and change in *NPL* and change in capital, suggesting more efficient banks increase capital holdings and take on greater credit risk (*NPL*), supporting the skimping hypothesis. This finding is contrary to the results by Kwan and Eisenbeis (1996) but consistent with Altunbas et al. (2007). When risk is measured by *RWA*, efficiency and change in *RWA* is related negatively, implying that less-efficient banks take on greater overall risk, supporting Hypothesis 1, which is the moral hazard hypothesis.

The results also show the parameter estimates of lagged capital and risk are negative and highly significant. The coefficients show the expected negative sign and lie in the required interval $[0, -1]$. This can be interpreted as the speed of capital and risk adjustment toward banks' target level (Stolz et al., 2003). The speed of risk adjustment is significantly slower than the capital adjustment, which is in line with findings by Stolz et al. (2003).

Capital buffers are negatively related to adjustment in RWA. This finding is consistent with Vallascas and Hagendorff (2013), who say it might be a sign that banks under-report their portfolio risk.

6.2.2 Impact of Regulatory Pressures on Changes in Capital and Risk

One important goal of this study is to assess what impact the risk-based capital standards had on changes in bank capital ratios, portfolio risk, and efficiency levels. To answer this question, an examination of the dummy *REG* and its interaction term provides some interesting insights. The negative coefficients of *REG* on both capital equations suggest that banks with low capital buffers increase capital by less than banks with large capital buffers. This result reflects the desire of well-capitalized banks to maintain a large buffer stock of capital, and the regulatory capital requirement was effective in raising capital ratios among banks that were already in compliance with the minimum risk-based standards. The parameter estimates of *REG* are negative and significant on ΔNPL but positive and significant on ΔRWA, suggesting that banks with low capital buffers reduce their level of nonperforming loans by more than banks with high capital buffer but decrease overall risk-weighted assets by less. The dummy *REG* has a positive sign on both efficiency equations, implying banks with lower capital buffer have higher cost efficiency than banks with higher capital buffer.

The interaction terms $REG \times Risk_{t-1}$ and $REG \times Cap_{t-1}$ shed further light on how the speed of adjustment towards the target level depends on the size of the capital buffer. The coefficients on $REG \times Cap_{t-1}$ are significant and positive, indicating that banks with low capital buffer adjust capital toward their targets faster than better capitalized banks. This is in line with the study by Berger, DeYoung, Flannery, Lee, and Oztekin (2008) in which they find that poorly capitalized and merely adequately capitalized banks adjust toward their capital targets at a faster speed than already well-capitalized banks. With respect to risk, we find that the coefficient of $REG \times Risk_{t-1}$ has the negative sign when risk is measured by *RWA* but becomes positive when risk is measured by *NPL*. The results suggest that banks with low capital buffer adjust *NPL* faster but adjust *RWA* slower than banks with high capital buffers.

The interaction terms of $REG_{i,t} \times \Delta Cap_{i,t}$ and $REG_{i,t} \times \Delta Risk_{i,t}$ represent the impact of capital buffer on the management of short-term risk and capital adjustments. We find that the coefficient on $REG_{i,t} \times \Delta Cap_{i,t}$ is insignificant when risk is measured by *NPL* but is significant and negative when risk is measured *RWA*. This finding indicates that banks with low capital buffer reduce overall risk-taking when capital is increased. We also find the coefficient on $REG_{i,t} \times \Delta Risk_{i,t}$ is significant and negative when risk is measured by *NPL* but is significant and positive when risk is measured *RWA*, suggesting that banks with low capital buffer reduce capital holding when *NPL* is increased but increase capital holding when *RWA* is increased. In sum, the findings are in line with the capital buffer theory hypothesis.

6.2.3 Variables Affecting Target Capital and Risk, and Efficiency Levels

We find that larger banks (in terms of total assets) tend to be less cost efficient, implying diseconomies of scale for banks. These results are contrary to previous studies that found large institutions tend to exhibit greater efficiency associated with higher scale economies (Wheelock & Wilson, 2012); Hughes & Mester, 2013). Bank size (*SIZE*) has a significant and negative effect on changes in capital and *RWA* but positive effect on changes in *NPL*. The finding is consistent with literature that larger banks generally have lower degrees of capitalization (Shrieves & Dahl, 1992; Aggarwal & Jacques, 2001; Rime, 2001; Stolz et al., 2003; and others). Larger banks have larger investment opportunity sets and are granted easier access to capital markets (Ahmad, Ariff, & Skully, 2008), which renders their target capital level smaller than the target capital levels of smaller banks. The negative relationship between size and change in *RWA* can be explained because larger banks are believed to be more diversified and could contribute to a reduction of their overall risk exposure (Lindquist, 2004). The results also show that size has a positive impact on change in *NPL*, suggesting larger banks tend to increase credit risk (*NPL*) more than smaller banks. This can be attributed to their too-big-to-fail position, whereby larger banks believe any distress will be bailed out by government assistance.

The results also support the findings of Stolz et al. (2003) and Altunbas et al. (2007) that profitability (measured by ROA) and capital are strongly positively related. Therefore, banks seem to rely strongly on retained earnings in order to increase capital. The coefficients of loan loss provision ratio on Δ*NPL* ratio is positive but negative on Δ*RWA* ratio. The results are contrary to the findings of Aggarwal and Jacques (2001), who determined that US banks with higher loan loss provision have higher risk-weighted assets. Liquidity (measured by loan-deposit ratio) appears to be negatively related to change in capital and positively related to efficiency. There is a strong significant positive relationship between liquidity and change in *RWA*. Banks with more liquid assets need less insurance against a possible breach of the minimum capital requirements. Therefore, banks with higher liquidity generally have smaller target capital levels and also might be willing to take on more risk.

6.3 The Spatial Effects

As a benchmark, we estimate Eq. (9) by nonspatial FE, and test for the presence of spatial correlation in the regression residuals by using the aforementioned weights matrices. Estimation results using the weights matrices constructed by *k*-nearest neighbors where $k = 10$ are reported in Table D.3–Table D.8. Columns 1–3 report estimates from spatial FE, FE, and GMM FE respectively. To minimize the impact of selection bias, the regressions reported are re-estimated using a Heckman type two-step procedure (Heckman, 1979) to control for the likelihood of surviving long enough to remain in the sample. The results using Heckman correction are reported in columns 5–7 in the table.

As suggested by Elhorst (2010), two measures of goodness-of-fit are reported for each model, R^2 and $Corr^2$. The R^2 reported for SFE differs from the R^2 for an OLS regression with a disturbance variance–covariance matrix $\sigma^2 I$. According to Elhorst (2010), there is no precise counterpart of the R^2 for an OLS regression for a generalized regression with a disturbance variance-covariance matrix $\sigma^2 \Omega$, where $we \neq \Omega$. We also report the squared correlation coefficient between actual and fitted values $corr^2 (Y, \hat{Y})$. This measure ignores the variation explained by spatial fixed-effects (Verbeek, 2000). Therefore, the difference between R^2 and $corr^2$ indicates how much variation is explained by spatial fixed-effects.

The presence of spatial correlation is tested by applying Moran's statistic to the residuals after regression in Section 6.2. Here we report two Moran's I statistics. The first Moran's I is obtained by applying Moran's statistic to the residuals after GMM FE regression obtained in Section 6.2. The second Moran's I is obtained by applying Moran's statistic to the residuals after spatial fixed-effect regression using weight matrices constructed. The null hypothesis of absence of spatial correlation in the errors is rejected for all weights matrices I used, suggesting the validity of applying the spatial error model in the first place. The second Moran's I's statistics are nonsignificant in all models, suggesting there is zero spatial autocorrelation present in the residuals after FE spatial error regression.

Table 4 reports results from the spatial error fixed-effect model with estimates of the spatial dependency parameter λ, the implied average network multiplier $\frac{1}{1-\lambda}$, and the $Corr^2$ of the regression. Full coefficient estimates are reported in Table D.3–Table D.8 in the Appendix. The autocorrelation term λ captures unobserved dependencies arising from links in the interbank network. The importance of the spatial dependence phenomenon is confirmed by the positive significant value of λ (significant at 1%) in all models, indicating the presence of a substantial network multiplier effect. For example, the estimated λ on Tier 1 ratio is about 0.152, suggesting that a \$1 idiosyncratic capital shock to one bank would result in a \$1.179 shock to aggregate change in capital in the banking network.

Parameter estimates resemble to a large extent those obtained in the previous section. For the risk equation (measured by *NPL*), the coefficients on Δ*Capital* and *efficiency* have the expected positive sign for all columns. This is also consistent with the results in Section 6.2. When risk is measured by *RWA*, the coefficients on Δ*Capital* and *efficiency* become negative for all columns. Banks increase *NPL* (decreases *RWA*) when capital increases and vice versa.

The high significance of the inverse Mills ratio suggests that controlling for survival bias is important. For the risk equation, the coefficient on the inverse

TABLE 4 Spatial Error Model Estimation

	Model Where Risk = NPL		
	Y = NPL	Y = Tier 1 Ratio	Y = Efficiency
Network effect λ	0.0974***	0.152***	0.797***
Average network multiplier	1.108	1.179	4.926
$Corr^2$	0.115	0.924	0.622
Number of banks	889	889	889
	Model Where Risk = RWA		
	Y = RWA	Y = Tier 1 Ratio	Y = Efficiency
Network effect λ	0.189***	0.135***	0.797***
Average network multiplier	1.233	1.156	4.926
$Corr^2$	0.235	0.924	0.621
Number of banks	889	889	889

***$P \leq 0.001$.

Mills ratio is positive, suggesting positive selection has occurred, meaning that without the correction, the estimate would have been upward-biased.

The coefficients on *REG* measure the impact of the risk-based capital standards had on changes in bank risk-taking. In Section 6.2, the parameter estimates of *REG* are negative and significant on ΔNPL but positive and significant on ΔRWA, suggesting that banks with low capital buffers reduce their level of nonperforming loans by more than banks with high capital buffer but decrease overall risk-weighted assets by less. Although the coefficients on *REG* are not significant when risk is measured by *NPL* as seen in Table D.3 columns 1–3 and become significant and negative after Heckman correction.

The interaction terms $REG \times Risk_{t-1}$ shed further light about how the speed of adjustment toward the target level depends on the size of the capital buffer. In Section 6.2, the coefficient is positive and significant, however, in this case all coefficients are nonsignificant, suggesting size of capital buffer does not affect the speed of risk *(NPL)* change. The positive effect of size on the change of *NPL* is in line with the too-big-to-fail notion that larger banks are more likely to take more risks.

For the capital equation (risk measured by *NPL*), the coefficients on $\Delta Risk$ are negative without correction but become positive and highly significant with Heckman correction. Results in columns 4–6 are consistent with the results obtained in Section 6.2. When risk is measured by *RWA*, the coefficients on $\Delta Risk$ are negative in all specifications and comparable with results in Section 6.2.

Size initially has a nonsignificant impact on changes in capital without correction term but has a negative impact on changes in capital when the correction term is included. The negative sign of size is in line with findings in Section 6.2, suggesting that larger banks generally have lower degrees of capitalization. The coefficients on *REG* are negative in all specifications and on both capital equations, suggesting that banks with low capital buffers increase capital by less than banks with large capital buffers. The magnitude of the *REG* coefficients is smaller after correction for selection bias and smaller in the case of spatial fixed-effect error model.

In sum, the fixed-effect spatial error model fits the data well, as the spatial interaction terms are both statistically and economically significant and both pseudo R^2 and $corr^2$ give reasonable goodness-of-fit. The comparison of FE, GMM models with spatial fixed effects models provides clear evidence about the existence of unobserved spatial effects in the interbank network on individual bank risk, capital, and efficiency levels and that such effects can be captured by the error term in the form of the nonsystematic risk of neighboring banks.

6.4   Robustness Checks

One skepticism about spatial econometric methods is that the results are said to depend on the choice of the weighting matrix. As mentioned previously, there is no clear guidance in the literature as to what the best weighting matrix might be. In order to check the robustness of the results, we also estimated spatial models for alternative weight matrices using hierarchical clustering methods. These results are consistent with estimations using *KNN* clustering.

7   Concluding Remarks

In this paper, we investigate the drivers of banks' risk-taking in the United States, and test how they respond to an increase in capital requirements. We use the most recent dataset of US banks from 2001 to 2016 and model risk, capital, and banks' best business practices (proxied by cost efficiency) in a robust framework. Controlling for endogeneities among risk, capital, and cost efficiency, we propose a method to construct the network based on clustering of residuals from GMM estimates. We then re-estimate the model in a spatial error framework to further address the issue of spatial correlation among banking networks.

Our findings suggest that a stricter capital requirement causes banks to reduce investments in risk-weighted assets, but at the same time, increase ex-post nonperforming loans, suggesting the unintended effects of higher capital requirements on credit risk. We also find capital buffer has important impact on capital, risk adjustments, and cost efficiency. Banks with low capital buffer adjust capital toward their targets faster than better capitalized banks. In addition, our results show that unobserved spatial effects exist in the interbank network and such effects can be captured by the error term in the form of the nonsystematic risk of neighboring banks.

This study has important policy implications and will shed light about how a more risk-sensitive capital regulation (i.e. Basel III) could influence banks' behavior. The different signs on nonperforming loans (*NPL*) and risk-weighted assets (*RWA*) raise concern whether risk-weighted assets are a credible measure of risk. It might be the case that banks under-report *RWA* to minimize regulatory burdens. Because the risk-weighting methodology remains essentially unchanged in Basel III, banks still will have the incentive to game the system by reallocating portfolios away from assets with high risk weights to assets with low risk weights.

The results also imply that current capital requirements still are not sufficient to ensure effective loss absorption during stress scenarios such as those experienced during the financial crisis. Basel III introduces a conservation buffer of 2.5%. Our study finds that the majority of banks actually maintained capital buffer levels that significantly exceeded Basel III requirements. Therefore, the introduction of an additional capital buffer might not be as effective in affecting bank's risk-taking as expected.

Taken as a whole, these results suggest that the effectiveness of the Basel III to increase capital and reduce risk-taking might be limited because it does not properly address the shortcomings of Basel II. Therefore, policymakers will have to carefully revise the risk-weighting approach and conduct tight and efficient supervision to minimize banks' ability to game the system.

Appendix A: A Stochastic Frontier Model

In the same spirit as Schmidt and Sickles (1984) and Cornwell, Schmidt, and Sickles (1990), we specify a panel data application of stochastic frontier model. Let y_{it} and x_{it} represent, respectively, the scalar output level and the input vector of k inputs for firm i at time t. The model has the general form:

$$y_{it} = \alpha_t + f(x_{it}; \beta) + v_{it} - u_{it}, \ i = 1,2,...,N, \ t = 1,2,...,T_i$$
$$= \alpha_{it} + f(x_{it}; \beta) + v_{it}$$
$$v_{it} \sim_{iid} N(0, \sigma_v^2)$$

where α_t is the frontier intercept, i.e. the maximum possible value for α_{it}. v_{it} is a two-sided symmetric, idiosyncratic component. Normal distribution usually is assumed for v_{it}. $u_{it} \geq 0$ is a firm effect representing technical inefficiency of firm i at time t. $f(x_{it}; \beta)$ is a log-linear production function (e.g., Cobb-Douglas, translog or Fourier flexible form). The fundamental idea of stochastic frontier technical efficiency can be formalized as the ratio of realized output, given a specific set of inputs, to maximum attainable output:

$$TE_{it} = \frac{y_{it}}{y_{it}^*} = \frac{f(x_{it}; \beta)e^{-u_{it}}e^{v_{it}}}{f(x_{it}; \beta)e^{v_{it}}} = e - u_{it} \in (0, 1]$$

with y_{it}^* is the maximum attainable output for unit i given x_{it}.

Cornwell, Schmidt, and Sickles (1990) proposed a model that the technical inefficiency term u_{it} is a quadratic function over time. They assumed that the intercepts depend on a vector of observables W_t in the following way:

$$\alpha_{it} = \delta_i W_t = \delta_{i1} + \delta_{i2}t + \delta_{i3}t^2$$

where the parameters $\delta_{i1}, \delta_{i2}, \delta_{i3}$ are firm specific and t is the time trend variable. Following a slightly different strategy, Lee and Schmidt (1993) specifies u_{it} as the form of $g(t)u_i$ in which

$$g(t)u_i = \left(\sum_{t=1}^{T} \beta_t d_t \right) u_i$$

where d_t is a time dummy variable and one of the coefficients is set equal to 1.

Numerous similarly motivated specifications have been proposed for u_{it}. Two that have proved useful in applications are Kumbhakar (1990)'s model,

$$g(t) = \left(1 + \exp\left(\eta_1 t + \eta_2 t^2 \right) \right)^{-1}$$

and Battese and Coelli (1992)'s time-decay model (the model of choice in many recent applications),

$$g(t) = \exp\left[-\eta(t - T_i) \right]$$

where T_i is the last period in the i_{th} panel, η is the decay parameter. The decay parameter gives information about the evolution of the inefficiency. When $\eta > 0$, the degree of inefficiency decreases over time; when $\eta < 0$, the degree of inefficiency increases over time. If η tends to 0, then the time-varying decay model reduces to a time-invariant model.

The specifications of u_{it} are summarized below.

TABLE A.1 Different Specifications of u_{it}

Model	Specification of u_{it}
CSS(1990)	$\alpha_{it} = \theta_{i1} + \theta_{i2}t + \theta_{i3}t^2, \hat{u}_{it} = \max \hat{\alpha}_{it} - \hat{\alpha}_{it}$
Kumbhakar (1990)	$u_{it} = (1 + \exp(\eta_1 t + \eta_2 t^2))^{-1} u_i$
Battese and Coelli (1992)	$u_{it} = \exp[-\eta(t - T_i)]u_i$
Lee and Schmidt (1993)	$u_{it} = (\sum_{t=1}^{T} \beta_t d_t) u_i$

The main purpose of the stochastic frontier analysis is to estimate inefficiency u_{it} or efficiency $TE_{it} = \exp(-u_{it})$. Because only the composed error term $\epsilon_{it} = v_{it} - u_{it}$ is observed, the firms inefficiency is predicted by the conditional mean $\hat{u}_{it} = E[u_{it}|\epsilon_{it}]$. Jondrow, Lovell, Materov, and Schmidt (1982) (JLMS) present the explicit result of $E[u_{it}|\epsilon_{it}]$ for the half-normal model

$$E[u_{it}|\epsilon_{it}] = \left[\frac{\sigma\lambda}{1+\lambda^2}\right]\left[\hat{\mu}_{it} + \frac{\phi(\tilde{\mu}_{it})}{\Phi(\tilde{\mu}_{it})}\right], \quad \tilde{\mu}_{it} = \frac{-\lambda\epsilon_{it}}{\sigma}$$

where $\sigma^2 = (\sigma_u^2 + \sigma_v^2)$, $\lambda = \sigma_u^2/\sigma_v^2$ and $\phi(\cdot)$ and $\Phi(\cdot)$ are the density and CDF of the standard normal distribution. With these in hand, estimates of technical efficiency $E[TE_{it}|\epsilon_{it}] = E[\exp(-u_{it})|\epsilon_{it}]$ also is obtained.

TABLE A.2 Recent Empirical Studies on Risk, Capital and Efficiency of Banks

Authors	Period of Study	Countries	Methodology	Main Empirical Results
Kwan and Eisenbeis (1996)	1986–1991	254 large US BHCs	2SLS	Less efficient banks took on more risk to offset the inefficiency; less efficient banks tend to be less well capitalized
Berger and DeYoung (1997)	1985–1994	US commercial banks	Granger causality OLS	Increases in NPL is followed by reductions in cost efficiency; decreases in cost efficiency are followed by increases in NPL; for the most efficient banks, increases in cost efficiency is followed by increases in NPL; thinly capitalized banks have incentive (moral hazard) to take increased risks
Williams (2004)	1990–1998	European savings banks	Granger causality OLS	Poorly managed banks (lower cost efficiency) tend to make more risky loans, supporting the bad management hypothesis; results are sensitive to the number of lags included
Altunbas et al. (2007)	1992–2000	Large sample of banks from 15 European countries	SUR	Positive relationship between capital and risk; inefficient banks appear to hold more capital and take on less risk; relationships vary depending on types of banks

Continued

TABLE A.2 Recent Empirical Studies on Risk, Capital and Efficiency of Banks—cont'd

Authors	Period of Study	Countries	Methodology	Main Empirical Results
Deelchand and Padgett (2009)	2003–2006	263 Japanese cooperative banks	2SLS	Negative relationship between risk and capital; inefficient banks appear to operate with larger capital and take on more risk; larger banks holding less capital take on more risk and are less efficient
Fiordelisi et al. (2011)	1995–2007	Commercial banks from EU-26 countries	Granger causality GMM	Subdued bank efficiency (cost or revenue) Granger causes higher risk supporting the bad management hypothesis; more efficient banks seem to eventually become more capitalized; higher capital also tends to have a positive effect on efficiency levels
Tan and Floros (2013)	2003–2009	101 Chinese banks	3SLS	Positive and significant relationship between risk and efficiency; relationship between risk (Z-score) and capital is negative and significant

Appendix B: Derivation

Quasi-Maximum Likelihood Formulation

Eq. (11) can be rewritten as

$$Y = X\beta + (I_n - \lambda W)^{-1}\epsilon$$

Because $\epsilon \sim N(0, \sigma^2 I_N)$, then $u \sim N(0, \Omega)$ where $\Omega = \sigma^2(I_n - \lambda W)'(I_n - \lambda W) - 1$. $(I_n - \lambda W)^{-1}$ should be nonsingular, this imposes restrictions on the value of λ. If

W is row standardized, so that the influence of neighbors can be represented in terms of averages, then $1/r_{min} < \lambda < 1$, where r_{min} is the smallest negative eigenvalue of W (Ord, 1975; Anselin, 1982).

The log-likelihood of the spatial error model if the spatial specific effects are assumed to be fixed can be obtained as:

$$\ln L = -\frac{NT}{2}\ln(2\pi\sigma^2) + T\ln|I_n - \lambda W| - \frac{1}{2\sigma^2}\sum_{i=1}^{N}\sum_{t=1}^{T}v'_{it}v_{it} \qquad (B.1)$$

where $v = (I_n - \lambda W)(y - X\beta).\beta$, σ^2 and λ can be estimated jointly using (quasi) maximum likelihood methods:

$$\hat{\beta} = \left(\widetilde{X}'\widetilde{X}\right)^{-1}\widetilde{X}'\widetilde{Y}, \quad \hat{\sigma}^2 = \frac{\hat{v}'\hat{v}}{NT}$$

where $\widetilde{X} = X^* - \lambda(I_T \otimes W)X^*$ and $\widetilde{Y} = Y^* - \lambda(I_T \otimes W)Y^*$.

Y^* and X^* are demeaned form of X and Y. The maximization of Eq. (B.1) can be done by searching over a grid values for λ. The asymptotic variance matrix of the parameters is:

$$\text{Asy.Var}\left(\beta, \lambda, \sigma^2\right) = \begin{bmatrix} \frac{1}{\sigma^2}X^{*'}X^* & 0 & 0 \\ 0 & T^*tr\left(\widetilde{W}\widetilde{W} + \widetilde{W}'\widetilde{W}\right) & 0 \\ 0 & \frac{T}{\sigma^2}tr\left(\widetilde{W}\right) & \frac{NT}{2\sigma^4} \end{bmatrix}$$

where $\widetilde{W} = W(I_N - \lambda W)^{-1}$.

Appendix C: Variable Definitions

TABLE C.1 Input and Output Description

Variable	Symbol	Description
Total cost	TC	Interest + noninterest expenses
Outputs		
Total securities	Y1	Securities held to maturity + securities held for sale
Total loans	Y2	Net loans (Gross loans—reserve for loan loss provisions)
Inputs prices		
Price of physical capital	W1	Expenditures on premises and fixed assets/premises and fixed assets
Price of labor	W2	Salaries/full-time equivalent employees
Price of borrowed funds	W3	Interest expenses paid on deposits/total deposits

TABLE C.2 Description of Variables Used in the Study

Variables	Descriptions
Capital	
Tier 1 risk-based ratio	Core capital (Tier 1)/risk-weighted assets
Total risk-based ratio	Core capital (Tier 1)+tier 2 capital/risk-weighted assets
Tier 1 leverage ratio	Core capital (Tier 1)/total assets
Risk	
NPL ratio	Nonperforming loans/total assets
RWA ratio	Risk-weighted assets/Total assets
Bank-specific variables	
Size	The natural logarithm of banks total assets
ROA	Annual net income/total assets
ROE	Annual net income/total equity
LLP ratio	Loan loss provisions/total assets
Cash ratio	Noninterest-bearing balances, currency, and coin/total assets
Loan-deposit ratio	Total loans/total deposits
Buffer	Total risk weighted capital ratio −8%
REG (regulatory pressure)	1 if a bank has a capital buffer ≤10th percentile capital buffer over all observations, and zero otherwise
Macro indicators	
GDPG	Growth rate of real GDP for the United States
Crisis	1 if year is between 2007 and 2009 and 0 otherwise
Case-Shiller Home Price Index Growth	rate of 20-city composite constant-quality house price indices

Appendix D: Tables

TABLE D.1 Parameter Estimates of the Translog Cost Functions on the Full Sample

Dependent	Total Cost	
	Parameter	*SE*
lny_1	0.066***	0.005
lny_2	−0.009	0.009
lnw_1	−0.063***	0.007
lnw_2	0.454***	0.0l0
lnw_3	0.593***	0.006
$lny_1 lny_2$	−0.049***	0.000
$lnw_1 lnw_2$	0.036***	0.001
$lnw_1 lnw_3$	−0.011***	0.001
$lnw_2 lnw_3$	−0.102***	0.001
$1/2\ ln\ y_1^2$	0.068***	0.000
$1/2\ ln\ y_2^2$	0.099***	0.001
$1/2\ ln\ w_1^2$	−0.03l***	0.001
$1/2\ ln\ w_2^2$	0.041***	0.002
$1/2\ ln\ w_3^2$	0.119***	0.001
$lny_1\ ln\ w_1$	0.000	0.000
$lny_1\ ln\ w_2$	−0.005***	0.00l
$lny_1\ ln\ w_3$	0.006***	0.000
$lny_2\ ln\ w_1$	0.007***	0.001
$lny_2\ ln\ w_2$	−0.007***	0.001
$lny_2\ ln\ w_3$	0.005***	0.001
t	0.016***	0.000
t^2	0.000***	0.000
$lny_1 t$	−0.001***	0.000
$lny_2 t$	−0.001***	0.000
$lnw_1 t$	−0.001***	0.000
$lnw_2 t$	0.001***	0.000

Continued

TABLE D.1 Parameter Estimates of the Translog Cost Functions on the Full Sample—cont'd

Dependent	Total Cost	
	Parameter	*SE*
lnw_3t	0.001***	0.000
Constant	1.302***	0.056
μ	0.555***	0.006
η	−0.008***	0.000
γ	0.888	
σ_{u_2}	0.099	
σ_{v_2}	0.013	
Estimated inefficiencies $\hat{u}_{it}$		
Mean	0.508	
SD	0.243	
Min	0.006	
Max	1.290	
Estimated cost efficiency $\hat{C}E_{it}$		
Mean	0.619	
SD	0.149	
Min	0.275	
Max	0.994	
Observations	330,790	

Note: The top and bottom 5% of inefficiencies scores are trimmed to remove the effects of outliers.
***P ≤ 0.001.

TABLE D.2 Two-Step GMM Estimations (FE) for the Relationships Between Bank Capital, Cost Efficiency, and Risk-Taking

Variables	Model Where Risk = NPL			Model Where Risk = RWA		
	Y = ΔNPL	Y = ΔTier1 ratio	Y = Efficiency	Y = ΔRWA	Y = ΔTier1 ratio	Y = Efficiency
ΔCapital	0.0243***		0.0517***	−0.987***		0.0378***
	(0.00313)		(0.00612)	(0.00615)		(0.00694)
ΔRisk		0.00686***	−0.00509		−0.00866***	−0.00967***
		(0.00246)	(0.00456)		(0.000192)	(0.00236)
Efficiency	0.00439***	0.00117***		−0.114***	0.000474***	
	(0.00103)	(0.000214)		(0.00192)	(0.000174)	
RISK$_{t-1}$	−0.263***			−0.320***		
	(0.00139)			(0.00122)		
Cap$_{t-1}$		−0.947***			−0.934***	
		(0.00129)			(0.000497)	
Buffer	0.00139	0.937***	−0.266***	−0.223***	0.925***	−0.265***
	(0.00126)	(0.00136)	(0.00243)	(0.00263)	(0.000494)	(0.00244)
Size	0.124***	−0.00482	−8.505***	−1.099***	−0.0156***	−8.507***
	(0.0124)	(0.00318)	(0.0175)	(0.0232)	(0.00210)	(0.0175)
ROA	−0.175***	0.0184***	0.761***	0.0972***	0.0175***	0.760***
	(0.00545)	(0.00111)	(0.0106)	(0.0100)	(0.000910)	(0.0106)

Continued

TABLE D.2 Two-Step GMM Estimations (FE) for the Relationships Between Bank Capital, Cost Efficiency, and Risk-Taking—cont'd

Variables	Model Where Risk = NPL			Model Where Risk = RWA		
	Y = ΔNPL	Y = ΔTier1 ratio	Y = Efficiency	Y = ΔRWA	Y = ΔTier1 ratio	Y = Efficiency
LLP ratio	0.323***	−0.0451***	0.275***	−0.400***	−0.0477***	0.270***
	(0.00583)	(0.00122)	(0.0111)	(0.0105)	(0.000955)	(0.0112)
LTD	−0.000540*	−0.00145***	0.0150***	0.163***	−0.000988***	0.0155***
	(0.000305)	(5.88e−05)	(0.000605)	(0.000683)	(5.29e−05)	(0.000620)
REG	−0.111***	−0.298***	0.773***	2.000***	−0.234***	0.773***
	(0.0143)	(0.0413)	(0.0217)	(0.214)	(0.0229)	(0.0217)
Crisis	0.0300***	0.0313***	1.474***	0.293***	0.0322***	1.473***
	(0.00886)	(0.00144)	(0.0173)	(0.0166)	(0.00150)	(0.0173)
REG* RISK$_{t-1}$	0.0344***			−0.0223***		
	(0.00387)			(0.00268)		
REG* ΔCAP	0.00301			−0.151***		
	(0.0154)			(0.0290)		
REF* Cap$_{t-1}$		0.0357***			0.0286***	
		(0.00418)			(0.00232)	

	(1)	(2)	(3)	(4)	(5)	(6)
REF* ΔRisk	−11.81***	−0.0122***			0.00731***	
	(0.476)	(0.00273)			(0.000520)	
GDP growth	−2.418***	−0.316***	25.04***	11.99***	0.0444	12.32***
	(0.142)	(0.0838)	(0.888)	(0.946)	(0.0808)	(0.947)
Spcs growth		−0.108***	3.186***	23.31***	−0.0779***	23.34***
		(0.0229)	(0.264)	(0.277)	(0.0240)	(0.277)
Hansen J statistic	0.063	0.097	1.403	0.217	0.92	0.233
	(0.8019)	(0.7553)	(0.1084)	(0.6414)	(0.3374)	(0.6295)
No. of observations	265,905	265,905	265,905	265,985	265,905	265,985
Number of banks	7644	7644	7644	7725	7644	7725

Notes: Standard errors in parentheses.
***P < 0.01, **P < 0.05, *P < 0.1.

TABLE D.3 Estimation Results Using KNN: Risk Equation (Risk = NPL)

Variables	Without Correction			Heckman Correction		
	Spatial FE	FE	GMM FE	Spatial FE	FE	GMM FE
$\Delta Capital$	0.0342***	0.0601***	0.0349***	0.0313***	0.0631***	0.0350***
	(0.00649)	(0.00553)	(0.00671)	(0.00632)	(0.00552)	(0.00648)
Efficiency	0.0231***	0.00633***	0.0224***	0.0295***	0.0101***	0.0164***
	(0.00291)	(0.000981)	(0.00279)	(0.00286)	(0.000997)	(0.00113)
$RISK_{t-1}$	−0.319***	−0.314***	−0.315***	−0.352***	−0.348***	−0.356***
	(0.00322)	(0.00315)	(0.00331)	(0.00320)	(0.00318)	(0.00327)
Buffer	0.00448*	0.00206	0.00349	0.00867***	0.00479**	0.00738***
	(0.00237)	(0.00228)	(0.00250)	(0.00231)	(0.00230)	(0.00241)
Size	0.0787***	0.0162	0.0961***	0.638***	0.540***	0.659***
	(0.0229)	(0.0175)	(0.0254)	(0.0247)	(0.0209)	(0.0231)
ROA	−0.131***	−0.139***	−0.138***	0.291***	0.282***	0.361***
	(0.0122)	(0.0116)	(0.0121)	(0.0143)	(0.0138)	(0.0145)
LLP ratio	0.338***	0.351***	0.341***	0.0991***	0.118***	0.0661***
	(0.0144)	(0.0139)	(0.0146)	(0.0147)	(0.0145)	(0.0148)
LTD	4.06e-05	−0.000261	−0.000333	−0.0192***	−0.0199***	−0.0240***
	(0.000607)	(0.000591)	(0.000629)	(0.000691)	(0.000692)	(0.000728)
REG	−0.0313	−0.0237	−0.0322	−1.554***	−1.560***	−1.890***
	(0.0416)	(0.0412)	(0.0430)	(0.0494)	(0.0498)	(0.0523)
Crisis	0.0343*	0.0157	0.0489***	0.0167	−0.0150	−0.0105
	(0.0190)	(0.0168)	(0.0181)	(0.0186)	(0.0166)	(0.0167)
$REG^* RISK_{t-1}$	−0.00668	−0.00885	−0.00966	−0.00197	−0.00683	−0.00798
	(0.0151)	(0.0150)	(0.0155)	(0.0147)	(0.0148)	(0.0150)
$REG^* \Delta CAP$	−0.0244	−0.0447	−0.0229	0.0111	−0.0209	0.0106
	(0.0444)	(0.0439)	(0.0461)	(0.0433)	(0.0436)	(0.0445)
GDP growth	−12.67***	−11.78***	−12.33***	−34.51***	−34.26***	−38.92***
	(1.003)	(0.895)	(0.929)	(1.064)	(0.984)	(1.006)
Home index growth	−1.903***	−2.150***	−1.812***	−4.460***	−4.804***	−5.327***
	(0.297)	(0.270)	(0.276)	(0.295)	(0.268)	(0.269)
Invmills				4.001***	4.025***	4.869***
				(0.0741)	(0.0749)	(0.0831)

TABLE D.3 Estimation Results Using KNN: Risk Equation (Risk = NPL)—cont'd

Variables	Without Correction			Heckman Correction		
	Spatial FE	FE	GMM FE	Spatial FE	FE	GMM FE
Constant		0.453*	−1.124***		−10.23***	−12.80***
		(0.233)	(0.393)		(0.318)	(0.353)
λ	0.0912***			0.0974***		
	(0.00944)			(0.00942)		
$\frac{1}{1-\lambda}$	1.100**			1.108***		
Moran's I (1)	0.9481***			0.9481***		
Moran's I (2)	0.02			0.03		
Observations	55,118	55,118	52,451	55,118	55,118	52,451
R-squared (within)	0.164	0.164	0.163	0.203	0.203	0.210
$Corr^2$	0.0907	0.0908	0.0886	0.115	0.117	0.123
Number of banks	889	889	889	889	889	889

Notes: ***$P < 0.01$, **$P < 0.05$, *$P < 0.1$.

TABLE D.4 Estimation Results Using KNN: Risk Equation (Risk = RWA)

Variables	Without Correction			Heckman Correction		
	Spatial FE	FE	GMM FE	Spatial FE	FE	GMM FE
$\Delta Capital$	−1.191***	−1.213***	−1.200***	−1.164***	−1.182***	−1.160***
	(0.0136)	(0.0116)	(0.0140)	(0.0134)	(0.0115)	(0.0137)
Efficiency	−0.0477***	−0.0149***	−0.0588***	−0.0406***	−0.00937***	−0.0475***
	(0.00647)	(0.00200)	(0.00548)	(0.00633)	(0.00198)	(0.00543)
$RISK_{t-1}$	−0.290***	−0.281***	−0.288***	−0.313***	−0.304***	−0.314***
	(0.00259)	(0.00255)	(0.00268)	(0.00261)	(0.00257)	(0.00271)
Buffer	−0.198***	−0.180***	−0.192***	−0.214***	−0.197***	−0.212***
	(0.00536)	(0.00520)	(0.00556)	(0.00529)	(0.00514)	(0.00548)
Size	−0.222***	0.137***	−0.197***	0.675***	0.949***	0.714***
	(0.0510)	(0.0371)	(0.0499)	(0.0543)	(0.0420)	(0.0559)
ROA	−0.0454*	−0.114***	−0.0955***	0.652***	0.543***	0.648***
	(0.0263)	(0.0227)	(0.0235)	(0.0309)	(0.0279)	(0.0298)
LLP ratio	−0.423***	−0.533***	−0.493***	−0.851***	−0.937***	−0.958***
	(0.0289)	(0.0265)	(0.0275)	(0.0303)	(0.0281)	(0.0296)
LTD	0.142***	0.142***	0.144***	0.120***	0.121***	0.120***
	(0.00147)	(0.00143)	(0.00149)	(0.00154)	(0.00151)	(0.00158)

REG	1.095	1.198*	1.036	−1.127*	−0.940	−1.459**
	(0.668)	(0.659)	(0.690)	(0.660)	(0.652)	(0.680)
Crisis	−0.0251	0.0750**	−0.0713**	−0.0342	0.0577*	−0.0919***
	(0.0428)	(0.0334)	(0.0356)	(0.0418)	(0.0329)	(0.0349)
REG*RISK$_{t-1}$	−0.0135	−0.0144*	−0.0124	−0.0150*	−0.0153*	−0.0131
	(0.00848)	(0.00836)	(0.00873)	(0.00835)	(0.00824)	(0.00857)
REG*ΔCAP	−0.197**	−0.175*	−0.170*	−0.144	−0.132	−0.134
	(0.0909)	(0.0896)	(0.0922)	(0.0895)	(0.0883)	(0.0906)
GDP growth	25.50***	26.38***	23.84***	−9.029***	−6.238***	−13.64***
	(2.272)	(1.806)	(1.824)	(2.373)	(1.963)	(2.024)
Home index growth	−0.299	1.151**	0.231	−4.063***	−2.518***	−4.017***
	(0.671)	(0.529)	(0.541)	(0.661)	(0.530)	(0.539)
Invmills		8.544***	14.68***	6.258***	5.901***	6.761***
		(0.504)	(0.781)	(0.152)	(0.150)	(0.169)
Constant					−6.721***	−2.754***
					(0.630)	(0.923)
λ	0.194***			0.189***		
	(0.00907)			(0.00907)		
$\frac{1}{1-\lambda}$	1.241***			1.233***		
Moran's I (1)	0.975***			0.975***		

Continued

TABLE D.4 Estimation Results Using KNN: Risk Equation (Risk = RWA)—cont'd

Variables	Without Correction			Heckman Correction		
	Spatial FE	FE	GMM FE	Spatial FE	FE	GMM FE
Moran's I (2)	0.01			0.01		
Observations	55,118	55,118	52,451	55,118	55,118	52,451
R-squared (within)	0.411	0.412	0.412	0.427	0.428	0.430
$Corr^2$	0.223	0.216	0.209	0.235	0.226	0.220
Number of banks	889	889	889	889	889	889

Notes: ***P < 0.01, **P < 0.05,*P < 0.1.

TABLE D.5 Estimation Results Using KNN: Capital Equation (Risk = NPL)

Variables	Without Correction			Heckman Correction		
	Spatial FE	FE	GMM FE	Spatial FE	FE	GMM FE
$\Delta Risk$	-0.000277	-0.00131**	-9.97e-05	0.00204***	0.00288***	0.00258***
	(0.000692)	(0.000635)	(0.000712)	(0.000675)	(0.000623)	(0.000695)
Efficiency	-0.000634***	-0.000673***	-0.00139***	-0.000988***	-0.00127***	-0.00195***
	(0.000226)	(0.000159)	(0.000224)	(0.000222)	(0.000155)	(0.000218)
Cap_{t-1}	-0.954***	-0.953***	-0.955***	-0.955***	-0.955***	-0.957***
	(0.000851)	(0.000858)	(0.000873)	(0.000829)	(0.000836)	(0.000846)
Buffer	0.941***	0.941***	0.942***	0.942***	0.942***	0.943***
	(0.000852)	(0.000860)	(0.000874)	(0.000830)	(0.000838)	(0.000847)
Size	-0.00443	-0.00545*	-0.0154***	-0.0886***	-0.0890***	-0.108***
	(0.00327)	(0.00294)	(0.00335)	(0.00355)	(0.00326)	(0.00365)
ROA	0.00510***	0.00665***	0.00668***	-0.0622***	-0.0613***	-0.0715***
	(0.00194)	(0.00180)	(0.00184)	(0.00227)	(0.00216)	(0.00225)
LLP ratio	-0.0506***	-0.0522***	-0.0527***	-0.00799***	-0.00862***	-0.00244
	(0.00217)	(0.00210)	(0.00213)	(0.00225)	(0.00220)	(0.00225)
LTD	-0.00211***	-0.00196***	-0.00195***	0.000804***	0.000964***	0.00146***
	(9.47e-05)	(9.44e-05)	(9.68e-05)	(0.000107)	(0.000107)	(0.000111)

Continued

TABLE D.5 Estimation Results Using KNN: Capital Equation (Risk = NPL)—cont'd

Variables	Without Correction			Heckman Correction		
	Spatial FE	FE	GMM FE	Spatial FE	FE	GMM FE
REG	-0.407***	-0.447***	-0.491***	-0.187***	-0.223***	-0.228***
	(0.0574)	(0.0580)	(0.0586)	(0.0560)	(0.0566)	(0.0569)
Crisis	0.0456***	0.0448***	0.0408***	0.0482***	0.0475***	0.0455***
	(0.00306)	(0.00265)	(0.00268)	(0.00300)	(0.00258)	(0.00260)
REG* Cap_{t-1}	0.0487***	0.0526***	0.0570***	0.0499***	0.0536***	0.0582***
	(0.00579)	(0.00586)	(0.00592)	(0.00564)	(0.00570)	(0.00573)
REG* $\Delta Risk$	-0.00172	-0.000728	-0.00303	0.000791	-2.43e-05	-0.00107
	(0.00368)	(0.00371)	(0.00378)	(0.00358)	(0.00362)	(0.00366)
GDP growth	0.0740	0.0551	0.0285	3.441***	3.488***	4.025***
	(0.166)	(0.144)	(0.143)	(0.174)	(0.154)	(0.156)
Home index growth	-0.220***	-0.222***	-0.248***	0.146***	0.151***	0.205***
	(0.0485)	(0.0420)	(0.0418)	(0.0480)	(0.0415)	(0.0412)
Invmills				-0.614***	-0.620***	-0.725***
				(0.0114)	(0.0116)	(0.0127)
Constant		6.909***	7.072***		8.623***	9.007***
		(0.0398)	(0.0470)		(0.0502)	(0.0576)

λ	0.146***		0.152***		
	(0.00930)		(0.00928)		
$\frac{1}{1-\lambda}$	1.171**		1.179***		
Moran's I (1)	0.9371***		0.9371***		
Moran's I (2)	0.06		0.06		
Observations	55,118	52,451	55,118	55,118	52,451
R-squared (within)	0.961	0.962	0.963	0.963	0.964
$Corr^2$	0.917	0.916	0.924	0.923	0.923
Number of banks	889	889	889	889	889

Notes: ***P < 0.01, **P < 0.05, *P < 0.1.

TABLE D.6 Estimation Results Using KNN: Capital Equation (Risk = RWA)

Variables	Without Correction			Heckman Correction		
	Spatial FE	FE	GMM FE	Spatial FE	FE	GMM FE
$\Delta Risk$	−0.00798***	−0.00549***	−0.00796***	−0.00726***	−0.00428***	−0.00694***
	(0.000361)	(0.000317)	(0.000373)	(0.000352)	(0.000310)	(0.000363)
Efficiency	−0.000617***	−0.000757***	−0.00140***	−0.000981***	−0.00130***	−0.00194***
	(0.000223)	(0.000159)	(0.000224)	(0.000218)	(0.000155)	(0.000218)
Cap_{t-1}	−0.942***	−0.945***	−0.943***	−0.944***	−0.948***	−0.946***
	(0.00101)	(0.000980)	(0.00104)	(0.000984)	(0.000958)	(0.00101)
Buffer	0.930***	0.933***	0.930***	0.932***	0.936***	0.934***
	(0.000991)	(0.000968)	(0.00102)	(0.000967)	(0.000945)	(0.000992)
Size	−0.00378	−0.00589**	−0.0158***	−0.0859***	−0.0868***	−0.104***
	(0.00323)	(0.00293)	(0.00334)	(0.00350)	(0.00325)	(0.00364)
ROA	0.00473**	0.00520***	0.00504***	−0.0607***	−0.0602***	−0.0694***
	(0.00192)	(0.00180)	(0.00184)	(0.00224)	(0.00215)	(0.00224)
LLP ratio	−0.0547***	−0.0551***	−0.0569***	−0.0129***	−0.0124***	−0.00839***
	(0.00216)	(0.00210)	(0.00214)	(0.00224)	(0.00221)	(0.00226)
LTD	−0.00162***	−0.00166***	−0.00151***	0.00118***	0.00112***	0.00171***
	(9.61e−05)	(9.57e−05)	(9.87e−05)	(0.000108)	(0.000107)	(0.000112)

REG	-0.413***	-0.438***	-0.463***	-0.192***	-0.221***	-0.209***
	(0.0590)	(0.0599)	(0.0605)	(0.0577)	(0.0585)	(0.0588)
Crisis	0.0449***	0.0442***	0.0399***	0.0475***	0.0472***	0.0446***
	(0.00301)	(0.00264)	(0.00268)	(0.00293)	(0.00258)	(0.00260)
$REG^{*}Cap_{t-1}$	0.0491***	0.0515***	0.0538***	0.0496***	0.0526***	0.0548***
	(0.00598)	(0.00607)	(0.00613)	(0.00583)	(0.00591)	(0.00594)
$REG^{*}\Delta Risk$	0.00164	0.00119	0.00301**	0.00235*	0.00125	0.00331**
	(0.00141)	(0.00144)	(0.00150)	(0.00138)	(0.00141)	(0.00145)
GDP growth	0.316*	0.245*	0.261*	3.547***	3.483***	4.022***
	(0.163)	(0.143)	(0.143)	(0.170)	(0.153)	(0.155)
Home index growth	-0.189***	-0.205***	-0.220***	0.162***	0.154***	0.210***
	(0.0476)	(0.0419)	(0.0418)	(0.0469)	(0.0414)	(0.0412)
Invmills				-0.599***	-0.601***	-0.693***
				(0.0113)	(0.0115)	(0.0126)
t						
Constant	6.833***	6.956***			8.512***	8.824***
	(0.0399)	(0.0471)			(0.0504)	(0.0579)
λ	0.135***			0.135***		
	(0.00849)			(0.00848)		
$\frac{1}{1-\lambda}$	1.156**			1.156***		
Moran's I (1)	0.949***			0.949***		

Continued

TABLE D.6 Estimation Results Using KNN: Capital Equation (Risk = RWA)—cont'd

Variables	Without Correction			Heckman Correction		
	Spatial FE	FE	GMM FE	Spatial FE	FE	GMM FE
Moran's I (2)	0.03			0.03		
Observations	55,118	55,118	52,451	55,118	55,118	52,451
R-squared (within)	0.961	0.961	0.962	0.963	0.963	0.964
$Corr^2$	0.918	0.918	0.917	0.924	0.924	0.924
Number of banks	889	889	889	889	889	889

Notes: ***$P < 0.01$, **$P < 0.05$, *$P < 0.1$.

TABLE D.7 Estimation Results Using KNN: Efficiency Equation (Risk = NPL)

Variables	Without Correction Spatial FE	FE	GMM FE	Heckman Correction Spatial FE	FE	GMM FE
ΔRisk	−0.0193	0.0703***	−0.334***	−0.0234	0.0887***	−0.461***
	(0.0758)	(0.0173)	(0.118)	(0.0758)	(0.0173)	(0.121)
ΔCap	−0.00383	0.125***	0.0461	−0.00301	0.108***	0.0602**
	(0.0184)	(0.0240)	(0.0284)	(0.0184)	(0.0240)	(0.0283)
Buffer	0.0325***	0.0156	−0.00219	0.0299***	−0.00897	−0.0580***
	(0.00682)	(0.00999)	(0.0102)	(0.00682)	(0.0101)	(0.0104)
Size	−6.583***	−3.437***	−4.249***	−6.835***	−4.921***	−6.114***
	(0.0854)	(0.0754)	(0.0790)	(0.0924)	(0.0890)	(0.102)
ROA	1.009***	−0.431***	−0.460***	0.847***	−1.036***	−0.817***
	(0.0503)	(0.0500)	(0.0498)	(0.0552)	(0.0607)	(0.0744)
LLP ratio	0.351***	0.619***	0.624***	0.451***	1.012***	1.101***
	(0.0469)	(0.0582)	(0.0583)	(0.0489)	(0.0618)	(0.0696)
LTD	0.0405***	−0.00145	−8.38e−05	0.0476***	0.0234***	0.00946***
	(0.00176)	(0.00258)	(0.00262)	(0.00202)	(0.00300)	(0.00336)
REG	0.330***	−0.0541	−0.0771	0.893***	1.889***	1.567***
	(0.0775)	(0.119)	(0.120)	(0.111)	(0.171)	(0.219)
Crisis	−2.442***	−1.224***	−1.585***	−2.445***	−1.572***	−2.060***
	(0.228)	(0.0732)	(0.0731)	(0.228)	(0.0723)	(0.0717)
GDP growth	3.030	49.62***	17.34***	10.95	50.78***	21.13***
	(12.82)	(3.916)	(4.202)	(12.86)	(4.315)	(5.465)
Home index growth	−28.41***	−18.56***	−17.57***	−27.72***	−14.25***	−15.67***
	(3.648)	(1.174)	(1.155)	(3.647)	(1.164)	(1.168)
Invmills				−1.488***	−5.216***	−4.495***
				(0.208)	(0.324)	(0.487)
Constant		79.02***	89.21***		103.1***	118.2***
		(0.961)	(1.005)		(1.317)	(1.640)
λ	0.797***			0.797***		
	(0.00274)			(0.00274)		
$\frac{1}{1-\lambda}$	4.926**			4.926***		
Moran's I (1)	0.995***			0.995***		
Moran's I (2)	0.003			0.004		

Continued

TABLE D.7 Estimation Results Using KNN: Efficiency Equation (Risk = NPL)—cont'd

	Without Correction			Heckman Correction		
Variables	Spatial FE	FE	GMM FE	Spatial FE	FE	GMM FE
Observations	55,118	55,118	52,451	55,118	55,118	52,451
R-squared	0.0467	0.046	0.0523	0.0468	0.066	0.0822
$Corr^2$	0.618	0.609	0.630	0.622	0.623	0.641
Number of banks	889	889	889	889	889	889

Notes: ***$P < 0.01$, **$P < 0.05$, *$P < 0.1$.

TABLE D.8 Estimation Results Using KNN: Efficiency Equation (Risk = RWA)

	Without Correction			Heckman Correction		
Variables	Spatial FE	FE	GMM FE	Spatial FE	FE	GMM FE
$\Delta Risk$	0.267**	−0.0608***	0.435***	0.265**	−0.0534***	0.416**
	(0.107)	(0.00857)	(0.164)	(0.107)	(0.00854)	(0.162)
ΔCap	0.433**	0.0314	0.753***	0.431**	0.0283	0.719***
	(0.176)	(0.0276)	(0.270)	(0.176)	(0.0275)	(0.266)
Buffer	0.0108	0.0197**	−0.0887***	0.00838	−0.00524	−0.0912***
	(0.0111)	(0.0100)	(0.0175)	(0.0111)	(0.0101)	(0.0175)
Size	−6.579***	−3.441***	−5.527***	−6.830***	−4.883***	−6.363***
	(0.0854)	(0.0754)	(0.0871)	(0.0923)	(0.0889)	(0.104)
ROA	1.072***	−0.444***	−0.260***	0.910***	−1.012***	−0.996***
	(0.0565)	(0.0500)	(0.0609)	(0.0609)	(0.0604)	(0.0644)
LLP ratio	0.522***	0.577***	1.094***	0.621***	0.951***	1.548***
	(0.0826)	(0.0584)	(0.119)	(0.0837)	(0.0620)	(0.143)
LTD	0.0264***	0.00184	−0.0365***	0.0336***	0.0249***	−0.00313
	(0.00590)	(0.00262)	(0.00919)	(0.00599)	(0.00302)	(0.00751)
REG	0.334***	−0.0536	−0.139	0.897***	1.770***	2.441***
	(0.0775)	(0.119)	(0.124)	(0.111)	(0.170)	(0.239)
Crisis	−2.439***	−1.221***	−2.103***	−2.442***	−1.570***	−2.050***
	(0.228)	(0.0731)	(0.0739)	(0.228)	(0.0722)	(0.0739)

TABLE D.8 Estimation Results Using KNN: Efficiency Equation (Risk = RWA)—cont'd

Variables	Without Correction			Heckman Correction		
	Spatial FE	FE	GMM FE	Spatial FE	FE	GMM FE
GDP growth	−5.232	50.76***	−10.57*	2.779	49.68***	27.10***
	(13.23)	(3.919)	(6.257)	(13.27)	(4.297)	(5.133)
Home index growth	−29.23***	−18.37***	−19.92***	−28.53***	−14.28***	−15.53***
	(3.663)	(1.174)	(1.263)	(3.662)	(1.164)	(1.200)
Invmills				−0.296***	−1.598***	−1.310***
				(0.0742)	(0.170)	(0.181)
Constant		78.79***	97.13***		90.95***	110.4***
		(0.961)	(1.011)		(1.275)	(1.326)
λ	0.797***			0.797***		
	(0.00274)			(0.00274)		
$\frac{1}{1-\lambda}$	4.926**			4.926***		
Moran's I (1)	0.970***			0.970***		
Moran's I (2)	0.0023			0.003		
Observations	55,118	55,118	52,451	55,118	55,118	52,451
R-squared	0.0332	0.046	0.0776	0.172	0.050	0.0818
$Carr^2$	0.618	0.610	0.630	0.621	0.623	0.641
Number of banks	889	889	889	889	889	889

Notes: ***P < 0.01, **P < 0.05, *P < 0.1.

References

Aggarwal, R., Jacques, K.T., 2001. The impact of FDICIA and prompt corrective action on bank capital and risk: estimates using a simultaneous equations model. Journal of Banking & Finance 25 (6), 1139–1160.

Ahmad, R., Ariff, M., Skully, M.J., 2008. The determinants of bank capital ratios in a developing economy. Asia-Pacific Financial Markets 15 (3–4), 255–272.

Aigner, D., Lovell, C.K., Schmidt, P., 1977. Formulation and estimation of stochastic frontier production function models. Journal of Econometrics 6 (1), 21–37.

Almanidis, P., Qian, J., Sickles, R.C., 2014. Stochastic frontier models with bounded inefficiency. In: Festschrift in honor of Peter Schmidt. Springer, pp. 47–81.

Altunbas, Y., Carbo, S., Gardener, E.P., Molyneux, P., 2007. Examining the relationships between capital, risk and efficiency in European banking. European Financial Management 13 (1), 49–70.

Altunbas, Y., Carbo Valverde, S., Molyneux, P., 2003. Ownership and performance in European and us banking—a comparison of commercial, co-operative and savings banks. Fondacion de las Cajas de Ahorros working paper, (180).

Anselin, L., 1982. A note on small sample properties of estimators in a first-order spatial autoregressive model. Environment and Planning A 14, 1023–1030.

Arellano, M., Bond, S., 1991. Some tests of specification for panel data: Monte Carlo evidence and an application to employment equations. The Review of Economic Studies 58 (2), 277–297.

Arnold, M., Stahlberg, S., Wied, D., 2013. Modeling different kinds of spatial dependence in stock returns. Empirical Economics 44, 1–14.

Asgharian, H., Hess, W., Liu, L., 2013. A spatial analysis of international stock market linkages. Journal of Banking & Finance 37 (12), 4738–4754.

Bai, J., 2003. Inferential theory for factor models of large dimensions. Econometrica 71, 135–171.

Bai, J., 2003. Inferential theory for factor models of large dimensions. Econometrica 71, 135–171.

Bai, J., 2009. Panel data models with interactive fixed effects. Econometrica 77 (4), 1229–1279.

Barth, J.R., Caprio, G., Levine, R., 2004. Bank regulation and supervision: what works best? Journal of Financial Intermediation 13 (2), 205–248.

Battese, G., Coelli, T., 1992. Frontier production functions, technical efficiency and panel data: with application to paddy farmers in India. Journal of Productivity Analysis 3 (1-2), 153–169.

BCBS, 2011. Basel iii: A global regulatory frame work for more resilient banks and banking systems. Basel Committee on Banking Supervision (BCBS).

Bech, M.L., Atalay, E., 2010. The topology of the federal funds market. Physica A: Statistical Mechanics and its Applications 389 (22), 5223–5246.

Berger, A.N., DeYoung, R., 1997. Problem loans and cost efficiency in commercial banks. Journal of Banking & Finance 21 (6), 849–870.

Berger, A.N., DeYoung, R., Flannery, M.J., Lee, D., Oztekin, O., 2008. How do large banking organizations manage their capital ratios? Journal of Financial Services Research 34 (2-3), 123–149.

Blundell, R., Bond, S., 1998. Initial conditions and moment restrictions in dynamic panel data models. Journal of Econometrics 87 (1), 115–143.

Camara, B., Lepetit, L., Tarazi, A., 2013. Ex ante capital position, changes in the different components of regulatory capital and bank risk. Applied Economics 45 (34), 4831–4856.

Cornwell, C., Schmidt, P., Sickles, R.C., 1990. Production frontiers with cross-sectional and time-series variation in efficiency levels. Journal of Econometrics 46 (1), 185–200.

Craig, B.R., Koetter, M., Kruger, U., 2014. Interbank lending and distress: observables, unobservables, and network structure. Bundesbank discussion paper no. 18/2014.

Craig, B., Von Peter, G., 2014. Interbank tiering and money center banks. Journal of Financial Intermediation 23 (3), 322–347.

Deelchand, T., Padgett, C., 2009. The relationship between risk, capital and efficiency: Evidence from Japanese cooperative banks. Capital and Efficiency: Evidence from Japanese Cooperative Banks (December 18, 2009).

Demirguc-Kunt, A., Detragiache, E., 2011. Basel core principles and bank soundness: does compliance matter? Journal of Financial Stability 7 (4), 179–190.

Denbee, E., Julliard, C., Li, Y., Yuan, K., 2017. Network risk and key players: a structural analysis of interbank liquidity. Working Paper.

De-Ramon, S., Francis, W., Harris, Q., 2016. Bank capital requirements and balance sheet management practices: has the relationship changed after the crisis? p. 635Bank of England Staff Working Paper No. 635.

Elhorst, J.P., 2003. Specification and estimation of spatial panel data models. International Regional Science Review 26 (3), 244–268.

Elhorst, J.P., 2010. Spatial panel data models. In: Fischer, M., Getis, A. (Eds.), Handbook of applied spatial analysis. Heidelberg: Springer, Berlin, pp. 377–407.

Fernandez, V., 2011. Spatial linkages in international financial markets. Quantitative Finance 11 (2), 237–245.

Fiordelisi, F., Marques-Ibanez, D., Molyneux, P., 2011. Efficiency and risk in European banking. Journal of Banking & Finance 35 (5), 1315–1326.

Frye, J., Pelz, E.A., 2008. BankCaR (Bank Capital-at-Risk): a credit risk model for US commercial bank charge-offs. Federal Reserve Bank of Chicago Working Paper 2008-03.

Furfine, C., 2003. Interbank exposures: quantifying the risk of contagion. Journal of Money, Credit, and Banking 35 (1), 111–128.

Heckman, J., 1979. Sample selection bias as a specification error. Econometrica 47 (1), 153–162.

Hughes, J.P., Lang, W., Mester, L.J., Moon, C.-G., et al., 1995. Recovering technologies that account for generalized managerial preferences: An application to non-risk-neutral banks. Wharton School Center for Financial Institutions, University of Pennsylvania.

Hughes, J.P., Mester, L.J., 2013. Who said large banks don't experience scale economies? Evidence from a risk-return-driven cost function. Journal of Financial Intermediation 22 (4), 559–585.

Jablecki, J., et al., 2009. The impact of basel i capital requirements on bank behavior and the efficacy of monetary policy. International Journal of Economic Sciences and Applied Research 2 (1), 16–35.

Jacques, K., Nigro, P., 1997. Risk-based capital, portfolio risk, and bank capital: a simultaneous equations approach. Journal of Economics and Business 49 (6), 533–547.

Kane, E.J., 1995. Three paradigms for the role of capitalization requirements in insured financial institutions. Journal of Banking & Finance 19 (3), 431–459.

Kelejian, H.H., Prucha, I.R., 1998. A generalized spatial two-stage least squares procedure for estimating a spatial autoregressive model with autoregressive disturbances. The Journal of Real Estate Finance and Economics 17 (1), 99–121.

Kneip, A., Sickles, R.C., Song, W., 2012. A new panel data treatment for heterogeneity in time trends. Econometric Theory 28 (03), 590–628.

Kumbhakar, S.C., 1990. Production frontiers, panel data, and time-varying technical inefficiency. Journal of Econometrics 46 (1), 201–211.

Kwan, S.H., Eisenbeis, R.A., 1996. An analysis of inefficiencies in banking: a stochastic cost frontier approach. Economic Review 2, 16.

Kwan, S., Eisenbeis, R.A., 1997. Bank risk, capitalization, and operating efficiency. Journal of Financial Services Research 12 (2–3), 117–131.

Lall, R., 2012. From failure to failure: the politics of international banking regulation. Review of International Political Economy 19 (4), 609–638.

Lee, L.-F., 2004. Asymptotic distributions of quasi-maximum likelihood estimators for spatial autoregressive models. Econometrica 72 (6), 1899–1925.

Lee, Y.H., Schmidt, P., 1993. A production frontier model with flexible temporal variation in technical efficiency. In: Fried, H., Lovell, C.A.K., Schmidt, S. (Eds.), The measurement of productive efficiency; techniques and applications. Oxford University Press, Oxford, pp. 237–255.

Lindquist, K.-G., 2004. Banks' buffer capital: how important is risk. Journal of International Money and Finance 23 (3), 493–513.

Liu, X., Prucha, I.R., 2018. A robust test for network generated dependence. Journal of Econometrics 207 (1), 92–113.

Meeusen, W., Van den Broeck, J., 1977. Efficiency estimation from cobb-douglas production functions with composed error. International Economic Review 18, 435–444.

Milne, A., Whalley, A.E., 2001. Bank capital regulation and incentives for risk-taking. Bank of England Working Paper 90.

Moran, P., 1950. Notes on continuous stochastic phenomena. Biometrika 37, 17–23.

Ord, K., 1975. Estimation methods for models of spatial interaction. Journal of the American Statistical Association 70 (349), 120–126.

Qu, X., Lee, L.-f., 2015. Estimating a spatial autoregressive model with an endogenous spatial weight matrix. Journal of Econometrics 184 (2), 209–232.

Rime, B., 2001. Capital requirements and bank behaviour: empirical evidence for Switzerland. Journal of Banking & Finance 25 (4), 789–805.

Roodman, D., 2009. A note on the theme of too many instruments. Oxford Bulletin of Economics and Statistics 71 (1), 135–158.

Schmidt, P., Sickles, R.C., 1984. Production frontiers and panel data. Journal of Business & Economic Statistics 2 (4), 367–374.

Sealey, C.W., Lindley, J.T., 1977. Inputs, outputs, and a theory of production and cost at depository financial institutions. The Journal of Finance 32 (4), 1251–1266.

Shrieves, R.E., Dahl, D., 1992. The relationship between risk and capital in commercial banks. Journal of Banking & Finance 16 (2), 439–457.

Stock, J.H., Yogo, M., 2002. Testing for weak instruments in linear iv regression. National Bureau of Economic Research Cambridge, Mass., USA.

Stolz, S., Heid, F., Porath, D., 2003. Does capital regulation matter for bank behavior? Evidence for German Savings Banks. EFMA 2004 Basel Meetings Paper, December.

Tan, Y., Floros, C., 2013. Risk, capital and efficiency in Chinese banking. Journal of International Financial Markets Institutions and Money 26, 378–393.

Upper, C., Worms, A., 2004. Estimating bilateral exposures in the German interbank market: is there a danger of contagion? European Economic Review 48 (4), 827–849.

Vallascas, F., Hagendorff, J., 2013. The risk sensitivity of capital requirements: evidence from an international sample of large banks. Review of Finance 17 (6), 1947–1988.

Van Roy, P., 2005. The impact of the 1988 Basel Accord on banks' capital ratios and credit risk-taking: an international study. European Center for Advanced Research in Economics and Statistics (ECARES).

Verbeek, M., 2000. A guide to modern econometrics. John Wiley & Sons, Chichester, p. 320.

Weng, Y., Gong, P., 2016. Modeling spatial and temporal dependencies among global stock markets. Expert Systems with Applications 43, 175–185.

Wheelock, D.C., Wilson, P.W., 2012. Do large banks have lower costs? New estimates of returns to scale for us banks. Journal of Money, Credit and Banking 44 (1), 171–199.

Williams, J., 2004. Determining management behaviour in European banking. Journal of Banking & Finance 28 (10), 2427–2460.

Further Reading

Haldane, A., 2009. Rethinking the financial network, April 2009. Speech Delivered at The Financial Student Association, Amsterdam.

Jondrow, J., Lovell, C.K., Materov, I.S., Schmidt, P., 1982. On the estimation of technical inefficiency in the stochastic frontier production function model. Journal of Econometrics 19 (2-3), 233–238.

Chapter 14

Panel Data in Educational Research

Geraint Johnes* and Jill Johnes[†]
*Lancaster University Management School, Lancaster University, Lancaster, United Kingdom,
[†]Huddersfield Business School, University of Huddersfield, Huddersfield, United Kingdom

Chapter Outline

1 Introduction

One sector of the economy in which considerable gains have been realized through the application of panel data methods concerns education. Indeed, given the nature of education—whose very purpose is to effect changes in the attributes of individuals as they pass through time—this is a natural context in which to apply data that are longitudinal in nature. Given the institutional arrangements that are commonly in place in the sector, it is also a context in which large scale administrative data sets, following individual pupils through time, are available (Figlio, Karbownik, & Salvanes, 2017). Meanwhile, researchers long have been aware of challenges that are posed by the nesting of pupils within classes that are themselves nested within schools and within localities. This gives models of the education system a multilevel structure often modeled in a random effects framework.

In this chapter, we will consider a number of areas in the sphere of education where panel data have been used to enhance our understanding. Our survey is intended to highlight studies that are representative of the main areas in which the literature has been developed, rather than to be encyclopedic. Much research effort in the economics of education in recent years has focused on the issue of causality, with methods such as propensity score matching, regression discontinuity design, and difference-in-difference models being at the fore (Card, 2001). Of these, the last is particularly pertinent, because it requires the use of panel data. We begin in the next section by focusing on

Panel Data Econometrics. https://doi.org/10.1016/B978-0-12-815859-3.00014-7

models drawn from the literature that has grown in recent years around the availability of administrative pupil level data; several of these studies exploit the possibilities afforded by panel data to use difference-in-difference methods. In Section 3, we examine a further group of difference-in-difference studies that have been conducted at organization level (e.g., school or university). Section 4 highlights the opportunities that panel data present to separate age effects from cohort effects. This is particularly important when investigating the impact of education on subsequent earnings, because analyses based on cross-section data, while very common in the literature, conflate these two effects. In Section 5, we examine the role played by panel data in improving our understanding of peer effects in an educational setting. This is followed, in Section 6, by consideration of a group of studies that uses longitudinal data to investigate the role played by education in explaining intergenerational socioeconomic mobility. Section 7 introduces applications of panel data analysis at a higher level, namely organization level (e.g., school or university); this section concerns the use of longitudinal data in evaluating the efficiency of educational institutions. Section 8 concerns the family of structural dynamic discrete choice models, applications of which have allowed substantial new insights to be gained about the likely effects of policy interventions on individuals' education and subsequent labor market histories. Conclusions are drawn in Section 9.

2 Pupil Level Analyses

An early review of studies that are based on pupil level data is that of Levačić and Vignoles (2002). Using the Coleman et al. (1966) report, in which the educational production function was made the cornerstone of the analysis, as a starting point, these authors identify a number of econometric problems that must be overcome, and provide a set of criteria that should be met by serious analyses of the production process in educational institutions. Given issues of endogeneity bias (where schools with poorer quality intakes might be allocated more resources) and omitted variables (leading to unobserved heterogeneity), it is highly desirable that studies should use panel data (or at least use prior attainment as a control) and that they should ideally involve some instrumentation.

The early studies in the United Kingdom took advantage of the existence of cohort data sets such as the National Child Development Study (Blundell, Dearden, & Sianesi, 2001; Dearden, Ferri, & Meghir, 1997; Dolton & Vignoles, 1999, 2000, 2002a, 2002b; Dustmann, Rajah, & van Soest, 1998, 2003; Feinstein & Symons, 1999; Harmon & Walker, 2000) or the Millennium Cohort Study (Burgess, Greaves, Vignoles, & Wilson, 2011, 2015). These allow scholastic outcomes to be modeled at the level of the individual as a function of various resources and, crucially, of previous achievement. Although these allowed new insights to be gained, the measures of past attainment generally are quite limited—typically reading and mathematics ability test scores at a base age are used. More serious application of panel data methods had to await the development of administrative data sets.

Such data arrived, in the United Kingdom, in the form of the Pupil Level Annual School Census (PLASC). The requirement for each school in England and Wales to return data that included some pupil level information was introduced in the 1996 Education Act and was extended over the next 5 years. This resulting data set, now forming the National Pupil Database and available to researchers through the UK Data Service at the University of Essex, has spawned a large amount of literature.

In their investigation of the effectiveness of strategies used by parents in choosing their children's secondary school, Allen and Burgess (2011, 2013) examine how, within each school, pupil characteristics (including prior attainment) affect outcome. Consistent with other work in the school choice literature, they find that parents' use of league tables of schools in deciding where to send their children results in considerably better outcomes than would random choice.

Allen and Vignoles (2016) use panel data from the National Pupil Database to estimate achievement functions for 16-year-old students, controlling for prior achievement and, through fixed effects at individual level, correct for unobserved heterogeneity. They look for, but fail to find, an impact on value added of the presence of Roman Catholic faith schools in the pupils' locality.

In a pair of papers, Machin, McNally, and Meghir (2004, 2010) examine the impact on pupil performance and attendance of the Excellence in Cities program, a policy intervention designed to improve outcomes in inner cities. They use panel data from the National Pupil Database with fixed effects at individual and school level in a difference-in-difference model,[1] and find a positive effect for the policy on attendance and on performance, particularly in mathematics. The Excellence in Cities program also is evaluated by Bradley and Migali (2011), using the same data set. In this case, however, they also evaluate the impact of the introduction of specialist schools. In so doing, they develop the matching and difference-in-difference approach (see Imbens & Wooldridge, 2009 for an overview) to accommodate the case in which multiple policies are being assessed simultaneously. Their findings indicate that specialist schools, in particular, have a pronounced effect on pupil performance, and that there is some measure of complementarity between the policies, such that specialist schools covered by the Excellence in Cities program are particularly effective.

---

1. A useful presentation of the difference in difference approach is offered by Ashenfelter and Card (1985). Useful references on the matching approach include Heckman, Ichimura, and Todd (1997), Rosenbaum and Rubin (1983), Rubin (1979), and Todd (2010).

The National Pupil Database also has been used in several studies to evaluate the extent to which selective secondary schools affect the change in pupil performance, controlling for pupils' attainment on entry (Andrews, Hutchinson, & Johnes, 2016; Burgess, Crawford, & Macmillan, 2017). These studies take advantage of the fact that, under current arrangements in England, selective secondary education is available only in a few localities. The studies typically find small effects, with students enrolling at selective schools achieving slightly higher value added (than similar students in a nonselective area), while those attending other schools in selective areas achieve lower gains (again, in comparison with students in a nonselective area).

A particularly neat example of the use of difference-in-difference methods, from Metcalfe, Burgess, and Proud (2011), involves an investigation of the impact of study time on academic performance. They use National Pupil Database to examine the impact on pupils' scholastic performance of participation by the England national football team in major international competitions. The final stages of the World Cup are played every 4 years, most recently in 2014, while the final stages of the European Championship are also played every 4 years, most recently in 2016. England failed to qualify for the 2008 European Championship finals. In a specification with a control for prior attainment, the authors find that performance (as measured by GCSE score) is worse in tournament years than other years, this gap being greater for boys than for girls. The performance impact of the reduced effort amounts to about 0.12 of a standard deviation.

The United States is similarly rich in national cohort data sets. For studying early childhood effects, there is the Early Childhood Longitudinal Study (ECLS). One of these, ECLS-B, follows a sample of children born in 2001 through to entry to kindergarten; another takes a sample of children entering kindergarten in 1998–99 and follows through to eighth grade; and the most recent takes a sample of children entering kindergarten in 2010–11 with the intention of following through to fifth grade. In the context of compulsory education, there is the National Education Longitudinal Study (NELS) of eighth graders in 1988, and the Educational Longitudinal Study (ELS) of tenth graders in 2002.

Buscha, Maurel, Page, and Speckesser (2012) use panel data from NELS:88 in order to investigate the possible effect on school grades of pupils working part time. They apply a combination of propensity score matching and difference-in-difference to control for differences in unobservable characteristics and find, in contrast to studies that fail to make such controls, no significant effect on reading or mathematics scores of part-time working in grade 12.

The term panel data frequently involves repeated measurement of the same observations over time. However, there are situations when (a) the observations are not the same in each time period, or (b) measurements are available only for one time period but across various dimensions (e.g., subjects). For example, the international pupil level data provided by the Program for International Student

Assessment (PISA) collects data about pupils across subjects in different time periods, but the observations in each period are different. The problem highlighted in the first scenario has been approached by constructing pseudo-panel data at organization level from the pupil data (more details on this approach can be found in Deaton, 1985 and Verbeek & Nijman, 1993), and we discuss this further in Section 3. In the case of the second scenario, the time dimension can be replaced by an alternative dimension, allowing panel data methods—fixed effects, for example—to be used even in the absence of the time dimension. An important example of this is provided by Lavy (2015), who makes use of the fact that PISA data provide information about pupils' performance across a range of different subjects in a given time period. Therefore, it is possible to replace performance at different points in the calendar with performance in different subjects in constructing a panel. Lavy uses panel data methods, including pupil fixed effects, in examining the impact of instructional time on individual test performance across subjects. His findings confirm that additional instructional time contributes to stronger performance. Although it would be desirable to have a longitudinal element to PISA data, Lavy's work is important as an example both of how panel data methods can be used on the main international data sets and of how, more generally, panel data do not necessarily have a time dimension.

3   School Level Studies

Other studies are unable to take advantage of the option of an analysis at the level of the individual student, instead employing school level data, while still using a panel of data (which, in this case, is schools across time). Examples include Bradley and Taylor (2009)—in a precursor of the Bradley and Migali (2011) paper—who find positive, albeit not huge, effects on pupil performance of various policies, including the encouragement of competition between schools, the introduction of specialist schools, and the Excellence in Cities program. Their work includes fixed effects both at school and district level. Using Australian data, Pugh, Mangan, Blackburn, and Radicic (2015) use school level data to analyze the impact of expenditures on performance, and find that an additional 1% of expenditure per pupil would lead to a 0.7% pupil improvement on the typical pupil's median score on the Australian Tertiary Admission Rank (ATAR—the main measure used for admission to undergraduate university programs).

An important group of studies by Steve Machin and co-authors (Eyles, Machin, & Silva, 2018; Machin & Vernoit, 2011) consider the impact of the academy program in England. On gaining the designation of an academy, schools gain considerable autonomy over curriculum, finance, and staffing issues; the conversion of a school to an academy also has often (but not necessarily) entailed the installation of a new leadership team. The research studies involve school-level difference-in-difference exercises, in which the conversion of existing schools into academies has been staggered over time, thus providing a clear identification strategy.[2] The findings suggest that, at least in its early years, the program was successful in improving educational outcomes.[3]

More recently, the flexibility afforded by academy status has been extended also to primary schools. Difference-in-difference methods, using the National Pupil Database, also have been used in this context, though the literature has not arrived at consistent findings, with McDool (2016) reporting positive effects, particularly at the bottom end of the ability distribution; Regan-Stansfield (2016) and Eyles, Machin, and McNally (2016), however, fail to find any overall benefit.

School cohorts offer an effective data source from which to evaluate various policy initiatives. The Teach First program in the United Kingdom, for example, has, since 2003, been allocating high-flying university graduates to schools facing various challenges such as difficulties in recruiting teachers and high teacher turnover. It is similar to programs elsewhere, such as Teach for America and Teach for All, and so can assess its effectiveness is important beyond the United Kingdom. Using a matched difference-in-difference panel estimation approach whereby 168 schools that participated in the Teach First scheme early on are matched with schools in the same region that participate at a later date, Allen and Allnutt (2017) find that there are benefits arising from the program in terms of small but significant schoolwide gains in GCSE results.

The PISA database, where (as highlighted in Section 2) the individual pupils within the database differ from one wave to the next, provides an interesting source from which to create pseudo-panel data at the school level. Pedraja-Chaparro, Santín, and Simancas (2016) create their cohort of schools by taking data for 35 randomly selected pupils in each school in each of two waves (2003 and 2009). They apply a difference-in-difference approach to investigate the effect of the concentration of immigrants in schools on grade retention, and find that higher concentrations have a negative effect on grade retention amongst immigrant pupils, but the effect on grade retention among native pupils is negative only after the concertation rises above 15%.

An alternative international pupil data base is the Trends in International Mathematics and Science Study (TIMMS) collected by the International Association for the Evaluation of Education Achievement (IEA), which reports on performance of fourth and eighth grade pupils every 4 years. De Simone (2013) uses the data from two waves of TIMMS relating to Italian pupils to form a pseudo panel in order to explore learning divides in mathematics and science and attribute them to primary and/or secondary education. It appears that the

---

2. Eyles, Hupkau, and Machin (2016a) conduct a similar exercise at pupil level.
3. Similar policy initiatives in other countries include charter schools in the United States and free schools in Sweden. Studies that evaluate these have been surveyed by Eyles, Hupkau, and Machin (2016b).

gender gap in mathematics observed at secondary level actually is rooted in primary provision. In contrast, the learning divide between students with different family backgrounds is more attributable to secondary education than primary.

Researchers also have taken advantage of country-specific pupil-level databases to create pseudo panels in order to examine specific issues. Contini and Grand (2017) use a database of Italian pupils in fifth and sixth grades to explore the same issue as in De Simone (2013). They find that inequalities in gender widen at secondary school level in reading but not in mathematics, which is in contrast to the earlier study. They find a similar result for inequalities relating to family background.

Sprietsma (2012) uses a data set of Brazilian pupils to examine the effect of the use and availability of ICT on pupil performance in Brazil. She finds that, although the use of the Internet has a positive impact on pupils' test scores, the availability of a computer lab, in contrast, is detrimental to pupils' test performance in both mathematics and reading.

Spencer, Polachek, and Strobl (2016) use pupil level data over the period 1993–2010 in 13 Caribbean countries to create average test scores by school/examination center. A difference-in-difference approach is used to identify the effect of hurricanes on test scores. Although hurricanes have a significantly negative effect on achievement when striking during the academic year, there is no effect when they strike outside of school time. There appears to be a differential effect by subject, a finding that is confirmed in the context of earthquakes in Chile (Sarmiento, 2017).

4   Cohort Analyses

A common result in the literature about labor economics, deriving from the work of Mincer (1974), is that log earnings are a function of schooling and of a polynomial term in labor market experience. Many studies based on cross-section data suggest that earnings rise as the typical worker ages, up to a point, and then fall. But cross-section data are not ideally suited to this type of analysis, because, in such data, workers differ not only in terms of their ages and experience but also in terms of the environment (for instance, the quality of schooling) during their formative years. That the earnings of workers approaching retirement appear to be lower than those of prime-age workers might reflect a cohort effect rather than an indication that a given worker can expect to see her earnings fall over time.

This issue has been studied recently by Charni and Bazen (2017), who use British Household Panel Data to separate out cohort effects from age effects. The virtue of panel data in this context is clear: The link between age (or experience) and earnings can be evaluated separately for different cohorts of workers, in essence allowing the impact of aging on members of a single cohort to be followed through over time. The authors find that earnings do not tend to decline as workers approach the end of their working lives, and that any apparent decline that emerges from the analysis of cross-section data is likely to be because a cohort effect.

Even with the benefit of panel data, however, difficulties attached to separating out age and cohort effects remain. In early contributions, Ryder (1965), Feinberg and Mason (1979), and Heckman and Robb (1985) highlighted that a third effect can be of importance in determining outcomes, namely time. The addition of an extra dimension through the use of panel data is insufficient fully to resolve what has come to be known as the age-period-cohort (APC) problem. A variety of approaches has emerged that impose some structure on this problem and allow researchers to disentangle the three effects. For example, Browning, Crawford, and Knoef (2012) show that, where the outcome variable is bounded, APC models are partially identified and point identification of the parameters can be achieved using a maximum entropy estimator.[4] They illustrate this with some empirical examples, including one in which the impact of age, period, and cohort on the labor force participation of women—a function also of education—is examined.

Some further studies partially address the APC issue using pseudo-panel data (Bhattacharya & Sato, 2017; Himaz & Aturupane, 2016; Warunsiri & McNown, 2010). These focus on age (or experience) and cohort, or age and period only.

Ultimately, the best prospect for resolution of the APC problem is to await the emergence of richer panel data that allow an additional dimension. As we have seen earlier, the dimensions in panel data are not restricted to individuals and time. A data set that included, for example, observations about individuals in different time periods and across different dimensions of activity (with testing of each individual in each period on, say, manual and mental dexterity) conceivably could be used to separate out the age, period, and cohort effects without recourse to restrictive assumptions.

5 Peer Effects

Production, in the context of education, is unusual in several respects. It typically is provided as a club benefit, with many students receiving tuition from the same teacher at the same time. This means that experience of education depends in part on spillover effects from one student to another. Analysis of such peer effects is complicated by several considerations: assignment of students into classes is rarely random; a student might not only be influenced by her peers but also influences them; and detection of any effects of this kind necessarily relies on the availability of longitudinal data that allow examination of changes in individuals' performance over time.

A particularly influential study of peer effects, notable for its reliance on random assignment of peers, is from Sacerdote (2001), who uses data about

---

4. Alternative solutions are discussed by O'Brien (2011, 2014) and Luo (2013).

room sharing among undergraduate students at Dartmouth College. Because peers' characteristics are uncorrelated with each other, this greatly simplifies the identification of the effect that one student's characteristics might have on the roommate's outcomes. The data come from the college's database of students, allowing comparison of academic performance pre- and posttreatment. During the freshman year, an increase of 1 in roommate's grade point average (GPA) results, on average, in an increase of a little more than 0.1 in a student's own GPA. This is a small, but statistically highly significant result, deemed by Sacerdote to be plausible given the highly selective nature of the institution from which the data are drawn. Other studies based on data from a single institution likewise find small positive peer effects (see, for example, Arcidiacono, Foster, Goodpaster, & Kinsler, 2012).

Causal studies typically rely on a discontinuity to establish the effect on outcomes of a change in a driving variable. An interesting such discontinuity is used by Hoxby and Weingarth (2005), who note that the school district of Wake County in North Carolina has reassigned large numbers of students among schools as a response to rapid population growth. This reassignment means that many students, apparently at random, are moved from one set of peers in the classroom to a different set. The structure of these natural experiments makes possible an analysis of nonlinear peer effects. This is important because peer effects are really interesting only when they operate nonlinearly, that is, when the move of a student from one class to another involves peer gains and losses that do not cancel each other out. Using panel data for third- through eighth-grade students from 1994–95 through 2002–03 provide data that include around 4000 students who switch schools each year. Using means of explanatory variables obtained from simulated peer groups as instrumental variables, Hoxby and Weingarth's results indicate a substantial positive peer effect in a student fixed effects model, with a student's own achievement being increased by around a quarter of a point as a consequence of a one-point improvement in the mean achievement of her classmates.[5] There are, however, substantial nonlinearities, with the impact of peer effects varying across the distribution. These imply support for two models of peer effects: the boutique model, in which students benefit most from being in a group of peers with characteristics similar to themselves, and the focus model, in which peer homogeneity is beneficial even if the student herself is not similar to her peer group. The importance of nonlinear effects also is emphasized in work by Burke and Sass (2013), who, using a 6-year panel of 3rd through 10th-grade students in Florida, also find support for the boutique and focus models.

A similar (arguably) random reallocation to peer groups occurs when students move from primary to secondary education. Gibbons and Telhaj (2016)

---

5. Instrumentation is important in analyzing peer effects because of the reflection problem (Manski, 1993), that is, if a student is influenced by her peers then so, presumably, does she influence her peers.

use data about this transition in England from the National Pupil Database, focusing on four cohorts of students and, controlling for prior attainment, investigating the effect on performance of peer group quality. They find that increases in peer group attainment are associated with a positive but small increase in a student's own achievement. In common with other work discussed above, they find nonlinear effects, with, for example, peer effects being greater for students in receipt of free school meals than for others.

A recent reform in Poland's school system, which has extended elementary schooling to 8 years and abolished middle schooling, permits an analysis of peer effects on achievement using 6 years of data (Herbst, Wójcik, & Sobotka, 2017). They find that the instability of peer group composition is detrimental to achievement in mathematics and science, and is particularly so for students at extremes of the performance spectrum.

The existence or otherwise of peer effects is clearly important in determining class composition, and this is the focus of an instructive study by Gottfried and Graves (2014). Using data from the Early Childhood Longitudinal Study (Kindergarten Class), they find interesting results about the importance of peer effects across grades, genders, and subjects. For example, although gender balance typically is conducive to good performance, gender-specific instruction might be optimal in mathematics. A related result is derived from a study that uses Teach for America data and a pseudo-panel approach (Eren, 2017). Having a higher proportion of own gender in the classroom is particularly beneficial for girls' mathematics scores; peer achievement is more important in benefitting male than female academic performance.

A pseudo-panel approach also is used by Tonello (2016) to investigate the effects of the presence of nonnative peers in the classroom on native students' performance. In the context of Italian junior high schools, the picture is mixed: although an increase in the nonnative peer group in the classroom has a detrimental effect on the language score of the native students, it has no effect on mathematics outcomes.

Most analyses of peer effects have been confined to single country studies, but Zimmer and Tona (2000) use data from a cross-national study conducted by the International Association for the Evaluation of Educational Achievement (IEA), focusing on student performance in mathematics. Twenty countries took part in the survey, and eight of these collected data about students' performance both before the start of the school year and at the end. This allows the authors to evaluate the impact on the change in performance, at individual student level, of various explanatory variables, including peer influence. Therefore, they test to examine whether individual student performance is enhanced by raising the mean performance of other students at the same school. They use a fixed effects model within each country (Zimmer & Tona, 2000, p. 82, footnote 10), though their main results are reported as a regression in which the data are pooled across countries with country fixed effects. Their findings confirm the existence of positive peer effects.

Another international study is from Ammermueller and Pischke (2009), who use Progress in International Reading Literacy Study (PIRLS) data for France, Germany, Iceland, the Netherlands, Norway, and Sweden, and who, for identification, rely on an assumption that classes within schools are formed randomly. Their data about student characteristics are not extensive, however, and no information about prior achievement is available; background is therefore proxied by the number of books at home. Because these data lack the properties of a panel, this study is not described further here.

An alternative cross-country study takes advantage of PISA (specifically the 2003 wave) and examines the effects of peer composition on educational outcomes in Japan, Finland, Germany, Italy, and the United Kingdom (Mostafa, 2010). Multilevel modeling reveals that social peer effects are positively and nonlinearly related to outcomes, but, as with the paper by Ammermueller and Pischke (2009), the analysis does not use a panel-data approach.

Although most of the literature about peer effects identifies quite small positive effects, one recent study is worth noting because it finds negative effects (Antecol, Eren, & Ozbeklik, 2016). This study uses data from the Teachers Trained Through Different Routes to Certification (TTTDRC) files produced by Mathematica; this provides a panel over the period 2004–06. The study focuses specifically on schools located in disadvantaged neighborhoods, which likely explains the unusual findings.

It is appropriate to end this section with a caveat. The widespread finding that peer effects exist and are highly nonlinear can be both intuitively appealing and compelling, but most studies find them to be small. Moreover, as Angrist (2014) has argued, truly random assignment is rare and many studies suffer from weak instruments. Nevertheless, this is a topic of policy relevance, and is one that can be addressed only using panel data.

6   Intergenerational Analysis

Another strand of work in the area of the economics of education that has exploited the availability of panel data concerns the effect that education can have on intergenerational mobility. This area has received a significant boost in recent years following the assembly of a panel of administrative data covering college students in the United States from 15 years beginning in 1999 (Chetty, Friedman, Saez, Turner, & Yagan, 2017). The data comprise all those born between 1980 and 1991 who have either a Social Security number or an individual taxpayer identification number and who can be linked to parents for whom (nonnegative) data are available from federal income tax returns. The sample comprises more than 30 million students.

Chetty et al. (2017) investigate, in particular, how patterns of intergenerational income mobility vary across the institutions of higher education attended by the younger generation. They find that access to elite institutions varies markedly by parental income, being much greater for those students whose parents are in the top quintile. Conditional on the school attended by the younger generation, however, parental income exerts little influence on children's income. Plotting success rate (the percentage of children achieving incomes in the top quintile) against access (the percentage of parents whose incomes are in the bottom quintile) for each institution of higher education is particularly revealing. The Ivy League and (to a somewhat lesser extent) public flagship schools generally perform poorly on access but well on success rate, reflecting the characteristics of their intake. Although it might be tempting to introduce measures to enhance access to such institutions, there is another group of institutions that can be characterized as having a high mobility rate, in which a relatively high proportion of students come from low quintile backgrounds but achieve high quintile outcomes. Further expanding access to these schools, including, for example, the City University of New York, and California State in Los Angeles, might be a more gainful route to enhancing intergenerational mobility.

Elsewhere, the role played by education in intergenerational mobility also has been studied by Blanden, Gregg, and Macmillan (2007). Drawing primarily on data from the British Cohort Study (BCS), a repeated series of surveys of a cohort of just more than 17,000 people born between April 5 and 11, 1970,[6] they find evidence of a strong association of incomes across generations. Regressing earnings at age 30 against parental income (averaged across measures obtained when the child was 10 and 16) provides a regression coefficient of 0.32. This is because in some measure to a large number of inherited noncognitive characteristics and to decisions made about investments in education. Controlling for a large number of such characteristics allows the authors to explain a little more than one-half of the relationship between parental income and subsequent offspring income (0.17 of the abovementioned 0.32). Comparing the results from the BCS with those from earlier data from the NCDS suggests that intergenerational persistence increased between the two cohorts; this is primarily because of an increase in the explained component, with (among other things) the expansion of higher education and the link between higher education and parental income being a major factor.[7] This finding has clear implications for social and educational policy.

Some interesting aspects of intergenerational mobility have been examined in some focused studies. Using a pseudo panel of data across 25 countries in sub-Saharan Africa, Delprato, Akyeampong, and Dunne (2017) explore the effect that the early marriage of the mother can have on children's schooling

6. They also use data from the National Child Development Study (NCDS), a similar cohort data set based on those born between March 3–9, 1958.
7. These results build on earlier work for the United Kingdom, based on the British Household Panel Study, by Nicoletti and Ermisch (2005). Although the latter use panel data, the panel is relatively short, and the information about parental income is based on recall data about parents' occupations.

outcomes. While early marriage has had a detrimental on educational outcomes, it appears that the effect might be decreasing over time. In another focused study, Huebener (2015) exploits the German Socio-Economic Panel Study data to investigate the effect of a father being risk averse has on his son's educational and income mobility. Sons with risk-averse fathers are less mobile with respect to education and income than their peers who have risk-taking fathers.

The impact of noncognitive skills on subsequent outcomes also is studied in depth by Gensowski (2014), who likewise uses data that allow her to control extensively for parental background. In this case, the data set was initiated by a Stanford University psychologist, Lewis Terman (1925), and originally was called the Genetic Studies of Genius. The study sampled children of high IQ who, in 1921, were between the ages of 8 and 15, and so (albeit to a limited extent) analysis of separate age cohorts within the group is possible. Although limited to a highly untypical group comprising only the top 0.5% of performers on intelligence test, the Terman study provides the earliest cohort study available and allows analysis during the subjects' entire working lives. Gensowski (2014) exploits the richness of these data to find considerable variation over the life cycle in the extent to which earnings respond to personality traits such as conscientiousness and extraversion, and to acquired characteristics such as education.

7 Efficiency Analysis

Educational institutions provide a wealth of data about inputs and outputs that have made this sector a particularly fertile laboratory for examining the nature of the production process. Much recent work has focused on the opportunity that such rich data present for research that opens up the black box of production (see, for example, Johnes & Taylor, 1990; Johnes, 2013; Johnes, Tsionas, & Izzeldin, 2019). In doing so, many studies have examined the efficiency with which schooling is provided, often in a context where multiple inputs are used to produce multiple outputs.

Drawing on the seminal contribution of Farrell (1957), two main approaches have been developed to analyze efficiency. Stochastic frontier analysis (Aigner, Knox Lovell, & Schmidt, 1977) is a statistical approach in which the standard assumption of a normal residual term in a regression of output against inputs is replaced, in the basic SFA model, by a composite residual made up of normal disturbances and an asymmetric component designed to capture variation in efficiency across observations. There are various extensions of the basic model. Data envelopment analysis (Charnes, Cooper, & Rhodes, 1978) uses linear programming to derive an efficiency frontier, and measures the efficiency of decision-making units in relation to that frontier. It is a nonparametric method that allows input and output weights to vary across decision-making units in a manner that, subject to some constraints, maximizes the efficiency score for each unit. As with SFA, there are various extensions of the basic DEA model.

Panel data about education have come to be widely used in applications of both stochastic frontier analysis (SFA) and data envelopment analysis (DEA). Extensive surveys of the applications of these methods in education have been published by De Witte and López-Torres (2017) and by Thanassoulis et al. (2016); the survey of operational research applications in education by Johnes (2015) also covers relevant material. Because of these surveys, this section is concise and focuses solely on applications that involve the use of panel data.

A suite of papers uses panel data drawn from a variety of countries to estimate parametric cost frontiers in higher education—see Johnes and Salas-Velasco (2007) for Spain; Johnes, Camanho, and Portela (2008) for Portugal; Johnes, Camanho, et al. (2008), Johnes, Johnes, et al. (2008), and Johnes and Johnes (2009) for England; Johnes and Schwarzenberger (2011) for Germany; Agasisti and Johnes (2015) for the United States. These studies all draw on the insights of Baumol, Panzar, and Willig (1982), as well as some earlier work on panel-cost frontiers (Johnes, Johnes, Thanassoulis, Lenton, & Emrouznejad, 2005; Stevens, 2005) to estimate costs using a functional form that appropriately captures the multiproduct nature of production in this sector, and therefore can allow subsequent analysis of returns to scale and scope. In each case, the studies use a stochastic frontier formulation with random parameters at institution level. In the simplest case, a random parameter on the intercept term is tantamount to a random effects model, and allows for unobserved heterogeneity (in the inefficiency component) across institutions in the standard way. Many of these studies, however, extend the random parameters beyond the intercept, allowing variation across institutions also in the slope terms. This brings the parametric stochastic frontier approach much closer to the nonparametric approach of data envelopment analysis, in which each institution has a distinct set of input and output weights.

The latent class stochastic frontier iis another panel data method that has been used to accommodate unobserved heterogeneity in this context. Here, rather than allowing the parameters of the cost function to differ across all institutions, the institutions are divided into two (or more) groups—the latent classes—and separate parameters are estimated for each class. The allocation of institutions into one class or the other is determined, alongside the parameter values, by maximizing the likelihood function. This approach is used by Agasisti and Johnes (2015). Parenthetically, we note that a particularly appealing feature of the latent-class approach is that it can be used to allow for unobserved heterogeneity even when the data are cross-section rather than panel in nature—see, for example, Johnes and Johnes (2013, 2016).

Typically, these studies have found that instruction is costlier to deliver in laboratory-based subjects than in classroom-based subjects, and that costs rise with the level of qualification. In many cases, product-specific returns to scale are unexhausted, suggesting that some reallocation of activity across institutions within the sector could lead to economies. The evidence about economies of scope is more mixed. Frontier estimation often results in an estimate of the fixed costs parameter (intercept) that is low relative to that obtained by least squares regression, and this erodes the cost saving associated with joint production of several outputs.

SFA also has been applied in the production context, although in the issue of multiple inputs and multiple outputs requires various assumptions to be overcome. Johnes (2014) assumes a translog production function with homogeneity in outputs to estimate a production function with multiple inputs and outputs. A random effects SFA model reveals interesting differences in average efficiencies between merging and nonmerging universities.

Johnes and Soo (2017) have a single output production model, but use the true random effects variant of the stochastic frontier model to evaluate grade inflation over time in UK universities. Each university in each year from 2004 through 2012 represents a data point, with the dependent variable—proportion of good degrees awarded—modeled as a function of entry qualifications, a variety of resource variables, and time dummies. They find little evidence of grade inflation at the boundary between upper and lower second-class degrees; they do, however, find, other things being equal, an increase in the proportion of first-class degrees awarded. This paper builds on the earlier work of Johnes (2004).

An important recent development in the application of stochastic frontier methods to panel data is from Tsionas and Kumbhakar (2014). This exploits the presence of data over an extended period to allow the asymmetric residual measuring inefficiency to be separated into two components, respectively reflecting persistent (relating to long-term or structural issues) and transient (relating to short-term fluctuations) inefficiency. Several recent contributions in the education sphere include Papadimitrou and Johnes (2016) and Gralka (2016). In the former study, inefficiency in English universities is found to be more a consequence of structural problems rather than short-term issues. This suggests that only by addressing, for example, deep-rooted management practices or government regulations can improvements in efficiency be seen.

The nonparametric method of DEA also has allowed use of panel data. In particular, the availability of longitudinal data allows change in the relative efficiency of decision-making units over time to be analyzed. The Malmquist (1953) index, further developed by Caves, Christensen, and Erwin Diewert (1982) and popularized by Färe, Grosskopf, Norris, and Zhang (1994), is the tool of choice, and has been used in many studies of efficiency in education including: in the context of universities, Flegg, Allen, Field, and Thurlow (2004); Worthington and Lee (2008); Johnes (2008); Johnes, Johnes, and

Thanassoulis (2008); Ng and Li (2009); Rayeni and Saljooghi (2010); Margaritis and Smart (2011); Thanassoulis, Kortelainen, Johnes, and Johnes (2011); Barra and Zotti (2013); García-Aracil (2013); in the context of post-compulsory schooling, Bradley, Johnes, and Little (2010); and, in the context of schools, Ouellette and Vierstraete (2010); Essid, Ouellette, and Vigeant (2014). In essence this allows the efficiency of each decision-making unit to be evaluated within each period using standard DEA methods, and then changes in both the efficiency frontier and in the relative position of each unit over time can be assessed. As might be expected owing both to technological change and learning about how best to manage organizations, these studies typically find that productivity rises over time, often in terms of the location of the production frontier rather than in terms of a reduced dispersion in performance across units, although there are exceptions where the productivity growth is more a conse-quence of efficiency rather than technology improvements (García-Aracil, 2013; Rayeni & Saljooghi, 2010).

Education has provided the backdrop against which the Malmquist index has been extended to measure both differentials in performance between groups and in identifying the evolutionary patterns of change in these differ-entials over time. In particular, the application of the Malmquist approach applied in the context of cross-section data to compare DMUs over two (or more) groupings rather than over two (or more) time periods (Camanho & Dyson, 2006) is extended to a panel data setting. Aparicio, Crespo-Cebada, Pedraja-Chaparro, and Santín (2017) use this extended Malmquist to compare public and private government-dependent secondary schools in the Basque country using four waves of PISA data to form pseudo panels. They find that privately run schools are persistently better in terms of performance because of technological superiority. de la Torre et al. (2017) use the same approach to compare public and private universities in Spain during the period 2009–10 to 2013–14. In this case, private universities out-perform public universities at the start of the period, but the Malmquist decomposition applied to groups within panel data reveals that public univer-sities catch up over the period.

In a study of Ohio school districts that also applies the Malmquist approach to groups (the five groups are graded by the harshness of their environment) over time, Johnson and Ruggiero (2014) find that environmental harshness largely explains growth in productivity. Furthermore, although all schools expe-rience technological progress, environmental harshness appears to hinder the technological progress of schools operating in the poorest environments relative to those at the other end of the spectrum. Clearly, this extended Malmquist decomposition provides insights with policy relevance.

Although much of the efficiency work in the context of panel data examines performance of organizations (such as schools or universities) within a country over time, some rare studies look at performance across countries over time. Such international comparisons have the advantage that lessons in efficiency (good practice) can be learned across nations. A caveat of these studies, however, relates to whether the data definitions and production conditions are comparable across countries. With this caveat in mind, two studies use the Malmquist approach to make international comparisons in productivity. The first of these studies (Agasisti & Pérez-Esparells, 2010) uses university-level data in Italy and Spain over two time periods to find rising productivity. Closer inspection reveals that technological progress is the dominant force for increasing productivity in Italy; while it is efficiency changes in Spain. The analysis also uncovers in both countries some interesting regional differences that are of policy relevance. The second study (Agasisti, 2014) is particularly novel because the level of analysis is country. In a comparison of national expenditure on schooling in 20 countries, data from PISA highlight the most efficient countries (Switzerland and Finland) and least efficient countries (Spain and Portugal). Much more work needs to be undertaken in this context to ensure comparisons are valid and policy recommendations are meaningful.

8 Dynamic Discrete Choice Models

The decisions that people make about education are inherently dynamic in nature. Investment in education, often viewed from a human capital perspective, involves sacrificing earnings opportunities in one period in order to enhance productive potential for the future. As students study, they acquire new information about their ability to learn, and so there is a stochastic element to their investment decision. Likewise, as they progress from education into the labor market, they are faced with new information about the extent of their productivity in whatever occupations they pursue. The stochastic and dynamic features of this process have been captured in a family of structural dynamic discrete choice models. These have been usefully surveyed by Aguirregabiria and Mira (2010), and, specifically in the context of education and labor markets, by Keane and Wolpin (2009) and Keane (2010).

A particularly interesting early attempt to apply such models in the context of education and the labor market is from Keane and Wolpin (1994, 1997). These authors set up a problem in which each individual is able to choose between several actions in each period of their life. They can undertake skilled work, unskilled work, work in the military, study, or remain at home. In any period in which they work, their return to employment depends on the human capital that they have acquired up to that period, and so is influenced by their past education and their past experience of work in each sector. But their decision in any given period depends also upon the impact that that decision will have on expected returns to any and all possible subsequent career paths. This means that the state space that needs to be considered in this type of problem is huge. Keane and Wolpin develop an approximation method that reduces the computational burden associated with this problem.

In the context of a dynamic optimization problem solved by backward recursion—solving for the choice of outcome in the final period first—maximizing behavior in the penultimate (and earlier) periods requires evaluation of the outcomes associated with all possible subsequent career paths. This is approximated by using a small sample of points in the state space to fit a curve that then is used to provide an estimated value for the outcomes at all other points.

Keane and Wolpin subsequently fit their model to panel data from the National Longitudinal Survey of Youth, and find that it performs well as long as it incorporates nonpecuniary element of returns to each occupation, mobility costs across outcomes, depreciation of skills during periods of inactivity, and some initial heterogeneity across respondents. Of particular relevance in the context of education is the finding that schooling raises the probability of more favorable occupational outcomes. Moreover, the authors find that the provision of tuition subsidies increases participation in education, particularly for respondent types who are initially relatively unlikely to attend higher education, but that a high proportion of the cost of such subsidy is dead weight because it supports largely respondents who would have attended higher education anyway.

Other papers that employ this type of approximation include further analysis of the interface between education and occupational destination (Altonji, Blom, & Meghir, 2012), examination of the labor market for teachers, in which policies for reducing attrition are assessed (Stinebrickner, 1998, 2000, 2001a, 2001b), and analyses of education and labor markets in India and Brazil (Aggarwal, Johnes, Freguglia, & Spricigo, 2013; Johnes, Aggarwal, Freguglia, & Spricigo, 2016).

As Keane (2010) has noted, the rate of adoption by researchers of models of this kind has not been high. This is largely because the code needed to estimate such models is highly specific to the particular structural model, with even very minor changes to the model requiring substantial changes in programming. Under certain conditions, however, a shortcut from Hotz and Miller (1993), and refined further in Hotz, Miller, Sanders, and Smith (1994), can be used. The central insight is that, given information that often is available to the analyst in this context, conditional choice probabilities (CCP) can be evaluated and inferences drawn about the shape of the value function, thus obviating the need to use dynamic programming methods to evaluate that function. Indeed, use of what has come to be known as the Hotz-Miller inversion allows dynamic discrete choice models to be estimated using a two-step method that can be implemented using just a few lines of code in standard statistical software packages such as Stata. The first step involves nonparametric estimation of a model that explains the CCPs; the Hotz-Miller inversion straightforwardly allows the predictions of this model to be mapped into estimates of the value function. The second step uses these estimates to evaluate the parameters of the dynamic discrete choice model.

In the specific context of education, the Hotz-Miller inversion has been used by Declercq (2016) to investigate outcomes in each year of study for higher education students. The dynamic discrete choice model used here is one in which the outcome for students is modeled as a function of their gender, age, high school background, and study choices. The model is effective in predicting which students succeed in progressing from year to year and which drop out. His data follow a cohort of more than 50,000 Flemish students who enter higher education after graduating from high school in 2005. A particularly interesting feature of the higher education system in Flanders is that institutions of higher education cannot set their own admission standards. A consequence is that there is a high rate of attrition at the end of students' first year, with many moving from challenging courses at universities to less-challenging options in colleges.

Dynamic discrete choice models of this kind often are used to simulate the impact of policy changes that are not observed in the data. Declercq (2016) uses his findings to evaluate the likely effects of introducing a variety of policies. These include ex post selection (whereby students are excluded from their studies if they fail to meet a threshold level of performance) and the award of subsidies to high-performing students. The former policy reduces costs, but discourages potentially successful students from enrolling in higher education; the second policy encourages both enrolment and progression. A combination of both policies can improve outcomes while remaining fiscally neutral. This paper thus provides a fine example of the way in which dynamic discrete choice models, the parameters of which are estimated using panel data, can be used in a policy context.

9 Conclusions

Further advances in the use of panel data are likely in the near future as opportunities to link data sets increase. In particular, linking panel data about individuals with data about educational institutions and workplaces offers researchers the prospect of analyzing complete work histories with data on both sides of the labor market. In the United Kingdom, for example, further opportunities to conduct sophisticated analyses in the sphere of education come from the recent linking of the higher education student loan book data to Her Majesty's Revenue and Customs (HMRC) data on income tax records (Britton, Dearden, Shephard, & Vignoles, 2016) and also from the new Longitudinal Educational Outcomes (LEO) data set. The latter links, at the level of the individual, data about primary and secondary school career (from the National Pupil Database), university (from the Higher Education Statistics Agency), or further education (from the Individualised Learner Record), and subsequently on employment (from HMRC) and welfare payments (from the Department for Work and Pensions). These data became available to researchers in December 2016; an early study to make use of this resource is that of Hupkau, McNally, Ruiz-Valenzuela, and Ventura (2017).

The coverage of this chapter has necessarily been selective, but it is representative of the broader range of studies that have made use of panel data in the sphere of education. The number of pupil-level analyses have increased considerably since rich data have become available, and these have allowed insights to be gained into what works in education. At the same time, the availability of big data has allowed us to learn much about the dynamics of social change. And, at the institutional level, our understanding of the educational production function has been enhanced by studying producers as networks.

The very nature of education is one in which people undergo change; they acquire human capital that equips them to become more productive, but this acquisition itself takes time and resources. Intervention in the form of schooling quintessentially brings about a change in states. This being so, there is no area of study for which the use of panel data is more appropriate.

References

Agasisti, T., 2014. The efficiency of public spending on education: an empirical comparison of EU countries. European Journal of Education 49, 543–557.

Agasisti, T., Johnes, G., 2015. Efficiency, costs, rankings and heterogeneity: the case of US higher education. Studies in Higher Education 40, 60–82.

Agasisti, T., Pérez-Esparells, C., 2010. Comparing efficiency in a cross-country perspective: the case of Italian and Spanish state universities. Higher Education 59, 85–103.

Aggarwal, A., Johnes, G., Freguglia, R., Spricigo, G., 2013. Education and labour market outcomes; evidence from India. The Indian Journal of Labour Economics 56, 331–347.

Aguirregabiria, V., Mira, P., 2010. Dynamic discrete choice structural models: a survey. Journal of Econometrics 156, 38–67.

Aigner, D., Knox Lovell, C.A., Schmidt, P., 1977. Formulation and estimation of stochastic frontier production function models. Journal of Econometrics 6, 21–37.

Allen, R., Allnutt, J., 2017. The impact of Teach First on pupil attainment at age 16. British Educational Research Journal 43 (4), 627–646.

Allen, R., Burgess, S., 2011. Can school league tables help parents choose schools. Fiscal Studies 32, 245–261.

Allen, R., Burgess, S., 2013. Evaluating the provision of school performance information for school choice. Economics of Education Review 34, 175–190.

Allen, R., Vignoles, A., 2016. Can school competition improve standards? The case of faith schools in England. Empirical Economics 50, 959–973.

Altonji, J.G., Blom, E., Meghir, C., 2012. Heterogeneity in human capital investments: high school curriculum, college major and careers. Annual Review of Economics 4, 185–223.

Ammermueller, A., Pischke, J.-S., 2009. Peer effects in European primary schools: evidence from the Progress in International Reading Literacy Study. Journal of Labor Economics 27, 315–348.

Andrews, J., Hutchinson, J., Johnes, R., 2016. Grammar schools and social mobility. Education Policy Institute, London. https://epi.org.uk/wp-content/uploads/2016/09/Grammar-schools-and-social-mobility_.pdf. (Accessed 7 June 2017).

Angrist, J.D., 2014. The perils of peer effects. Labour Economics 30, 98–108.

Antecol, H., Eren, O., Ozbeklik, S., 2016. Peer effects in disadvantaged primary schools. Journal of Human Resources 51, 95–132.

Aparicio, J., Crespo-Cebada, E., Pedraja-Chaparro, F., Santín, D., 2017. Comparing school ownership performance using a pseudo-panel database: a Malmquist-type index approach. European Journal of Operational Research 256 (2), 533–542.

Arcidiacono, P., Foster, G., Goodpaster, N., Kinsler, J., 2012. Estimating spillovers using panel data, with an application to the classroom. Quantitative Economics 3, 421–470.

Ashenfelter, O., Card, D., 1985. Using the longitudinal structure of earnings to estimate the effect of training programs. Review of Economics and Statistics 67, 648–660.

Barra, C., Zotti, R., 2013. Measuring teaching and research efficiency in higher education using data envelopment analysis. A case study from the University of Salerno. University of Salerno CELPE, Interdepartmental Centre for Research in Labour Economics and Economic Policy. Working Papers Number 3/2013, https://www.academia.edu/4905831/Measuring_teaching_ and_research_efficiency_in_higher_education_using_data_envelopment_analysis._A_case_ study_from_the_University_of_Salerno. (Accessed 1 December 2018).

Baumol, W., Panzar, J.C., Willig, R.D., 1982. Contestable markets and the theory of industry structure. Harcourt Brace Jovanovich, San Diego.

Bhattacharya, P., Sato, T., 2017. Estimating regional returns to education in India: a fresh look with pseudo-panel data. Progress in Development Studies 17, 282–290.

Blanden, J., Gregg, P., Macmillan, L., 2007. Accounting for intergenerational income persistence: noncognitive skills, ability and education. Economic Journal 117, C43–C60.

Blundell, R., Dearden, L., Sianesi, B., 2001. Estimating the returns to education: Models, methods and results. Discussion Paper no 16, Centre for the Economics of Education, LSE, London.

Bradley, S., Johnes, J., Little, A., 2010. The measurement and determinants of efficiency and productivity in the further education sector in England. Bulletin of Economic Research 62, 1–30.

Bradley, S., Migali, G., 2011. The joint evaluation of multiple educational policies: the case of specialist schools and excellence in cities policies in Britain. Education Economics 20, 322–342.

Bradley, S., Taylor, J., 2009. Diversity, choice and the quasi-market: an empirical analysis of secondary education policy in England. Oxford Bulletin of Economics and Statistics 72, 1–26.

Britton, J., Dearden, L., Shephard, N., Vignoles, A., 2016. How English domiciled graduate earnings vary with gender, institution attended, subject and socioeconomic background. Institute for Fiscal Studies Working Paper W16/06. http://wonkhe.com/wp-content/uploads/2016/04/ Graduate-earnings-IFS.pdf. (Accessed 22 June 2017).

Browning, M., Crawford, I., Knoef, M., 2012. The age-period-cohort problem: Set identification and point identification. CENMAP Working Paper CWP02/12. https://www.econstor.eu/bitstream/ 10419/64757/1/68481806X.pdf. (Accessed 20 June 2017).

Burgess, S., Crawford, C., Macmillan, L., 2017. Assessing the role of grammar schools in promoting social mobility. University College London. Department of Quantitative Social Science Discussion Paper 17-09. http://repec.ioe.ac.uk/REPEc/pdf/qsswp1709.pdf. (Accessed 7 June 2017).

Burgess, S., Greaves, E., Vignoles, A., Wilson, D., 2011. Parental choice of primary school in England: what types of school do different types of family really have available to them? Policy Studies 32, 531–547.

Burgess, S., Greaves, E., Vignoles, A., Wilson, D., 2015. What parents want: school preferences and school choice. Economic Journal 125, 1262–1289.

Burke, M.A., Sass, T.R., 2013. Classroom peer effects and student achievement. Journal of Labor Economics 31 (1), 51–82.

Buscha, F., Maurel, A., Page, L., Speckesser, S., 2012. Effect of employment while in high school on educational attainment: a conditional difference-in-differences approach. Oxford Bulletin of Economics and Statistics 74 (3), 380–396.

Camanho, A.S., Dyson, R.G., 2006. Data envelopment analysis and Malmquist indices for measuring group performance. Journal of Productivity Analysis 26, 35–49.

Card, D., 2001. Estimating the return to schooling: progress on some persistent econometric problems. Econometrica 69, 1127–1160.

Caves, D.W., Christensen, L.R., Erwin Diewert, W., 1982. The economic theory of index numbers and the measurement of input, output and productivity. Econometrica 50, 1393–1414.

Charnes, A., Cooper, W.W., Rhodes, E., 1978. Measuring the efficiency of decision making units. European Journal of Operational Research 2, 429–444.

Charni, K., Bazen, S., 2017. Do earnings really decline for older workers? International Journal of Manpower 38, 4–24.

Chetty, R., Friedman, J.N., Saez, E., Turner, N., Yagan, D., 2017. Mobility report cards: The role of colleges in intergenerational mobility. http://www.equality-of-opportunity.org/papers/coll_mrc_paper.pdf. (Accessed 7 June 2017).

Coleman, J.S., Campbell, E., Hobson, C., McPartland, J., Mood, A., Weinfeld, F., et al., 1966. The 'Coleman Report': Equality of educational opportunity. US Office of Education, Washington, DC.

Contini, D., Grand, E., 2017. On estimating achievement dynamic models from repeated cross sections. Sociological Methods & Research 46 (4), 988–1017.

de la Torre, E.M., et al., 2017. Comparing university performance by legal status: a Malmquist-type index approach for the case of the Spanish higher education system. Tertiary Education and Management 23 (3), 206.

De Simone, G., 2013. Render unto primary the things which are primary's: inherited and fresh learning divides in Italian lower secondary education. Economics of Education Review 35, 12–23.

De Witte, K., López-Torres, L., 2017. Efficiency in education: a review of the literature and a way forward. Journal of the Operational Research Society 68, 339–363.

Dearden, L., Ferri, J., Meghir, C., 1997. The effects of school quality on educational attainment and wages. Review of Economics and Statistics 84, 1–20.

Deaton, A., 1985. Panel data from time series of cross-sections. Journal of Econometrics 30 (1), 109–126.

Declercq, K., 2016. Study progression in higher education: The impact of ex post selection. Mimeo, KU Leuven. http://bit.ly/2qV0Vqx. (Accessed 24 May 2017).

Delprato, M., Akyeampong, K., Dunne, M., 2017. Intergenerational education effects of early marriage in Sub-Saharan Africa. World Development 91, 173–192.

Dolton, P., Vignoles, A., 1999. The impact of school quality on labour market success in the UK. University of Newcastle Discussion Paper.

Dolton, P., Vignoles, A., 2000. The effects of school quality on pupil outcomes: an overview. In: Heijke, H. (Ed.), Education, training and employment in the knowledge-based economy. Macmillan, Basingstoke .

Dolton, P., Vignoles, A., 2002a. Is a broader curriculum better? Economics of Education Review 21, 415–429.

Dolton, P., Vignoles, A., 2002b. The return on post-compulsory school mathematics study. Economica 69, 113–141.

Dustmann, C., Rajah, N., van Soest, A., 1998. School quality, exam performance and career choice. https://pure.uvt.nl/portal/files/528739/16.pdf. (Accessed 6 June 2017) .

Dustmann, C., Rajah, N., van Soest, A., 2003. Class size, education and wages. Economic Journal 113, F99–F120.

Eren, O., 2017. Differential peer effects, student achievement, and student absenteeism: evidence from a large-scale randomized experiment. Demography 54 (2), 745–773.

Essid, H., Ouellette, P., Vigeant, S., 2014. Productivity, efficiency, and technical change of Tunisian schools: a bootstrapped Malmquist approach with quasi-fixed inputs. Omega 42 (1), 88–97.

Eyles, A., Hupkau, C., Machin, S., 2016a. School reforms and pupil performance. Labour Economics 41, 9–19.

Eyles, A., Hupkau, C., Machin, S., 2016b. Academies, charter and free schools: do new school types deliver better outcomes. Economic Policy 31, 453–501.

Eyles, A., Machin, S., McNally, S., 2016. Unexpected school reform: Academisation of primary schools in England. London School of Economics Centre for Economic Performance Discussion Paper 1455, http://cep.lse.ac.uk/pubs/download/dp1455.pdf. (Accessed 7 June 2017).

Eyles, A., Machin, S., Silva, O., 2018. Academies 2: the new batch—the changing nature of academy schools in England. Fiscal Studies 39, 121–158.

Färe, R., Grosskopf, S., Norris, M., Zhang, Z., 1994. Productivity growth, technical progress, and efficiency change in industrialized countries. American Economic Review 84, 66–83.

Farrell, M.J., 1957. The measurement of productive efficiency. Journal of the Royal Statistical Society A 120, 253–290.

Feinberg, S.E., Mason, W.M., 1979. Identification and estimation of age-period-cohort models in the analysis of discrete archival data. Sociological Methodology 10, 1–67.

Feinstein, L., Symons, J., 1999. Attainment in secondary school. Oxford Economic Papers 51, 300–321.

Figlio, D., Karbownik, K., Salvanes, K., 2017. The promise of administrative data in education research. Education Finance and Policy 12, 129–136.

Flegg, T., Allen, D., Field, K., Thurlow, T.W., 2004. Measuring the efficiency of British universities: a multi-period data envelopment analysis. Education Economics 12 (3), 231–249.

García-Aracil, A., 2013. Understanding productivity changes in public universities: evidence from Spain. Research Evaluation 22 (5), 351–368.

Gensowski, M., 2014. Personality, IQ and lifetime earnings. IZA Discussion Paper 8235, https://papers.ssrn.com/sol3/Delivery.cfm/dp8235.pdf?abstractid=2450426&mirid=1&type=2. (Accessed 20 June 2017).

Gibbons, S., Telhaj, S., 2016. Peer effects: evidence from secondary school transition in England. Oxford Bulletin of Economics and Statistics 78, 548–575.

Gottfried, M.A., Graves, J., 2014. Peer effects and policy: the relationship between classroom gender composition and student achievement in early elementary school. Journal of Economic Analysis & Policy 14, 937–977(Berkeley Electronic).

Gralka, S., 2016. Persistent effects in the efficiency of the higher education sector. http://www.qucosa.de/fileadmin/data/qucosa/documents/21129/CEPIE_WP_06_16-1.pdf. (Accessed 31 May 2017)

Harmon, C., Walker, I., 2000. The returns to the quantity and quality of education: evidence for men in England and Wales. Economica 67, 19–35.

Heckman, J., Ichimura, H., Todd, P., 1997. Matching as an econometric evaluation estimator: evidence from evaluating a job training program. Review of Economic Studies 64, 605–654.

Heckman, J., Robb, R., 1985. Using longitudinal data to estimate age, period and cohort effects in earnings equations. In: Mason, W.M., Feinberg, S.E. (Eds.), Cohort analysis in social research: Beyond the identification problem. Springer-Verlag, New York .

Herbst, M., Wójcik, P., Sobotka, A., 2017. The effect of peer group stability on student achievement in the context of school grade configuration: Evidence from Poland. University of Warsaw, Educational Research Institute.

Himaz, R., Aturupane, H., 2016. Returns to education in Sri Lanka: a pseudo-panel approach. Education Economics 24, 300–311.

Hotz, V.J., Miller, R.A., 1993. Conditional choice probabilities and the estimation of dynamic models. Review of Economic Studies 60, 497–529.

Hotz, V.J., Miller, R.A., Sanders, S., Smith, J., 1994. A simulation estimator for dynamic models of discrete choice. Review of Economic Studies 61, 265–289.

Hoxby, C.M., Weingarth, G., 2005. Taking race out of the equation: School reassignment and the structure of peer effects. https://www.pausd.org/sites/default/files/pdf-faqs/attachments/TakingRaceOutOfTheEquation.pdf. (Accessed 9 June 2017).

Huebener, M., 2015. The role of paternal risk attitudes in long-run education outcomes and intergenerational mobility. Economics of Education Review 47 (August), 64–79.

Hupkau, C., McNally, S., Ruiz-Valenzuela, J., Ventura, G., 2017. Post-compulsory education in England: choices and implications. National Institute Economic Review 240, R42–R57.

Imbens, G.W., Wooldridge, J.M., 2009. Recent developments in the econometrics of program evaluation. Journal of Economic Literature 47 (1), 5–86.

Johnes, G., 2004. Standards and grade inflation. In: Johnes, G., Johnes, J. (Eds.), International Handbook on the Economics of Education. Edward Elgar, Cheltenham, pp. 462–483.

Johnes, G., 2013. Efficiency in English higher education institutions revisited: a network approach. Economics Bulletin 33 (4), 2698–2706.

Johnes, J., 2008. Efficiency and productivity change in the English higher education sector from 1996/97 to 2004/5. The Manchester School 76, 653–674.

Johnes, J., 2014. Efficiency and mergers in English higher education 1996/97 to 2008/9: parametric and non-parametric estimation of the multi-input multi-output distance function. The Manchester School 82 (4), 465–487.

Johnes, J., 2015. Operational research in education. European Journal of Operational Research 243, 683–696.

Johnes, G., Aggarwal, A., Freguglia, R., Spricigo, G., 2016. Education and occupational outcomes: evidence from Brazil. International Journal of Manpower 37, 1304–1321.

Johnes, G., Camanho, A.S., Portela, M.S., 2008. Assessing efficiency of Portuguese universities through parametric and non-parametric methods. Portuguese Journal of Management Studies 13 (1), 39–66.

Johnes, G., Johnes, J., 2009. Higher education institutions' costs and efficiency: taking the decomposition a further step. Economics of Education Review 28, 107–113.

Johnes, J., Johnes, G., 2013. Efficiency in the higher education sector: A technical exploration. Department for Business Innovation and Skills, London.

Johnes, G., Johnes, J., 2016. Costs, efficiency and economies of scale and scope in the English higher education sector. Oxford Review of Economic Policy 32, 596–614.

Johnes, G., Johnes, J., Thanassoulis, E., 2008. An analysis of costs in institutions of higher education in England. Studies in Higher Education 33 (5), 527–549.

Johnes, G., Johnes, J., Thanassoulis, E., Lenton, P., Emrouznejad, A., 2005. An exploratory analysis of the cost structure of Higher Education in England. Department for Education and Skills, London, p. 641. Research Report.

Johnes, G., Salas-Velasco, M., 2007. The determinants of costs and efficiencies where producers are heterogeneous: the case of Spanish universities. Economics Bulletin 4 (15), 1–9.

Johnes, G., Schwarzenberger, A., 2011. Differences in cost structure and the evaluation of efficiency: the case of German universities. Education Economics 19, 487–500.

Johnes, G., Soo, K.T., 2017. Grades across universities over time. The Manchester School 85, 106–131.

Johnes, J., Taylor, J., 1990. Performance indicators in higher education. Society for Research into Higher Education and Open University Press, Buckingham.

Johnes, G., Tsionas, M., Izzeldin, M., 2019. Network stochastic frontier analysis. Mimeo.

Johnson, A.L., Ruggiero, J., 2014. Nonparametric measurement of productivity and efficiency in education. Annals of Operations Research 221, 197–210.

Keane, M.P., 2010. Structural v atheoretic approaches to econometrics. Journal of Econometrics 156, 3–20.

Keane, M.P., Wolpin, K.I., 1994. The solution and estimation of discrete choice dynamic programming models by simulation and interpolation: Monte Carlo evidence. Review of Economics and Statistics 76, 648–672.

Keane, M.P., Wolpin, K.I., 1997. The career decisions of young men. Journal of Political Economy 105, 473–522.

Keane, M.P., Wolpin, K.I., 2009. Empirical application of discrete choice dynamic programming models. Review of Economic Dynamics 12, 1–22.

Lavy, V., 2015. Do differences in schools' instruction time explain international achievement gaps? Evidence from developed and developing countries. Economic Journal 125, F397–F424.

Levačić, R., Vignoles, A., 2002. Researching the links between school resources and student outcomes in the UK: a review of issues and evidence. Education Economics 10, 313–331.

Luo, L., 2013. Assessing validity and application scope of the intrinsic estimator approach to the age-period-cohort problem. Demography 50, 1945–1967.

Machin, S., McNally, S., Meghir, C., 2004. Improving pupil performance in English secondary schools: excellence in cities. Journal of the European Economic Association 2, 396–405.

Machin, S., McNally, S., Meghir, C., 2010. Resources and standards in urban schools. Journal of Human Capital 4, 365–393.

Machin, S., Vernoit, J., 2011. Changing school autonomy: Academy schools and their introduction to England's education. London School of Economics Centre for the Economics of Education Discussion Paper 123. http://files.eric.ed.gov/fulltext/ED529842.pdf. (Accessed 6 June 2017).

Malmquist, S., 1953. Index numbers and indifference surfaces. Trabajos de Estatistica 4, 209–242.

Manski, C.F., 1993. Identification of endogenous social effects: the reflection problem. Review of Economic Studies 60, 531–542.

Margaritis, D., Smart, W., 2011. Productivity changes in Australasian universities 1997-2005: a Malmquist analysis. In: 52nd Annual Conference of the New Zealand Association of Economics, Wellington, New Zealand, 29 June–1 July .

McDool, E., 2016. The effect of primary converter academies on pupil performance. University of Sheffield Economic Research Paper Series 2016013, https://www.sheffield.ac.uk/polopoly_fs/1.670238!/file/paper_2016013.pdf. (Accessed 7 June 2017).

Metcalfe, R., Burgess, S., Proud, S., 2011. Student effort and educational attainment: Using the England Football Team to identify the education production function. Centre for Market and Public Organisation 11/276Department of Economics, University of Bristol, Bristol, UK.

Mincer, J., 1974. Schooling, experience and earnings. National Bureau of Economic Research, New York.

Mostafa, T., 2010. Decomposing inequalities in performance scores: the role of student background, peer effects and school characteristics. International Review of Education 56 (5), 567–589.

Nicoletti, C., Ermisch, J., 2005. Intergenerational earnings mobility: changes across cohorts in Britain. Journal of Economic Analysis & Policy. 7 (2) (article 9 (Berkeley Electronic). https://www-degruyter-com.ezproxy.lancs.ac.uk/downloadpdf/j/bejeap.2007.7.2/bejeap.2007.7.2.1755/bejeap.2007.7.2.1755.pdf. (Accessed 14 June 2017).

Ng, Y.C., Li, S.K., 2009. Efficiency and productivity growth in Chinese universities during the post-reform period. China Economic Review 20, 183–192.

O'Brien, R.M., 2011. The age-peiod-cohort conundrum as two fundamental problems. Quality and Quantity 45, 1429–1444.

O'Brien, R.M., 2014. Estimable functions in age-period-cohort models: a unified approach. Quality and Quantity 48, 457–474.

Ouellette, P., Vierstraete, V., 2010. Malmquist indexes with quasi-fixed inputs: an application to school districts in Québec. Annals of Operations Research 173 (1), 57–76.

Papadimitrou, M., Johnes, J., 2016. Persistent and transient cost inefficiency in the English higher education sector: a generalised true random effects model. In: Paper presented at the OR58 Conference, Operational Research Society, Portsmouth, 6 September.

Pedraja-Chaparro, F., Santín, D., Simancas, R., 2016. The impact of immigrant concentration in schools on grade retention in Spain: a difference-in-differences approach. Applied Economics 48 (21), 1978–1990.

Pugh, G., Mangan, J., Blackburn, V., Radicic, D., 2015. School expenditure and school performance: evidence from New South Wales schools using a dynamic panel analysis. British Educational Research Journal 41, 244–264.

Rayeni, M.M., Saljooghi, F.H., 2010. Network data envelopment analysis model for estimating efficiency and productivity in universities. Journal of Computer Science 6 (11), 1235–1240.

Regan-Stansfield, J., 2016. Do good primary schools perform even better as academies. Lancaster University Economics Working Paper Series 2016/020. http://eprints.lancs.ac.uk/83311/7/LancasterWP2016_020.pdf. (Accessed 7 June 2017).

Rosenbaum, P.R., Rubin, D.B., 1983. The central role of the propensity score in observational studies for causal effects. Biometrika 70, 49–55.

Rubin, D.B., 1979. Using multivariate matched sampling and regression adjustment to control bias in observational studies. Journal of the American Statistical Association 74, 318–328.

Ryder, N.B., 1965. The cohort as a concept in the study of social change. American Sociological Review 30, 843–861.

Sacerdote, B., 2001. Peer effects with random assignment: results for Dartmouth roommates. Quarterly Journal of Economics 116, 681–704.

Sarmiento, B.P., 2017. Causal effect of time spent by students at school on academic performance. In: Workshop on Education Economics, Maastricht University, December 13.

Spencer, N., Polachek, S., & Strobl, E. (2016). How do hurricanes impact achievement in school? A Caribbean perspective. IZA Discussion Paper 10169.

Sprietsma, M., 2012. Computers as pedagogical tools in Brazil: a pseudo-panel analysis. Education Economics 20 (1), 19–32.

Stevens, P.A., 2005. A stochastic frontier analysis of English and Welsh universities. Education Economics 13 (4), 355–374.

Stinebrickner, T.R., 1998. An empirical investigation of teacher attrition. Economics of Education Review 17, 127–136.

Stinebrickner, T.R., 2000. Serially correlated variables in dynamic discrete choice models. Journal of Applied Econometrics 15, 595 624.

Stinebrickner, T.R., 2001a. Compensation policies and teacher decisions. International Economic Review 42, 751–779.

Stinebrickner, T.R., 2001b. A dynamic model of teacher labor supply. Journal of Labor Economics 19, 196–230.

Terman, L.M., 1925. Mental and physical traits of a thousand gifted children. Stanford University Press, Stanford, CA.

Thanassoulis, E., De Witte, K., Johnes, J., Johnes, G., Karagiannis, G., Conceição, M., et al., 2016. Applications of data envelopment analysis in education. In: Zhu, J. (Ed.), Data envelopment analysis: A handbook of empirical studies and applications. Springer, New York .

Thanassoulis, E., Kortelainen, M., Johnes, G., Johnes, J., 2011. Costs and efficiency of higher education institutions in England: a DEA analysis. Journal of the Operational Research Society 62, 1282–1297.

Todd, P., 2010. Matching estimators. In: Durlauf, S., Blume, L. (Eds.), Microeconometrics: The New Palgrave economics collection. Palgrave Macmillan, London .

Tonello, M., 2016. Peer effects of non-native students on natives' educational outcomes: mechanisms and evidence. Empirical Economics 51 (1), 383–414.

Tsionas, M.E.G., Kumbhakar, S.C., 2014. Firm heterogeneity, persistent and transient technical inefficiency: a generalised true random effects model. Journal of Applied Econometrics 29, 110–132.

Verbeek, M., Nijman, T., 1993. Minimum MSE estimation of a regression model with fixed effects from a series of cross-sections. Journal of Econometrics 59 (1), 125–136.

Warunsiri, S., McNown, R., 2010. The returns to education in Thailand: a pseudo-panel approach. World Development 38, 1616–1625.

Worthington, A., Lee, B.L., 2008. Efficiency, technology and productivity change in Australian universities, 1998–2003. Economics of Education Review 27, 285–298.

Zimmer, R.W., Tona, E.F., 2000. Peer effects in private and public schools across countries. Journal of Policy Analysis and Management 19, 75–92.

Further Reading

Allen, R., Allnutt, J., 2013. Matched panel data estimates of the impact of Teach First on school and departmental performance. In: University College London Institute of Education DoQSS Working Paper 13-11. http://repec.ioe.ac.uk/REPEc/pdf/qsswp1311.pdf. (Accessed 5 June 2017).

Dancer, D., Morrison, K., Tarr, G., 2015. Measuring the effects of peer learning on students' academic achievement in first-year business statistics. Studies in Higher Education 40 (10), 1808–1828.

Feng, H., Li, J., 2016. Head teachers, peer effects, and student achievement. China Economic Review 41, 268–283.

Foster, G., Frijters, P., 2010. Students' beliefs about peer effects. Economics Letters 108 (3), 260–263.

Lu, F., 2014. Testing peer effects among college students: evidence from an unusual admission policy change in China. Asia Pacific Education Review 15 (2), 257–270.

Sansone, N., Ligorio, M.B., Buglass, S.L., 2016. Peer e-tutoring: effects on students' participation and interaction style in online courses. Innovations in Education and Teaching International 1–10.

Ullmer, J., 2012. Student characteristics, peer effects and success in introductory economics. Journal of Economics and Economic Education Research 13 (1), 79–86.

Chapter 15

Panel Data in Energy Economics[☆]

Scott E. Atkinson

Department of Economics, University of Georgia, Athens, GA, United States

Chapter Outline

1 Introduction

In 2016, the electric-power sector consumed 39% of all energy resources, the transportation sector 29%, the industrial sector 22%, and the residential/commercial sector 11%. The use of panel data to study energy economics is so vast that this chapter focuses on econometric analyses since the 1960s of three of the largest and most widely studied consumers of energy resources—the fossil-fueled electric-power sector, railroads, and airlines.

To fully understand the advantages (and potential pitfalls) of panel data analysis, we review the cross-sectional estimation of the production, input demand, cost, and profit functions for electric utilities that began in the 1960s. Analysts rightly criticize early production function estimation for using homogeneous functional forms, ignoring the endogeneity of explanatory variables, and often employing macro data that obscures causality. Responding to these criticisms, researchers in the 1970s use cross-sectional micro data to estimate flexible functional forms for input demand, cost, and profit systems (where cost and profit systems include derived demand or share equations).

[☆] I wish to thank Chris Cornwell, Rong Luo, Tom Quan, and Mike Tsionas, for helpful comments about an earlier draft.

Panel Data Econometrics. https://doi.org/10.1016/B978-0-12-815859-3.00015-9

These analysts assume that arguments of their functions (inputs prices, output prices, and output quantities) are exogenous. Panel data in the late 1970s allows the calculation of the fixed effects (FE) estimator, which eliminates time-invariant unobserved heterogeneity and therefore reduces the potential for endogeneity. Panel data also enable the calculation of firm- and input-specific price-inefficiency parameters. The researcher also can compute firm-specific measures of technical efficiency (TE), technical change (TC), efficiency change (EC), and productivity change (PC). Although TE measures the distance of the firm from the production frontier, EC is the change in this measure over time, TC is the shift in the frontier over time, and PC is the sum of the latter two measures. In the 1980s, interest focuses on multiproduct cost functions and economies from vertical integration (EVI) of production, transmission, and generation of electricity.

In the late 1980s, econometricians return to estimate production functions. Researchers now use panel data and specify multiple-output production functions. Some formulate distance and directional distance functions for electric utilities, in which multiple outputs are either good (such as residential and commercial/industrial generation) or bad (such as SO_2, CO_2, and NO_x emissions). Researchers often avoid direct estimation of cost and profit functions, because many good inputs (such as capital, labor, and energy) and bad outputs lack market prices. When exogenous prices are available, some analysts specify distance and directional distance systems (distance and directional distance functions together with first-order conditions from cost-minimization or profit-maximization problems). Typically, researchers compute an instrumental variable (IV) estimator, in which prices comprise a subset of their instruments. In some cases, econometricians employ Bayesian analysis via Gibbs sampling with instruments to facilitate the imposition of constraints, estimation of input- and firm-specific price inefficiencies, and residual-based calculation of firm-specific TE, EC, TC, and PC. Many researchers formulate multiple-output production functions for railroads and airlines. Other studies introduce control functions into production functions to model unobserved productivity directly, as part of a potential solution to the endogeneity problem. This approach is especially useful to achieve identification in the absence of exogenous input and output prices. This approach also improves upon the older residual-based method for calculating PC and its associated measures. Because the control-function approach requires strong assumptions to achieve identification, however, it is another tool rather than a panacea in the treatment of endogeneity. More recently, a number of studies use macro data, employ homogeneous functional forms, or ignore the potential endogeneity of inputs. In these cases, we have come full circle to repeat the errors of the production function estimation from the 1960s, now using panel rather than cross-sectional data.

Substantial agreement exists among studies of the electric power, railroad, and airline industries. For the electric power sector, this is true regardless of the choice between utility-level versus plant-level data, cross-sectional versus panel data, and pooled-data analysis versus FE estimation. A general consensus also exists across estimates of cost, profit, and distance functions, as well as systems including these functions. Scale economies appear to be exhausted for the largest firms, rates of productivity growth are moderate, and substantial EVI exists for the generation, transmission, and distribution sectors. Cost saving can accrue from a competitive generating sector. Although allocative inefficiency appears to exist, substantial disagreement persists regarding the existence and magnitude of an Averch and Johnson (1962) (AJ) effect and the relative efficiency of public versus private utilities. The AJ effect occurs when the firm over-capitalizes because of rate-of-return regulation, as long as the allowed rate of return exceeds the market return on capital. Railroads exhibit increasing returns to scale (RTS), substantial inefficiencies, and low productivity growth. Airlines operate close to constant RTS and enjoy modest productivity growth. Substantial inefficiencies decrease with deregulation. A valuable alternative to FE is a control function approach to model productivity, which allows one to control for endogeneity and compute partial effects from a productivity function.

2   Cross-Sectional Modeling of Electric Utilities

2.1   Production Functions Without Instruments

Initial examination of a number of cross-sectional studies allows comparison with the results from later panel studies of similar topics. The consensus from these cross-sectional studies is that RTS are nearly exhausted for the largest firms, that allocative inefficiency is moderate for some inputs, that the AJ effect exists, and that EVI are substantial. Douglas (1976) references early estimates of the Cobb-Douglas production function using macro data without concern for endogeneity of inputs, a practice that is criticized by Griliches and Mairesse (1998) (GM). Cowing and Smith (1978) survey a number of early studies by Komiya (1962), Galatin (1968), and Courville (1974) that use micro cross-sectional data on US utilities for various time periods to fit electric utility production functions. However, they estimate a homogeneous production function and ignore the endogeneity of inputs. Generally, they obtain evidence of substantial technical progress and moderate scale economies.

2.2   Cost, Derived Demand, and Profit Functions

Nerlove (1963) is among the first to address endogeneity by recognizing that the inputs of an electric utility production function are endogenous. Instead, he estimates a Cobb-Douglas cost function, whose arguments are output quantity and input prices for capital, labor, and energy. These variables are arguably exogenous for a regulated firm buying inputs in competitive markets and selling output at prices determined by regulators. Using a cross-sectional sample of 145 US firms in 1955, Nerlove obtains evidence of a marked degree of increasing

RTS for smaller firms, where $\text{RTS} = 1 - (\partial \ln C / \partial \ln y)$, C is cost, and y is output. Thus, positive numbers indicate scale economies, and negative numbers indicate scale diseconomies. He finds that RTS falls from 0.91 to -0.03 as output increases. Extending this work, Dhrymes and Kurz (1964), Cowing (1974), and Boyes (1976) use cross-sectional data on new US plants installed over time to estimate more flexible input demand models, assuming either cost-minimization or profit-maximization. The consensus result is that RTS declines with firm size to nearly zero.

One of the first studies to employ a second-order flexible functional form is Christensen and Greene (1976), who specify a translog cost system for cross sections of US utilities in 1955 and 1970. They find significant increasing RTS for nearly all firms in the earlier group, but essentially constant RTS for the latter group of larger firms. They reject the null hypotheses of homothetic and homogeneous technologies. Nearly all studies from this point forward specify a second-order flexible functional form for cost, profit, distance, and directional distance functions. Only the use of the Cobb-Douglas function will warrant specific mention. In a related study, Christensen and Greene (1978) estimate a cost system for 138 US firms in 1970 and find no evidence of systematic cost savings from power pooling. Commonly owned firms, however, exhibit lower average costs than comparable individual firms.

Atkinson and Halvorsen (1984) generalize this work by formulating a shadow cost system for 123 US private utilities in 1970, where shadow costs are a parametric function of shadow prices. These are virtual prices to the firm that might differ from actual or market prices because of regulatory constraints, labor union rules, or other forces that impede free markets from efficiently setting prices. Using cross-sectional data, shadow cost systems (and profit systems to be addressed) allow direct estimation of input-specific allocative efficiency (AE) parameters. Atkinson and Halvorsen find that RTS are nearly exhausted for the largest firms, evidence of an AJ effect, and moderate allocative inefficiency. Two studies formulate shadow cost systems to examine the relative efficiency of public and private utilities using cross-sectional data. Atkinson and Halvorsen (1986) employ 1970 data for 123 private and 30 public US electric utilities, concluding that the two ownership types are equally cost efficient. Other cross-sectional studies summarized in their paper are divided in their assessments of relative efficiency. Following the methodology of Atkinson and Halvorsen (1984), Koh, Berg, and Kenny (1996) use a 1986 cross-section of 121 private and 61 public US utilities. They find that public utilities are more efficient at low output levels.

A number of studies estimate profit functions as a dual alternative to cost functions. Atkinson and Halvorsen (1976) specify a normalized restricted profit system (a profit function plus derived share equations), whose arguments are input prices, output prices, and quantities of fixed inputs. They assumed exogeneity of these prices, because individual plants arguably are price takers in both input and output markets. For 108 US power plants in 1972, they find that

RTS are close to zero. Cowing (1978) estimates a profit system for 150 new private US plants constructed between 1947 and 1965. He provides general support for the effectiveness of rate-of-return regulation and the existence of an AJ effect. Atkinson and Halvorsen (1980) generalize previous work by estimating AE parameters using a normalized shadow profit system for a set of 38 US power plants in 1973. Shadow profits are a parametric function of shadow prices. They find that these plants do not generally achieve relative and absolute price efficiency.

Meyer (2012a) surveys a number of cross-sectional studies of EVI for US utilities. The consensus conclusion is that separating generation from transmission, distribution, and retail services substantially increases costs. Using data on US firms, Roberts (1986), Kaserman and Mayo (1991), and Gilsdorf (1995) generally agree that a reduction in average cost results from increasing output to existing customers, with no substantial savings from increasing the number of customers. They also find substantial EVI. Huettner and Landon (1978) estimate cost functions for production, transmission, and distribution for a cross-section of 74 US electric utilities in 1971. They find diseconomies of scale beyond moderate firm sizes for all three activities. They also find that holding companies do not generate cost savings. Using data for 1999, Bushnell, Mansur, and Saravia (2008) explain the cost, price, and residual supply of electricity for three market areas in the United States. They find that the prevention by regulators of the long-term price commitments associated with vertical arrangements (as in California) increases prices by 45%.

3   Pooled and Fixed-Effects Panel Data Modeling

Most research about electric utilities employs panel data. Consider the estimation of a linear panel data model for firm i in period t:

$$y_{it} = x_{it}\beta + c_i + e_{it}, \quad i = 1,...,N; t = 1,...,T, \tag{1}$$

where y_{it} is the dependent variable, x_{it} is a $(1 \times K)$ vector of regressors, β is a $(K \times 1)$ coefficient vector, and the error term is composed of c_i, which is firm-specific, time-invariant unobserved heterogeneity, and an idiosyncratic error term, e_{it}.

One advantage of panel over cross-sectional data occurs in the treatment of endogeneity. Endogeneity occurs if c_i or e_{it} is correlated with the explanatory variables. With panel data, one can remove c_i from the error term by computing the FE estimator of β, through time-demeaning the data or estimating c_i directly. With a linear model, the FE estimator also is termed the "within" estimator. Alternatively, one can assume away endogeneity by employing the random-effects (RE) estimator, which requires that the composite error term, $c_i + e_{it}$, is orthogonal to x_{it}. Using linear equations analogous to Eq. (1), the analyst can compute the within estimator for linear cost, profit, or distance functions. For cost, profit, or distance systems, one directly estimates c_i using FE. Clearly,

FE methods do not eliminate the time-varying correlation between e_{it} and $\mathbf{x}_{it}$. As an alternative to FE and RE estimation, one can simply pool the untransformed panel data (ignoring c_i) and compute what is termed the "pooled" estimator.

A second advantage of panel over cross-sectional data is in the calculation of firm-level productivity growth and efficiency over time. Early cross-section estimates of cost and production functions do compare estimated models for each cross section of firms over time. Panel data, however, allows efficiency gains in estimation and the computation of firm-specific parameters determining AE, EC, TC, and PC.

In spite of the ability of the FE estimator to remove c_{it} from the error term, GM argue against its use. They provide evidence that FE estimates of RTS vary substantially from those obtained using pooled panel data. They argue that the FE estimator does more harm than good by eliminating a rich source of variation, failing to eliminate time-varying endogeneity, and increasing measurement error. Also, they speculate that the econometrician can more precisely estimate productivity by avoiding the FE estimator in favor of a control function approach, which we consider later.

3.1 Electric Utilities

3.1.1 Single-Output Input Demand, Cost, and Production Functions

Early studies using panel data either specify input demand equations, presumably avoiding endogeneity, or estimate production functions while ignoring endogeneity. Barzel (1964) employs a panel of 220 US plants from 1941 to 1959 and uses pooled data to compute input demand equations as functions of price and other controls. He obtains evidence of increasing RTS that are most pronounced for labor and less so for capital and fuel. On this basis, he argues that a Cobb-Douglas production function is inadequate to study the electric power industry. Belinfante (1978) estimates a production function using a pooled unbalanced panel of 80 US electric utility plants from 1947 to 1959 and calculates that average embodied TC is 3% and disembodied TC is 0.5%. This study ignores endogeneity.

Many panel data studies of single-output production by private electric utilities since the 1980s formulate pooled cost system models. They universally assume that the arguments of the cost function are exogenous. A nearly universal consensus from panel and previously summarized cross-sectional studies is that RTS are close to zero for the largest firms. In addition, the panel data studies generally find that productivity growth is slowing, and that TC has become small over time. Petersen (1975) estimates a cost function for a pooled panel of 56 US private plants that experience substantial expansion from 1966-68. He finds evidence of an AJ effect and increasing RTS for all but the largest plants. Gollop and Roberts (1981) formulate a cost system for a pooled sample of 11 private, vertically integrated US firms from 1958 to 1975. They calculate that increasing RTS range from 0.31 to 0.1, but that RTS falls substantially in the last year. The rate of TC generally declines over their sample to negative levels in that year. Nelson and Wohar (1983) estimate total factor productivity (TFP) growth using a cost system by pooling data about 50 private US utilities from 1950 to 1978, where TFP is the ratio of real output to a Divisia index of real factor inputs. Including a measure of the allowed rate of return, they find evidence of an AJ effect, consistent with cross-sectional studies references noted previously. They also estimate that TC is the primary source of TFP growth that averaged 2.5%, and that RTS is stable over time at small positive levels. In contrast, Baltagi and Griffin (1988) compute a general index of TC after estimating a cost system using panel data with firm FE for 30 private US utilities from 1951 to 1978. They first calculate TC (the negative of the difference in log costs between the present and a previous period) from 1971 to 1978. Then they regress this measure on vintage, SO_2 restrictions, regulatory tightness, and capacity use. The biggest factor decreasing TC is a restriction on SO_2 production, enacted in the 1970s, along with reduced use rates. Because these measures are arguably correlated with variables in the first-stage cost function, however, the caveats of Wang and Schmidt (2002) (WS) apply. They show via Monte Carlo simulation that regression of first-step residuals on second-step explanatory variables—when these are correlated with first-step explanatory variables but omitted from that step—generates substantial bias in both steps. Using a cost system and a pooled panel from 1995 and 1996 for 775 US private plants, Maloney (2001) estimates that the largest plants exhaust RTS. Law (2014) summarizes a number of studies of US utilities that examine the existence of an AJ effect and criticizes most studies that confirm its existence.

Knittel (2002) estimates a stochastic production frontier including FE for an unbalanced panel of investor-owned gas and coal-fired electric generating plants from 1981 to 1986. Using 951 and 5040 observations, respectively, he examines the effects of alternative regulatory methods on firm efficiency, finding that programs tied to generator performance and ones that modify traditional fuel pass-through clauses result in greater efficiency. Concerns about the untreated endogeneity of inputs, however, must apply.

Two subsequent studies about electric utilities employ an IV estimator with FE for distance systems. A popular choice to model single-output production is the input-oriented distance function, which is dual to a cost function. Atkinson and Dorfman (2009) specify an input distance system with firm FE to explain total generation for a panel of 13 Chilean hydroelectric power plants from 1986 to 1997. Panel data allow calculation of a full set of input- and plant-specific AE parameters using Gibbs sampling, which draws sequentially from conditional Generalized Method of Moments (GMM) IV estimates. They compute substantially differing degrees of efficiency across plants, with measures of PC ranging from 2% to 12%. Over time, TE improves for most plants. Atkinson and

Cornwell (2011) estimate firm FE for a panel of 78 privately owned electric utilities from 1988 to 1997 using a dynamic shadow input distance system that integrates dynamic adjustment costs into a long-run shadow cost-minimization problem. They formulate a system composed of the first-order conditions from the short-run shadow cost-minimization problem for the variable shadow inputs, a set of Euler equations, and the input distance function, expressed in terms of shadow quantities. Estimates indicate that adjustment costs represent about 0.42% of total cost and about 1.26% of capital costs. Instruments include exogenous input prices. Compared to the static model, the dynamic model finds that over-use of capital and labor is less severe and annual PC is more stable and higher, about 1.7% on average.

Three studies examine the efficiency of public utilities or compare the efficiency of public and private utilities. Nelson and Primeaux (1988) examine a pooled panel of 23 US municipally owned utilities from 1961 to 1976. They formulate a cost function for total distribution costs and find that substantial scale economies with respect to output exist throughout most of the sample. They calculate that RTS, with respect to simultaneous increases in output and the number of customers, however, appear to have been exhausted by the larger firms. This result is consistent with cross-sectional studies of US utilities by Huettner and Landon (1978) and by Roberts (1986). Pescatrice and Trapani (1980) estimate a cost system for a pooled sample of 23 public and 33 private US utilities from 1965 to 1976. In contrast to Atkinson and Halvorsen (1986), they calculate that public firms minimize costs and have 24%–33% lower per unit costs than private firms. They attribute the cost differential to rate-of-return regulation of the latter. Nemoto, Nakanishi, and Madono (1993) formulate a variable cost system using pooled data for nine vertically integrated Japanese firms from 1981 to 1983. They obtain evidence of short-run economies of scale and long-run diseconomies of scale plus evidence supporting the AJ effect.

Restructuring the generation sector so that it is competitive appears to reduce costs. Rather than estimate a production function directly, Fowlie (2010) examines the effect of restructuring on plant input efficiency and emissions of NO_x, using a pooled panel of 702 coal-fired US electric generating plants from 2000 to 2004. Estimates from a random coefficients logit model indicate that deregulated plants in restructured electricity markets are less likely to install more capital intensive pollution control technologies compared to similar regulated and public plants. And damages to health and the environment would have been less under symmetric economic regulation (universal restructuring or universal regulation), with relatively more of the permitted NO_x emitted in relatively low damage areas. In a review of papers examining the effects of electricity restructuring on rates, Hiebert (2002) specifies a variable cost stochastic frontier (with a two-component error term as in Eq. (1)) for an unbalanced panel of 432 plants burning coal and 201 plants burning natural gas and oil in the United States from 1988 to 1997. He rejects the Cobb-Douglas form and finds evidence of greater efficiency as plant utilization rises, as the number of plants owned by a utility increases, as investor-owned status increases, and as coal plants are restructured. Kwoka (2008) critiques a number of panel data studies about restructuring. One of the more convincing studies is by Joskow (2006), who examines nearly all US states for 34 years. Estimating price regressions that include state FE, he finds that restructuring significantly reduces the price of electricity in the residential and industrial markets by 5%–10%. Rungsuriyawiboon and Stefanou (2007) formulate a dynamic FE efficiency model of shadow cost minimization for 72 private US utilities from 1986 to 1999. They treat net investment demand as endogenous and find that TE of inputs improves for utilities in restructured jurisdictions. They also determine that capital is overused relative to other inputs, but differences in allocative inefficiencies of variable inputs are not significantly different for deregulated versus regulated utilities. Estimated RTS (defined as the elasticity of output with respect to all inputs) ranges from 1.22 to 1.37, with higher RTS for the pre-deregulation period.

Chan, Fell, Lange, and Li (2017) estimate a production function using FE to determine the efficiency and environmental impacts of restructuring. They examine changes in fuel efficiency, cost of coal purchases, and utilization for a panel data set of coal-fired power plants from 1991 to 2005. Their data cover several years after the implementation of restructuring and their regressions include between 3700 and 5400 observations. They find that restructuring has led to approximately a 15 percent reduction in operating expenses and up to a 7.5 percent reduction in emissions. Although the authors consider many different sources of endogeneity, they rely on state-level (rather than plant-specific) variables for instruments. They do not report tests of the validity and relevance of their instrument set and do not directly model the production of SO_2. The latter, however, would require the estimation of a distance or directional distance function.

Llorca, Orea, and Pollitt (2016) examine the effect of environmental factors (such as wind and precipitation) on the efficiency of the US electricity transmission industry for the period 2001–09, using a pooled panel of 59 US electricity transmission companies. The authors recognize the caveats of WS and examine a number of alternative random-effects frontier models in which firm inefficiency is a function of external variables such as weather. They find that the cost elasticity with respect to network length evaluated at the sample mean is 0.89. More than half of the firms in their sample exhibit increasing RTS based on this measure. Further, the cost elasticity with respect to density ranges from 0.70 to 0.75. Together these imply the existence of important economies of density in electricity transmission. Finally, they find that adverse weather reduces firm efficiency.

A number of recent studies ignore the concerns of GM regarding the use of macro variables and endogeneity in production functions. Zhang, Parker, and Kirkpatrick (2008) assess the effects of privatization, competition, and regulation on the performance of the electricity generation industry using panel data for 36 developing and transitional countries from 1985 to 2003. They estimate country FE for a model in which the dependent variables are electricity generation and explanatory variables measure regulation, competition, privatization, and other controls. They do not, however, address potential remaining endogeneity. Pompei (2013) regresses Malmquist measures of TFP on TC, EC, and measures of regulatory stringency in the electricity sectors of 19 EU countries from 1994 to 2007. He computes pooled regressions in which many of the explanatory variables are arguably endogenous. Oh and Lee (2016) estimate a firm FE production function for a panel of five Korean utilities from 2001 to 2012, without addressing potential remaining endogeneity. Growth of TFP is 0.33%, and RTS are small but positive. Polemis and Stengos (2017) explain generation, capacity, and productivity using aggregate variables and country-specific FE for 30 OECD countries from 1975 to 2013. For already economically liberalized countries, the level of economic freedom does not affect levels of production. Again, the authors do not address potential remaining endogeneity and the use of macro data clouds causal inference.

3.1.2 Multiple-Output Cost and Production Functions

A large body of literature estimates two different types of multiproduct cost systems. With the first system, the outputs are generation, transmission, and distribution (and sometimes retail) of electricity. With the second system, the outputs are residential, commercial, and industrial electricity generation, possibly also including bad outputs. Most studies compute pooled cost system regressions, assuming that the arguments of their cost functions are exogenous. A few studies estimate production functions, employ instruments, and specify FE.

Cost Savings From Economies of Vertical Integration

A number of studies examine EVI for generation, transmission, and distribution of electricity in the United States and other countries. The strong consensus is that substantial EVI exist. Ramos-Real (2005) provides a survey of cost function estimation, arguments in favor of restructuring, and evidence of EVI. In the first of a series of studies of EVI for the United States, Thompson (1997) formulates a cost system based on the total cost of production, procurement, and delivery of power using a pooled panel consisting of all major investor-owned US electric utilities for the years 1977, 1982, 1987, and 1992. He calculates substantial scale economies for expanding sales (with a given customer base) but no economies for expanding the customer base (for a given level of sales). He also finds substantial EVI. Hayashi, Goo, and Chamberlain (1997) examine 50 private vertically integrated US utilities from 1983 to 1987 by estimating firm FE with a cost function for both electricity supply and generation. Estimates of scale economies for generation are about 10% for smaller firms and fall by half for larger firms. They also reject the null hypothesis of separability of generation and transmission/distribution implying that vertical integration could reduce total costs. Meyer (2012b) estimates a FE cost function in which generation, transmission, and distribution are outputs, using a sample of 143 US utilities from 2001 to 2008. He determines that separating generation from networks and retail is the costliest alternative with an average cost increase of 19% to 26%. If generation and transmission remain integrated but separate from distribution and retail, costs would increase by 8% to 10%. Finally, separating transmission from the remaining supply stages would increase costs by approximately 4%.

A number of studies of EVI focus on OECD and European countries. Hattori and Tsutsui (2004) analyze the impact of regulatory reform on the level of the industrial price and the ratio of the industrial to residential price, using panel data for 19 OECD countries from 1987 to 1999. They calculate country-specific FE, finding that expanded retail access lowers the industrial price and increases the price differential between industrial and household customers. Unbundling generation from transmission and introducing a wholesale spot market do not necessarily lower the price and might increase it. Steiner (2001) estimates firm FE to explain the impact of industry structure and regulation on efficiency and prices, using panel data for 19 OECD countries from 1986 to 1996. The calculated benefits from unbundling are problematic, however, because explanatory variables are macro (which might not be the actual causal factors) and the model ignores the potential endogeneity of many explanatory variables.

Other studies examine Spanish, Japanese, Italian, and New Zealand electric utilities, generally finding substantial EVI. Martínez-Budría, Jara-Díaz, and Ramos-Real (2003), Jara-Díaz and Ramos-Real (2004), and Jara-Díaz and Ramos-Real (2011) formulate aggregate, multi-output (generation and distribution), and multistage-multioutput (coal, oil, hydraulic, nuclear, and distribution) cost functions for the Spanish electric sector using a panel of 12 Spanish utilities from 1985 to 1996. This sample includes a period of regulatory reform. Aggregation bias for the multistage-multioutput function, because of combining such disparate production technologies, is a paramount concern. They compute firm FE and find EVI of about 9% as well as essentially constant RTS at the multistage level. Nemoto and Goto (2004) formulate a shadow cost system using a pooled panel data set on the transmission/distribution stages of nine Japanese electric utilities from 1981 to 1988. The results indicate EVI for these two stages. They also calculate a negative externality effect of generation facilities on the cost of the transmission/distribution stage. This implies that vertical integration of generation and transmission/distribution facilities will generate EVI by internalizing these externalities.

Fraquelli, Piacenza, and Vannoni (2005) specify a multiproduct cost system using a pooled sample of 25 Italian electric utilities from 1994 to 2000. They include generation and distribution as separate outputs, finding overall increasing RTS for large utilities because of the presence of vertical economies. The latter counterbalance the effects of decreasing RTS in the generation phase. For the average firm, the authors find weak but statistically significant EVI (3%) as well as multistage RTS of about 1.015, using the same formula as Atkinson and Primont (2002), where $RTS = \frac{1}{\sum_m (\partial \ln C / \partial y_m) y_m}, m = 1, ..., M$, for M outputs and C is cost. Numbers greater (less) than one indicate increasing (decreasing) RTS. Utilities that generate and distribute more than average amounts of electricity benefit from both EVI and increasing RTS, while the cost advantages increase up to 40% for large operators.

Studies in New Zealand generally indicate substantial EVI. Scully (1998) formulates a pooled cost system for New Zealand electrical supply authorities from 1982 to 1994. He includes controls for engineering characteristics, whether the supply authority is municipal, and the degree of horizontal integration, finding that deregulation substantially reduces costs, with the real price of electricity falling 16.4% over the period. Scale economies decline to small levels as output expands. Negative TC through 1984 increases to about 1% in 1994. Nillesen and Pollitt (2011) estimate firm FE and RE models using a Cobb-Douglas cost function for 28 New Zealand utilities from 1995 to 2007. They determine that deregulation swaps one form of vertical integration (retail-distribution) for another form of vertical integration (retail-generation). Ownership unbundling in New Zealand substantially reduces costs and increases quality of service, while overall competition falls and prices rise.

The potential exists for endogeneity in cost-system studies of EVI. In a cost-system framework, estimating input demand equations by regressing inputs on input prices and output might suffer from endogeneity. The production function specified by GM, p. 172, is

$$y = az + \beta x + u, \tag{2}$$

where y is the log of output, z the log of capital (or a fixed input), and x is the log of labor (or a variable input). They then assume that product prices are equal for different producers and therefore are normalized to unity. Equating the price of labor to the marginal product of x, derived from Eq. (2), and taking logs yields the following marginal productivity equation:

$$y = x + w + v - \ln(\beta), \tag{3}$$

where w is the log of the wage and v is the error in the marginal product equation.

Solving Eqs. (2), (3) for their reduced-form equations, GM obtain (dropping constant terms):

$$x = (1 - \beta)^{-1}(az - w + u - v) \tag{4}$$

$$y = (1 - \beta)^{-1}(az - \beta w + u - \beta v). \tag{5}$$

Therefore, x and y are correlated with both u and v, so that input demand equations, whose arguments are input prices and output, suffer from endogeneity.

As GM point out, if utilities operate within a regulatory environment, the assumption that y is exogenous might be valid. In a restructured environment, where output is no longer determined by a regulatory commission, however, output is most likely endogenous to the firm.

Single or Multiple Good Outputs With Bads

A number of studies examine the joint production of good and bad outputs. Gollop and Roberts (1983) measure the effect of restrictions on SO_2 emissions for productivity growth in the electric power industry from 1973 to 1979. They formulate a cost system for 56 pooled US private firms, assuming the exogeneity of the arguments of the cost function—prices of labor, capital, low-sulfur fuel, high-sulfur fuel, output, regulatory intensity, and time. In addition to rejecting the null of constant RTS, they find that the smallest firms enjoy substantial scale economies, while the largest firms exhibit scale diseconomies. The mean RTS in 1979 is about 0.08. They also conclude that the biggest factor reducing TC is the restriction on SO_2 emissions enacted in the 1970s. Carlson, Burtraw, Cropper, and Palmer (2000) estimate a firm-FE translog cost function, in which generation of electricity and SO_2 are outputs, to examine the gains from trading SO_2 emission allowances by coal-fired generating units. Examining 829 such units from 1985 to 1994, they conclude that these gains are lower than expected because of declines in the price of low-sulfur coal and improvements in technology that has lowered the cost of fuel switching. Although they assume cost-minimization at the firm level, much of their data is at the unit level, where this assumption might be more difficult to justify. Because the plant is the cost-minimizing unit, individual generating units might fail to minimize costs.

Many other studies examine the production of goods and bads using distance and directional distance functions. Färe, Grosskopf, Noh, and Weber (2005) estimate an output-oriented directional distance function to measure the TE of 209 US utilities in 1993 and 1997 observed at the boiler level. Performing separate cross-section regressions, they model two outputs, electricity and SO2, as a function of standard inputs. Although their approach produces reasonable shadow prices for SO_2, they ignore endogeneity. Atkinson and Dorfman (2005) compute firm FE for an input-oriented distance system. They model a good output (electricity generation) and a bad output (SO_2 production) using a panel of 43 private US electric utilities for 1980, 1985, 1990, and 1995. Using Bayesian GMM with instruments, Gibbs sampling allows easy imposition of monotonicity. Assuming cost minimization, they compute reasonable shadow values for SO_2 and find declining levels of PC and TC in addition to negative EC. A substantial portion of PC and TC is due to a reduction of the bad. Assuming profit maximization, Atkinson and Tsionas (2016) use Bayesian methods with FE to estimate optimal firm-specific directions for a technology-oriented directional distance system. They examine 77 US utilities from 1988 to 1997, where production is a function of good inputs and outputs as well as bad inputs and outputs (SO_2, CO_2, and NO_x). Estimated firm-specific directions for each input and output are quite different from those normally assumed. The computed firm-specific TE, TC, and PC using estimated optimal directions are substantially higher than those calculated using fixed directions.

Three papers estimate multiple outputs for the residential the industrial/ commercial sectors. Estimates of RTS and inefficiencies are in general agreement with those from previous studies. Atkinson, Cornwell, and Honerkamp (2003) estimate an input distance function with firm FE, using a GMM estimator with instruments, examining 43 private US utilities from 1961 to 1992. Outputs are residential and industrial/commercial generation. Estimates of RTS range from 0.8 to 1.13, with an average of 1.04, using the Atkinson and Primont (2002) formula. They also find small positive weighted-average PC computed from residuals. Atkinson and Primont (2002) generalize previous work by estimating multiple-output cost and production systems. The multiple outputs are residential and commercial/industrial production. They specify firm FE for shadow cost and shadow distance systems. Their data is a balanced panel of 43 private US electric utilities from 1961 to 1997. The authors include instruments and find moderate allocative inefficiency, evidence of an AJ effect, very small productivity growth, and increasing RTS from about 1.13–1.15. Hayashi, Sevier, and Trapani (1985) estimate a rate-of-return cost system for residential, commercial, and industrial electricity. They employ a pooled panel of 32 private, vertically integrated US firms in 1965 and 1970, finding evidence of an AJ effect. Their results are problematic, however, because they did not impose linear homogeneity in prices, which is a required accounting identity for a cost function, either in actual prices or in shadow prices.

3.2 Railroads

Although many panel data studies examine the efficiency of railroads and their RTS, the only generally robust conclusions are that RTS are modest and that substantial differences in firm efficiencies exist. Kumbhakar (1987) compares the estimates of a Cobb-Douglas production system to those of a Cobb-Douglas cost system to determine the TE and AE for a set of 13 Class-I US railroads from 1951 to 1975. He assumes that both outputs—freight-ton miles and passenger miles—are exogenous and that the production system (cost share equations estimated jointly with the production function) is free of endogeneity. This is in contrast to the conclusions of GM that are drawn from Eqs. (4), (5). Because of considerable differences between the results of the cost and production systems, Kumbhakar advocates against the latter.

Atkinson, Färe, and Primont (2003) include firm FE to formulate a shadow input distance system for 12 US Class-I railroads from 1951 to 1975, using a GMM IV procedure. Their shadow input distance equation is a function of input shadow quantities and output quantities. They include the first-order conditions from the dual shadow cost-minimization problem, computing firm- and input-specific AE parameters that are time-varying. Because input and output quantities are endogenous, instruments that over-identify the model are firm dummies, time dummies, and interactions of firm with time dummies. They find substantial allocative inefficiencies for capital and energy. The average RTS is 1.17 for their sample, which is similar to that obtained by Caves, Christensen, and Swanson (1981), who compute a variable multiple-output cost system using a pooled sample with more US railroads but fewer years. For the full 1955 to 1974 period, they calculate an average annual rate of productivity growth of 1.8%.

A number of studies about railroads formulate production or factor requirement functions but fail to adequately address the potential endogeneity of inputs. Perelman and Pestieau (1988) estimate a production function for a pooled sample of 19 non-US railroads for 1970 to 1983 and perform a second-stage regression to explain the sources of productivity growth. The caveats of WS apply to the second-stage regression. Perelman and Pestieau do not address the potential endogeneity of inputs and outputs. Coelli and Perelman (1999) formulate input and output-oriented distance functions, pooling annual data on 17 EU railway companies observed from 1988 to 1993. They find increasing RTS at the mean of their data. Their work is subject to the same concerns regarding the potential endogeneity of inputs and outputs. Gathon and Perelman (1992) estimate FE and RE factor requirements functions for 19 EU railway companies from 1961 to 1988. They make strong assumptions about exogeneity that might be invalid. Friebel, Ivaldi, and Vibes (2010) examine the effects of reforms on railroad efficiency for 11 pooled EU countries for approximately 20 years. They estimate a Cobb-Douglas production frontier as a function of capital, labor, a deregulation dummy, and country FE, where the latter two are scaled by time. After controlling for endogeneity using the interaction of time with the firm dummy and a deregulation dummy, they find that efficiency levels increase because of market reforms. These include third-party network access, introduction of an independent regulator, and vertical separation. One must question whether their FE approach accounts for all potential endogeneity.

3.3   Airlines

Many studies investigate RTS and productivity growth in airlines using panel data. The consensus is that roughly constant RTS prevail, that productivity growth is positive but modest, that deregulation reduces costs, and that substantial differences in firm efficiencies exist. Many studies, however, use a two-step method to explain productivity growth while others fail to carefully address endogeneity.

Caves, Christensen, and Tretheway (1981) formulate a model of TFP for 11 trunk US airline carriers from 1972 to 1977. In the first step, they compute indices of the log of TFP and differences in the logs of TFP in successive years. In the second step, they regress these measures on time and firm dummies, output, average stage length, and load factor. Clearly, one must consider the caveats of WS about the potential bias from two-step estimation.

Nearly all succeeding studies estimate a FE model, sometimes in conjunction with other models. Schmidt and Sickles (1984) formulate a stochastic frontier production function for 12 US airlines with quarterly data from 1971 to 1978. Inputs are capital, labor, energy, and materials, while output is capacity ton miles. They compare the within, generalized least squares (GLS), and maximum likelihood (ML) estimators. For the GLS estimator, they assume the independence of the firm effects and the explanatory variables. For the ML estimator, they assume independence of the firm effects and the idiosyncratic error term from themselves and from the regressors. They also assume a distribution for each component of the error. Estimated technical efficiencies are relatively constant across specifications. Productivity growth ranges from 1.5% to 2%. A Hausman (1978) test of the null hypothesis of no correlation between the effects and the regressors is accepted. The low power of this test, however, implies a low probability of rejecting a false null. We also must consider the possibility of other sources of endogeneity not eliminated by their FE approach.

Park, Sickles, and Simar (1988) specify airline production functions using a panel of US and European airlines from 1976 to 1990 to explain capacity ton-mile service. They compute a within, semiparametric efficient IV estimator, in which the random effects and the regressors have certain patterns of correlation. Their results indicate constant RTS in the provision of service capacity and that productivity growth is slightly more than 2%.

Cornwell, Schmidt, and Sickles (1990) consider efficient IV estimation of a frontier production function for ton-miles using a panel of quarterly data about eight US airlines from 1970 to 1981. They allow coefficients and intercepts to vary over firms and measure time-varying technical efficiency levels for individual firms. Their approach avoids strong distributional assumptions for technical inefficiency and random noise by including in the production function a flexible function of time and firms. The authors compare the within estimator, a GLS estimator, and an extension of the Hausman and Taylor (1981) IV estimator, assuming that seasonal dummies, a time trend, labor, and materials are exogenous. Estimates from the within transformation, GLS, and efficient IV are similar. The computed RTS are not significantly different from unity. Productivity growth rates average slightly greater than 1% for the first and third methods.

Good, Röller, and Sickles (1995) compute a FE estimator for a frontier production function using a panel of the eight largest EU and US airlines from 1976 to 1986. Although the US industry is deregulated, the EU industry is not totally deregulated but has become increasingly more competitive. The authors employ many of the same variables used by Schmidt and Sickles (1984). Good et al. find that the American carriers are more productively efficient, however, endogeneity might be a problem with both studies.

Sickles, Good, and Johnson (1986) estimate a FE profit function for a panel of 13 US airlines observed quarterly from 1970 to 1981. They obtain prices for passenger and cargo revenue ton-miles as well as capital, labor, energy, and materials inputs. Because the profit function includes service output characteristics (service quality and stage length), the authors specify for them reduced-form equations that are functions of prices and time. They formulate a system composed of these equations, the profit function, and the output supply and input demand equations. Following the methods of Atkinson and Halvorsen (1980, 1984), they include parameters to measure allocative distortions. A firm-specific error-component term measures time-invariant unobserved heterogeneity. They conclude that deregulation reduces both the total cost of allocative distortions and their relative levels for input and outputs.

Two studies estimate FE cost systems. Atkinson and Cornwell (1994) formulate a firm FE shadow cost system explaining capacity ton-miles for a panel of 13 US airlines using quarterly data from 1970 to 1984. They measure firm-specific TE and calculate firm- and input-specific parameters measuring AE. Substantial inefficiencies exist. Potential cost savings from achieving TE and AE vary from 14% to 48% across airlines. Baltagi, Griffin, and Rich (1995) specify firm FE using a short-run cost system (capital is fixed) with panel data for 24 US airlines from 1971 to 1986. They separate cost changes into categories attributable to technical change, economies of scale and density, and input prices. After a first-step estimation of a general index of industry TC, a second-step regression explains the sources of TC. They determine that deregulation stimulates technical change because of more efficient route structures. Their two-step methodology, however, is subject to the WS caveats.

Gerardi and Shapiro (2009) formulate FE and cross-sectional models using quarterly panel data on nine major US airline carriers from 1993 to 2006 to explain price dispersion. They determine that competition has a negative effect on price dispersion, which is the expected result. These results contrast with those of Borenstein and Rose (1994), who find that price dispersion increases with competition, based on a 10% random sample of US airfares for the second quarter of 1986. Using cross-sectional data, Gerardi and Shapiro basically reproduce the Borenstein-Rose results. After controlling for route-carrier characteristics, however, their FE estimator yields the opposite result. A reasonable conclusion is that this estimator eliminates the omitted variable bias induced by time-invariant, route-carrier effects. Unfortunately, few other studies carry out such a comparison, which would help greatly in determining the relative value of the two approaches.

A number of studies fail to employ instruments where endogeneity seems to be clearly problematic. Liu and Lynk (1999) formulate a variable cost function using a panel of 11 US airlines for the post-deregulation period 1984 to 1991. They include stage length and load factor, which are arguably endogenous, but do not use instruments. Although they fail to reject the null of exogeneity using a Hausman test, the power of the Hausman test is low, as mentioned previously.

Sun (2017) investigates the impact of airline deregulation on air travel demand and competition using pooled panel data for three Korean routes from 2006 to 2010. The explanatory variables for market shares are arguably endogenous. Whalen (2007) includes firm FE in regressions explaining price and the number of passengers using an 11-year panel data set of US and EU airlines. He investigates code sharing, antitrust immunity, and the open skies treaties. The use of lagged instruments might be problematic and the inclusion of a number of macro variables, such as population and income, make inference difficult.

4 A Control Function Approach

As an alternative to the estimation of firm FE, an important line of research specifies a two-component error term that is different from that of Eq. (1). The first is an idiosyncratic shock that is a surprise to the firm and therefore cannot be predicted or observed. The second is an error that is potentially observable or predictable productivity, which is at least in part known by the firm but is unknown to the econometrician. If the firm at least partially takes this error into account in its choice of inputs, it is correlated with the explanatory variables. As indicated previously, GM argue that the within estimator distorts computed RTS, eliminates important identifying information, will not eliminate time-varying endogeneity, and increases measurement error. Alternatively, Olley and Pakes (1996) (OP), Levinsohn and Petrin (2003) (LP), and Ackerberg, Caves, and Frazer (2015) (ACF) consider a Cobb-Douglas panel-data model for firm i in period t that explicitly models the productivity component of the error term rather than resorting to time-demeaning of the data.

These three papers use a control function approach to model the productivity shock component of the error term. They introduce a monotonic function for productivity into a Cobb-Douglas production function:

$$\mathbf{y}_{it} = \mathbf{x}_{it}\boldsymbol{\beta} + \omega_{it} + e_{it}, \quad i = 1,\ldots,N; t = 1,\ldots,T, \tag{6}$$

where $\mathbf{y}_{it}$ is the dependent variable, $\mathbf{x}_{it}$ is a $(1 \times K)$ vector of regressors, $\boldsymbol{\beta}$ is a $(K \times 1)$ vector of coefficients, ω_{it} is a productivity shock, and e_{it} is an idiosyncratic error term. The major contribution of this approach is to replace c_i in Eq. (1) with ω_{it} and to create a proxy for ω_{it} by introducing a new function, which for OP is the investment function and for LP is an intermediate input demand function, to control for the unobserved productivity shock. Assuming a monotonic relationship between investment or intermediate demand and ω_{it}, one can invert the investment or intermediate demand function and solve for ω_{it} as an unknown function of observed variables. The resulting control function then is substituted for ω_{it} in Eq. (6) before the model is estimated. Differing from OP and LP, ACF argue that labor is a deterministic function of the set of variables in the OP/LP procedures, upon which one must condition. Thus, ACF suggest inverting investment or intermediate demand functions that are conditional on the labor input. With OP/LP/ACF, ω_{it} is not fixed over time, allowing calculation of time-varying partial effects of explanatory variables directly from the estimated control function.

The control function approach is not without its own potential problems. The analyst must specify a functional form for ω_{it} and specify moment conditions to identify the parameters of the model. This requires assumptions about the lagged dependence of productivity and the validity of additional instruments such as input prices. Additionally, as pointed out by GM, one assumes that the control function is completely specified and, before inversion of the investment function or the intermediate demand function, that ω_{it} rather than its change from last period is an argument in these functions. If these assumptions are incorrect, the control function approach does not model endogeneity correctly.

Borrowing the control function approach of OP/LP/ACF, Atkinson, Primont, and Tsionas (2018) use Gibbs sampling to estimate a technology-oriented directional distance function together with price equations derived from profit-maximization and cost-minimization models. They employ a balanced panel of 77 US utilities from 1988 to 2005. Their Bayesian approach allows joint estimation of a generalized control function, a second-order flexible production function, and shadow price equations, in which the latter allow measurement of firm-specific price inefficiency. The authors also compute optimal firm-specific directions. Employing input prices as part of their instrument set, these authors reach four major conclusions: the profit-maximization model is superior to its cost-minimization counterpart; only weak support exists for the AJ effect; mean productivity change is slightly less than 1%; and the partial effects of productivity with respect to its arguments are largest for lagged productivity and energy prices.

Following OP/LP/ACF, Atkinson and Luo (2018) formulate a Cobb-Douglas production function for electricity generation which includes a control function for productivity, using a panel of the 80 largest and almost exclusively coal-fired US electric power plants from 1995 to 2005. They extend OP/LP/ACF by modeling the optimal control of a major pollutant, SO_2. Subject to a given level of electricity production, they compute the cost-minimizing solution for the firm, which must either purchase emission permits or directly control this pollutant. They include input prices and lagged inputs as instruments, calculating partial effects of inputs on productivity from the fitted control function.

Both ACF and GM question whether input and output prices are valid instruments. If the Law of One Price holds, variation in prices occurs only because of unobserved quality differences, rendering prices correlated with the error term, which contains these quality measures. With electric utilities, however, omitted quality differences are minimal. For wages, unmeasured quality differences should be important only for higher-level management. Other tasks are highly mechanized in a very capital-intensive process. The price of energy is in terms of thermal content, so no quality differential is omitted. The price of capital is typically a function of the price index for equipment and structures, the yield on utility bonds, tax rates, the ratio of equity to total capitalization, and depreciation. This calculation includes all important quality differentials. Finally, the price of output is measured as price per kilowatt hour in terms of a standardized voltage, which includes the relevant quality measure. To a large extent, similar arguments can be made for the use of nonlabor input prices as instruments in the analysis of railroads and airlines.

What factors might cause exogenous input price variation across time and firms? Four exogenous market imperfections vary across firms and time: the degree of union power, which is greater in the Northeast, but which has diminished nationwide over time; increased availability of natural gas in the Northeast, which historically receives less than the South, because of recent fracking; recent state subsidies for the purchase of high-sulfur coal if made within same-state boundaries; and increasingly strict state air quality implementation plans in states such as California, which affect the choice of fuel relative to pollution-control equipment.

5   Conclusion

A consensus emerges for three important sectors of panel data energy economics. Substantial agreement exists among studies of the electric power industry, whether the unit of observation is the utility or plant and whether the data is cross-sectional or panel. With the latter, general agreement exists among studies that pool panel-data and those that estimate firm FE to remove time-invariant unobservables. A consensus of results also is found across a variety of behavioral assumptions: cost minimization, profit maximization, distance functions without behavioral assumptions, and systems of equations that append first-order conditions to cost, profit, and distance functions. Generally, studies reject homogeneous and homothetic functional forms and find that RTS are nearly constant for the largest firms. And productivity growth, computed as a residual, declines over time to small but positive levels. Nearly all panel studies examining vertical integration find substantial EVI, which argues against restructuring of the generation, transmission, and distribution sectors. Cost saving can accrue from a competitive generating sector. Substantial controversy remains regarding the existence of an AJ effect and the relative efficiency of public versus private utilities. Railroads appear to enjoy increasing RTS but exhibit substantial allocative inefficiency through 1975, with low productivity growth. Airlines appear to operate close to constant RTS, while TE and allocative inefficiency are substantial for many firms. Both decrease with deregulation. With renewed interest in production function estimation, the approach of OP/LP/ACF is a potentially valuable method for dealing with endogeneity by directly estimating the unknown productivity term using a control function. Some of their identifying assumptions, however, might be problematic. Bayesian methods are important tools to facilitate the estimation of more complex models of this variety. Unfortunately, many recent studies of production functions ignore much of this literature, assume a homogeneous technology, and ignore possible endogeneity, much like the initial production function literature for the electricity sector in the 1960s. The major difference is that the new studies employ panel rather than cross-sectional data.

References

Ackerberg, D.A., Caves, K., Frazer, G., 2015. Identification properties of recent production function estimators. Econometrica 83 (6), 2411–2451.

Atkinson, S.E., Cornwell, C., 1994. Parametric measurement of technical and allocative inefficiency with panel data. International Economic Review 35 (1), 231–244.

Atkinson, S.E., Cornwell, C., 2011. Estimation of allocative efficiency and productivity growth with dynamic adjustment costs. Econometric Reviews 30, 337–357.

Atkinson, S.E., Cornwell, C., Honerkamp, O., 2003. Measuring and decomposing productivity change: Stochastic distance function estimation vs. DEA. Journal of Business and Economic Statistics 21, 284–294.

Atkinson, S.E., Dorfman, J.H., 2005. Bayesian measurement of productivity and efficiency in the presence of undesirable outputs: Crediting electric utilities for reducing air pollution. Journal of Econometrics 126, 445–468.

Atkinson, S.E., Dorfman, J.H., 2009. Feasible estimation of firm-specific allocative inefficiency through bayesian numerical methods. Journal of Applied Econometrics 24, 675–697.

Atkinson, S.E., Färe, R., Primont, D., 2003. Stochastic measurement of firm inefficiency using distance functions. Southern Economic Journal 69, 596–611.

Atkinson, S.E., Halvorsen, R., 1976. Interfuel substitution in steam-electric power generation. Journal of Political Economy 84 (5), 959–978.

Atkinson, S.E., Halvorsen, R., 1980. A test of relative and absolute price efficiency in regulated utilities. Review of Economics and Statistics 62 (1), 81–88.

Atkinson, S.E., Halvorsen, R., 1984. Parametric efficiency tests, economies of scale, and input demand in U.S. electric power generation. International Economic Review 25 (3), 647–662.

Atkinson, S.E., Halvorsen, R., 1986. The relative efficiency of public and private utilities in a regulated environment: the case of U.S. electric utilities. Journal of Public Economics 29 (3), 281–294.

Atkinson, S.E., Luo, R., 2018. Productivity, abatement cost efficiency, and restructuring of coal-fired power plants. Working paper, Department of Economics, University of Georgia.

Atkinson, S.E., Primont, D., 2002. Measuring productivity growth, technical efficiency, allocative efficiency, and returns to scale using distance functions. Journal of Econometrics 108 (2), 203–225.

Atkinson, S.E., Primont, D., Tsionas, M.G., 2018. Statistical inference in efficient production with bad inputs and outputs using latent prices and optimal directions. Journal of Econometrics 204, 131–146.

Atkinson, S.E., Tsionas, M.G., 2016. Directional distance functions: optimal endogenous directions. Journal of Econometrics 190 (2), 301–314.

Averch, H., Johnson, L.L., 1962. Behavior of the firm under regulatory constraint. American Economic Review 52 (5), 1052–1069.

Baltagi, B.H., Griffin, J.M., 1988. A general index of technical change. Journal of Political Economy 96 (1), 20–41.

Baltagi, B.H., Griffin, J.M., Rich, D.P., 1995. Airline deregulation: The cost pieces of the puzzle. International Economic Review 36 (1), 245–258.

Barzel, Y., 1964. The production function and technical change in the steam-electric industry. Journal of Political Economy 72 (2), 133–150.

Belinfante, A., 1978. The identification of technical change in the electricity generating industry. In: Fuss, M.A., McFadden, D.L. (Eds.), Production economics: A dual approach to theory and applications. North Holland, Amsterdam.

Borenstein, S., Rose, N., 1994. Competition and price dispersion in the U.S. airline industry. Journal of Political Economy 102 (4), 653–683.

Boyes, W.J., 1976. An empirical examination of the Averch-Johnson effect. Economic Inquiry 14 (1), 25–35.

Bushnell, J.B., Mansur, E.T., Saravia, C., 2008. Vertical arrangements, market structure, and competition: An analysis of restructured US electricity markets. American Economic Review 98 (1), 237–266.

Carlson, C., Burtraw, D., Cropper, M., Palmer, K.L., 2000. Sulfur dioxide control by electric utilities: What are the gains from trade? The Journal of Political Economy 108 (6), 1292–1326.

Caves, D.W., Christensen, L.R., Swanson, J., 1981. Productivity growth, scale economies, and capacity utilization in U.S. railroads, 1955-74. American Economic Review 71 (5), 994–1002.

Caves, D.W., Christensen, L.R., Tretheway, M., 1981. U.S. trunk air carriers, 1972–1977: A multilateral comparison of total factor productivity. In: Cowing, T.G., Stevenson, R.E. (Eds.), Productivity measurement in regulated industries. Academic Press, New York, pp. 47–76.

Chan, H.R., Fell, H., Lange, I., Li, S., 2017. Efficiency and environmental impacts of electricity restructuring on coal-fired power plants. Journal of Environmental Economics and Management 81, 1–18.

Christensen, L.R., Greene, W.H., 1976. Economies of scale in U.S. electric power generation. Journal of Political Economy 84 (4), 655–676.

Christensen, L.R., Greene, W.H., 1978. An econometric assessment of cost savings from coordination in US electric power generation. Land Economics 54 (2), 139–155.

Coelli, T.J., Perelman, S., 1999. A comparison of parametric and non-parametric distance functions: with applications to European railways. European Journal of Operational Research 117 (2), 326–339.

Cornwell, C., Schmidt, P., Sickles, R., 1990. Production frontiers with cross-sectional and time-series variation in efficiency levels. Journal of Econometrics 46 (1-2), 185–200.

Courville, L., 1974. Regulation and efficiency in the electric utility industry. Bell Journal of Economics and Management Science 5 (1), 53–74.

Cowing, T.G., 1974. Technical change and scale economies in an engineering production function: the case of steam electric power. Journal of Industrial Economics 23 (2), 135–152.

Cowing, T.G., 1978. The effectiveness of rate-of-return regulation: An empirical test using profit functions. In: Fuss, M.A., McFadden, D.L. (Eds.), Production economics: A dual approach to theory and applications. North Holland, Amsterdam.

Cowing, T.G., Smith, V.K., 1978. The estimation of a production technology: A survey of econometric analyses of steam electric generation. Land Economics 54 (2), 156–186.

Dhrymes, P.J., Kurz, M., 1964. Technology and scale in electricity generation. Econometrica 32 (3), 287–315.

Douglas, P.H., 1976. The Cobb-Douglas production function once again: Its history, its testing, and some new empirical values. Journal of Political Economy 84 (5), 903–916.

Färe, R., Grosskopf, S., Noh, D., Weber, W., 2005. Characteristics of a polluting technology: Theory and practice. Journal of Econometrics 126 (2), 469–492.

Fowlie, M., 2010. Emissions trading, electricity restructuring, and investment in pollution abatement. American Economic Review 100 (3), 837–869.

Fraquelli, G., Piacenza, M., Vannoni, D., 2005. Cost savings from generation and distribution with an application to italian electric utilities. Journal of Regulatory Economics 28 (3), 289–308.

Friebel, G., Ivaldi, M., Vibes, C., 2010. Railway (de)regulation: A european efficiency comparison. Economica 77 (305), 77–91.

Galatin, M., 1968. Economies of scale and technological change in thermal power generation. North Holland, Amsterdam.

Gathon, H.-J., Perelman, S., 1992. Measuring technical efficiency in European railways: A panel data approach. Journal of Productivity Analysis 3 (1/2), 131–151.

Gerardi, K.S., Shapiro, A.H., 2009. Does competition reduce price dispersion? New evidence from the airline industry. Journal of Political Economy 117 (1), 1–37.

Gilsdorf, K., 1995. Testing for subadditivity of vertically integrated electric utilities. Southern Economic Journal 62 (1), 126–138.

Gollop, F.M., Roberts, M.J., 1981. The sources of economic growth in the US electric power industry. In: Cowing, T.G., Stevenson, R.E. (Eds.), Productivity measurement in regulated industries. Academic Press, New York, p. 1981.

Gollop, F.M., Roberts, M.J., 1983. Environmental regulations and productivity growth: The case of fossil-fueled electric power generation. Journal of Political Economy 91 (4), 654–674.

Good, D.H., Röller, L.-H., Sickles, R.C., 1995. Airline efficiency differences between Europe and the U.S.: Implications for the pace of EC integration and domestic regulation. European Journal of Operational Research 80 (3), 508–518.

Griliches, Z., Mairesse, J., 1998. Production functions: The search for identification. In: Strøm, S. (Ed.), Econometrics and economic theory in the 20th century. Cambridge University Press, pp. 169–203.

Hattori, T., Tsutsui, M., 2004. Economic impact of regulatory reforms in the electricity supply industry: A panel data analysis for OECD countries. Energy Policy 32 (6), 823–832.

Hausman, J., Taylor, W., 1981. Panel data and unobservable individual effects. Econometrica 49 (6), 1377–1398.

Hausman, J.A., 1978. Specification tests in econometrics. Econometrica 46, 1251–1271.

Hayashi, P.M., Goo, J.Y., Chamberlain, W.C., 1997. Vertical economies: the case of US electric utility industry, 1983-87. Southern Economic Journal 63 (3), 710–725.

Hayashi, P.M., Sevier, M., Trapani, J.M., 1985. Pricing efficiency under rate of return regulation: Some empirical evidence for the electric utility industry. Southern Economic Journal 51 (3), 776–792.

Hiebert, L.D., 2002. The determinants of the cost efficiency of electric generatings plants: a stochastic frontier approach. Southern Economic Journal 68 (4), 935–946.

Huettner, D.A., Landon, J.H., 1978. Electric utilities: Scale economies and diseconomies. Southern Economic Journal 44 (4), 883–912.

Jara-Díaz, S., Ramos-Real, F.J., 2004. Economies of integration in the Spanish electricity industry using a multistage cost function. Energy Economics 26 (6), 995–1013.

Jara-Díaz, S., Ramos-Real, F.J., 2011. The effect of output specification on the optimal policy design for electric utilities. Journal of Regulatory Economics 40 (1), 62–81.

Joskow, P., 2006. Markets for power in the United States: An interim assessment. Energy Journal 27 (1), 1–36.

Kaserman, D.L., Mayo, J.W., 1991. The measurement of vertical economies and the efficient structure of the electric utility business. The Journal of Industrial Economics 39 (5), 483–503.

Knittel, C.R., 2002. Alternative regulatory methods and firm efficiency: Stochastic frontier evidence from the U.S. electricity industry. Review of Economics and Statistics 84 (3), 530–540.

Koh, D.S., Berg, S., Kenny, W., 1996. A comparison of costs in privately owned and publicly owned electric utilities: The role of scale. Land Economics 72 (1), 56–65.

Komiya, R., 1962. Technical progress and the production function in the United States steam power industry. Review of Economics and Statistics 44 (2), 156–166.

Kumbhakar, S., 1987. Production frontiers and panel data: an application to U.S. class 1 railroads. Journal of Business and Economic Statistics 5 (2), 249–255.

Kwoka, J., 2008. Restructuring the U.S. electric power sector: a review of recent studies. Review of Industrial Organization 32 (3-4), 165–196.

Law, S.M., 2014. Assessing the Averch-Johnson-Wellisz effect for regulated utilities. International Journal of Economics and Finance 6 (8), 41–67.

Levinsohn, J., Petrin, A., 2003. Estimating production functions using inputs to control for unobservables. Review of Economic Studies 70 (2), 317–342.

Liu, Z., Lynk, E.L., 1999. Evidence on market structure of the deregulated US airline industry. Applied Economics 31 (9), 1083–1092.

Llorca, M., Orea, L., Pollitt, M.G., 2016. Efficiency and environmental factors in the US electricity transmission industry. Energy Economics 55 (issue C), 234–246.

Maloney, M.T., 2001. Economies and diseconomies: Estimating electricity cost functions. Review of Industrial Organization 19 (2), 165–180.

Martínez-Budría, E., Jara-Díaz, S., Ramos-Real, F.J., 2003. Adapting productivity theory to the quadratic cost function: An application to the Spanish electric sector. Journal of Productivity Analysis 20 (2), 213–229.

Meyer, R., 2012a. Vertical economies and the costs of separating electricity supply—A review of theoretical and empirical literature. Energy Journal 33 (4), 161–185.

Meyer, R., 2012b. Economies of scope in electricity supply and the costs of vertical separation for different unbundling scenarios. Journal of Regulatory Economics 42 (1), 95–114.

Nelson, R.A., Primeaux Jr., W.J., 1988. The effects of competition on transmission and distribution costs in the municipal electric industry. Land Economics 64 (4), 338–346.

Nelson, R.A., Wohar, M.E., 1983. Regulation, scale economies and productivity in steam-electric generation. International Economic Review 24 (1), 57–79.

Nemoto, J., Goto, M., 2004. Technological externalities and economies of vertical integration in the electric utility industry. International Journal of Industrial Organization 22 (1), 67–81.

Nemoto, J., Nakanishi, Y., Madono, S., 1993. Scale economies and over-capitalization in Japanese electric utilities. International Economic Review 34 (2), 431–440.

Nerlove, M., 1963. Returns to scale in electricity supply. In: Christ, C.F. (Ed.), Measurement in economics: Studies in mathematical economics and econometrics in memory of Yehuda Grunfeld. Stanford University Press, Palo Alto, CA.

Nillesen, P.H.L., Pollitt, M.G., 2011. Ownership unbundling in electricity distribution: Empirical evidence from new zealand. Review of Industrial Organization 38 (1), 61–93.

Oh, D., Lee, Y.G., 2016. Productivity decomposition and economies of scale of Korean fossil-fuel power generation companies: 2001-2012. Energy 100 (1), 1–9.

Olley, G.S., Pakes, A., 1996. The dynamics of productivity in the telecommunications equipment industry. Econometrica 64 (6), 1263–1297.

Park, B.U., Sickles, R.C., Simar, L., 1988. Stochastic panel frontiers: A semiparametric approach. Journal of Econometrics 84 (2), 273–301.

Perelman, S., Pestieau, P., 1988. Technical performance in public enterprises: A comparative study of railways and postal services. European Economic Review 32 (2/3), 432–441.

Pescatrice, D.R., Trapani, J.M., 1980. The performances and objectives of public and private utilities operating in the United States. Journal of Public Economics 13 (2), 259–276.

Petersen, H.C., 1975. An empirical test of regulatory effects. Bell Journal of Economics 6 (1), 111–126.

Polemis, M.L., Stengos, T., 2017. Electricity sector performance: A panel threshold analysis. Energy Journal 38 (3), 141–158.

Pompei, F., 2013. Heterogeneous effects of regulation on the efficiency of the electricity industry across European Union countries. Energy Economics 40, 569–585.

Ramos-Real, F.J., 2005. Cost functions and the electric utility industry. A contribution to the debate on deregulation. Energy Policy 33 (1), 69–87.

Roberts, M.J., 1986. Economies of density and size in the production and delivery of electric power. Land Economics 62 (4), 378–387.

Rungsuriyawiboon, S., Stefanou, S.E., 2007. Dynamic efficiency estimation an application to U.S. electric utilities. Journal of Business and Economic Statistics 25 (2), 226–238.

Schmidt, P., Sickles, R., 1984. Production frontiers and panel data. Journal of Business and Economic Statistics 2 (4), 367–374.

Scully, G.W., 1998. Reform and efficiency gains in the New Zealand electric supply industry. Journal of Productitviy Analysis 11 (2), 133–147.

Sickles, R.C., Good, D., Johnson, R.L., 1986. Allocative distortions and the regulatory transition of the U.S. airline industry. Journal of Econometrics 33 (1/2), 143–163.

Steiner, F., 2001. Regulation, industry structure and performance in the electricity supply industry. OECD Economic Studies 32 (1), 143–182.

Sun, J.Y., 2017. Airline deregulation and its impacts on air travel demand and airline competition: evidence from Korea. Review of Industrial Organization 51 (3), 343–380.

Thompson, H.G., 1997. Cost efficiency in power procurement and delivery service in the electric utility industry. Land Economics 73 (3), 287–296.

Wang, H.-J., Schmidt, P., 2002. One-step and two-step estimation of the effects of exogenous variables on technical efficiency levels. Journal of Productivity Analysis 18 (3), 129–144.

Whalen, T.W., 2007. A panel data analysis of code-sharing, antitrust immunity, and open skies treaties in international aviation markets. Review of Industrial Organization 30 (1), 39–61.

Zhang, Y.-F., Parker, D., Kirkpatrick, C., 2008. Electricity sector reform in developing countries: an econometric assessment of the effects of privatization, competition and regulation. Journal of Regulatory Economics 33 (2), 159–178.

Chapter 16

Panel Data Analysis Based on Lab Evidence in Auction Market Experiments

Georgia Kosmopoulou, Daniel Nedelescu and Fletcher Rehbein
University of Oklahoma, Norman, OK, United States

Chapter Outline

1 Introduction

In the natural sciences, researchers have long been replicating in the laboratory naturally occurring phenomena to isolate effects based on the underpinnings of theoretical models. In economics, on the other hand, most of the empirical work is based on field socioeconomic data. Economic researchers started to develop a methodology—experimental economics—to run experiments, in the same spirit as those run only by physicists in the second half of the 20th century. One of the first economics experiment was in fact a market game run by Edward Chamberlin at Harvard University in the 1940s during one of his lectures. In his experiment, Chamberlin used a pit market to show that, contrary to theoretical predictions pertaining to full efficiency of a perfectly competitive markets, experimental findings deviate as we now know for a variety of market related reasons. One of the fathers of experimental economics, Vernon Smith, is a graduate student of Chamberlin's.

Smith is one of the economists who created the foundation for experimental economics as a methodology to study markets. Articles such as

Panel Data Econometrics. https://doi.org/10.1016/B978-0-12-815859-3.00016-0

"Microeconomic Systems as an Experimental Science" (Smith, 1982) and "Economics in the Laboratory" (Smith, 1994) are seminal in experimental economics. His initial work focused on double auction mechanisms, an improvement of the pit market experiment by Chamberlin. These auction mechanisms were shown to increase market efficiency to more than 90%.

Considering the number of published articles, experimental economics does not have a long history and it evolved rapidly in recent years. In the 1960s, just a few articles were published annually, while currently more than 100 articles appear in print per year. The most impactful journal dedicated to the field, *Experimental Economics*, had its first issue only in 1998. In its rapid evolution, it is important to understand how the econometric analysis of lab experiments has evolved to allow for better controls within data leading to rigorous analysis of research questions.

In the next sections, we offer details related to the experimental design in the laboratory and how a careful treatment can help answer research questions more accurately. In spite of its tight control on many aspects of the environment that cannot be controlled in naturally occurring socioeconomic data such as the underlying distribution of bidder values, an experiment still cannot control for all the factors affecting economic agents in their interactions. As a result, we need to use the same methods that econometricians use when they deal with panel data based on field observations. When unobserved group level characteristics affect a variable of interest, the traditional tools of regression analysis lead to inefficient and likely biased estimates. The use of random or fixed effects models is common among economic experimentalists to control for unobserved variability in individual characteristics and explore the panel structure of an experimental design. Our focus for the remainder of this chapter will be on experimental papers in auction starting with the nuances of different experimental environments designed to test economic hypotheses and then explaining how econometric analysis can help us control and refine our search taking a step toward answering fundamental economic questions.

2 Why Do Economists Conduct Experiments?

Smith (1994) lists seven main reasons as an answer to this question tied closely to the methodological treatment of data collected.

1. Test a theory, or discriminate between theories

Researchers produce new theories/economic models. Running an experiment is one way to examine how much we can rely on the theoretical modeling and how their predictions project to real world outcomes. Smith provides as relevant examples, experiments from auction theory, in which different mechanisms allow us to capture and differentiate attitudes toward risk. Creating a mapping between theory and relevant data is easier in an experimental setting than in the field. In most experiments, for example, a careful design can control for most typically unobserved heterogeneity, limit selection, or endogeneity issues that can be met in the field, thus requiring the use of simpler panel data techniques and avoiding bias.

2. Explore the causes of a theory's failure

Smith offers an example context of common value auctions on circumstances where one can explore the failure of theoretical predictions. Kagel and Levin (1986) study the winner's curse effect by differentiating between a situation when the number of experienced subjects is small, and they reach the Nash equilibrium outcome, and when it is large and the Nash equilibrium is not reached as bidders bid aggressively, generate negative profits, and fall prey to the winner's curse. Careful control of the environment, participation, values, and risk preferences allows use of now-mainstream econometric techniques.

3. Establish empirical regularities as a basis for new theory

The double auction institution was studied in the laboratory before an economic model was proposed (see Friedman (1991)).

4. Compare environments

In common value auctions, we observe how the number of subjects can change market outcomes. In a laboratory experiment, the researcher can control for many variables, which makes it easier to isolate the impact of a factor on theoretical predictions.

5. Compare institutions

Keeping the same environment, the researcher can change the type of auction institution (English vs Dutch or vs first-price sealed bid auction) to provide comparisons unaffected by issues of selection. Controlling the environment in terms of values and participation, we can study, for example, which auction framework gives the highest revenue.

6. Evaluate policy proposals

Experimental economics offers the option to evaluate different policies before these policies are implemented. Plott (1987) offers a discussion about how experimental economics is used in actual policy decision-making. When considering designs to accommodate policy effects such as the difference-in-difference model, an effort to address concerns, such as those raised by Bertrand, Duflo, and Mullainathan (2004) about empirical work that does not account for correlated errors, should be made.

7. The laboratory as a testing ground for institutional design

Smith gives as an example early experiments that study uniform-price sealed bid auctions for Treasury securities. He states that these experiments were the reason why Henry Wallich motivated the Treasury in the early 1970s to offer some long-term bonds using these mechanisms.

3 Controlling for Factors Through Experimental Design

An advantage in running an economic experiment is that a researcher can control for a plethora of factors through careful design. It is easy in a controlled experiment to change the valuation of a subject, to assign different treatments to each subject, or change the institution. These changes make the analysis of data easier and the conclusions clearer. For example, there are situations in which a good experimental design can ensure that the basic assumptions of the OLS estimation model are satisfied.

The balk of the statistical analysis using experimental data range from the use of a basic Student's *t*-test when considering simple hypothesis testing about the mean under the assumption of normally distributed observations, a nonparametric Wilcoxon rank-sum test and ANOVA testing. A number of those papers use complementary pooled data analysis such as List and Lucking-Reiley (2000), List (2001), Kosmopoulou and De Silva (2007), Kagel, Pevnitskaya, and Ye (2007), Filiz-Ozbay and Ozbay (2007), Shahriar and Wooders (2011), and Pagnozzi and Saral (2017). An experimental design, however, cannot control for all factors that influence the results of our analysis. Much like in a field study, the researcher can use more rigorous econometric techniques to account for unobserved heterogeneity and the issue of potential bias. Fixed effects and random effects models help researchers to control for unobservable characteristics of subjects or the environment within an experimental study in the same way that they help an applied econometrician in the analysis of field data. In this section, we pay attention more to the experimental design and how a researcher can control for factors, while in the next sections we show how avoiding selection issues simple fixed and random effects models are applied in experimental economics.

Assume that a researcher would like to study whether the Dutch auction is strategically equivalent to the first-price sealed auction. An example for such study is Coppinger, Smith, and Titus (1980), in which the authors compare the classical auction formats. If the researcher uses field socioeconomic data, she needs to control for a few factors that can change how a bidder behaves: the reservation value for the good, individual characteristics, number of bidders in the auction, expectations, the experience of the bidders, etc. In the econometric model, the researcher should include all these variables to avoid bias in the estimated effects of the treatment variables. More often than not, data sets do not include variables such as the reservation value for the goods auctioned off or risk preference that critically influence the bid submitted and can help answer the research question.

Using an economic experiment, these problems can be avoided. First, the researcher does not have to deal with the problem that reservation values are not observable for the bidders. The bidders are allocated values that represent their fictitious valuations for each commodity. The payment to each participant depends on her reservation value and the price she will pay if she wins the auction.

Other individual characteristics are typically unobservable in a field auction, but they are important in the determination of a bid. An example is risk preferences. In experiments, risk preferences can be elicited introducing lottery choices similar to the method proposed by Holt and Laury (2002). Other individual characteristics can be determined with ease and relative accuracy through a survey at the end of each experiment.

In field auctions, it is not easy to observe or control if a bidder participates in the two types of auctions (Dutch and first-price) under consideration. In contrast, in an experiment, the researcher can randomly allocate one of the two types of auction to each subject that participates in a session. By randomly assigning the type of auction (treatment), we ensure that there is no selection issue. The design might require a larger number of participants, which can be costly, but it is feasible and the researcher can draw reliable conclusions.

Based on such a design, we can run a simple OLS regression. The depended variable is the bid value, and some independent variables can be identifying the type of auction (dummy D_{it}), reservation value, risk preferences, individual characteristics (X_{it}), and auction-related effects (Z_{at}).

$$Y_{iat} = \beta_1 D_{it} + \beta_2 X_{it} + Z_{at} + \varepsilon_{iat}$$

If the error terms ε_{iat} are independent across time (t), individuals (i), and auctions (a) with $E\varepsilon_{iat} = 0$ and $V\varepsilon_{iat} = \sigma^2$, the model can be estimated via OLS, constituting a pooled regression. If there are still unobservable individual characteristics that can influence the value of the bid, a fixed or random effects model can be employed. If we think that some of these unobservable characteristics are correlated with one of our independent variables (e.g., we did not collect information about education that might affect the bid, but we have information about age), then a fixed effects model is deemed more appropriate. If unobservable individual effects are not correlated to the extent possible with any of the independent variables, however, then a random effects model is better under considerations of efficiency. Using random effects under the generalized least squares estimation (GLS) rather than fixed effects or within group estimators to account for unobserved auction heterogeneity has been a common practice in experiments, partly because of the ability to control for a number of factors that typically are unobservable in the field and partly because of limitations in the number of bids available per auction. Fixed effects estimators are not consistent when data are limited (e.g., see Bajari, Houghton, & Tadelis, 2014). Ultimately, a Hausman test can provide guidance about which of the two models is better for our econometric specification.

The experimental design could allow us to collect more independent observations regarding both types of auction if we allocate both types of auction to all subjects. This design is called within-subject design. Compared to between-subject design in which subjects participate in one auction format at random, this design allows for a smaller number of subjects (so a lower cost to run the experiment) for the same number of independent observations from both auctions. This, however, implies repeated measurements and can affect how a subject behaves. For example, the subject might have certain behavior if initially exposed to the Dutch auction and then to a first-price sealed bid auction, compared to the situation when the participant is exposed to first-price sealed bid auction initially. This is called the order effect. To control for this effect, the researcher can run multiple sessions and change the order of the treatment.

Statistical experimental designs help us control for this kind of variation. A few designs that can help control for one or two factors such as order of the treatments follow:

(a) *Randomized complete block design.* This design controls for variations of one nuisance factor, such as the order of the treatment within a session. The results from a treatment might be different if the treatment is run at the beginning of the session or at the end of the session.

(b) *Latin square design.* This design controls for variations of two nuisance factors.

(c) *Incomplete block design.* There are situations when we cannot allocate all our treatments within a session.

(d) *2k factorial design.* This type of design is for a situation when you try to control for a few factors that all have only two options/levels.

No matter which design a researcher chooses, in the end it is impossible to control or measure all the factors that might influence the results of our experiment. All these designs help us to control for some of the factors and allow us to use simple econometric models to answer our research question. But even the simplest research question cannot have an experimental design that takes everything into consideration. This is the reason why it is quite common to use fixed or random effects to account for unobservable (individual or auction) characteristics. One persistent observation is that the random effects model is much more common in experimental papers than in pure empirical papers that are dominated by the use of fixed effects. Considerations of the number of observations and controls can be critical in this selection. In the next section, we present a small representative sample of experimental articles in auctions and discuss how the authors use these two models that are prevalent in empirical analysis.

4   The Panel Structure of Experimental Data in Auctions

Auction experiments have a panel structure characterized by cross sections of participants observed interacting over a sequence of rounds. Each of the cross-sectional units is observed repeatedly in a balanced panel structure. Interactions over time are affected by bidder characteristics, initial resource allocation, and the outcome of previous rounds. Some of the individual characteristics are unobservable, potentially time invariant, and share a common influence over the bids submitted by subjects. This influence leads to inefficiency of traditional linear regression techniques and is likely to bias the estimated effect of observable characteristics and treatments (unless the included predictors and excluded individual level effects are independent).

The model that reflects this panel structure is:

$$Y_{iat} = \beta_1 D_{iat} + \beta_2 X_{iat} + u_{iat} \tag{1}$$

$$u_{iat} = \delta_a + \mu_i + \varepsilon_{iat},$$

$$i = 1,...,N, \quad a = 1,...,M, \quad t = 1,...,T$$

where δ_a and μ_i assumes time invariant heterogeneity specifically related to the auction and individual related characteristics. Ignoring δ_a and μ_i creates a composite error that no longer satisfies the *i.i.d.* condition. Potential correlation between unobserved effects and explanatory variables could lead to problems of endogeneity and bias.

Experimental researchers typically have two ways to gain insight about those unobserved effects, namely by introducing fixed or random effects within the model. A fixed effects model allows a researcher to explore the relationship between the predictor and the response variable controlling explicitly for unobserved individual characteristics of a subject or the auction environment that might influence outcomes. Focusing on individual effects, the fixed effects model is designed to remove the effects of time-invariant characteristics of experimental subjects to provide an unbiased estimate of the effect of a predictor on the response variable. It is intended to estimate the causes of change in bidding behavior within a subject and assumes that all μ_i's are fixed unknown values. A simple estimation framework assumes that $E\varepsilon_{iat} = 0$ and $V\varepsilon_{iat} = \sigma^2$ with $\sum_{i=1}^{N} \mu_i = 0$ while a useful generalization would incorporate heteroscedasticity across the individual dimension $V\varepsilon_{iat} = \sigma_i^2$. The pooled OLS estimator in the fixed effects model is not merely inefficient but biased as well. Typically, within group estimators or fixed effects estimators, however, are unbiased and consistent. The random effects model is based on a strong assumption that those unobserved time invariant characteristics are uncorrelated to other observables. The random effects model does not explicitly model the unobserved effects, and it is unbiased only in the absence of correlation between the observable controls and the unobservable characteristics.

The model now can be written as:

$$Y_{iat} = \beta_1 D_{iat} + \beta_2 X_{iat} + u_{iat} \tag{2}$$

$$u_{iat} = \delta_a + \mu_i + \varepsilon_{iat},$$

$$\delta_a \sim i.i.d.(0, \sigma_\delta),$$

$$\mu_i \sim i.i.d.(0, \sigma_\mu)$$

$$\varepsilon_{iat} \sim i.i.d.(0, \sigma_\varepsilon)$$

$$i = 1,...,N, \quad a = 1,...,M, \quad t = 1,...,T$$

The errors are assumed to be independent of each other. If the standard assumptions of the OLS model hold, the fixed effects model is unbiased and consistent for large samples; if the additional assumption of independence between the explanatory variables and unobservable factors holds the random effects model estimated via a Generalized Least Squares estimation method produces not only unbiased and consistent estimates but also efficient. Therefore, there is a clear tradeoff between the two models that depends on the nuances of the environment. In typical experimental research in auctions, the unobservable characteristics of randomly selected subjects are less likely to be correlated with the treatment effects of interest than in the field because of selection, and the random effects model has been the model of choice. The limited number of observations of a typical experiment favors the use of random effects models because of potential inconsistency of the fixed effects model estimation results.

Setting aside the issue of unbiased, efficient, or consistent estimation of parameters, datasets with observations that are grouped naturally into clusters can reduce the precision of the standard errors or estimates. The introduction of clustered robust standard errors is relevant in panel data estimation, but it has had more limited use in the experimental work in the laboratory surveyed here. Cameron and Miller (2015) provide a practitioner's guide to cluster robust inference and focus on getting accurate statistical inferences through estimation of clustered robust standard errors in regression models, in which observations are grouped into clusters, with errors that are uncorrelated across clusters but correlated within clusters. In auction panel data, for example, there could be clustering at the individual level across time or clustering at the auction level. Failure to control for within-cluster error correlation can lead to underestimation of the variance and misleading confidence interval construction. Bertrand et al. (2004) pointed out that many difference-in-difference models fail to account for correlated errors and often cluster standard errors at the incorrect level with consequences in estimation.

4.1 Random Effects

A few examples of papers that use random effects models can help explain their widespread use in the analysis of experimental data.

4.1.1 Common or Private Value Auctions and Sequential Single Unit Sales

Nishimura, Cason, Saijo, and Ikeda (2011) study behavioral factors such as spite and reciprocity in auctions. The main factors controlled by the experiment were the type of auction (second price, or ascending bid auction), and the information dissemination in the auction environment (complete, or incomplete information). The reservation values were provided as part of the experimental design. The experiment had seven sessions of 12 subjects each, and in four of them the subjects participated in all four formats. In the remaining three sessions, they participated in a second price auction with complete information. Subjects submitted bids for 6–10 periods within each treatment configuration.

There is no entry selection issue here. In the field, bidders can choose the auction in which they would like to participate. In this experiment, like in most other laboratory experiments related to auctions, the subjects are allocated to an auction exogenously and their participation is guaranteed. In order to offer an example of modeling considerations and choices, we consider one of the hypotheses that were tested in this environment: *In the complete information environment, overbidding is more common for low-value bidders than for high-value bidders.* To test this hypothesis, the authors estimate four econometric models. The dependent variable was either the difference between the bid and the reservation value (for two GLS models), or a dummy variable that was equal to 1 if the bid exceeded the reservation value (in two Probit models). The independent variables include a dummy identifying the bidder with the lower reservation value, a dummy variable indicating if the bidder was matched with the same counterpart in the entire session (fixed paring), and a time trend (using the standard form 1/period). The estimation model is:

$$(y = 1 \,|\, Bid > Value)_{iat} = \beta_0 + \beta_1 D^{Low}{}_{iat} + \beta_2 D^{Fix}{}_{iat} + \beta_3 (1/period)_{iat} + \mu_i + \varepsilon_{iat}.$$

In order to account for subjects' unobserved individual characteristics, the author could use fixed or random effects models depending on the appropriateness of use. We can observe that the independent variables in the econometric model that are controlled by the experimental design are not likely related to individual characteristics. In that sense, a random effects model is likely to offer more advantages relative to the fixed effects model. The number of observations used in this analysis ranges from 39 to 84, which is low relative to the typical number from a field study. In a similar data set from a field auction, the dummy variable D^{Low} might be correlated to unobservable individual characteristics, because reservation values are not controlled and values could be critically determined by bidder characteristics. Coupled with the availability of larger data sets in the field, a fixed effect model potentially could be preferred.

For the Probit models, the coefficient β_1 is significantly different from zero at the one-percent level. This implies that in the complete information environment (when the bidders know the valuation of the other bidder) the bidders with lower valuations overbid more than the higher valuation bidders. This overbidding pattern is seen more often in a second-price auction compared to an ascending price auction. These patterns are not found under the incomplete information environment.

Isaac and Schnier (2005) analyze data from three field fundraising auctions (silent auctions), and six sessions of similar auctions performed through laboratory experiments. There were eight participants in each lab session, 16 goods auctioned off, and five auctions per session. Although the authors did not use fixed or random effects for the field data, they controlled for random effects for the panel data obtained from the experiment. Many of the variables are constructed in the same fashion as in the field (e.g., number of bidders) and some are modified (e.g., values) reflecting the flexibility that a laboratory experiment can provide to study ultimately perturbations to the institutional environment.

Schram and Onderstal (2009) perform experiments to compare three mechanisms used for charitable giving: the first-price winner-pay auction, the first-price all-pay auction, and lotteries. The results support the theoretical predictions that the first-price all-pay auction raises the most revenue and is the preferred mechanism to raise proceeds for charity. Each treatment is separated into four blocks of seven rounds. In two blocks, revenue wins are transformed into a public good for participants, representing charity. Revenues in general are higher when there is a charity than when there is not. Subjects were allocated to groups in each round and those groups constitute a unit of observation that is considered statistically independent. In order to test the hypothesis about revenue, they estimated a model with random effects introduced at the group level. The maximum likelihood estimation results confirm that the order of rounds does not affect revenue.

Corrigan and Rousu (2006) perform a series of experiments to test whether posting a price in an early auction affects bidding in subsequent lettings. Two distinct type of items were auctioned in a second-price sealed-bid auction setting. Participation took place in ten rounds of bidding with 28 and 36 participants taking part in each treatment respectively. The paper also analyzes the effect of gender and student performance on bidding behavior, employing a random effects model to capture variations between group. They controlled for time and treatment and bidder characteristics such as income, gender, and GPA. Posted prices have a significant impact on bids submitted through time.

In Ham and Kagel (2006), the authors study differences in bidding between men and women in a private-value auction setting. The auction process called indicative bidding is a two-stage game commonly followed in field settings to purchase assets. Based on nonbinding first-stage bids, a short list of bidders is selected to make bids in a first-price sealed-bid auction. In each of the experimental sessions, there were two auction markets with six bidders operating simultaneously. There were 25 auction periods were planned, with two auction markets operating simultaneously. They use a random effects Probit model, with subject as the random component, pooling the data across sessions to study bidding aggressiveness. The main result is that in a two-stage indicative bidding framework, women were more likely to enter the second stage with lower first-stage values than men. Estimating a bidding function of the second-stage bids, women were more aggressive bidding when their values were in the upper three-quarters of their support. Everything else equal, women are more likely to go bankrupt than men.

Casari, Ham, and Kagel (2007) are testing cognitive ability, as well as gender and college major, on ability to avoid winner's curse in a first-price sealed-bid common value auction. The experimental environment identifies a standard common value structure, two different levels of starting cash balances, and two different levels of both starting cash balances and subject returning incentives. The authors use random effects instrumental variable estimation to account for the correlations across periods for a given subject and the potential endogeneity of cash balances. The variables included here typically represent unobservable factors that if ignored could bias duration dependence. They find that those with ability below the median level bid more aggressively and go bankrupt more quickly, inexperienced women bid substantially higher than inexperienced men, and economics/business majors bid most aggressively.

Armantier and Treich (2009) test the effect of subjective probabilities and preferences on overbidding in a first-price private-value auction. The experimental design identifies two treatments, one with no feedback and one with feedback on bidder prediction accuracy and information on the objective winning probability. The authors conducted four experimental sessions with 10 subjects and 15 rounds each. They employ individual random effects to control for unobserved factors affecting subject predictions over time. They find that bidders who receive feedback about prediction accuracy make better predictions and overbid less than those with no feedback.

Li and Plott (2009) study tacit collusion in an environment in which each auction consists of eight subjects and eight items offered in simultaneously functioning, continuous ascending first-price auctions. The paper shows that tacit collusion is reached in the laboratory environment and develops over time as the subjects continue to bid on subsequent rounds. Tacit collusion is measured by a decrease in average prices, a decrease in number of bids, and a decrease in the duration of auctions. The econometric modeling used alternative specifications with prices, bids, duration, and the logarithms of those variables employed as dependent variables, and the auction round as an independent variable. All six models use random effects, and the estimated coefficient is negative and statistically significant. Each model is estimated based on 30 observations. The experimental results show that once tacit collusion develops, it is not easy to disrupt it.

Corrigan and Rousu (2011) test whether value affiliation leads to a breakdown of incentive compatibility in second-price auctions. The experimental procedure outlines a second-price treatment and a noncompetitive Becker-DeGroot-Marschak mechanism treatment. Both treatments were given private and common value signals. The second-price treatment included posted prices to mirror current auction trends. A random effects model is used to control for individual effects. As expected, the authors find modest evidence that bidders in second-price auctions initially adjust bids downward. They also find, however, that bidders in second-price auctions rapidly begin to overbid in subsequent rounds, suggesting that affiliation plays a relatively minor role.

Ivanova-Stenzel and Salmon (2011) test how bidders choose to enter an auction and its impact using the sealed-bid first-price auction and an English auction. The experimental procedure identifies an initial learning phase, and two auction choice phases, one where some bidders are forced into one of the two auctions while the others choose endogenously (FB). Random effects models are used to analyze the results of the data with and without selection. A first econometric model includes two dummy variables (one for the last 10 periods, and one for FB treatment), and the interaction between these variables. Also used is a random effects logit panel regression, which includes risk aversion, valuation, and interactions between them. The paper provides evidence that knowledge about one's own value has an impact on the auction format choice. They find that when endogenous entry is allowed the revenue advantage of the sealed-bid auction disappears. Bidders with lower values prefer the sealed-bid first-price auction, while those with higher values choose the English auction.

Hu, Kagel, Xu, and Ye (2013) study auction environments where competition imposes negative externalities that can improve market conditions. The paper investigates auctions in which an entrant imposes negative externalities on incumbents, conditional on winning the auction. The negative externality does not exist when an incumbent wins the auction. This setting tries to simulate a situation in which the characteristics of competitors affect market outcomes. They study this effect under English auction and first-price sealed-bid auction. Under an English auction, as theory predicts, the incumbent bidder that remains in the auction bids above her private value by a value equal to the negative externality. Under first-price auction, the two incumbents cannot coordinate, so the bids become more aggressive. This behavior will induce the entrant to bid more aggressively as well. While the incumbent bids are close to theoretical predictions, the entrant bids are not. The econometric model uses a random effects regression with the bid value as the dependent variable and identifiers of incumbent or entrant status, the private value, its square, and interaction between these variables as independent variables. We can observe that all independent variables are allocated randomly by experimental design, so there is no expected correlation with unobservables, which is the requirement for using a random effects model.

In Grosskopf, Rentschler, and Sarin (2018), the authors test the effect of access to private vs public information about bidding and the winner's curse in a first-price common-value auction. The experimental environment identifies: an asymmetric information structure, a symmetric structure with public information access, and a symmetric structure without public information access. To study what determines bidding behavior in this setting, they employ random effects Tobit estimation models to control for correlation of participants' behavior over time. They find that bidders who possess private information tend to overbid, but those observing public information underbid systematically.

Ariely, Ockenfels, and Roth (2005) compare eBay and Amazon auctions to study how the ending rule governing online auctions might change bidding behavior. Although both websites use second-price auctions, they differ by their ending rule. On eBay there is a fixed deadline, but on Amazon an auction ends only after 10 minutes pass without bidding activity. The paper presents results on the economic experiment used to control for other differences between the auctions bidding on the two websites (such as self-selection of sellers and buyers). The economic experiment has four treatments comparing eBay, Amazon, and second-price auctions (They introduce two eBay treatments that differ by the probability that a bid submitted at the last moment will be transmitted successfully.) In all four treatments, two bidders participate and each of them received a reservation value drawn independently from a uniform distribution. The highest bidder wins the auction, and pays the bid of the opponent.

The empirical analysis of the panel data focuses on time trends in bidding, considering the number of late bids received across auction formats. The main result of this study is that the null hypothesis that the number of bids submitted late is coming from the same distribution for the three treatments used to simulate the eBay and Amazon environment is rejected based on Kruskal-Wallis H-testing. A random-effects Probit model offers the same conclusion. The use of the random-effects model is based on a Hausman test. In both eBay treatments, there is a tendency to bid later as bidders gain experience, but in Amazon experienced bidders submit relatively fewer bids toward the end of the auction.

Cason and Turocy (2015) study auctions with independent signaling and interdependent values under first-price and second-price auction settings. They change the degree of interdependence of the values, with the extreme cases being the private-values model and common-values model. Contrary to Bayesian-Nash equilibrium and to cursed equilibrium, the revenues of an auction are the highest for intermediate values of interdependence. The authors analyze also how the pricing rule (first-price or second-price auction) or valuation structure affects response time. This is one of the first papers that study this correlation. The econometric model is a random-effects model at participant level, with clustered standard errors at the session level. The dependent variable is the response time, while the independent variables are the signal value, one over the number corresponding to the time period ($1/t$), and dummy variables for gender (women = 1), if participant is English native speaker, and if the major of the participant is economics. The results show that under first-price auction the response time is positively correlated with the signal level (higher signal leads to longer response time), while under second-price auction these two variables are independent.

4.1.2 Procurement Auctions

Cason, Kannan, and Siebert (2011) run an experiment in which they control for the amount of information that is provided after an auction, revealing in some cases only the winner's bid and in other cases all bids. Their intent is to study the trade-off that exists between learning enough from the auction process, and not revealing too much information to rivals. One result is that procurers pay less under the treatment with less information only when the market is very competitive. The bids are higher than the risk-neutral prediction, which can be explained by the degree of risk-aversion. The main independent variable of interest is a dummy that accounts for the treatment: incomplete or complete information about bids. The regressions to test the main hypotheses are Probit and Tobit models, both using subject random effects. The independent variables are the inverse of the period ($1/t$), a variable capturing order, a dummy variable identifying the information policy treatment, and another dummy related to the competitive treatments.

Chang, Chen, and Salmon (2015) compare a standard low-price procurement auction with an average bid auction, where the contract is awarded to the bidder whose bid is closest to the average of all bids. This was done using a between-subject design, in which subjects participated in only one of the two auction types. Bidder behavior is determined using bidder cost signal, dummies for an average auction, if the auction was in the second half of the session, cost realization type, and interaction terms. A random effects model is used at the subject level. The average bid mechanism is more successful in preventing winner's curse and in preventing seller losses.

Chang, Salmon, and Saral (2016) examine the effect of renegotiation on solving winner's curse in procurement auctions. They compare four treatments, with the presence and absence of weak bidders, and the presence and absence of renegotiation. Random effects models are used to test whether a behavioral difference with renegotiation exists. Bids are regressed on combined cost signals, and dummy variables for renegotiation, strong sellers, and low cash balances. In anticipation of successful renegotiation, bidders will lower bids to win and provide credible possibility of default.

4.1.3 Auction in Environmental Economics

Cason (1995) studies the auction mechanism used by the Environmental Protection Agency to allocate emission allowances according to Clean Air Act Amendments of 1990. The hypotheses tested by the experiment are related to how the number of bidders affects the winning bids and the bids summited. The experiment had 10 sessions. In two sessions, the opponent were robots, while in the other eight they were humans. Within the session with a human opponent, using an ABA design (in this design, they switch back and forth between two treatments A and B, in which in general A is the base treatment, and B is main treatment), the number of bidders with an auction changed from three bidders (treatment A) to six bidders (treatment B). The estimated models used a random-effects specification to control for bidder heterogeneity. A dummy variable is used to capture the difference in the number of bidders. Because assignment of bidders to treatments was random, selection was not an issue. Based on the analysis, the mean winning bid for the auction involving six bidders was higher than the one involving three bidders. Bids were above the risk-neutral Nash prediction. The risk-averse behavior would predict lower bids. Because most of the literature consistently accepts that most of the people are either risk-neutral or risk-averse, risk attitude cannot explain this deviation from the theoretical prediction.

In a series of papers also related to environmental economics, Cason, Gangadharan, and Duke (2003), Cason and Gangadharan (2004 and 2005) study auctions used for reducing nonpoint source pollution. For each of these papers, the sessions are run in the United States and in Australia. In their econometric estimation, the authors use random effects models at the session level. In their first paper related to how auctions might reduce the nonpoint source pollution, the main results show that when environmental quality of a project is revealed, the sellers misrepresent their cost for high-quality projects. The policy implication is that not revealing such information can improve regulatory efficiency. In the subsequent papers, the authors compare two distinct types of auctions (uniform and discriminatory) used to reduce the nonpoint source pollution. Although the offers made are in line with costs under the uniform price auction, some inefficiency occurred because there is the same price per unit. With the discriminatory price auction, the offers are above cost, creating inefficiencies but less than those of the uniform price auction.

Jog and Kosmopoulou (2014) study first-price asymmetric auctions with resale opportunities in secondary trading inspired by the market for emission trading permits. They compare outcomes in terms of bidding and efficiency between a buyer's and a seller's market. They find a price/efficiency tradeoff between the two regimes with higher bids submitted in the primary market when the secondary market is seller-advantaged. To explain bidding behavior, the econometric specification uses a random effects model and controls for values, asymmetries, attitudes toward risk, gender, academic level, and previous participation. A simple quantile regression model also is used to investigate the effect of key control variables across the conditional distribution of bids.

4.1.4 Multiunit Auctions

In Kagel and Levin (2001), the authors test the sensitivity of bidders to the demand reduction possibilities inherent in uniform price auctions when bidders have nonincreasing demand for multiple units. The experimental environment identifies behavior under five types of auctions: a sealed-bid auction, an English clock auction with dropout price feedback, a uniform price clock auction with no feedback, sealed-bid auction where dropout information of the clock auction is exogenously provided, and a dynamic Vickrey auction. The authors use subject-specific and auction-specific random effects. They find clear demand reduction in uniform price auctions, with demand reduction limited in the Vickrey auction, and closer to equilibrium in the ascending bid auction with dropout information than in a sealed-bid auction and ascending-bid auction with no information.

Kagel and Levin (2005) look at multiunit auction with synergies, and they ran the auction under two settings: ascending (open-outcry) and sealed-bid uniform-price auctions. Their main focus is on bidding behavior, however, without omitting a discussion about efficiency and revenue. A random effect Tobit model is estimated in order to show how values affect bids. In each of the econometric models, the independent variables include controls related to the valuation levels that were controlled by the experiment. The main result, which is supported by the estimated Tobit model, shows that, although the bids increase with the value as theory predicts, the bids are higher than predicted for the lower valuations, and lower for higher valuations.

Anderson and Holland (2006) tested the effects of different auction mechanisms on market outcomes. The experimental environment outlines a uniform price auction, a Kth price auction, and a $K + 1$st price auction. A random effects Tobit to control for auction-specific effects is used because of efficiency levels being at or near the maximum value of 1. The authors find that different auction types significantly affect market outcomes because of differing bidding strategies.

In Drichoutis, Nayga, and Lazaridis (2011), the authors test the role of subject training on bidding behavior in experimental auctions. They used a Vickrey auction to assess valuation for a number of lotteries. The experimental procedure outlines a 2×2 design varying the extent of training (minimal vs extensive) and the practice of posting market clearing prices (posting vs not posting the second-highest price). Standard sociodemographic data were collected regarding the subjects' age, household size, and a self-assessment of their economic position. The authors use a random effects Tobit model and find that extensive training increases one's willingness to pay.

In Armantier, Holt, and Plott (2013), the authors test distinctive features of the reference price auction adopted by the US Treasury with use in the TARP (Troubled Asset Relief Program). The experimental procedure outlines a grand auction, an announced accurate reference price auction, an announced noisy reference price auction, and a secret noisy reference price auction. They use random effects to capture individual, auction, and individual/auction effects. They find that a reference price auction can effectively promote competition and mitigate adverse selection. Beyond the TARP auction, these results are relevant to the various multiobject auctions in which value heterogeneity and informational asymmetries often pose serious efficiency challenges.

4.1.5 Auction as an Elicitation Method

Lusk, Ty, and Schroeder (2004) compare different auction mechanisms as methods to elicit the willingness to pay (valuations) for new products. In their experiment, there are nine different treatments. The differences between treatments are based on a subject's initial endowment, the auction type (second-price, random nth price, English, or Becker-DeGroot-Marschak auction), and the number of goods available for exchange (two or five different items). The theory shows that under the four auctions, the willingness to pay should be the same. A random effects Tobit is employed to control for bidder preferences. They also control for bidder gender, age, education, income, student status, and for the presence of all five types in a treatment. The main result is that second-price auctions were found to generate the highest willingness to pay, and random nth price auctions generated the lowest.

Gracia, Loureiro, and Nayga (2011) compare willingness to pay estimates from the most common elicitation tasks used to uncover willingness to pay, namely experimental auctions and real choice experiments (RCE). The design identifies an RCE in which participants choose between goods of different quality and prices and a random nth price auction in which participants bid simultaneously on each quality of goods. A random effects model is used. The same sociodemographic variables are included in determining the effect of each treatment to provide a direct comparison. The results indicate that willingness to pay estimates differ in experimental auctions and RCE.

4.2 Fixed Effects

In Ivanova-Stenzel and Salmon (2008), the authors provide revenue comparisons between the first-price sealed-bid and ascending-bid auctions in an independent private value setting. The experimental procedure identifies the learning phase in which subjects participate in both auctions exogenously and the main phase in which subjects choose which auction to participate.

The average revenue for the ascending auction is 54.9 ECUs (experimental currency units), and for the sealed-bid auction average revenue is 51.95 ECUs. A t-test and a Wilcoxon signed-rank test cannot reject the null hypothesis that the means of the two distributions are not statistically significantly different. The authors run a fixed-effects regression model clustering the standard errors by the groups of individuals that participate together in the same auctions. The estimated model of revenue includes identifiers for the type of auction and time.

We can observe that in this experiment, differently from most of the laboratory experiments regarding auctions, the subjects will choose in which type of auction they would like to participate. Because the subjects are presented with a choice, the authors use fixed effects to control for preference over auction types in time. The dummy variable identifying auction preference likely is correlated to the individual unobservable characteristics. This possible correlation potentially leads to violation of one of the assumptions for the random-effects model, giving a comparative advantage to the fixed-effects alternative. Most of the papers that analyze field data use fixed-effects model, and not random-effects model, which is different from what we observed in the typical laboratory experiment in auctions.

The main conclusion of the paper is that when endogenous entry is allowed, ascending auction revenue is high enough to reach the level of those of first-price sealed-bid auctions (this contradicts conventional wisdom in experiments in which the first-price auctions surpass ascending auctions in revenue likely because of individual attitudes toward risk but are less efficient). The two types of auctions lead to the same level of efficiency.

Salmon and Iachini (2007) compare the revenue and efficiency of the English auction and the pooled multi-unit auction. They find that overbidding in pooled auctions creates substantially higher revenue than the continuous ascending-bid auction, although both auction mechanisms have comparable efficiency. Experimentally, subjects participate in both types of auctions. The econometric model regresses a bid on a predicted risk neutral estimate for each bidder to make this partially a structural regression and includes a series of other variables to account for deviations from the risk-neutral prediction. These variables include a dummy for the last half of the experiment, interactions to test for bid changes over time, and controls for the pooled auctions occurring first. A dummy identifying high-valued goods is used to determine if overbidding is confined to those values, and variables for wealth and change in wealth are included. Although accumulated wealth during the experiment is correlated to the reservation value that is controlled by the experiment, this variable might be correlated to unobservable characteristics of the bidder, so a fixed effects model is used.

Elbittar (2009) studies the impact of valuation ranking information on bidding behavior. The experimental environment identifies a first-price sealed-bid auction under symmetric conditions and asymmetric conditions, in which bidders are informed of the rank order of their valuation. Two sessions of each treatment are performed, with 10 rounds of single-auction markets and 20 rounds of dual-auction markets in each session. In dual-auction markets, subjects are informed about rank order after submitting a bid and asked to submit a second, binding bid. A fixed effects model is used, separately controlling for individual effects and for session effects. Individual bidding price as a proportion of reserve value in a session is determined by the deviation of individual i and session s from the mean, and dummy variables are used to identify high- and low-value bidders bidding after the information was released. As theory predicts, low-value bidders bid more aggressively under asymmetric conditions. Contrary to theory, high-value bidders submit lower bids, and expected seller revenue does not increase because of high-value bidders submitting lower bids.

Saral (2012) considers an ascending clock auction with a resale opportunity in which the resale price is determined by the bargaining power held by the final buyer. She examines how the existence of a secondary market affects price in the primary auction market. Sixteen subjects participated in eight sessions with an automatic resale market run to control the environment and focus on strategic behavior in the primary market. Introducing controls for bidder values and the resale environment that identifies who has the advantage at the second stage of the experiment, she estimated several panel fixed effects models with clustered standard errors at the auction level to analyze bidding behavior relative to the equilibrium. Demand reduction (or bidding below the equilibrium level) is observed when the bargaining power is with the final buyer in resale; speculation is observed when it is with the seller in the secondary market.

4.3 Fixed Effects and Random Effects

Shogren, List, and Hayes (2000) ask why experimental subjects pay high premia for new food products in laboratory experiments. The paper attributes early overbidding to preference learning and not experimental inexperience. The experimental design consists of three stages within four sessions, with each subject participating in each session. In all those stages, a sealed-bid second-price auction took place to reveal bidders' preferences for three different items. The panel data collected across the four different sections are analyzed by considering the bids for subject i in trial t introducing fixed and random effects to control for individual specific time invariant effects potentially reflecting private values or risk tendencies. The independent variables used are dummy variables for each session, a lagged price, and a dummy variable that indicates if the bidder was the winner in the previous session. The estimates reported are only for the fixed-effects model, because the random-effects model provides very similar results.

Ham, Kagel, and Lehrer (2005) test the effect of cash balances on bidding behavior in affiliated first-price private-value auctions. The experimental environment identifies a standard private-value structure with a lottery at the end of each trading period to randomize cash balances. The authors use both random effects and fixed effects to provide estimates of the cash balance effect. Assuming the modeling assumptions hold, the random-effects model is used to increase efficiency, but fixed effects also are used to address potential endogeneity in cash balances that could be affected by previous bidding behavior. Using the Hausman-Wu test, random effects are shown to be preferred. They find that randomized data suggest cash balance plays a stronger role on behavior than previously thought. They also find 2SLS estimates to be imprecise and might suffer from small sample bias.

In Shogren, Parkhurst, and Mcintosh (2006), the authors test bidding sincerity in second-price auctions and auction tournaments. The experimental environment identifies a standard second-price auction and a standard second-price auction tournament. The authors use a two-way random effects model. Trial-specific effects, which include learning and other trends, and subject-specific effects are drawn from a bivariate normal distribution. They also use fixed effects to control for bidding patterns and ordering of experiment types. The Hausman-Wu test provides evidence that the random-effects model is more appropriate. They find that a tournament setting induces more bidding rationality than its single-auction counterpart.

Isaac, Pevnitskaya, and Salmon (2010) perform two sets of experiments to test the effect of preferences for charitable giving on raising auction seller revenue. In the first experiment, different levels of charitable preferences are induced. In the second, a laboratory/field hybrid is performed, in which proceeds are donated to real charities in half of the auctions. Random-effects models are used in the regressions of auction revenue on dummy variables for bonus regime, auction form, and interaction terms, as well as the two highest bids by round. Fixed effects are used in multiple regressions, including the regressions of auction revenue on revenue prediction interacted with bonus regime. Random and fixed effects are at the group level in the first two estimated models because the group is the unit of observation for revenue. For the remaining estimated models, the authors use individual fixed-effects models. The main finding of the paper is that charitable giving preferences do not substantially raise revenue for auctioneers.

Jog and Kosmopoulou (2015) study first-price auctions with resale opportunities. The paper uses an asymmetric value structure and explores the impact of the form and characteristics of the secondary market on prices and efficiency in the primary market. They find that bidders bid higher in the primary market if the secondary market is a seller's market, and they bid lower if it is a buyer's market. The basic econometric model reflects the relationship between values and bids for both bidder types that is derived directly from the equilibrium strategies. In estimating the bidding function, they use as controls the values of the bidders, indicators for bidder type (strong and weak), measures of bidders' attitudes toward risk, and bidder demographic characteristics and experience. The model includes indicators of the order of an auction in the experimental sequence, and the number of available bidders of each type in a session. Random- and fixed-effects models are estimated with clustered robust standard errors at the bidder level; testing leads to the selection of the random-effects model as the most appropriate to use.

4.4 Mixed Effects

Salmon and Wilson (2008) study a mechanism in which the highest losing bidder has a chance to buy a unit in a postauction stage. For example, eBay has the option for a second-chance offer when an item is not sold, or the original seller has a second unit to sell. The experimental environment has two stages. The first stage is a second-price or ascending-clock auction for a unit. The second stage is an ultimatum bargaining stage in which the seller makes a take-it-or-leave-it offer to the bidder with the highest bid that lost the auction in the first stage. This is English-Ultimatum game (EU). The experiment has three treatments: a two-bidder EU treatment, a four-bidder EU treatment, and a four-bidder English-English game (EE) as a benchmark. For the EE treatment, the second stage is another auction similar to the one in stage one. The main two findings are that sellers have higher profits under EU institution compared to EE institution, although the two institutions are the comparable in performance from the efficiency point of view. The econometric models use first-unit price, second-unit price, and seller profit as dependent variables. The independent variables are a dummy variable for EE institution, a dummy variable for the first 10 periods of the treatment (first half), deviations of the relevant valuations from their theoretical expected values, and two- and three-term interactions. The econometric model is a linear mixed effects model to compare EU and EE institutions and explain price variations across units. The primary treatment effect (fixed effect) is set to one for an EE session and zero otherwise. They use random losing bidder effects for the first-unit prices and random-seller effects for the second-unit prices to identify the decision makers in each relevant setting.

Filiz-Ozbay, Lopez-Vargas, and Ozbay (2015) study multiobject auctions with the possibility of resale in which bidders can be global (interested in all units) or local (interested in one unit). They consider Vickrey auctions in which packaged bidding is allowed and simultaneous second-price auctions with sales conducted for each unit separately. In the secondary market, winners can make a take-it-or-leave-it offer. They consider prices and efficiency achievement and show that the overall efficiency is not different if the final outcomes of the two-stage market and the single-market outcome are compared. In the second-price auction, preventing resale does not hurt or benefit auction revenue. The bidding results are based on a model with mixed effects, introducing random effects at the individual level and fixed effects at the session level.

5 Conclusion

A plethora of papers in experimental economics focus on auction outcomes. They use a variety of statistical tools to analyze data ranging from simple parametric and nonparametric tests to pooled data analysis using the classical OLS method. Most of the recent papers, however, exploit the panel structure to introduce either fixed-effects or random-effects models depending on the characteristics of the auction environment. A few papers test the appropriate framework via a Hausman-Wu test or use mixed effects to study a multilayered problem. This survey of common methods provides some representative examples in the auction literature in an effort to highlight the value of panel data techniques in the analysis of experimental data obtained in the laboratory. The majority of work is done using random effects models, when researchers are mindful of the challenge of obtaining a significant number of observations to maintain consistency in estimation while exploiting the ability to control for factors that typically are unobserved, such as valuations and risk attitudes and being able to avoid the challenge of selection.

We suggest two potential avenues that could enhance the learning process from the analysis of auction data obtained through laboratory experiments. The first relates to the use of panel data quantile regression techniques similar to those proposed by Koenker (2004, 2005) and Lamarche (2010) to investigate whether the treatment effects applied in experimental analysis vary across the distribution of bids in auctions. This is appropriate in asymmetric environments or in interventions that do not affect all bidders uniformly and in cases in which the impact is restricted in particular quantiles with scale effects varying across the range. Such techniques would require larger datasets but would enhance the richness of analysis and the ability to study distributional effects.

There is also a lot of room for expansion in the techniques that are used to analyze auction data in a way that explores more broadly the dynamic nature of strategic interactions. This is the second proposed avenue for enhancement of experimental auction analysis. Branas-Garza, Bucheli, and Garcia-Munoz (2018) argue in their paper that using panel data techniques that incorporate temporal dependency (lag) explicitly in a model becomes crucial to control for the dynamics of the process to unravel paths of behavior more accurately and explore evolving relationships. In an auction setting, the probability of success might depend on the history of bidding at the auction, which can be tied to budget availability. If this dynamic aspect is critical in a setting, the GLS and OLS estimators are biased and inconsistent. The model suffers from the endogeneity problem because of its dynamic structure. Branas-Garza et al. (2018) propose the use of difference GMM estimators proposed by Arellano and Bond (1991). The presence of heteroscedasticity requires a modification to the two-step GMM model of Windmeijer (2005). In the presence of other time invariant explanatory variables in the model, Arellano and Bover (1995) and Blundell and Bond (1998) proposed alternative methods.

References

Anderson, C., Holland, D., 2006. Auctions for initial sale of annual catch entitlement. Land Economics 82 (3), 333.

Arellano, M., Bond, S., 1991. Some tests of specification for panel data: Monte Carlo evidence and an application to employment equations. Review of Economic Studies 58, 277–297.

Arellano, M., Bover, O., 1995. Another look at the instrumental variables estimation of error components models. Journal of Econometrics 68, 29–51.

Ariely, D., Ockenfels, A., Roth, A.E., 2005. An experimental analysis of ending rules in internet auctions. RAND Journal of Economics 36 (4), 890–907.

Armantier, O., Holt, C.A., Plott, C.R., 2013. A procurement auction for toxic assets with asymmetric information. American Economic Journal: Macroeconomics 5 (4), 142–162.

Armantier, O., Treich, N., 2009. Subjective probabilities in games: an application to the overbidding puzzle. International Economic Review 50 (4), 1079–1102.

Bajari, P., Houghton, S., Tadelis, S., 2014. Bidding for incomplete contracts: an empirical analysis of adaptation costs. The American Economic Review 104 (4), 1288–1319.

Bertrand, M., Duflo, E., Mullainathan, S., 2004. How much should we trust differences-in-differences estimates? Quarterly Journal of Economics 119 (1), 249–275.

Blundell, R., Bond, S., 1998. Initial conditions and moment restrictions in dynamic panel-data models. Journal of Econometrics 87, 115–143.

Branas-Garza, P., Bucheli, M., Garcia-Munoz, T., 2018. Dynamic panel data: a useful technique in experiments. In: Working paper. Universidad de Granada, Spain.

Cameron, C., Miller, D.L., 2015. A practitioner's guide to cluster-robust inference. Journal of Human Resources 50, 317–372.

Casari, M., Ham, J.C., Kagel, J.H., 2007. Selection bias, demographic effects, and ability effects in common value auction experiments. American Economic Review 97 (4), 1278–1304.

Cason, T.N., 1995. An experimental investigation of the seller incentives in the EPA's emission trading auction. The American Economic Review 85 (4), 905–922.

Cason, T., Gangadharan, L., 2004. Auction design for voluntary conservation programs. American Journal of Agricultural Economics 86, 1211–1217.

Cason, T., Gangadharan, L., 2005. A laboratory comparison of uniform and discriminative price auctions for reducing non-point source pollution. Land Economics 81 (1), 51–70.

Cason, T., Gangadharan, L., Duke, C., 2003. A laboratory study of auctions for reducing non-point source pollution. Journal of Environmental Economics and Management 46, 446–471.

Cason, T., Kannan, K., Siebert, R., 2011. An experimental study of information revelation policies in sequential auctions. Management Science 57 (4), 667–688.

Cason, T., Turocy, T.L., 2015. Bidding in first-price and second-price interdependent-values auctions: a laboratory experiment. In: Working paper series, University of East Anglia, Centre for Behavioural and Experimental Social Science (CBESS). School of Economics, University of East Anglia, Norwich, UK, pp. 15–23.

Chang, W.S., Chen, B., Salmon, T., 2015. An investigation of the average bid mechanism for procurement auctions. Management Science 61 (6), 1237–1254.

Chang, W.S., Salmon, T., Saral, K., 2016. Procurement auctions with renegotiation and wealth constraints. Economic Inquiry 54 (3), 1684–1704.

Coppinger, V., Smith, V., Titus, J., 1980. Incentives and behavior in English, Dutch and sealed-bid auctions. Economic Inquiry 18 (1), 1–22.

Corrigan, J.R., Rousu, M.C., 2006. Posted prices and bid affiliation: evidence from experimental auctions. American Journal of Agricultural Economics 88 (4), 1078–1090.

Corrigan, J.R., Rousu, M.C., 2011. Are experimental auctions demand revealing when values are affiliated? American Journal of Agricultural Economics 93 (2), 514–520.

Drichoutis, A.C., Nayga, R.M., Lazaridis, P., 2011. The role of training in experimental auctions. American Journal of Agricultural Economics 93 (2), 521–527.

Elbittar, A., 2009. Impact of valuation ranking information on bidding in first-price auctions: a laboratory study. Journal of Economic Behavior and Organization 69 (1), 75–85.

Filiz-Ozbay, E., Lopez-Vargas, K., Ozbay, E.J., 2015. Multi-object auctions with resale: theory and experiment. Games and Economic Behavior 89, 1–16.

Filiz-Ozbay, E., Ozbay, E.J., 2007. Auctions with anticipated regret: theory and experiment. American Economic Review 94 (4), 1407–1418.

Friedman, D., 1991. Simple testable model of double auction markets. Journal of Economic Behavior and Organization 15 (1), 47–70.

Gracia, A., Loureiro, M.L., Nayga, R.M., 2011. Are valuations from nonhypothetical choice experiments different from those of experimental auctions? American Journal of Agricultural Economics 93 (5), 1358–1373.

Grosskopf, B., Rentschler, L., Sarin, R., 2018. An experiment on first-price common-value auctions with asymmetric information structures: the blessed winner. Games and Economic Behavior 109, 40–64.

Ham, J.C., Kagel, J., 2006. Gender effects in private value auctions. Economics Letters 92, 375–382.

Ham, J.C., Kagel, J.H., Lehrer, S.F., 2005. Randomization, endogeneity and laboratory experiments: the role of cash balances in private value auctions. Journal of Econometrics 125 (1), 175–205.

Holt, C.A., Laury, S.K., 2002. Risk aversion and incentive effects. American Economic Review 92 (5), 1644–1655.

Hu, Y., Kagel, J., Xu, X., Ye, L., 2013. Spite and reciprocity in auctions. Games and Economic Behavior 82, 269–291.

Isaac, M., Pevnitskaya, S., Salmon, T., 2010. Do preferences for charitable giving help auctioneers? Experimental Economics 13, 14–44.

Isaac, M., Schnier, K., 2005. Silent auctions in the field and in the laboratory. Economic Inquiry 43 (4), 715–733.

Ivanova-Stenzel, R., Salmon, T.C., 2008. Revenue equivalence revisited. Games and Economic Behavior 64 (1), 171–192.

Ivanova-Stenzel, R., Salmon, T., 2011. The high/low divide: self-selection by values in auction choice. Games and Economic Behavior 73, 200–214.

Jog, C., Kosmopoulou, G., 2014. Experimental evidence on the performance of emission trading schemes in the presence of an active secondary market. Applied Economics 46, 527–538.

Jog, C., Kosmopoulou, G., 2015. Auctions with resale opportunities: an experimental study. Economic Inquiry 53, 624–639.

Kagel, J.H., Levin, D., 1986. The winner's curse and public information in common value auctions. The American Economic Review 76 (5), 894–920.

Kagel, J.H., Levin, D., 2001. Behavior in multi-unit demand auctions: experiments with uniform price and dynamic Vickrey auctions. Econometrica 69 (2), 413–454.

Kagel, J., Levin, D., 2005. Multi-unit demand auctions with synergies: behavior in sealed-bid versus ascending-bid uniform-price auctions. Games and Economic Behavior 53, 170–207.

Kagel, J.H., Pevnitskaya, S., Ye, L., 2007. Survival auctions. Economic Theory 33, 103–119.

Koenker, R., 2004. Quantile regression for longitudinal data. Journal of Multivariate Analysis 91 (1), 74–79.

Koenker, R., 2005. Quantile regression. Cambridge Books, New York, NY.

Kosmopoulou, G., De Silva, D., 2007. The effect of shill bidding upon prices: experimental evidence. International Journal of Industrial Organization 25, 291–313.

Lamarche, C., 2010. Robust penalized quantile regression estimator for panel data. Journal of Econometrics 157, 396–408.

Li, J., Plott, C., 2009. Tacit collusion in auctions and conditions for its facilitation and prevention: equilibrium selection in laboratory experimental markets. Economic Inquiry 74 (3), 425–448.

List, J.A., 2001. Do explicit warnings eliminate the hypothetical bias in elicitation procedures? evidence from field auctions for sportscards. American Economic Review 91 (5), 1498–1507.

List, J.A., Lucking-Reiley, D., 2000. Demand reduction in multiunit auctions: evidence from a sportscard field experiment. American Economic Review 90 (4), 961–972.

Lusk, J.L., Ty, F., Schroeder, T.C., 2004. Experimental auction procedure: impact on valuation of quality differentiated goods. American Journal of Agricultural Economics 86 (2), 389–405.

Nishimura, N., Cason, T., Saijo, T., Ikeda, Y., 2011. Spite and reciprocity in auctions. Games 2, 365–411.

Pagnozzi, M., Saral, K., 2017. Demand reduction in multi-unit auctions with resale: an experimental analysis. Economic Journal 127, 2702–2729.

Plott, C., 1987. Some policy applications of experimental method. In: Roth, A.E. (Ed.), Laboratory experimentation in economics. Cambridge University Press, Cambridge, pp. 193–219.

Salmon, T., Iachini, M., 2007. Continuous ascending vs. pooled multiple unit auctions. Games and Economic Behavior 61, 67–85.

Salmon, T., Wilson, B., 2008. Second chance offers versus sequential auctions: theory and behavior. Economic Theory 34, 47–67.

Saral, J., 2012. Speculation and demand reduction in English clock auctions. Journal of Economic Behavior and Organization 84, 416–421.

Schram, A.J.H.C., Onderstal, S., 2009. Bidding to give: an experimental comparison of auctions for charity. International Economic Review 50 (2), 431–457.

Shahriar, Q., Wooders, J., 2011. An experimental study of auctions with a buy price under private and common values. Games and Economic Behavior 72 (2), 558–573.

Shogren, J.F., List, J.A., Hayes, D.J., 2000. Preference learning in consecutive experimental auctions. American Journal of Agricultural Economics 82 (4), 1016–1021.

Shogren, J.F., Parkhurst, G.M., Mcintosh, C., 2006. Second-price auction tournament. Economics Letters 92 (1), 99–107.

Smith, V., 1982. Microeconomic systems as an experimental science. The American Economic Review 72 (5), 923–955.

Smith, V., 1994. Economics in the laboratory. Journal of Economic Perspectives 8 (1), 113–131.

Windmeijer, F., 2005. A finite sample correction for the variance of linear two-step GMM estimators. Journal of Econometrics 126, 25–51.

Further Reading

Menkhaus, D.J., Phillips, O.R., Coatney, K.T., 2003. Shared agents and competition in laboratory English auctions. American Journal of Agricultural Economics 85 (4), 829–839.

Phillips, O.R., Menkhaus, D.J., Coatney, K.T., 2003. Collusive practices in repeated English auctions: experimental evidence on bidding rings. The American Economic Review 93 (3), 965–979.

Chapter 17

Maximum Likelihood for Cross-Lagged Panel Models With Fixed Effects*

Paul D. Allison*, Richard Williams[†] and Enrique Moral-Benito[‡]
*University of Pennsylvania, Philadelphia, PA, United States, †University of Notre Dame, Notre Dame, IN, United States, ‡Bank of Spain, Madrid, Spain

Chapter Outline

1 Introduction

Panel data have two big attractions for making causal inferences with nonexperimental data:

- The ability to control for unobserved, time-invariant confounders.
- The ability to model the direction of causal relationships.

Controlling for unobservables can be accomplished with fixed-effects methods that are now well known and widely used (Allison, 2005a, 2009; Firebaugh, Warner, & Massoglia, 2013; Halaby, 2004). To examine causal direction, the most popular approach has long been the cross-lagged panel model, originating with the two-wave, two-variable model proposed by Duncan (1969) and elaborated by many others (e.g., Finkel, 1995; Hamaker, Kuiper, & Grasman, 2015; Kenny & Judd, 1996; Kessler & Greenberg, 1981; Markus, 1979; McArdle & Nesselroade, 2014). In these models, x and y at time t affect both x and y at time $t + 1$.

---

*This chapter is an updated version of a previously published paper, Allison et al. (2017).

Panel Data Econometrics. https://doi.org/10.1016/B978-0-12-815859-3.00017-2

Unfortunately, attempting to combine fixed-effects models with cross-lagged panel models leads to serious estimation problems that are well known in the econometric literature. Economists typically refer to such models as dynamic panel models because of the lagged effect of the dependent variable on itself. The estimation difficulties include error terms that are correlated with predictors, the so-called incidental parameters problem, and uncertainties about the treatment of initial conditions. For reviews of the extensive literature about dynamic panel data models, see Wooldridge (2010), Baltagi (2013), or Hsiao (2014).

The most popular econometric method for estimating dynamic panel models has long been the generalized method of moments (GMM) that relies on lagged variables as instruments. This method been incorporated into several widely available software packages, including SAS, Stata, LIMDEP, RATS, and plm (an R package), usually under the name of Arellano-Bond (AB) estimators. While the AB approach provides consistent estimators of the coefficients, there is evidence that the estimators are not fully efficient, have considerable small-sample bias, and often perform poorly when the autoregressive parameter (the effect of a variable on itself at a later point in time) is near 1.0.

In recent years, econometricians have explored maximum likelihood (ML) estimation as a way to overcome some of the limitations of the GMM methodology. These efforts have culminated in the work of Moral-Benito (2013), who developed an ML method that effectively addresses the key problems of dynamic panel data models. Unfortunately, little software is currently available to implement his method. In this chapter, we show that the model and method of Moral-Benito fall within the framework of linear structural equation modeling (SEM), and that it therefore can be estimated in a straightforward way with widely available SEM packages. Using simulated data, we show that the ML-SEM method outperforms the AB method with respect to bias and efficiency under most conditions. ML-SEM also has several other advantages over the AB method:

- Error variances can easily be allowed to vary with time.
- The unobserved, time-invariant factor can have different effects at different times.
- Missing values on predictors can be handled easily by full information maximum likelihood (FIML).
- Many goodness-of-fit measures are available to assess the over-identifying restrictions of the model.
- There is no need to choose among many possible instrumental variables.
- Latent variables with multiple indicators can be incorporated into the model.
- Time-invariant variables can be included in the model.

ML-SEM, however, does have a few downsides:

- Programming can be complex and tedious (although this problem essentially has been solved with the new **xtdpdml** command for Stata).
- Convergence failures sometimes occur.

- Computation can be noticeably slower than with AB, especially when using FIML to handle unbalanced or other forms of missing data.

This chapter proceeds in several steps:

- Section 2 explores the relationship between the dynamic panel data models of econometrics and the cross-lagged panel models used in other social sciences.
- Section 3 reviews GMM estimation of dynamic panel data models and examines its limitations.
- Section 4 reviews the development of ML methods for dynamic panel data models.
- Section 5 shows how the ML method of Moral-Benito can be implemented in the SEM framework.
- Section 6 presents an empirical example.
- Section 7 presents results from a Monte Carlo study comparing the AB method and the ML-SEM method.
- Section 8 offers a conclusion.

2 Cross-Lagged Panel Models Versus Dynamic Panel Data Models

2.1 Cross-Lagged Panel Models

We begin with a cross-lagged panel model that is specified in a way that facilitates comparisons with the dynamic panel models of econometrics. The data consist of a sample of N individuals, each of whom is observed at T points in time ($t = 1, \ldots, T$). Thus, the data set is balanced, having the same number of observations for each individual. Although the methods to be considered can be extended to unbalanced data, the initial development is simpler if we exclude that possibility. We also presume that the number of time points is substantially smaller than the number of individuals.

At each time point, we observe two quantitative variables, x_{it} and y_{it}, and we want to allow for the possibility that they have a lagged, reciprocal causal relationship. We also observe a column vector of control variables w_{it} that vary over both individuals and time (possibly including lagged values), and another column vector of control variables z_i that vary over individuals but not over time.

Consider the following equation for y, with $i = 1, \ldots, N$ and $t = 2, \ldots, T$:

$$y_{it} = \mu_t + \beta_1 x_{it-1} + \beta_2 y_{it-1} + \delta_1 w_{it} + \gamma_1 z_i + \alpha_i + \varepsilon_{it} \tag{1}$$

where μ_t is an intercept that varies with time, β_1 and β_2 are scalar coefficients, δ_1 and γ_1 are row vectors of coefficients, ε_{it} is a random disturbance, and α_i represents the combined effects on y of all unmeasured variables that are both constant over time and have constant effects. The lags for x and y are shown here as lags of one time unit, but the lags could be greater and could be different for each variable.

We also specify an analogous equation for x:

$$x_{it} - \tau_t + \beta_3 x_{it-1} + \beta_4 y_{it-1} + \delta_2 w_{it} + \gamma_2 z_i + \eta_i + v_{it} \tag{2}$$

where τ_t, is an intercept that varies with time, β_3, and β_4 are scalar coefficients, δ_2 and γ_2 are row vectors of coefficients, v_{it} is a random disturbance, and η_i is a set of individual effects analogous to α_i in Eq. (1). Eqs. (1), (2) do not allow for simultaneous causation, which would require problematic assumptions in order to estimate and interpret the causal effects.

These two equations differ from the classic cross-lagged panel model in two ways: first, by the introduction of the unobserved individual effects, α_i and η_i, and, second, by the presumption that the coefficients for all variables are constant over time. The constancy assumption can be relaxed easily, but we retain it now for simplicity.

The individual effects α_i and η_i can be specified either as random variables or as sets of fixed parameters. Outside of economics, they usually are treated as random variables that are independent of all other exogenous variables (e.g., Hamaker et al., 2015).

More needs to be said about the random disturbance terms, ε_{it} and v_{it}. We assume that they are independent of each other (both within and between time points) and normally distributed with means of 0 and constant variance (at least across individuals, although we will allow for variances that change over time). We also assume that w_{it} and z_i are strictly exogenous, meaning that for any t and any s, w_{it} and z_i are independent of ε_{is} and v_{is}. With respect to x and y, we cannot assume strict exogeneity because both variables appear as dependent variables. In fact, Eqs. (1), (2) together imply that ε_{it} and v_{it} are correlated with all future values of x and y.

2.2 Dynamic Panel Data Models

The basic dynamic panel data model found in the econometric literature is essentially the same as Eq. (1), above, but with a few changes in meaning:

- x is typically a vector rather than a scalar.
- x is usually not lagged.
- α_i is treated as a set of fixed constants rather than as a set of random variables.

The first two differences are relatively unimportant, but the third is crucial. Treating α as a set of fixed constants (fixed effects) is equivalent to allowing for unrestricted correlations between α and all the time-varying predictors, both x and w. Allowing these correlations supports a claim that these models control for all time-invariant confounders, either observed or unobserved.

As in the cross-lagged panel model, w_{it} and z_i are assumed to be strictly exogenous. But x_{it} is assumed to be predetermined (Arellano, 2003) or, equivalently, sequentially exogenous (Wooldridge, 2010). This means that for all

$s > t$, x_{it} is independent of ε_{is}. That is, the x variables are independent of all future values of ε but can be correlated with past values of ε.

The assumption that x_{it} is predetermined allows for the existence of Eq. (2), but it also allows for a much wider range of possibilities. In particular, Eq. (2) could be modified to have multiple lags of y, or it could be a nonlinear equation. For example, if x is dichotomous (as in the example in Section 6), a logistic regression equation could substitute for Eq. (2).

It should now be fairly clear that the cross-lagged panel model can be regarded as a special case of the dynamic panel data model. We can get from the latter to the former by lagging x and reducing it from a vector to a scalar, converting fixed effects into random effects, and imposing the structure of Eq. (2) on the dependence of x on prior y's.

We agree with economists that the less restricted model is a better way to go. The ability to control for unmeasured confounders is a huge advantage in making claims of causality. And not having to specify the functional form of the dependence of x on y both simplifies the estimation problem and reduces the danger of misspecification. If we are interested in the dependence of x on y, we can always specify a second dynamic panel data model for y and estimate that separately.

On the other hand, we believe that those working in the cross-lagged panel tradition have chosen the better approach to estimation. Except in the simple case of two-wave data, most cross-lagged models are formulated as structural equation modeling and estimated by maximum likelihood using standard SEM packages. Economists have taken a rather different path, one that has led to possibly inferior estimators and to a few dead ends.

3 GMM Estimation

Estimation of the dynamic panel data model represented by Eq. (1) is not straightforward for reasons that are well known in the econometric literature. First, the presence of the lagged dependent variable as a predictor implies that conventional fixed-effects methods will yield biased estimates of the β coefficients (Arellano, 2003). Second, even if the lagged dependent variable is excluded, the fact that the x's are merely predetermined, not strictly exogenous, implies that conventional fixed effects methods will yield biased estimates of the coefficients whenever $T > 3$ (Wooldridge, 2010).

Until recently, econometricians focused almost exclusively on instrumental variable methods. The dominant method usually is attributed to Arellano and Bond (1991), although there were important earlier precedents (Anderson & Hsiao, 1982; Holtz-Eakin, Newey, & Rosen, 1988). To remove the fixed effects (α) from the equations, the model is reformulated in terms of first differences: $\Delta y_{it} = y_{it} - y_{it-1}$, $\Delta x_{it} = x_{it} - x_{it-1}$, and $\Delta w_{it} = w_{it} - w_{it-1}$. The first differencing not only removes α from the equation, but also removes z, the vector of time-invariant predictors. Lagged difference scores for y, x, and w then are used as instrumental variables for Δy and Δx, and the resulting system of equations is estimated by the generalized method of moments (GMM).

Models with instrumental variables imply multiple restrictions on the moments in the data, specifically, that covariances between instruments and certain error terms are 0. GMM chooses parameter estimates that minimize the corresponding observed moments. Because there are multiple moment restrictions, the method requires a weight matrix that optimally combines the observed moments into a unidimensional criterion. In many settings, GMM requires iteration to minimize that criterion. For the moments used in the AB method, however, minimization is accomplished by solving a linear equation that requires no iteration.

AB estimators come in two forms, the one-step method (the usual default in software) and the two-step method. The latter uses results from the first step to reconstruct the weight matrix, but there is little evidence that its performance is any better than the one-step method (Judson & Owen, 1999). Another extension is the GMM system estimator of Blundell and Bond (1998), which uses both levels and first differences of the lagged variables as instruments. This method produces more efficient estimators, but at the cost of making the rather unrealistic assumption that the initial observations reflect stationarity of the process generating the data.

AB estimators are believed to suffer from three problems:

1. *Small sample bias.* AB estimators are consistent, that is, they converge in probability to the true values as sample size increases. Simulation evidence, however, indicates that they are prone to bias in small samples, especially when the autoregressive parameter (the effect of y_{t-1} on y_t) is near 1.0 (Blundell & Bond, 1998; Kiviet, Pleus, & Poldermans, 2014).

2. *Inefficiency.* AB estimators do not make use of all the moment restrictions implied by the model. As a consequence, they are not fully efficient. Ahn and Schmidt (1995) proposed an efficient GMM estimator that does make use of all restrictions, but its nonlinear form makes it more difficult to implement. In any case, their method is not generally available in commercial software packages.

3. *Uncertainty about the choice of instruments.* Anyone who has attempted to use the AB method knows that there are many choices to be made regarding what variables to use as instruments and whether they are to be entered as levels or first differences. In principle, it would make sense to use all possible instruments that are consistent with the model. Available evidence, however, suggests that too many instruments can be just as bad as too few, leading to additional small-sample bias (Roodman, 2009). This problem is especially acute when T is large, in which case the number of potential instruments is also large.

4 ML Estimation of Dynamic Panel Models

In an effort to solve some of these problems, quite a bit of work in the econometric literature has been on ML estimation of dynamic panel models. That work, however, has yet to have a significant impact on empirical applications. Bhargava and Sargan (1983) considered ML estimation of dynamic panel models, but they assumed that the time-varying predictors were uncorrelated with the fixed effects, which is precisely what we do not want do. The seminal paper of Hsiao, Pesaran, and Tahmiscioglu (2002) proposed a ML estimator that does allow the predictors in each equation to be correlated with the fixed effects. In their view, accomplishing this was difficult for two reasons:

There are two issues involved in the estimation of the fixed effects dynamic panel data model when the time-series dimension is short. One is the introduction of individual-specific effects that increase with the number of observations in the cross-section dimension. The other is the initial value problem. Both lead to the violation of the conventional regularity conditions for the MLE of the structural parameters to be consistent because of the presence of "incidental parameters." (p. 139)

The issue of incidental parameters is a well-known problem in maximum likelihood estimation. It's what happens when the number of parameters increases with the sample size, thereby invalidating the usual asymptotic arguments for consistency and efficiency of ML estimators (Nickell, 1981).

Hsiao et al. dealt with the incidental parameters problem by using the same device as Arellano and Bond—taking first differences of the time-varying variables, thereby eliminating the individual-specific fixed effects. The likelihood then was formulated in terms of the difference scores. To deal with the initial value problem, they introduced assumptions of stationarity for the generation of the initial values from some, prior, unobserved process, assumptions that they admitted might be controversial. They also presented simulation evidence indicating that the performance of their ML estimator was somewhat better than that of several different GMM estimators.

Although the use of first differences solves the incidental parameters problem for the fixed effects, it greatly complicates the subsequent development of the method. Moreover, Han and Phillips (2013) argued that the first-difference likelihood is not a true likelihood function and that, consequently, it can behave in pathological ways, especially when the autoregressive coefficients have values near 1.0.

For many years, no software was readily available to implement the ML method of Hsiao et al. Grassetti (2011), however, showed that implementation is possible with conventional random effects software by working with variables that are differences from initial values instead of differences between adjacent time points. Kripfganz (2016) introduced a Stata command, **xtdpdqml**, that implements both the method of Hsiao et al. and the random effects model of Bhargava and Sargan (1983). Kripfganz, however, also pointed out that that the method of Hsiao et al. does not yield consistent estimators for models with predetermined variables.

In contrast to Hsiao et al., Moral-Benito (2013) showed that parameters in Eq. (1) or (2) can be estimated directly by maximum likelihood without first differencing and without any assumptions about initial conditions. The key insight is that α_i and η_i do not have to be treated as fixed parameters. As pointed out by Mundlak (1978) and elaborated by Chamberlain (1982, 1984), the fixed effects model is equivalent to a random effects model that allows for unrestricted correlations between the individual-specific effects (α_i and η_i) and the time-varying predictors. After that approach is adopted, there is no longer any need to impose arbitrary assumptions on the initial observations, y_1 and x_1. They can be treated as strictly exogenous, which is entirely appropriate given the lack of knowledge about what precedes those observations.

5 ML Estimation Via SEM

In this section, we show how Moral-Benito's method can be implemented with SEM software. The essential features of the ML-SEM method for cross-lagged panel models with fixed effects were described by Allison (2000, 2005a, 2005b, 2009), but his approach was largely pragmatic and computational. Moral-Benito provided a rigorous theoretical foundation for this method.

The justification for using SEM software rests on the fact that Eqs. (1), (2) are a special case of the linear structural equation model proposed by Jöreskog (1978) and generalized by Bentler and Weeks (1980). In its most general form, the model can be specified compactly as

$$\mathbf{y} = \boldsymbol{\mu} + \mathbf{B}\mathbf{y} + \boldsymbol{\Gamma}\mathbf{x} \tag{3}$$

where $\mathbf{y}$ is a $p \times 1$ vector of endogenous variables that can be either observed or latent, $\mathbf{x}$ is a $k \times 1$ vector of exogenous variables that, again, can be either observed or latent (including any disturbance terms in the model), $\boldsymbol{\mu}$ is a vector of intercepts, and $\mathbf{B}$ and $\boldsymbol{\Gamma}$ are matrices of coefficients. The endogenous vector $\mathbf{y}$ and any latent variables in $\mathbf{x}$ are assumed to have a multivariate normal distribution conditional on the observed exogenous variables. The $\mathbf{B}$ matrix has zeros on the main diagonal, and both $\mathbf{B}$ and $\boldsymbol{\Gamma}$ might have many additional restrictions. Most commonly, these restrictions take the form of setting certain parameters equal to 0, but there also can be equality restrictions. The remaining parameter Θ is the variance matrix for $\mathbf{x}$, which usually has many elements set to 0.

Several widely available software packages will estimate any special case of this model via maximum likelihood. These include LISREL, EQS, Amos, Mplus, PROC CALIS (in SAS), sem (in Stata), lavaan (for R), and OpenMx (for R). Remarkably, the earliest version of LISREL, introduced in 1973, probably could have estimated the dynamic panel models considered here, albeit with considerably more programming effort than with contemporary packages.

How does this model relate to the cross-lagged Eqs. (1), (2)? Although Eqs. (1), (2) can be estimated simultaneously, we follow the econometric tradition of focusing only on Eq. (1), while allowing Eq. (2) to determine certain constraints (or lack thereof) on Θ, the variance matrix for the exogenous variables.

Eq. (1) is a special case of Eq. (3), in the following sense. Without loss of generality, we treat w_{it} and z_i as scalars rather than vectors. We then have, $\mathbf{y}' = (y_{i2}, \ldots, y_{iT})$, $\mathbf{x}' = (\alpha_i, z_i, y_{i1}, x_{i1}, \ldots, x_{i(T-1)}, w_{i2}, \ldots, w_{iT}, \varepsilon_{i2}, \ldots, \varepsilon_{iT})$ and $\boldsymbol{\mu}' = (\mu_2, \ldots, \mu_T)$. For $\boldsymbol{\Gamma}$ we have

$$\boldsymbol{\Gamma} = \begin{bmatrix} 1 & \gamma_1 & \beta_2 & \beta_1 & 0 & \cdots & \delta_1 & 0 & \cdots & 1 & 0 & \cdots \\ 1 & \gamma_1 & 0 & 0 & \beta_1 & \cdots & 0 & \delta_1 & \cdots & 0 & 1 & \cdots \\ 1 & \gamma_1 & 0 & 0 & 0 & \cdots & 0 & 0 & \cdots & 0 & 0 & \cdots \\ \vdots & \vdots & \vdots & \vdots & \vdots & \vdots & \vdots & \vdots & \ddots & \vdots & \vdots & \ddots \\ 1 & \gamma_1 & 0 & 0 & 0 & \cdots & 0 & 0 & \cdots & 0 & 0 & \cdots \end{bmatrix}$$

and for $\mathbf{B}$,

$$\mathbf{B} = \begin{bmatrix} 0 & 0 & 0 & \cdots \\ \beta_2 & 0 & 0 & \cdots \\ 0 & \beta_2 & 0 & \cdots \\ \vdots & \vdots & \vdots & \ddots \end{bmatrix}$$

For Θ, the following covariances are set to 0:

- α with z
- α with all ε
- z with all ε
- all w with all ε
- all ε with each other
- x_{it} with ε_{is} whenever $s \geq t$.

All other elements of Θ are left unrestricted. Note that α is allowed to correlate with both w and x. And x is allowed to correlate with all prior realizations of ε, as a consequence of Eq. (2). The restriction that $\text{cov}(\alpha, z) = 0$, while perhaps undesirable, is essential for identification. That is, we must assume that the fixed effects are uncorrelated with any time-invariant variables.[1]

Fig. 1 displays a path diagram of this model for the case in which $T = 4$, with no w variables and no z variables.[2] That is, we have only the endogenous y variables and the predetermined x variables. Notice that all the x variables are

---

1. For an alternative parameterization and a derivation of the likelihood function, see Moral-Benito, Allison, and Williams (2018).
2. The path diagrams in Figs. 1 and 3 were produced by Mplus, version 7.4.

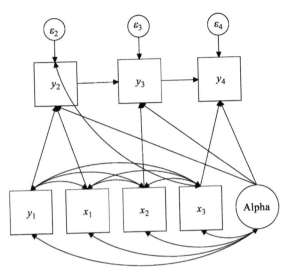

FIG. 1 Path diagram for four-period dynamic panel model.

allowed to freely correlate with each other, as well as with y_1, which is treated like any other exogenous variable. Similarly, the latent variable alpha (enclosed in a circle) is allowed to correlate with all the exogenous variables, including y_1. Alpha affects each y variable (with a coefficient of 1, not shown). The coefficients for the effects of the x's on the y's are constrained to be the same at all three time points, but this constraint can be easily relaxed.

What makes x predetermined in this diagram is the correlation between x_3 and ε_2. If this correlation were omitted, x would be strictly exogenous rather than predetermined. Again, the rule is that, for any predetermined variable, x at time t is allowed to correlate with the error term for y at any prior time point.

How do the assumptions of ML-SEM differ from those of AB? ML-SEM makes stronger assumptions in three respects. First, and most importantly, ML-SEM assumes multivariate normality for all endogenous variables, but AB makes no distributional assumptions. ML-SEM, however, produces consistent estimators even when the normality assumption is violated (Moral-Benito, 2013). And if there is concern about normality, robust standard errors can be used for constructing confidence intervals and hypothesis tests. Second, in order to identify the effects of time-invariant variables, we introduced the assumption that $\text{cov}(\alpha, z) = 0$. But if we have any reason to doubt that assumption, we can just exclude time-invariant variables from the model. They still will be controlled as part of the α term. Lastly, ML-SEM makes use of the moment restrictions implied by the assumption that there is no serial correlation in the error terms in Eq. (1). Although the use of these restrictions was recommended by Ahn and Schmidt (1995) to improve efficiency, they generally have not been incorporated into AB estimation because they imply nonlinear estimating equations.

ML-SEM, however, makes it possible relax many assumptions that are built into AB. Most notably, the default in ML-SEM is to allow for an unrestricted effect of time itself, and for different error variances at each time point. It also is possible to allow α, the latent variable for the individual effects, to have different coefficients at different time points.

6 Empirical Example

As an example of how to implement ML-SEM for dynamic panel models, we reanalyze data described by Cornwell and Rupert (1988) for 595 household heads who reported a nonzero wage in each of 7 years from 1976 to 1982. For purposes of illustration, we use only the following variables from that data set:

$y =$ WKS $=$ number of weeks employed in each year
$x =$ UNION $= 1$ if wage set by union contract, else 0, in each year
$w =$ LWAGE $=$ ln(wage) in each year
$z =$ ED $=$ years of education in 1976

Let's suppose that our principal goal is to estimate the effect of UNION at time t on WKS at time $t + 1$. However, we also want to allow for the possibility that UNION is itself affected by earlier values of WKS. That is, we want to treat UNION as a predetermined variable. We also want to control for LWAGE, a time-varying variable, and we want to estimate the effect of ED, a time-invariant variable, on WKS. If we suspected that LWAGE was affected by earlier values of WKS, we also could treat it as predetermined. But for simplicity, we will assume that it is strictly exogenous.

Our goal, then, is to estimate Eq. (1), reproduced here as

$$y_{it} = \mu_t + \beta_1 x_{i,t-1} + \beta_2 y_{i,t-1} + \delta_1 w_{it} + \gamma_1 z_i + \alpha_i + \varepsilon_{it} \tag{4}$$

with x treated as predetermined, and w and z treated as strictly exogenous. By specifying UNION as predetermined, we allow for the possibility that number of weeks worked at time t could affect union status at time $t + 1$ or, indeed, at any future time. However, we don't have to specify the functional form of that relationship. Because UNION is dichotomous, a logistic regression model might be a natural first choice for this dependence. We don't have to make that choice, however, because the model is agnostic regarding the dependence of x on y.

Note that although we have lagged the effect of x in Eq. (4) in order to be consistent with the cross-lagged panel approach, the ML-SEM method does not require x to be lagged. We could have written x_t rather than x_{t-1}, and the estimation would have been equally straightforward. If we choose not to lag x, however, it would be problematic to estimate another model in which x depends on unlagged y. That would imply a model with simultaneous, reciprocal causation, which would not be identified without additional instrumental variables.

```
1    proc calis data=my.wagewide;
2    path
3    wks2 <- wks1 union1 lwage1 ed alpha = a b c d 1,
4    wks3 <- wks2 union2 lwage2 ed alpha = a b c d 1,
5    wks4 <- wks3 union3 lwage3 ed alpha = a b c d 1,
6    wks5 <- wks4 union4 lwage4 ed alpha = a b c d 1,
7    wks6 <- wks5 union5 lwage5 ed alpha = a b c d 1,
8    wks7 <- wks6 union6 lwage6 ed alpha = a b c d 1,
9    alpha <-> ed = 0,
10   wks2 <-> union3 union4 union5 union6,
11   wks3 <-> union4 union5 union6,
12   wks4 <-> union5 union6,
13   wks5 <-> union6,
14   <-> wks2 wks3 wks4 wks5 wks6 wks7 = v v v v v v;
14   run;
```

FIG. 2 SAS Program for estimating dynamic panel model with fixed effects.

We use PROC CALIS in SAS to illustrate the estimation of Eq. (4) because CALIS has a syntax and default settings that are particularly well-suited to dynamic panel models. Like most SEM packages, CALIS requires that the data be in the wide form rather than the long form.[3] For our example, the wide-form data set has one record per person, with seven variables corresponding to each conceptual variable at the seven time points. Thus, we have WKS1, WKS2, ..., WKS7, and LWAGE1, LWAGE2, ..., LWAGE7, etc. Of course, there is only one variable for ED, which did not vary over time. In contrast, most software packages for the analysis of panel data (including those for the AB method) expect the data to be in the long form, with separate records for each individual at each point in time.

Because the setup for this kind of model will be unfamiliar to most readers, it is worth examining in some detail. Fig. 2 shows the CALIS program for estimating the model. (Equivalent code for Stata, Mplus, and lavaan can be found in Appendix B.) Line 1 invokes the CALIS procedure for the data set MY. WAGEWIDE. Line 2 begins the PATH statement, which continues until the end of Line 13. Lines 3–8 specify an equation for each of the six time points. Note that no equation is specified for WKS1 because at time 1 we do not observe the lagged values of the predictor variables.

The variable ALPHA refers to the fixed effects variable α_i that is common to all equations. When CALIS encounters a variable name such as ALPHA that is not on the input data set, it presumes that the name refers to a latent variable. After the equals sign on each line, there is a list of coefficient names or values corresponding to the predictor variables in the equation. Because the coefficient names are the same for each equation, the corresponding coefficients are also

---

3. Mplus can analyze long form data using a multilevel add-on, but its multilevel mode is not suitable for the dynamic panel models considered here. Version 8 of Mplus allows for dynamic panel analysis in long form, but only with a Bayesian estimator.

constrained to be the same. The coefficient of ALPHA is constrained to have a value of 1.0 in each equation, consistent with Eq. (4).

By default in PROC CALIS, latent exogenous variables such as ALPHA are allowed to covary with all observed exogenous variables, including WKS1 and all the LWAGE and UNION variables. This is exactly what we want to achieve in order for ALPHA to truly behave as a set of fixed effects (Allison & Bollen, 1997; Bollen & Brand, 2010; Teachman, Duncan, Yeung, & Levy, 2001). Because ED does not vary over time, however, the correlation between ALPHA and ED is not identified, so it is constrained be 0 in Line 9. Lines 10–13 allow the error term ε in each equation to be correlated with future values of UNION. This is the key device that allows UNION to be a predetermined (sequentially exogenous) variable.[4]

By default, CALIS allows the intercept to differ for each equation, which is equivalent to treating time as a set of dummy variables. It is easy to constrain the intercepts to be the same if desired. With a little more difficulty, one can impose constraints that correspond to a linear or quadratic effect of time.

Also by default, the error variances are allowed to differ across equations, which is not the case for most AB software. Line 14 constrains the error variances to be the same for each equation in order to produce results that can be compared directly with AB estimates. This line assigns names to the error variances for each variable. Because they are given the same name (v), the corresponding parameter estimates are constrained to be the same. In most applications, however, it is probably better to leave the variances unconstrained.

Fig. 3 is a path diagram for the model. Here are a few key points to note about this diagram:

- There is no correlation between ALPHA and ED.
- All other observed exogenous variables are freely correlated with one another.
- All error terms are correlated with future values for UNION. This implicitly allows for the possibility that y affects future x, with no restrictions on that relationship.

Table 1 displays the numerical results in the first four columns. Not surprisingly, there is a highly significant effect of WKS($t-1$) on WKS(t), although the magnitude of the effect is not large. There is also a significant negative effect (at the 0.05 level) of UNION($t-1$) on WKS(t), and a not quite significant negative effect of ED on WKS(t). By constraint, these coefficient estimates are the same for all six equations.

This is only a small portion of the output from PROC CALIS. The full output also contains estimates of the variances and covariances for all the exogenous

---

4. An equivalent method is to specify five additional regressions for UNION2 through UNION6 as dependent variables, with predictor variables that include all values of LWAGE, prior values of WKS, prior values of UNION, and ALPHA.

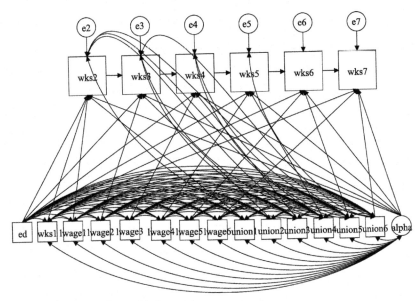

FIG. 3 Path diagram for empirical example.

TABLE 1 Alternative Estimates for Dynamic Model With Fixed and Lagged Effects

Predictor	ML-SEM			Arellano-Bond		
	Estimate	SE	z	Estimate	SE	z
wks($t-1$)	0.188	0.020	9.59	0.163	0.039	4.18
lwage($t-1$)	0.588	0.488	1.20	-1.276	0.462	-2.76
union($t-1$)	-1.206	0.522	-2.31	-1.175	0.513	-2.29
ed	-0.107	0.056	-1.89			

variables, including ALPHA and the error terms for each equation. As with all SEM software, there is also a likelihood ratio chi-square statistic comparing the fitted model with a saturated or just-identified model that perfectly reproduces the covariance matrix for all the variables. This example has a value of 138.48 with 76 degrees of freedom, yielding a P-value <0.0001. The 76 degrees of freedom correspond to 76 over-identifying restrictions on the covariance matrix of the observed variables that are implied by the model.

Because this is a goodness-of-fit statistic, higher P-values indicate a better fitting model. Therefore, by conventional significance standards, the model does not fit the data. The consensus in the SEM literature, however, is that with large sample sizes, it might be hard to find any reasonably parsimonious model that yields a P-value >0.05. There are numerous alternative measures of fit that are relatively insensitive to sample size, and many of these are reported by PROC CALIS. For example, Bentler's Comparative Fit Index is 0.995 while Bentler and Bonnet's nonnormed index (also known as the Tucker-Lewis index) is 0.987.[5] Values near 1.0 are desirable, so these measures suggest a very good fit to the data. One of the most popular measures of fit is the root mean squared error of approximation (RMSEA). For this example, it has a value of 0.037. Anything <0.05 is considered to be a good fit.

For comparison, we also estimated the same model using the standard AB method, as implemented with the Stata command **xtdpd**. The last three columns of Table 1 display the results. This method—because it is based on difference scores—cannot produce any estimates for the effect of ED, which does not change over time.[6] The lagged effects of UNION and WKS (on itself) are similar to the estimates produced by PROC CALIS. The coefficient for the lagged effect of LWAGE, however, is dramatically different from the ML estimate. This naturally raises the question of which method performs better, in general.

7   Monte Carlo Study

To evaluate the performance of the ML-SEM method and compare it with the AB method, we generated observations from the following cross-lagged panel model:

$$y_{i1} = c\alpha_i + gu_{i1}$$

$$x_{i1} = c\eta_i + gv_{i1}$$

$$y_{it} = \beta_1 x_{it-1} + \beta_2 y_{it-1} + c\alpha_i + gu_{it}$$

$$x_{it} = \beta_3 x_{it-1} + \beta_4 y_{it-1} + c\eta_i + gv_{it}$$

for $i = 1, ..., N$ and $t = 2, ..., T$. The time-invariant fixed effects, α_i and η_i, were generated as bivariate standard normal variates with correlation ρ. The time-specific disturbances u_{it} and v_{it} each were standard normal and independent of all other exogenous variables. Parameters and data structures were varied as shown in Table 2.

---

5. Stata, Mplus, and lavaan report somewhat lower values of these measures because they define the baseline model in a different way.

6. The **xtdpd** model also includes dummy variables for time in order to ensure comparability with the ML-SEM estimates.

TABLE 2 Parameter Values for Monte Carlo Simulation

N	50, 100, **400**, 1600
T	4, **5**, 7, 10
ρ	0, 0.25, 0.50, **0.75**, 0.90
β_1	0, **0.25**, 0.50, 0.75, 1.00
β_2	0, 0.25, 0.50, **0.75**, 1.00, 1.25
β_4	**−0.25**, 0, 0.25
g	0.75, **1.00**, 1.50, 2.00
c	0.50, **1.00**, 1.50 2.00

The numbers in bold are the values for the baseline model. Each parameter was varied in turn, while keeping all others at their baseline values. For each condition, 1000 samples were generated, with a total of 30 different conditions.

For each sample, we estimated the parameters in the equation for y as the dependent variable using both ML-SEM and AB. We used Stata both to generate the data and to estimate the models. The **sem** command[7] was used for ML-SEM and the **xtdpd** command was used for AB. For the latter, we used the default one-step method with all available instruments.[8] Program code for the Monte Carlo simulations is available in an online appendix.

We will focus on the estimates for β_1, the cross-lagged effect of x on y, and β_2, the autoregressive effect of y on itself. For each of those parameters and for each condition, Table A1 reports the mean and the standard deviation of the estimates for β_1 across the 1000 samples, as well as the coverage—the proportion of nominal 95% confidence intervals (calculated in each sample using the conventional normal approximation) that actually includes the true values. If a method is performing well, the coverage should be close to 0.95.

Unlike AB, ML-SEM requires an iterative algorithm, and that algorithm sometimes fails to converge, especially with small samples and more extreme parameter values. Of the 30 conditions in the simulation, 12 had convergence failures for at least one of the 1000 samples. For each condition, Table A1 gives

---

7. We actually used the user-written command, **xtdpdml**, which serves as a simplifying shell for the **sem** command. For details, see Williams, Allison, and Moral-Benito (2018).

8. The ML models are less restrictive than the AB models. Specifically, the ML-SEM models allow for a different intercept and a different error variance at each point in time, while the AB models constrain those estimates to be the same for all time points. Because the data generating process embodied those constraints, both AB and ML-SEM should produce consistent estimates. The fact that AB estimated fewer parameters, however, might have given it some advantage in assessing the relative efficiency of the two estimators.

the number of convergence failures. Of those conditions that had convergence failures, the number of failures range from 1 to 23 (out of 1000 samples). Thus, in the worst case, only about 2% of the samples suffers convergence failures.

Samples with convergence failures are likely to be more extreme or unusual than those without such failures, and the exclusion of those samples could give an unfair advantage to ML-SEM. To avoid that possibility, we also exclude the same nonconvergent samples from the AB estimation.

In Table A1, both ML-SEM and AB estimators appear, at first glance, to produce approximately unbiased point estimates of β_1 (the cross-lagged effect of x on y) under all 30 conditions. The AB estimator, however, actually shows a small downward bias under many conditions. Specifically, for AB, 11 of the 30 95% Monte Carlo confidence intervals (not shown) do not include the true value because the upper confidence limit is less than the true value. For ML-SEM, on the other hand, every 95% Monte Carlo confidence interval includes the true value. In spite of the downward bias in AB, the two estimators did about equally well for interval estimation. For both ML-SEM and AB, the median coverage over the 30 conditions was 0.949. ML-SEM coverage ranged from 0.934 to 0.957. For AB, the coverage ranged from 0.937 to 0.958.

For β_2 (the lagged effect of y on itself), AB does substantially worse than ML-SEM, as shown in Table A2. Again, ML-SEM produces approximately unbiased estimates of β_2 under all conditions. Every 95% Monte Carlo confidence interval includes the true value. AB estimates, however, are persistently smaller than the true values, and only one of the 95% Monte Carlo confidence intervals includes the true value. This downward bias is generally small, however, except for the smaller sample sizes of $N = 50$ and $N = 100$ where it is quite apparent. Somewhat surprisingly, given earlier literature, the bias is small even when β_2 is at or close to 1.0.

The bias in AB for β_2 translates into slightly worse coverage for interval estimates. For ML-SEM, the median coverage over the 30 conditions is 0.951 with a range from 0.937 to 0.965. For AB, the median coverage is 0.941, ranging from 0.890 (for $N = 50$) to 0.961.

Next, we examine the relative efficiency of ML-SEM and AB. We calculate relative efficiency as the ratio of the estimated mean squared error for ML-SEM to the estimated mean squared error for AB. Mean squared error is the sampling variance plus the square of the bias. Across 30 different conditions, the relative efficiency of AB compared with ML-SEM for estimating β_1 ranges from 0.83 (AB did 17% worse) to 1.12 (AB did 12% better), with a median of 0.96. Therefore, there was no clear winner for the cross-lagged effect. For β_2, however, the relative efficiency ranged from 0.34 (AB did 66% worse) to 0.87 (AB did 13% worse) with a median of 0.68. To put this in perspective, if the relative efficiency is 0.50, then using AB rather than ML would be equivalent to discarding half of the sample.

What affects relative efficiency? Although the relative efficiencies for all conditions are shown in the last column of Tables A1 and A2, we also present

TABLE 3 How Number of Time Points Affects Relative Efficiency of the AB Method

	β_1	β_2
$T = 4$	1.040	0.827
$T = 5$	0.944	0.708
$T = 7$	0.939	0.505
$T = 10$	0.832	0.337

some of them here to highlight key results. Table 3 gives the relative efficiencies of the estimators for β_1 and β_2 as a function of the number of time points.

For both β_1 and β_2, the relative efficiency of AB declines with the number of time points, although the decline is much more precipitous for β_2, the autoregressive coefficient. These declines are consistent with the literature suggesting that when there are many time points—and therefore many instruments—AB is vulnerable to overfitting.

Unfortunately, there is a potential problem with the results in Table 3. Because our data generating model is not constrained to be stationary, the variances and covariances at later time points might differ from those at earlier time points. Therefore, the declines in efficiency observed in Table 3 could reflect not the number of time points but rather changes over time in the pattern of variances and covariances. To avoid this possible confounding, we first produce approximate stationarity by generating data from 1000 time points. Then, for the $T = 4$ condition, we use the data from the next four time points to estimate the model. The same strategy is used for $T = 5, 7,$ and 10. Results in Table 4

TABLE 4 Number of Time Points and Relative Efficiency Under Approximate Stationarity

	β_1	β_2
$T = 4$	0.982	0.562
$T = 5$	0.989	0.527
$T = 7$	1.038	0.371
$T = 10$	1.029	0.305

show that the ML and AB estimators do about equally well for β_1 regardless of the number of time points. For β_2, however, the efficiency of AB is quite low at all time points and declines noticeably as the number of time points grows larger. In this case, the inferiority of AB stems both from downward bias in the coefficients and from larger standard errors.

Previous work (Kiviet, 2005) has suggested that the ratio of the fixed effects variance to the error variance might be an important factor in the efficiency of AB. Table 5 confirms this for β_2 but not for β_1. When the standard deviations of α and η are held constant at 1.0, increases in the standard deviations of ε and ν are associated with declines in the relative efficiency of AB for β_2 but not for β_1. The direction is reversed when the standard deviation of ε is held constant and the standard deviation of α is varied—higher standard deviations of α result in higher relative efficiency of AB for β_2.

TABLE 5 How Relative Efficiency Depends on the Variance of ε and α

	β_1	β_2
$SD(\varepsilon) = 0.25$	0.924	0.716
$SD(\varepsilon) = 1.0$	0.944	0.708
$SD(\varepsilon) = 1.5$	0.974	0.640
$SD(\varepsilon) = 2.0$	0.964	0.570
$SD(\alpha) = 0.5$	0.981	0.629
$SD(\alpha) = 1.0$	0.944	0.708
$SD(\alpha) = 1.5$	0.989	0.814
$SD(\alpha) = 2.0$	0.974	0.863

TABLE 6 How Relative Efficiency Depends on ρ

	β_1	β_2
$\rho = 0$	0.936	0.378
$\rho = 0.25$	1.044	0.467
$\rho = 0.50$	0.881	0.535
$\rho = 0.75$	0.944	0.708
$\rho = 0.90$	0.942	0.759

TABLE 7 How Relative Efficiency Depends on β_1

	β_1	β_2
$\beta_1 = 0$	0.978	0.483
$\beta_1 = 0.25$	0.944	0.708
$\beta_1 = 0.50$	0.959	0.750
$\beta_1 = 0.75$	0.875	0.814
$\beta_1 = 1.00$	0.938	0.779

Table 6 shows how relative efficiency is affected by the value of ρ, the correlation between the two fixed effects, α and η. For β_1 there is no apparent trend. For β_2, however, the relative efficiency of AB increases substantially as the correlation goes from 0 to 0.90.

Finally, Table 7 shows how relative efficiency is affected by the magnitude of β_1, the cross-lagged coefficient. As in the previous two tables, the relative efficiencies of AB estimates for β_1 are virtually unaffected. For β_2, relative efficiency increases substantially as β_1 gets larger.

Three other factors have no apparent effect on relative efficiency: the sign of β_4 (the cross-lagged effect of y on x), sample size, and the magnitude of β_2 (the autoregressive coefficient). The absence of a relationship with sample size and β_2 is somewhat surprising. We expected ML-SEM to do better in smaller samples, and we expected AB to perform worse when β_2 is close or equal to 1.0. In fact, AB did quite well when $\beta_2 = 1$, both in absolute terms and relative to ML-SEM.

Because ML-SEM is based on the assumption of multivariate normality, it has been suggested that it might do worse than AB when distributions are not normal. To check this out, for the baseline set of parameter values, all the random draws are made from a chi-square distribution with two degrees of freedom, a distribution that is highly skewed to the right. The last rows of Tables A1 and A2 show that both estimators do well under this condition, but ML-SEM does better. The relative efficiency of AB is 0.908 for β_1 and 0.619 for β_2.

8 Discussion and Conclusion

Panel data have a lot of potential for improving our ability to make causal inferences from nonexperimental data, but appropriate methods are needed take advantage of such data. The linear dynamic panel model of econometrics protects against two major threats to valid causal inference: unmeasured confounders and reverse causation. The Arellano-Bond method can produce approximately unbiased estimates of the parameters of that model under a wide range of conditions. One of our goals is to show that cross-lagged panel models can be estimated within this econometric framework by estimating each side of the cross-lagged model separately. Compared with simultaneous estimation, this approach has the advantage of producing estimates that are robust to misspecification of the lag structure or the functional form of the other side.

Unfortunately, the AB method is reputed to be problematic when the autoregressive parameter is near 1.0, and its efficiency also has been questioned. Maximum likelihood methods based on first differences have been offered as an alternative, but they rely on questionable assumptions about the initial conditions.

In this chapter, we have shown that the linear dynamic panel model with predetermined regressors is a special case of the well-known linear structural equation modeling. Instead of relying on difference scores to eliminate the fixed effects, maximum likelihood estimation of this model is accomplished by allowing the fixed effects to have unrestricted correlations with the time-varying predictors. The initial observations of the dependent variable are treated just like any other exogenous variables. Cross-lagged causation is accommodated by allowing the error term in each equation to correlate with future values of the time-dependent predictors. Many different statistical packages, both freeware and commercial, can implement the ML-SEM method.

Monte Carlo simulations show that ML-SEM produced approximately unbiased estimates under all the conditions studied. Confidence interval coverage is also excellent. The AB estimator also does very well for the cross-lagged parameter, although with some downward bias. For the autoregressive parameter, however, the downward bias in AB is much more substantial, and its efficiency (relative to ML-SEM) is poor under most conditions. For this parameter, the efficiency of AB relative to ML-SEM also declines markedly as the number of time points increases.

One key conclusion from the simulations is that if we are primarily interested in the cross-lagged coefficients, AB and ML-SEM have statistical properties that are about equally good. Nevertheless, there are still plenty of reasons why one might prefer ML-SEM. As detailed by Bollen and Brand (2010), the ML-SEM method can be extended in several ways. Although maximum likelihood is the default estimator for all SEM packages, most packages offer alternative methods, including the asymptotic distribution free method of Browne (1984). Many packages also have options for robust standard errors. Many of the constraints that are implied by the linear dynamic panel model can be relaxed easily in the SEM setting. We showed how the error variances can be allowed to vary with time; the coefficients also could be allowed to vary with time.

It is even possible to allow the coefficient of α, the fixed effect, to vary with time instead of being constrained to 1 for every time point. This option is attractive because it removes one of the principal limitations of the classic fixed effects estimator: that it does not control for unmeasured time-invariant variables when their effects change over time. It is also possible to allow for individual-specific trends that are correlated with the time-varying predictors (Teachman, 2014).

With regard to unbalanced samples and missing data more generally, most SEM packages have the option of handling missing data by FIML. Unlike AB, FIML can easily handle missing data on predictor variables.[9]

Although we have not considered models with simultaneous reciprocal effects, such effects certainly can be built into SEM models if appropriate instruments are available. Finally, some SEM packages (such as Mplus or the **gsem** command in Stata) can estimate similar models for categorical dependent variables.

Are there any downsides to ML-SEM? As noted earlier, ML-SEM is not suitable when T is large relative to N. This is easily seen from the fact that ML-SEM operates on the full covariance matrix for all the variables at all points in time. For example, if the predictors in the model consist of nine time varying variables and $T = 11$, then the covariance matrix will be 101×101. And unless $N > 101$, that matrix will not have full rank, causing the maximization algorithm to break down. As also noted earlier, ML-SEM sometimes will fail to converge. And even if it converges, computation time can be considerably greater than for AB, especially when using FIML to handle missing data.

As can be seen from Fig. 2 and Appendix B, program code for ML-SEM can be more complex than for the AB method. Not only are ML-SEM programs typically longer, but it also can be challenging for the analyst to figure out exactly how to specify the model so that the correct covariances are either set to 0 or left unconstrained. This challenge is exacerbated by the fact that different packages have different defaults for the covariances and different ways of overriding those defaults.

Of course, this is just a programming issue, and it certainly would be feasible to write a Stata command, an SAS macro, or an R function that would automatically set up the correct model with minimal input from the user. As noted earlier, we have already developed a Stata command called **xtdpdml** that does exactly that (Williams et al., 2018). This command radically reduces the programming needed for ML-SEM, and is actually simpler to use than the built-in Stata commands for AB estimation (**xtabond**, **xtdpd**, or **xtdpdsys**).

---

9. For examples of the use of FIML to handle missing data, see Williams et al. (2018) and Moral-Benito et al. (2018).

A   Results From Monte Carlo Simulations

TABLE A1 Performance of ML and AB Estimators of β_1, the Lagged Effect of x on y

Condition	True[a]	Nonconverge[b]	Maximum Likelihood			Arellano–Bond			Relative Efficiency
			Mean[c]	SD[d]	Coverage[e]	Mean[c]	SD[d]	Coverage[e]	
$N = 50$	0.25	19	0.256	0.0975	0.934	0.240	0.0918	0.939	1.121
$N = 100$	0.25	23	0.250	0.0664	0.946	0.242	0.0664	0.943	0.985
$N = 400$	0.25		0.250	0.0314	0.949	0.249	0.0323	0.952	0.944
$N = 1600$	0.25		0.250	0.0161	0.947	0.250	0.0164	0.952	0.964
$\beta_2 = 0$	0.25		0.250	0.0325	0.950	0.252	0.0324	0.955	1.004
$\beta_2 = 0.25$	0.25		0.251	0.0322	0.947	0.252	0.0310	0.954	1.076
$\beta_2 = 0.50$	0.25		0.251	0.0313	0.950	0.249	0.0318	0.949	0.969
$\beta_2 = 0.75$	0.25		0.250	0.0314	0.949	0.249	0.0323	0.952	0.944
$\beta_2 = 0.90$	0.25		0.251	0.0324	0.953	0.248	0.0343	0.943	0.890
$\beta_2 = 1.0$	0.25		0.249	0.0328	0.949	0.249	0.0346	0.949	0.900
$\beta_2 = 1.25$	0.25		0.249	0.0335	0.957	0.248	0.0345	0.941	0.942
$\beta_1 = 0$	0.00	2	0.000	0.0331	0.947	−0.002	0.0334	0.947	0.978
$\beta_1 = 0.25$	0.25		0.250	0.0314	0.949	0.249	0.0323	0.952	0.944

Continued

TABLE A1 Performance of ML and AB Estimators of β_1, the Lagged Effect of x on y—cont'd

Condition	True	Nonconverge	Maximum Likelihood			Arellano–Bond			Relative Efficiency
			Mean	SD	Coverage	Mean	SD	Coverage	
$\beta_1 = 0.50$	0.50		0.500	0.0310	0.953	0.498	0.0316	0.958	0.959
$\beta_1 = 0.75$	0.75		0.750	0.0304	0.954	0.749	0.0325	0.957	0.875
$\beta_1 = 1.00$	1.00		1.001	0.0300	0.948	1.000	0.0310	0.948	0.938
$\beta_4 = -0.25$	0.25		0.250	0.0314	0.949	0.249	0.0323	0.952	0.944
$\beta_4 = 0$	0.25	4	0.250	0.0337	0.948	0.250	0.0336	0.949	1.007
$\beta_4 = 0.25$	0.25	23	0.250	0.0311	0.950	0.251	0.0309	0.949	1.014
$\rho = 0$	0.25	4	0.251	0.0325	0.947	0.248	0.0336	0.941	0.936
$\rho = 0.25$	0.25		0.250	0.0337	0.939	0.248	0.0329	0.949	1.044
$\rho = 0.50$	0.25		0.250	0.0315	0.954	0.247	0.0334	0.951	0.881
$\rho = 0.75$	0.25		0.250	0.0314	0.949	0.249	0.0323	0.952	0.944
$\rho = 0.90$	0.25		0.252	0.0321	0.940	0.249	0.0331	0.953	0.942
$SD(\varepsilon) = 0.25$	0.25	15	0.251	0.0305	0.950	0.249	0.0317	0.944	0.924
$SD(\varepsilon) = 1.0$	0.25		0.250	0.0314	0.949	0.249	0.0323	0.952	0.944
$SD(\varepsilon) = 1.5$	0.25	1	0.250	0.0325	0.954	0.247	0.0328	0.951	0.974
$SD(\varepsilon) = 2$	0.25	13	0.250	0.0318	0.949	0.247	0.0322	0.954	0.964

SD(α) = 0.5	0.25		0.250	0.0336	0.938	0.247	0.0338	0.937	0.981
SD(α) = 1.0	0.25	21	0.250	0.0314	0.949	0.249	0.0323	0.952	0.944
SD(α) = 1.5	0.25		0.251	0.0315	0.949	0.250	0.0318	0.955	0.989
SD(α) = 2.0	0.25	2	0.251	0.0317	0.945	0.250	0.0322	0.941	0.974
T = 4	0.25		0.250	0.0402	0.947	0.249	0.0394	0.948	1.040
T = 5	0.25		0.250	0.0314	0.949	0.249	0.0323	0.952	0.944
T = 7	0.25	8	0.251	0.0247	0.952	0.248	0.0254	0.949	0.939
T = 10	0.25		0.250	0.0188	0.949	0.246	0.0203	0.941	0.832
Chi-square	0.25		0.252	0.0315	0.941	0.250	0.0331	0.947	0.908

[a] True value of the coefficient in the model producing the data.
[b] Number of nonconvergent samples for ML.
[c] Mean of 1000 parameter estimates.
[d] Standard deviation of 1000 parameter estimates.
[e] Percentage of nominal 95% confidence intervals that include the true value.

TABLE A2 Performance of ML and AB Estimators of β_2, the Lagged Effect of y on Itself

Condition	True[a]	Maximum Likelihood			Arellano-Bond			Relative Efficiency
		Mean[b]	SD[c]	Coverage[d]	Mean[b]	SD[c]	Coverage[d]	
$N = 50$	0.75	0.752	0.0917	0.953	0.680	0.1021	0.890	0.549
$N = 100$	0.75	0.752	0.0675	0.951	0.716	0.0760	0.914	0.657
$N = 400$	0.75	0.750	0.0325	0.953	0.742	0.0377	0.950	0.708
$N = 1600$	0.75	0.750	0.0159	0.955	0.748	0.0195	0.946	0.656
$\beta_2 = 0$	0.00	0.001	0.0327	0.948	−0.005	0.0377	0.955	0.738
$\beta_2 = 0.25$	0.25	0.248	0.0322	0.964	0.241	0.0456	0.951	0.554
$\beta_2 = 0.50$	0.50	0.499	0.0378	0.952	0.488	0.0492	0.947	0.554
$\beta_2 = 0.75$	0.75	0.750	0.0325	0.953	0.742	0.0377	0.950	0.708
$\beta_2 = 0.90$	0.90	0.901	0.0257	0.961	0.895	0.0289	0.952	0.769
$\beta_2 = 1.0$	1.00	0.999	0.0219	0.956	0.996	0.0243	0.940	0.798
$\beta_2 = 1.25$	1.25	1.250	0.0150	0.947	1.249	0.0160	0.942	0.867
$\beta_1 = 0$	0.25	0.752	0.0425	0.960	0.730	0.0577	0.936	0.483
$\beta_1 = 0.25$	0.25	0.750	0.0325	0.953	0.742	0.0377	0.950	0.708
$\beta_1 = 0.50$	0.75	0.750	0.0249	0.953	0.747	0.0286	0.952	0.750
$\beta_1 = 0.75$	0.75	0.750	0.0208	0.956	0.748	0.0229	0.946	0.814
$\beta_1 = 1.00$	0.75	0.751	0.0175	0.948	0.748	0.0198	0.933	0.779

$\beta_4 = -0.25$	0.75	0.750	0.0325	0.953	0.742	0.0377	0.950	0.708
$\beta_4 = 0$	0.75	0.751	0.0303	0.953	0.743	0.0344	0.942	0.749
$\beta_4 = 0.25$	0.75	0.749	0.0294	0.938	0.743	0.0323	0.938	0.788
$\rho = 0$	0.75	0.753	0.0418	0.948	0.727	0.0640	0.919	0.378
$\rho = 0.25$	0.75	0.752	0.0380	0.948	0.736	0.0540	0.929	0.467
$\rho = 0.50$	0.75	0.750	0.0352	0.948	0.737	0.0464	0.925	0.535
$\rho = 0.75$	0.75	0.750	0.0325	0.953	0.742	0.0377	0.950	0.708
$\rho = 0.90$	0.75	0.751	0.0305	0.950	0.742	0.0343	0.949	0.759
$SD(\varepsilon) = 0.25$	0.75	0.751	0.0254	0.942	0.745	0.0296	0.944	0.716
$SD(\varepsilon) = 1.0$	0.75	0.750	0.0325	0.953	0.742	0.0377	0.950	0.708
$SD(\varepsilon) = 1.5$	0.75	0.751	0.0455	0.951	0.731	0.0536	0.935	0.640
$SD(\varepsilon) = 2$	0.75	0.750	0.0519	0.965	0.723	0.0632	0.934	0.570
$SD(\alpha) = 0.5$	0.75	0.752	0.0552	0.948	0.725	0.0650	0.919	0.629
$SD(\alpha) = 1.0$	0.75	0.750	0.0325	0.953	0.742	0.0377	0.950	0.708
$SD(\alpha) = 1.5$	0.75	0.751	0.0232	0.946	0.747	0.0256	0.943	0.814
$SD(\alpha) = 2.0$	0.75	0.751	0.0176	0.951	0.749	0.0189	0.961	0.863
$T = 4$	0.75	0.752	0.0483	0.944	0.744	0.0529	0.946	0.827
$T = 5$	0.75	0.750	0.0325	0.953	0.742	0.0377	0.950	0.708
$T = 7$	0.75	0.750	0.0224	0.938	0.739	0.0295	0.928	0.505

Continued

TABLE A2 Performance of ML and AB Estimators of β_2, the Lagged Effect of y on Itself—cont'd

| Condition | True | Maximum Likelihood | | | Arellano-Bond | | | Relative Efficiency |
		Mean	SD	Coverage	Mean	SD	Coverage	
$T = 10$	0.75	0.750	0.0157	0.950	0.736	0.0231	0.898	0.337
Chi-square	0.75	0.750	0.0317	0.959	0.744	0.0398	0.941	0.619

[a] True value of the coefficient in the model producing the data.
[b] Mean of 1000 parameter estimates.
[c] Standard deviation of 1000 parameter estimates.
[d] Percentage of nominal 95% confidence intervals that include the true value.

B   Example Program Code for Other Software Packages

Stata

```
1  use c:\wagewide.dta, clear
2  sem(wks2 <- lwage1@a wks1@b union1@c ed@d Alpha@1 E2@1) ///
3    (wks3 <- lwage2@a wks2@b union2@c ed@d Alpha@1 E3@1) ///
4    (wks4 <- lwage3@a wks3@b union3@c ed@d Alpha@1 E4@1) ///
5    (wks5 <- lwage4@a wks4@b union4@c ed@d Alpha@1 E5@1) ///
6    (wks6 <- lwage5@a wks5@b union5@c ed@d Alpha@1) ///
7    (wks7 <- lwage6@a wks6@b union6@c ed@d Alpha@1), ///
8  var(e.wks2@0 e.wks3@0 e.wks4@0 e.wks5@0) ///
9  cov(Alpha*(ed E*)@0) cov(_OEx*(E2 E3 E4 E5)@0) ///
10 cov(E2*(E3 E4 E5)@0) cov(E3*(E4 E5)@0) cov(E4*(E5)@0) ///
11 cov(E2*(union3 union4 union5 union6)) ///
12 cov(E3*(union4 union5 union6)) ///
13 cov(E4*(union5 union6)) cov(E5*union6) noxconditional ///
14 var(E2-E5@f e.wks6@f e.wks7@f)
```

Explanation

- Line 1 reads the wide-form data into memory.
- Lines 2–13 are all one single **sem** command. The /// at the end of each line allows the command to be spread across multiple lines in a DO file.
- Lines 2–7 specify the linear equations for years 2–7.
- The rule is that variable names (such as **lwage1**) that begin with lowercase letters are observed variables, while variable names that begin with upper-case letters (such as **Alpha**) are latent.
- @a assigns the name **a** to the coefficient for **lwage1**. Giving parameters the same name constrains them to be equal. Alpha@1 constrains the coefficient of Alpha to be 1.0.
- An unfortunate limitation of the **sem** command is that it does not allow the error term in an equation to be correlated with observed, exogenous variables. But that is exactly what we need to do for the dynamic panel model: allow error terms to be correlated with future values of the time-dependent predictors, in this case **union**. The workaround is to suppress the original error terms (by setting their variances equal to 0 in line 8), and introducing new latent error terms E2-E5 in lines 2–5. There is no need to do that at times 6 and 7 because there are no future values of **union** in the model.
- In line 9, the first **cov** option sets to 0 the covariance between **Alpha** and the time-invariant predictor **ed**, as well as the covariances between **Alpha** and

the new error terms. The second **cov** option sets to 0 the covariances between the new error terms and all of the observed, exogenous variables (_OEx).

- Line 10 constrains the all the new error terms to be uncorrelated with each other.
- Lines 11–13 allow the new error terms to be correlated with future values of the predetermined predictor, **union**.
- The **noxconditional** option on line 13 requests that the means, variances, and covariances of the observed exogenous variables be included in the parameters. For unknown reasons, the model will not run correctly without this option.
- Line 14 constrains the error variance to be the same at all time points. This is generally not advisable, but was done here to ensure comparability with the AB method.

This model also can be estimated in Stata with the user-written **xtdpdml** command, which acts as a simplifying shell for the **sem** command (Williams et al., 2018). The code for this example is:

```
use c:\wages.dta, clear
xtset id t
xtdpdml wks L.lwage, pre(L.union) inv(ed) errorinv
```

Mplus

```
 1 data: file = 'C:\wagewide.csv';
 2 variable: names =
 3    id ed fem blk wks1 wks2 wks3 wks4 wks5 wks6 wks7
 4    lwage1 lwage2 lwage3 lwage4 lwage5 lwage6 lwage7
 5    union1 union2 union3 union4 union5 union6 union7
 6    ms1 ms2 ms3 ms4 ms5 ms6 ms7;
 7 usevar=ed wks1 wks2 wks3 wks4 wks5 wks6 wks7
 8    lwage1 lwage2 lwage3 lwage4 lwage5 lwage6
 9    union1 union2 union3 union4 union5 union6;
10 model:
11    alpha by wks2@1 wks3@1 wks4@1 wks5@1 wks6@1 wks7@1;
12    wks2 on lwage1 (1)
13             wks1 (2)
14           union1 (3)
15               ed (4);
16    wks3 on lwage2 (1)
17             wks2 (2)
18           union2 (3)
19               ed (4);
```

```
20   wks4 on lwage3 (1)
21           wks3 (2)
22           union3 (3)
23             ed (4);
24   wks5 on lwage4 (1)
25           wks4 (2)
26           union4 (3)
27             ed (4);
28   wks6 on lwage5 (1)
29           wks5 (2)
30           union5 (3)
31             ed (4);
32   wks7 on lwage6 (1)
33           wks6 (2)
34           union6 (3)
35             ed (4);
36   alpha with wks1 lwage1-lwage6 union1-union6;
37   wks2 with union3-union6;
38   wks3 with union4-union6;
39   wks4 with union5 union6;
40   wks5 with union6;
41   ed on wks1 lwage1-lwage6 union1-union6;
42   wks2-wks7 (5);
```

Explanation

- Line 1 specifies the location of the data file. It must be a text file in free format: one record per person, no variable names, and spaces between values.
- Lines 2–6 assign names to the variables in the order in which they appear on the data file.
- Lines 7–9 restrict the variables to those that actually appear in the model.
- Line 10 begins the model specification.
- Line 11 defines the latent variable **alpha** by specifying its indicators, each of which has a factor loading constrained to be 1.0.
- Lines 12–15 specify the first regression equation. In order to constrain coefficients to be the same across equations, the predictors must be on different lines, with a number in parentheses at the end of each line.
- Lines 16–35 specify the regressions for the remaining time points. Coefficients for variables followed by the same numbers are constrained to be the same.
- Line 36 allows the latent variable **alpha** to be correlated with the predictor variables, except for **ed**.

- Lines 37–40 allow the error term in each equation to be correlated with future values of the predetermined variable **union**.
- Line 41 allows **ed** to be correlated with all the other exogenous variables. It accomplishes this by specifying a regression with **ed** as the dependent variable.
- Line 42 constrains the error variances to be the same at all time points. This is generally not advisable, but was done here to ensure comparability with the AB method.

lavaan (R package)

```
1 wage <- read.table("C:/wagenames.txt",header=T)
2 wagemod <-'
3 alpha =~ 1*wks2 + 1*wks3 + 1*wks4 + 1*wks5 + 1*wks6 + 1*wks7
4 wks2 ~ a*wks1 + b*union1 + c*lwage1 + d*ed
5 wks3 ~ a*wks2 + b*union2 + c*lwage2 + d*ed
6 wks4 ~ a*wks3 + b*union3 + c*lwage3 + d*ed
7 wks5 ~ a*wks4 + b*union4 + c*lwage4 + d*ed
8 wks6 ~ a*wks5 + b*union5 + c*lwage5 + d*ed
9 wks7 ~ a*wks6 + b*union6 + c*lwage6 + d*ed
10 wks2 ~~ union3 + union4 + union5 + union6
11 wks3 ~~ union4 + union5 + union6
12 wks4 ~~ union5 + union6
13 wks5 ~~ union6
14 alpha ~ wks1+lwage1+lwage2+lwage3+lwage4+lwage5+lwage6+
15     union1+union2+union3+union4+union5+union6
16 union6 ~ ed+wks1+lwage1+lwage2+lwage3+lwage4+lwage5+lwage6+
17     union1+union2+union3+union4+union5
18 union5 ~ ed+wks1+lwage1+lwage2+lwage3+lwage4+lwage5+lwage6+
19     union1+union2+union3+union4
20 union4 ~ ed+wks1+lwage1+lwage2+lwage3+lwage4+lwage5+lwage6+
21     union1+union2+union3
22 union3 ~ ed+wks1+lwage1+lwage2+lwage3+lwage4+lwage5+lwage6+
23     union1+union2
24 wks2 ~~ f*wks2
25 wks3 ~~ f*wks3
26 wks4 ~~ f*wks4
27 wks5 ~~ f*wks5
28 wks6 ~~ f*wks6
29 wks7 ~~ f*wks7 '
30 wagefit <- sem(wagemod,data=wage)
31 summary(wagefit)
```

Explanation

- Line 1 reads the data from a text file in free format with variable names in the first row. This data set is assigned the name **wage**.
- Lines 2–23 specify the model, which is stored in the object **wagemod**. The model specification is a literal that is demarcated by single quotes.
- Line 3 defines the latent variable **alpha** by naming its indicators, each with a factor loading of 1.0. The symbol $= \sim$ means "is measured by".
- Lines 4–9 specify the six regression equations. The symbol $\sim$ means "is regressed on." The letters preceding each variable are the names of the coefficients. Coefficients with the same names are constrained to be equal.
- Lines 10–13 allow the error terms in each of the equations to be correlated with future values of the predetermined variable **union**. The symbol $\sim\sim$ means "is correlated with."
- Lines 14–15 allow the latent variable **alpha** to be correlated with other exogenous variables, except for **ed**.
- Lines 16–23 allow the **union** variables to be correlated with other exogenous variables. This is necessary because lines 10–13 caused the **union** variables to be treated as endogenous, and the default in lavaan is to presume that endogenous and exogenous variables are uncorrelated.
- Lines 24–29 impose the constraint that error variances are the same at all time points. This is not generally advisable but was done here to ensure comparability with the AB method.
- Line 30 calls the **sem** function that actually fits the model, using the **wage** data and the **wagemod** model specification.
- Line 31 reports the estimates and associated statistics.

References

Ahn, S.C., Schmidt, P., 1995. Efficient estimation of models for dynamic panel data. Journal of Econometrics 68, 5–27.

Allison, P.D., 2000. Inferring causal order from panel data. In: Paper presented at the ninth international conference on panel data, June 22, Geneva, Switzerland.

Allison, P.D., 2005a. Fixed effects regression methods for longitudinal data using SAS. The SAS Institute, Cary, NC.

Allison, P.D., 2005b. Causal inference with panel data. In: Paper presented at the annual meeting of the American Sociological Association, August, Philadelphia.

Allison, P.D., 2009. Fixed effects regression models. Sage Publications, Thousand Oaks, CA.

Allison, P.D., Bollen, K.A., 1997. Change scores, fixed effects, and random effects: a structural equation approach. In: Paper presented at the annual meeting of the American Sociological Association, August, Toronto, Canada.

Allison, P.D., Richard, W., Enrique, M.-B., 2017. Maximum likelihood for cross-lagged panel models with fixed effects. Socius: Sociological Research for a Dynamic World 3, 1–17.

Anderson, T.W., Hsiao, C., 1982. Formulation and estimation of dynamic models using panel data. Journal of Econometrics 18, 67–82.

Arellano, M., 2003. Panel data econometrics. Oxford University Press, Oxford.

Arellano, M., Bond, S., 1991. Some tests of specification for panel data: Monte Carlo evidence and an application to employment equations. The Review of Economic Studies 58, 277–297.

Baltagi, B.H., 2013. Econometric analysis of panel data, 5th ed. Wiley, New York.

Bentler, P.M., Weeks, D.G., 1980. Linear structural equations with latent variables. Psychometrika 45 (3), 289–308.

Bhargava, A., Sargan, J.D., 1983. Estimating dynamic random effects models from panel data covering short time periods. Econometrica 51, 1635–1659.

Blundell, R., Bond, S., 1998. Initial conditions and moment restrictions in dynamic panel data models. Journal of Econometrics 87, 115–144.

Bollen, K.A., Brand, J.E., 2010. A general panel model with random and fixed effects: a structural equations approach. Social Forces 89, 1–34.

Browne, M.W., 1984. Asymptotically distribution-free methods for the analysis of covariance structures. British Journal of Mathematical and Statistical Psychology 37, 62–83.

Chamberlain, G., 1982. Multivariate regression models for panel data. Journal of Econometrics (1), 5–46.

Chamberlain, G., 1984. Panel data. In: Griliches, Z., Intriligator, M. (Eds.), Handbook of econometrics. North-Holland, Amsterdam, pp. 1247–1318.

Cornwell, C., Rupert, P., 1988. Efficient estimation with panel data: an empirical comparison of instrumental variables estimators. Journal of Applied Econometrics 3, 149–155.

Duncan, O.D., 1969. Some linear models for two-wave, two-variable panel analysis. Psychological Bulletin 72, 177–182.

Finkel, S.E., 1995. Causal analysis with panel data. Sage, Thousand Oaks, CA.

Firebaugh, G., Warner, C., Massoglia, M., 2013. Fixed effects, random effects, and hybrid models for causal analysis. In: Morgan, S.L. (Ed.), Handbook of causal analysis for social research. Springer, New York, pp. 113–131.

Grassetti, L., 2011. A note on transformed likelihood approach in linear dynamic panel models. Statistical Methods & Applications 20 (2), 221–240.

Halaby, C.N., 2004. Panel models in sociological research: theory into practice. Annual Review of Sociology 30, 507–544.

Hamaker, E.L., Kuiper, R.M., Grasman, R.P., 2015. A critique of the cross-lagged panel model. Psychological Methods 20 (1), 102–116.

Han, C., Phillips, P.C., 2013. First difference maximum likelihood and dynamic panel estimation. Journal of Econometrics 175 (1), 35–45.

Holtz-Eakin, D., Newey, W., Rosen, H.S., 1988. Estimating vector autoregressions with panel data. Econometrica 56, 1371–1395.

Hsiao, C., 2014. Analysis of panel data (No. 54). Cambridge University Press.

Hsiao, C., Pesaran, M.H., Tahmiscioglu, A.K., 2002. Maximum likelihood estimation of fixed effects dynamic panel data models covering short time periods. Journal of Econometrics 109 (1), 107–150.

Jöreskog, K.G., 1978. Structural analysis of covariance and correlation matrices. Psychometrika 43 (4), 443–477.

Judson, R.A., Owen, A.L., 1999. Estimating dynamic panel data models: a guide for macroeconomists. Economics Letters 65, 9–15.

Kenny, D.A., Judd, C.M., 1996. A general procedure for the estimation of interdependence. Psychological Bulletin 119, 138–148.

Kessler, R.C., Greenberg, D.F., 1981. Linear panel analysis: models of quantitative change. Academic Press, New York.

Kiviet, J.F., 2005. Judging contending estimators by simulation: tournaments in dynamic panel data models. In: Tinbergen Institute discussion paper, No. 05-112/4.

Kiviet, J.F., Pleus, M., Poldermans, R., 2014. Accuracy and efficiency of various GMM inference techniques in dynamic micro panel data models. In: Amsterdam School of Economics discussion paper, No. 2014/9.

Kripfganz, S., 2016. Quasi-maximum likelihood estimation of linear dynamic short-T panel-data models. The Stata Journal 16, 1013–1038.

Markus, G.B., 1979. Analyzing panel data. Sage Publications, Thousand Oaks, CA.

McArdle, J.J., Nesselroade, J.R., 2014. Longitudinal data analysis using structural equation modeling. American Psychological Association, Washington, DC.

Moral-Benito, E., 2013. Likelihood-based estimation of dynamic panels with predetermined regressors. Journal of Business & Economic Statistics 31, 451–472.

Moral-Benito, E., Allison, P.D., Williams. R. 2018. Dynamic panel data modelling using maximum likelihood: an alternative to Arellano-Bond. Applied Economics 51, 2221–2232.

Mundlak, Y., 1978. On the pooling of time series and cross section data. Econometrica 46, 69–85.

Nickell, S., 1981. Biases in dynamic models with fixed effects. Econometrica 49, 1417–1426.

Roodman, D., 2009. A note on the theme of too many instruments. Oxford Bulletin of Economics and Statistics 71, 135–158.

Teachman, J., 2014. Latent growth curve models with random and fixed effects. In: McHale, S., Amato, P., Booth, A. (Eds.), Emerging methods in family research. National symposium on family issues. In: Vol. 4. Springer, Cham.

Teachman, J., Duncan, G.J., Yeung, W.J., Levy, D., 2001. Covariance structure models for fixed and random effects. Sociological Methods & Research 30, 271–288.

Williams, R., Allison, P.D., Moral-Benito, E., 2018. xtdpdml: linear dynamic panel-data estimation using maximum likelihood and structural equation modeling. The Stata Journal 18, 293–326.

Wooldridge, J.M., 2010. Econometric analysis of cross section and panel data. MIT Press, Cambridge, MA.

Chapter 18

Panel Data in Transportation Research

Rico Merkert and Corinne Mulley
The University of Sydney Business School, NSW, Sydney, Australia

Chapter Outline

1 Introduction

Little activity can take place without involving transport, both in terms of mobility for passengers and supply chain services for freight. Transport is typically a means to an end, allowing goods to move from their manufacture to their destination and people to move from their origin to an activity center or destination where they consume goods or services.

Many studies about transport have focused on the use of aggregate data. Studies about freight movements often are limited by the use of aggregate statistics about trade and freight or national surveys of shippers because more disaggregate data is confidential to manufacturers or not available at all (such as the type and number of commodities carried in trucks). For passenger movements, travel demand models were initially, and in many cases remain, calibrated by aggregate data. For example, aggregate models for trip generation and trip distribution are commonplace, particularly in early travel planning models.

Research about transport, like other domains, is constrained by the availability of data. The trend, however, is to examine questions at a more disaggregate level, often building to the aggregate level through the summation of individual

Panel Data Econometrics. https://doi.org/10.1016/B978-0-12-815859-3.00018-4

data, which can be problematic in the panel data context. Broadly, studies about transport can be divided into demand or supply/cost studies, each of these needing different types of data to analyze research questions to inform an aspect of the transport domain.

Moving from aggregate to disaggregate statistics carries with it a number of challenges—particularly methodologically—but comes with significant benefits. For demand side or for travel behavior, and particularly for distinguishing between short-run and long-run effects, genuine panel data of individual records are the ideal data. Real panel data, however, including panels that are large enough for modeling or analyzing human behavior are not common because of the high costs associated with large sample size and sample attrition problems. There are few genuine mobility studies—the German Mobility Panel (from 1994) and the Puget Sound Panel (1989–2002)—are two notable panels. As compared to genuine panel data, repeated cross-sectional travel and travel behavior surveys are commonly undertaken but do not allow individuals to be traced over time, so that the difference between short-run and long-run effects, necessary to understand from a policy perspective, cannot be distinguished. This can be overcome by the use of pseudo-panel data.

In contrast, supply side and cost studies in transportation tend to be panel data investigations with data more readily available. Both aggregate and disaggregate data for an individual firm over time can provide the basis of a research investigation because the number of records often is not as demanding as when investigating individual behavior. Nevertheless, panel data related to the supply side comes with its own challenges related to implementing and interpreting of the results. For example, efficiency analysis results based on panels can be misleading, as unobserved heterogeneity as well as a lack of comparability of the data and distortions both in the longitudinal (e.g., change of uncontrolled variables such as a merger with another firm over time) and cross-sectional (i.e., international) context need to be accounted for (if possible).

Combining aspects of both demand and supply-side factors is demand forecasting literature that aims to use panel data related to exogenous variables such as GDP or disposable income and also supply-side data such as frequency of provided services (such as flights per week) to explain changes in observed panel data related to transport demand or transport activity (Hakim & Merkert, 2019). Of interest and importance in such studies are causal effects and time lags. For example, Baker, Merkert, and Kamruzzaman (2015) have shown a bidirectional relationship between air transport activity and economic development for developed countries, which does not exist in the low-income context of many developing countries. For the latter, panel data Granger causality analysis has shown (Hakim & Merkert, 2016) that only a unidirectional impact runs from economic development to transport demand, which allows for further investigation (and multivariate panel data analysis) of other determinants of transport demand in that context.

This chapter is structured as follows. The next section looks at demand-side studies. It provides an overview of the key true panels in transport that exist and reviews the type of studies for which the panel data has been essential. This demand-side section also considers the use of pseudo-panel data and looks at studies in which pseudo panels have been created and used to look at research questions that otherwise would require true panel data. This is followed by a section on supply or cost/efficiency/productivity-based studies, often (but not exclusively) used to underpin sensible discussions about benchmarking. The penultimate section presents a supply-side case study in the use of panel data in transport—the development of a framework for the benchmarking of railways in different contextual settings (and thereby for the first time accounting for rail operating firms in the regional context being very different from those that operate in the urban context).

2 Demand-Side Studies

This section first considers key transport panel surveys before turning to studies that have been facilitated by the data offered by the panel surveys. The final section addresses pseudo panels use in the estimation of transport demand. It will show that not only do the panel surveys vary, but also the opportunities they offer to researchers in supporting empirical studies.

2.1 Panel Surveys

This section is concerned with surveys collecting panel data with a specific transport or mobility focus. It is, of course, recognized that more general panel data collection, seeking to provide a representative view of the population of a particular society, does take place, such as the Panel Study of Income Dynamics (United States), the British Household Panel Study (United Kingdom), and the German Socio-Economic Panel (Germany). These will have some transport questions but not the in-depth focus on transport and mobility of surveys dedicated to this topic. The need for continuous data collection—not necessarily as panel data—is reviewed carefully by Ortúzar, Armoogum, Madre, and Potier (2011) and contains much information about survey design and its impact on eventual analysis.

The German Mobility Panel (MOP) started collecting data in 1994 and has been collecting data annually since then. Initially, just under 1000 households were contacted, but this number has been rising steadily, with the most recent data (2014) showing just under 1700 households included. Its inception was motivated by a need to make reliable and evidence-based decisions about mode choice in transport planning, forecasting transport demand into the longer term to understand the likely longer-term requirements of transport supply and providing the everyday understanding of mobility decisions to support intelligent intermodal transport solutions. The MOP is undertaken in conjunction with large cross-sectional travel surveys that are more infrequent.

The MOP was designed as a rotating panel survey in which households participate for three consecutive years, after which they are replaced by newly recruited households. The survey collects data in the autumn using a 1-week travel diary, thus providing multiday and multiperiod data about daily travel from each of the household members (from the age of 10 upward). The diary records each trip made during the week, the mode used, the trip purpose, and trip distance. A second part of the survey is collected in the spring for respondents with private cars who record odometer readings for 8 weeks and provide information about fuel consumption. The data provide insights into individual longitudinal patterns of behavior and how this might change over time. In contrast to a single-day survey, the MOP as a multiday, multiperiod survey provides the potential to see how behavior can vary over a week, whereas a single-day diary might be just the day the respondent stays at home (Zumkeller, 2009). The Puget Sound Transportation Panel (PSTP) collected data for the four counties in the northwest of the United States between 1989 and 2002. Although the MOP recruitment was random (through random digit telephone dialing), the PSTP deliberately included households in which one member was a regular bus traveler and households in which one member was a regular car pooler. Initially, about 1700 households were included, and the same households were included in each of the 10 waves of data collection. This required approximately 20% replacement of households because of attrition; the replacements were chosen to reflect those leaving the study.

The PSTP used a two-day travel diary for all trips for each member of the household to elicit information about trip purpose, mode choice, travel time, travel distance, and whether the travel was alone or with others. In the first couple of waves, attitude questions were asked of some respondents, but for most of the waves all respondents answered all questions Kilgren (2017). The PSTP, however, was not undertaken regularly (with a gap of up to 2 years between waves), nor at the same time as year as with the MOP, which limits some of the comparability between patterns.

While the PSTP was being implemented, a large cross-sectional study also was implemented in 1999. This study used a large sample (6000 households) with the specific purpose of providing data to develop, and presumably calibrate, the Regional Travel Demand Forecasting Model and to support the development of the Metropolitan Transportation Plan Update. More recently, the Puget Sound Regional Council took the first of a three-wave survey in 2017, with two further waves in 2019 and 2021, if funds allow (Kilgren, 2014).

The Netherlands was one of the first countries to implement a mobility panel in the 1980s alongside its cross-sectional surveys. The Longitudinal Mobility Survey (LVO) had a sample size of about 1500 households and required all members of the household age 12 years or older to keep a seven-day travel diary and take part in a personal interview. Unusually, the LVO was designed as a universal instrument for data supply and analysis rather than being driven by a specific purpose. The sample frame did not aim to be representative but, like the PSTP, it oversampled interesting groups from a mobility point of view. The travel diary was repeated twice annually until it was discontinued in 1989. Various reasons were advanced for stopping the survey: Expense was one because the travel diaries were paper-based and needed to be postprocessed by hand, but the respondent burden also must have been a factor (Kilgren, 2017). At the time, it was considered state of the art, with many of the results passed to the MOP.

Recognizing the need for longitudinal data for the calibration of large-scale strategic transport models that reinforce transport policy, exante investment decisions, and describing travel behavioral dynamics, the Netherlands has undertaken a new mobility panel. The Mobiliteits Panel Nederland (MPN) first collected data in 2013 and was committed for the following 4 years. The sample consists of 2500 households, in which all members of the household older than 12 complete a three-day web-based travel diary. The screening questionnaire and a household questionnaire is completed by the head of household, and two additional questionnaires are completed in alternative waves to collect demographic information and attitudinal information. In order to reduce the response burden, the data are matched to administrative data to provide information about, for example, car ownership, spatial characteristics, and post code information (Hoogendoorn-Lanser, Schaap, & Oldekalter, 2015).

The panels described so far have been designed to monitor travel behavior generally or, in some cases, by interesting cases, monitor how travel behavior is trending. Many panels, typically intended to be short-term at the outset, have been created to investigate specific transport-related phenomena. The following sections give some idea of the reasons for setting out to create a panel dataset.

In Santiago, Chile, a transformational change was planned for the public transport system, known as Transantiago. As identified by Kitamura (1990), panels have significant advantages in evaluating changes, especially if the scale of change proposed is large. In Santiago, the panel was created to understand and allow the modeling of changes in mode choice that ensued from the wide changes to the public transport system. Although the public transport change was planned for the summer 2007, the first wave of the panel survey began in December 2006, with three additional waves in May 2007, December 2007, and October 2008. The sample (of just more than 300 in wave 1 reducing to 258 by wave 4) was based on individuals working at one of the six universities in Santiago. Because the intention was to capture how regular trips changed, the survey looked only at the journey to work using a five-day pseudo diary with the data collected through a personal digital assistant. Other panels to investigate major change include the investigation of the impact of a free bus service in the United States (Parody, 1977) and a before-and-after study in Amsterdam (Kroes, Daly, Gunn, & van der Hoorn, 1996). In addition, Ortúzar et al. (2011) refers to a panel survey in Japan to look at travel behavior changes as a result of the introduction of an automated railway between the suburbs and CBD of Hiroshima (seven waves, 1987–97).

Panels also have been created to look at specific questions. One panel survey, for example, was created to look at the impact on commuting in urban areas from flexible working and, in particular, ICT dependent teleworking. The panel was created from an annual Internet-based survey, repeated four times with a sample of about 1000 individuals in paid employment, taken from a panel of 120,000 members. Each wave retained about 1000 individuals, but attrition was an issue with only 96 individuals taking part in all four waves (864 participated in more than one wave) (CTS, 2009). Another example of a specific question was the Australian panel built to understand whether travel behavior change resulted from voluntary travel demand management measures (Stopher & Swann, 2008). This was followed by further panels based on GPS data, investigating the impact of voluntary travel demand measures in different states. Ortúzar et al. (2011) identifies panel surveys in Spain (a relatively small panel of three waves and 143 respondents looking at season ticket use in Valuencia and a longitudinal study looking at long distance travel between Madrid and Barcelona).

In summary, only a handful of ongoing panel data collections, in which the data are being selected from substantial number of households, are in the transport domain. Indeed, currently, there are only two: the MOP and the newly introduced MPN in the Netherlands, if it continues beyond the first agreed 4 years. In contrast, many short panels with a transport or mobility element have been created either to monitor change or to investigate specific questions. The next section provides an overview of the empirical work facilitated by the major panel surveys—the MOP in Germany, the PSTP in the United States, and the LVO and MPN in the Netherlands.

2.2 Panel Survey Studies

This section presents some of the studies undertaken with data from the major panel data sets we have identified. The aim is to provide a cross section of studies, rather than to be exhaustive.

One of the objectives of the MOP was to provide an evidence base to make sound judgments about future supply of transport infrastructure. Chikaraishi, Fujiwara, Zhang, Axhausen, and Zumkeller (2011) investigated a method for capturing changes in travel time expenditure and, in particular, for identifying how travel time expenditure varies around the average. The link to infrastructure evaluation is captured by Metz (2008) who argues that because travel time expenditure is stable, then transport investment brings benefits through enhanced access rather than through reduced travel times (i.e., if there is an investment that improves travel times), people will just travel farther. This view, however, is not universally held. Chikaraishi et al. aimed to use the

MOP data to resolve this point so as to provide for better transport planning and decisions about investment.

The multiday and multiperiod panel, such as the MOP, allows variations and changes in activity travel behavior to be analyzed. For example, it allows a distinction to be made between a constant average travel time expenditure that is made up from unchanging times of journeys to be distinguished from a constant average travel time made from the commute journey becoming longer but journeys to other activities being shorter. The study had two major results. First, although average travel time expenditures appear stable over time, the intraindividual variations in travel time expenditure have increased, and the interindividual variations in travel time expenditure have decreased. The authors suggest this implies that the factors that influence travel time expenditure are changing from the dominant influence being socioeconomic, geographic, or demographic to more situational factors, such as changing plans following a phone call and changes in the weather. Second, differences in the variation of travel time expenditure between the groups of mobility tool owners (car owners, public transport pass holders) become smaller over time. Chikaraishi et al. (2011) suggest that because an underlying variation is not captured by the average travel time expenditure, the analysis not only confirms travel time savings might not be the best way to capture the benefits of transport investment, but also shows some of the factors that have been subject to change over the previous decade.

Frondel, Peters, and Vance (2008) used MOP to examine the rebound effect, which is the increase in service demand that occurs when a car driver becomes an owner of a more fuel-efficient car and drives more in response to the lower per-kilometer costs relative to other modes. The rebound effect is not restricted to transport but is a more general economic phenomenon that relates to the reduction in the potential gains of a cost-reducing innovation. Investigating three different definitions of rebound and using a number of different econometric techniques, Frondel et al. (2008) find stable results of a rebound effect between 57% and 67%. These results are robust to alternative panel estimators and to alternative definitions of the rebound but considerably higher than previously found estimates, most derived in the United States. The authors suggest that the better European access to public transport might explain the difference between the evidence from MOP and from the United States, especially because typical trips in the United States tend to be longer, particularly for commuting, which then would have a lower impact on how drivers respond to changes in automobile efficiency. In a recent study that is more of a follow-up study, Frondel, Ritter, and Vance (2012) examine the heterogeneity associated with the rebound effect specifically in relation to how this affects vehicle emissions reduction. Their conclusions suggest that fuel efficiency appears to be considered as simply a way of decreasing the unit cost of driving, which in turn suggests that the European Community's reliance on efficiency standards as a means to reduce pollution might not be effective and that increased fuel taxes might prove more successful. Related papers about car driving behavior include an examination of what determines automobile travel and quantify the impact of fuel prices and fuel economy using 10 years of data from the MOP (Frondel & Vance, 2009). Treating automobile behavior as a two-stage practice (the decision to own a car and then the decision to use it), the paper found positive correlations between fuel economy and distance traveled and that increasing fuel taxes would be more effective in reducing vehicle miles traveled and, consequently, emissions, than imposing fuel efficiency standards. Also using a two-stage approach, Vance and Hedel (2007) look at 8 years of individual panel data to investigate the relationship between urban transport and car travel. The methodology is interesting for the way in which endogeneity arises from the potential simultaneity of residential and mode choice with instrumental variables. The study includes that urban form has a statistically significant and positive effect on the vehicle kilometers traveled (VKT).

Travel behavior research has moved from an interest in the aggregate behavior of individuals to an interest in how individuals travel. This, of course, is what has driven the development of many of the panel data collection exercises. The studies by Kuhnimhof, Buehler, and Dargay (2011) and Kuhnimhof, Buehler, and Wirtz (2012) carry out such investigations. Kuhnimhof et al. (2011) compares the experience of the United Kingdom and Germany using pooled data from MOP to overcome small sample issues and the National Travel Survey from the United Kingdom (an annual cross-section survey). The paper is interesting for the way in which the MOP was harmonized with the irregular cross-section survey in Germany (the Kontiv) and compared with annual cross-section survey in the United Kingdom. The results show similarities with other industrialized countries with people between 20 and 29 years old owning fewer cars, driving fewer miles, and using other modes of travel more. Kuhnimhof et al. (2012) is a more typical panel study using the MOP with the 10 years pooled into two 4-year samples and the 1976 cross-sectional Kontiv survey as the baseline. The study was concerned with 19- to 29-year-olds and found similar results to the 2011 study: between 1976 and 1996, adults younger than 40 had the highest VKT, but from 1996, adults between 18 and 29 had 20% lower VKT, and the VKT for the 30- to 40-year-old cohort had stagnated.

Studies using the PSTP appear to be generally focused on the analysis of data of the area and are naturally more dated than the MOP studies. Nevertheless, Yee and Niemeier (1996, 2000) used the panel to discuss and implement methodological approaches necessitated by the longitudinal and panel nature of the data. Yee and Niemeier (1996) are concerned with the benefits and costs of longitudinal versus repeated cross-section data. They conclude that there are benefits of increased statistical power from the panel study, but that repeated cross-section studies might be more cost effective and benefit from larger sample sizes because they are not prone to attrition. Yee and Niemeier (2000) consider the potential for model misspecification in the context of examining activity generation and activity duration. They conclude that, during the four waves of data considered, activity durations did change and were associated particularly with increasing numbers of children in the family.

Farsi, Filippini, and Kuenzle (2006) used the PSTP to examine the interaction between the built environment and emissions. The study posits that the development of suburban neighborhoods with more curvy roads and lack of connectivity by foot to nearby locations affects the vehicle miles traveled (VMT) by design. The paper specifically considers interactions between a number of built environment variables, household travel demand, vehicle emissions, and demographic variables, thereby combining PSTP data with other secondary data. By showing how land use affects the degree and nature of emissions, the study argues that land-use policy should play a more important role in regional air quality strategy.

In summary, it can be seen that panel data in transport has been used to examine a wide variety of demand-led questions providing directly and indirectly an evidence base for policy. Panel data has been increasingly used to focus on the travel behavior of the individual in which the repeated nature of the panel data can provide particular insights. As some of the studies identify, however, the sample sizes from a wave of a panel study might not be big enough so successive waves have to be pooled for analysis, resulting in a loss of many of the specific benefits of a longitudinal panel in following the same households. However, few general transportation panel surveys with many more repeated cross-section surveys are available. Pseudo panels, discussed in the next section, are used to create longitudinal data from repeated cross-section surveys in order to examine the dynamic impacts over time in relation to the demand for transport.

2.3 Pseudo Panels

As identified by Yee and Niemeier (1996) and others, repeated cross-section data collection, or even one-off data collections, can reveal some travel demand aspects. Given the importance of time effects in the decision-making process, however, it is sometimes important to understand the dynamics of travel behavior. In these cases, panel data is ideal because the way in which the same individual responds over time can be identified and a number of the previously mentioned studies, such as those looking at the behavioral change of millennials, have benefited from using a true panel data (Kuhnimhof et al., 2011, 2012). True panel data, however, is expensive to collect and transport, with the exception of the MOP, has not had large numbers of waves. Moreover, attrition and respondent burden are significant, which, in turn, lead to higher levels of attrition.

In the transport domain, Dargay and Vythoulkas (1999) were the first to suggest that using pseudo-panel data could provide a way of making data more available for analysis. Deaton (1985) introduced the idea of pseudo-panel data in consumer economics and showed how existing repeated cross-sectional data could be used to group individuals or households into cohorts using time invariant variables such as birth date and household characteristics. The created dataset allows the identification of the patterns of travel behavior to be examined by considering each cohort to be represented by the cohort mean. Although looking at the cohort level loses individual information, this can be minimized if the intracohort variation is less than the intercohort variation (Verbeek & Nijman, 1992). The great advantage of pseudo panels is the way in which they provide the potential to create a disaggregate approach using aggregate data.

Pseudo-panel studies in transport, as with the true panel studies, have been more focused on car travel studies. Dargay and Vythoulkas (1999) looked at the determinants of car ownership in the United Kingdom between 1970 and 1994 using the Family Expenditure Survey and estimated the long-run elasticity to be three times greater than short-run elasticities. This study was extended to look at differences in urban and rural car ownership in which the different sensitivities to motoring costs were identified, and found that the long-run elasticities were still consistently higher than short-run elasticities (Dargay, 2002). Dargay (2007) followed her earlier studies by looking at the relationships among car travel, car ownership, and household income. The study found the relationship with income to be asymmetric because rising income encouraged car ownership, but falling incomes did not cause households to abandon their cars.

Weis and Axhausen (2009) used a pseudo-panel data set built from the Swiss National Travel survey to estimate a structural equations model examining induced travel emerging from interactions among the share of mobiles, number of trips, and travel distance. The results confirm the importance of generalized cost in the traveler's mobility, and the study showed that SEM could be applied to pseudo-panel data as if they were true panel data.

In spite of not having real individual information, as with a true panel, a pseudo panel provides a deeper insight into variations over time as compared to aggregate data. Although pseudo-panel data overcomes the restrictions on empirical investigations from a lack of true panel data, however, the data requirements still demand that the cohort size is sufficiently large and meets the requirements of group-specific variations.

3 Supply-Side Studies

The literature about supply-side studies using panel data has grown during the last decade and is mainly concerned with either changes in costs, service offerings (including both quantity and quality), and/or performance (inefficiency) usually relating the former two aspects. A number of methods for performance evaluation have been developed in the literature, with Coelli, Rao, O'Donnell, and Battese (2005), Fried, Knox Lovell, and Schmidt (2008), or Greene, Khalaf, Sickles, Veall, and Voia (2016), being particularly useful and applicable to the transportation context. Although there might be industry characteristics that will demand different inputs, outputs, or model specifications (such as assumptions on input/output orientation or cost minimization), the principal methods of efficiency analysis can be applied across all modes of transport and industries. Merkert, Odeck, Bråthen, and Pagliari (2012) and more recently Merkert and Cowie (2018) provide good overviews of the methods applied not only to mainstream transport, but also to the regional and remote context (where more sophisticated econometric methods also can be used). Although Daraio et al. (2016) have produced a good overview of public transport efficiency studies, Yu (2016) provides an overview of the main concepts and methods of airline efficiency analysis (for a more recent study see Kottas & Madas, 2018). Their findings are of high relevance to all modes of transport, and their proposed methods have been applied across the board, including innovative transport modes such as BRT systems (Merkert, Mulley, & Hakim, 2017). Table 1 provides an overview of a sample of supply-side panel data (efficiency) studies. Given that the selection of the papers was based on their impact (measured in number of citations) to the literature of each mode of transport that they cover, we find it useful to illustrate some key trends in relation to supply-side transport literature that uses panel data.

As shown in Table 1, using panel data for efficiency assessment in transport goes beyond the evaluation of simple characteristics of firm size, business models, or market shares. The methods range from simple partial productivity measures (PPM), to data envelopment analysis (DEA) for nonparametric analysis and stochastic frontier approaches (SFA) for larger data sets. As for other industries, productivity/efficiency changes over time usually are analyzed using Tornqvist or Malmquist indices. From reviewing the extant transport literature, we find that the quality of the data appears to determine the choice of the appropriate estimation method, with DEA used where data are considered to be of lower quality, and other approaches used where better data are obtained. Even with high-quality data, some functions are difficult to estimate, particularly the translog cost function (for a recent example in the air cargo context see Balliauw, Meersman, Onghena, & Van de Voorde, 2018), and therefore need careful evaluation before being used to generate efficiency estimates. Also influenced by the data availability, extant studies in the transport context usually have focused on technical efficiency (TE), although some examples such as Merkert and Hensher (2011) have included cost efficiency (CE) and allocative efficiency (AE). Merkert and Assaf (2015) focused on the differences between technical and allocative efficiency, but because data about input prices is often not available or is distorted in the transport context many studies have refrained from going beyond technical efficiency (productivity). Although many transport-related studies are limited to domestic data (which help with availability and comparability) or unbalanced panels (or only very few years of data), it is remarkable that those that have used international samples were able to evaluate all three types of efficiency. Nevertheless, for transport it is common that cost and price evaluations often are not possible, therefore productivity studies are more popular and reliable when it comes to panel data analysis. Obtaining reliable panel data generally is problematic for transport, although it could be

TABLE 1 Well Cited Examples of Efficiency Studies Using Panel Data

	DMUs	Period	Method	Focus	Inputs	Prices	Outputs	Exogenous Variables
Cornwell, Schmidt, and Sickles (1990)	8 US airlines	1970–81	SFA/TFP	TE/AE/CE	Capital, labor, energy, materials	–	Ton-miles	Stage length, service quality
Merkert and Hensher (2011)	54 airlines globally	2007–08	DEA	TE/AE/CE	FTE, ATK	FTE price, ATK price	RPK, RTK	Airline size, stage length, seats, fleet age & commonality
Sarkis (2000)	44 US airports	1990–94	DEA	TE	Opcost, employees, gates, runways	–	Op.rev., ATM, general aviation, pax, cargo	Hub status, multiairport-system, snow belt
Gillen and Lall (1997)	21 US airports	1989–93	DEA	TE	Runways, gates, terminal, FTE, baggage belts, parking spots	–	pax, cargo	Residual financing, general aviation, limits on ops, airline hubs
Oum, Yan, and Yu (2008)	109 airports globally (unbalanced)	2001–04	SFA	CE	FTE, runways, terminal size, nonlabor variable cost	Nonlabor input price, wage rate	pax, ATM, nonaero. revenue	Ownership, labor cost share, location, cargo share, int. pax share
Odeck (2008a)	17 Norwegian bus operators	1995–2002	DEA/Malmquist	TE	Seats, fuel, labor	–	seat-km	Mergers

Study	DMU	Period	Method	Efficiency	Inputs	Input prices	Outputs	Other
Farsi, Filippini, and Greene (2005)	94 Swiss bus operators (unbalanced)	1986–97	SFA	CE	Network length, employees, seats	Labor price, capital price/seat	seat-km	
Coelli and Perelman (2000)	17 European railways	1988–93	COLS/Tornqvist	TE	Labor, rolling stock and lines	–	pkm, ton-km	Time
Farsi et al. (2005)	45 Swiss train operators (unbalanced)	1985–97	SFA (FE + RE)	CE	Network length, employees	Average cost, capital, labor, electricity	pkm, ton-km	
Merkert, Smith, and Nash (2010)	43 UK, Swedish & German railways	2006–07	DEA	TE	FTE, transaction & production staff, material	–	train-km, pkm, ton-km	HHI, vertical separation, type of ops, relative transaction costs
Cullinane, Song, and Gray (2002)	15 Asian container ports/terminals	1989–98	SFA	TE	Quay length, terminal area, cargo handling equipment	–	TEUs	
Odeck (2008b)	82 Norwegian ferries	2003–05	SFA/Malmquist	TE	Fuel, maint. cost, labor cost, capital (vehicle capacity)	–	pkm	Type of waters, type of ferry, age of ferry

DMU, decision making unit; TE, technical efficiency/productivity; AE, allocative efficiency; CE, cost efficiency.

argued that some modes such as aviation (in the United States) and railways provide easier access to data than others, such as ocean shipping lines.

As with other industries, transport research usually assumes a trade-off between capital and labor. Typical input variables are unsurprisingly around full-time employees (FTEs) for labor and vehicles/aircraft or other proxies for capital. In terms of outputs, maritime and bus operation studies benefit from simpler industry characteristics because freight and passenger operations are undertaken separately. In contrast, aviation and rail studies use not only passenger and freight volumes, but also how far those commodities have been carried. In particular for aviation, the inclusion of nonaeronautical revenues as a key output has gained in importance (e.g., Oum et al., 2008) because they are becoming a major source of revenue for airports and airlines. Another recent trend in transport-related efficiency studies is to include and account for bad business outputs, such as airline delays (Tsionas, Chen, & Wanke, 2017). Overall, we find that benchmarking efficiency scores of transport operators is a very powerful tool because it allows to identify how firms perform over time, in comparison to their peers, and, if data are available, over time against their peers. What is potentially even more informative is to try to explain the differences in revealed inefficiency of otherwise (at face value) relatively similar operations. Although SFA incorporates this into the functional approach, DEA typically uses exogenous variables of efficiency such as firm size, vehicle size (e.g., Merkert & Hensher, 2011), fleet heterogeneity, ownership, network configuration, market structure, and business models. Similarly, a number of cost studies have evaluated the effect of various aspects (such as the impact of M&A activity) on cost structures of transport operating firms (e.g., Gudmundsson, Merkert, & Redondi, 2017).

In summary, we find that transport supply-side studies that use panel data are not different from other industries. The majority of studies consist of only a small number of years and lack international (balanced) panel data, mainly because of data availability and comparability. What also is missing, even in the most recent studies (e.g., Zuidberg, 2017), is a clustering of operators into market segments that account for the spatial, demographic, and business characteristics of urban/hub versus regional/small scale operations. We argue that just adding an urban/regional dummy into the second stage of efficiency studies is insufficient. The following section provides a case study illustrating why we think that using context specific samples matters when benchmarking rail transport service efficiency.

4 Case Study Illustrating Why Supply-Side Panel Analysis Context Matters

4.1 Case Study Background, Methodology, and Data

Given the close relationship between efficiency performance and fare determination, rigorous examination of performance across urban rail systems globally can produce results that are of interest to both stakeholders and regulators. In spite of having different spatial settings, rail-based technology and rail regulation (particularly in relation to safety) impose similar operational frameworks on operators across national and international boundaries, which in turn facilitates effective comparisons about train operating efficiency and effectiveness. As will be discussed in this case study, however, such analysis benefits from using context-specific samples that control for the spatial environment of the transport operation.

The definition of efficiency for public transport has been discussed widely since the 1980s. The most commonly used framework (developed by Fielding et al. (1985) and extended by Merkert et al. (2017)) distinguishes between efficiency and effectiveness in evaluating the performance of a public transport operator. Efficiency in this framework refers to the total service outputs, usually measured by car-km traveled or car-hour operated with respect to service inputs (labor, fuel consumption, or operating cost) for rail-based systems, whereas effectiveness represents the service consumption by passengers, such as number of passengers or passenger-km against service inputs. The ratio of service consumption to service outputs is defined as service-effectiveness, with the distinction between efficiency and effectiveness highlighting the different aspects of performance evaluation from the operator and consumer perspective, respectively.

As discussed in the previous section, a number of methods to evaluate efficiency and effectiveness performance have been developed in the literature. The simplest approach is a partial factor productivity (PFP), also called partial productivity measure (PPM) method, which we use to measure the ratio of a public transport system's output (e.g., number of passengers) to a single input (e.g., FTE). The advantage of this approach is that it is easy to collect data, analyze, and understand, and is favored by managers and consultants in the rail business when developing key performance indicators (KPIs). A PFP methodology, however, takes account of only one input against one output and, as a result, multiple and often conflicting KPIs are computed without any rationale for the way in which they can be combined to give a conclusive indication of overall performance nor of sensible prognosis for improvement. In this case study, a PFP approach is used to supplement a two-stage DEA to make a commentary about effectiveness, specifically service effectiveness. The PFP approach also is useful in the sense that, after total performance measures are obtained, it is possible to establish whether partial measures might be good proxies for overall performance. A two-stage DEA model is used to identify the linear production (efficient) frontier and inefficiency scores (distance of individual observation from efficient frontier) for each firm or transport operator in each of the two samples. A key advantage of DEA compared to parametric approaches such as SFA is that it can be performed with much smaller data samples and its application has been popular in the transport literature. The DEA approach is flexible, allowing the selection of multiple inputs and outputs. It also allows for nonconstant returns to scale (Banker, Charnes, & Cooper, 1984), which is important in the context of transport, in particular when one aims to identify differences between the urban and regional context, where variable returns to scale are prevalent. Moreover, when historical data are available, DEA can identify changes in efficiency arising from institutional reform or technical change, thus providing an understanding (for operators and policy-makers alike) as to whether the operating strategy has improved efficiency per-formance. These DEA models determine the relative efficiency of the train operators in each of their benchmarking group (urban versus regional). As typ-ical in transportation, we use a two-stage DEA efficiency approach in which efficiency scores estimated in the first-stage DEA models are used as dependent variables in a truncated (censored at 0) second-stage regression model to pro-vide an understanding about the determinants of efficiency. Bootstrapping (with 2000 iterations) of the first-stage DEA scores is used to minimize bias and unre-liable second-stage regression results (Simar & Wilson, 2000, 2008). From a policy point of view, the regression results that identify the determinants of inef-ficiencies form the evidence base to provide recommendations for the improve-ment of cost efficiency and effectiveness. This approach not only can identify technical efficiency (productivity), but also identify allocative (optimal mix of multiple inputs) and cost efficiency, and scale efficiency. Both cost efficiency and cost effectiveness are analyzed by using DEA models, in which labor and a proxy of capital employed is used as inputs and car-km (for cost efficiency) and pax-km (for cost effectiveness) as outputs.

To appropriately account for the difference between urban and regional train operations, the benchmarking analysis consists of two samples. The first sample focuses on peers (other train operating companies (TOCs)) that are comparable to urban operators. Table 2 shows the international urban train operators who are members of the sample. This is a similar, but larger sample, to that of the ISBeRG benchmarking group (http://www.isberg-web.org/).

The choice of peers is important when using DEA analysis because the lin-ear programming approach means that efficiency is measured relative to the members of the peer group. This means that comparisons can be made only within the peer group and not between operators from the regional peer group (illustrated in Table 3) and the operators from the Metropolitan TOCs peer group.

Data were collected for three annual periods (financial years 2011–12 to 2013–14) on the items shown in Table 4. Data primarily were collected from annual accounts and other secondary sources with the finer details being pro-vided by the operators on request or through freedom of information requests. Already at this point it is apparent that the two samples are different not only in terms of the size of their operations, but also in regards to the type of their net-works, cost structures, and measurements they use (e.g., car-km for urban train operators while train-km is used in the regional context).

TABLE 2 The Metropolitan TOC Peer Group

Region	Metro Operator	City (and Country)
North America	Bay Area Rapid Transit	San Francisco, United States
	LACMTA	Los Angeles, United States
	Long Island Railroad	New York City, United States
	MBTA	Boston, United States
	Metro North	New York City, United States
	New York City Transit	New York City, United States
	SEPTA	Philadelphia, United States
	Transit Chicago	Chicago, United States
	WMATA	Washington D.C., United States
Europe	FGC	Barcelona, Spain
	Lisbon Metro	Lisbon, Portugal
	London Overground	London, United Kingdom
	London Underground	London, United Kingdom
	Madrid Metro	Madrid, Spain
	Merseyrail	Liverpool, United Kingdom
	Newcastle Nexus	Newcastle Tyne and Wear, UK
	Transports Met. de Barcelona	Barcelona, Spain
Asia	Delhi Metro	Delhi, India
	MTR	Hong Kong, China
	SMRT	Singapore, Singapore
	Taipei Metro	Taipei, Taiwan
Australasia	Adelaide Metro	Adelaide, Australia
	Auckland Metro	Auckland, New Zealand
	Metro Trains Melbourne	Melbourne, Australia
	QR Citytrain	Brisbane, Australia
	Sydney Trains	Sydney, Australia
	Transperth	Perth, Australia
	TranzMetro	Wellington, New Zealand

TABLE 3 The Regional TOC Peer Group

Region	Operator	Country of Operation
Asia	Israel Railway, IsR	Israel
	Central Japan Railway Company, JR Central	Japan
	West Japan Railway Company, JR West	Japan
	Korea Railroad Corporation, Korail	South Korea
Australasia	NSW TrainLink	Australia
	Queensland Rail, QR	Australia
	V/line	Australia
Europe	ÖBB trains	Austria
	Societe Nationale des Chemins de fer Belges, SNCB	Belgium
	České dráhy, CD	Czech Republic
	Danish State Railways, DSB	Denmark
	Iarnród Éireann, Irish Rail	Ireland
	Nederlandse Spoorwegen, NS	Netherlands
	Norges Statsbaner AS, NSB	Norway
	Polish State Railways, PKP	Poland
	Swedish State Railways, SJ	Sweden
	Swiss Federal Railways, SBB/CFF/FFS	Switzerland
	Arriva Trains Wales	UK
	East Midlands Trains, EMT	UK
	Northern Rail	UK
	ScotRail	UK
	Southeastern Railway	UK
	Southern Railway	UK
	South West Trains	UK
	XC Trains	UK
North America	Amtrak	USA
	Metra	USA
	Metrolink	USA
	New Jersey Transit	USA
	Southeastern Pennsylvania Transportation Authority, SEPTA	USA

TABLE 4 Descriptive Statistics Comparison of Our Two Samples

	Network Size (Route kms)	Train_km (m)	Car_km (m)	Pax_km (m)	Total Operating Pax Revenue (m PPP A$)	Total Operating Costs (m PPP A$)	Number of Employees	Staff Costs (m PPP A$)	Fleet Size (Units)	Nonstaff Opex (m GDP PPP A$)
3FY Average Metropolitan TOCs Peer Group										
Mean	223.2	18.1	108.4	3900.5	1044.6	1619.2	5138.1	684.1	1111.9	935.1
Standard deviation	148.4	16.9	118.7	4786.6	1426.6	1903.5	6121.2	1092.2	1334.9	905.7
Count	27	27	27	27	27	27	27	27	27	27
3FY Average Regional TOCs Peer Group										
Mean	3656.4	51.3	–	9644.1	2769.8	2528.2	7575.1	712.5	1925.3	1815.7
Standard deviation	3884.7	46.6	–	14768.3	3893.8	2951.0	7808.4	861.6	1990.0	2315.5
Count	30	30	30	30	30	30	30	30	30	30

For the different TOC peer groups, different variables were used in the second stage. For example, freight operations and vertical organization of the operator are more relevant to regional than urban rail operations (Tsai, Mulley, & Merkert, 2015).

4.2 Case Study Results

The main focus on partial productivity measures has been considering punctuality, service reliability, and safety. The data collection was complicated, however, by a number of TOCs that did not monitor punctuality and reliability in a way that was comparable to the majority, which considered thresholds of between 3 and 6 min. Nevertheless, what we were able to observe is much more variability in the punctuality of the regional operator compared to urban train operators. A comparison of safety also has proved difficult, with different definitions being used in different TOCs and with changes of definitions over time. Panel data analysis of international peer groups, therefore, appears difficult with regard to these KPIs.

What proved more realistic and doable in terms of benchmarking the two samples was a comparison of cost and service effectiveness, which required a comparison of service consumption with service outputs. For each of the peer groups, this was done by using two measures of service consumption (farebox revenue and revenues) and car-km as the measure of service outputs for the Metropolitan Peer Group, and train-km for the measure of service outputs for the Regional Peer Group. In regards to farebox revenue per passenger and in terms of EBIT per train/car-km, metropolitan operators perform better than their regional counterparts.

In regards to DEA efficiencies, our data suggest that the metropolitan/urban train operators had on average with TE = 0.84, not only a higher technical efficiency, but with AE = 0.93 and CE = 0.78, also a higher allocative and cost efficiency than the average regional operator (who was associated with, on average, TE = 0.75; AE = 0.89 and CE = 0.68). Although we argue that operators from the two samples are not really comparable and therefore it is not meaningful to directly compare their averages, it has become apparent that both groups of operators do better in allocative efficiency than they do in regards to technical efficiency, as shown in Figs. 1 and 2. In order to avoid possible yearly fluctuations and to show trends, both figures show the 3-year average for all types of efficiency.

Because the efficiency measured for each operator is relative to the peers in the each sample, it is more meaningful to analyze the second-stage regression results than to compare efficiency scores (including economies of scale) across the two groups of train operators. As shown in Table 5, for the metropolitan peer group, private ownership is good for efficiency, and multiple operators sharing track has a negative effect on technical and cost efficiencies. For the regional

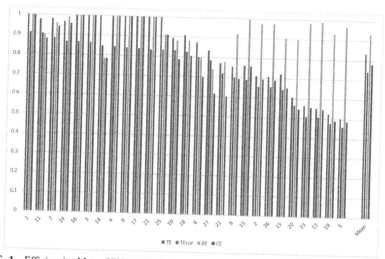

FIG. 1 Efficiencies Metro 3FY (2011/12-2013/2014) averages (ranked by TEcor).

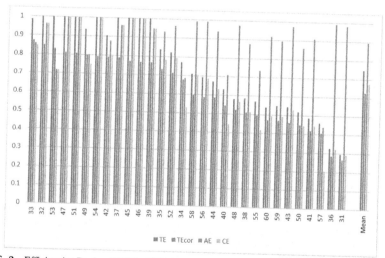

FIG. 2 Efficiencies Regional TOCs 3FY (2011/12-2013/2014) averages (ranked by TEcor).

peer group, vertical integration has a negative impact on efficiency but for this group the distance between stations and GDP/capita are relevant determinants.

For metropolitan train operators, the most important driver (most significant at the 1% level) of TE, AE, and CE is ownership, with private ownership on average contributing up to 25% higher efficiency. Competition on the tracks, however, appears to be negative for both TE and CE because operators who share the tracks with other operators tend to have lower average efficiency

TABLE 5 Summary of Results

	Metropolitan TOC Group	Regional TOC Peer Group
Number stations	No significant impact	Positive impact on TE and CE
Station distance	No significant impact	No significant impact
GDP/capita	No significant impact	Positive impact on TE
Ownership (private)	Positive impact on TE, AE, and CE	n/a
Vertical integration (yes)	n/a	Negative impact on TE and CE
Freight (part of the same company)	n/a	No significant impact
Multiple operators on track	Negative impact on TE and CE	No significant impact
Australasia (yes)	Positive impact on TE, AE, and CE	n/a

scores than their counterparts. The number of stations, distance between stations, and GDP/capita have no significant impact on metropolitan train operating company efficiency. Because population density is highly correlated with GDP/capita for this sample (and therefore not included in the regression), it is concluded that population density has no significant impact on efficiency. Vertical integration of the infrastructure manager also does not have an impact on efficiency, simply because this variable did not have much variation in the metropolitan TOC peer group.

For Regional TOC Peer Group results, vertical integration of the infrastructure has the most significant effect. This suggests that, although there is no impact on AE from vertically separated railways, they are associated with higher average technical and cost efficiency. Because vertical integration is correlated with ownership, it can be inferred that, as with the Metropolitan TOC Peer Group, private ownership results on average in higher efficiency scores. A separate model confirmed ownership impacts on TEcor at the 5% significance level. In contrast to the Metropolitan TOC Peer Group, stations and GDP/capita (and therefore population density) have a significant positive impact on TE for the Regional TOC Peer Group. While the former also has a significant impact on CE, GDP/capita also is close to being significant for CE. Having a freight division with the same train operating company/group, distance between stations or multiple operators on the tracks do not have a significant impact on regional train operator's efficiency. The second stage of the DEA analysis has shown that, when using panel data to evaluate the determinants of transport operators' efficiency, it is beneficial if not mandatory to use samples that accurately reflect the spatial context and nature of the transport operation in question.

5 Conclusions

In summary, this chapter has shown that panel data have been used widely to analyze both the demand and supply side of transport operations. Obtaining true panels at the international level, however, appears to be difficult for various reasons. For the demand side, our peer review of the transport literature has demonstrated that pseudo-panel data can be treated as if it is true panel data. The supply side is more complicated and results in many studies using unbalanced panels. In terms of methods, we find that the DEA approach overcomes the problems of conflicting KPIs when considering overall cost efficiency while providing a robust tool for implementing change through the understanding of the key determinants of efficiency. Our case study, however, has evidenced that context matters for the sample composition of DEA analysis in transport. Metropolitan/urban operators are different from regional train operators and therefore should be treated in different samples rather than mixed into an aggregate sample that controls for the spatial context via a dummy variable in the second-stage regression models.

References

Baker, D., Merkert, R., Kamruzzaman, M., 2015. Regional aviation and economic growth: cointegration and causality analysis in Australia. Journal of Transport Geography 43, 140–150.

Balliauw, M., Meersman, H., Onghena, E., Van de Voorde, E., 2018. US all-cargo carriers' cost structure and efficiency: a stochastic frontier analysis. Transportation Research Part A: Policy and Practice 112, 29–45.

Banker, R.D., Charnes, A., Cooper, W.W., 1984. Some models for estimating technical and scale inefficiencies in data envelopment analysis. Management Science 30, 1078–1092.

Chikaraishi, M., Fujiwara, A., Zhang, J., Axhausen, K., Zumkeller, D., 2011. Changes in variations of travel time expenditure: some methodological considerations and empirical results from German mobility panel. Transportation Research Record: Journal of the Transportation Research Board 2230, 121–131.

Coelli, T., Perelman, S., 2000. Technical efficiency of European railways: a distance function approach. Applied Economics 32, 1967–1976.

Coelli, T.J., Rao, P.D.S., O'Donnell, C.J., Battese, G.E., 2005. An introduction to efficiency and productivity analysis. Springer, New York.

Cornwell, C., Schmidt, P., Sickles, R.C., 1990. Production frontiers with cross-sectional and time-series variation in efficiency levels. Journal of Econometrics 46 (1–2), 185–200.

CTS, 2009. Research briefing sheet 009. Retrieved from: https://www.google.com.au/search?q=teleworker+panel+data+uwe&ie=utf-8&oe=utf-8&client=firefox-b-ab&gfe_rd=cr&dcr=0&ei=ZaJwWteSFY6C8AXdobzAAw#. (Accessed 30 January 2018).

Cullinane, K., Song, D.-W., Gray, R., 2002. A stochastic frontier model of the efficiency of major container terminals in Asia: assessing the influence of administrative and ownership structures. Transportation Research Part A: Policy and Practice 36, 743–762.

Daraio, C., Diana, M., Di Costa, F., Leporelli, C., Matteucci, G., Nastasi, A., 2016. Efficiency and effectiveness in the urban public transport sector: a critical review with directions for future research. European Journal of Operations Research 248, 1–20.

Dargay, J., 2007. The effect of prices and income on car travel in the UK. Transportation Research Part A: Policy and Practice 41 (10), 949–960.

Dargay, J.M., 2002. Determinants of car ownership in rural and urban areas: a pseudo-panel analysis. Transportation Research Part E 38 (5), 351–366.

Dargay, J.M., Vythoulkas, P.C., 1999. Estimation of dynamic car ownership model: a pseudo-panel approach. Journal of Transport Economics and Policy 33 (3), 287–302.

Deaton, A., 1985. Panel data from time series of cross-sections. Journal of Econometrics 30 (1-2), 109–126.

Farsi, M., Filippini, M., Greene, W., 2005. Efficiency measurement in network industries: application to the Swiss railway companies. Journal of Regulatory Economics 28 (1), 69–90.

Farsi, M., Filippini, M., Kuenzle, M., 2006. Cost efficiency in regional bus companies–an application of alternative stochastic frontier models. Journal of Transport Economics and Policy 40 (1), 95–118.

Fielding, G.J., Babitsky, T.T., Brenner, M.E., 1985. Performance evaluation for bus transit. Transportation Research Part A 19 (1), 73–82.

Fried, H.O., Knox Lovell, C.A., Schmidt, S.S., 2008. The measurement of productive efficiency and productivity growth. Oxford University Press, Oxford, New York.

Frondel, M., Peters, J., Vance, C., 2008. Identifying the rebound: evidence from a German household panel. The Energy Journal 29 (4), 145–163.

Frondel, M., Ritter, N., Vance, C., 2012. Heterogeneity in the rebound effect: further evidence for Germany. Energy Economics 34 (2), 461–467.

Frondel, M., Vance, C., 2009. Do high oil prices matter? Evidence on the mobility behavior of German households. Environmental and Resource Economics 43, 81–94.

Gillen, D., Lall, A., 1997. Developing measures of airport productivity and performance: an application of data envelopment analysis 1997. Transportation Research Part E: Logistics and Transportation Review 33 (4), 261–273.

Greene, W.H., Khalaf, L., Sickles, C., Veall, R., Voia, M.-C., 2016. Productivity and efficiency analysis. Springer Proceedings in Business and Economics, Switzerland.

Gudmundsson, S.V., Merkert, R., Redondi, R., 2017. Cost functions and determinants of unit cost effects in horizontal airline M&As. Transportation Research Part A: Policy and Practice 103, 444–454.

Hakim, M.M., Merkert, R., 2016. The causal relationship between air transport and economic growth: empirical evidence from South Asia. Journal of Transport Geography 56, 120–127.

Hakim, M.M., Merkert, R., 2019. Econometric evidence on the determinants of air transport in South Asian countries. Transport Policy (in press).

Hoogendoorn-Lanser, S., Schaap, N.T.W., Oldekalter, M.-J., 2015. The Netherlands mobility panel: an innovative design approach for web-based longitudinal travel data collection. Transportation Research Procedia 11, 311–329.

Kilgren, N., 2014. 1999 Puget sound household travel survey. Puget Sound Regional Council, Seattle. Retrieved from: https://www.psrc.org/travel-surveys-1999-puget-sound-household-travel-survey.

Kilgren, N., 2017. Overview of the Puget sound transportation panel 1989–2002. Puget Sound Regional Council, Seattle. Retrieved from: https://www.psrc.org/sites/default/files/pstp_summary.pdf. (Accessed 30 January 2018).

Kitamura, R., 1990. Panel analysis in transportation planning: an overview. Transportation Research Part A: Policy and Practice 24, 401–415.

Kottas, A.T., Madas, M.A., 2018. Comparative efficiency analysis of major international airlines using data envelopment analysis: exploring effects of alliance membership and other operational efficiency determinants. Journal of Air Transport Management 70, 1–17.

Kroes, E.P., Daly, A.J., Gunn, H.F., van der Hoorn, A.I.J.M., 1996. The opening of the Amsterdam ring road: a case study on short-term effects of removing a bottleneck. Transportation 23, 71–82.

Kuhnimhof, T., Buehler, R., Dargay, J., 2011. A new generation. Transportation Research Record 2230, 58–67.

Kuhnimhof, T., Buehler, R., Wirtz, M., 2012. Travel trends among young adults in Germany: increasing multimodality and declining car use for men. Journal of Transport Geography 24, 443–450.

Merkert, R., Assaf, A.G., 2015. Using DEA models to jointly estimate service quality perception and profitability—evidence from international airports. Transportation Research Part A 75, 42–50.

Merkert, R., Cowie, J., 2018. Efficiency assessment in transport service provision. In: Cowie, J., Ison, S. (Eds.), The Routledge handbook of transport economics. Routledge, Abingdon, United Kingdom, pp. 251–267.

Merkert, R., Hensher, D.A., 2011. The impact of strategic management and fleet planning on airline efficiency—a random effects Tobit model based on DEA efficiency scores. Transportation Research Part A: Policy and Practice 45 (7), 686–695.

Merkert, R., Mulley, C., Hakim, M., 2017. Determinants of bus rapid transit (BRT) system revenue and effectiveness—a global benchmarking exercise. Transportation Research Part A: Policy and Practice 106, 75–88.

Merkert, R., Odeck, J., Bråthen, S., Pagliari, R., 2012. A review of different benchmarking methods in the context of regional airports. Transport Reviews 32 (3), 379–395.

Merkert, R., Smith, A.S.J., Nash, C.A., 2010. Benchmarking of train operating firms—a transaction cost efficiency analysis. Journal of Transportation Planning and Technology 33 (1), 35–53.

Metz, D., 2008. The myth of travel time saving. Transport Reviews 28, 321–336.

Odeck, J., 2008a. The effect of mergers on efficiency and productivity of public transport services. Transportation Research Part A: Policy and Practice 42, 696–708.

Odeck, J., 2008b. Efficiency measurement of ferries serving road networks in Norway: a stochastic frontier approach. Maritime Economics & Logistics 10 (4), 409–428.

Ortúzar, J.d.D., Armoogum, J., Madre, J., Potier, F., 2011. Continuous mobility surveys: the state of practice. Transport Reviews 31 (3), 293–312.

Oum, T.H., Yan, J., Yu, C., 2008. Ownership forms matter for airport efficiency: a stochastic frontier investigation of worldwide airports. Journal of Urban Economics 64 (2), 422–435.

Parody, T., 1977. Analysis of predictive qualities of disaggregate modal-choice models. Transportation Research Record 637, 51–57.

Sarkis, J., 2000. An analysis of the operational efficiency of major airports in the United States. Journal of Operations Management 18, 335–351.

Simar, L., Wilson, P.W., 2000. A general methodology for bootstrapping in non-parametric frontier models. Journal of Applied Statistics 27, 779–802.

Simar, L., Wilson, P.W., 2008. Statistical inference in nonparametric frontier models: recent developments and perspectives. In: Fried, H.O., Lovell, C.A.K., Schmidt, S.S. (Eds.), The measurement of productive efficiency and productivity change. Oxford University Press, New York, pp. 421–522.

Stopher, P., Swann, N., 2008. Six-wave odometer panel for evaluation of voluntary travel behaviour change programs. Transportation Research Record 2049, 119–127.

Tsai, C., Mulley, C., Merkert, R., 2015. Measuring the cost efficiency of urban rail systems: an international comparison using DEA and tobit models. Journal of Transport Economics and Policy 49 (1), 17–34.

Tsionas, M.G., Chen, Z., Wanke, P., 2017. A structural vector autoregressive model of technical efficiency and delays with an application to Chinese airlines. Transportation Research Part A: Policy and Practice 101, 1–10.

Vance, C., Hedel, R., 2007. The impact of urban form on automobile travel: disentangling causation from correlation. Transportation 34, 578–588.

Verbeek, M., Nijman, T., 1992. Can cohort data be treated as genuine panel data? Empirical Economics 17 (9), 9–23.

Weis, C., Axhausen, K.W., 2009. Induced travel demand: evidence from a pseudo panel data based structural equations model. Research in Transportation Economics 25 (1), 8–18.

Yee, J.L., Niemeier, D.A., 1996. Advantages and disadvantages: longitudinal vs. repeated cross-section surveys. Project Battelle, pp. 94–116.

Yee, J.L., Niemeier, D.A., 2000. Analysis of activity duration using the Puget sound transportation panel. Transportation Research Part A: Policy and Practice 34, 607–624.

Yu, C., 2016. Airline productivity and efficiency: concept, measurement, and applications. In: Bitzan, J.D., Peoples, J.H., Wilson, W.W. (Eds.), Airline efficiency. In: Advances in airline economics5, Emerald Group Publishing Limited, Bingley, UK, pp. 11–53.

Zuidberg, J., 2017. Exploring the determinants for airport profitability: traffic characteristics, low-cost carriers, seasonality and cost efficiency. Transportation Research Part A: Policy and Practice 101, 61–72.

Zumkeller, D., 2009. The dynamics of change: latest results from the German mobility panel. In: Paper presented at the 12th international conference on travel behaviour research, Jaipur, India. 13–18 December 2009.

Chapter 19

Panel Data in Banking: Research Issues and Data Peculiarities

David Humphrey

Florida State University, Tallahassee, FL, United States

Chapter Outline

1 Introduction

Data on banking is quite detailed, voluminous, and at times peculiar. It is detailed since considerable bank asset and liability information as well as income and expense data are available for individual banks. It is voluminous because in the United States, where much banking research is focused, it can cover over 5100 commercial banks and is publicly available from banking regulators. There are also 800 thrift institutions and almost 6000 credit unions but, as they account for only 5.5% of all US banking-type assets, they are little studied. Importantly, banking data have peculiarities that can affect research results, such as scale and scope economies as well as analyses of profitability, competition, and productivity. In addition, the data contain strange outliers (e.g., banks with no loans, others with no deposits,) that if not adjusted for can skew results.

Time-series banking data exist but are quite limited relative to the number of parameters typically specified in banking studies using translog, Fourier, spline, or distance functions. Thus analyses of individual banks over time is rare and research focuses on sets of banks (usually by size-class) using panel or cross-section data to expand sample size. Panel data are preferred since results are likely more stable than from a single cross-section. There were 8300

☆ Comments by the Editor, Jaap Bos, and Phillip Molyneux are acknowledged and appreciated.

Panel Data Econometrics. https://doi.org/10.1016/B978-0-12-815859-3.00019-6

commercial banks in 2000 but only 5113 by 2016 due to mergers, acquisitions, failures, and new entry. Rather than deleting missing banks and generating an unbalanced panel, most studies apply one of two methods to obtain a balanced panel. Unfortunately, one popular method can bias certain results.

In what follows we outline important issues associated with generating a banking panel data set and outline the ways it can go wrong for the unwary. We also illustrate the major ways banking panel data has been applied in practice. This concerns traditional issues such as estimating scale and scope economies, technical change, efficiency measurement, and banking productivity, but also the functional forms specified and their focus on cost, profit, or revenue. The theoretical and technical aspects of econometric estimation using panel data are covered in earlier chapters of this book.

2   Generating a Panel Data Set

Screening the Data. If we were assessing scale economies or productivity of the airline or energy industries, we probably would not want to include airlines that have no planes or energy firms with no output. The same applies to banking since there are "banks" with no deposits, others with no loans, or one employee but multiple millions in assets, and other unexpected anomalies. These are shell banks, special purpose banks, or banks acting as placeholders for a banking charter. They are not at all representative of normal banking operations performed by all the other banks. Although small in number, the extreme nature of their outlier values can bias results and policy conclusions. One screen that can be employed is to delete all banks with specified variables that fall outside plus or minus five (or more) standard deviations of their respective means. If one is worried about screening the data in this manner, their model can be estimated first with and then without the screened data and the results compared.[1]

Data Availability. There are large differences in availability of banking data between countries, even between the US and Europe. Partly this is due to differences in the number of banks in different countries and a different view about what data should be made public. As empirical analysis seems to follow data availability (e.g., for stock markets today or on SIC code industries in earlier production function analyses), most banking research has focused on US banks.

A problem with European banking data is that the most used source (Bank Scope, a private firm) covers only the larger banks, rather than all banks. Also, it does not contain enough information to compute a standard bank-specific price of labor (an important variable in cost function estimation). A workaround of sorts is to use the average price of labor in a country to approximate the price of labor for banks in that country or the ratio of labor costs to total assets. European bank panel data are usually within a country as well as across countries.

---

1. We know of no case where this has been done. Even so, researchers should note if their data has been screened and the type of screen used.

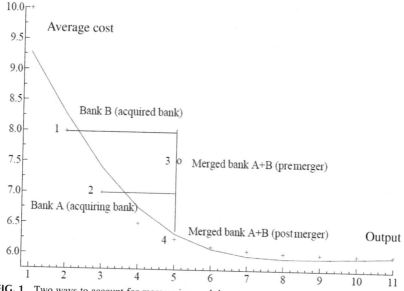

FIG. 1 Two ways to account for mergers in panel data.

Unlike the United States where bank regulation and enforcement is the same across states, both can differ across European countries. Country dummy variables (or a fixed or random effects framework) have been used to address this concern.

Handling Mergers. In generating a panel data set, the existence of mergers and acquisitions will yield an unbalanced panel. Bank mergers are actually quite numerous: between 1980 and 1998 there were 8000 of them (Rhoades, 2000). More recently, as suggested above, a net 3200 banks disappeared between 2000 and 2016. Mergers and acquisitions eliminated some 4300 banks, an additional 200 failed outright, but around 1300 newly entered the industry. Fortunately the vast majority of this churn is among smaller banks with assets less than $1 billion which, as a group, account for less than 10% all bank assets. Mergers and acquisitions do occur among the largest US banks: in fact this is how they became "largest" in the first place.[2]

Most studies employ one of two methods to generate a balanced panel. A common approach simply aggregates all premerger entities as if they were actually "combined" in the premerger period. For example, if panel data covers 2008–12 and Bank A is in the panel in 2012 but merged with or acquired Bank B in 2010 (after which Bank B no longer exists), then the premerger data for Banks A and B would be added together as if they were the same bank in the year of the merger (2010) and all prior years (2008 and 2009). This creates

---

2. Even in 1985, 85% of asset growth of the 20 largest US banks was achieved through a merger or acquisition (Rhoades, 1985). Today, the percentage would be even larger.

a balanced panel but also can bias any scale effect estimated since these two banks will, if scale economies are important, show higher costs per unit of output than would occur for banks that actually were this size during the premerger period. This is illustrated in Fig. 1.

In Fig. 1, points 1 and 2 reflect the average cost (Y-axis) and asset size (X-axis) of Banks A and B in the premerger period. Combining these banks as if they were merged in the premerger period yields point 3. If scale economies are important, the average cost (and other variables) of the combined premerger banks at point 3 can be quite different from other banks of a similar overall size at point 4 on the average cost curve.

There is a simple way to address this issue: Bank B would just be deleted from the sample. Bank A would be observed to be the actual size it was during the premerger 2008–09 period (point 2), but expands in 2010 due to the merger, and is observed to be its actual reported size in 2011–12 as well as 2010 (maybe close to point 4). This is consistent with how Bank A actually grows from a merger or acquisition. Even so, there will be a transition period to absorb the merger and it may be advisable to specify a dummy variable for at least 2010 to adjust for this.[3]

Most mergers or acquisitions strongly affect bank size: Bank A could easily grow by 50%–100% from a merger. Thus the misstatement of scale influences on costs using the first procedure to obtain a balanced panel can be significant. The second approach would show (correctly) that Bank A experiences a jump in size over 2010–12 compared to the premerger time period.

Annual Versus Quarterly Data. How could there be any confusion here? As expected, annual bank balance sheet and income and expense information is reported in the 4th quarter Call Reports available from bank regulators. This represents the sum of all income and expenses over all four quarters together and the end of year position of all liabilities and assets on the bank balance sheet. Quarterly data are available in separate Call Reports for each quarter. And like the 4th quarter data, balance sheet data for the 1st quarter is the sum of income and expenses and the balance sheet position at the end of 1st quarter. The same holds for the 2nd and 3rd quarters.

If you were expecting to see only the income and expenses for the 2nd quarter alone, and only 3rd and 4th quarters alone, you will have to compute them separately to obtain these values. For example, income and expenses only for the 2nd quarter is found by subtracting 1st quarter income and expenses from those reported for the 2nd quarter. Separate information the 3rd and 4th quarters are obtained similarly. Balance sheet information does not need any adjustment since it reflects the level of liabilities and assets on the quarterly reporting date but the income and expense information are sums of the prior quarters.

---

3. A dummy variable for a single observation is just a different way to delete the observation from the sample.

TABLE 1 Illustration of How Not to Compute Quarterly Bank Data

Data for 2010	Q1	Q2	Q3	Q4
Wage bill ($ millions)	$72.1	$148.4	$221.5	$296.1
Number of employees	3177	3216	3242	3367
Average price of labor	$18,072	$35,854	$53,665	$71,579
Business loan revenue ($ millions)	$117.2	$236.0	$354.4	$472.5
Value of business loans ($ billions)	$10.3	$10.2	$10.2	$10.3
Average business loan rate	1.35%	2.70%	4.05%	5.41%

If one wants data separately by quarter to see how labor prices or loan rates may have changed and mistakenly uses the summed quarterly information from the Call Report, the specification of a quarterly dummy can control for the quarterly jumps in the data. This is not a small issue, as is illustrated in Table 1. While the total wage bill and business loan revenue (income and expense variables) rise markedly over four quarters for US banks in 2010, the number of bank (FTE) employees and the value of business loans (from the balance sheet) do not.[4] The result is a set of inaccurate quarterly labor prices and business loan rates.[5]

Getting the Panel Data. If you want data on all or even most banks in the United States, you will have to go to two separate reports—Call Report 041 for banks with domestic and foreign offices and Call Report 031 for banks with only domestic offices. Matching a list of bank ID numbers you want to each Call Report will select the banks and then matching a list of the variables wanted against the bank data selects the variables required for these banks. The resulting data sets then are stacked, giving a single data set ready for estimation. Sometimes there are changes in the variables reported in the Call Reports but data from 2000 to today are little changed.

Size Distribution of Banks. Of the 5113 commercial banks in 2016, the 604 largest institutions (with $1 billion or more in total assets accounted for 93% of all bank asset value and 92% of all bank deposits. Adding in 3,155 more banks with assets of $100 million to $1 billion, raises these two coverage ratios to 99.5% and 99.4%, respectively. The goal of most banking research is to be able

---

4. The data are from a balanced panel of 4284 US commercial banks with more than $100 million in total assets for 2010 (author's calculation).
5. When the FDIC reports quarterly information elsewhere, the quarterly data are adjusted to reflect data by quarter, not data summed over the quarters.

to generalize results to the banking system as a whole and for this purpose restricting the banking panel to only billion dollar banks is usually sufficient. Indeed, when especially large samples are used covering the vast majority of banks, this can importantly bias results when determining scale economies, a result of the functional form used and a peculiarity of the data, as discussed next.

3 Measuring Scale and Scope Economies

3.1 Scale Economies and Technical Change

Scale Economies. Estimation of cost curves has been around since Jacob Viner and his draftsman. More recently, some 35 years ago, there was much interest in using panel data to estimate bank scale economies and to disentangle scale effects from technical change. In a cost function with panel data, the cross-section variation identifies scale economies while the time-series variation identifies technical change. A standard specification for a bank cost function is $C = f(Q_i, P_i)$ where $C =$ total operating and interest expenses, $Q_i =$ total assets, or today, a selection of separate bank balance sheet asset values (a stock) covering major loan categories and security holdings, and $P_i =$ the prices of factor inputs (labor and physical capital) along with funding inputs. Some researchers include an estimate of equity cost in C (Hughes, Mester, & Moon, 2001) but most take equity capital levels as being largely required by regulators and not subject to being minimized by banks and thus are excluded from the cost function. With constant average costs, the cost elasticity $\Sigma \, \partial \ln C / \partial \ln Q_i$ would be 1.00. Separate identification of technical change usually just means that some function of time (t) is added to the cost function.

A common estimate of bank scale economies evaluated at the mean of the data in the past would be around .96.[6] This suggests that for every doubling of bank assets, total costs rise by only 96% and average cost would fall. If a bank with $100 million in assets (a relatively small bank) grew to almost $2.5 trillion (the current size of JP Morgan Chase), that bank would have doubled some 15 times to get there. The average cost per $1 of bank assets in 2015 was 2.9¢.[7] Assume average cost at a $100 million dollar bank is 3¢. Doubling assets 15 times would imply that a $2.5 trillion dollar bank would have average costs of 2.2¢, an apparent reduction of 27% compared to a $100 million dollar bank.

If this were true, only very large banks would probably exist. The problem is that the average scale estimate of .96 was used, neglecting the fact that bank scale economies are larger for small banks (with a cost elasticity below .96) and smaller for larger banks (closer to 1.0). Early academic studies found that

---

6. Although scale estimates from translog and Fourier functional forms differ across bank size-classes (as illustrated below) they typically are quite close when evaluated at the mean of the data.
7. The ratio of total bank costs—noninterest expenses of $385 billion (mostly labor and capital) plus interest costs of $40 billion—to total assets of $14.9 trillion is 2.9¢. Labor is currently the single largest component of all bank costs but this can change with relatively high interest rates.

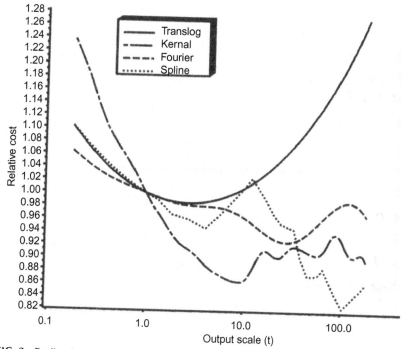

FIG. 2 Predicted average cost from different functional forms.

economies are indeed greater for smaller banks, as expected, but was markedly reduced as banks became larger. Indeed, using a translog cost function and a sample of almost all banks, a common result in the past was either no scale economies at all for the very largest banks or weak but significant scale diseconomies. Bankers at large banks, however, did not agree. Their view was that scale economies were still being realized, and used this argument to justify the many mergers they undertook to become larger still.[8]

To a degree, the bankers' view was supported in the few studies that had separately estimated their samples by bank size-classes and found both economies and slight diseconomies for different groups, including large banks. The issue was resolved when McAllister and McManus (1993) showed how predicted average cost can differ depending on the functional form used in estimating the cost function when all or the vast majority of banks are in the sample. They estimated translog, kernel, Fourier, and spline cost functions using bank data for 1984–90 and generated the predicted average cost curves shown in Fig. 2. The translog form treats all observations and their squared

---

8. Regulators require that the benefit of a proposed merger be noted but little empirical information is required for support. Merger studies find cost changes from a merger are small and only about half of the time are costs reduced.

errors equally and the curvature of predicted average cost is affected by where the mass of the observations lie which is with the smaller banks. The other functional forms are more like what the results would be if the translog was separately estimated for different bank size-classes and the pieces of predicted average cost stitched together into a single cost curve, like a spline function does.

A peculiarity of panel banking data is that it is highly skewed. As noted above, there are thousands of small banks, multiple hundreds of large banks, and only tens of the very largest.[9] Estimating scale economies using a translog cost function with the vast majority of all banks will minimize the overall sum of squared errors but the squared errors for the much more numerous smaller banks will dominate the process and affect the curvature of predicted average cost for the far less numerous largest banks. The result was that scale economies for the largest banks appeared to be quite flat or, worse, generated scale diseconomies.

A recent policy issue related to large bank scale economies was the Durbin Amendment to the Dodd-Frank financial reform legislation of 2010. It effectively stipulated that debit card interchange fees be equal to the incremental cost (marginal cost) of debit card transaction growth for only large banks (who dominate debit card issuance and processing). Scale economies are equal to the ratio of marginal to average cost. If the time period used for measurement is one month, even with some monthly or seasonal transaction variation the measured marginal cost would likely be zero. Like electricity generation, there is always excess capacity to handle small variations in card transaction demand.

If the time period is one year (which it was), the change in total debit card cost (and transaction volume) will be smaller than if a multiple-year time period is used. More of what appear to be fixed costs for this service over one year will become variable over multiple years and add to marginal cost. An additional issue is that nothing was said about including a normal return on invested capital covering fixed investment. Short-run marginal cost was legislated to be the debit card interchange fee and, because the data collected only covered one year rather than a longer time period, this became the estimate. The end result was that the $17 billion in debit interchange fee revenue was cut almost in half.

---

9. The skew is quite large. Out of a total of 5113 banks in 2016 the distribution is:

Banks	Assets (B = Billion)
4509	<$1B
506	$1B to $10B
89	$10B to $250B
9	>$250B

This illustrates why it is important to estimate bank scale economies using the cross-section component of a bank panel which effectively reflects the cost involved in changing the scale of a bank's operation over multiple years.[10] The underlying assumption for using a cross-section to estimate scale effects is that a smaller bank will "look like" a larger bank as it grows over time and is assumed to face the same level of costs as that larger bank.

Finally, as a caution, it is noted that virtually all panel data analysis of bank scale, scope, technical change, productivity, and profitability have assumed that the flow of banking output is proportional to the (stock) values shown in the balance sheet. If the balance sheet value of loans is three times the value of securities (close to what it actually is), it is assumed that the value of the output flow from loans is also three times that for securities. This may not be the case as there are alternative ways to measure banking output. Indeed, banking output is measured differently in the national accounts. This issue is raised when bank productivity is discussed below.

Technical Change. Technical change can be measured many different ways: exponential in time with/without interaction with other variables, a generalization of Solow's index of technical change (Baltagi & Griffin, 1988), or even through upward/downward shifts in annual predicted average cost curves (Humphrey, 1993). Using these different approaches in equilibrium or disequilibrium (fixed capital) models, technical change has fluctuated between 1% and 1.4% annually in the past. Although the passage of time is the standard approach, more informative results are possible when one is able to specify the specific type and time sequence of technical change in the estimating function.

Addressing a 2009 conference on the future of finance, Paul Volker suggested that "The only thing useful banks have invented in 20 years is the ATM" (New York Post, 2009). This reflected his view that the invention and use of credit default swaps, CDOs, and similar financial engineering products were risk-shifting instruments rather than productivity improvements. In addition to ATMs, one could add the shift to lower cost and often more convenient electronic payments, such a debit cards at the point-of-sale and ACH electronic bill payments. While credit cards are also convenient they are generally the most expensive consumer payment instrument. Banks will soon provide 24/7 electronic payer-initiated credit transfer services for person-to-person transactions as well as consumer and business bill payments.[11] Such a bank-provided service is already in place in the United Kingdom.

---

10. Two additional reasons are (1) it is not easy to collect bank cost data over long periods and (2), even if such information were easily available, other influences on cost are occurring at the same time and would have to be accounted for.

11. Other providers currently offer these services but they are little used. A standardized service from a bank will likely be more acceptable.

The real benefit is not 24/7 person-to-person payments. Rather, it is business-to-business and person-to-business bill payments that combine the electronic payment with electronic invoices. This eliminates the cost and errors involved in going from a biller's internal electronic account receivable files, to a paper invoice mailed to a customer, having the customer manually adjust the invoice (special discounts, missing items, breakage, etc.), copying this information into the customer's electronic account payable files, mailing the adjusted invoice to the biller with a check, and having the biller update its electronic account receivable files when the payment and invoice are received. The 24/7 aspect here is not usually important since, among businesses, trade credit is given so bills remain unpaid for 15 to 45 days or more (unless a discount for early payment is offered and taken). The benefits of Electronic Business Data Interchange (EBDI) is in the electronic connections between the biller's electronic accounts receivable file and the customer's electronic accounts payable file for both the payment and the invoice.

ATMs were supposed to reduce the bank cost of depositor cash acquisition, check deposits, and balance inquiry, compared to dealing with tellers at branch offices for these services. ATMs also provide greater convenience: they are more numerous than branches and operate 24/7. Unfortunately, bank Call Reports do not report this information by bank but aggregate information on the number of ATMs is available elsewhere. There is also information on the number and type of branch offices that ATMs were to replace in the FDIC's annual Survey of Deposits. This shows, by bank, the number of full service standalone offices and the number of offices in supermarkets or other retail outlets. Supermarket offices have lower capital costs and "produce" more deposits per employee (Radecki, Wenninger, & Orlow, 1996). Just as the number of ATMs or the number of ATM transactions are not available by bank, neither are transaction volumes for check, card, or wire transfers.

Today, many banks are closing some offices and/or making them more automated with video connections to a banker to handle standard depositor questions and requests. This form of bank-specific technical change reduces branch operating cost. Other technical or operational changes are at times available in bank annual reports which announce major computer upgrades and/or advances in telecommunications, but this information is almost never used. The default option in almost all efforts to assess technical change in banking is to specify time as a variable but the aggregate ratio of ATMs to branch offices could be a better indicator. At least one knows what this variable refers to, a clarity not achieved by using time alone or fixed or random effects.[12]

---

12. Sometimes specific information on technical or organizational change is available. One example was the analysis of the Federal Reserve's effort to consolidate its wire transfer offices (Hancock, Humphrey, & Wilcox, 1999). Another was the effect that digitalization of deposited checks had on Federal Reserve and bank operating costs, as well as on float reduction in check bill payments to businesses (Humphrey & Hunt, 2013).

3.2   Scope Economies

Interest in scope economies followed scale economies (Jagtiani & Khanthavit, 1996; Lawrence, 1989). Panel data applications attempted to determine the cost effects of banks producing both deposits and loans. While many view deposits as an input, since it provides low cost funding for intermediation into loans and securities, there is also an output service flow of transaction processing, cash acquisition, and safekeeping for depositors. Thus the cost effects of jointly producing deposits and loans can lead to more loans since: (i) deposits are often a lower cost and more stable funding source than purchased funds; and (ii) most branch offices have a (small) dual use in meeting depositor transaction needs as well as soliciting, making, and monitoring loans to borrowers, thereby generating cost complementarities.

This is not just of academic interest. At the time, policy makers had been considering "narrow banking" proposals to separate insured deposits from most types of bank lending, effectively protecting the payment system from risky banking activities and the on-going cross-subsidization of these activities with underpriced FDIC deposit insurance.[13] The idea was that insured deposits would only be invested in safe assets while risky loans and other assets would be supported with more costly uninsured purchased funds. Scope economies between two deposit (Q_1, Q_2) and three loan categories (Q_3, Q_4, Q_5) in a cost function framework $C(Q_1, Q_2, ... Q_m, P_i)$ could be determined from:

$$SCOPE = [C(Q_1, Q_2, 0, 0, 0, P_i) + C(0, 0, Q_3, Q_4, Q_5, P_i) \\ - C(Q_1, Q_2, ..., Q_m, P_i)]/C(Q_1, Q_2, ... Q_m, P_i) \qquad (1)$$

where P_i represents a set of factor input and funding prices and Q_m represents liabilities and assets in addition to Q_1 to Q_5.[14] $SCOPE$ equals the total cost of specializing in producing only deposits plus the cost of producing only loans (the first two cost functions in the equation) minus the current total joint cost of producing both together, as a percent of this joint cost. If $SCOPE = 10\%$, joint production versus specialized production presumedly reduces cost by ten percent.

Although complete specialization as well as joint production across firms may exist in other industries or in farming, a peculiarity of banking data is that

---

13. It is well recognized that FDIC deposit insurance rates are lower than if this insurance was provided by the private sector. The FDIC has a line of credit with the US Treasury and the government would be expected to provide funds if bank losses exceed the liquidity of the deposit insurance fund (a fund generated through deposit insurance fees on banks).

14. Other possibilities exist, such as producing each of the Q_1 to Q_5 outputs separately. This is rather speculative: no banks even come close to doing this in practice so it has little empirical support in the data.

complete or close to complete specialization in production of different banking services rarely occurs.[15] Thus evaluating the first two cost functions in Eq. (1) assuming complete specialization—inserting zeros or very small values where zeros are now—is not appropriate. To minimize bias and "strange results", the zeros should be replaced with values that are not too far away from their actual values experienced by a reasonable subset of banks in the panel. Extrapolating SCOPE results much beyond the point where they have some empirical support typically leads to unstable and insignificant SCOPE estimates. Regardless of the estimating form used—translog, Box-Cox transformed translog, or a composite quadratic function (Pulley & Braunstein, 1992)—it is useful to evaluate at different levels of separated output and examine the results for stability and significance. For banks, the closer the evaluation is to zero and complete specialization, the more unstable and insignificant are the SCOPE values.

Estimates of bank deposit-loan scope economies have ranged from 4% to 5% and is primarily due to reduced opportunities to spread fixed costs over both deposits and loans together. The effect from cost complementarities was insignificant. Multiplying the increase in fixed cost by total banking cost suggested that production costs could rise by $16 billion. While FDIC deposit insurance rates could fall for deposits now invested in safe assets, the extra cost of purchasing funds to invest in the remaining (and more risky) assets could be $12 billion (using the spread between uninsured CDs and Treasury bills). All in, narrow banking could cost banks some $28 billion annually.[16] The alternative is to expand equity capital enough to achieve the same level of protection for the payment system, which has been the current approach following the recent financial crisis.

The scope economy concept could also be applied to assess differences in performance when bank holding companies diversify into nonbank financial activities (e.g., insurance, securities brokerage, REITs, servicing activities, etc.). Relating performance to the degree of diversification across bank holding companies in a regression format can illustrate the types of diversification associated with greater performance as the regulation of permissible nonbank activities has expanded (Cetorelli, Jacobides, & Stern, 2017).[17] A more formal

---

15. True, there are other types of financial entities that take small value uninsured deposits and hold only safe assets (short-term money market mutual funds) or raise investments from private sources and hold risky assets (private equity firms). However, these entities do not offer the wide range of deposit or loan services supplied by banks and their funding and asset values are small. Even so, combining their cost information with banking data could be interesting but we know of no study that has done so.
16. These values reflect 1990 prices (Pulley & Humphrey, 1993).
17. A similar analysis focusing on the risk and joint production effects of interest earning activities (primarily loans and securities) and noninterest or fee-based activities (underwriting, investment banking, and venture capital along with service charges on deposit accounts) is also possible (Abedifar, Molyneux, & Tarazi, 2017).

exercise that substitutes profits for costs in Eq. (1) and defines Q_i as the value of various bank as well as nonbank activities is also possible.

4 Assessing Bank Efficiency Using Frontier Models

More recently, panel data has been employed to focus on banking efficiency using upwards of five different frontier models. Bayesian analysis has also been used (Malikov, Kumbhakar, & Tsionas, 2016). The workhorse frontier model has been the cost function but later was extended to standard profit and alternative profit functions.

Frontier Models. There are two main approaches: linear programming (LP) versus a parametric frontier. The most used LP technique is data envelopment analysis (DEA) with free disposal hull (FDH) used occasionally. On the parametric side, the stochastic frontier approach (SFA) assumes that most banks are either on or very close to the efficiency frontier. Inefficiency—being away from the frontier—is assumed to have a half-normal distribution, allowing it to be separated from normal error in a composed error model. Its use is encouraged by being offered as a command in popular econometric packages.[18]

A different composed error model is the distribution-free approach (DFA). It is called "distribution-free" because, unlike the SFA, it makes no assumption about the distribution of bank inefficiency. In a panel data set, the composed error terms of separate DFA cross-section estimations are averaged. The random error component is assumed to average close to zero so the average error that remains for individual banks gives the distribution of inefficiency across banks. Since this resembles a Gamma distribution, it either calls into question the SFA assumption that most banks lie close to the efficient frontier and forms a half-normal distribution skewed away from the frontier or it raises the question of whether averaging the estimated composed error takes care of random error in the DFA model.[19]

A well-known drawback of the LP approach is that there is no real statistical test of the constraints specified in a DEA linear program. And specifying more constraints, either well-considered or not, should always reduce estimated inefficiency. However, if the same information were used as a variable in a parametric model, its statistical significance can be determined to see if it is important or not. Specifying more variables in a parametric model need not expand R^2 and reduce measured inefficiency, but this feedback is not available when specifying constraints in the LP approach.

---

18. Early on, a Gamma distribution was assumed to reflect inefficiency. However, It was difficult to separate this assumed distribution of inefficiency from normal error in the composed error model (Greene, 1993).

19. There is also a thick frontier approach (TFA) that does not require a composed error and instead divides up a panel data set into average cost quartiles, estimates each one separately, and uses the difference in between the highest and lowest quartile estimate as an indicator of average cost inefficiency.

The parametric approach has its own well-known drawback and this concerns assuming a particular functional form on how the specified variables may affect the dependent variable. The LP approach imposes no functional form and is less restrictive in this sense. Even so, if the LP model is set up assuming constant costs, scale effects will not occur even if they are in the data, and vice versa if the program is set up for scale economies. While the possible existence of scale effects has to be determined a priori, in banking it seems a safe guess that this is the case.

The results from over 20 European bank frontier efficiency studies are surveyed in Weill (2004). A broader and earlier survey covering some 130 studies focused mostly US and European banks is in Berger and Humphrey (1997). Mean estimates of bank inefficiency range between 20% and 25% across 21 countries and covers DEA, SFA, and DFA (the three most used empirical models). Generally, the linear programming approach finds greater bank inefficiency than do the regression-based models.

Later analyses attempted to reduce unexplained inefficiency by adding balance sheet variables to these models either directly or in side regressions relating measured inefficiency to these variables. This had almost no effect. However, adding branch and labor productivity variables to DEA and DFA models reduced unexplained operating cost and interest cost inefficiency (the two sources of bank costs) to only 5%–7% (Carbo, Humphrey, & Lopez, 2007).[20] Thus previously unexplained inefficiency may have an apparent explanation after all.

Estimating LP and Parametric Models With the Same Data

Frontier models (DEA, FDH, SFA, and TFA) can be applied to a single cross section as well as to panel data. Only the DFA model requires panel data since the composed error terms from separate cross-section estimations are averaged to obtain inefficiency. Some studies have contrasted the results from these different frontier models using the same panel data set. Mostly, the contrast is between DEA and SFA, finding them to give different values of inefficiency and a moderately different ranking of banks by their measured level of inefficiency.

One study contrasted the results from four models estimated different ways—for single years or using a 12-year panel—but using the same functional forms and variable definitions. The distributions of cost efficiency for the three parametric models (SFA, DFA, and TFA) had similar means and standard deviations, ranked banks in generally the same order, and mostly identified the same banks with high or low efficiency. The DEA model, estimated different ways, generated lower average efficiencies, ranked the banks differently, and identified different high and low efficient banks compared to the parametric models.

---

20. Two other studies focusing on adding productivity indicators are Berger and Mester (1997) and Frei, Harker, and Hunter (2000).

Finally, the parametric models were more consistent with nonfrontier measures of bank performance such as ROE and ROE (Bauer, Berger, Ferrier, & Humphrey, 1998). Overall, differences among the LP and parametric approaches to determining frontier efficiency have not been great enough to induce partisans to switch and both approaches are still in use.

Have Frontier Models Helped Banks Improve Efficiency? As detailed as the Call Reports are, the data available are not detailed enough to clearly show the way to improve bank efficiency. One needs detailed cost accounting data and other nonpublic information to do this properly. Academic frontier studies basically just say that Bank A is estimated to have 25% cost or profit inefficiency compared to only 15% for Bank B. And both are being compared to the bank or banks (in truncated data) that define the efficiency frontier.

With some additional analysis, it may be found that Bank A employs more workers or pays higher wages or produces fewer deposits per branch office than banks close to the frontier. However, there is no information on just where the apparent excess employment may be since there is no information on employment by specific bank service line or a breakout of actual full time versus part time (peak load) employment or where branch offices could be better located or combined. Higher average wages at a bank can be affected by the local cost of living, or overbranching, or the result of too many layers of management. If Bank A has a lower deposit/branch ratio, "producing" fewer deposits per unit of capital, this may reflect the fact that many/most of its offices are located in a lower income area or in a low growth location. It is known that high income depositors tend to hold higher idle demand balances and use more banking services. The same is true in areas where economic growth is more rapid.

An additional complication is that only end-of-day deposit balances are reported. Large firms sweep most of their deposits out of their banks to earn interest overnight. Consumers and small businesses lack the ability to do this. Thus the composition of depositors can affect the deposit/branch ratio productivity measure (which is like an output/capital ratio). The same holds for the labor/branch ratio (like a labor/capital ratio). A high labor/branch ratio can identify banks that are less reliant on ATMs, Internet banking, and other automated services than others.

In sum, if a bank wants actionable information on how it can reduce its cost and/or earn a higher ROE, it needs to conduct a benchmarking exercise with a consulting firm that specializes in this type of peer comparison analysis.[21] This requires much more detailed cost accounting and other information than is contained in publicly available banking data. In sum, due to a lack of publicly available data, frontier efficiency studies have been of limited use in helping banks

---

21. Sherman and Ladino (1995) describe one such banking benchmarking study.

improve their efficiency. Such a conclusion does not apply to the use of panel data to determine scale, scope, and (sometimes) technical change for policy purposes as the data requirements are more easily met.

5 Bank Competition

Frontier analysis and less complex models have used panel data to assess banking competition (surveyed in Degryse, Acevedo, & Ongena, 2015). The focus to date has always been on competition measures evaluated at the level of the entire bank (Bikker, Shaffer, & Spierdijk, 2012; Koetter, Kolari, & Spierdijk, 2012). This does not apply to the Herfindahl-Herschman Index (HHI). The FDIC makes a special effort to collect deposit information at each bank branch to compute this local market concentration measure. All other reported bank information is at the bank, not branch, level and can cover multiple local markets.

Almost all academic competition analyses have used the HHI, or the H-Statistic, or the Lerner Index, or some other preferred measure (e.g., a Boone model) and relate one of these measures to other variables (profitability, cost efficiency, financial fragility) that could be affected by competition or may have affected the competition measure itself (bank deregulation, changes in branching laws). Rarely are the different competition measures compared with each other. But when comparisons are made, it is typically just between the HHI and some other single measure as different researchers have their own favorite competition measure. This is unfortunate since there seems to be very little correlation between one competition measure and any of the others.[22] This suggests that competition results are probably "measure specific" in that use of one measure can give results that differ from using another measure, especially in terms of the strength of the estimated relationship with other variables.

The HHI focus on market shares does not account for how these shares may have been achieved—through lower costs or by uncompetitive behavior (Demsetz, 1973). This led to the efficient structure controversy and the finding that cost efficiency (measured from a cost frontier) and the HHI are about equally important in explaining differences in bank profitability (Berger, 1995).

Recently, competition measures have been compared for five individual banking services: consumer and business loans, savings and small time deposits (time deposits less than $100,000), and payment activities (Bolt & Humphrey, 2017). The results suggest that the Herfindahl-Herschman Index (HHI) and the Panzar and Rosse H-Statistic are not significantly predictive of relatively high or relatively low bank prices for these services. The best results were obtained using a simple service line mark-up (similar to a Lerner Index) and a competition efficiency frontier measure (similar to a theoretical model in Boone, 2008).

Overall, researchers have almost always preferred the Lerner Index or the H-Statistic, probably because of a relatively strong theoretical foundation—directly relating price to underlying cost as a markup or via correlation—versus

---

22. This holds for Europe (Carbo, Humphrey, Maudos, & Molyneux, 2009) and the United States.

the HHI which is a more indirect indicator where price and cost are not explicit but the existence of concentrated markets allow for the possibility that price may rise to a uncompetitive level regardless of cost. Even so, regulators and antitrust authorities still rely on the HHI (and additional market information) for assessing competition due to the legal history and the importance of legal precedent in antitrust enforcement.

Assume the empirical evidence is overpowering that (say) the ex ante Lerner Index is far better than the ex post HHI (calculated ex ante) as an ex post indicator of market competition. This raises two related issues for antitrust authorities. First, their legal remit is focused on preventing a merger that would importantly reduce competition. This requires a measure that can predict, in some fashion, the likely effect of a merger before it occurs. The HHI provides such a prediction, assuming that bank market concentration at some point does significantly affect market prices. For the Lerner Index to be useful here, one would have to show that a higher than average premerger Lerner measure consistently predicts a higher postmerger value (not the same or a lower value, although that too would be useful information).

Second, past Supreme Court decisions have used market concentration as the reason to prevent a merger, not information that the size of a firm's markup over cost prior to a merger is "too high". In the end, it may portend the same result but has not been the stated basis for court decisions. Academic studies of competition typically neglect these two practical issues.

Even so, there has been some effort by regulators to incorporate mark-up issues along with the need for an a priori measure. Called GUPPI (Gross Upward Pricing Pressure Index), it attempts to assess the likelihood that a proposed merger among firms producing imperfectly substitute goods may have the opportunity to raise prices and increase postmerger revenues (see Shapiro, 2010). In brief, two firms each producing one popular but imperfectly substitutable product merge (e.g., Coca Cola and Pepsi). After merging, the combined firm raises one price shifting some demand to the other good sufficient to raise total revenue from both goods.

It is not clear that banks could do this effectively, raising deposit fees or loan prices at the acquiring bank to shift some deposit and loans to the acquired bank rather than to some third bank in the same market. Banking services/products are, in principle, highly substitutable. However, this would work if there were almost no other banks nearby, which returns us to the HHI to assess the likelihood of this occurring. Anecdotal information indicates that merged banks do change some prices but mostly by making them more similar within the merged institution which usually now has a single name rather than maintaining their separate premerger identity.

If prices are raised after a merger, management is judging that few depositors or borrowers would move to other institutions due to (1) the merged institution's large size and/or more convenient locations or (2) the role it plays as a price leader with other banks following suit. Credit unions consistently offer depositors slightly lower loan rates and slightly higher deposit rates and are viewed as being the strongest competitor to local banks. Even so, due to a lack of numerous convenient locations, their market shares are typically small even though they effectively place a lid on fees and rates charged/paid by banks in their local market.

Regardless of the competition measure used, a problem for researchers is that bank mergers that have been rejected (or were not proposed in the first place because of possible rejection) do not occur so the power of tests to see how well various competition measures would be able to identify strong uncompetitive behavior is likely reduced. This is important: in 2010 the value of the HHI used in the merger guidelines to signal an uncompetitive merger was almost 40% higher than the pre-2010 HHI value. Thus past mergers that would have passed muster today would not have done so prior to 2010. One is left with trying to distinguish between competitive and uncompetitive banks when the sampled banks have already been deemed by the authorities as being sufficiently competitive to begin with.

6   Productivity Analysis

Productivity is typically measured as output per unit of input. Academics have long used growth accounting index models or a Solow residual regression approach to measure productivity as the deflated value of output unexplained by the growth in the deflated value of factor inputs. Adjusting for output quality and education of the labor input, along with advances in index number theory, have improved this methodology.[23] Following this path, many banking panel studies have used cost function estimates of technical change (often a simple quadratic function of time) or shifts in predicted average costs from a cost function to indicate changes in productivity. Here productivity is the change in total or average cost unexplained by output levels or input prices.

A similar approach to bank productivity measurement uses frontier analysis. Here a bank's deviation from the efficient frontier is reflective of its relative productivity (Bauer, Berger, & Humphrey, 1993). Expanding this to include shifts in the efficient frontier, along with movements of banks toward or away from the frontier, Casu, Girardone, and Molyneux (2004) looked at European banks between 1994 and 2000. They found that productivity growth was mostly due to technical change, interpreted as the outward shift in the efficient frontier rather than the general movement of banks closer to the frontier over time. This study contrasted productivity estimates from a parametric cost function and a nonparametric (DEA) estimate of a Malmquist Index, finding that the two approaches yielded generally consistent results.[24] Another study used a shadow price cost function to investigate the effects of deregulation on bank productiv-

---

23. Hulten (2001) provides a comprehensive survey of TFP developments, focusing on aggregate measures.
24. Their Malmquist Index did not include deposits, or any bank liability, as an input, which can create a problem as discussed below.

ity (Kumbhakar & Sarkar, 2003). Many times it is possible to decompose a productivity estimate into technology improvements, scale effects, and input cost adjustments. Unfortunately, only anecdotal information really exists regarding what the technological improvements might be (see The Economist, 2017, for one—machine learning in finance).

More recently, academic productivity models have used multi-output, multi-input distance functions or a Malmquist Index approach—essentially a production function framework—to identify the portion of productivity associated with a shift in the best-practice production frontier versus a shift of banks moving closer to this frontier, as well as other decompositions. Importantly, none of these models rely on a physical (flow) measure of banking output. Indeed, information on the number of deposit/loan accounts and/or payment transaction data do not exist for individual banks. Instead, balance sheet values (stocks) are commonly assumed to be representative of the underlying output flows as noted above when scale economies were discussed. At the aggregate level, however, account and transaction data can be approximated and is used by the US Bureau of Labor Statistics (BLS) to measure bank productivity.

Model Specification. Theoretical models of banking and the implementation of monetary policy through the banking system focus on the intermediation of liabilities into assets and the consequent effects on economic activity. As well, almost all bank cost function models relate costs to major asset categories (balance sheet values of different types of loans and securities) as well as prices of selected liabilities (deposits, purchased funds) and factor inputs. And profit functions are estimated using the prices of both outputs and inputs. Given this history, many distance function analyses of bank productivity specify that banks produce asset outputs (Q_{Ai}) using balance sheet values of liability inputs (Q_{Li}) as well as factor inputs (Q_L, Q_K) and determine productivity from something like $Q_{Ai} = f(Q_{Li}, Q_L, Q_K)$.

For econometric estimation, an output distance function composed of three asset outputs ($A1, A2, A3$) and one liability/equity input such as deposits ($L1$), as well as factor inputs, is represented as $D_O(A1, A2, A3, L1, Q_L, Q_K) = 0$. Imposing homogeneity of degree 1.0 and assuming a logarithmic functional form, one of the outputs is factored out and the estimated function becomes $-\ln A1 = \ln D_O(A2/A1, A3/A1, L1, Q_L, Q_K) + v + u$, where v is normal error and u is an indicator of frontier inefficiency. A difficulty here is that not only can there be no productivity from liability inputs "producing" asset outputs, due to the balance sheet constraint, but any productivity measured may be biased. The same problem exists in a nonparametric Malmquist Index which can be expressed as ratios of distance functions (specified as above) in two time periods.

Let the three asset outputs be C&I loans, consumer loans, and security holdings and the liability/equity funding input be deposits. If the deposit input falls and the value of C&I loans falls by a smaller amount with the remaining asset reduction absorbed by agricultural loans or some other asset category not specified in the model, this can appear to be a productivity gain. Productivity will also appear to rise if equity capital (which is not a specified liability) expands and some of it is used to purchase securities or any of the other specified assets.

Due to the balance sheet constraint where total assets equals total liabilities plus equity, a $1 change in bank liabilities will always result in a $1 change in some asset. Specifying bank liabilities as inputs in a multi-output, multi-input distance function or Malmquist Index model unfortunately can have no productivity in producing assets (e.g., Wheelock & Wilson, 1999; Feng & Serletis, 2010, and others). In addition, these productivity studies specify only the main assets and liabilities as outputs and inputs. As a result, the productivity estimates can be biased up or down as illustrated above. One way around the balance sheet constraint is to not specify any liabilities in these models, returning us to how productivity was assessed in the past via $Q_{Ai} = f(Q_L, Q_K)$.[25]

However, this neglects recent developments in how the banking sector is now represented in the national accounts by the Bureau of Economic Analysis and how the Bureau of Labor Statistics measures aggregate banking productivity (Royster, 2012). Based on multiyear government/academic discussions of how to treat services in the national accounts, it was concluded that bank deposit services—payments, cash acquisition, and savings safekeeping—are just as much a banking service output as loans.[26] If the balance sheet value of deposits is used to represent deposit output, it can be highly collinear (due to the balance sheet constraint) with the other specified outputs. What is needed is something similar to the approach adopted in the national accounts which measures banking output differently.[27]

7 Other Banking Topics

Many other banking topics are addressed using panel data. While these analyses are typically descriptive and involve standard econometric techniques, often the difficulty for researchers is in obtaining enough detailed data to investigate policy issues regarding risk, bank lending, securitization, and payment activities. For bank profitability, the problem is the extent of negative values in the data which varies over time.

Risk. Panel data on bank risk exists but has many facets, incorporating liquidity, credit assessment, as well as levels of equity capital and profits to cover expected losses. Indeed, if risk can be reasonably assessed a priori, it should be best reflected in the price being charged. One summary measure is the value of funds available to cover losses (a flow of profits relative to assets

---

25. For example, Casu et al. (2004) estimated a Malmquist Index using DEA but did not specify a bank liability as an input in addition to factor inputs.
26. The main arguments are outlined in Griliches (1992) for banking and other services. Changes to the national accounts were announced in 2003.
27. See Fixler, Reinsdorf, and Smith (2003) for the user cost approach in the national accounts and Hancock (1985) or Humphrey (2019) for a panel data application.

plus the stock of existing capital relative to assets) divided by the standard deviation of the return on assets. Bank examiners have devised more detailed risk indicators associated with asset liquidity, the growth of loan charge-offs, and the ability to absorb earnings reductions from loan losses (similar to the summary risk measure just noted). Examiners also look at rapid loan growth and outsize reliance on purchased funds (which can "run" when they are needed most). Focusing on loan-price uncertainty, a structural model has been estimated for a number of European countries and functions as an early warning for the recent financial crisis (Tsionas, 2016). Banks have their own internal risk measures, of which value-at-risk models are the most well-known. These models deal with large unexpected shocks that lie in the tail of ill defined probability distributions (Allen & Saunders, 2015).

The source of risk differs by bank on- and off-balance sheet activity, with certain derivatives of particular concern (interest rate swaps and futures, credit default swaps, forward exchange contracts). While they are used to hedge against risk of loss, they still face liquidity and counterparty default risk in times of financial market disruption when they are needed most. Systemic risk also exists among banks due to their daily financing and interbank payment flows through national wire transfer networks and other settlement venues (De Bandt, Hartmann, & Alcalde, 2015). Panel data has been used to model these interactions (Bech & Hobijn, 2007) and the ECB has outlined how systemic risk from different sources can be assessed (European Central Bank, 2010).

The hourly/daily interbank funds flows are primarily an effort to minimize the cost of holding a pool of uninvested funds to meet hard to predict deposit withdrawals or additions as well as unexpected loan takedowns. Although shifting all overnight federal funds contracts to a one week holding period was shown to basically eliminate systemic risk on large value payment networks (CHIPS and Fedwire), the current solution has been to collateralize and cap net debit exposures on these networks. In some cases, central bank funding is used to provide a free or low cost positive balance at the opening of business so almost all subsequent payment transactions can be settled in good funds and net debit exposures dramatically reduced.

Lending. Considerable panel information exists on different types of loans, covering real estate, C& I, consumer, and agricultural loans. Income and balance sheet information, including loan size, maturity, and collateralization, are available along with loan losses and types of borrowers (e.g., small businesses), but not costs. Indeed, the allocation of operating cost (labor and capital expenses) to bank service lines does not exist so covariation analysis could be used to approximate this allocation using panel data.[28]

---

28. It would be nice to re-test the accuracy of this procedure. With cost accounting data already allocated to outputs or services for a panel of banks, the costs would be summed and regressed on the mix of outputs to see how well the estimated parameters matched the actual operating cost shares.

Loan research has largely focused on bank loans made to small businesses due their importance for employment growth in both Europe (Casey & O'Toole, 2014) and the United States (Berger & Black, 2011). Surveys suggest that bank loans to small businesses account for close to 60% of their debt financing. However, "debt financing" must not cover trade credit since Federal Reserve Flow of Funds data show that for each $1 of bank loans to businesses, there is about $2 in trade credit given to businesses. For small businesses, trade credit is easier to get than a bank loan and is outstanding for a shorter period. Importantly, trade credit substitutes for bank funding just as commercial paper does when issued by large credit-worthy firms.

Much research focuses on the major impediments to making small businesses loans, such as a lack of standardized credit information (Agarwal & Hauswald, 2010) and insufficient collateral. Trade credit, like bank credit, is important for managing firm growth. Receiving trade credit and not having to pay an account payable (A/P) until 32 days later (the average time in the United States and northern Europe) adds to a firm's working capital while giving trade credit as an account receivable (A/R) is an incentive that helps sell a firm's output (Ferrando & Mulier, 2012). In some southern European countries, an average A/R may not be received for four months or more. Since about one-third of firms that go bankrupt have had serious problems with late or nonpayment of their A/Rs, the EU issued a directive on late payments to the effect that public entities should pay their A/Ps in 30 days (with 60 days for private firms).

Regulators have focused on consumer loans (auto, installment, credit card, mortgage) from both banks and retailers. This takes the form of mandating greater disclosure of loan terms and rates charged as well as providing an avenue for complaints so that potentially unfair practices can be investigated and, if found to be widespread, dealt with. Discriminatory behavior in providing access to consumer loans has also been legislated (c.f., Community Reinvestment Act) requiring certain enforcement requirements on regulators and the assessment of penalties if warranted (Avery, Brevoort, & Canner, 2006). Panel data has been used to identify such situations as well as explain other loan practices like credit rationing and the incidence of credit card fees by income group.[29]

Securitization. Like loans, there is a considerable amount of information available about securitization by individual banks, from which panel data sets can be formed. Securitization basically transforms relatively illiquid bank assets, such as mortgages and other types of bank loans (auto loans, credit card receivables, student loans, etc.) into a pool of assets that are taken off a bank's balance sheet and securities sold backed by these assets.

---

29. Another example concerns deposit account overdraft fees. The average fee is around $35 for each overdraft and raised $12 billion in 2015. This can be unfair since the debits and deposits to an account at some banks are re-ordered to maximize the probability of an overdraft, rather than using the actual time of their occurrence.

In effect, assets which previously were held on the balance sheet and tied up available deposit funding until the assets matured, are sold to investors before maturity freeing up bank funds for making more loans. This has a multiplier effect on the ability of banks to issue credit that did not exist before, with consequent effects on loan growth during recent economic expansions. It also passes default risk to the purchaser of the securities and, in the recent financial crisis, is believed to have led to reduced bank credit standards (Dell'Ariccia, Igan, & Laeven, 2012; Mian & Sufi, 2009).

Payment Services. Panel data are quite limited here. While some information on revenues from payment services are available for individual banks in the Call Report (service charges on deposit accounts, ATM income, and bank debit and card fees and interchange income), no corresponding payment transaction (output) data are available for individual banks. Transaction data, however, does exist at the national level (as noted above when the BLS approach to productivity measurement was outlined). As well, operating costs are not allocated to any bank service line and only a few nonfactor payment-related costs are available. It is pretty much a desert for payment panel data for the United States, less so for Europe. Payment transaction, cost, and price information are available for individual banks in a few countries but almost all have this information at the national level.[30] This means that cross-country panel data are available to assess payment instrument substitution and cost economies (Humphrey, Willesson, Bergendahl, & Lindblom, 2006).

Profitability. Data on bank profits and the cost, revenue, and tax components of profits (yielding bank net income), either absolutely or as computable ROA or ROE values, are reported in the Call Report. The problem is that many models are in double log form, such as standard or alternative profit functions, which can't accept zero or negative values. Profit functions have been used to determine whether inefficiency is greater for outputs or inputs as well as how bank mergers may have affected subsequent profitability (Akhavein, Berger, & Humphrey, 1997). Banks with negative net income can be dropped from a sample but then the analysis is truncated and the parameter results may be unrepresentative.

One common workaround is to retain banks with negative profits in the data set but identify the bank with the highest negative profit, increase this negative value by one, change the sign to positive, add this value to all banks' net income, take logs, and run the logarithmic model. This "works" but, in a comparative analysis of profit function estimation results, seems to affect the estimation results more than just deleting the negative profit observations (Bos & Koetter, 2011). The same authors suggest a third method that appears to

---

30. For example, national level data have been used to see how per transaction pricing has hastened the shift to electronic payments in Norway relative to the Netherlands, which did not price (Bolt, Humphrey, & Uittenbogaard, 2008).

improve their results.[31] As illustrated below, this involves no change in model specification for observations where profits are positive.[32] For observations with negative profits, the dependent variable is moved to the RHS where its absolute value becomes an additional variable with a parameter restricted to 1.0. The estimating equation then becomes the stacked equation:

$$\text{positive profit} = f\left(\beta_i^1 \text{RHS variables}\right) + 1.0$$

$$1.0 = f\left(\beta_i^2 \text{RHS variables} + |\text{negative profit}|\right).$$

Correlation between positive profit and the original RHS variables determines β_i^1. Covariation among the RHS variables and the positive value of negative profit determines β_i^2 and the stacked nature of the equation imposes the restriction $\beta_i^1 = \beta_i^2$ in estimation.

Cost, Profit, and Revenue Functions. Most empirical banking studies have used the cost function: minimizing cost given output levels (Q_O) and input prices (P_I) by varying input quantities in $C = f(Q_O, P_I)$. Some studies have used profit functions maximizing profit given output (P_O) and input prices, by varying output and input quantities in $PFT = f(P_O, P_I)$. Fewer still have used a revenue function maximizing revenue given output prices and input quantities (Q_I) by varying output quantities in $R = f(P_O, Q_I)$. In sum, almost all banking analyses have used models assuming that the banking system is competitive.

What might be a way for allowing some imperfect competition? The assumption of price exogeneity applies to such nationally-traded bank assets as government securities and federal funds purchased or sold, and also likely applies for most commercial loans to low-risk large corporate borrowers. To a degree, however, price setting behavior exists through deposit overdraft fees, minimum balance requirements, rates on consumer installment and credit card loans, as well as rates charged on agricultural and small business loans. Indeed, the Loan Pricing Corporation provides subscribing banks with detailed (anonymous) information on loan prices for borrowers grouped by SIC code and geographic area and loan rates show considerable dispersion for the same type of borrower and location. Overall, perhaps two-thirds of bank revenues may be generated from services where banks have a rather small to moderate degree of control over price (Radecki, 1999).

For small business loans and middle market loans, a bank can raise or lower the borrower's required compensating balance and adjust the fee on the unused portion of the loan. If the loan amount is $500,000, a portion (say 10%) may be held idle in a demand deposit account paying no interest. The borrower pays interest on all of the loan but only has use of $450,000. This raises the effective loan rate and is negotiated between the borrower and the bank and is not public

---

31. "Appears" is the correct word here. The true result of estimating a double log profit model with positive and negative profits is unknown.
32. Aside from adding 1.0 on the RHS to complete the last column vector for the two equations.

information. It is not unlike a bank using a borrower's credit rating to set the loan rate on an auto, installment, or a credit card loan as the correspondence between a credit rating and the loan rate need not be the same for all banks.

Allowing for imperfect competition and a degree of price-setting behavior, the so-called alternative profit and alternative revenue functions have been specified as: $PFT^A = f(Q_O, P_I)$ and $R^A = f(Q_O, P_I)$. This is just the cost function above but with a different dependent variable.[33] As a contrast to studies estimating cost efficiency, standard and alternative profit functions have been used to investigate frontier efficiency in the United States as well as Europe (Maudos, Pastor, Perez, & Quesada, 2002). The general result is that estimated profit efficiency is substantially lower than cost efficiency but there is not much difference between the standard and alternative profit function results (Berger & Mester, 1997). Investigating a different issue, an alternative revenue function has been used to compute revenue scope economies. The question was, do consumers pay for one-stop banking? This concerns the revenue from joint provision of banking services to customers as opposed to the cost savings to banks for providing these services jointly. Studies have found the joint production of deposits and loans saves costs, but the associated revenue is not significantly different (Berger, Humphrey, & Pulley, 1996).

8 Summary

Over the last thirty five years, the main bank issues investigated with panel data have been scale and scope economies, technical change and productivity, profitability and efficiency (frontier or otherwise), competition and payments, and lending to small businesses plus assessments of risk. Some of the models used in these investigations, along with their typical results, are reported in the text. Mostly, however, we have focused on data issues in this paper and how they may affect the topics investigated. As the task of forming a panel data set over a long time period can be difficult due to changes in the reported data and the incidence of mergers, most banking studies use a single cross-section or panel data over a short period of time. Have the banking topics studied been of some use in informing legislative or regulatory decisions or assisted practitioners in improving their operations? Generally, yes, except for frontier efficiency analysis. The detailed cost accounting data needed are not publicly available to usefully benchmark ways to improve bank cost or profit efficiency.

Fortunately, publicly available data on banks is quite extensive and detailed. Even so, its peculiarities can cause problems for the unwary. It is important to decide how to deal with extreme outliers in the data. Examples are banks with no deposits or no loans, or unrealistically high average wages, or billions in

---

33. In truth, the proper specification should be a mixture of price-setting and price-taking behavior but this is not usually seen in the banking literature.

assets but one or two employees. Many researchers screen their data but some do not report the criteria used.

Researchers know that the size distribution of banks is highly skewed: thousands of small banks, hundreds of large banks, but only tens of the very largest banks. This did not prevent academics from finding that the largest banks had no scale economies, or worse, had diseconomies even though bankers argued otherwise. The problem was that a translog (or simpler) functional form was being applied to a sample of the vast majority of all banks and the skewed data biased the resulting scale estimates. The correction was either to separate the data and estimate by bank size class or retain a large sample but apply a Fourier or spline function in estimation. This showed that the bankers were correct. As the goal of most banking research is to be able to generalize to the industry as a whole, it is usually sufficient to focus only on the 600 banks with more than $1billion in total assets that account for 92% of assets or deposits rather than over 5000 banks that account for 100%.

There were 4300 bank mergers or acquisitions between 2000 and 2016. Although most of them were among smaller banks, quite a few were among the very largest institutions. Indeed, M&A was the way the currently very largest banks got that way. This does not pose a problem for assembling an unbalanced panel, but is an issue if a balanced panel is desired. There are two ways to deal with mergers: one can bias results if capturing scale effects is important to the question at hand while the other simply replicates how banks are observed to expand—by mergers that can increase assets and services by 50%–100% each time. If quarterly data are being used, it is important to know that the primary source reports the sum of income and expense items across quarters, not the value for each quarter separately (so some recalculation is necessary).

In a bank balance sheet, the value of all assets equals the value of liabilities plus equity capital. A common way to determine industry productivity is to measure the change in output associated with a change in inputs. In banking, this can be difficult to do if the value of assets produced is specified to be a function of the value of liability and factor inputs. In some industries this may be reasonable but not in banking since $1 of liabilities or equity will always "produce" $1 of assets. This can lead to biased estimates of productivity. One solution is to define bank output as they do in the national accounts, rather than use the reported values in the balance sheet. Other problems associated with banking data are covered in the text, along with the workarounds that can be applied.

References

Abedifar, P., Molyneux, P., Tarazi, A., 2017. Non-interest income and bank lending. Working Paper, College of Business Administration, University of Sharjah, Sharjah, UAE.

Agarwal, S., Hauswald, R., 2010. Distance and private information in lending. Review of Financial Studies 23 (7), 2757–2788.

Akhavein, J., Berger, A., Humphrey, D., 1997. The effects of megamergers on efficiency and prices: Evidence from a bank profit function. Review of Industrial Organization 12 (1), 95–139.

Allen, L., Saunders, A., 2015. Risk management in banking. In: Berger, A., Molyneux, P., Wilson, J. (Eds.), The Oxford handbook of banking. 2nd ed. Oxford University Press, Oxford, UK, pp. 160–183.

Avery, R., Brevoort, B., Canner, G., 2006. Higher-priced home lending and the 2005 HMDA data. Federal Reserve Bulletin 92 (September 8), A123–A166.

Baltagi, B., Griffin, J., 1988. A general index of technical change. Journal of Political Economy 96 (1), 20–41.

Bauer, P., Berger, A., Ferrier, G., Humphrey, D., 1998. Consistency conditions for regulatory analysis of financial institutions: A comparison of frontier efficiency methods. Journal of Economics and Business 50 (2), 85–114.

Bauer, P., Berger, A., Humphrey, D., 1993. Efficiency and productivity growth in U.S. banking. In: Fried, H., Smith, S., Schmidt, S., Lovell, C.A.K. (Eds.), The measurement of productive efficiency: Techniques and applications. Oxford University Press, pp. 386–413.

Bech, M., Hobijn, B., 2007. Technology diffusion within central banking: the case of RTGS. International Journal of Central Banking 3 (September), 147–181.

Berger, A., 1995. The profit–structure relationship in banking: Tests of the market-power and efficient-structure hypotheses. Journal of Money, Credit and Banking 27 (2), 404–431.

Berger, A., Black, K., 2011. Bank size, lending technologies, and small business finance. Journal of Banking & Finance 35 (3), 724–735.

Berger, A., Humphrey, D., 1997. Efficiency of financial institutions: International survey and directions for future research. European Journal of Operational Research 98 (2), 175–212.

Berger, A., Humphrey, D., Pulley, L., 1996. Do consumers pay for one-stop banking? Evidence from an alternative revenue function. Journal of Banking & Finance 20 (9), 1601–1621.

Berger, A., Mester, L., 1997. Inside the black box: What explains differences in the efficiencies of financial institutions. Journal of Banking & Finance 21 (7), 895–947.

Bikker, J., Shaffer, S., Spierdijk, L., 2012. Assessing competition with the Panzar-Rosse model: The role of scale, costs, and equilibrium. Review of Economics and Statistics 94 (4), 1025–1044.

Bolt, W., Humphrey, D., 2017. Competition and price conduct by bank service line. In: Bikker, J., Spierdijk, L. (Eds.), Handbook of competition in banking and finance. Edward Elgar Publishing.

Bolt, W., Humphrey, D., Uittenbogaard, R., 2008. Transaction pricing and the adoption of electronic payments: A cross-country comparison. International Journal of Central Banking 4 (1), 89–123.

Boone, J., 2008. A new way to measure competition. Economic Journal 118, 1245–1261. No. 531 August).

Bos, J., Koetter, M., 2011. Handling losses in translog profit models. Applied Economics 43 (3), 307–312.

Carbo, S., Humphrey, D., Lopez, R., 2007. Opening the black box: Finding the source of cost inefficiency. Journal of Productivity Analysis 27 (3), 209–220.

Carbo, S., Humphrey, D., Maudos, J., Molyneux, P., 2009. Cross-country comparisons of competition and pricing power in European banking. Journal of International Money and Finance 28 (1), 115–134.

Casey, E., O'Toole, C., 2014. Bank lending constraints, trade credit and alternative financing during the financial crisis: evidence from European SMEs. Journal of Corporate Finance 27 (August), 173–193.

Casu, B., Girardone, C., Molyneux, P., 2004. Productivity change in European banking: A comparison of parametric and non-parametric approaches. Journal of Banking & Finance 28 (10), 2521–2540.

Cetorelli, N., Jacobides, M., Stern, S., 2017. Transformation of corporate scope in US banks: patterns and performance implications. Federal Reserve Bank of New York Staff Reports. Staff Report No. 813, May, 2017.

De Bandt, O., Hartmann, P., Alcalde, J., 2015. Systemic risk in banking after the great financial crisis. In: Berger, A., Molyneux, P., Wilson, J. (Eds.), The Oxford handbook of banking. 2nd ed. Oxford University Press, Oxford, UK, pp. 667–699.

Degryse, H., Acevedo, P., Ongena, S., 2015. Competition in banking. In: Berger, A., Molyneux, P., Wilson, J. (Eds.), The Oxford handbook of banking. 2nd ed. Oxford University Press, Oxford, UK, pp. 589–616.

Dell'Ariccia, P., Igan, D., Laeven, L., 2012. Credit booms and lending standards: Evidence from the subprime mortgage market. Journal of Money, Credit and Banking 44 (2-3), 367–384.

Demsetz, H., 1973. Industry structure, market rivalry, and public policy. Journal of Law and Economics 16 (1), 1–10.

European Central Bank, 2010. Analytical models and tools for the identification and assessment of systemic risk. In: Financial stability review, pp. 138–146. June.

Feng, G., Serletis, A., 2010. Efficiency, technical change, and returns to scale in large U.S. banks: Panel data evidence from an output distance function satisfying theoretical regularity. Journal of Banking & Finance 34 (1), 127–138.

Ferrando, A., Mulier, K., 2012. Do firms use the trade credit channel to manage growth?. ECB Working Paper Series, No. 1502, December.

Fixler, D., Reinsdorf, M., Smith, G., 2003. Measuring the services of commercial banks in the US national accounts: changes in concepts and methods. In: Paper prepared for OECD National Accounts Experts Meeting. October, STD/NAES(2003)20.

Frei, F., Harker, P., Hunter, L., 2000. Inside the black box: What makes a bank efficient? In: Harker, P., Zenios, S. (Eds.), Performance of financial institutions: Efficiency, innovation, regulation. Cambridge University Press, Cambridge.

Greene, W., 1993. The econometric approach to efficiency analysis. In: Fried, H., Lovell, C.A.K., Schmidt, S. (Eds.), The measurement of productivity efficiency: Techniques and applications. Oxford University Press, Oxford, UK.

Griliches, Z. (Ed.), 1992. Output measurement in the service sectors, studies in income and wealth. In: Vol. 56. National Bureau of Economic Research, University of Chicago Press.

Hancock, D., 1985. The financial firm: Production with monetary and nonmonetary goods. Journal of Political Economy 93 (5), 859–880.

Hancock, D., Humphrey, D., Wilcox, J., 1999. Cost reductions in electronic payments: The roles of consolidation, economies of scale, and technical change. Journal of Banking & Finance 23 (2-4), 391–421.

Hughes, J., Mester, L., Moon, C., 2001. Are scale economies in banking elusive or illusive? Evidence obtained by incorporating capital structure and risk-taking into models of bank production. Journal of Banking & Finance 25 (12), 2169–2208.

Hulten, C., 2001. Total factor productivity: A short biography. In: Hulten, C., Dean, E., Harper, M. (Eds.), New developments in productivity analysis, national bureau of economic research. University of Chicago Press. ISBN: 0-226-36062-8, pp. 1–54.

Humphrey, D., 1993. Cost and technical change: Effects of bank deregulation. Journal of Productivity Analysis 4 (1-2), 9–34.

Humphrey, D., 2019. An improved measure of banking productivity. Working Paper, Florida State University.

Humphrey, D., Hunt, R., 2013. Cost savings from check 21 electronic payment legislation. Journal of Money, Credit and Banking 45 (7), 1415–1429.

Humphrey, D., Willesson, M., Bergendahl, G., Lindblom, T., 2006. Benefits from a changing payment technology in European banking. Journal of Banking & Finance 30 (6), 1631–1652.

Jagtiani, J., Khanthavit, A., 1996. Scale and scope economies at large banks: Including off-balance sheet products and regulatory effects, 1984-1991. Journal of Banking & Finance 20 (7), 1271–1287.

Koetter, M., Kolari, J., Spierdijk, L., 2012. Enjoying the quiet life under deregulation? Evidence from adjusted Lerner indices for U.S. banks. Review of Economics and Statistics 94 (2), 462–480.

Kumbhakar, S., Sarkar, S., 2003. Deregulation, ownership, and productivity growth in the banking industry: Evidence from India. Journal of Money, Credit and Banking 35 (3), 403–424.

Lawrence, C., 1989. Banking costs, generalized functional forms, and estimation of economies of scale and scope. Journal of Money, Credit and Banking 21 (3), 368–379.

Malikov, E., Kumbhakar, S., Tsionas, M., 2016. A cost system approach to the stochastic directional technology distance function with undesirable outputs: The case of US banks in 2001–2010. Journal of Applied Econometrics 31 (7), 1407–1429.

Maudos, J., Pastor, J., Perez, F., Quesada, J., 2002. Cost and profit efficiency in European banks. Journal of International Financial Markets Institutions and Money 12 (1), 33–58.

McAllister, P., McManus, D., 1993. Resolving the scale efficiency puzzle in banking. Journal of Banking & Finance 17 (2-3), 389–405.

Mian, A., Sufi, A., 2009. The consequences of mortgage credit expansion: Evidence from the U.S. mortgage default crisis. Quarterly Journal of Economics 124 (4), 1449–1496.

New York Post newspaper, 2009. December 13, 2009. http://nypost.com/2009/12/13/the-only-thing-useful-banks-have-invented-in-20-years-is-the-atm/. (Accessed 14 October 2007).

Pulley, L., Braunstein, Y., 1992. A composite cost function for multiproduct firms with an application to economies of scope in banking. Review of Economics and Statistics 74 (2), 221–230.

Pulley, L., Humphrey, D., 1993. The role of fixed costs and cost complementarities in determining scope economies and the cost of narrow banking proposals. Journal of Business 66 (3), 437–462.

Radecki, L., 1999. Banks' payments-driven revenues. Economic Policy Review 5 (2), 53–70. Federal Reserve Bank of New York.

Radecki, L., Wenninger, J., Orlow, D., 1996. Bank branches in supermarkets. Current Issues 2 (13), 1–6. Federal Reserve Bank of New York.

Rhoades, S., 1985. Mergers of the 20 largest banks and industrials, all bank mergers, 1960-1993, and some related issues. Antitrust Bulletin 30 (3), 617–649.

Rhoades, S., 2000. Bank mergers and banking structure in the United States, 1980-98, Staff Study 174. Board of Governors of the Federal Reserve System.

Royster, S., 2012. Improved measures of commercial banking output and productivity. Monthly Labor Review, pp. 3–17.

Shapiro, C., 2010. The 2010 horizontal merger guidelines: From hedgehog to fox in forty years. Antitrust Law Journal 77 (1), 49–107.

Sherman, D., Ladino, G., 1995. Managing bank productivity using data envelopment analysis, DEA. Interfaces 25 (2), 60–73.

The Economist, 2017. Machine-learning in finance: Unshackled algorithms. p. 68.

Tsionas, M., 2016. Parameters measuring bank risk and their estimation. European Journal of Operational Research 250 (1), 291–304.

Weill, L., 2004. Measuring cost efficiency in European banking: A comparison of frontier techniques. Journal of Productivity Analysis 21 (2), 133–152.

Wheelock, D., Wilson, P., 1999. Technical progress, inefficiency, and productivity change in U.S. banking, 1984-1993. Journal of Money, Credit, and Banking 31 (2), 212–234.

Chapter 20

Quantile Panel Estimation of Financial Contagion Effects

Christoph Siebenbrunner*,† and Michael Sigmund‡,a

*University of Oxford, Mathematical Institute, Oxford, United Kingdom, †Institute for New Economic Thinking, Oxford, United Kingdom, ‡Oesterreichische Nationalbank (OeNB), Vienna, Austria

Chapter Outline

1 Introduction

A key topic in financial regulation is the identification of "systemically important" institutions that would cause high losses for the financial system if they were to fail. As the recent financial crisis has shown, many lessons are to be learned for policymakers and researchers. For example, many standard macroeconomic models lacked a banking sector, and contagion effects between economic sectors, in particular banks, were not adequately addressed. On the policy side, most countries did not have a clear path for bank recovery and resolution to prevent bank crises and ensure the orderly resolution of failing banks while minimizing their impact on the real economy and the financial sector. The devastating cascading effects observed during the financial crisis of 2008 have shown

---

a. The views expressed in this paper are those of the authors and do not necessarily reflect those of the Eurosystem or the OeNB.

Panel Data Econometrics. https://doi.org/10.1016/B978-0-12-815859-3.00020-2

that even crises in moderately sized institutions and markets can put global financial stability at risk (Fratzscher & Rieth, 2015; Haldane & May, 2011).

The ability to identify systemically important institutions for the purpose of regulatory scrutiny is key to addressing the problem of moral hazard inherent in any institution that cannot be allowed to fail. This insight has, in part, triggered a paradigm shift in financial regulation, which, instead of trying to identify institutions that are "too big to fail," now focuses on institutions that are "too interconnected to fail" (Haldane & May, 2011). This new approach is most visible in the capital add-ons for globally and domestically systemically important institutions (see BIS, 2012, 2013; FED, 2015; EBA, 2014—henceforth referred to as SII regulations). These regulations define weighted scorecard metrics aimed at quantifying not only an institution's size, but also its interconnectedness and systemic importance within the global and domestic financial system.

Studies of systemic interconnectedness, however, are plagued by scarce availability of data bilateral interbank relations, which are both highly confidential and rarely collected comprehensively. International projects of significant scale have been undertaken to try to close some of those data gaps (Anand et al., 2018). In this study, we use a unique data set that combines both time series of the complete network of interbank relations of the entire banking system of a country and of the indicators used in the SII regulations. This allows us both to assess the weighting scheme used by current regulations and to provide regulators who do not have access to such data with additional guidance. In our approach, we aim to capture some peculiar features of interconnected financial systems, which are said to exhibit "robust-yet-fragile" tendencies (Gai & Kapadia, 2010). Most of the time, small shocks are absorbed easily by the system and do not cause significant systemic losses. In a very few instances, however, even small, isolated shocks have the capacity to affect huge parts of the system. This leads to highly skewed loss distributions, focusing this chapter, in particular, on the importance of tail events in the context of systemic risk.

Our tool of choice for this approach is quantile regression. The origins of quantile regression date back to some of the first works about regression in the mid-18th century. Its application in modern econometrics can be attributed to Koenker and Bassett (1978). Quantile regression differs from standard, least-squares regression in that it provides conditional forecasts of the quantiles rather than the mean of the distribution of a dependent variable. Its application is particularly warranted in the case of highly skewed distributions, such as those describing the systemic losses in robust-yet-fragile systems (Koenker, 2005).

The rest of this chapter is structured as follows. In Section 2, we briefly review the literature about financial contagion and systemic risk analysis. In Section 3, we discuss the panel quantile estimators used in our analysis. In Section 4, the application to systemic risk analysis is presented. In Section 5, we conclude and derive a set of policy recommendations.

2   Literature Review

The study of systemic risk can be traced back to the work by Allen and Gale (2000), who extended the seminal model of bank runs by Diamond and Dybvig (1983) to multiple regions, showing the potential for financial contagion from insolvent to solvent banks. Other early contributions about the role of the network formed by interbank lending relationships include Freixas, Parigi, and Rochet (2000), Angelini, Maresca, and Russo (1996), and Rochet and Tirole (1996). Eisenberg and Noe (2001) show how to compute the equilibrium effects of financial contagion even in the presence of cycles in the network, which can lead to potentially infinitely many rounds of revaluations. On the empirical side, Elsinger, Lehar, and Summer (2006) provide one of the first implementations of the model of Eisenberg and Noe (2001) with real-world data, with an earlier version of the data set used in this study.

As mentioned in the introduction, quantile regression has been identified and adopted as an appropriate tool for the empirical study systemic risk analysis by many authors in the literature, most notably by Adrian and Brunnermeier (2016), who develop the popular CoVaR metric, which has become a widely used measure of systemic importance for publicly traded financial institutions. Publicly traded institutions are also the focus of other popular systemic risk measures such as SRISK (Brownlees & Engle, 2015) and the Marginal Expected Shortfall (Brownlees & Engle, 2012).

Our goal, however, is also to study the systemic importance of nonlisted institutions and to provide insights to regulators using data sets that are available for all institutions, such as those used in the SII regulations. Our work is related in spirit to that of Siebenbrunner, Sigmund, and Kerbl (2017), who also studies the relationship between SII indicators and systemic importance with fixed effects linear panel models. In particular, they have shown that metrics based on market measures such as CoVaR and SRISK cannot be applied for about 90% of banks in Europe and the United States. We want to improve upon their work by combining a contagion model in the spirit of Eisenberg and Noe (2001) with quantile regression techniques popularized by Adrian and Brunnermeier (2016) for the study of systemic risk. The strength of the approach of Eisenberg and Noe (2001) is that it imposes a causal model of how losses are transmitted through the system, and thus allows for an analysis of counterfactuals, which are particularly important for policy applications. Furthermore, the model can be computed for all banks and is not restricted to publicly traded banks, as is the CoVaR metric. The advantage of the approach taken by Adrian and Brunnermeier (2016) is that it puts the focus on high quantiles of the loss distribution, which are of particular interest in the case of systemic risk, which deals with the potential downfall of entire financial systems. We argue that our approach combines the advantages of these two approaches by allowing for counterfactual analysis of tail risks in high quantiles. In a similar vein, Klomp and De Haan (2012) use quantile regression to estimate the impact of banking regulation on banking risk. Their measures for bank risk combine multiple aspects of risk using factor analysis, their data set, however, is restricted to bank-specific variables and does not include the network data necessary for computing systemic contagion losses in the spirit of Eisenberg and Noe (2001). Covas, Rump, and Zakrajsek (2014) take a similar approach, using a dynamic panel quantile estimator to estimate capital shortfalls in US banks. Other related works include Anand, Craig, and Von Peter (2015); Glasserman and Young (2015); and Caccioli, Farmer, Foti, and Rockmore (2015).

On the methodological side, the nature of our research question and data set call for the application of panel estimation techniques, which in the case of quantile regression are from Koenker (2004).

3 Methodologies for Quantile Panel Estimation

In this section, we describe the methodological toolkit that we will employ to study the questions discussed in Section 1. Much of our methodology is taken from the literature, some parts are adaptions of existing methodologies to the panel setting and some parts go—to the best of our knowledge—beyond what can be found in the literature to date.

3.1 Quantile Panel Estimators

Following Koenker and Bassett (1978), we define the piecewise linear check function:

$$\rho_\tau(y) = y\big(\tau - \mathbb{I}_{y<0}\big) \tag{1}$$

where $\tau \in [0,1]$ is the quantile in consideration and $\mathbb{I}$ is the indicator function. We wish to estimate a classic, linear fixed effects model

$$y_{it} = \alpha_i + X_{it}\beta + u_{it}, \quad i = 1...N, \quad t = 1...T, \tag{2}$$

for a dependent variable $y \in \mathbb{R}^{NT}$ capturing information for $N \in \mathbb{N}$ individuals over $T \in \mathbb{N}$ observation periods. $\alpha \in \mathbb{R}^N$ is a vector of time-constant, individual specific effects, $X \in \mathbb{R}^{NT \times K}$ is a matrix of $K \in \mathbb{N}$ independent variables with coefficients $\beta \in \mathbb{R}^K$, and $u \in \mathbb{R}^{NT}$ is an error term.[1] We will denote by $\mathbf{1}^N$ an N-dimensional vector of ones and by $A \otimes B$ the Kronecker product of A and B and write the model in matrix notation:

$$y = a \otimes \mathbf{1}^T + X\beta + u, \tag{3}$$

---

1. X_{it} refers to the K-dimensional row vector representing the row of X corresponding to individual i at time t. For consistency with the matrix notation, X will be assumed to contain all T entries for the ith individual in rows $(i-1)T + 1 \dots iT$. Other than this exception, vectors here in general are column vectors and A' denotes the transpose of A.

We will denote by $\begin{pmatrix} \alpha^{\tau} \\ \beta^{\tau} \end{pmatrix}$ the coefficients for a given quantile τ. The conditional quantile of y for a given set of coefficients and data is given by $Q\left(\begin{pmatrix} \alpha^{\tau} \\ \beta^{\tau} \end{pmatrix}, X\right) = \alpha^{\tau} \otimes 1^{T} + X\beta^{\tau}$. The unconstrained estimator for these coefficients, which we denote the *dummy-variable*[2] estimator $DV \in \mathbb{R}^{N+K}$, is given by Kato, Galvao, and Montes-Rojas (2012):

$$DV^{\tau} = \begin{pmatrix} \hat{\alpha}^{\tau}_{DV} \\ \hat{\beta}^{\tau}_{DV} \end{pmatrix} = \min_{\alpha,\beta} \; \arg\min_{\alpha,\beta} f_{\tau}(\alpha\beta) \tag{4}$$

where

$$f_{\tau}(\alpha, \beta) = \sum_{i=1}^{N} \sum_{t=1}^{T} \rho_{\tau}(y_{it} - \alpha_i - X_{it}\beta) \tag{5}$$

While the problem as posed is not linear, because of the nonlinearity of ρ, it can be solved using methods of linear programming by exploiting its properties. The objective function $f: \mathbb{R}^{K+1} \rightarrow \mathbb{R}$ is an addition of $(N*T)$ ρ − functions. Because ρ is a convex, continuous, and piece-wise linear function that is bounded below by zero, f itself has these properties. The feasible region of the minimization problem, therefore, is a convex polytope that is bounded below and at least one (though not necessarily exactly one, as we will discuss shortly) of its corners defines a minimum of f. The corners are given by the points of nondifferentiability of the objective function, which are the roots of the $(N*T)$ ρ-functions. The basic solutions of the optimization problem are given by coefficient combinations that fit a regression line exactly through one or more observations (setting their corresponding ρ-functions to 0). The uniqueness of the global solution here, however, is not guaranteed by the usual condition that the number of linearly independent observations be no less than the number of coefficients: rank$(XX') \geq K+1$. When $\tau*N*T$ is an integer (e.g., when there is an even number of observations in the case of a median estimator), the slopes of the $t_1 = \tau*N*T$ and $t_2 = (1 - \tau)*N*T$ ρ-functions cancel out each other in the interval between the t_1th- and $(t_1 + 1)$th-largest observations (unless the two fall together), creating a compact affine subspace of $\mathbb{R}^{K+1}$ with slope $t_1*(\tau - 1) + t_2*\tau = 0$. Because of the convexity of f each point on the affine subspace is a minimum of the objective function and defines a continuum of estimators. It is conventional in the literature to use the lowest coefficient values to obtain a uniquely defined estimator DV^{τ} in this case, bringing us to the second

---

2. The reason for choosing the name *dummy variable* rather than the more commonly used term *fixed effect* is the equivalence between dummy variable and fixed effect regression, and the fact that the within transformation associated with fixed effect estimation is generally not feasible for quantile estimators, because these are not linear operators, unlike least-squares estimators.

operator $\min_{\alpha,\beta}$ in Eq. (4). The solution to the optimization problem can be found by solving the following linear program (Koenker, 2005):

$$\min_{u^+,u^- \in \mathbb{R}^{N*T}} \quad (\tau u^+ + (1-\tau)u^-)' \mathbf{1}^{N*T}$$
$$\text{s.t.} \quad \forall i \in \{1...N\}, \forall t \in \{1...T\} : y_{it} = \alpha_i + X_{it}\beta + u_{it}^+ - u_{it}^- \quad u^+, u^- \geq 0 \tag{6}$$

where the vectors $u^+ = \max(0,u)$ and $u^- = -\min(0,u)$ split the errors into their positive and negative components.

One potentially important problem with the DV^τ estimator is the incidental parameter problem (Neyman & Scott, 1948), because the number of individual-specific intercepts grows with N. It is important to note that, in contrast to mean regression, to our knowledge, there is no general transformation that can suitably eliminate the individual effects in the DV^τ model. Asymptotically, if $N \to \infty$ and T fixed, the DV^τ estimator has a potentially important bias. Fixing this incidental parameter problem has drawn a lot of attention in recent literature (Galvao & Kato, 2016). For empirical applications, however, no uniquely accepted method to remove the bias has been established yet. Our argument for the consistency of the DV^τ estimator in our setting relies on two results. First, the asymptotic result of Fernández-Val (2005) shows that the DV^τ estimator is consistent for $N \to \infty$, $T \to \infty$, and $\log(N)/T \to 0$. Second, Kato et al. (2012) perform a simulation exercise, and in their setting ($N = 200$, $T = 50$) closest to our setting ($N = 716$, $T = 32$), they show that the bias is extremely small.

Koenker (2004) suggests fixing the individual-specific effects α for all quantiles and letting only the slopes β depend on the quantile. Under this assumption, which we denote the *quantile-independence hypothesis*, the location shift effect of the individual-specific effects on the distribution of the response is the same for all quantiles. Estimating the coefficients under this restriction requires choosing a set of quantiles $P = \{p \mid p \in [0,1]\}$ of finite cardinality $|P|$ and a vector of corresponding weights $W \in [0,1]^{|P|}$ with the property that $W'\mathbf{1}^{|P|} = 1$. The *quantile-independent dummy* estimator $QID \in \mathbb{R}^{N+K}$ of the coefficients for a given quantile $\tau \in P$ under a given quantile set P and weighting scheme W is then given by:

$$QID_{P,W}^\tau = \begin{pmatrix} \hat{\alpha}_{QID_{P,W}}^{p=\tau} \\ \hat{\beta}_{QID_{P,W}}^{p=\tau} \end{pmatrix} = \min_{\alpha^{p_1},...,\alpha^{p_{|P|}},\beta^{p_1},...,\beta^{p_{|P|}}} \operatorname*{arg\,min}_{\alpha^{p_1},...,\alpha^{p_{|P|}},\beta^{p_1},...,\beta^{p_{|P|}}}$$

$$\sum_{p \in P} \sum_{i=1}^{N} \sum_{t=1}^{T} w(p)\rho_p\left(y_{it} - \alpha_i^p - X_{it}\beta^p\right)$$

$$\text{s.t.} \quad \forall p_1, p_2 \in P, \; i \in \{1...N\} : \alpha_i^{p_1} = \alpha_i^{p_2} \tag{7}$$

where the map $w : P \to [0,1]$ returns the element of W corresponding the respective quantile of P. Note that QID can be seen as a generalization of the DV estimator, which can be recovered by setting $P = \{\tau\}$ and $W = 1$. In the following, we will sometimes assume—without loss of generality—a uniform weighting scheme $W_i = \frac{1}{|P|} \forall i \in \{1 \dots |P|\}$ and drop the subscript W for notational convenience.

Note that every quantile set P uniquely determines a set of estimators $QID_P = \{QID_P^\tau | \tau \in P\}$, where the estimators QID_P^τ and $LS_{P'}^\tau$, for the same quantile τ under different quantile sets $P \neq P'$ can differ.[3] Hence, while $\hat{\alpha}_{QID_P}^\tau$ by construction does not depend on which quantile $\tau \in P$ is considered, both $\hat{\alpha}_{QID_P}^\tau$ and $\hat{\beta}_{QID_P}^\tau$ do depend on the set of sample quantiles P, and thus $\hat{\beta}_{QID_P}^\tau$ can differ from the unconstrained estimate $\hat{\beta}_{DV}^\tau$.[5] This raises questions about the consistency of the QID estimator in the case that the quantile-independence hypothesis does not hold. Testing for the validity of this assumption is of particular concern to us, because the individual-specific effect carries an important interpretation in our application (see Section 4). We will discuss the question of how to test this hypothesis in greater detail in Section 3.2.

Analyzing the incidental parameter problem in the $QIDp$, w^τ estimator, Koenker (2004) has shown that the estimator is consistent and asymptotically normally distributed when $N^a/T \to \infty$ for $a > 0$.

The idea of fixing parameters across quantiles also can be applied differently, e.g., by fixing the slopes across quantiles and letting only the individual-specific effects depend on the quantile, or fixing both of them across quantiles. Versions of these estimators can sometimes be encountered in the literature, typically for nonpanel estimators (e.g., the *composite quantile estimator* by Zou & Yuan, 2008). We denote the panel-versions of such estimators as the *quantile-independent slopes* and *quantile-independent estimators*, respectively defined as:

$$
QIS_{P,W}^\tau = \begin{pmatrix} \hat{\alpha}_{QIS_{P,W}}^{p=\tau} \\ \hat{\beta}_{QIS_{P,W}}^{p=\tau} \end{pmatrix} = \min_{\alpha^{p_1},\dots,\alpha^{p_{|P|}},\beta^{p_1},\dots,\beta^{p_{|P|}}} \underset{\alpha^{p_1},\dots,\alpha^{p_{|P|}},\beta^{p_1},\dots,\beta^{p_{|P|}}}{\arg\min}
$$

$$
\sum_{p\in P}\sum_{i=1}^{N}\sum_{t=1}^{T} w(p)\rho_p\left(y_{it} - \alpha_i^p - X_{it}\beta^p\right)
$$

$$
\text{s.t. } \forall p_1, p_2 \in P : \beta^{p_1} = \beta^{p_2} \tag{8}
$$

$$
QI_{P,W} = \begin{pmatrix} \hat{\alpha}_{QI_{P,W}} \\ \hat{\beta}_{QI_{P,W}} \end{pmatrix} = \min_{\alpha,\beta} \underset{\alpha,\beta}{\arg\min} \sum_{p\in P}\sum_{i=1}^{N}\sum_{t=1}^{T} w(p)\rho_p\left(y_{it} - \alpha_i - X_{it}\beta\right) \tag{9}
$$

Note that QIS and QI are again generalizations of the DV estimator. Every quantile set P again determines a set QIS_P of quantile-independent slope estimators, while the QI estimator is unique for every quantile set and weighting

---

3. Examples proving these claims are constructed easily. They also hold true in the data set that we use.

scheme. One still can choose to interpret the QI estimator for a given quantile, e.g., by centering the quantile set P symmetrically around this quantile (e.g., by considering $QI_{\{0.25,0.5,0.75\}}$ an augmented median estimator).

3.2 Statistical Tests

Tests exist in the literature to test whether individual coefficients or all coefficients jointly vary between two or more quantiles. The null hypothesis:

$$H_0 : DV^{p_i} = DV^{p_j} \ \forall p_i \neq p_j \in P \tag{10}$$

can be tested by considering the following test statistic (Koenker & Bassett, 1982) for a subset $\underline{P} \subseteq P$ of quantiles that are compared jointly:

$$Tn = (N+K)(|\underline{P}| - 1)(H*\underline{DV})'(H*V(\underline{DV})*H')^{-1}(H*DV) \tag{11}$$

where the matrix H expresses the linear hypothesis H_0 for the $|\underline{P}|$ quantiles that are compared jointly and $V(\cdot)$ denotes the variance-covariance matrix of the composite estimator $\underline{DV} = (DV^1, ..., DV^{|\underline{P}|})'$ (Koenker & Bassett, 1982). We choose to make pairwise comparisons of two quantiles, hence $H = (-\mathbf{I}^{N+K}, \mathbf{I}^{N+K})$, where $\mathbf{I}^{N+K}$ is an $N + K$-dimensional identity matrix. Koenker and Bassett (1982) show that Tn asymptotically follows a noncentral χ^2 distribution with $\text{rank}(H) = N + K$ degrees of freedom under common regularity assumptions.

We wish to test, however, whether the quantile-independence hypothesis causes the coefficients $\hat{\alpha}^\tau_{QID_{P,W}}$ and $\hat{\beta}^\tau_{QID_{P,W}}$ to be inconsistent for a given quantile. Our rationale for performing such a test is based on the argument that the DV estimator is consistent (at least weakly) and asymptotically normal regardless of whether the hypothesis of quantile-independent individual-specific effects holds or not. Weak consistency under fairly standard assumptions and asymptotic normality under slightly stricter assumptions, which we will assume to hold here, of the DV estimator has been shown by Kato et al. (2012). The QID estimator would be consistent only in the case where this assumption holds, but it would be more efficient in this case, because the restrictions placed on the coefficients should reduce the variance of the estimator. We, therefore, are comparing a potentially inconsistent but more efficient estimator with a consistent one. This situation resembles the case of the classical Hausmann test for fixed versus random effects in least-squares regression. We propose the following test statistic to test the null hypothesis that both the QID and DV estimator are consistent against the alternative hypothesis that only the DV estimator is consistent:

$$S^\tau_P(QID^\tau_P) = (DV^\tau - QID^\tau_P)'(V(DV^\tau) - V(QID^\tau_P))^\dagger (DV^\tau - QID^\tau_P) \tag{12}$$

where † denotes the Moore-Penrose inverse.[4] Note that every estimator set QID_P determines a set of test statistics $Sp = \{S_P^\tau \mid \tau \in P\}$, therefore consistency has to be established separately for each quantile in P.[5] We note that both QID and DV are asymptotically normally distributed; Kato et al. (2012) show both weak consistency and asymptotic normality for the DV estimator, and Lamarche (2010) shows asymptotic normality for the QID estimator, under slightly different but compatible assumptions. Therefore, every element in S_P follows a χ^2 distribution with degrees of freedom equal to the rank of $V(DV^\tau) - V(QID^\tau)$. This allows applying a Wald test (Wald, 1945) with the null hypothesis that the quantile estimate QID_P^τ is consistent and the alternative hypothesis that it is inconsistent.

Test statistics $S_P^\tau(QIS_P^\tau)$ and $S_P^\tau(QI_P)$ for the alternatively restricted estimators QIS and QI can be computed analogously to $S_P^\tau(QIS_P^\tau)$. Although QI technically does not depend on the quantile, consistency still has to be established against a reference quantile of DV^τ, as the restricted coefficients $\hat{\alpha}_{QI_{P,w}}$ and $\hat{\beta}_{QI_{P,w}}$ might be consistent with regards to some quantiles and inconsistent when compared to others. One has to make a choice which quantile one wants to compare the QI estimator against, e.g., by interpreting it as an augmented estimator for the central quantile in P, as discussed in Section 3.1.

3.3 Goodness of Fit Measures for Quantile Panel Estimators

Extending the ideas from Koenker and Machado (1999) to the panel setting, we define a benchmark estimator B containing only individual-specific effects, which can be seen as the panel analogue of an intercept:

$$B^\tau = \begin{pmatrix} \hat{\alpha}_B^\tau \\ \mathbf{0}^K \end{pmatrix} = \min_\alpha \arg\min_\alpha \sum_{i=1}^N \sum_{t=1}^T \rho_\tau(y_{it} - \alpha_i) \tag{13}$$

We then define the sum of prediction errors $E_B = \rho_\tau^{NT}(y - Q(B^\tau, X))' \mathbf{1}^{NT}$, where $\rho_\tau^{NT} : \mathbb{R}^{NT} \to \mathbb{R}^{NT}$ describes the element-wise application of the ρ_τ-map to the elements of a vector. We further define the sum of errors for the DV estimator $E_{DV} = \rho_\tau^{NT}(y - Q(DV^\tau, X))' \mathbf{1}^{NT}$ to define an R^1-measure as suggested by Koenker and Machado (1999):

$$R_{DV}^1 = 1 - \frac{E_{DV}}{E_B} \tag{14}$$

---

4. Refer to Kato et al. (2012) and Lamarche (2010) for the variance-covariance matrix of the DV and QID estimators, respectively. In the case of estimators of multiple quantiles, we refer to the $(N + K) \times (N + K)$ submatrix corresponding to the tested quantile.
5. This can be interpreted in the sense that, even for a fixed quantile set P, it is possible that the estimate $\hat{\beta}_{QID_P}^\tau$ for one quantile $\tau \in P$ is consistent while the estimate $\hat{\beta}_{QID_P}^\tau$ for a different quantile $\tau' \in P \backslash \tau$ might be inconsistent.

We apply the same idea of the R^1 measure by Koenker and Machado (1999) to the *QID* estimator by replicating the restrictions placed on the individual-specific coefficients in the benchmark estimator $BQID \in \mathbb{R}^N$:

$$BQID_{P,W}^{\tau} = \begin{pmatrix} \hat{\alpha}_{BQID_{P,W}}^{p=\tau} \\ \mathbf{0}^K \end{pmatrix} = \min_{\alpha^{p_1},...,\alpha^{P|P|}} \arg\min_{\alpha^{p_1},...,\alpha^{P|P|}} \sum_{p \in P}^{N} \sum_{i=1}^{T} \sum_{t=1}^{T} w(p)\rho_p\left(y_{it} - \alpha_i^p\right)$$

s.t. $\forall p_1, p_2 \in P, \ i \in \{1...N\} : \alpha_i^{p_1} = \alpha_i^{p_2}$

We then define the error sum and R_{DV}^1-measure for the restricted benchmark model:

$$E_{BQID} = \rho_{\tau}^{NT}\left(y - \hat{\alpha}_{BQID_{P,W}}^{\tau} \otimes \mathbf{1}^T\right)' \mathbf{1}^{NT} \tag{15}$$

$$R_{QID}^1 = 1 - \frac{E_{QID}}{E_{BQID}} \tag{16}$$

where E_{QID} is defined in analogy to E_{DV}. The same considerations can be applied to the *QI* estimator. For the *QIS* estimator, a direct analogue of R_{DV}^1 can be employed, because the restrictions in this case do not affect the benchmark model. One should be cautious, however, when comparing the goodness of fit R_{DV}^1 and R_{QID}^1 of the different estimators, because these relate to different benchmark models.

4   Application to Systemic Risk

The main idea behind capital-based systemic risk regulations, such as the SII regulations, is that the extent of regulatory scrutiny or pressure that a financial institution receives should be proportional to the risk posed to the financial system by this particular institution.[6] The indicator set of the SII regulations aims to proxy this systemic relevance using a set of bank-specific indicators. These indicators have the advantage of ready availability to regulators. However, they do not explicitly incorporate aspects of interconnectedness, which is a main driver of systemic contagion effects and robust-yet-fragile dynamics (Gai & Kapadia, 2010).

The remainder of this section is structured as follows: in Section 4.1, we briefly outline our approach to measuring systemic risk and describe the resulting contagion losses, and in Section 4.2 we present the application of the methodological toolkit presented in Section to 3 to this data set. In Section 4.3, we discuss our results and compare them to the regulatory regime defined in EBA (2014).

---

6. For simplicity, we will refer to all financial institutions covered by the appropriate regulations such as EBA (2014) as banks.

4.1   Systemic Risk Measurement

It is common in the literature to measure the systemic risk contribution of a bank as the sum of losses by all system participants that are caused by the idiosyncratic default of a particular bank (Glasserman & Young, 2015). Such losses can arise through multiple channels, and there exists a rich amount of literature about how to model and measure these effects. In this study, we will use the framework developed by Siebenbrunner et al. (2017), which has the advantage of being able both to incorporate multiple contagion channels and to consistently separate the contribution of individual channels.

We use the seminal model of Eisenberg and Noe (2001), which has been adopted widely in the literature (Barucca et al., 2016; Elsinger et al., 2006; Upper, 2011) to compute systemic contagion effects. The model considers the balance sheets of N banks, reporting for each bank the liabilities it has toward other banks, its claims on other banks, and other assets and liabilities (the latter are included as liabilities toward a "sink node"). The financial system in this model is fully described by a tupel of a matrix $L \in \mathbb{R}_+^{N+1 \times N+1}$ of bilateral loans and a vector $e \in \mathbb{R}_+^{N+1}$ of external assets. Using the vector $\bar{p}_i = \sum_{j=1}^n L_{ij}$ and the matrix of relative liabilities

$$\Pi_{ij} = \begin{cases} \dfrac{L_{ij}}{\bar{p}j} & \text{if } \bar{p}_i > 0 \\ 0 & \text{otherwise} \end{cases}, \tag{17}$$

we can compute the value of interbank claims, assuming that all claims are repaid fully, as $\Pi'\bar{p}$. If a bank is insolvent, however, it cannot repay its liabilities in full. Assuming that in this case banks distribute the remaining values of their assets proportionally among their creditors, we then can write the payments of bank i as:

$$p_i = \begin{cases} \bar{p}_i & \text{if } i \neq s \wedge \bar{p}_i \leq e_i + (\Pi'p)i \\ e_i + (\Pi'p)_i & \text{otherwise} \end{cases}, \tag{18}$$

Eisenberg and Noe (2001) show that Eq. (18) has a unique solution under mild conditions, which they call the **clearing payment vector**. We use this framework to study the effect of an idiosyncratic shock to one institution $s \leq N - 1$ that wipes out all of its assets and compute the clearing payment vector:

$$p_i = \begin{cases} 0 & \text{if } i = s \\ \bar{p}_i & \text{if } i \neq s \wedge \bar{p}_i \leq e_i + (\Pi'p)_i \\ e_i + (\Pi'p)_i & \text{otherwise} \end{cases} \tag{19}$$

We arrive at the **systemic contagion losses** caused by the default of institutions by summing up the losses received by each bank at each point in time $t, y_{s,t} = \sum_{i \neq s}^N \Pi'(\bar{p}_t - p_t)_i$, where p is the clearing payment vector as defined in

Eq. (19). We repeat the computation for each time point $t \in \{1, \ldots, T\}$, yielding the dependent variable $y_{i, t}$ for our estimations. We will estimate this dependent variable using the indicators from the SII regulations presented in Table 1. This data set includes 9 out of the 10 indicators used in the current SII regulations, which we will discuss in greater detail in Section 4.3. The one missing variable, value of payment transactions, could not be reconstructed retroactively for the time series we consider here.

We use data for the Austrian banking system, taken from the regulatory reporting system and the central credit registry. The time series of quarterly observations ranges from the second quarter of 2008 to the first quarter of 2016, yielding a panel of $N = 716$ banks and $T = 32$ points in time. Table 2 provides summary statistics for all variables.

TABLE 1 Description of Variables

Variable Name	Description	Unit
Total assets	Total assets	EUR
Private sector deposits	Deposits taken from domestic and foreign nonbanks (no public sector), all currencies	
Private sector loans	Loans to foreign and domestic nonbanks (no public sector)	EUR
Face value of derivatives	Notional value of OTC derivatives	EUR
Cross border loans	Loans to foreign domiciled nonbanks and banks	EUR
Cross border deposits	Deposits from foreign domiciled nonbanks and banks	EUR
Bank deposits	Deposits taken from domestic and foreign banks, all currencies	EUR
Bank loans	Loans to domestic and foreign banks, all currencies	EUR
Securitized debt	Liabilities in the form of securitized debt obligations and transferable certificates	EUR

All indicators, except for value of private domestic payment transactions, are taken from the regulatory reporting data, which are available on a quarterly basis. Because of data restrictions, we cannot include value of domestic payment transactions in our analysis on a quarterly basis and before 2014. We therefore decided to exclude this variable from our analysis.
The data set covers the periods 2008Q1–2016Q1, yielding a panel of N = 716 banks and T = 32 points in time.
Source: Oesterreichische Nationalbank.

TABLE 2 Summary Statistics of Included Variables

Var. Name	Min.	1st Qu.	Median	Mean	3rd Qu.	Max.	StD	Data C.
Contagion losses	0	1699	8896	370,402	33,863	79,732,168	2,619,878	90%
Total assets	301	67,580	147,461	1,271,509	343,526	157,220,135	7,277,256	90%
Private sector deposits	0	52,394	111,725	485,265	246,644	54,007,704	2,339,717	89%
Private sector loans	0	33,405	81,529	601,138	195,482	73,111,936	3,267,999	89%
Face value of deriv.	0	0	0	4,039,725	7878	1,513,070,221	46,117,293	89%
Cross border deposits	0	901	2825	198,405	11,051	43,498,252	1,515,197	89%
Cross border loans	0	844.50	4065	378,031	17,729	67,202,424	2,990,777	89%
Bank deposits	0	2957	10,731	394,504	39,718	190,752,720	3,082,595	88%
Bank loans	0	16,291	29,847	371,660	64,939	162,070,592	2,857,894	89%
Securitized debt	0	0	0	258,292	0	37,764,072	1,875,005	89%

Regulatory reporting data and credit registry data for the observation span 2008Q2–2016Q1. This table shows the summary statistics of the included variables. To improve readability, all variables are expressed in Tsd. EUR. Data C. refers to data coverage.
Source: OeNB.

4.2 Estimation and Results

We estimate a linear model with individual-specific effects, as introduced in Section 3.1 to estimate the contagion losses as described in Section 4.1:

$$y_{it} = \alpha_i + X_{it}\beta + u_{it}, \quad i = 1...N, \quad t = 1...T, \tag{20}$$

The dependent variable y_{it} is the sum of losses incurred by all other banks in the system following an idiosyncratic default of bank i at time t. The explanatory variables X_{it} are the contemporaneous SII indicators for bank i, as presented in Table 1. We consider the quantiles $P = \{0.25, 0.50, 0.75, 0.9, 0.95, 0.99\}$, which we also use as the quantile set for the constrained estimators.

As described in the introduction to Section 4, we are particularly interested in studying the individual-specific effects because they can be interpreted as the contribution of network effects that cannot be captured by the SII indicators. We first estimate the system described previously using the DV estimator with Koenker (2018). Next, we employ the Anova-test described by Koenker and Bassett (1982) to test whether the coefficients differ between each pair of quantiles in our quantile set P. Table A.1 in the appendix reports the results of this test applied to each combination of two or more quantiles in the set P. As can be seen from the results, the null hypothesis is rejected for all quantile combinations, showing that the parameters (including the individual-specific effects) jointly differ between quantiles.

We then proceed to estimating the system using the QID estimator with Koenker and Bache (2014) in order to be able to apply the test introduced in Section 3.2. Table 3 reports the results of these tests. As can be seen, the null hypothesis of consistency of the QID estimator is rejected for all quantiles except $\tau = 0.25$, as one would expect given that the Anova-test shows that the coefficients differ across quantiles. If the individual-specific effects differ across quantiles, then the restrictions imposed by the quantile-independence hypothesis cause the coefficients of QID to be biased. It is interesting to note,

TABLE 3 Quantile-Independence Hypothesis Test

	S Statistic	P-value
$\tau = 0.25$	350.72	0.96
$\tau = 0.5$	1019.27	0.00
$\tau = 0.75$	1989.68	0.00
$\tau = 0.9$	2076.93	0.00
$\tau = 0.95$	2795.07	0.00
$\tau = 0.99$	1306.87	0.00

Results for the Hausmann-type test in Eq. (12) for the models presented in Tables 4 and 5.
Source: OeNB, own calculations.

however, that the two tests do not necessarily agree on their results, as can be seen from the test result for the $\tau = 0.25$ quantile. This is because the Anova-test also might be rejected because of differing values of the slope coefficients across quantiles. In this case, the QID estimator, which does allow for the slope coefficients to vary across quantiles, still might be consistent, showing the importance of testing separately for the consistency of the QID estimator.

Summarizing our findings so far, we can infer all coefficients, including the individual-specific effects, vary across quantiles. We do not report the values of the individual-specific effects for confidentiality reasons, but we can say that we observe a nonmonotonic relationship between the value of their coefficients and the quantile level for many banks.

In Table 4, the coefficient for Total assets is highly significant and positive for all quantiles. The coefficient increases for higher quantile, indicating that big banks simply cause more contagion losses and that this relationship is highly quantile dependent. This result, however, is not driven only by a few (large) banks that cause high contagion losses, but it also holds true for banks that do not cause high contagion losses. As expected, private sector deposits reduce contagion losses, because these deposits are supplied outside the interbank market. Also, private sector loans should not significantly influence contagion losses, which holds true for most of the quantile estimation results. The coefficients of the face value of derivatives are not significant. In our data set, only a few banks hold such derivatives and this balance sheet item does not contribute significantly to contagion losses. The interpretation of the coefficient of cross-border deposits is similar to that of private-sector deposits, although it is economically less important, it still reduces contagion losses significantly. Cross-border loans tend to reduce contagion losses, especially for banks that cause large contagion losses, because losses on such deposits are materialized outside the financial system under investigation. Regarding bank deposits, we find a positive coefficient that, however, is not significant. The coefficient for bank deposits decreases for higher quantiles, which makes sense when we consider that the highest contagion losses are driven by higher-order contagion rounds rather than first-round effects stemming directly from the deposits of the defaulted bank (see Section 4.1). For bank loans, we can find a similar explanation as for private sector loans. Finally, the coefficient of securitized debt is negative. Securitized debt is an outside refinancing source of banks that should reduce contagion losses in the financial system.

In Table 4, we also see that the fixed effects model appears to be driven largely by the higher quantiles of the loss distribution, unsurprisingly for highly skewed data. We also note that there are differences regarding the sign and significance for several variables, e.g., for bank deposits. Bank deposits are highly significant with a negative sign in the fixed-effects model, while having a positive sign (albeit not being significant) for all quantiles. This could be explained by the decreasing contribution of bank deposits for higher quantiles discussed previously. The fixed-effects coefficient in this case might have been distorted by the extreme values of high losses, which are of particular importance and

TABLE 4 Dummy Variable (Unrestricted) Model

	FE-Model	τ: 0.25	τ: 0.5	τ: 0.75	τ: 0.9	τ: 0.95	τ: 0.99
Total assets	0.9693***	0.6223***	0.7247***	0.8136***	0.8513***	0.9641***	1.1958***
	(0.0078)	(0.1056)	(0.1264)	(0.1209)	(0.1433)	(0.1645)	(0.1998)
Private sector deposits	−1.0790***	−0.7751***	−0.7101***	−0.8024***	−0.7643***	−0.8327***	−1.1574***
	(0.0198)	(0.1114)	(0.1417)	(0.1443)	(0.1638)	(0.1724)	(0.1991)
Private sector loans	0.4608***	0.1620*	0.0413	0.0291	0.0131	−0.0311	−0.0184
	(0.0192)	(0.0730)	(0.0613)	(0.0679)	(0.0822)	(0.0937)	(0.0974)
Face value of derivatives	−0.0084***	−0.0045	−0.0036	−0.0042	−0.0019	−0.0059	−0.0077
	(0.0004)	(0.0044)	(0.0049)	(0.0042)	(0.0052)	(0.0052)	(0.0058)
Cross border deposits	−0.5432***	−0.5765***	−0.5427***	−0.7153***	−0.6569***	−0.7017***	−0.7011***
	(0.0170)	(0.1384)	(0.1529)	(0.1561)	(0.1516)	(0.1524)	(0.1536)
Cross border loans	−0.3177***	0.0116	−0.0634	−0.1003	−0.2323	−0.2416	−0.4899**
	(0.0114)	(0.1154)	(0.1236)	(0.0924)	(0.1197)	(0.1494)	(0.1847)
Bank deposits	−0.2951***	0.0219	0.1406	0.1431	0.1410	0.1083	0.0575
	(0.0119)	(0.0754)	(0.0910)	(0.0887)	(0.1027)	(0.0900)	(0.1101)

Bank loans	0.4170***	0.0837	−0.0136	0.0502	−0.0257	−0.0773	−0.0465
	(0.0137)	(0.0725)	(0.0693)	(0.0634)	(0.0674)	(0.0777)	(0.0988)
Securitized debt	−0.4693***	−0.2256*	−0.2253*	−0.3270***	−0.3407**	−0.3027*	−0.3833*
	(0.0132)	(0.0897)	(0.0972)	(0.0915)	(0.1268)	(0.1352)	(0.1650)
Goodness of fit	0.70	0.26	0.27	0.33	0.37	0.37	0.40

The dependent variable is the systemic contagion loss (see Section 4.1). The independent variables are described in Table 1. The FE-model is estimated with the least-squares dummy variable estimator. All other models are estimated with the DV quantile estimator given in Eq. (4) for the 0.25, 0.5, 0.75, 0.9, 0.95 and the 0.99 quantile. For the FE-model, we use the within R^2. For the quantile regressions, we calculate the goodness of fit measure suggested by Koenker and Machado (1999) and defined in Eq. (14).
***$P < 0.001$.
**$P < 0.01$.
*$P < 0.05$.
Source: OeNB, own calculations.

TABLE 5 Quantile-Independent Dummies (Restricted) Model

	τ : 0.25	τ : 0.5	τ : 0.75	τ : 0.9	τ : 0.95	τ : 0.99
Total assets	0.7261***	0.7547***	0.8069***	0.8444***	0.8794***	1.0743***
	(0.1155)	(0.1249)	(0.1338)	(0.1544)	(0.1664)	(0.1589)
Private sector deposits	−0.7704***	−0.7404***	−0.8285***	−0.8729***	−0.8926***	−0.9873***
	(0.1622)	(0.1399)	(0.1495)	(0.1708)	(0.1842)	(0.2099)
Private sector loans	0.0780	0.0163	0.0540	0.0673	0.0501	0.0225
	(0.0904)	(0.0838)	(0.0848)	(0.0856)	(0.0941)	(0.1843)
Face value of derivatives	−0.0051	−0.0054	−0.0063	−0.0065	−0.0069	−0.0075*
	(0.0040)	(0.0037)	(0.0038)	(0.0039)	(0.0036)	(0.0034)
Cross border deposits	−0.5144*	−0.4882*	−0.4904*	−0.4338	−0.3869	−0.0895
	(0.2186)	(0.2156)	(0.2254)	(0.2226)	(0.2116)	(0.2117)
Cross border loans	−0.1216	−0.1321	−0.1097	−0.1202	−0.1311	−0.3391*
	(0.0932)	(0.1135)	(0.1091)	(0.1126)	(0.1182)	(0.1400)

Bank deposits	0.0115	0.1113	0.0895	0.0665	0.0736	0.0105
	(0.1009)	(0.1006)	(0.1048)	(0.1272)	(0.1445)	(0.1795)
Bank loans	0.0720	0.0152	0.0584	0.0702	0.0637	−0.0127
	(0.0987)	(0.0824)	(0.0917)	(0.0987)	(0.1086)	(0.1931)
Securitized debt	−0.3066*	−0.2444*	−0.3031**	−0.3187*	−0.3276*	−0.2756
	(0.1437)	(0.1173)	(0.1137)	(0.1279)	(0.1369)	(0.1647)
Goodness of fit	0.22	0.15	0.32	0.61	0.76	0.92

The dependent variable is the systemic contagion loss (see Section 4.1). The independent variables are described in Table 1. All models are estimated with the QID quantile estimator given in Eq. (7) for the 0.25, 0.5, 0.75, 0.9, 0.95 and the 0.99 quantile. We calculate the goodness of fit measure as defined in Eq. (16).
***P < 0.001.
**P < 0.01.
*P < 0.05.

cannot be discarded as outliers. Quantile regression performs better at judging both the sign and the significance of these effects. Those variables that are significant with a negative under quantile regression are variables that indeed direct losses away from the financial system under consideration, such as cross-border deposits. We conclude that quantile regression is the better-suited method to analyze financial contagion effects than least-squares regression.

4.3 Discussion and Policy Implications

One of the main benefits of this analysis is that it allows a quantitative assessment of the current regulatory practice for assigning SII risk scores. This process is defined in Article 131(3) of Directive 2013/36/EU (CRD) for domestic systemically important institutions (OSII). It works by computing a weighted sum of scores of individual indicators, which are averaged over the sum of the values of that indicator in the same country:

$$\text{OSII} - \text{Score}_i = 10,000 * \sum_{ind. \in \text{OSII-Indicators}} W^{Ind.} \frac{Ind._i}{\sum_{j=1}^n Ind._j} \qquad (21)$$

This normalization is meant to allow for comparing OSII-Scores across countries. The indicators are grouped into four categories and can be seen together with the respective weights in Table 6.

Comparing these scores to the results in Table 4, the first thing that we notice is that, although the regulatory score has only positive weights, the coefficients in all the models for different quantiles and fixed effects have negative weights. We also see that the Total assets line has a far higher coefficient than its weight in the OSII score, and this effect is exacerbated when one moves to higher quantiles of the loss distribution. This hints at the fact that interconnectedness and size are more strongly interrelated than the debate about whether banks are "too big" or "too interconnected" to fail (see Section 1) suggests.

One interesting question is to what extent the overemphasis on components other than size distorts the explanatory power of the OSII indicator for systemic contagion effects. For this purpose, we reconstructed the OSII-score in Eq. (21) for the available data and performed the same regressions using this score. Table 7 reports the results of these regressions. As can be seen from Table 8, the quantile independence hypothesis is rejected for all quantiles, so we focus our analysis on the unrestricted model. We observe that the value of the OSII coefficient is barely significant, and mostly for the highest quantiles. We observe a far lower explanatory power from the model induced by the OSII weights as compared to the models in Table 4. Both findings suggest that the weighting of the OSII scores could be improved by moving closer to the coefficients in Table 4. In particular, our analysis suggests that size, as measured by Total Assets, should be given a higher weight. We also note the negative coefficients of some of the variables, which raises the question whether these coefficients should be kept in the indicator set at all.

TABLE 6 Scoring Process

Criterion	Indicators	Weight (%)
Size	Total assets	25
Importance	Value of domestic payment transactions	8.33
	Private sector deposits from depositors in the EU	8.33
	Private sector loans to recipients in the EU	8.33
Complexity/cross-border activity	Value of OTC derivatives (notional)	8.33
	Cross-jurisdictional liabilities	8.33
	Cross-jurisdictional claims	8.33
Interconnectedness	Intra financial system liabilities	8.33
	Intra financial system assets	8.33
	Debt securities outstanding	8.33

Source: EBA (2014). On the criteria to determine the conditions of application of Article 131(3) of Directive 2013/36/EU (CRD) in relation to the assessment of other systemically important institutions (O-SIIs). EBA Guideline, European Banking Authority.

Looking further at the results of the tests for quantile independence, we see that the assumption of constant intercepts across quantiles generally is rejected, and the consistency of the restricted estimator is rejected for all quantiles except the lowest one, $\tau = 0.25$. The individual-specific intercepts describe the influence of unobserved time-constant effects. In the context of our analysis, we argue that these effects capture at least some of the contribution of the network effects that cannot be explained by the OSII indicators. These indicators look only at node-specific characteristics, without accounting for the structure of the interbank network. It would be surprising if this contribution were constant across quantiles. The importance of network effects would be expected to increase with higher losses, because as the size of the cascade grows more second-round and higher-order contagion effects are observed. We cannot show the values of the individual-specific effects for confidentiality reasons, but we can report that their contribution increases as one moves to higher quantiles, confirming this reasoning. Therefore, the rejection of the quantile-independence hypothesis highlights the particular importance of network effects.

All unrestricted models are estimated with the DV quantile estimator given in Eq. (4) for the 0.25, 0.5, 0.75, 0.9, 0.95 and the 0.99 quantile. All restricted models are estimated with the QID quantile estimator given in Eq. (7) for the 0.25, 0.5, 0.75, 0.9, 0.95 and the 0.99 quantile.

TABLE 7 Contagion Losses vs. OSII Score: Unrestricted vs. Restricted Models

	FE-Model	τ: 0.25	τ: 0.5	τ: 0.75	τ: 0.9	τ: 0.95	τ: 0.99
Unrestricted models							
OSII score	3169.93***	1081.34	2656.78	4596.66	9913.70*	9913.70*	9063.73*
	(297.38)	(1070.35)	(2870.32)	(4580.90)	(4159.86)	(4010.04)	(4437.10)
Goodness of fit	0.01	0.01	0.02	0.02	0.04	0.05	0.06
Restricted models							
OSII Score		1367.11	4859.60	8670.85	13303.28**	17852.00***	28303.68***
		(3901.28)	(4936.98)	(5127.06)	(4397.19)	(4068.11)	(4923.81)
Goodness of fit		0.12	0.03	0.21	0.50	0.67	0.89

***$P < 0.001$.
**$P < 0.01$.
*$P < 0.05$.
Source: OeNB, own calculations.

TABLE 8 Quantile-Independence Hypothesis Test Results for OSII Score

	S Statistic	P-Value
$\tau = 0.25$	491.08	0.00
$\tau = 0.5$	1087.36	0.00
$\tau = 0.75$	932.87	0.00
$\tau = 0.9$	1240.10	0.00
$\tau = 0.95$	980.57	0.00
$\tau = 0.99$	922.15	0.00

Results for the Hausmann-type test in Eq. (12) for the models presented in Table 7.
Source: OeNB, own calculations.

5 Conclusion

In this chapter, we present a new framework for systemic risk analysis combining the strengths of two different approaches to systemic risk analyses. The popularity of the CoVaR method based on quantile regression shows that the focus on the tails of the loss distribution helps to identify the most systemically important banks. CoVaR and other similar methods relying on market-based information, however, are not applicable for the vast majority of banks, which are generally not listed. We combine the idea of focusing on the tails of the loss distribution with a model based on network theory that allows computing losses for all banks in a given system. The resulting systemic risk measure describes the risk of large crises in the financial system being triggered by initially idiosyncratic shocks. Although we are not able to elaborate about individual results for confidentiality reasons, we observe that nonlisted institutions can cause and transmit high contagion losses.

We estimate these contagion losses using panel quantile estimation. We discuss two types of panel quantile estimators, an unrestricted dummy-variable estimator, and a restricted estimator, which forces the individual-specific intercepts to be constant across quantiles. In our analysis, we interpret the intercept as part of the network effects that cannot be explained by the bank-specific regulatory variables alone. Therefore, the rejection of the quantile independence hypothesis can be seen as a confirmation of the importance of network effects. We further compare the results of the quantile regression with a standard fixed-effects regression and find that the latter appears to be distorted by extreme losses, which in our context cannot be discarded as outliers. These distortions lead to highly significant coefficients and to economically less meaningful signs compared to the quantile estimation results. We therefore prefer the results of the quantile estimation for describing systemic risk effects, in line with the approaches in the literature mentioned previously.

We use this framework to perform an assessment of the current approach to regulating systemic risk regulations. In particular, we look at the OSII regulations by EBA (2014) for capital buffers for systemically important institutions, based on the global recommendations by BIS (2012, 2013). We find that the OSII score alone has very weak explanatory power for the contagion losses in the contagion model. This can be explained by comparing the weightings used in the OSII scoring system with the coefficients in the resulting models. We find, in particular, that the size of the bank, as measured by Total Assets, is given a too-low weight in the regulatory score. Giving a lower score to size might be motivated by the desire to focus on banks that are too highly connected rather than banks that are just too large. As our results from a network-based contagion model show, however, the two concepts might be more strongly related than the regulators thought.

Appendix A Anova Tables

In this section, we test whether the coefficients for each contagion channel and tau-specific models are jointly different. The tests include all combinations of tau-specific models (also combinations of more than two.) These following Anova tables are estimated with Koenker (2018).

TABLE A.1 Anova Test Results

Models	ndf	ddf	Tn	P-value
$\tau = 0.25$, $\tau = 0.5$	736	36,070	14087.62	0.00
$\tau = 0.25$, $\tau = 0.75$	736	36,070	36560.74	0.00
$\tau = 0.25$, $\tau = 0.9$	736	36,070	50759.71	0.00
$\tau = 0.25$, $\tau = 0.95$	736	36,070	53154.73	0.00
$\tau = 0.25$, $\tau = 0.99$	736	36,070	119001.65	0.00
$\tau = 0.5$, $\tau = 0.9$	736	36070	17898.26	0.00
$\tau = 0.5$, $\tau = 0.95$	736	36,070	16900.33	0.00
$\tau = 0.5$, $\tau = 0.99$	736	36,070	53313.77	0.00
$\tau = 0.75$, $\tau = 0.9$	736	36,070	12579.44	0.00
$\tau = 0.75$, $\tau = 0.95$	736	36,070	14958.96	0.00
$\tau = 0.75$, $\tau = 0.99$	736	36,070	30577.63	0.00
$\tau = 0.9$, $\tau = 0.95$	736	36,070	1258.42	0.00
$\tau = 0.9$, $\tau = 0.99$	736	36,070	3258.30	0.00
$\tau = 0.95$, $\tau = 0.99$	736	36,070	1555.21	0.00

Models refers to the set of models to be tested. ndf refers to the number of parameters. ddf refers to the degrees of freedom. Tn returns an F-like statistic in the sense that an asymptotically chi-squared statistic is divided by its degrees of freedom and the reported P-value is computed for an F statistic based on the numerator degrees of freedom equal to the rank of the null hypothesis and the denominator degrees of freedom is taken to be the sample size minus the number of parameters of the maintained model.

References

Adrian, T., Brunnermeier, M.K., 2016. CoVaR. American Economic Review 106 (7), 1705–1741.

Allen, F., Gale, D., 2000. Financial contagion. Journal of Political Economy 108 (1), 1–33.

Anand, K., Craig, B., Von Peter, G., 2015. Filling in the blanks: network structure and interbank contagion. Quantitative Finance 15 (4), 625–636.

Anand, K., van Lelyveld, I., Banai, Á., Friedrich, S., Garratt, R., Halaj, G., et al., 2018. The missing links: a global study on uncovering financial network structures from partial data. Journal of Financial Stability 35, 107–119.

Angelini, P., Maresca, G., Russo, D., 1996. Systemic risk in the netting system. Journal of Banking & Finance 20 (5), 853–868.

Barucca, P., Bardoscia, M., Caccioli, F., D'errico, M., Visentin, G., Battiston, S., et al., 2016. Network valuation in financial systems. (SSRN working paper).

BIS, 2012. A framework for dealing with domestic systemically important banks. Basel Committee on Banking Supervision Publication, Basel Committee on Banking Supervision.

BIS, 2013. Global systemically important banks: Updated assessment methodology and the higher loss absorbency requirement. Basel Committee on Banking Supervision Publication, Basel Committee on Banking Supervision.

Brownlees, C.T., Engle, R., 2012. Volatility, correlation and tails for systemic risk measurement. Available at: SSRN, 1611229.

Brownlees, C.T., Engle, R.F., 2015. SRISK: A conditional capital shortfall measure of systemic risk. (Working paper).

Caccioli, F., Farmer, J.D., Foti, N., Rockmore, D., 2015. Overlapping portfolios, contagion, and financial stability. Journal of Economic Dynamics and Control 51, 50–63.

Covas, F.B., Rump, B., Zakrajsek, E., 2014. Stress-testing US bank holding companies: a dynamic panel quantile regression approach. International Journal of Forecasting 30, 691–713.

Diamond, D., Dybvig, P., 1983. Bank runs, deposit insurance, and liquidity. Journal of Political Economy 91 (3), 401–419.

EBA, 2014. On the criteria to determine the conditions of application of Article 131(3) of Directive 2013/36/EU (CRD) in relation to the assessment of other systemically important institutions (O-SIIs). EBA Guideline, European Banking Authority.

Eisenberg, L., Noe, T.H., 2001. Risk in financial systems. Management Science 47 (2), 236–249.

Elsinger, H., Lehar, A., Summer, M., 2006. Risk assessment for banking systems. Management Science 52 (9), 1301–1314.

FED, 2015. Calibrating the GSIB surcharge. Fed Publication, Board of Governors of the Federal Reserve System.

Fernández-Val, I., 2005. Bias correction in panel data models with individual specific parameters.

Fratzscher, M., Rieth, M., 2015. Monetary policy, bank bailouts and the sovereign-bank risk nexus in the euro area. (DIW Discussion Papers, No. 1448).

Freixas, X., Parigi, B., Rochet, J., 2000. Systemic risk, interbank relations, and liquidity provision by the central bank. Journal of Money, Credit and Banking 32 (3(2)), 611–638.

Gai, P., Kapadia, S., 2010. Contagion in financial networks. Proceedings of the Royal Society A: Mathematical, Physical and Engineering Sciences 466 (2120), 2401–2423.

Galvao, A.F., Kato, K., 2016. Smoothed quantile regression for panel data. Journal of Econometrics 193 (1), 92–112.

Glasserman, P., Young, H.P., 2015. Contagion in financial networks (OFR Working Paper)., pp. 15–21.

Haldane, A.G., May, R.M., 2011. Systemic risk in banking ecosystems. Nature 469 (7330), 351.

Kato, K., Galvao, A.F., Montes-Rojas, G.V., 2012. Asymptotics for panel quantile regression models with individual effects. Journal of Econometrics 170, 76–91.

Klomp, J., De Haan, J., 2012. Banking risk and regulation: does one size fit all? Journal of Banking & Finance 36, 3197–3212.

Koenker, R., 2004. Quantile regression for longitudinal data. Journal of Multivariate Analysis 91, 74–89.

Koenker, R., 2005. Quantile regression. Cambridge University Press, Cambridge.

Koenker, R., 2018. Quantreg: Quantile regression (R Package Version 5)., p. 35.

Koenker, R., Bache, S.H., 2014. RQPD: Regression quantiles for panel data. (R Package Version 0.6/r10).

Koenker, R., Basset, G., 1978. Regression quantiles. Econometrica 46 (1), 33–50.

Koenker, R., Bassett, G., 1982. Robust tests for heteroscedasticity based on regression quantiles. Econometrica 50 (1), 43–61.

Koenker, R., Machado, J.A.F., 1999. Goodness of fit and related inference processes for quantile regression. Journal of the American Statistical Association 94 (448), 1296–1310.

Lamarche, C., 2010. Robust penalized quantile regression estimation for panel data. Journal of Econometrics 157, 396–408.

Neyman, J., Scott, E.L., 1948. Consistent estimates based on partially consistent observations. Econometrica: Journal of the Econometric Society 16, 1–32.

Rochet, J., Tirole, J., 1996. Interbank lending and systemic risk. Journal of Money, Credit and Banking 28 (4), 733–762.

Siebenbrunner, C., Sigmund, M., Kerbl, S., 2017. Can bank-specific variables predict contagion effects? Quantitative Finance 17 (12), 1805–1832.

Upper, C., 2011. Simulation methods to assess the danger of contagion in interbank markets. Journal of Financial Stability 7 (3), 111–125.

Wald, A., 1945. Statistical decision functions which minimize the maximum risk. Annals of Mathematics 46 (2), 265–280.

Zou, H., Yuan, M., 2008. Composite quantile regression and the oracle model selection theory. Source: The Annals of Statistics The Annals of Statistics 36 (3), 1108–1126.

Chapter 21

Application of Panel Data Models for Empirical Economic Analysis

Keshab Bhattarai

University of Hull Busines School, Hull, United Kingdom

Chapter Outline

Panel Data Econometrics. https://doi.org/10.1016/B978-0-12-815859-3.00021-4

665

1 Introduction

Many economic issues require cause-effect analyses of cross-sections of individuals, households, or countries over time. The major objective of this section is to illustrate economic issues in which the application of panel data model is helpful in quantifying cause and effect relations among $x_{i,t}$ and $y_{i,t}$ variables with observations on $i = 1$ to N individuals over $t = 1$ to T time periods.

What makes growth rates differ across countries at a particular year and of the same country over time? Are wages and earnings linked to characteristic of workers and other environmental factors over time? Do profits vary systematically by firms and by production periods? Why is share of labor in income declining? How is foreign aid linked to trade and economic growth across countries? Is there any trade-off between unemployment and inflation across OECD economies? Are trade and growth interlinked across emerging economies of South Asia? Has FDI contributed to the economic growth in advanced countries? How is expenditure on food linked to income across regions of the United Kingdom? How is growth influencing the level and space of globalization in the last three decades? Do cognitive skills matter for economic growth? What is the significance of panel unit root tests, panel cointegration tests, panel VAR, and threshold panel models in process inference in these issues? When confronted with these questions, an appropriate econometric method requires interactions of all observations across individuals for each time period under investigation; emphasis lies on decomposing total variation within a group and among various groups. Theoretical and empirical literature about the panel data model is developing very fast.[1] This article reviews 10 applications of panel data model to test causal relationship among economic variables using panel data estimation routines in STATA, Eviews, and PCgive softwares.

---

1. See works by Wallace and Hussain (1969), Balestra and Nerlove (1966), Hausman (1978), Chamberlain (1982), Arulampalam and Booth (1998), Blundell and Smith (1989), Chesher (1984), Hansen (1982), Hausman (1978), Heckman (1979), Im, Pesaran, and Shin (2003), Imbens and Lancaster (1994), Keifer (1988), Kao (1999), Kwaitkowski, Phillips, Schmidt, and Shin (1992), Larsson, Lyhagen, and Lothgren (2001), Levin, Lin, and Chu (2002), Pedroni (1999), Pesaran and Smith (1995) Phillips (1987), McCoskey and Kao (1999), Johansen (1988), Staigler Stock (1997), Lancaster (1979), Lancaster and Chesher (1983), Zellner (1985), Windmeijer (2005). More work about dynamic panel data models and use of instrumental variables in panel data analysis is found in Nickell (1981), Arellano and Bond (1991), Arellano and Bover (1995), Kiviet (1995), Islam (1995), Mankiw, Romer, and Weil (1992), Caselli, Esquivel, and Lefort et al. (1996), Blundell and Bond (1998), Judson and Owen (1999), Hahn and Kuersteiner (2002), Ho (2006), Windmeijer (2005), Roodman (2009), Wooldridge (2010); Hansen (1999), Kleibergen and Paap (2006), Hayakawa(2009), Baltagi et al. (2012), Su and Lu (2013), Kapetanios et al. (2014), Lee (2014); Cornwell and Rupert (1988), Robertson and Symons (1992), Hansen (1999), Bai and Ng (2005). Wooldridge (2005), Kleibergen and Paap (2006), Sentana (2009), Carriero et al. (2009), Semykina and Wooldridge (2013), Koop (2013). Excellent texts include Johnston (1960), Baltagi (1995), Davidson and MacKinnon (2004), Greene (2008), Hsiao (1993), Lancaster (1990), Ruud (2000), Verbeek (2008), Wooldridge (2002).

TABLE 1 Average Labor Share by Decades

Years	$\bar{\beta}$	$\sigma\ (\beta)$	Countries
1950	0.588	0.116	48
1960	0.570	0.1280	87
1970	0.556	0.146	107
1980	0.547	0.137	109
1990	0.548	0.139	127
2000	0.530	0.134	127
2011	0.514	0.137	127

Average share $\beta = \frac{WL}{Y}$; $Y = AK^{\alpha}L^{\beta}$
Data source: Penn World Tables v8; Maddison dataset.

2 Global Empirical Evidence on Declining Labor Share

It is clear that average share of labor is declining for each decade as shown in Table 1. Labor share in income was about 59 percent of GDP in 1950, and it has declined by 9 percentage points to 51.4 percent by 2011. The dispersion in these shares have increased as the standard deviation has increased from 0.116 to 0.137. Maddison and EU KLEMs dataset provide more information.

We construct panel data set for 127 countries for year 1990 to 2011 for labor income share (labshare), consumption share (consshare), capital share (capshare), government consumption share (govconshare), import share (impshare), exports share (expshare), and real trade share (rtrdshare). We estimate the fixed effect and random effect panel data models and results are reported in Table 2. As is clear, the labor share is decreasing as the shares of capital and exports are rising. Increase in private and public consumption, imports have positive and significant impacts. The process of substitution of labor by capital as discussed in Karabarbounis and Neiman (2013) and Picketty and Goldhammer (2014) have increased the capital share, causing reduction in labor share of about 10 percent magnitude.

3 Impacts of Trade and Aid on Growth: Panel Data Analysis

Advanced countries provide foreign aid to developing countries. Some economists think such aid raises investment and creates positive impacts in the recipient economies, and others think that the aid is tied to exports of goods and services from advanced to developing economies, reversing the flows of resources from developing to advanced countries. In this context, we investigate whether aid from the United Kingdom has promoted trade and growth in Asian countries. This hypothesis that growth rates $(gr_{i,t})$ at time t depend on trade

TABLE 2 Static Panel Regression Estimates for the Share of Labour in GDP (1990:1–2014:4)

Dep Variable: Labor Share	Fixed Effect	Random Effect
Consumption share	0.559***	0.548***
Capital share	−0.004***	−0.104***
Gov cons share	0.088***	0.088***
Import share	0.034***	0.033***
Exports share	−0.033***	−0.033***
Real Trade share	0	0
Constant	0.520***	0.520***
Tests	$F(12,270) = 58.21$ (0.000)	Wald: $\chi^2 = 290.7$ (0.000)
Sample	$N = 127$; $NT = 2794$	$N = 127$; $NT = 2794$
Within	0.0986	0.0986
Between	0.0160	0.0160
Overall	0.0218	0.0218

Hausman Test for random effect model $\chi^2 = 24.46$ (0.000)

$(trd_{i,t})$, investment $(Inv_{i,t})$, and foreign aid $(Aid_{i,t})$ is tested using the panel data for Bahrain, Bangladesh, Bhutan, Cambodia, China, India, Indonesia, Iran, Japan, Jordan, Korea, Kuwait, Lebanon, Malaysia, Maldives, Mongolia, Nepal, Oman, Pakistan, Philippines, Qatar, Saudi Arabia, Singapore, Sri Lanka, Thailand, United Arab Emirates, Vietnam, and Yemen from 2003 to 2014.

$$gr_{i,t} = \gamma_0 + \gamma_1 trd_{i,t} + \gamma_2 Inv_{i,t} + \gamma_3 Aid_{i,t} + \varepsilon_{gr,i,t} \tag{1}$$

In theory, investment ratio and foreign aid should contribute positively to the growth rate. Whether imports from the donor country raise or lower growth should depend on the nature of such exports. If exports are used to purchase raw materials or technical knowhow, it should promote growth; it should not have much impact if it is spent on consumption. Gravity model has been used in analysis of trade in many studies:

$$\ln(T_{dr}) = \beta_1 \ln\left(\frac{Y_d Y_r}{Y_W}\right) + \beta_2 \ln\left(\frac{Y_d}{P_d}\right) + \beta_3 \ln\left(\frac{Y_r}{P_r}\right) + \beta_4 \ln(D_{dr})$$
$$+ \beta_5 \ln(REM_d) + \beta_6 \ln(REM_r) + \beta_7 \ln(LAN_{dr}) + \varepsilon_{dr}$$

See results in Table 3.

$$\ln(A_{dr}) = \beta_1 \ln(Y_d) + \beta_1 \ln(Y_r) + \beta_3 \ln(D_{dr}) + \beta_4 \ln\left(\frac{Y_d}{P_d}\right)$$

$$+ \beta_5 \ln\left(\frac{Y_r}{P_r}\right) + \beta_6 \ln(LAN_{dr}) + \beta_7 \ln(MILSR_{dr}) + C + \varepsilon_{dr}$$

$$\ln(T_{dr}) = \ln\Gamma_{dr} + \beta_8 \ln(\max\{1, A_{dr}\}) + \beta_9 \ln(NAD_{dr}) + \varepsilon_{dr}$$

$$REM_r = \frac{1}{\sum_d \left(\frac{\left(\frac{Y_d}{Y_W}\right)}{D_{dr}}\right)}$$

http://www.distancefromto.net/countries.php;   http://www.cepii.fr/CEPII/en/bdd_modele/models.asp

Table 3 illustrates impact on growth of investment, aid-conditioned imports and aid: static panel regression estimates of the UK.

Table 4 contains system Dynamic panel data estimation of aid on trade and growth: Arellano-Bover/Blundell-Bond Estimation.

Econometric estimates in this section generally support the analytical results in the previous section: that an influx of aid can raise or lower the growth rate in the recipient country depending on the size of the aid relative to investment needs, and whether the aid is tied to trade or how much it affects the technical progress in the recipient countries. Multilateral global interaction model is required to assess the impacts of development cooperation. We expand the

TABLE 3 Impact on Growth of Investment, Aid-Conditioned Imports and Aid: Static Panel Regression Estimates of the UK Aid Influx to Asian Countries

Dep Variable: Growth	Fixed Effect	Random Effect
log AID	1.40e-06	2.91e-06
Investment	0.002***	0.001***
Imports (cond.)	−4.02e-09***	−6.49e-09
Constant	−0.01047	0.032***
Tests	$F(3, 173) = 5.92$ (0.000)	Wald: χ^2 (Arellano & Bover, 1995) = 10.8 (0.013)
Sample	$N = 22$; $NT = 198$	$N = 22$; $NT = 198$
Within	0.093	0.066
Between	0.000	0.031
Overall	0.0411	0.010

Hausman test for random effect model χ^2 (Arellano & Bonhomme, 2012) = 8.19 (0.017)

TABLE 4 System Dynamic Panel Data Estimation of Aid on Trade and Growth: Arellano-Bover/Blundell-Bond Estimation

Dep Variable: Growth	Coefficient	Z-value	$P > |z|$
Growth, lag 1	0.019	0.27	0.78
log Aid	−5.84e-07***	−0.17	0.86
Inv ratio	0.002	4.19	0.00
log UK exports	−0.011***	−3.05	0.00
Constant	0.124	2.57	0.010

Wald χ^2 (Arulampalam et al., 2004) = 28.79(0.000).

Sample size $N = 22$; NT= 176

scope of this study covering aid flow from G7 countries separately, and the OECD as whole, for countries in Asia, Africa, Latin America, and Oceania.

Foreign aid might or might not raise growth rates in receiving countries (compare estimates in Tables 5 and 7). In general, it can increase investment, but if the amount of aid is conditional on exports, it will have negative impacts on growth rates. Simulation of the analytical model shows that if TFP grows faster in the recipient countries than the donor countries, they can converge in capital output ratios and investment saving ratios with similar growth patterns over the long term. If the resource flows out of the developing countries in return for aid, it might have harmful effects in growth of developing economies. Econometric estimates show that investment, rather than aid, was a factor contributing to growth. Exports tied to aid are always harmful for growth of recipient countries. British exports to developing economies in Asia have promoted investments and raised growth rates in per capita income, irrespective of the amount of aid. Exports can be promoted by targeted aid (Table 6).

Trade Impacts of Aid for the UK: Do file and panel settings

- Import Excel "C:\AIEFS\tdata\Aidpanel UK 2014.xlsx", Sheet1, first row
- Xtset ID tt, yearly
- Generate aidd1 = Aid+1
- Xtreg exp YYUKYA ypuk dist Aid, re
- Xtreg exp YYUKYA ypuk dist Aid, fe
- Xtdpdsys exp YYUKYA ypuk yp dist aidd1, lags(Arellano & Bond, 1991) twostep artests(Arellano & Bonhomme, 2012)
- Xtreg lexp lyyuka lyp lypuk ldist laidd1, re
- Xtreg lexp lyyuka lyp lypuk ldist laidd1, fe
- Xtabond lexp lyyuka lyp lypuk ldist laidd1, lags(Arellano & Bond, 1991) twostep artests(Arellano & Bonhomme, 2012)

Data sources: exp YYUKYA ypuk yp WBDI; distance from the Google map and Gleditsch (2002); AID from OECD

See FE and RE, Arrelano-Bond, and dynamic paned data model results in Tables 5, 6, and 7, respectively.

TABLE 5 Impact of Aid Static Panel Regression Estimates for Exports on Aid

Dep Variable: Exports	Fixed Effect	Random Effect
YYUKYA	0.00003***	0.00003***
YPUK	23.56*	62.804*
DIST	0	−89.481
AID	33.973	85.967
Constant	−1,744,498*	−2,012,530
Tests	$F(3, 212) = 469$ (0.000)	Wald: χ^2 (Arellano & Bonhomme, 2012) $= 724.5$ (0.000)
Sample	$N = 22$; NT = 237	$N = 22$; NT = 237
Within	0.8691	0.8639
Between	0.8785	0.8834
Overall	0.8199	0.8240

Hausman test for random effect model χ^2 (Arellano & Bonhomme, 2012) $= 11.75$ (0.019)

TABLE 6 System Dynamic Panel Data Estimation of Exports on Aid and Income: Arellano-Bover/Blundell-Bond Estimation

Dep Variable: Exports	Coefficient	Z-value	$P > |z|$
Exp, lag 1	1.005***	4412.5	0.00
YYUKYA	−1.76e-0.6***	−178.5	0.00
YPUK	2.0892***	64.37	0.002
YP	0	0	0.00
DIST	0	4.95	0.00
AID	1.9852	52.22	0.00
Constant	0	0	0

Wald χ^2 (Arellano & Bonhomme, 2012) $= 6.55 + 08(0.000)$.

Sample size $N = 22$; NT = 216

TABLE 7 Dynamic Panel Data Model for Impact on Trade of Income, Trade, and Aid (Elasticity Form): Arellano-Bover/Blundell-Bond Estimation

Dep Variable: Growth	Coefficient	Z-value	$P > \mid z \mid$
log Exp, lag 1	−0.179***	4.63	0.000
log YYUKYA	−1.562***	−1.87	0.061
log YPUK	2.764***	7.97	0.000
log YP	−1.766	2.59	0.000
DIST	1.309	1.04	0.297
log AID	−0.0252	−7.65	0.00
Constant	0	0	0

Wald χ^2 (Arellano & Bonhomme, 2012) = 155168 (0.000).

Sample size $N = 22$; $NT = 216$

4 Unemployment Inflation Tradeoffs Across OECD Countries

We take the quarterly data series about inflation, unemployment rate, and growth rate for OECD economies from 1991:1–2014:4 from the database available on the OECD webpage (https://data.oecd.org/price/inflation-cpi.htm) to investigate trade-offs between inflation and unemployment. Nature of correlations between inflation and unemployment (Phillips curve), between growth and unemployment rate (Okun's curve), and the inflation and growth rate of output (aggregate supply curve) for this period are given in Table 8. Out of 3240 possible pairs of correlations, there is evidence for both positive ($\rho+$)

TABLE 8 Correlations for the Phillips Curve, Aggregate Supply, and Okun's Curves in the OECD (1990:1–2014:4)

	Number of Positive and Negative Correlations		
	N	$\rho+$	$\rho-$
Phillips curve	3240 (1.000)	1705 (0.54)	1535 (0.46)
Okuns curve	3240 (1.000)	2232 (0.68)	1008 (0.32)
Aggregate supply	3240 (1.000)	2129 (0.66)	1111 (0.44)

TABLE 9 Cointegration Test Between Unemployment and Inflation in the OECD (1990:1–2014:4)

	Tau-test	Prob	Zstat	Prob
Unemployment	−8.64	0.00	−197.43	0.00
Inflation	−4.21	0.00	−50.58	0.00

*Mackinnon (1996) P-values; H_0:no cointegration.

TABLE 10 Granger Causality Test Between Unemployment and Inflation in the OECD (1990:1–2014:4)

	F-test	Prob*
Unemployment does not cause inflation	14.49	0.00
Inflation does not cause unemployment	9.22	0.00

N = 2243; H_0: no causality; lags 2.

and negative $(\rho-)$ correlations. Contrary to our expectation, about 54 percent of the correlations were positive for inflation and unemployment. Similarly, about 32 percent correlations were positive between growth and unemployment. This might indicate the lack of unambiguous relationship between these variables, but correlations do not imply any causality.

Further empirical analysis of the relationships among inflation, unemployment, and growth rates requires checking on their stationarity. Growth rate series were stationary for almost all countries, inflation was stationary for most countries, but the unemployment rates were stationary only in the first differences for most countries. Cointegrating relations between inflation and unemployment, however, were significant for all of these countries as shown by the cointegration test in Table 9. Bidirectional Granger causality was found in the inflation and unemployment series as shown by F-test statistics in Table 10. Full results of stationarity and cointegration tests are not reported because of space constraints. It seems statistically acceptable to conduct simple OLS regression analyses between inflation and unemployment rate series among these countries (Table 11).

4.1 Inflation and Unemployment Trade-Offs: Country-Specific Phillips Curves

Country-specific regression in Table 11 are estimates for a simple OLS of inflation on unemployment, $\pi_t = \beta0 + \beta_1 u_t + e_{i,t}$ because our objective is to find

TABLE 11 Phillips Curve: Regression of Inflation on Unemployment in the OECD Countries, 1990–2014 (Quarterly Series)

	Coefficients	t-prob	R^2	F-prob	Constant	t-prob
Australia	-0.385	0.015	0.086	0.015	4.940	0.000
Austria	-0.166	0.239	0.020	0.024	2.690	0.000
Belgium	-0.879	0.000	0.254	0.000	8.840	0.000
Brazil	0.160	0.155	0.030	0.155	4.760	0.000
Canada	-0.533	0.000	0.171	0.000	5.787	0.000
Chile	-0.347	0.038	0.063	0.000	6.205	0.000
Czech Republic	-0.319	0.073	0.051	0.073	4.710	0.000
Denmark	-0.151	0.035	0.065	0.035	2.850	0.000
Estonia	-0.292	0.003	0.139	0.003	6.797	0.000
Euro area (Hansen, 1999)	-0.296	0.003	0.213	0.003	4.745	0.000
European Union (Johansen, 1988)	-0.338	0.003	0.205	0.003	5.218	0.000
Finland	-0.391	0.001	0.153	0.001	5.090	0.000
France	-0.587	0.000	0.307	0.000	6.845	0.000
Germany	-0.031	0.501	0.006	0.501	1.721	0.000
Greece	-0.207	0.000	0.557	0.000	5.532	0.000
Hungary	-0.555	0.002	0.147	0.002	9.898	0.000
Iceland	0.255	0.356	0.019	0.356	4.350	0.000
Ireland	-0.400	0.000	0.419	0.000	5.513	0.000
Israel	-0.098	0.566	0.005	0.566	3.180	0.025

Italy	−0.136	0.006	0.104	0.007	3.317	0.000
Japan	−1.475	0.000	0.575	0.000	6.666	0.000
Korea	0.351	0.035	0.065	0.035	1.630	0.017
Luxembourg	−0.374	0.017	0.062	0.168	3.990	0.006
Mexico	−2.236	0.000	0.306	0.000	14.920	0.000
Netherlands	−0.282	0.000	0.175	0.000	3.218	0.000
New Zealand	−0.461	0.000	0.230	0.000	4.770	0.000
Norway	−0.389	0.157	0.034	0.157	3.299	0.000
Poland	−0.501	0.005	0.940	0.005	64.700	0.003
Portugal	−0.183	0.000	0.244	0.000	3.830	0.000
Russia	8.369	0.000	0.625	0.000	−47.158	0.000
Slovak Republic	0.632	0.000	0.253	0.000	−4.588	0.027
Slovenia	−0.687	0.001	0.158	0.001	8.731	0.000
Spain	−0.133	0.000	0.351	0.000	4.576	0.000
Sweden	−0.611	0.000	0.346	0.000	5.602	0.000
United Kingdom	0.535	0.000	0.386	0.000	−1.094	0.005
United States	−0.284	0.000	0.194	0.000	4.059	0.000

trade-offs between these two variables. We use Doornik and Hendry (1996) routines in PcGive to estimate slope coefficients reported in Table 11. As results show, Phillips curve relations seem to be significant for 28 of 37 countries (including averages for the Euro area and the European Union) in this table. Demand for labor is derived from the demand for output. When an economy grows quickly, demand for labor leads to lower rates of unemployment. In contrast, during recessionary periods, many workers are ready to work but do not find jobs. The main structural reason for an excess supply of labor is the rigidity in the nominal wage rates in spite of falling prices. When workers demand high wages, cost-conscious employers cannot afford to hire them and so many workers are likely to remain unemployed. When firms put a higher mark-up (over the wage rate) on the prices of goods and services they sell, workers are likely to demand higher wages that they apply to the higher prices of commodities to maintain their real wage rates. Such behavior creates imperfections in the labor market that often sets a process of wage-price spiral and disequilibrium in the labor market, which manifests itself in higher unemployment rates. The Keynesian remedy of creating additional demand by expansionary fiscal or monetary policy, however, can push the aggregate demand beyond the productive capacity of the economy. This causes both inflation and an upward movement in the Phillips curve, eroding the trade-offs even further and shifting this curve toward the right. Analysis of Phillips curve effects should be complemented by analysis of the tax-benefit system, technological progress and efficiency of the job market in matching employees and employers. The explanatory power of this model is quite weak, as shown by low value of R-square despite significant F-statistic.

4.2 Panel Data Model for Inflation and Unemployment Trade-Offs

Although the evidence is mixed for individual economies, there appears to be trade-offs between unemployment and inflation in the panel of these OECD countries as shown by the random- and fixed-effect models in Table 12; Hausman test is in favor of random-effect model. GMM estimation for the dynamic panel accounts of unobserved heterogeneity among countries and estimates are given in Table 13. Both of these panel estimates were from panel model routines in STATA for a panel regression of inflation on unemployment of the form $\pi_{i,t} = \beta_{i,0} + \beta_1 u_{i,t-1} + \gamma_t + e_{i,t}$ with $\beta_{i,0}$ as individual-specific effects and γ_t as the time-specific effects.

The slopes of the Phillips curves are significant in all panel data models and have expected negative signs, but the GMM coefficients are smaller than those in random- or fixed-effects models because these are corrected for unobserved heterogeneity. Therefore, there are trade-offs between inflation and unemployment when one regresses inflation on unemployment rates.

We now regress inflation on growth rates for an idea about underlying aggregate supply functions implied in the data, and regress unemployment

TABLE 12 Static Panel Regression Estimates for the OECD Countries (1990:1–2014:4)

Dep Variable: Inflation	Fixed Effect	Random Effect
Unemployment rate	−0.163***	−0.140***
Constant	4.088***	3.888***
Tests	$F(1, 2270) = 99.49$ (0.000)	Wald: χ^2 (Arellano & Bonhomme, 2012) $= 71.7$ (0.000)
Sample	$N = 38$; NT$= 2309$	$N = 38$; NT$= 2309$
Within	0.0408	0.0408
Between	0.1344	0.1344
Overall	0.0059	0.0059

Hausman Test for random effect model χ^2 (Arellano & Bonhomme, 2012) $= 24.46$ (0.000)

TABLE 13 Dynamic GMM Panel Regression of the Phillips Curve: Arellano-Bover/Blundell-Bond Estimation

Dep Variable: Inflation	Coefficient	Z-value	$P > |z|$
Inflation (−1)	0.8925***	132.73	0.00
Unemployment rate	−0.0431	−3.08	0.002
Constant	0.5934***	4.95	0.00

Wald χ^2 (Arellano & Bonhomme, 2012) $= 21156.27$ (0.000).

Sample size $N = 38$; NT$= 2,221$.

on growth rates for estimation of Okun coefficients. Phillips curve, aggregate supply, and Okun's curves are used in stabilization model and loss function minimizing inflation choice models.

4.3 Regressions of Inflation on Growth Rates: Country Specific Supply Functions

Thinness of the trade-off between unemployment and inflation results prompt us to estimate aggregate supply functions for these economies in the form of

$\pi_t = \beta 0 + \beta_1 g_t + e_t$ where growth rate (g_t) is regressed to inflation (π_t). This is a short-run aggregate supply function. The slopes of coefficients were significant in only six of 37 countries as shown in Table 14. This also indicates the weakness of demand-oriented policies to create growth and employment. The aggregate supply function does not work well with rigidity in prices and wages in the short run. Expansionary monetary or fiscal policies might be able to raise aggregate demand but might not be significant in reducing unemployment rates. Such effects occur because prices and wages adjust at slower rates than the output or employment after an expansionary program (Bailey, 1956; Aghevli, 1977; Phelps & Taylor, 1977; Ball, Mankiw, & Romer, 1988; Dixon, 1988; Ball & Romer, 1990; Nickell, 1998; Barro, 1995; Ball, 1999). Then, as argued in the classical and new classical theories of employment, perfect flexibility of wages and prices means an expansionary policy is more likely to raise the price level than reduce unemployment. Equilibrium unemployment rates are less affected by a stimulus of demand because of the neutrality of money; it requires supply-side reforms (Yellen, 1984; Manning, 1995; Layard & Nickell, 1990; Nickell & Quintini, 2003; Roed & Zhang, 2003).

4.4 Regressions of Unemployment on Growth Rates: Estimation of Okun's Curves

How much less growth occurs because of more unemployment? This is an issue addressed by the Okun's curve. We estimate and test this proposition using a simple function, $u_t = \beta 0 + \beta_1 g_t + e_t$. In Okun's original estimate for the US economy, a 3 percent reduction in unemployment reduced growth rate by 1 percent. We use our data to estimate this relationship and find that the coefficients of Okun's curve for growth on unemployment had expected negative signs and was significant only in 13 countries. These results are given in Table 15.

4.5 Panel VAR Model of Inflation and Unemployment Trade-Offs in OECD Countries

Variables in a VAR model are determined simultaneously and rely more on historic patterns of data to establish relations between unemployment and inflation than economic theories. VAR models are becoming popular because of big controversies about theories regarding unemployment and inflation, and violation of exogeneity assumption is contained in the single equation models estimated previously. A simple VAR model with two lags on inflation $(\pi_{i,t})$ and unemployment $(u_{i,t})$ shows persistence of inflation and unemployment rates among the OECD economies as shown in Table 16 estimated with VAR routines in Eviews. Here also, the trade-offs between inflation and unemployment are thin, as shown by the impulse responses to inflation and unemployment shocks as shown in Fig. 1.

TABLE 14 Supply Curve: Regression of Inflation on Growth Rates in the OECD Countries, 1990–2014 (Quarterly Series)

	Coefficients	t-prob	R²	F-prob	Constant	t-prob
Australia	−0.010	0.886	0.000	0.887	2.767	0.000
Austria	−0.252	0.241	0.021	0.241	2.108	0.000
Belgium	−0.041	0.748	0.001	0.784	1.977	0.000
Brazil	−0.768	0.173	0.028	0.173	6.571	0.000
Canada	−0.092	0.313	0.015	0.313	2.004	0.000
Chile	−0.901	0.029	0.070	0.029	3.877	0.000
Czech Republic	−0.369	0.152	0.031	0.152	3.238	0.000
Denmark	−0.091	0.393	0.011	0.393	2.037	0.000
Estonia	−0.020	0.218	0.023	0.218	4.297	0.000
Euro area (Hansen, 1999)	−0.090	0.580	0.005	0.580	1.936	0.000
European Union (Johansen, 1988)	0.114	0.585	0.005	0.585	2.470	0.000
Finland	−0.126	0.268	0.019	0.269	1.792	0.000
France	−0.145	0.420	0.010	0.420	1.550	0.000
Germany	−0.022	0.819	0.000	0.820	1.478	0.000
Greece	0.037	0.793	0.001	0.793	2.721	0.000
Hungary	0.567	0.217	0.023	0.217	5.666	0.000
Iceland	−0.276	0.056	0.054	0.057	5.396	0.000
Ireland	0.207	0.303	0.016	0.300	2.676	0.000

Continued

TABLE 14 Supply Curve: Regression of Inflation on Growth Rates in the OECD Countries, 1990–2014 (Quarterly Series)—cont'd

	Coefficients	t-prob	R^2	F-prob	Constant	t-prob
Israel	−0.304	0.300	0.016	0.300	2.676	0.000
Italy	−0.182	0.193	0.025	0.197	2.077	0.000
Japan	−0.311	0.006	0.108	0.006	0.039	0.784
Korea	−0.568	0.000	0.268	0.000	3.597	0.000
Luxembourg	−0.095	0.164	0.029	0.164	2.206	0.000
Mexico	−0.152	0.775	0.001	0.775	6.221	0.000
Netherlands	−0.327	0.028	0.070	0.029	2.183	0.000
New Zealand	−0.543	0.009	0.099	0.009	2.576	0.000
Norway	−0.185	0.114	0.037	0.114	2.084	0.000
Poland	−0.481	0.387	0.011	0.387	4.289	0.000
Portugal	−0.107	0.608	0.004	0.608	2.299	0.000
Russia	3.589	0.021	0.076	0.021	13.704	0.000
Slovak Republic	−0.010	0.617	0.003	0.672	4.912	0.000
Slovenia	0.470	0.093	0.042	0.093	3.931	0.000
Spain	0.584	0.013	0.090	0.013	2.221	0.000
Sweden	−0.260	0.095	0.042	0.093	1.312	0.000
United Kingdom	−0.771	0.000	0.239	0.000	2.501	0.000
United States	0.058	0.791	0.001	0.791	2.287	0.000

TABLE 15 Okun's Curve: Regression of Unemployment Rate on Growth Rates in the OECD Countries, 1990–2014 (Quarterly Series)

	Coefficients	t-prob	R²	F-prob	Constant	t-prob
Australia	−0.177	0.000	0.157	0.001	5.794	0.000
Austria	−0.232	0.213	0.023	0.213	4.870	0.000
Belgium	0.137	0.173	0.030	0.173	7.770	0.000
Brazil	4.677	0.005	0.112	0.005	8.782	0.000
Canada	−0.032	0.652	0.003	0.652	7.243	0.000
Chile	0.141	0.641	0.003	0.641	8.202	0.000
Czech Republic	0.234	0.080	0.049	0.080	6.940	0.000
Denmark	0.601	0.739	0.012	0.739	5.508	0.000
Estonia	0.195	0.336	0.016	0.336	9.899	0.000
Euro area (Hansen, 1999)	−0.175	0.607	0.007	0.607	9.705	0.000
European Union (Johansen, 1988)	0.064	0.872	0.000	0.872	9.058	0.000
Finland	0.300	0.006	0.106	0.007	8.422	0.000
France	0.193	0.355	0.019	0.355	8.911	0.000
Germany	0.142	0.579	0.005	0.579	8.045	0.000
Greece	−1.261	0.102	0.096	0.010	13.677	0.000
Hungary	−0.849	0.000	0.169	0.001	8.436	0.000
Iceland	−0.161	0.115	0.053	0.114	4.708	0.000
Ireland	−0.459	0.064	0.051	0.064	8.307	0.000

Continued

TABLE 15 Okun's Curve: Regression of Unemployment Rate on Growth Rates in the OECD Countries, 1990–2014 (Quarterly Series)—cont'd

	Coefficients	t-prob	R^2	F-prob	Constant	t-prob
Israel	−0.062	0.769	0.001	0.769	8.077	0.000
Italy	0.133	0.694	0.002	0.694	9.188	0.000
Japan	0.108	0.068	0.049	0.069	4.505	0.000
Japan	0.165	0.091	0.042	0.091	3.750	0.000
Korea	−0.113	0.216	0.051	0.216	5.099	0.000
Luxembourg	0.011	0.084	0.000	0.933	3.921	0.000
Mexico	−0.080	0.723	0.002	0.723	4.143	0.000
Netherlands	0.044	0.842	0.000	0.842	5.502	0.000
New Zealand	0.066	0.296	0.012	0.296	3.407	0.000
Norway	0.017	0.948	0.002	0.947	10.799	0.000
Poland	−1.855	0.000	0.164	0.001	8.855	0.000
Portugal	0.545	0.002	0.143	0.002	6.969	0.000
Russia	0.067	0.722	0.002	0.722	14.828	0.000
Slovak Republic	−0.082	0.093	0.042	0.093	3.931	0.000
Slovenia	−5.087	0.000	0.332	0.000	17.612	0.000
Spain	0.132	0.422	0.012	0.422	6.924	0.000
Sweden	−0.465	0.043	0.065	0.043	6.310	0.000
United Kingdom	−0.522	0.118	0.037	0.119	6.422	0.000
United States						

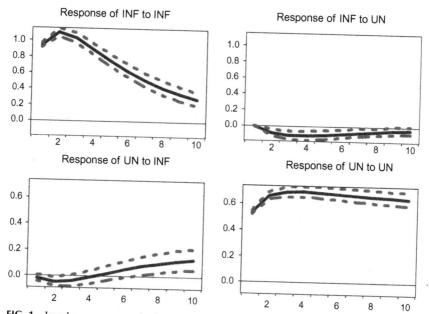

FIG. 1 Impulse responses to shocks.

$$\pi_{i,t} = \beta_{1,0} + \beta_{1,1}\pi_{i,t-1} + \beta_{1,2}\pi_{i,t-2} + \beta_{1,3}u_{i,t-1} + \beta_{1,4}u_{i,t-1} + e_{i,t} \qquad (2)$$

$$u_{i,t} = \beta_{2,0} + \beta_{2,1}\pi_{i,t-1} + \beta_{2,2}\pi_{i,t-2} + \beta_{2,3}u_{i,t-1} + \beta_{2,4}u_{i,t-1} + e_{i,t} \qquad (3)$$

The inflation targeting policies adopted by most of the OECD countries have reduced changes in inflation in recent years, but there are still wide variations in unemployment rates. Enough statistical evidence exists for the persistence hypothesis, either in line with the theory of frictional unemployment, insider-outsider hypothesis, efficiency wage theory, job mismatch, or lottery theory of unemployment, or the structural theory of so-called hysteresis and Eurscelosis hypothesis. The estimates from the vector autoregressive model of order two are enough to prove this persistence in unemployment rates among these countries as presented in Table 16. The problem, however, is that it cannot explain the reason for unemployment in the first place because the current unemployment rate depends only on past values. Initial starting values, or historical accidents are important for such models. Nevertheless when existing theories are unable to explain unemployment rates or inflation rates, it is common for a researcher to turn to time-series models to predict the likely effects of supply or demand shocks in unemployment rates and inflation, tracing the marginal and cumulative impacts of shocks over years as evidenced from the impulse response diagrams in Sims' (1981) spirit of "let the data speak for themselves" (see also Holly & Weale, 2000). Even here, however, the data generating processes can be very different among countries, giving different values

TABLE 16 Phillips Curve: Regression of Inflation on Unemployment in the OECD Countries, 1990–2014 (Quarterly Series)

	Inflation Equation		Unemployment Equation	
	Coefficients	t-prob	Coefficients	t-prob
Inflation (−1)	0.146	18.93	0.170	10.99
Inflation (−2)	0.135	6.168	−0.045	−2.94
Unemployment (−1)	−0.139	−4.704	1.254	60.28
Unemployment (−2)	0.164	5.463	−0.335	−15.93
Constant	0.973	9.280	0.313	4.25
Tests				
R²	0.273		0.898	
F-statistic	198.7		4633.2	
Log-Likelihood	−4500		−3748	
AIC	4.250		3.528	
Swarz SC	4.24		3.54	

of coefficients. Then even unit shocks of same size generate significantly different cumulative effects on unemployment rate and inflation.

5 Determinants of Trade and Growth in South Asia

Time series on economic growth rates are available from international comparison projects such as the Summers-Heston Penn world tables, Asian Development Bank, and World Development Indicators of the World Bank. Correlations and panel data regression estimates mostly support the theoretical simulations presented elsewhere. See correlations in Table 17.

Consider a dynamic panel data model of the form where growth rate of output of country i at time t, $y_{i,t}$ is explained by its lagged values and a set of exogenous explanatory variables $x_{i,t}$. Here α_i is individual-specific effects, and λ_t represents the time-specific effects.

$$y_{i,t} = \gamma y_{i,t-1} + \alpha_i + \beta_i x_{i,t} + \lambda_t + e_{i,t} \quad \gamma < 1 \tag{4}$$

A generalized method of moments (GMM) as proposed by Hansen (1982) for a panel data model generates the unbiased estimate of γ and α_i solving endogeneity and bias in estimation because of the presence of correlation between the lagged values of dependent variables $y_{i,t-1}$ and errors terms $e_{i,t}$. Right

TABLE 17 Pairwise Correlation in Growth Rates in SAARC Countries, 1980–2014

	gr_IND	gr_NPL	gr_LKA	gr_BGL	gr_PAK	gr_MLD	gr_BTN
gr-IND	1.0000						
gr-NPL	0.0516	1.0000					
gr-LKA	0.2917	0.4385	1.0000				
gr-BGL	0.4001	0.4109	0.4749	1.0000			
gr-PAK	0.3725	0.0593	0.3236	0.4513	1.0000		
gr-MLD	0.0281	−0.1574	0.0210	0.0991	0.0980	1.0000	
gr-BTN	−0.0004	−0.1949	−0.0109	−0.126	0.0291	−0.1711	1.0000

instrument for lagged $y_{i,t-1}$ by $y_{i,t-2}$ solves this inconsistency and generates unbiased estimator (ignoring $x_{i,t}$ and λ_t):

$$\hat{\gamma}_{IV} = \frac{\sum\limits_{t}^{T}\sum\limits_{i}^{N} y_{i,t-2}\left(y_{i,t-1} - \bar{y}_{i,t-2}\right)}{\sum\limits_{t}^{T}\sum\limits_{i}^{N} y_{i,t-2}\left(y_{i,t-1} - y_{i,t-2}\right)} \tag{5}$$

where $y_{i,t-2}$ is used as instrument of $(y_{i,t-1} - y_{i,t-2})$.

GMM method includes the most efficient instrument, Z_i:

$$\gamma_{GMM} = \left(\left(\sum_{i=1}^{N}\Delta y_{i,t}Z_i\right) W_N \left(\sum_{i=1}^{N}Z_i'\Delta y_{i,t}\right)\right)^{-1} \times$$
$$\left(\left(\sum_{i=1}^{N}\Delta y_{i,t}Z_i\right) W_N \left(\sum_{i=1}^{N}Z_i'\Delta y_{i,t}\right)\right) \tag{6}$$

Arellano and Bond (1991), Windmeijer (2000), Blundell and Smith (1989), Verbeek (2004), and Wooldridge (2002), among others, have more extensive analyses of the GMM estimation. The essence of the GMM estimation remains in finding a weighting matrix that can guarantee the most efficient estimator. This should be inversely proportional to transformed covariance matrix.

$$W_N^{opt} = \left(\left(\frac{1}{N}\right)\sum_{i=1}^{N}Z_i'\Delta e_{i,t}\Delta e'_{i,t}Z_i\right)^{-1} \tag{7}$$

TABLE 18 GDP on Capital and Labor in SAARC Countries, 1980–2014 (Double Log)

Dep Variable: ln(Y)	Fixed Effect	Random Effect
lnk	0.614***	0.614***
lnpop	0.332***	0.332***
ltfp	1.000***	0
Constant	0.000	0.000
Tests	$F(3, 235) =$ (0.000)	Wald: χ^2 (Arellano & Bonhomme, 2012) = 4621 (0.000)
Sample	$N = 7$; $T = 35$, $NT = 245$	$N = 7$; $T = 35$, $NT = 245$
Within	1.00	0.949
Between	1.00	0.981
Overall	1.00	0.979

Hausman Test for random effect model χ^2 (Arellano & Bonhomme, 2012) = 0.09 (0.957)

The GMM estimator with instruments (levels, first differences, orthogonal deviations, deviations from individual means, combination of first differences and levels) used in PcGive is:

$$\hat{\delta} = \left(\left(\sum_{i=1}^{N} W_i^* Z_i \right) A_N \left(\sum_{i=1}^{N} Z_i' W_i \right) \right)^{-1} \left(\left(\sum_{i=1}^{N} W_i^* Z_i \right) A_N \left(\sum_{i=1}^{N} Z_i' y_i^* \right) \right) \quad (8)$$

where $A_N = \left(\sum_{i=1}^{N} Z_i' H_i Z_i \right)^{-1}$ is the individual-specific weighting matrix.

Doornik and Hendry (2001, chap. 7–10) provide a procedure for how to estimate coefficients using fixed-effect, random-effect, and the GMM methods, including a lagged term of dependent variable among explanatory variables for a dynamic panel data model: $y_{i,t} = \sum_{i=1}^{p} a_k y_{i,t-s} + \beta^t(L) x_{i,t} + \lambda_t + \alpha_i + e_{i,t}$ or, in short, $y_{i,t} = W_i \delta + \iota_i a_i + e_i$. It will be relevant to study the process of convergence among states in India and SAARC countries using this type of growth model in coming years.

Table 18 provides panel regressions for SAARC countries: growth accounting

Table 19 provides panel regressions for SAARC countries: with human capital

Table 20 provides elasticity of output with respect to capital, labor, and TFP among SAARC countries.

TABLE 19 Growth Accounting in SAARC Countries, 1980–2014

Dep Variable: ln(Y)	Fixed Effect	Random Effect
grk	0.614***	0.614***
grpop	0.332***	0.332***
grtfp	1.000***	0
Constant	0.000	0.000
Tests	$F(3, 228) =$ (0.000)	Wald: χ^2 (Arellano & Bonhomme, 2012) = 4621 (0.000)
Sample	$N = 7$; $T = 34$, NT = 245	$N = 7$; $T = 34$, NT = 238
Within	1.00	0.1028
Between	1.00	0.4578
Overall	1.00	0.1074

Hausman Test for random effect model χ^2 (Arellano & Bonhomme, 2012) = 31.5 (0.000)

Estimated coefficients of the dynamic panel data model of growth for South Asian economies confirm the basic results of the simulation. These show the share of capital to be about 60 percent, that of labor and human capital, 25 percent and 15 percent, respectively. There are also country- and time-specific factors at play because growth rates vary significantly across countries and over time. Although these results are consistent, as in Table 20 here, with panel data estimates of growth for other countries, such as presented by Barro and Sala-i-Martin, additional factors such as cognitive skill and openness and joint responsibility of public and private sectors to educate children are examined in other studies (Basu and Bhattarai, 2012).

6   Empirical Literature on FDI and Growth

Among empirical studies about FDI, Wallis (1968) had looked at the increase in inflows of FDI from the United States to the European Union and assessed the importance of FDI in enhancing economic growth. Feldstein and Horioka (1980) had estimated impacts of FDI on saving and investment. Desai, Foley, and Hines (2005) had found an almost one-to-one positive relationship between FDI inflows and saving GDP ratios and investment, and negative relationship between FDI outflows and reduction in investment among OECD countries in the 1990s. Borensztein, De Gregorio, and Lee (1998) found domestic absorptive capacity is needed to make FDI an important factor on economic growth in a study of FDI flows from industrialized countries to 69 developing

TABLE 20 GDP on Capital and Labor in SAARC Countries, 1980–2014 (Double Log)

Dep Variable: ln(Y)	Fixed Effect	Random Effect
lnk	0.603***	0.699***
lnpop	0.248***	0.280***
human capital	0.151***	0.133***
Constant	3.080	3.040
Tests	$F(3, 201) =$ (0.000)	Wald: χ^2 (Arellano & Bonhomme, 2012) = 3849 (0.000)
Sample	$N = 6$; $T = 35$, $NT = 210$	$N = 6$; $T = 35$, $NT = 210$
Within	0.943	0.943
Between	0.989	0.989
Overall	0.986	0.986

Hausman Test for random effect model χ^2 (Arellano & Bonhomme, 2012) = 3.93(0.26)

countries. de Mello (1999) used the panel data model to conclude that growth and FDI nexus are sensitive to country-specific factors and generally supports a positive relationship between FDI and growth in the long run. Balasubramanyam, Salisu, and Sapsford (1996) use a panel data study of 46 developing countries to find support for the Bhagwati hypothesis that the impact of FDI is larger in countries that have adopted export-led growth strategies. Similar findings are reported in country-specific studies such as Ram and Zhang (2002) and Binh and Haughton (2002). Wang and Zhao (2008) look at the technology spillover effect across vertically and horizontally integrated firms and industries in China and find ownership of FDI to be an important variable in assessing externalities of FDI. Many other studies aim to measure the impact of foreign aid on a particular country (Helpman, 2006). Lensink and Morrissey (2006) have shown how the volatility of investments has detrimental impacts on economic growth. A sample of 84 countries from 1987 to 2001 shows that the effects of greenfield investments and merger and acquisition (M&A) have different impacts on actual economic growth. In most cases, greenfield investments raise economic growth, whereas M&A can be beneficial only when the host country has adequate human capital (Wang and Wong, 2009). Taking account of these findings, this section will test the predictions of these theories, particularly the impact of FDI inflows and outflows on investment and growth in 31 OECD countries for 1990 to 2004.

TABLE 21 Common Unit Root Test of Panel Data with Levin, Lin, Chu (LCC) Test

	Test-Statistics	Probability
Growth	−10.60	0.00
Investment ratio	−5.01	0.00
Inflow ratio	−2.11	0.02
Outflow ratio	−2.05	0.02
Cross sections: 30; No of observations: 390		

Inflows and outflows relative to total domestic investment were extremely high in Luxembourg (40 times higher) and noticeably higher in the South Korea (two to three times higher) than in other countries.

All variables used here are stationary on the basis of Levin, Lin and Chu test statistics in Eviews in Table 21.

6.1 Panel Regression Analysis on Impacts of FDI in Growth and Investment

We obtained the data for our analysis from the OECD database on FDI, available from the economic and social database for the United Kingdom (http://www.esds.ac.uk/International/international) for 1990 to 2004. We regress growth rate of output across OECD countries $y_{i,t}$ on FDI inflow or outflow and other explanatory variables, $x_{i,t}$ as:

$$y_{i,t} = \alpha_i + x_{i,t}\beta + e_{i,t} \quad e_{i,t} \sim IID(0, \sigma_e^2) \tag{9}$$

where parameter α_i picks up the fixed effects that differ among individuals but constant over time, β is the vector of coefficients on explanatory variables, $x_{i,t}$. The random term $e_{i,t}$ takes all other effects. The model is estimated by the least square dummy variable method as:

$$\bar{y}_i = \alpha_i + \bar{x}_i\beta + e_i \quad \bar{y}_i = T^{-1}\sum_i y_{i,t} \tag{10}$$

$$y_{i,t} - \bar{y}_i = (x_{i,t} - \bar{x}_i)\beta + (e_{i,t} - e_i) \tag{11}$$

The estimator of parameters from the mean difference then is given by:

$$\beta_{FE} = \left(\sum_t^T \sum_i^N (x_{i,t} - \bar{x}_i)(x_{i,t} - \bar{x}_i)'\right)^{-1} \sum_t^T \sum_i^N (x_{i,t} - \bar{x}_i)(y_{i,t} - \bar{y}_i)' \tag{12}$$

$$\alpha_i = \bar{y}_i - \bar{x}_i\beta_{FE} \tag{13}$$

These estimators are unbiased, consistent, and efficient. Their significance is tested based standard errors obtained from:

$$\text{cov}(\beta_{FE}) = \sigma_e^2 \left(\sum_t^T \sum_i^N (x_{i,t} - \bar{x}_i)(x_{i,t} - \bar{x}_i)' \right)^{-1} \tag{14}$$

$$\sigma_e^2 = \frac{1}{N(T-1)} \sum_t^T \sum_i^N (y_{i,t} - \alpha_i - x_{i,t}\beta_{FE}) \tag{15}$$

The data about GDP and GFCF are taken using the currency for each country and then converting to US dollars using the exchange rate of the national currency to the US dollar. The authors compute growth rates of GDP, investment, and FDI. Variables used in this analysis are stationary (Table 21). We do not find any evidence of reverse causality from growth to investment ratio as indicated by Blomström and Kokko (1996).

Results, presented in Tables 22–24, are estimated using the PcGive and reveal several interesting facts regarding the impact of FDI on growth and investment.

TABLE 22 Growth Rate of Output on Investment Ratio in OECD Countries

	Coefficient	Standard Error	t-value	t-prob
Growth	0.30686	0.130	−2.360	0.019
FDI ratio	0.00049	0.000	4.680	0.000
Tax rate	−0.00042	0.000	−2.010	0.045
Invratio	0.86255	0.202	4.270	0.000
Invratio (−1)	−0.85115	0.182	−4.670	0.000
Constant	0.03319	0.014	2.400	0.017

$R^2 = 0.42, \chi^2 = 399.2 \ [0.000], \ T = 14, \ N - 31.$

TABLE 23 Determinants of FDI Inflows in OECD Countries

	Coefficient	Standard Error	t-value	t-prob
openk	0.047	0.018	2.550	0.011
infract	0.001	0.000	2.440	0.015
Constant	−8.732	3.276	−2.670	0.008

$R^2 = 0.59, \chi^2 = 7.68 \ [0.021], \ T = 14, \ N = 31.$

TABLE 24 Determinants of FDI Outflows in OECD Countries

	Coefficient	Standard Error	t-value	t-prob
openk	0.051	0.021	2.460	0.014
infract	0.001	0.000	2.320	0.021
Constant	−9.366	3.690	−2.540	0.011

$R^2 = 0.57$, $\chi^2 = 7.09$ [0.029], $T = 14$, $N = 31$.

TABLE 25 Contribution of FDI Inflows and Outflows to Domestic Investment in OECD Countries

	Coefficient	Standard Error	t-value	t-prob
Invratio (−1)	0.881728	0.01695	52.00	0.019
ki	0.000476	0.00011	4.170	0.000
Tax rate	−0.000185	0.00009	−2.110	0.045
oflwinvratio	0.000212	0.00007	3.190	0.000
GDP_PPP	−0.00000	0.00000	−2.160	0.000
Constant	0.020043	0.00567	3.540	0.017

$R^2 = 0.89$, $\chi^2 = 1068$ [0.000], $T = 14$, $N = 31$.

First, the ratio of investment to GDP is a significant determinant of growth rates across OECD countries as shown in Table 22, exactly what is expected from the theory of economic growth. Net investment adds to capital accumulation, and more capital associated with labor generates more output. The negative sign in the lagged term shows cyclical pattern of the investment ratio. FDI contributes positively to growth, and higher tax rates cause lower growth rates, as expected. Overall fit of the model is good, with R^2 is 42 percent.

Inflows of FDI in OECD countries relate positively to the openness of the country (openk) and the size of the country (interaction of investment ratio and per capita GDP in PPP) as shown in Table 23. Openness (openk) and size (intract) are also significant determinants of outflows as shown in Table 24.

In Table 25, we show that domestic investment ratio falls with a rise in the tax rate (taxrate) but responds positively to a share of capital in output (ki) and the ratios outflows to investment (oflwinvratio) and are a bit lower for countries

TABLE 26 Contribution of FDI Inflows and Outflows to Growth Rate of Output in OECD Countries

	Coefficient	Standard Error	t-value	t-prob
growth (−1)	0.214	0.110	1.940	0.053
infinnvratio	0.006	0.002	3.760	0.000
infinnvratio (−1)	−0.004	0.001	−4.520	0.000
infinnvratio (−3)	−0.002	0.001	−2.070	0.039
intract	0.000	0.000	−3.170	0.002
intract (−1)	0.000	0.000	3.350	0.001
tax*GDP	0.001	0.000	2.790	0.006
tax*GDP (−1)	−0.001	0.000	−2.890	0.004
invratio	1.558	0.380	4.100	0.000
invratio (−1)	−1.576	0.357	−4.410	0.000
Constant	0.045	0.016	2.750	0.006

$R^2 = 0.49$, $\chi^2 = 233.2$ [0.000], $T = 14$, $N = 31$.

with higher per capita income (GDP PPP). All these findings correspond to the neoclassical theory of capital accumulation and are consistent with the findings of Desai et al. (2005). The panel regression analysis clearly reveals little influence of FDI outflows on aggregate investment ratios and but good influence on growth rates as shown in Table 26.

Foreign investment substitutes for domestic investment a bit, and there is some justification in this empirical analysis for popular sentiments against foreign capital. The contribution of FDI to economic growth is both direct and indirect. Inflows or outflows make the economy more sensitive to foreign capital, so domestic firms have to be more competent, which enhances economic growth. Similarly, the amount of investment and the growth rate are influenced through indirect channels. This is clear from the result in Table 26 where inflows seem to influence growth rates in a similar way as the domestic investment, having both positive and cyclical effects. Country size and investment interaction effect (intract) is positive, but tax GDP interaction term is negative, as expected.

We also tried to disentangle the country- and time-specific effects of FDI on investment and growth rates across OECD countries. When controlled for time-specific and country-specific factors, outflows have negative impacts on domestic investment ratio, but the corresponding impacts of inflows are not very significant. Country-specific and time-specific factors are more dominant in determining the investment ratio or growth rates than inflows or outflows of FDI. Countries with more liberal FDI policies, such as Ireland, South Korea, Slovakia, and Spain, had more positive impacts of FDI on growth rate than in other OECD countries. FDI contributed positively on growth rates from 1994 to 2001 but had either positive or negative effects on growth in other years.

7   Expenditure on Food in the UK

Consider the cross-regional variation of expenditure on food in the United Kingdom. For simplicity, it is assumed that food expenditure depends only on wage and salary income in each region. We can formulate a model relating expenditure on food (F) and income (Y) that takes account of region specific effects. The equations for each region are independent, but contemporaneous correlation exists among the error terms across the regions. We represent the model in terms of a system of stacked regressions that takes into account both individual- and system-specific effects. The SURE or GLS estimator system can be applied to estimate the structural parameters of this model. Their covariance structure can be written in matrix form. This model has been estimated using a pooled-time series and cross-section data set (with the sample size of $T = 14$ and $N = 13$) available from the website of the Office of the National Statistics (food exp UK regional panel.csv: http://www.statistics.gov.uk). The estimated coefficients, by region, are given in the following table.

$$F_{i,t} = \alpha_i + \beta_1 y_{i,t} + e_{i,t} \quad e_{i,t} \sim IID\left(0, \sigma_e^2\right) \quad (16)$$

Readers can see Panel Data Model Food Expenditure in UK in Table 27.

8   House Prices by Regions in UK

Estimating the model by 3SLS (using HousePrice_regional.csv). See Table 28.

9   Panel Regressions of Trade Ratios in the Global Economy

To check further for robustness of the relationship, we run panel regressions covering a sample period of 1971–2006 for 14 categories of countries after controlling for fixed and random effects. These 14 groups, based on the World Bank (2007), include countries with low income, middle income, lower middle income, upper middle income, high income, high income OECD and highly indebted ones. Each country has 36 years of observation from 1971 to 2006. One degree of freedom is lost for each country in the dynamic panel regression. List of countries included in each of these 14 categories is given in Basu and Bhattarai (2012).

TABLE 27 Food Expenditure on Income: Stacking Data for SURE)l

	Coefficient	t-value	t_Prob
Emp_income	0.511	69.4	0.000
Constant	−252.126	−2.18	0.031
NW	−28.2405	−0.178	0.859
YH	−362.599	−2.29	0.023
EM	359.178	2.27	0.025
WM	2034.03	12.8	0.000
EA	1715.26	10.3	0.000
GL	753.455	4.77	0.000
SE	−700.345	−4.36	0.000
SE_R	−326.693	−2.02	0.045
SW	412.537	2.61	0.010
WL	710.626	4.49	0.000
SCT	580.688	3.65	0.000
NI	2374.79	4.66	0.000

$R^2 = 0.99$; N =182; T = 14; Chi^2 = 4815. [0.000] **

Tables 29 and 30 report static panel regressions of export share $\left(\frac{x}{y}\right)$, import share $\left(\frac{m}{y}\right)$ on education share (*Educ*) and growth rate (*g*).[2] Although both models are significant on the basis of F and χ^2 tests, the random effect model is recommended by the Breusch-Pagan LM test (Table 29).[3]

We find clear evidence of positive impacts of education spending ratio (*Educ*) and growth rates (*g*) on ratios of exports $\left(\frac{x}{y}\right)$ and imports $\left(\frac{m}{y}\right)$. Fixed- and random-effect estimates presented in Tables 29 and 30 provide strong empirical evidence for the central hypothesis of this chapter: Countries that spend more on education and grow faster are more open. The Breusch-

---

2. These regression results are robust on the grounds of stationarity and cointegration criteria. We have performed common panel unit root tests and Pedroni's (1999) panel cointegration tests involving $\frac{m}{y}$, $\frac{x}{y}$, *Educ* and *g* and found a long-run relationship. These results are available from the authors upon request.

3. The panel regression results reported here show only long-run relationships among openness, education, and growth. Many factors could contribute to an endogenous long-run relationships among these three variables. In this section, we focus on cognitive skills.

TABLE 28 Determinants of House Price in UK: SURE (3SLS) Estimation

	Coefficient	t-value	t_Prob
Rincome	4.64	45.2	0.000
Pop	1.25	0.55	0.054
MRT_RT	−11.51	−0.022	0.982
M/H_Ratio	−237240	−19.9	0.000
CRNTDP	1.94	5.85	0.000
SVDEP	1.10	3.72	0.000
NE	22845.3	2.04	0.042
NW	8064.9	2.85	0.005
YH	14615.8	2.37	0.018
SW	9939.4	1.50	0.134
EN	−148092	−1.66	0.097
EM	12868.1	1.61	0.108
WM	12404.2	2.20	0.029
EE	16599.7	2.84	0.005
GL	5454.8	2.00	0.046
Constant	101298.1	5.31	0.000

$F(90, 373) = 7.09\ (0.00)$; $N = 480$; Chi^2 (Arellano & Bonhomme, 2012) $= 59.2$. [0.000] **

Pagan LM test suggests that the random-effect model is more appropriate, although there is little difference in the estimates between these two models.

In these panel regressions, there is a potential problem of endogeneity of regressors because of correlation of the unobserved panel-level effects with the lagged dependent variables, which could lead to inconsistency of estimates. Arellano and Bover (1995) and Blundell and Bond (1998) employ a GMM method to remove the inconsistency, which is appropriate for a large panel and fewer periods. Estimations based on the Blundell-Bond (1998) system method are reported in Tables 31 and 32. Both Arellano-Bover and Blundell-Bond estimation methods perform better than the Arellano and Bond (1991) estimator for our sample. A robust and significant dynamic panel relationship holds between the overall trade share and growth. Although education spending ratio has a positive sign as expected, it is not statistically significant. This issue could be investigated further as richer and better data sets become available (Tables 30 and 31).

TABLE 29 Static Panel Regression of Export Ratio on Education Spending Ratio and Growth Rate

Dep Variable: $\frac{x}{y}$	Fixed Effect	Random Effect
Educ	2.707***	2.550***
g	81.056***	80.558***
Constant	8.335***	8.927***
Tests	F(2,488) = 36.44 (0.000)	Wald: χ^2 (Arellano & Bonhomme, 2012) = 71.7 (0.000)
Sample	N =14; T = 36; NT = 504	N = 14; T = 36; NT = 504
Within	0.1299	0.1299
Between	0.006	0.006
Overall	0.0556	0.0556

Breusch-Pagan LM Test for random effect model χ^2 (Arellano & Bonhomme, 2012) = 1545.0 (0.000)

See notes in Table 1 for definitions of variables.

TABLE 30 Static Panel Regression of Import Ratio on Education Spending Ratio and Growth Rate

Dep Variable: $\frac{m}{y}$	Fixed Effect	Random Effect
Educ	2.462***	2.329***
g	72.089***	70.907***
Constant	10.590***	11.110***
Tests	F(2,488) = 35.3 (0.000)	Wald: χ^2 (Arulampalam & Booth, 1998) = 7933.6 (0.000)

Sample size N =14; T=33; NT =462

10 Cognitive Skill and Economic Growth

We explore the causal relation between cognitive skills and the previously identified variables using a cross-section regression of averages of growth rate (g), education ratios (*Educ*), imports $\left(\frac{m}{y}\right)$, and exports shares $\left(\frac{x}{y}\right)$ with cognitive

TABLE 31 Dynamic Panel Regression of Trade Ratio on Education Spending Ratio and Growth Rate: Arellano-Bover/Blundell-Bond Estimation

Dep Variable: $\frac{x+m}{y}$	Coefficient	Z-value	p>|z|
$\frac{x+m}{y}(-1)$	1.119***	33.47	0.00
$\frac{x+m}{y}(-2)$	−0.177	−3.11	0.00
$\frac{x+m}{y}(-3)$	0.035***	0.83	0.41
Educ	0.167	0.70	0.49
g	31.003***	5.40	0.00
Constant	0.554	0.57	0.571

Wald χ^2 (Arulampalam & Booth, 1998) = 11013.6 (0.000).

Sample size $N = 14$; $T = 33$; $NT = 462$

TABLE 32 Dynamic Panel Regression of Import Ratio on Education Spending Ratio and Growth Rate: Arellano-Bover/Blundell-Bond Estimation

Dep Variable: $\frac{m}{y}$	Coefficient	Z-value	$P > \|z\|$
$\frac{m}{y}(-1)$	1.151***	34.33	0.00
$\frac{m}{y}(-2)$	−0.338***	−5.89	0.00
$\frac{m}{y}(-3)$	−0.124***	2.94	0.00
Educ	0.093	0.71	0.48
g	15.226***	5.00	0.00
Constant	1.135**	2.11	0.04

Wald χ^2 (Arulampalam & Booth, 1998) = 7933.6 (0.000)

Sample size $N = 14$; $T = 33$; $NT = 462$

skill as a right-side variable. The effects of cognitive skills on openness and growth are found to be positive and significant at the 5% level as shown in Table 33. The coefficient of cognitive skill on education spending ratio regression is negative but is not statistically significant at the 5% level. When splitting the sample between low cognitive skills and high cognitive skills (using the median as the cut-off point), however, a positive relationship, although not statistically significant, emerges between these two variables for low cognitive-skill countries (Table 33).

TABLE 33 Regression of Growth Rate, Export and Import Shares on Cognitive Skills

	g	Educ	Educ_low	Educ_high	$\frac{x}{y}$	$\frac{m}{y}$
Constant	−18.95	18.62**	3.35	16.88**	−558.0*	−470.8*
Cognitive-skill (Q)	4.50***	−2.76	0.11	−2.41	120.0**	102.0**
R2	0.18	0.10	0.02	0.08	0.20	0.18
F	4.2**	3.4*	0.05	2.86	7.7***	6.9**
DW	2.6	1.75	2.04	1.71	2.70	2.60
N	33	33	41	34	33	33

See notes on Table 1. *Educ_low* and *Educ high* stand for education ratios of low and high cognitive skill countries respectively.

Reverse regressions of cognitive skill on growth or openness measures (not reported here for brevity) are not found to be statistically significant, which suggests that cognitive skill is the driving force in determining the three important macroeconomic variables. Although such static regressions do not necessarily lead us to conclude anything about the causal ordering, it provides enough motivation for our endogenous growth model in which cognitive skill is a driver of the cross-country relationship between openness and growth (Table 33).

In addition to these applications, much literature can be found about the panel limited dependent variable models.

11 Panel Unit Root Test

Estimators are inefficient if the variables in a panel data are nonstationary unless they are cointegrated. How can one ascertain whether variables are stationary or cointegrated? Are the unit root processes the same across sections or different? How is cointegration affected by these cross-sectional characteristics of the unit root? These issues have been investigated extensively in the literature. Although Pesaran (2015) classifies first and second generations of the panel unit as root test models, panel cointegration models also have become popular in recent years. First generation panel unit root test models such as Maddala and Wu (1999), Hadri (2000), Levin et al. (2002, LLC), and Im et al. (2003, IPS) assume that all cross sections in $\Delta y_{i,t} = \alpha_i + \rho y_{i,t-1} + \sum_{k=1}^{n} \phi_i \Delta y_{i,t-1} + \delta_i t + \theta_t + u_{i,t}$ have same panel unit root process with $H_0: \rho < 1$ against $H_A: \rho \geq 1$. The null hypothesis of panel unit root test assumes that Y series are stationary, and alternative hypothesis is that Y series is nonstationary.

Heterogeneity in unit roots: against no unit root, $t_{IPS} =$

$$\frac{\sqrt{N}\left(t - \frac{1}{N}\sum_{k=1}^{n} E[t_{iT}| \rho_i = 0]\right)}{\sqrt{\frac{1}{N}\sum_{k=1}^{n} \mathrm{var}[t_{iT}| \rho_i = 0]}} \Rightarrow N(0,1)$$ Fisher, Phillip-Peron, Fisther test $\Pi =$

$-2\sum_{k=1}^{n} \ln \pi_i$ with χ^2 distribution where π_i is the probability limit of ADF test. Kwaitkowski, Phillips, Schmidt, and Shin (LM test, $KPSS = \sum_{t=1}^{T} \frac{S_t^2}{\hat{\sigma}^2}$ and $LM_2 =$ $\frac{1}{N}\left(\sum_{i=1}^{N}\left(\frac{1}{T^2}\right)\sum_{i=1}^{N}\frac{S_i^2}{\hat{\sigma}^2}\right)$ where $S_t^2 = \sum_{t=1}^{T} e_t$ is the partial sum of errors in a regression of Y on an intercept and time trend. LLC, IPS, PKSS, Hadri, Harris-Tzavalis, Breitung, Fisher tests of unit root are defined in STATA routine for longitudinal data series. Pane unit root test summary in Eviews as presented in this box.

Panel unit root test: Summary
Series: INFINVRATIO
Date: 11/12/17 Time: 06:39
Sample: 1990 2004
Exogenous variables: Individual effects, individual linear trends
User-specified lags: 1
Newey-West automatic bandwidth selection and Bartlett kernel
Balanced observations for each test

Method	Statistic	Prob.**	Cross-section...	Obs
Null: Unit root (assumes common unit root process)				
Levin, Lin & Chu t*	0.13702	0.5545	30	390
Breitung t-stat	0.08598	0.5343	30	360
Null: Unit root (assumes individual unit root process)				
Im, Pesaran and Shin W-stat	0.77237	0.7801	30	390
ADF - Fisher Chi-square	51.2256	0.7829	30	390
PP - Fisher Chi-square	88.8932	0.0091	30	420

** Probabilities for Fisher tests are computed using an asymptotic Chi-square distribution. All other tests assume asymptotic normality.

11.1 Larsson, Fisher, Kao, and Pedroni Tests of Panel Cointegration

Kao (1999), Larsson et al. (2001) and Pedroni (1999) tests are popular for panel cointegration analysis. For this, start with $y_{i,t} = \alpha_i + x_{i,t}\beta + e_{i,t}$ where $e_{i,t} \sim IID\,(0, \sigma_e^2)$. For a residual-based cointegration, formulate $e_{i,t} = \rho e_{i,t-1} + v_{i,t}$. Then estimate $\rho = \frac{\sum_{t=1}^{T}\sum_{n=1}^{N}\hat{e}_{i,t}\hat{e}_{i,t-1}}{\sum_{t=1}^{T}\sum_{n=1}^{N}\hat{e}_{i,t}^2}$ and related t statistics $t_p = \frac{(\hat{\rho}-1)\sqrt{\sum_{t=1}^{T}\sum_{n=1}^{N}\hat{e}_{i,t}^2}}{\frac{1}{NT}\left(\sum_{t=1}^{T}\sum_{n=1}^{N}(\hat{e}_{i,t}^2 - \hat{\rho}\hat{e}_{i,t}^2)\right)}$

Larsen's test is based on Johansen's' maximum likelihood procedure; $\Delta Y_{i,t} = \Pi_i Y_{i,t-1} + \sum_{k=1}^{n}\Gamma_k \Delta y_{i,t-k} + u_{i,t}$ with H_0: $rank\,(\Pi_i) - r_i < r$ for all i from

1 to N and H_A: $rank\,(\Pi_i) = p$ for all i from 1 to N. The standard rank test statistics is defined in terms of average of the trace statistic for each cross section unit and mean and variance of trace statistics.

$$LR = \frac{\sqrt{N}(LR_{NT} - E(Z_k))}{\sqrt{var(Z_t)}} \tag{17}$$

Pedroni test for panel cointegration uses within group and between group t-statistics. Within group tests: Panel v statistic

$$T^2 N^3 Z_{vNT} = \frac{T^2 N^{\frac{3}{2}}}{\sum\limits_{t=1}^{T}\sum\limits_{n=1}^{N} L_{1,1}^{-2}(\hat{e}_{i,t}^2)} \tag{18}$$

Panel ρ statistic

$$T\sqrt{N}Z_\rho NT = \frac{T\sqrt{N}\left(\sum\limits_{t=1}^{T}\sum\limits_{n=1}^{N} L_{1,1}^{-2}(\hat{e}_{i,t}^2)\Delta\hat{e}_{i,t}^2 - \hat{\lambda}_i\right)}{\sum\limits_{t=1}^{T}\sum\limits_{n=1}^{N} L_{1,1}^{-2}(\hat{e}_{i,t}^2)} \tag{19}$$

Panel t statistic

$$Z_{tNT} = \sqrt{\sigma_{NT}^2 \sum\limits_{t=1}^{T}\sum\limits_{n=1}^{N} L_{11}^{-2}(\hat{e}_{i,t-1}^2)}\left(\sum\limits_{t=1}^{T}\sum\limits_{n=1}^{N} L_{1,1}^{-2}(\hat{e}_{i,t}^2)\Delta\hat{e}_{i,t}^2 - \hat{\lambda}_i\right) \tag{20}$$

Panel t statistic (parametric)

$$Z_{tNT} = \sqrt{\sigma_{NT}^2 \sum\limits_{t=1}^{T}\sum\limits_{n=1}^{N} L_{1,1}^{-2}(\hat{e}_{i,t-1}^2)}\left(\sum\limits_{t=1}^{T}\sum\limits_{n=1}^{N} L_{1,1}^{-2}(\hat{e}_{i,t}^2)\Delta\hat{e}_{i,t}^2 - \hat{\lambda}_i\right) \tag{21}$$

Between group tests: Group statistic

$$T\sqrt{N}Z_\rho NT = \frac{T\sqrt{N}\sum\limits_{t=1}^{T}\left(\hat{e}_{i,t}^2\Delta\hat{e}_{i,t}^2 - \hat{\lambda}_i\right)}{\sum\limits_{t=1}^{T}\sum\limits_{n=1}^{N}(\hat{e}_{i,t}^2)} \tag{22}$$

Group t statistic

$$\sqrt{N}Z_{tNT-1} = \sqrt{N}\sum\limits_{n=1}^{N}\sqrt{\sigma_i^2 \sum\limits_{t=1}^{T}\hat{e}_{i,t}^2 \sum\limits_{t=1}^{T}\left(\hat{e}_{i,t}^2\Delta\hat{e}_{i,t}^2 - \hat{\lambda}_i\right)} \tag{23}$$

Group t statistic (parametric)

$$\sqrt{N}Z_{tNT-1} = \sqrt{N}\sum_{n=1}^{N}\sqrt{\sigma_i^2\sum_{t=1}^{T}\hat{e}_t^2\sum_{t=1}^{T}\left(\hat{e}_{i,t}^2\Delta\hat{e}_{i,t}^2 - \hat{\lambda}_i\right)} \tag{24}$$

Fully or dynamic modified OLS (FMOLS/DOLS) are conducted after variables are found to be cointegrated in panel data models.

Pedroni Residual Cointegration Test
Series: INFINVRATIO GROWTH GROWTHREAL INFLOW INVRATIO
    OFLWINVRATIO
Date: 11/12/17   Time: 06:43
Sample: 1990 2004
Included observations: 450
Cross-sections included: 30
Null Hypothesis: No cointegration
Trend assumption: Deterministic intercept and trend
User-specified lag length: 1
Newey-West automatic bandwidth selection and Bartlett kernel

Alternative hypothesis: common AR coefs. (within-dimension)

	Statistic	Prob.	Weighted Statistic	Prob.
Panel v-Statistic	-1.322133	0.9069	-3.981340	1.0000
Panel rho-Statistic	3.977261	1.0000	6.633915	1.0000
Panel PP-Statistic	-10.41060	0.0000	-2.373715	0.0088
Panel ADF-Statistic	-4.576494	0.0000	-1.921041	0.0274

Alternative hypothesis: individual AR coefs. (between-dimension)

	Statistic	Prob.
Group rho-Statistic	7.888745	1.0000
Group PP-Statistic	-7.883788	0.0000
Group ADF-Statistic	-1.314522	0.0943

Here are steps for empirical estimations of Larsen, Kao, Fisher, and Pedroni cointegration tests in Eviews. First, format balanced or unbalanced panel from the data using File/new/workfile/balanced panel options. Then, select the variables and open them as a group. Select group estimation or cointegration. Then select views/panel cointegration option of the Johansen procedure.

11.2 Construction of Panel Data Workfile in Eviews

1. File/New/Workfile
2. Select Balanced panel give start and end dates.
3. Save this panel work file. For data
4. Open data file, e.g. unido panel.csv

5. Select variables and copy them in the new panel workfile.
6. Do panel tests including the panel unit root test, panel cointegration test. Panel Unit Root Test in Eviews,

Panel Cointegration in Eviews

Save data in excel/csv; import in Eviews as foreign data file/Select Basic structure as panel data (have panel id and year id variables in the data file); Quick/Group statistics/Johansen cointegration test; then list variables; select Pedroni (Engle-Granger based) and other specifications, then estimate. Get results as following.

Study the trace and max-eigen value tests.

Unrestricted Cointegration Rank Test (Trace and Maximum Eigenvalue)

Hypothesized No. of CE(s)	Fisher Stat.* (From Trace Test)	Prob.	Fisher Stat.* (From Max-Eigen Test)	Prob.
None	72.00	0.0000	65.75	0.0001
At most 1	27.83	0.4735	22.71	0.7477
At most 2	20.99	0.8256	17.79	0.9314
At most 3	32.79	0.2435	32.79	0.2435

12 Threshold Panel

Regime changes occur in the real world. The threshold panel model developed by Hansen (1997), Caner and Hansen (2004) handles such issues. Basic reason for this is:

$$y_i = \theta'_1 z_i + e_i \quad q_i \leq \gamma$$

$$y_i = \theta'_2 z_i + e_i \quad q_i > \gamma$$

$$y_i = \theta'_1 z_i | (q_i \leq \gamma) + \theta'_2 z_i | (q_i > \gamma) + e_i$$

To find a threshold:

$$x_i = g_i(x_i, \pi) + u_i$$

$$E(u_i / x_i) = 0$$

$$y_i = \theta'_1 g_i | (q_i \leq \gamma) + \theta'_2 g_i | (q_i > \gamma) + v_i$$

$$v_i = \theta'_1 u_i | (q_i \leq \gamma) + \theta'_2 u_i | (q_i > \gamma) + e_i$$

MATLAB Programme data.m THRESH P.m on web: http://www.ssc.wisc.edu/bhansen/.

13 Conclusion

This chapter reviews important applications of panel data models. The process of substitution of labor by capital as discussed in Karabarbounis and Neiman (2013) and Picketty and Goldhammer (2014) have increased the capital share, causing about a 10 percent reduction in the labor share, with impacts of trade and aid on economic growth. Fixed and random effect estimates show that investment rather than aid was a factor contributing to growth. Exports tied to aid are always harmful for growth of recipient countries. Although the evidence is mixed for individual economies, trade-offs exists between unemployment and inflation in the panel of OECD countries as shown by random- and fixed-effect models, with the Hausman test in favor of the random-effect model. A simple VAR model with two lags on inflation ($\pi_{i,t}$) and unemployment ($u_{i,t}$) show persistence of inflation and unemployment rates among the OECD economies. The ratio of investment to GDP is a significant determinant of growth rates across OECD countries, and FDI is found to contribute positively to growth. Higher tax rates have been found to cause lower growth rates, which supports the intuitive belief. Overall fit of this model is good because R^2 is 42 percent. Panel data model estimates of food expenditure and house prices in the United Kingdom are a good fit for the data.

Static panel regressions of export share $\left(\dfrac{x}{y}\right)$, import share $\left(\dfrac{m}{y}\right)$ on education share (*Educ*) and growth rate (*g*) are significant on the basis of F and χ^2 tests; the random-effect model is recommended by the Breusch-Pagan LM test. These regression results are robust on the grounds of stationarity and cointegration criteria. Common panel unit root tests and Pedroni's (1999) panel cointegration tests involving $\dfrac{m}{y}, \dfrac{x}{y}$, *Educ* and *g* and found a long-run relationship. The threshold panel model developed by Hansen (1997), Caner and Hansen (2004) shows how to study regime changes occurring in the real-world situation.

References

Aghevli, B.B., 1977. Inflationary finance and growth. Journal of Political Economy 85 (6), 1295–1307.

Arellano, M., Bond, S., 1991. Some tests of specification for panel data: Monte Carlo evidence and an application to employment equations. Review of Economic Studies 58, 277–297.

Arellano, M., Bonhomme, S., 2012. Identifying distributional characteristics in random coefficients panel data models. Review of Economic Studies 79 (3), 987–1020.

Arellano, M., Bover, O., 1995. Another look at the instrumental variable estimation of error-components models. Journal of Econometrics 68, 29–51.

Arulampalam, W., Booth, A.L., 1998. Learning and earning: do multiple training events pay? A decade of evidence from a cohort of young British men. Economica 68 (271), 379–400.

Arulampalam, W., Booth, A.L., Bryan, M.L., 2004. Training and the new minimum wage. The Economic Journal 114 (494), C87–C94.

Bai, J., Ng, S., 2005. Tests for skewness, kurtosis, and normality for time series data. Journal of Business and Economic Statistics 23, 49–60.

Bailey, M.J., 1956. The welfare cost of inflationary finance. Journal of Political Economy LXIV2 (April), 93–110.

Balasubramanyam, V.N., Salisu, M., Sapsford, D., 1996. Foreign direct investment and growth in EP and is countries. The Economic Journal 106 (434), 92–105.

Balestra, P., Nerlove, M., 1966. Pooling cross section and time series data in the estimation of a dynamic model: the demand for natural gas. Econometrica: Journal of the Econometric Society 34, 585–612.

Ball, L., 1999. Efficient rules for monetary policy. International finance 2 (1), 63–83.

Ball, L., Mankiw, G., Romer, D., 1988. The new Keynesian economics and output-inflation trade-off. Brookings Papers in Economic Activity 1, 1–65.

Ball, L., Romer, D., 1990. Real rigidities and the non-neutrality of money. Review of Economic Studies 57, 183–203.

Baltagi, B.H., 1995. Econometric analysis of panel data. 2Wiley, New York.

Baltagi, B.H., Feng, Q., Kao, C., 2012. A lagrange multiplier test for cross-sectional dependence in a fixed effects panel data model. Journal of Econometrics 170 (1), 164–177.

Barro, R.J., 1995. Inflation and economic growth. Bank of England Quarterly Bulletin 35 (2), 166–175.

Basu, P., Bhattarai, K., 2012. Cognitive skills, openness and growth. The Economic Record 88 (280), 18–38.

Binh, N., Haughton, J., 2002. Trade liberalisation and foreign direct investment in Vietnam. ASEAN Economic Bulletin 19 (3), 302–318.

Blomström, M., Kokko, A., 1996. The impact of foreign investment on host countries: a review of the empirical evidence. Policy Research Working Paper 1745.

Blundell, R., Bond, S., 1998. Initial conditions and moment restrictions in dynamic panel data models. Journal of Econometrics 87, 115–143.

Blundell, R.W., Smith, R.J., 1989. Estimation in a class of simultaneous equation limited dependent variable models. Review of Economic Studies 56, 37–38.

Borensztein, E., De Gregorio, J., Lee, J.W., 1998. How does foreign direct investment affect economic growth. Journal of International Economics 45 (1), 115–135.

Caner, M., Hansen, B.E., 2004. Instrumental variable estimation of a threshold model. Econometric Theory 20, 813–843.

Carriero, A., Kapetanios, G., Marcellino, M., 2009. Forecasting exchange rates with a large Bayesian VAR. International Journal of Forecasting 25, 400–417.

Caselli, F., Esquivel, G., Lefort, F., 1996. Reopening the convergence debate: a new look at cross-country growth empirics. Journal of Economic Growth 1 (3), 363–389.

Chamberlain, G., 1982. Multivariate regression models for panel data. Journal of Econometrics 18 (1), 5–46.

Chesher, A., 1984. Improving the efficiency of Probit estimators. Review of Economic Studies 66 (3), 523–527.

Cornwell, C., Rupert, P., 1988. Efficient estimation with panel data: An empirical comparison of instrumental variables estimators. Journal of Applied Econometrics 3 (2), 149–155.

Davidson, R., MacKinnon, J.G., 2004. Econometric theory and methods. 5Oxford University Press, New York.

de Mello, L.R., 1999. Foreign direct investment-led growth: evidence from time series and panel data. Oxford Economic Papers 51 (1), 133–151New Series.

Desai, M.A., Foley, C.F., Hines Jr, J.R., 2005. Foreign direct investment and the domestic capital stock. American Economic Review 95 (2), 33–38.

Dixon, H., 1988. Controversy: the macroeconomics of unemployment in the OECD. The Economic Journal 108, 779–781.

Doornik, J.A., Hendry, D.F., 2001. Modelling dynamic systems using PcGive 10. Timberlake Consultants.

Doornik, J.F., Hendry, D.F., 1996. Empirical econometric modelling: using PcGive for Windows. InternationalThomson Business Press.

Feldstein, M.S., Horioka, C.Y., 1980. Domestic saving and international capital flows. Economic Journal 90, 314–929.

Gleditsch, K.S., 2002. Expanded trade and GDP data. Journal of Conflict Resolution 46 (5), 712–724.

Greene, W., 2008. Econometric analysis, 6th ed. Pearson/Prentice Hall.

Hadri, K., 2000. Testing for stationarity in heterogeneous panel data. The Econometrics Journal 3 (2), 148–161.

Hahn, J., Kuersteiner, G., 2002. Asymptotically unbiased inference for a dynamic panel model with fixed effects when both n and T are large. Econometrica 70 (4), 1639–1657.

Hansen, B.E., 1999. Threshold effects in non-dynamic panels: Estimation, testing, and inference. Journal of Econometrics 93, 345–368.

Hansen, L.P., 1982. Large sample properties of generalized method of moment estimators. Econometrica 50 (4), 1029–1054.

Hausman, J.A., 1978. Specification tests in econometrics. Econometrica 46 (6), 1251–1271.

Hayakawa, K., 2009. On the effect of mean nonstationarity in dynamic panel data models. Journal of Econometrics 153 (2), 133–135.

Heckman, J.J., 1979. Sample selection bias as a specification error. Econometrica 47 (1), 153–161.

Helpman, E., 2006. Trade, FDI, and the organization of firms. Journal of Economic Literature 44 (3), 589–630.

Ho, T.W., 2006. Income thresholds and growth convergence: a panel data approach. The Manchester School 74 (2), 170–189.

Holly, S., Weale, M., 2000. Econometric modelling: techniques and applications. University Press, Cambridge, pp. 69–93.

Hsiao, C., 1993. Analysis of panel data. Cambridge University Press.

Im, K.S., Pesaran, M., Shin, Y., 2003. Testing for unit roots in heterogeneous panels. Journal of Econometrics 115, 53–74.

Imbens, G.W., Lancaster, T., 1994. Combining micro and macro data in microeconometric models. Review of Economic Studies 61 (4), 655–680.

Islam, N., 1995. Growth empirics: a panel data approach. The Quarterly Journal of Economics 110 (4), 1127–1170.

Johansen, S., 1988. Estimation and hypothesis testing of cointegration vectors in Gaussian vector autoregressive models. Econometrica 59 (6), 1551–1580.

Johnston, J., 1960. Econometric methods, 7th ed. McGraw Hill.

Judson, R.A., Owen, A.L., 1999. Estimating dynamic panel data models: a guide for macroeconomists. Economics Letters 65 (1), 9–15.

Karabarbounis, L., Neiman, B., 2013. The global decline of the labor share. The Quarterly Journal of Economics 129 (1), 61–103.

Kao, C., 1999. Spurious regression and residual-based tests for cointegration in panel data. Journal of Econometrics 90, 1–44.

Kapetanios, G., Mitchell, J., Shin, Y., 2014. A nonlinear panel data model of cross-sectional dependence. Journal of Econometrics 179, 134–157.

Keifer, N., 1988. Economic duration data and hazard functions. Journal of Economic Literature 26, 647–679.

Kiviet, J.F., 1995. On bias, inconsistency, and efficiency of various estimators in dynamic panel data models. Journal of Econometrics 68 (1), 53–78.

Kleibergen, F., Paap, R., 2006. Generalized reduced rank tests using the singular value decomposition. Journal of Econometrics 133, 97–126.

Koop, G.M., 2013. Forecasting with medium and large Bayesian VARS. Journal of Applied Econometrics 28 (2), 177–203.

Kwaitkowski, D., Phillips, P.C., Schmidt, P., Shin, Y., 1992. Testing the null hypothesis of stationarity against the alternative of a unit root. Journal of Econometrics 54, 159–178.

Lancaster, T., 1979. Econometric methods for the duration of unemployment. Econometrica: Journal of the Econometric Society 47, 939–956.

Lancaster, T., 1990. The analysis of transition data. Cambridge University Press.

Lancaster, T., Chesher, A., 1983. The estimation of models of labour market behviour. Review of Economic Studies 50 (4), 609–624.

Larsson, R., Lyhagen, J., Lothgren, M., 2001. Likelihood-based cointegration tests in heterogeneous panels. The Econometrics Journal 4, 109–142.

Layard, R., Nickell, S., 1990. Is unemployment lower if unions bargain over employment? Quarterly Journal of Economics 3, 773–787.

Lee, Y., 2014. Testing a linear dynamic panel data model against nonlinear alternatives. Journal of Econometrics 178, 146–166Part 1.

Lensink, R., Morrissey, O., 2006. Foreign direct investment: flows, volatility, and the impact on growth. Review of International Economics 14 (3), 478–493.

Levin, A., Lin, C., Chu, C., 2002. Unit root tests in panel data: Asymptotic and finite sample properties. Journal of Econometrics 108, 12–24.

MacKinnon, J.G., 1996. Numerical distribution functions for unit root and cointegration tests. Journal of Applied Econometrics 11 (6), 601–618.

Maddala, G.S., Wu, S., 1999. A comparative study of unit root test with panel data and a new simple test. Oxford Bulletin of Economics and Statistics 61, 631–652.

Mankiw, N.G., Romer, D., Weil, D.N., 1992. A contribution to the empirics of economic growth. The Quarterly Journal of Economics 107 (2), 407–437.

Manning, A., 1995. Development in labour market theory and their implications for macroeconomic policy. Scottish Journal of Political Economy. 42 (3)August.

McCoskey, S., Kao, C., 1999. Testing the stability of a production function with Urbanisation as a shift factor. Oxford Bulletin of Economics and Statistics 61, 671–690.

Nickell, S., 1981. Biases in dynamic models with fixed effects. Econometrica: Journal of the Econometric Society 49, 1417–1426.

Nickell, S., 1998. Unemployment: questions and some answers. Economic Journal 108, 803–816.

Nickell, S., Quintini, G., 2003. Nominal wage rigidity and the rate of inflation. Economic Journal 113 (490), 762–781.

Pedroni, P., 1999. Critical values for cointegration tests in heterogeneous panels with multiple regressors. Oxford Bulletin of Economics and Statistics 61, 653–670.

Pesaran, M.H., 2015. Time series and panel data econometrics. Oxford University Press.

Pesaran, M.H., Smith, R., 1995. Estimating long-run relationships from dynamic heterogeneous panels. Journal of Econometrics 68, 79–113.

Phelps, E.S., Taylor, J.B., 1977. Stabilisation powers of monetary policy under rational expectations. Journal of Political Economy 85 (1), 163–190.

Phillips, P.C.B., 1987. Time series regression with a unit root. Econometrica 55 (2), 277–301.

Picketty, T., Goldhammer, A., 2014. Capital in the 21st century. Harvard University Press.

Ram, R., Zhang, K.H., 2002. Foreign direct investment and economic growth: evidence fromcross-country data for the 1990s. Economic Development and Cultural Change 51 (1), 205–215.

Robertson, D., Symons, J., 1992. Some strange properties of panel data estimators. Journal of Applied Econometrics 7 (2), 175–189.

Roed, K., Zhang, T., 2003. Does unemployment compensation affect unemployment duration? Economic Journal 113 (484), 190–206.

Roodman, D., 2009. How to do xtabond2: an introduction to difference and system GMM in Stata. The Stata Journal 9 (1), 86–136.

Ruud, P.A., 2000. An introduction to classical econometric theory. OUP Catalogue.

Semykina, A., Wooldridge, J.M., 2013. Estimation of dynamic panel data models with sample selection. Journal of Applied Econometrics 28 (1), 47–61.

Sentana, E., 2009. The econometrics of mean-variance efficiency tests: A survey. The Econometrics Journal 12, C65–C101.

Sims, C.A., 1981. Macroeconomics and reality. Econometrica 48 (1 January), 1–48.

Staigler, D., Stock, J.H., 1997. Instrumental variables regression with weak instruments. Econometrica 65 (3), 557–586.

Su, L., Lu, X., 2013. Nonparametric dynamic panel data models: kernel estimation and specification testing. Journal of Econometrics 176 (2), 112–133.

The World Bank, 2007. World development indicators. The World Bank, Washington, DC.

Verbeek, M., 2004. A guide to modern econometrics. Southern Gate. In: Chichester. England Hoboken, West Sussex.

Verbeek, M., 2008. A guide to modern econometrics. John Wiley & Sons.

Wallace, T.D., Hussain, A., 1969. The use of error components models in combining cross section with time series data. Econometrica: Journal of the Econometric Society 37, 55–72.

Wallis, K.F., 1968. The EEC and United States foreign investment: some empirical evidence reexamined. The Economic Journal 78 (311), 717–719.

Wang, C., Zhao, Z., 2008. Horizontal and vertical spillover effect of foreign direct investment in Chinese manufacturing. Journal of Chinese Economic and Foreign Trade Studies 1 (1), 8–20.

Wang, M., Wong, M.C., 2009. What drives economic growth? The case of cross-border M&A and Greenfield FDI. KYKLOS 62, 316–330.

Windmeijer, F., 2000. Moment conditions for fixed effects count data models with endogenous regressors. Economics Letters 68 (1), 21–24.

Windmeijer, F., 2005. A finite sample correction for the variance of linear efficient twostep GMM estimators. Journal of Econometrics 126, 25–51.

Wooldridge, J.M., 2010. Econometric analysis of cross section and panel data. MIT Press.

Wooldridge, J.M., 2002. Econometric analysis of cross section and panel data. MIT Press.

Wooldridge, J.M., 2005. Simple solutions to the initial conditions problem in dynamic, nonlinear panel data models with unobserved heterogeneity. Journal of Applied Econometrics 20 (1), 39–54.

Yellen, J.L., 1984. Efficiency wage models of unemployment. American Economic Review 74 (2), 199–205.

Zellner, A., 1985. Bayesian econometrics. Econometrica 53, 253–269.

Further Reading

Arulampalam, W., Stewart, M.B., 1995. The determinants of individual unemployment durations in an era of high unemployment. The Economic Journal 105 (429), 321–332.

Baltagi, H., 2008. Econometric analysis of panel data, 4th ed. Blackwell.

Bhargava, A., 1991. Identification and panel data models with endogenous regressors. Review of Economic Studies 58 (1), 129–140.

Hall, A., 2003. Generalised methods of moments. In: Baltagi, (Ed.), Theoretical econometrics. Blackwell.

Kyriazidou, E., 2001. Estimation of dynamic panel data sample selection models. Review of Economic Studies 68 (3), 543–572.

Lancaster, T., 2002. Orthogonal parameters and panel data. Review of Economic Studies 69 (3), 647–666.

Phillips, P.C.B., Sul, D., 2007. Bias in dynamic panel estimation with fixed effects, incidental trends and cross section dependence. Journal of Econometrics 137, 162–188.

Chapter 22

The Income-Health Gradient: Evidence From Self-Reported Health and Biomarkers in Understanding Society

Apostolos Davillas*, Andrew M. Jones[†,‡] and Michaela Benzeval*
*Institute for Social and Economic Research, University of Essex, Colchester, United Kingdom, [†]Department of Economics and Related Studies, University of York, York, United Kingdom, [‡]Centre for Health Economics, Monash University, Clayton, VIC, Australia

Chapter Outline

1 Introduction

Economic studies that aim to explore the health-income gradient face a number of challenges (e.g., Benzeval & Judge, 2001; Deaton & Paxson, 1998; Ettner, 1996; Jones & Wildman, 2008; Van Doorslaer & Jones, 2003). First, most of these studies are based on self-reported health measures, such as the conventional self-assessed health (SAH). SAH is considered as an indirect indicator of underlying health, which can be subject to misreporting and are associated with comparability problems at both the individual level and among countries (Bago d'Uva, O'Donnell, & van Doorslaer, 2008; Jürges, 2007, 2008). If the reporting error is distributed randomly, this might not be an issue. Reporting bias, however, has been shown to vary systematically with income and other socioeconomic characteristics that often are used to explore health inequalities, which raises doubts about the robustness of such studies based on self-reported health indicators (Crossley & Kennedy, 2002; Dowd & Zajacova, 2010;

Panel Data Econometrics. https://doi.org/10.1016/B978-0-12-815859-3.00022-6

Ziebarth, 2010). The same issues hold true for other self-reported health measures, such as functional limitations, self-reported chronic conditions, and self-administered well-being measures (Baker, Stabile, & Deri, 2004; Daltroy, Larson, Eaton, Phillips, & Liang, 1999; Johnston, Propper, & Shields, 2009; Powdthavee, 2010).

Second, self-reported health indicators and other health proxies do not necessarily identify presymptom and predisease stages. Identifying the role of income in physiological processes that occur before a disease or condition manifests itself might be particularly important for better understanding the link between income and health (Dowd, Simanek, & Aiello, 2009; Jürges, Kruk, & Reinhold, 2013). Recent studies have explored the association between measures of socioeconomic status and more objective and proximal health measures such as blood-based or nurse-administered biomarkers (e.g., Banks, Marmot, Oldfield, & Smith, 2006; Johnston et al., 2009; Jürges et al., 2013; Muennig, Sohler, & Mahato, 2007; Murasko, 2008; Powdthavee, 2010). Biomarkers are measured and evaluated objectively as an indicator of normal biological processes, pathogenic processes, or pharmacologic responses to a therapeutic intervention (Biomarkers Definition Working Group, 2001).

A third challenge in income-health studies is how to measure income. Dating to Friedman (1957), a prolonged discussion about the importance of permanent versus short-term income levels, which can be found in the general economics literature, also might be relevant for health (Fuchs, 2004). According to the permanent income hypothesis, it might be anticipated that permanent income (as opposed to transitory) might be more relevant as a determinant of the demand for health services (Feldstein, 1966). From a life-course perspective, long-term socioeconomic position might be more relevant to health because it might better reflect cumulative disadvantage (see e.g., Benzeval & Judge, 2001; Singh-Manoux, Ferrie, Chandola, & Marmot, 2004). Moreover, employing measures of income based on long income histories might be better indicators of an individuals' economic status because they are less sensitive to temporary income variations, such as a brief spell of unemployment or hard times, and they help to reduce concerns regarding the role of any potential effects of health shocks on income (Menchik, 1993).

Fourth, studies about the link between income and health measures typically explore the effect of the former on the conditional mean of the health outcome (for instance, Johnston et al., 2009; Jürges et al., 2013; Powdthavee, 2010). Analyses based solely on the mean, however, might mask important information in other parts of the distribution (Bitler, Gelbach, & Hoynes, 2006). This is particularly important in the case of the health-income association, in which clinical concern typically is focused on the tails of the health distribution (Carrieri & Jones, 2016; Jolliffe, 2011). For example, individuals with higher income who experience ill-health might be more likely to initiate behavioral adjustments. Therefore, evaluating the income gradients at different points of the health distribution might be beneficial.

In this chapter, we seek to address all of these concerns by using both self-reported health outcomes and nurse-measured and blood-based biomarkers in an analysis that compares short-run and long-run measures of income and evaluates the health-income gradient at the mean and across the full distribution of the outcomes. The absorption of the British Household Panel Survey (BHPS) into the Understanding Society (the United Kingdom Household Longitudinal Study, UKHLS) gives us the rare opportunity of combining cross-sectional (UKHLS wave 3 data) and longitudinal (up to a maximum of 18 BHPS waves) household income data with a large set of self-reported and objective health measures. We estimate short- and long-run income gradients in health to explore the relative importance of permanent versus current measures of income. This is the first study, to our knowledge, that estimates the association of a large set of subjective and objective health measures with both cross-sectional and long-run income measures as well as employing econometric techniques that facilitate beyond the mean analysis. Over and above conventional regression models, the recently proposed unconditional quantile regression (UQR) technique—based on the recentered influence function (RIF) approach—is used to explore the potential heterogeneity of the income gradients at different points of the unconditional distribution of each of our continuous health measures (Firpo, Fortin, & Lemieux, 2009).

Our chapter contributes to the literature in two main ways. First, complementary to the conventional self-reported health measures, we also employ a number of nurse-administered and blood-based biomarkers, that is, adiposity measures, blood pressure, resting heart rate, inflammatory biomarkers, blood glucose (HbA1C), and cholesterol ratio. We believe that using these biomarkers in the analysis of the income gradient in health has its virtues. They capture different health dimensions and are considered as secondary physiological responses to stress, and, thus, they are more proximal outcomes in the process through which economic status gets "under the skin" (Glei et al., 2013; Turner, Thomas, & Brown, 2016). Stress has been considered as one of the causal pathways through which socioeconomic status can affect health (Acabchuk, Kamath, Salamone, & Johnson, 2017; Adler & Newman, 2002). Focusing on the relevant biomarkers, therefore, can provide information about important physiological links between income and health. For example, contrary to any self-reported psychosocial stress instrument, inflammatory biomarkers, such as C-reactive protein (CRP) and fibrinogen, are more objective indicators and capture the cumulative effect of long-run exposures to stress (e.g., Gémes, Ahnve, & Janszky, 2008; Jürges et al., 2013; Theorell, 2002). Moreover, because biomarkers provide direct information about predisease conditions by measuring physiological processes below the individual's level of perception, they also can be interpreted as markers of future health (Karlamangla, Gruenewald, & Seeman, 2012). Unlike the conventional self-reported health indicators that mainly capture current health, biomarkers can allow for revealing income associations when diseases have not yet become explicit.

In spite of these advantages of biomarkers and the subjective nature of the self-reported health measures, however, the latter also are relevant because they have been shown to be strong predictors of future mortality (Idler & Benyamini, 1997; Jürges et al., 2013; Jylhä, 2009). In this study, we employ a large set of both self-reported health measures (SAH, functional disabilities, and physical-health functioning (PCS-12)) and biomarkers that cover several different dimensions of health. Identifying differences in the income-gradients between these self-reported and objective health measures that might be attributed to reporting heterogeneity in the self-reported health could be of particular interest.

Second, beyond the mean estimation techniques allow us to explore: the potential heterogeneity in the short- and long-run income-health gradients across the distribution of the health measures of interest, and whether long-run, compared to short-run income, is more relevant to health toward the tails of the distribution, where elevated risks are prominent, implying greater burden of illness for individuals and possibly higher costs for the health care system. We find that long-run income gradients are much greater in magnitude and more statistically significant than those based on the cross-sectional income measure. Moreover, the corresponding UQR results reveal a more clearly increasing pattern toward the tails of the distribution that correspond to higher health risks, when long-term average income is used as opposed to cross-sectional income. This is particularly true for the self-reported PCS-12 and for biomarkers of adiposity, heart rate, inflammation (CRP), diabetes, and cholesterol.

2 Methods

In this section, we present the empirical strategy that we employ in this study. We first give a brief illustration of the regression models that we use to explore the association between income and our different health measures. This is followed by a presentation of the health specifications for the case of short-run and long-run income measures.

2.1 Health Outcome Regression Models

Ordered probit models and probit models are used to test the association of short-run and long-run household income with SAH and functional difficulties, respectively. The continuous health measures (PCS-12, nurse-measured, and blood-based biomarkers) are modeled initially using the conventional linear regression model (OLS). In this context, a general model specification can be written as:

$$H_i^* = \gamma' I_i + \delta' z_i + u_i \tag{1}$$

where H_i^* stands for the health outcome of interest, I_i represents the household income variable, z_i stands for the covariates, and γ and δ are the regression coefficients to be estimated. In the case of the continuous health outcomes

(OLS models), H_i^* coincides with the observed health measure (H_i). Regarding the probit models for functional difficulties and ordered probit models for SAH, H_i^* stands for latent variable.

We also apply quantile regression techniques that allow us to consider the entire distribution of the continuous health outcomes and to investigate the potentially differential effect of household income across different points of their distribution. UQR models are employed in this study (Firpo et al., 2009). Unlike the conventional conditional quantile regression models, which explore the effect of covariates on the conditional quantiles of the outcome variable (Koenker & Bassett, 1978), the UQR technique estimates unconditional quantile partial effects.

The estimation of the UQR is based on the RIF. This can be estimated directly from the data by computing sample quantiles of the health measure (q_τ) and then estimating the density of the distribution of health measures at those quantiles using kernel density methods. Specifically, for an observed quantile (q_τ), an RIF, which can take one of two values depending upon whether the observation's value of the health measure is less than or equal to the observed quantile (q_τ), is generated:

$$RIF(H_i; q_\tau) = q_\tau + \frac{\tau - 1[H_i \leq q_\tau]}{f_H(q_\tau)} \tag{2}$$

where, q_τ is the observed sample quantile, $1[H_i \leq q_\tau]$ is an indicator that equals to one if the observation value of the health measure of interest is less than or equal to the observed quantile q_τ and zero otherwise; $f_H(q_\tau)$ is the estimated kernel density of the particular health measure at the τth quantile. The RIF then is regressed on a set of covariates z_i using OLS; this constitutes a rescaled linear probability model. We use the bootstrap method with 500 replications to obtain unbiased estimates of the variance-covariance matrix of the parameter estimates (Buchinsky, 1998; Jolliffe, 2011).

2.2 Model Specifications

Cross-sectional regressions of health on income (specification 1) are estimated initially using current household income (collected at UKHLS wave 3). We then enhance this approach by using a long-run average measure of household income (within-individual mean of the natural logarithm of the household income) derived from the longitudinal income histories covering a long period (maximum of 18 BHPS waves) prior to the health outcomes (specification 2).

3 The UKHLS and BHPS Datasets

The data come from the BHPS subsample of UKHLS. At wave 2 (2010–11), BHPS sample members were absorbed into the UKHLS. The BHPS is a widely used representative longitudinal UK study that covered the period between 1991 and 2009 (18 waves) up to the time it was incorporated in the UKHLS.

For the BHPS respondents followed up in the UKHLS, a set of nurse-administered health measures and a nonfasted blood sample were collected, as part of the UKHLS wave 3 (Benzeval, Davillas, Kumari, & Lynn, 2014; McFall, Petersen, Kaminska, & Lynn, 2014). For our study, we merge BHPS waves 1–18 with UKHLS wave 3 data for the BHPS sample members who were followed up in the UKHLS wave 3. To exploit all the available observations, an unbalanced sample of the BHPS waves 1–18 is employed to calculate our long-run income measure, as the within-individual mean income (long-run income data are available for a potential sample of 8086 unique individuals across the 18 BHPS waves, with an average of 12 observations per individual).

For the health regression models, the self-reported health measures, and the relevant covariates (such as demographics, socioeconomic characteristics, etc.) were collected as part of the UKHLS wave 3 main survey. When available, bio-medical data from the nurse visits that followed UKHLS wave 3 also are included. Respondents were eligible for the nurse visits if they took part in the main survey, lived in Great Britain (not Northern Ireland), and were not pregnant (McFall et al., 2014). Blood sample collections were restricted further to those who had no clotting or bleeding disorders and had never had a seizure (Benzeval et al., 2014). The potential sample for our health regression models includes the BHPS sample members who participated at UKHLS wave 3, that is, cross-sectional data for 8086 individuals. Of those, 4512 took part in the nurse visits, while the blood-based biomarker data are available for 3020 respondents[1]. Excluding missing information of any of the covariates used in our regression models, the analysis sample is reduced from 8086 individuals to a maximum of 7979 individuals (depending on the specific self-reported health outcome considered); for the nurse-administered and the blood-based biomarkers, the nurse visit is required, so the available sample size is reduced to a maximum of 4474 and 3003 individuals, respectively.[2]

3.1 Health Measures

3.1.1 Self-Reported Health

Three self-reported health measures are used. SAH categorizes respondents on a five-category scale, ranging from excellent (value of 1) to poor (value of 5) health. We also consider a self-reported functional disability measure. A

---

1. Comparison of the summary statistics across different samples reveals similar results (Table A1, appendix), indicating that the implications of the reduction in the sample size (in the case of the nurse visits and the blood data) might be limited in our analysis.

2. Given these differences in the sample size between the self-reported health measures and the bio-markers, we implement sensitivity analysis for the case of self-reported health measures by restricting our analysis sample to the nurse visits subsample (Tables A2 and A3, appendix). Our results show that the conclusions of the study are robust to this choice of alternative samples.

dichotomous variable is constructed taking the value of one if the respondent reported any long-standing functional difficulty with any domain of life and zero otherwise. The SF-12 is a self-administered measure of health functioning. For this study, we use the physical component submeasure (PCS-12), which has values between zero and 100 and is standardized to have a mean of 50 and a standard deviation of 10. To facilitate consistency with the interpretation of our results, because we intend to measure ill-health, PCS-12 is inverted such as higher values indicate worse physical health functioning.

3.1.2 Adiposity Measures

Anthropometrics were measured during the nurse visits (McFall et al., 2014). We employ waist circumference (WC) to capture central adiposity, in addition to the conventional BMI. The mean of the WC measurements (the two closest, if there were three) is used for the purpose of our study (Davillas & Benzeval, 2016). Body weight and height are used to calculate BMI as the weight (in kilograms) over the square of height (in meters). It has been shown that there is a J-shaped association of BMI and WC with mortality risks; mortality risk is elevated for the underweight and it gradually increases with higher levels of BMI and WC (Pischon et al., 2008; Prospective Studies Collaboration, 2009).

3.1.3 Blood Pressure and Resting Health Rate

Systolic blood pressure (SBP) is the maximum pressure in an artery at the moment when the heart is pumping blood; diastolic blood pressure (DBP) is the lowest pressure in an artery in the moments between beats when the heart is resting. A large body of medical studies have demonstrated that the cardiovascular morbidity and mortality risks gradually increase with higher levels of SBP and DBP. Heart rate is an overall measure of heart function and cardiovascular fitness. Heart rate values above 90 heart beats per minute (bpm) are indicative of excess health risks (Seccareccia et al., 2001).

3.1.4 Blood-Based Biomarkers

Two biomarkers of inflammation are examined: CRP and fibrinogen. CRP (in mg/L) is an acute phase protein that mainly reflects general chronic or systemic inflammation. It has been shown that the risk of ischemic vascular disease, metabolic syndrome, and mortality gradually increase in CRP (Ferrari et al., 2015). CRP values greater than 5 mg/L are considered to be elevated, while CRP greater than 3 mg/L are a high risk for cardiovascular diseases (Ferrari et al., 2015); values greater than 10 mg/L are regarded as suggestive of acute infections (Ishii et al., 2012). Fibrinogen (in g/L) is a glycoprotein that stops bleeding by helping blood clots to form. As such, fibrinogen is directly related to coronary artery thrombosis, but, it also is regarded as an inflammatory biomarker. There is an approximately log-linear association of fibrinogen levels with cardiovascular conditions and mortality (Fibrinogen Studies Collaboration, 2005).

Glycated hemoglobin (HbA1c) is a validated diagnostic test for diabetes (WHO, 2011). Implications for health are not homogenous across the distribution of HbA1c because different levels suggest distinct conditions and severity. HbA1c levels between 42 mmol/mol and 48 mmol/mol indicate prediabetes risk, HbA1c $\geq$48 mmol/mol indicates diagnosis of diabetes, and higher HbA1c levels suggestive of more severe conditions (WHO, 2011).

Cholesterol concentrations measure the fat in the blood. For this study, the cholesterol ratio is calculated as the ratio of total cholesterol over high-density lipoprotein cholesterol. This is a stronger predictor of cardiovascular morbidity and mortality risks than either of the individual cholesterol concentrations, with a dose-response association (Prospective Studies Collaboration, 2007).

3.2 Household Income Variables

The monthly gross household income is used as the dependent variable in the panel household income model for BHPS waves 1–18. Current household income (i.e., UKHLS wave 3) is available as a derived variable in UKHLS.[3] The household income variables are transformed to natural logarithms in order to allow for the concavity of the health-income associations (e.g., Contoyannis, Jones, & Rice, 2004) and because of the skewness of the income distribution. To facilitate comparisons over time and between households, household income is deflated, using the Retail Price Index, to express income in January 2010 prices and equivalized (using the modified OECD scale).

3.2.1 Other Covariates

The covariates that are used to model our health outcomes are collected at the UKHLS wave 3 (Table A1, appendix presents a detailed description, along with summary statistics). The estimation models include 14 age dummies for each gender (age group dummies for five-year intervals and a dummy for those older than 84), to allow for a flexible association between health, age, and gender. Ethnicity dummies also are included in the health models. We include marital status, because it can affect household production of health and demand for health (Fuchs, 2004). Education also is included, given evidence showing the positive association between schooling and health (Contoyannis et al., 2004). Regional dummies are added to capture regional variations.

---

3. Questionnaires that are used to derive total household income variables are the same between the UKHLS and the BHPS dataset with the exception that there is no basis for estimating annual income in the case of the UKHLS. Böheim and Jenkins (2006) have shown that the income distributions for the monthly and annual income data are remarkably similar in the case of BHPS. For this reason, the monthly income measures (available in both BHPS and UKHLS) are used in our analysis. As a further test for the comparability of the wave 3 UKHLS and BHPS household income data, the quantile household income distributions from these datasets can be compared to the corresponding data from external sources, such as the Family Resources Survey (FRS). We find practically identical results between the UKHLS wave 3 and the FRS, also the case for BHPS sample (Jenkins, 2011).

Medications can affect the level of the biomarkers. Following previous literature (Godoy et al., 2007; Powdthavee, 2010; Rahkovsky & Gregory, 2013), we adjust for taking relevant medications. This allows exploration of the health-income gradients on the whole population, controlling for the role of medications. A dummy for antihypertensive medications is included in the blood pressure models, and dummies for statins and antiinflammatory medications are added to the CRP models. Antiinflammatory medications also are accounted for in fibrinogen models. The cholesterol ratio and the HbA1c regression models include indicators for statins and antidiabetic medications, respectively. Because an unbalanced BHPS sample is used to define long-run income, we also account for the number of BHPS waves that each individual is observed in the case of the regressions of health on long-run income (Verbeek & Nijman, 1992); this variable is not statistically significant at any conventional level across all the different models estimated.

4 Empirical Results

Income gradients for our different health indicators using cross-sectional (specification 1) and long-run (within-individual mean of the natural logarithm of the household income over up to 18 BHPS waves; specification 2) household income measures are presented in Tables 1–6.

Tables 1 and 2 present the results for our self-reported health measures. As expected, we find a strong cross-sectional income gradient in both SAH and functional disability; higher income is related to a better SAH (i.e., lower SAH values because SAH is coded from excellent [1] to poor health [5]) and to a lower probability of functional disability (specification 1, Table 1). There is also a negative association between higher cross-sectional income and poor physical health functioning (inverted PCS-12; specification 1, Table 2). The UQR estimates show that the gradient is more evident beyond the median of the PCS-12 distribution (corresponding to lower physical functioning). For instance, the income gradient at the 75th percentile is about five times higher than that at the 10th percentile (−1.922 vs. −0.391).

Employing our long-run income measure (proxy of permanent income) we find much higher income gradients (specification 2) than those based on cross-sectional income (specification 1). Specifically, the long-run income gradients in SAH and the functional disability (average partial effects) are 1.6–2 times higher than those based on cross-sectional income. Moreover, long-run, compared to current income, exhibits steeper patterns and greater heterogeneity in the income gradients in (inverted) PCS-12 (Table 2, specification 2). For example, the long-run income gradient at the 90th percentile is about eight times higher than at the 10th (inverted) PCS-12 percentile.

The income gradients in adiposity are presented in Table 3. Again, in the BMI models, the income coefficients are larger in magnitude for long-run versus cross-sectional income measures. Although there is no systematic association at the mean (OLS), the long-run income coefficient at the 95th BMI percentile

TABLE 1 Income Gradients in Self-Assessed Health and Functional Disabilities Using Cross-Sectional and Long-Run Income Measures

Panel A: Self-assessed health

	Coeff. (s.e.)[a]	Ordered Probit APE (s.e.)[a]				
		Excellent	Very Good	Good	Fair	Poor
Specification 1						
Ln(current income)	−0.233***	0.052***	0.033***	−0.021***	−0.037***	−0.027***
	(0.024)	(0.005)	(0.003)	(0.002)	(0.004)	(0.003)
Specification 2						
Long-run mean ln(income)	−0.406***	0.090***	0.057***	−0.035***	−0.063***	−0.048***
	(0.029)	(0.006)	(0.004)	(0.003)	(0.005)	(0.004)
Sample size				7978		

Panel B: Functional disabilities

	Probit	
	Coeff. (s.e.)[a]	APE (s.e.)[a]
Specification 1		
Ln(current income)	−0.176***	−0.048***
	(0.032)	(0.009)
Specification 2		
Long-run mean ln(income)	−0.388***	−0.105***
	(0.041)	(0.011)
Sample size	7724	

APE, average partial effects; Coeff., coefficients; s.e., standard errors.
[a]Robust standard errors in parenthesis.
*** P < .01.
** P < .05.
* P < .10.

TABLE 2 Income Gradients in (Inverted) PCS-12 Using Cross-Sectional and Long-Run Income Measures

| | OLS | Unconditional Quantile Regressions | | | | | |
| | | Q10 | Q25 | Q50 | Q75 | Q90 | Q95 |
	Coeff. (s.e.)[a]	Coeff. (s.e.)[b]	Coeff. (s.e.)[b]	Coeff. (s.e.)[b]	Coeff. (s.e.)[b]	Coeff. (s.e.)[b]	Coeff. (s.e.)[b]
Specification 1							
Ln(current income)	−1.310***	−0.391**	−0.916***	−1.523***	−1.922***	−1.696**	−1.145
	(0.231)	(0.166)	(0.157)	(0.249)	(0.516)	(0.725)	(0.735)
Specification 2							
Long-run mean ln (income)	−3.058***	−0.799***	−0.885***	−2.292***	−5.409***	−6.510***	−6.100***
	(0.294)	(0.196)	(0.182)	(0.299)	(0.710)	(1.039)	(1.037)
Sample size				7048			

Coeff., coefficients; OLS, ordinary least squares; s.e., standard errors.
[a]Robust standard errors in parenthesis.
[b]UQR standard errors are bootstrap estimates with 500 replications.
***$p < .01$.
**$p < .05$.
*$p < .10$.

TABLE 3 Income Gradients in Adiposity Using Cross-Sectional and Long-Run Income Measures

Panel A: Body mass index

	OLS	Unconditional Quantile Regressions[a]					
		Q10 (22.0 kg/m²)	Q25 (24.4 kg/m²)	Q50 (27.4 kg/m²)	Q75 (31.1 kg/m²)	Q90 (35.2 kg/m²)	Q95 (38.3 kg/m²)
	Coeff. (s.e.)[b]	Coeff. (s.e.)[c]	Coeff. (s.e.)[c]	Coeff. (s.e.)[c]	Coeff. (s.e.)[c]	Coeff. (s.e.)[c]	Coeff. (s.e.)[c]
Specification 1							
Ln(current income)	−0.091	0.099	−0.026	−0.078	−0.059	−0.282	−0.757*
	(0.154)	(0.197)	(0.187)	(0.199)	(0.256)	(0.367)	(0.430)
Specification 2							
Long-run mean ln (income)	−0.254	0.228	−0.115	−0.284	−0.476	−0.743	−1.414**
	(0.194)	(0.239)	(0.230)	(0.230)	(0.315)	(0.457)	(0.579)
Sample size				4224			

Continued

Panel B: Waist circumference

	OLS	Unconditional Quantile Regressions[a]					
		Q10 (76.2 cm)	Q25 (84.2 cm)	Q50 (93.7 cm)	Q75 (103.7 cm)	Q90 (113.6 cm)	Q95 (120 cm)
	Coeff. (s.e.)[b]	Coeff. (s.e.)[c]	Coeff. (s.e.)[c]	Coeff. (s.e.)[c]	Coeff. (s.e.)[c]	Coeff. (s.e.)[c]	Coeff. (s.e.)[c]
Specification 1							
Ln(current income)	−0.820**	−0.780	0.0300	−0.237	−1.310**	−1.821**	−2.110**
	(0.377)	(0.563)	(0.546)	(0.491)	(0.590)	(0.815)	(0.955)
Specification 2							
Long-run mean ln (income)	−1.377***	−0.543	−0.322	−0.682	−1.630**	−3.020***	−4.302***
	(0.493)	(0.770)	(0.670)	(0.614)	(0.689)	(1.036)	(1.251)
Sample size				4372			

Coeff., coefficients; OLS, ordinary least squares; s.e., standard errors.
[a]Body mass index and waist circumference values that correspond to each percentile of the distribution also are presented.
[b]Robust standard errors in parenthesis.
[c]UQR standard errors are bootstrap estimates with 500 replications.
***P < .01.
**P < .05.
*P < .10.

(corresponds to BMI values within the range of severe obesity, i.e., ≥ 35 kg/m^2; Prospective Studies Collaboration, 2009) is more than five times higher than the corresponding OLS coefficient. The income gradients in WC are more pronounced. This is broadly in accordance with previous studies that found stronger socioeconomic gradients for central adiposity measures rather than BMI, reflecting the fact that BMI is a noisy adiposity measure that cannot distinguish fat from lean body mass (Davillas & Benzeval, 2016; Ljungvall, Gerdtham, & Lindblad, 2015). Income gradients in WC are also higher in magnitude in the case of long-run versus current income measures, notably at the right tail of the WC distribution. A closer look at the long-run income gradients (specification 2) reveals that the OLS estimator averages out notable differences across the WC distribution. Specifically, the UQR models suggest no systematic income gradients at the lower percentiles of WC, but there are statistically significant and gradually increasing income gradients at higher percentiles (up to three times larger than the OLS estimate).

Table 4 presents the results for blood pressure and heart rate. There is some evidence of considerably higher income gradients at the right tails of the distribution for both systolic and diastolic blood pressure, especially in the case of long-run income measures, albeit only statistically significant at the 10% level. More pronounced income gradients are evident for our measure of overall cardiovascular fitness (heart rate). Long-run income gradients in heart rate are larger in magnitude and increase toward the right tail of the heart rate distribution than those for current income. No systematic gradients are found at the lowest percentiles of the heart rate distribution (up to 60 bmp; most likely reflecting athletic lifestyles), whereas gradually increasing negative income gradients are evident toward the higher percentiles, with a peak at the 95th percentile that is close to the clinical threshold for elevated health risks (>90 bmp; Seccareccia et al., 2001).

Income gradients in inflammatory biomarkers are also higher in magnitude for long-run versus cross-sectional income (Table 5). Analysis beyond the mean reveals that the differences between them are more evident at the tails of the CRP distribution, where both higher health risks and steeper income gradients are observed. For example, the long-run income gradient at the 95th percentile (reflecting acute inflammation; Ishii et al., 2012) is about seven times higher than the OLS coefficient. We find limited variation, however, in the magnitude of the negative income gradient in fibrinogen across its distribution; this result is in accordance with previous evidence (Carrieri & Jones, 2016).

The long-run income measure shows larger income gradients and a sharper increase in the income gradients toward the right tail of the distribution of our blood sugar (HbA1c) and fat in the blood (cholesterol ratio) biomarkers than current income measures (Table 6). For HbA1c, we find a steeper pattern across the HbA1c distribution for the long-run measure; with the gradient increasing almost linearly up to 90th percentile and much sharper after this point (95th HbA1c percentile, i.e., values close to the diabetes threshold). The long-run income gradient in cholesterol ratio (specification 2) gradually increases toward

TABLE 4 Income Gradients in Blood Pressure and Heart Rate Measurements Using Cross-Sectional and Long-Run Income Measures

Panel A: Systolic blood pressure

	OLS	Unconditional Quantile Regressions[a]					
		Q10 (106 mmHg)	Q25 (114.5 mmHg)	Q50 (124.5 mmHg)	Q75 (136.5 mmHg)	Q90 (148.5 mmHg)	Q95 (156.5 mmHg)
	Coeff. (s.e.)[b]	Coeff. (s.e.)[c]	Coeff. (s.e.)[c]	Coeff. (s.e.)[c]	Coeff. (s.e.)[c]	Coeff. (s.e.)[c]	Coeff. (s.e.)[c]
Specification 1							
Ln(current income)	-0.687	-0.508	-0.575	-0.211	-0.587	-0.613	-2.061
	(0.470)	(0.628)	(0.576)	(0.633)	(0.839)	(0.978)	(1.558)
Specification 2							
Long-run mean ln (income)	-0.050	1.023	-0.144	1.008	0.547	-0.610	-4.238*
	(0.608)	(0.312)	(0.773)	(0.765)	(0.975)	(1.396)	(2.390)
Sample size				3632			

Panel B: Diastolic Blood Pressure

| | OLS | Unconditional Quantile Regressions[a] | | | | | |
| | | Q10 (59.5 mmHg) | Q25 (65.5 mmHg) | Q50 (73 mmHg) | Q75 (80 mmHg) | Q90 (87 mmHg) | Q95 (91.5 mmHg) |
	Coeff. (s.e.)[b]	Coeff. (s.e.)[c]	Coeff. (s.e.)[c]	Coeff. (s.e.)[c]	Coeff. (s.e.)[c]	Coeff. (s.e.)[c]	Coeff. (s.e.)[c]
Specification 1							
Ln(current income)	−0.809**	−0.573	−0.971**	−0.707*	−1.002*	−1.049	−0.861
	(0.326)	(0.448)	(0.456)	(0.430)	(0.520)	(0.693)	(0.978)
Specification 2							
Long-run mean ln (income)	−0.478	0.258	−0.199	0.0385	−1.131*	−1.619*	−1.520
	(0.422)	(0.680)	(0.607)	(0.545)	(0.665)	(0.886)	(1.114)
Sample size				3632			

Continued

Panel C: Resting Heart Rate

	OLS	Unconditional Quantile Regressions[a]					
		Q10 (56 bmp)	Q25 (61.5 bmp)	Q50 (68.5 bmp)	Q75 (75.5 bmp)	Q90 (84 bmp)	Q95 (89 bmp)
	Coeff. (s.e.)[b]	Coeff. (s.e.)[c]	Coeff. (s.e.)[c]	Coeff. (s.e.)[c]	Coeff. (s.e.)[c]	Coeff. (s.e.)[c]	Coeff. (s.e.)[c]
Specification 1							
Ln(current income)	-1.425***	-0.673	-0.743*	-1.481***	-1.463***	-3.476***	-2.934***
	(0.348)	(0.535)	(0.434)	(0.467)	(0.534)	(0.848)	(0.869)
Specification 2							
Long-run mean ln (income)	-1.742***	-0.391	-0.992*	-1.712***	-2.118***	-4.078***	-5.061***
	(0.455)	(0.652)	(0.544)	(0.587)	(0.634)	(1.081)	(1.226)
Sample size				3636			

Coeff., coefficients; OLS, ordinary least squares; s.e., standard errors.
[a]Blood pressure and heart rate values that correspond to each percentile of the distribution are also presented.
[b]Robust standard errors in parenthesis.
[c]UQR standard errors are bootstrap estimates with 500 replications.
***P < .01.
**P < .05.
*P < .10.

TABLE 5 Income Gradients in Inflammatory Biomarkers Using Cross-Sectional and Long-Run Income Measures

Panel A: C-reactive protein

	OLS	Unconditional Quantile Regressions[a]					
		Q10 (0.3 mg/L)	Q25 (0.6 mg/L)	Q50 (1.4 mg/L)	Q75 (3.1 mg/L)	Q90 (6.7 mg/L)	Q95 (11 mg/L)
	Coeff. (s.e.)[b]	Coeff. (s.e.)[c]	Coeff. (s.e.)[c]	Coeff. (s.e.)[c]	Coeff. (s.e.)[c]	Coeff. (s.e.)[c]	Coeff. (s.e.)[c]
Specification 1							
Ln(current income)	−0.176	0.002	0.001	−0.048	−0.249	−1.195**	−2.151*
	(0.225)	(0.033)	(0.038)	(0.071)	(0.184)	(0.566)	(1.251)
Specification 2							
Long-run mean ln (income)	−0.815***	−0.031	−0.082*	−0.222**	−0.943***	−2.037***	−5.733**
	(0.280)	(0.048)	(0.049)	(0.089)	(0.234)	(0.730)	(2.378)
Sample size				2932			

Continued

Panel B: Fibrinogen

	OLS	Unconditional Quantile Regressions[a]					
		Q10 (2.1 g/L)	Q25 (2.4 g/L)	Q50 (2.8 g/L)	Q75 (3.2 g/L)	Q90 (3.6 g/L)	Q95 (3.8 g/L)
	Coeff. (s.e.)[b]	Coeff. (s.e.)[c]	Coeff. (s.e.)[c]	Coeff. (s.e.)[c]	Coeff. (s.e.)[c]	Coeff. (s.e.)[c]	Coeff. (s.e.)[c]
Specification 1							
Ln(current income)	−0.075***	−0.057**	−0.073***	−0.085***	−0.099***	−0.061	−0.046
	(0.020)	(0.025)	(0.025)	(0.025)	(0.031)	(0.045)	(0.059)
Specification 2							
Long-run mean ln (income)	−0.148***	−0.112***	−0.143***	−0.133***	−0.172***	−0.121**	−0.166**
	(0.025)	(0.033)	(0.034)	(0.031)	(0.038)	(0.060)	(0.069)
Sample size				2894			

Coeff., coefficients; OLS, ordinary least squares; s.e., standard errors.
[a]Biomarker values that correspond to each percentile of the biomarker distribution are also presented.
[b]Robust standard errors in parenthesis.
[c]UQR standard errors are bootstrap estimates with 500 replications.
***$p < .01$.
**$p < .05$.
*$p < .10$.

TABLE 6 Income Gradients in HbA1c and Cholesterol Ratio Using Cross-Sectional and Long-Run Income Measures

Panel A: HbA1c

	OLS	Unconditional Quantile Regressions[a]					
		Q10 (31 mmol/mol)	Q25 (33 mmol/mol)	Q50 (36 mmol/mol)	Q75 (39 mmol/mol)	Q90 (43 mmol/mol)	Q95 (50 mmol/mol)
	Coeff. (s.e.)[b]	Coeff. (s.e.)[c]	Coeff. (s.e.)[c]	Coeff. (s.e.)[c]	Coeff. (s.e.)[c]	Coeff. (s.e.)[c]	Coeff. (s.e.)[c]
Specification 1							
Ln (current income)	-0.673***	-0.342*	-0.455**	-0.347**	-0.450**	-0.308	-3.486*
	(0.227)	(0.197)	(0.181)	(0.166)	(0.228)	(0.602)	(1.865)
Specification 2							
Long-run mean ln (income)	-1.248***	-0.274	-0.488**	-0.774***	-0.938***	-1.123*	-5.549**
	(0.366)	(0.278)	(0.247)	(0.211)	(0.297)	(0.667)	(2.850)
Sample size	2779						

Continued

Panel B: Cholesterol ratio

	OLS	Unconditional Quantile Regressions[a]					
	Coeff. (s.e.)[b]	Q10 (2.35 units) Coeff. (s.e.)[c]	Q25 (2.81 units) Coeff. (s.e.)[c]	Q50 (3.5 units) Coeff. (s.e.)[c]	Q75 (4.45 units) Coeff. (s.e.)[c]	Q90 (5.55 units) Coeff. (s.e.)[c]	Q95 (6.3 units) Coeff. (s.e.)[c]
Specification 1							
Ln(current income)	−0.104**	−0.044	−0.096*	−0.138***	−0.231***	0.070	−0.085
	(0.046)	(0.039)	(0.050)	(0.052)	(0.077)	(0.119)	(0.157)
Specification 2							
Long-run mean ln (income)	−0.229***	−0.013	−0.122**	−0.221***	−0.379***	−0.305**	−0.475**
	(0.056)	(0.050)	(0.059)	(0.065)	(0.098)	(0.143)	(0.197)
Sample size				2932			

Coeff., coefficients; OLS, ordinary least squares; s.e., standard errors.
[a]Biomarker values that correspond to each percentile of the biomarker distribution are also presented.
[b]Robust standard errors in parenthesis.
[c]UQR standard errors are bootstrap estimates with 500 replications.
***P < .01.
**P < .05.
*P < .10.

the right tails of its distribution with two peak points: the first at around the 75th percentile (close to the clinical threshold of four; Millán et al., 2009) and another peak at the 95th percentile. The corresponding income gradient at the right tail of the cholesterol ratio distribution is 37 times higher compared to the bottom of the distribution (−0.475 vs. −0.013).

5   Conclusions

This chapter uses data from the BHPS subsample of the UKHLS, which allows for a large set of health measures and for both short- and long-run measures of income; we use a range of self-reported health measures, nurse-administered, and blood-based biomarkers. To our knowledge, this is the first study that explores income-health gradients using such a broad set of self-reported and objectively measured health indicators, both short-run and long-run income measures, and econometric techniques that facilitate beyond the mean analysis.

Our results show clear income gradients across all the self-reported health measures and most of the nurse-administered and blood-based biomarkers when we use cross-sectional income. We find that the cross-sectional association of current income with self-reported physical health functioning measures (PCS-12) and biomarkers of adiposity (BMI, WC), heart rate, inflammation (CRP), diabetes, and cholesterol varies across their distribution and is considerably larger at the tails of the distribution, where the health care risks are more evident. Employing permanent income measures (long-run income), however, the relevant income gradients are greater in magnitude (and statistical significance) and follow a steeper increasing pattern toward the tails of the distribution rather than the cross-sectional income measures.

A Descriptive Statistics

TABLE A1 Descriptive Statistics for the Variables Used in the Health Regression Models

	Maximum Possible Sample[a]		Nurse Visits Sample[b]		Blood Sample[c]	
	Mean	s.d.	Mean	s.d.	Mean	s.d.
Income measures						
Ln(current income)	7.364	0.579	7.363	0.579	7.378	0.580
Long-run mean ln (income)	7.302	0.490	7.308	0.486	7.330	0.481
Ethnicity						
White	0.968	0.177	0.969	0.174	0.975	0.156
Nonwhite (reference category)	0.032	0.177	0.031	0.174	0.025	0.156
Age-sex dummies						
Male (Age 19–24) (reference category)	0.030	0.170	0.019	0.137	0.016	0.125
Male (Age 25–29)	0.027	0.163	0.023	0.151	0.019	0.136
Male (Age 30–34)	0.035	0.184	0.032	0.176	0.027	0.163
Male (Age 35–39)	0.040	0.197	0.037	0.190	0.037	0.188
Male (Age 40–44)	0.046	0.210	0.045	0.208	0.044	0.205
Male (Age 45–49)	0.047	0.211	0.046	0.211	0.048	0.213
Male (Age 50–54)	0.043	0.203	0.044	0.205	0.049	0.216
Male (Age 55–59)	0.040	0.197	0.040	0.195	0.043	0.204
Male (Age 60–64)	0.038	0.192	0.039	0.193	0.039	0.194
Male (Age 65–69)	0.034	0.180	0.036	0.187	0.042	0.200
Male (Age 70–74)	0.027	0.163	0.029	0.167	0.031	0.174
Male (Age 75–79)	0.020	0.141	0.026	0.160	0.027	0.162
Male (Age 80–84)	0.016	0.124	0.015	0.123	0.016	0.124
Male (Age 85+)	0.009	0.097	0.011	0.102	0.008	0.091
Female (Age 19–24)	0.038	0.192	0.029	0.169	0.019	0.138
Female (Age 25–29)	0.032	0.177	0.030	0.169	0.022	0.147
Female (Age 30–34)	0.043	0.202	0.039	0.194	0.036	0.187

Continued

TABLE A1 Descriptive Statistics for the Variables Used in the Health Regression Models—cont'd

	Maximum Possible Sample		Nurse Visits Sample		Blood Sample	
	Mean	s.d.	Mean	s.d.	Mean	s.d.
Female (Age 35–39)	0.047	0.211	0.048	0.214	0.051	0.219
Female (Age 40–44)	0.051	0.220	0.053	0.224	0.056	0.230
Female (Age 45–49)	0.058	0.233	0.060	0.237	0.060	0.238
Female (Age 50–54)	0.052	0.223	0.051	0.219	0.055	0.227
Female (Age 55–59)	0.042	0.200	0.044	0.206	0.045	0.207
Female (Age 60–64)	0.049	0.215	0.056	0.230	0.060	0.237
Female (Age 65–69)	0.040	0.197	0.045	0.208	0.050	0.217
Female (Age 70–74)	0.030	0.170	0.033	0.179	0.034	0.182
Female (Age 75–79)	0.028	0.166	0.032	0.175	0.033	0.179
Female (Age 80–84)	0.021	0.142	0.022	0.148	0.022	0.146
Female (Age 85+)	0.015	0.122	0.015	0.121	0.012	0.109
Educational attainment						
Degree	0.298	0.458	0.309	0.462	0.321	0.467
A-level or equivalent	0.236	0.425	0.222	0.415	0.214	0.410
O-level or basic qualification	0.321	0.467	0.325	0.469	0.322	0.467
No qualification (reference category)	0.145	0.352	0.145	0.352	0.143	0.350
Marital status						
Single	0.154	0.361	0.128	0.334	0.107	0.309
Married (reference category)	0.695	0.460	0.702	0.457	0.713	0.453
Separated/divorced	0.077	0.267	0.087	0.282	0.092	0.289
Widowed	0.074	0.262	0.083	0.276	0.088	0.284
Household size	2.735	1.372	2.626	1.276	2.595	1.235
Number of kids in household	0.531	0.931	0.499	0.897	0.491	0.873

Continued

TABLE A1 Descriptive Statistics for the Variables Used in the Health Regression Models—cont'd

	Maximum Possible Sample		Nurse Visits Sample		Blood Sample	
	Mean	s.d.	Mean	s.d.	Mean	s.d.
Region						
North East	0.029	0.167	0.031	0.174	0.030	0.171
North West	0.084	0.278	0.092	0.289	0.096	0.295
Yorkshire & Humber	0.064	0.245	0.065	0.247	0.067	0.251
East Midlands	0.063	0.244	0.067	0.249	0.061	0.240
West Midlands	0.056	0.229	0.056	0.229	0.052	0.221
East of England	0.073	0.261	0.073	0.260	0.068	0.252
London	0.048	0.215	0.046	0.210	0.049	0.216
South East	0.102	0.302	0.105	0.307	0.102	0.303
South West	0.069	0.253	0.072	0.258	0.071	0.257
Wales	0.210	0.407	0.207	0.405	0.200	0.400
Scotland (reference category)	0.202	0.401	0.187	0.390	0.202	0.401
Sample size	7979		4474		3003	

[a]Sample size corresponds to the maximum possible sample size for the health regression models. Sample size varies in Tables 1–6 depending on the health outcome considered.
[b]Sample size corresponds to the nurse visits subsample.
[c]Sample size corresponds to the blood data subsample.

B **Income gradients in self-reported health measures for the nurse visits subsample**

TABLE A2 Income Gradients in Self-Assessed Health and Functional Disabilities for the Nurse Visits Sample

Panel A: Self-assessed health

	Coeff. (s.e.)[a]	Ordered Probit APE (s.e.)[a]				
		Excellent	Very Good	Good	Fair	Poor
Specification 1						
Ln(current income)	−0.264***	0.056***	0.041***	−0.022***	−0.043***	−0.032***
	(0.032)	(0.007)	(0.005)	(0.003)	(0.005)	(0.004)
Specification 2						
Long-run mean ln(income)	−0.409***	0.086***	0.062***	−0.034***	−0.066***	−0.048***
	(0.039)	(0.008)	(0.006)	(0.003)	(0.006)	(0.005)
Sample size				4474		

Continued

Panel B: Functional disabilities

	Probit	
	Coeff. (s.e.)[a]	APE (s.e.)[a]
Specification 1		
Ln(current income)	−0.174***	−0.050***
	(0.041)	(0.012)
Specification 2		
Long-run mean ln(income)	−0.379***	−0.108***
	(0.053)	(0.015)
Sample size	4474	

APE, average partial effects; Coeff., coefficients; s.e., standard errors.
[a]Robust standard errors in parenthesis.
***P < .01.
**P < .05.
*P < .10.

TABLE A3 Income Gradients in (Inverted) PCS-12 for the Nurse Visits Sample

	OLS	Unconditional Quantile Regressions					
		Q10	Q25	Q50	Q75	Q90	Q95
	Coeff. (s.e.)[a]	Coeff. (s.e.)[b]	Coeff. (s.e.)[b]	Coeff. (s.e.)[b]	Coeff. (s.e.)[b]	Coeff. (s.e.)[b]	Coeff. (s.e.)[b]
Specification 1							
Ln(current income)	−1.471***	−0.580***	−0.933***	−1.594***	−2.334***	−1.825**	−1.639**
	(0.299)	(0.203)	(0.188)	(0.325)	(0.701)	(0.906)	(0.810)
Specification 2							
Long-run mean ln (income)	−3.284***	−0.878***	−0.908***	−2.818***	−6.144***	−6.549***	−6.423***
	(0.397)	(0.263)	(0.243)	(0.421)	(1.007)	(1.308)	(1.154)
Sample size	4218						

Coeff., coefficients; OLS, ordinary least squares; s.e., standard errors.
[a]Robust standard errors in parenthesis.
[b]UQR standard errors are bootstrap estimates with 500 replications.
***P < .01.
**P < .05.
*P < .10.

Acknowledgments

Understanding Society is an initiative funded by the Economic and Social Research Council and various government departments, with scientific leadership by the Institute for Social and Economic Research, University of Essex, and survey delivery by NatCen Social Research and Kantar Public. The research data are distributed by the UK Data Service. We are grateful to the Economic and Social Research Council for financial support for this research via project "How can biomarkers and genetics improve our understanding of society and health?" (award no. ES/M008592/1). Andrew Jones acknowledges funding from the Leverhulme Trust Major Research Fellowship (MRF-2016-004). The funders, data creators, and United Kingdom Data Service have no responsibility for the contents of this paper.

References

Acabchuk, R.L., Kamath, J., Salamone, J.D., Johnson, B.T., 2017. Stress and chronic illness: the inflammatory pathway. Social Science & Medicine 185, 166–170.

Adler, N.E., Newman, K., 2002. Socioeconomic disparities in health: pathways and policies. Health Affairs 21 (2), 60–76.

Bago d'Uva, T., O'Donnell, O., van Doorslaer, E., 2008. Differential health reporting by education level and its impact on the measurement of health inequalities among older Europeans. International Journal of Epidemiology 37 (6), 1375–1383.

Baker, M., Stabile, M., Deri, C., 2004. What do self-reported, objective, measures of health measure. Journal of Human Resources 39 (4), 1067–1093.

Banks, J., Marmot, M., Oldfield, Z., Smith, J.P., 2006. Disease and disadvantage in the United States and in England. JAMA: The Journal of the American Medical Association 295 (17), 2037–2045.

Benzeval, M., Davillas, A., Kumari, M., Lynn, P., 2014. Understanding society-UK household longitudinal study: Biomarker user guide and glossary. University of Essex, Colchester.

Benzeval, M., Judge, K., 2001. Income and health: the time dimension. Social Science and Medicine 52 (9), 1371–1390.

Biomarkers Definition Working Group, 2001. Biomarkers and surrogate endpoints: preferred definitions and conceptual framework. Clinical Pharmacology & Therapeutics 69, 89–95.

Bitler, M.P., Gelbach, J.B., Hoynes, H.W., 2006. What mean impacts miss: distributional effects of welfare reform experiments. The American Economic Review 96 (4), 988–1012.

Böheim, R., Jenkins, S.P., 2006. A comparison of current and annual measures of income in the British Household Panel Survey. Journal of Official Statistics 22 (4), 733.

Buchinsky, M., 1998. Recent advances in quantile regression models: a practical guideline for empirical research. Journal of Human Resources 33 (1), 88–126.

Carrieri, V., Jones, A.M., 2016. The income-health relationship 'beyond the mean': new evidence from biomarkers. Health Economics 26 (7), 937–956.

Contoyannis, P., Jones, A.M., Rice, N., 2004. The dynamics of health in the British Household Panel Survey. Journal of Applied Econometrics 19 (4), 473–503.

Crossley, T.F., Kennedy, S., 2002. The reliability of self-assessed health status. Journal of Health Economics 21 (4), 643–658.

Daltroy, L.H., Larson, M.G., Eaton, H.M., Phillips, C.B., Liang, M.H., 1999. Discrepancies between self-reported and observed physical function in the elderly: the influence of response shift and other factors. Social Science & Medicine 48 (11), 1549–1561.

Davillas, A., Benzeval, M., 2016. Alternative measures to BMI: exploring income-related inequalities in adiposity in Great Britain. Social Science & Medicine 166, 223–232.

Deaton, A.S., Paxson, C.H., 1998. Aging and inequality in income and health. The American Economic Review 88 (2), 248–253.

Dowd, J.B., Simanek, A.M., Aiello, A.E., 2009. Socio-economic status, cortisol and allostatic load: a review of the literature. International Journal of Epidemiology 38 (5), 1297–1309.

Dowd, J.B., Zajacova, A., 2010. Does self-rated health mean the same thing across socioeconomic groups? Evidence from biomarker data. Annals of Epidemiology 20 (10), 743–749.

Ettner, S.L., 1996. New evidence on the relationship between income and health. Journal of Health Economics 15 (1), 67–85.

Feldstein, P.J., 1966. Research on the demand for health services. The Milbank Memorial Fund Quarterly 44 (3), 128–165.

Ferrari, M., Cuenca-Garcia, M., Valtuena, J., Moreno, L.A., Censi, L., González-Gross, M., et al., 2015. Inflammation profile in overweight/obese adolescents in Europe: an analysis in relation to iron status. European Journal of Clinical Nutrition 69 (2), 247–255.

Fibrinogen Studies Collaboration, 2005. Plasma fibrinogen level and the risk of major cardiovascular diseases and nonvascular mortality: an individual participant meta-analysis. JAMA: The Journal of the American Medical Association 294 (14), 1799–1809.

Firpo, S., Fortin, N.M., Lemieux, T., 2009. Unconditional quantile regressions. Econometrica 77 (3), 953–973.

Friedman, M., 1957. The permanent income hypothesis. In: A theory of the consumption function. Princeton University Press.

Fuchs, V.R., 2004. Reflections on the socio-economic correlates of health. Journal of Health Economics 23 (4), 653–661.

Gémes, K., Ahnve, S., Janszky, I., 2008. Inflammation a possible link between economical stress and coronary heart disease. European Journal of Epidemiology 23 (2), 95–103.

Glei, D.A., Goldman, N., Shkolnikov, V.M., Jdanov, D., Shalnova, S., Shkolnikova, M., et al., 2013. To what extent do biomarkers account for the large social disparities in health in Moscow? Social Science and Medicine 77, 164–172.

Godoy, R., Goodman, E., Gravlee, C., Levins, R., Seyfried, C., Caram, M., et al., 2007. Blood pressure and hypertension in an American colony (Puerto Rico) and on the USA mainland compared, 1886–1930. Economics and Human Biology 5 (2), 255–279.

Idler, E.L., Benyamini, Y., 1997. Self-rated health and mortality: a review of twenty-seven community studies. Journal of Health and Social Behavior 38 (1), 21–37.

Ishii, S., Karlamangla, A.S., Bote, M., Irwin, M.R., Jacobs Jr., D.R., Cho, H.J., et al., 2012. Gender, obesity and repeated elevation of C-reactive protein: data from the CARDIA cohort. PLoS One 7 (4), e36062.

Jenkins, S.P., 2011. Changing fortunes: Income mobility and poverty dynamics in Britain. OUP, Oxford.

Johnston, D.W., Propper, C., Shields, M.A., 2009. Comparing subjective and objective measures of health: evidence from hypertension for the income/health gradient. Journal of Health Economics 28 (3), 540–552.

Jolliffe, D., 2011. Overweight and poor? On the relationship between income and the body mass index. Economics and Human Biology 9 (4), 342–355.

Jones, A.M., Wildman, J., 2008. Health, income and relative deprivation: evidence from the BHPS. Journal of Health Economics 27 (2), 308–324.

Jürges, H., 2007. True health vs response styles: exploring cross-country differences in self-reported health. Health Economics 16 (2), 163–178.

Jürges, H., 2008. Self-assessed health, reference levels, and mortality. Applied Economics 40 (5), 569–582.

Jürges, H., Kruk, E., Reinhold, S., 2013. The effect of compulsory schooling on health-evidence from biomarkers. Journal of Population Economics 26 (2), 645–672.

Jylhä, M., 2009. What is self-rated health and why does it predict mortality? Towards a unified conceptual model. Social Science & Medicine 69 (3), 307–316.

Karlamangla, A.S., Gruenewald, T.L., Seeman, T.E., 2012. Promise of biomarkers in assessing and predicting health. In: Wolfe, B., Evans, W., Seeman, T.E. (Eds.), The biological consequences of socioeconomic inequalities. Russell Sage, New York.

Koenker, R., Bassett, G., 1978. Regression quantiles. Econometrica: Journal of the Econometric Society 46 (1), 33–50.

Ljungvall, Å., Gerdtham, U.G., Lindblad, U., 2015. Misreporting and misclassification: implications for socioeconomic disparities in body-mass index and obesity. The European Journal of Health Economics 16 (1), 5–20.

McFall, S.L., Petersen, J., Kaminska, O., Lynn, P., 2014. Understanding society—UK household longitudinal study: Waves 2 and 3 nurse health assessment, 2010-2012, guide to nurse health assessment. University of Essex, Colchester.

Menchik, P.L., 1993. Economic status as a determinant of mortality among black and white older men: does poverty kill? Population Studies 47 (3), 427–436.

Millán, J., Pintó, X., Muñoz, A., Zúñiga, M., Rubiés-Prat, J., Pallardo, L.F., et al., 2009. Lipoprotein ratios: physiological significance and clinical usefulness in cardiovascular prevention. Vascular Health and Risk Management 5, 757.

Muennig, P., Sohler, N., Mahato, B., 2007. Socioeconomic status as an independent predictor of physiological biomarkers of cardiovascular disease: evidence from NHANES. Preventive Medicine 45 (1), 35–40.

Murasko, J.E., 2008. Male-female differences in the association between socioeconomic status and atherosclerotic risk in adolescents. Social Science & Medicine 67 (11), 1889–1897.

Pischon, T., Boeing, H., Hoffmann, K., Bergmann, M., Schulze, M.B., Overvad, K., et al., 2008. General and abdominal adiposity and risk of death in Europe. New England Journal of Medicine 359 (20), 2105–2120.

Powdthavee, N., 2010. Does education reduce the risk of hypertension? Estimating the biomarker effect of compulsory schooling in England. Journal of Human Capital 4 (2), 173–202.

Prospective Studies Collaboration, 2007. Blood cholesterol and vascular mortality by age, sex, and blood pressure: a meta-analysis of individual data from 61 prospective studies with 55 000 vascular deaths. The Lancet 370 (9602), 1829–1839.

Prospective Studies Collaboration, 2009. Body-mass index and cause-specific mortality in 900 000 adults: collaborative analyses of 57 prospective studies. The Lancet 373 (9669), 1083–1096.

Rahkovsky, I., Gregory, C.A., 2013. Food prices and blood cholesterol. Economics and Human Biology 11 (1), 95–107.

Seccareccia, F., Pannozzo, F., Dima, F., Minoprio, A., Menditto, A., Lo Noce, C., et al., 2001. Heart rate as a predictor of mortality: the MATISS project. American Journal of Public Health 91 (8), 1258–1263.

Singh-Manoux, A., Ferrie, J.E., Chandola, T., Marmot, M., 2004. Socioeconomic trajectories across the life course and health outcomes in midlife: evidence for the accumulation hypothesis? International Journal of Epidemiology 33 (5), 1072–1079.

Theorell, T., 2002. Job stress and fibrinogen. European Heart Journal 23 (23), 1799–1801.

Turner, R.J., Thomas, C.S., Brown, T.H., 2016. Childhood adversity and adult health: evaluating intervening mechanisms. Social Science & Medicine 156, 114–124.

Van Doorslaer, E., Jones, A.M., 2003. Inequalities in self-reported health: validation of a new approach to measurement. Journal of Health Economics 22 (1), 61–87.

Verbeek, M., Nijman, T., 1992. Testing for selectivity bias in panel data models. International Economic Review 33 (3), 681–703.

WHO, 2011. Use of glycated haemoglobin (HbA1c) in the diagnosis of diabetes mellitus. World Health Organization, Geneva.

Ziebarth, N., 2010. Measurement of health, health inequality, and reporting heterogeneity. Social Science & Medicine 71 (1), 116–124.

Chapter 23

Application in Banking: Securitization and Global Banking

Andrada Bilan*, Hans Degryse[†,‡], Kuchulain O'Flynn* and Steven Ongena*,[†,‡]

*University of Zurich and Swiss Finance Institute, Zürich, Switzerland, [†]KU Leuven, Leuven, Belgium, [‡]CEPR, Washington, DC, United States

Chapter Outline

This chapter reviews the econometric techniques and findings regarding two recent developments in the banking literature—securitization and global banking. The banking industry has become more complex in its business models and in its geographic structure. First of all, banks have become more complex in scope. Securitization, for example, has allowed banks to diversify their traditional credit business, by selling the original loans to outside investors, and to create more complex financial products. At the same time, most banks are no longer local entities, lending to local firms and sensitive only to local shocks. Banks have become global in many aspects, and this new geographical structure is studied by the global banking literature.

The benefits of securitization and global banking are driven by the same forces: diversification and risk-sharing. The costs arise because of potential market failures, such as asymmetric information. Furthermore, the private costs might differ from the social costs stemming from contagion among the users of these innovations, which can be substantial as witnessed during the financial crisis.

Panel Data Econometrics. https://doi.org/10.1016/B978-0-12-815859-3.00023-8

In this chapter, we review recent empirical contributions that have relied on comprehensive data and panel data econometrics to study the effect that these two innovations have had on the traditional credit market. The first part of this chapter deals with securitization, which is followed by global banking. Each section includes a review of the econometric methodologies employed and a discussion of selected contributions. The following section provides an overview of the main sources of data employed in this chapter.

1 Data Sources

Most of the datasets used in this chapter have a panel structure, with a time and a cross-section dimension, typically across countries, banks, firms, or loans. More granular data leads to better identification.

Studies at the bank level typically rely on bank financial information, extracted from balance sheets and income statements. This is available either through regulatory reports (for example, the Federal Reserve's Report of Condition and Income or Call Reports), or from private data providers (such as Orbis Bank Focus or SNL). Indicators for the intensity of securitization can be obtained from private data provider Dealogic, which reports banks' involvement in different types of securitized assets (mortgages, corporate loans, covered bonds), or from rating agencies, such as Moody's. Trading data involving asset-backed securities, including commercial paper or bonds, can be found either in trade repositories, such as the Depository Trust and Clearing Corporation (DTCC), or by approaching the dealer banks that make markets for these products.

In many empirical analyses, bank data is supplemented with firm-level financial information, generally available either from Compustat (worldwide) or Bureau van Dijk and Moody's Analytics (European), and financial market indicators.

For loan-level analyses, the source of data depends on the type of credit product concerned. Most of the empirical research about mortgage lending has focused on the US market, where data is available either from the Home Mortgage Disclosure Act (HMDA) or the First American CoreLogic LoanPerformance databases. Detailed information is available, including mortgage rates, loan size, maturity, year of origination, contract types (hybrid, fixed-rate, adjustable-rate), default information, as well as borrower characteristics (credit scores, debt-to-income ratios) and loan application status (denied, approved, originated). Data aggregated at zip-code level also is available from Equifax, another data provider that maintains consumer credit history and related data about US households. Equifax provides annual aggregated data for outstanding credit and defaults, broken down by type of loan: mortgages, home equity lines, credit card debt, auto loans, student loans, and consumer loans.

Loan-level data about corporate credit has come from a variety of sources. The most widely used cross-country data source is Thomson Reuters' Dealscan database of syndicated loans, although information about securitized loans also is available from other providers, such as Creditex. In many countries, loan-level data is available through credit registries or bureaus, often organized at national central banks. Typically, they include all bank-firm lending above a certain threshold (e.g., Djankov, McLiesh, & Shleifer, 2007). As in the case of mortgages, these datasets offer an array of characteristics of the loan itself (maturity, interest rate, performance), or on the borrower.

Global banking requires data across countries. For instance, the "perfect" dataset to test the international transmission of monetary policy through banks would be a multicountry credit registry, combined with detailed data about banks and firms, and potentially enhanced with loan applications.[1] This unfortunately does not exist yet, because of the confidential nature of credit registries.

As a result, the datasets most frequently used for country-level studies are the Bank of International Settlements (BIS) Locational Banking Statistics (LBS) and, more recently, its Consolidated Banking Statistics (CBS). The LBS database contains data about the composition of banks' balance sheets by currency, and a geographical breakdown for their counterparties. The CBS database contains data about the worldwide consolidated country risk exposure of internationally active banks, with headquarters in countries that report to BIS. In addition, information about bank lending behavior across countries is sometimes available from surveys (an example being the Bank Lending Survey, carried out by the Eurosystem). Aggregation at country level (or even bank level), however, requires the strong assumption of homogeneous loan demand across banks. It is therefore crucial to control for borrower characteristics to avoid having to make this assumption.

Thus, a tension between internal and external validity is present in the global banking literature, even at the level of data comprehensiveness. To include the additional dimension of borrower information, the global banking literature has had to sacrifice coverage. For example, Morais, Peydró, and Ruiz (2019) make good use of the Mexican credit registry in order to identify the international credit channel of monetary policy. The data are rich enough to allow them to employ time-varying bank and firm effects, which benefits identification. Further, the granularity of the data allows the authors to test for heterogeneous real effects at firm level. The ability to measure real effects is important, because the transmission of monetary policy or other economic shocks matters only if there are real effects. All this consolidates the internal validity of their study, but the use of this data confines the analysis to a single country, which limits its external validity.

Syndicated loan datasets resolve this issue because they contain bank-firm data covering multiple countries. They have a different weakness, however. Although the data are sufficiently granular, syndicated loans tend to be large

---

1. See Jiménez, Ongena, Peydró, and Saurina (2012) for the use of loan application data in identifying the bank balance sheet channel of monetary policy transmission.

loans given to large firms. Using this data can hide credit supply effects on small and medium sized firms. Further, a key requirement for monetary policy to have real effects is imperfect substitutability between bank lending and other financing sources. Large firms are likely to have better access to outside financing. Thus, an analysis using this data is likely to underestimate the real effects of the bank lending channel.[2]

Recent contributions have found other ways to combine these datasets in ways that alleviate the tension between external and internal validity. Although not a multicountry credit registry, Ongena, Peydró, and van Horen (2015) employ granular data across countries and currency areas, combining multiple datasets[3] to obtain bank-firm data about SMEs, across 13 countries. This allows for the identification of the international bank lending channel and the analysis of its real effects, across a heterogeneous sample of firms. Popov and Ongena (2011) use the Business Environment and Enterprise Performance Survey (BEEPS) to create a synthetic panel dataset that can be merged with interbank market rates from the Global Financial database. This level of granularity in a panel structure allows modeling the effects of financial integration on firms' access to bank credit (borrowing constraints) and the cost of bank credit (loan rates).

2 Securitization and Lending

Although securitization dates to the 17th and 18th century in Holland (Goetzmann & Rouwenhorst, 2008), its massive usage is a relatively recent development in credit markets. Securitization implies that financial intermediaries that grant illiquid loans, subsequently pool them together, diversifying risks, and convert them into liquid assets or asset-backed securities (ABSs). These assets then are sold to outside investors, in exchange for wholesale funding. Although the largest share of ABSs cover home mortgage loans, other types of loans also have been securitized, including automobile credit, student loans, or corporate loans.

At the end of 2007, the US securitized mortgage loan market reached $6.42 trillion.[4] A liquid market for securitized assets has recognized benefits for the banking industry, such as improving risk sharing and reducing banks' cost of capital (Pennacchi, 1988). Credit to both households and firms should grow as a result. The global financial crisis of 2007–09, however, uncovered ways in which securitization could also hurt lending. It is well understood that the

---

2. Aggregated bank or country level data also suffers from this vulnerability, because lending to large firms drives aggregate loan volumes.
3. They combine the Bank-ownership database compiled by Claessens and van Horen (2014), bank funding data using Dealogic, bank balance sheet information from Bankscope, firm balance sheet information from Amadeus, and bank-firm connection information from Kompass.
4. See Loutskina (2011).

crisis started in the securitized subprime mortgage market, which collapsed after having accumulated an unmanageable amount of risks. This prompted both researchers in finance and policymakers to seek a better understanding of the benefits and the vulnerabilities of the markets for asset-backed securities. We offer a nonexhaustive review of the recent empirical literature addressing this need.

2.1 Methodology

The empirical literature investigating the relationships between securitization and bank lending uses extensively panel data econometrics. In general, the research design seeks to establish causality between securitization and the functioning of credit markets.

One way to look at establishing causality is to exploit cross-sectional heterogeneity between subjects along theoretical priors. At the country level, for example, Maddaloni and Peydró (2011) investigate whether monetary policy has a larger impact on lending standards in countries with a higher intensity of securitization. Or, at the bank level, Loutskina (2011) studies whether banks with a higher share of loans that can be securitized have lower holdings of liquid assets. Acharya, Schnabl, and Suarez (2013) investigate whether banks with lower levels of regulated capital engage more intensely in securitization. At the loan level, Benmelech, Dlugosz, and Ivashina (2012) and Albertazzi, Bottero, and Ongena (2016) argue that securitization does not negatively affect all credit markets, by showing that securitized corporate loans perform similarly to nonsecuritized ones. Other studies rely on the time pattern of correlations to suggest causality. Gorton and Metrick (2012), for example, use a panel in which the cross-sectional dimension is given by several prime and subprime financial markets. They exploit its time dimension, showing that the subprime market led the prime market in the run-up to the financial crisis. The panel structure of the data allows the researchers to include controls at subject-time level, but also fixed effects along each of the two dimensions.

Although many times a powerful tool, however, such correlational evidence still can be vulnerable to endogeneity. In the cross-sectional dimension, banks able to use securitization might be different from banks that are not, or securitized loans might be different from nonsecuritized ones, along characteristics that are unobservable to the econometrician. In the time series dimension, macroeconomic factors and policies might have a heterogeneous impact on lending, which might correlate with the intensity of securitization. For example, increasing house prices or extending government guarantees might lead to the securitization of riskier loans. Finally, observed loan volumes and spreads are the equilibrium result of transactions between banks and borrowers and, as such, they are subject to simultaneity between supply and demand.

The literature has addressed each of these issues in several ways. The recent availability of banking micro data allowed researchers to construct increasingly

homogeneous samples, thereby comparing individuals with similar characteristics, within the same product or geographical market segment (Albertazzi
et al., 2016; Benmelech et al., 2012; Demyanyk & Hemert, 2009; Mian &
Sufi, 2009). Other studies relied on established empirical techniques that specifically tackle endogeneity, such as difference-in-differences or regression discontinuity designs (Keys, Mukherjee, Seru, & Vig, 2010; Purnanandam, 2010).
Even when detailed micro data were not available, simultaneous estimation
helped disentangle supply and demand (Carbo-Valverde, Degryse, &
Rodríguez-Fernández, 2015).

We will review some of these contributions in more detail.

2.2 Securitization and Bank Business Models

The possibility to engage in loan securitization has changed the way banks do
business. The impact has been both direct, by altering bank management decisions, and indirect, because securitization affected the transmission of monetary
policy or bank regulation. In this section, we review selected empirical contributions that have documented these changes.

The direct benefits of securitization are put to the test in Loutskina (2011).
The author uses bank balance sheets and income statements extracted from the
Federal Reserve's Call Reports to study how securitization changes bank liquidity and funding management. Relying on panel data analysis conducted over
30 years (1976 to 2007), this study documents that securitization reduces banks'
needs for liquid assets. In turn, this increases banks' ability to extend credit. The
reason is clear: Loans that are long-term and illiquid now can be sold in the market, in exchange for new liquidity. Banks adapt their business from holding
loans on the balance sheet up to maturity to selling them to outside investors.

To capture this effect empirically, Loutskina (2011) constructs an index of
potential liquidity for each bank's portfolio. More precisely, this is a weighted
average of a bank's potential to securitize its own loans, based on the shares of
loans of the same type already securitized on the market. She then finds that the
index is inversely correlated with banks' holdings of liquid assets, measured as
the share of marketable assets and the federal funds sold, to total assets. Further
tests conducted around regulatory changes affecting liquidity for securitized
assets, confirm that a liquid ABS market offers a substitute to bank on-balance
sheet liquidity.

Securitization, however, can also have indirect effects on the banking market. One stems from its interaction with monetary policy. Expansionary monetary policy stimulates credit, but it can also increase risk-taking by banks. This
is known in the banking literature as the "risk-taking channel of monetary policy." Agency problems in banking, because of bailouts and liquidity assistance,
mean that low interest rates can induce banks to soften their lending standards
by improving banks' liquidity (Allen & Gale, 2007) and net worth (Adrian &

Shin, 2010). Moreover, low interest rates make riskless assets less attractive and might lead financial intermediaries to search for yield (Rajan, 2006).

We previously discussed how the possibility to securitize loans improves bank liquidity, but this additional liquidity could be excessive during a monetary expansion. Furthermore, loan securitization is also one way of creating assets that yield attractive returns for investors, but that are risky. As a result, although expansionary monetary policy alone could lead to softer lending standards, securitization might further amplify this phenomenon. To investigate the impact of securitization on the risk-taking channel of monetary policy, Maddaloni and Peydró (2011) use data from the Eurosystem's Bank Lending Survey (BLS).[5] The authors assemble survey data from 12 countries that are in the European Monetary Union between 2002:Q4 and 2008:Q3.[6]

Directly assessing the effects of monetary policy on bank lending standards can lead to biased estimates, because both tend to be endogenously determined, together with local economic conditions. The authors argue, however, that this is less concerning in the Euro-area. Here, monetary policy rates are set by the Governing Council of the European Central Bank (ECB) and are identical across countries, although significant national differences in terms of GDP and inflation persist. Based on this observation, the authors devise an identification strategy that exploits cross-country variation in monetary policy conditions and the intensity of securitization across Euro-area countries.

A first empirical specification confirms the effect of an expansionary monetary policy on lending standards:

$$LS_{t,i} = \alpha_i + \nu_t + \beta STrate_{t-1,i} + \gamma LTrate_{t-1,i} + \delta Controls_{t-1,i} + \epsilon_{t,i} \qquad (1)$$

where $LS_{t,i}$ is the net percentage of banks that report having tightened credit standards in quarter t and country i. $STrate_{t-1,i}$ captures the local effect of monetary policy conditions, proxied by country-specific residuals, from regressing the EONIA rate[7] on local GDP growth and inflation. A positive residual indicates contractionary monetary policy; a negative residual indicates expansionary policy. Therefore, if an expansionary monetary policy led to softer lending standards, then the β coefficient should be positive. The specification includes controls for long-term interest rates, GDP, inflation, as well as time- and country-fixed effects.

A second specification measures whether the effect of an expansionary monetary policy is amplified when securitization intensifies, by interacting the short-term rates with indicators for securitization. Maddaloni and Peydró

---

5. Jiménez, Ongena, Peydró, and Saurina (2014) and Ioannidou, Ongena, and Peydró (2015) provide loan-level empirical evidence for the existence of the risk-taking channel of monetary policy.
6. The 12 countries are: Austria, Belgium, France, Finland, Germany, Greece, Ireland, Italy, Luxembourg, the Netherlands, Portugal, and Spain.
7. The EONIA rate is the Euro OverNight Index Average, the short-term rate on the interbank market, targeted by ECB's monetary policy.

(2011) measure securitization activity using the ratio between all issuances of asset-backed and mortgage-backed securities in each quarter and country (as reported by Dealogic) and GDP.

$$LS_{t,i} = \alpha_i + \nu_t + \beta STrate_{t-1,i} + \zeta Securitization_{t-1,i} + \\ + \theta(STrate*Securitization)_{t-1,i} + \gamma LTrate_{t-1,i} + \delta Controls_{t-1,i} + \epsilon_{t,i} \quad (2)$$

The results confirm that low monetary policy rates soften lending standards for both firms and individuals. And, crucially, this softening is amplified by intense securitization activity, especially in the case of mortgages (the θ coefficient on the interaction term is positive and statistically significant).

Aside from its interaction with monetary policy, securitization can also dilute banking regulation. Acharya et al. (2013) argue that, prior to the financial crisis, commercial banks relied on securitization in order to circumvent regulatory capital constraints.

Banks can reduce capital requirements by securitizing and offloading loans.[8] Focusing on the asset-backed commercial paper (ABCP) market prior to 2007, Acharya et al. (2013) show that some banks use this product heavily to cut required capital, without adequately transferring the underlying risk of the loan exposures. As a result, these banks are more vulnerable when the crisis starts. Below, we first describe the most relevant institutional features of the ABCP market and then we review the empirical methods and findings of this study.

In the run-up to the financial crisis, banks set up conduits to purchase their loans. The conduits securitize the loans and finance them by issuing short-term ABCP to investors. Conduits, however, are subject to rollover risk: If the value of the assets in their portfolio deteriorates, they might not raise enough cash to refinance maturing commercial paper. Many of the investors in ABCP at the time, however, are money market funds, who prefer safe assets. To attract these investors, banks insure the new assets with explicit guarantees, structured such that investors get paid off even if the conduits' cash flow falls below the level of their claims. Crucially, even with such comprehensive guarantees, this type of securitization through conduits significantly reduces banks' capital requirements, to at most a tenth of the capital required to back on-balance sheet loans.

As a result, banks retain most of the credit risk even after securitizing the loans. When the financial crisis brings a sharp drop in the value of conduits,[9]

---

8. Capital regulation determines the level of capital that financial institutions have to hold against risk-weighted assets. Until 2013, this amount was set under the Basel II agreement at a minimum of 8% for banks.

9. In July 2007, the ABCP outstanding amount to $ 1.3 trillion. On August 9, 2007, the French bank BNP Paribas halts withdrawals from three funds invested in mortgage-backed securities, on the back of losses from the underlying assets. This has a profound impact on the ABCP market, which experiences a strong loss of investor confidence, with outstanding volumes dropping to $833 billion by December 2007.

losses to outside investors are small. The impact on banks, however, is negative and large, because they hold the financial responsibility of the conduits and have committed to repaying maturing ABCPs to investors at par.

To document these events empirically, the authors use comprehensive panel data. The main data source is ratings reports for all 938 conduits rated by Moody's Investors Service from January 2001 to December 2009, containing data about conduit sponsors, type, assets, and guarantees. This is enhanced with Moody's Weekly Announcement Reports of rating downgrades on conduits, from January 2007 to December 2008. In addition, the authors access a proprietary data set on all US ABCP transactions between January 2007 and February 2008, collected by the Depository Trust and Clearing Corporation (DTCC). Finally, they include bank financials and share prices.

The analysis follows three steps. The authors first investigate whether capital-constrained commercial banks, prior to the financial crisis, are more likely to sponsor conduits. They use panel regressions, and assess the relation between bank exposure to ABCP (measured as the ratio of ABCP relative to bank equity) and bank capital:

$$Exposure_{it} = \alpha_i + \delta_t + \beta CapitalRatio_{it} + \gamma X_{it} + \epsilon_{it} \tag{3}$$

where $Exposure_{it}$ measures the ABCP exposure of bank i at time t, $CapitalRatio_{it}$ is the capital ratio of bank i at time t, α_i are bank-fixed effects, δ_t are time-fixed effects, and X_{it} are controls for time-varying bank characteristics (size, return on assets, and short-term debt, deposits, loans, each weighted by assets). Bank capital is measured both as economic capital (book equity to assets) and regulatory capital (Tier 1 regulatory capital to risk-weighted assets). Economic capital is included because regulatory capital is vulnerable to reverse causality. If banks already had engaged in securitization to arrive at their existing capital ratios, then, in equilibrium, the econometrician would observe only relatively larger levels of regulated capital. In this case, economic capital might provide a better measure of capital constraints, because it is not monitored by bank supervisors.

A second specification looks into which conduits experience greater outflows, lower issuance, and higher spreads, as investors start fleeing risky assets in 2007. This analysis exploits cross-sectional variation in the strength of the guarantees: Although some guarantees completely cover credit and liquidity risks, others are weaker. The focus is on the period of four months before and after August 9, 2007, as follows:

$$y_{it} = \alpha + \beta_j Guarantee_{ij} + \gamma_j After_t Guarantee_{ij} + \delta After_t + \epsilon_{it} \tag{4}$$

where y_{it} is either the natural logarithm of the value of ABCP outstanding of conduit i in week t, or the overnight ABCP spread over the federal funds rate on new issues by conduit i on day t. $Guarantee_{ij}$ is an indicator variable for the guarantee of type j of conduit i and $After_t$ is an indicator variable that equals one after August 9, 2007. Additional specifications include time-fixed effects, conduit-fixed effects, and sponsor-time fixed effects. If the financial crisis worried investors about conduit risks, then conduits with weaker guarantees should have a relatively lower performance and less ability to roll over maturing assets (γ_j should be large and significant for relatively weaker guarantees).

For conduits that are fully guaranteed, the argument continues, investors should suffer no loss. In exchange, the negative shock should be absorbed by the sponsoring banks. A final specification tests whether these banks experience lower stock returns, in an event study around August 9, 2007. The baseline specification is:

$$R_i = a + \beta ConduitExposure_i + \gamma X_i + \epsilon_i \tag{5}$$

where R_i is the cumulative equity return of bank i, computed over the three-day period from August 8-10, 2007. $ConduitExposure_i$ is bank i's conduit exposure relative to equity in January 2007, and X_i are bank characteristics. Consistent with the hypothesis, we would expect a negative β.

The estimations show that, first, banks that are more capital-constrained have indeed larger ABCP exposures. Second, when asset quality deteriorates at the beginning of the crisis, ABCPs with weaker guarantees experience larger investor outflows. And, third, banks highly exposed to conduits appear to be the main losers from their underperformance: An increase in conduit exposure from 0% to 100% of bank equity reduces the stock return during the three-day event window by 1.4 percentage points.

2.3 Types of Securitization and Asymmetric Information

The increased risk-taking observed prior to 2007 and associated with securitization might stem from a shift in the distribution of new borrowers, when supply increases sufficiently to satisfy a credit demand of lower quality. Securitization, however, can also increase informational friction in the credit market.

In their traditional role as financial intermediaries, banks should reduce information asymmetries between lenders and borrowers. When the originator of a loan holds it to maturity, they have incentives to select the loans that perform best. This is done both by ex-ante screening borrowers and by monitoring them ex-post (Gorton & Pennacchi, 1995; Holmstrom & Tirole, 1997; Parlour & Plantin, 2008; Pennacchi, 1988; Petersen & Rajan, 1994). Securitization, however, changes the traditional lending market from an originate-to-hold to an originate-to-distribute model (Purnanandam, 2010). As banks offload loans shortly after origination, by securitizing them, their screening efforts might be reduced. In fact, if screening is costly and loans can be securitized easily, banks might screen borrowers only for hard information. This information can be observed easily by outside investors and contracted upon. Any soft information that could predict the future performance of a loan is costly to process and unobservable to outsiders and risks being overlooked.

The empirical evidence suggests that securitization did increase informational asymmetries, but this effect was limited to the subprime mortgage market. Researchers have sought to explain the increased risk-taking in this market segment by looking for causal evidence of, first, an increase in bank credit supply, and second, of a simultaneous reduction in screening efforts. We review this evidence in the following section. Then, we review studies involving corporate credit, showing that these markets are more resilient to informational friction.

2.3.1 Subprime Mortgage Lending

Among the first studies exploring the reasons behind the weakness of the securitized mortgage market in the run-up to the financial crisis are Demyanyk and Hemert (2009) and Mian and Sufi (2009).

Demyanyk and Hemert (2009) use loan-level data about subprime mortgages from LoanPerformance and document a decrease in loan quality in this market segment, between 2001 and 2007. They employ proportional odds duration models, estimating the probability of first-time delinquency on a subprime mortgage loan as a function of loan characteristics, borrower characteristics, macroeconomic conditions, and origination year effects. The evidence is consistent with a sustained increase in risk-taking in the market. Conditional on observables, loan quality deteriorates monotonically between 2001 and 2007, but it is masked by the simultaneous appreciation in house prices. As house prices start to decline in 2006, poor loan quality materializes into realized defaults in 2006 and 2007.

What is the driver behind this increased risk-taking in mortgage lending? Is it driven by demand or supply? And how is it linked to securitization? These questions are hard to address in the context of Demyanyk and Hemert (2009), because their study lacks a control group. Other lending segments might have behaved similarly. Mian and Sufi (2009) take the investigation further and show that the increased underperformance was supply-driven and specific to the securitized subprime mortgage sector. They employ data about lending activity at the level of US zip codes, by combining Equifax information on outstanding credit and defaults, with new mortgage lending from the HMDA dataset.

Their work sheds light onto how micro data is necessary to choose between competing theoretical explanations. The expansion in subprime mortgage credit after 2000, they argue, could have been caused by two factors. It could have been demand-based, if the income prospects of subprime borrowers had improved over the same period. Or, lenders could have increased their supply of credit to riskier borrowers, expecting to immediately offload the risk by securitizing the loans. The analysis starts at county level. County level trends are consistent with the demand-based hypothesis: Income growth is stronger in counties with a higher share of subprime consumers during 2002 to 2005. If this growth in incomes is concentrated among the prime segments of the population, however, the correlation could be spurious. And, indeed, zooming at zip code level supports the alternative hypothesis: During the same period, subprime borrowers experience negative income growth. This supports the hypothesis of increasing credit supply to the riskier subprime sector.

So far, the causal interpretation is still weak. Subsequent contributions tackle causality and further investigate the underlying economic mechanisms linking securitization and deteriorating lending standards.

Keys et al. (2010) employ a regression discontinuity design to establish causality between securitization and decreased loan performance, because of reduced screening incentives. They use individual data about subprime mortgages from LoanPerformance from January 2001 to December 2006.

The discontinuity is at a specific threshold in mortgage borrowers' credit scores, inducing exogenous variation in the probability that their loan is securitized. This threshold is based on governmental guidelines advising against lending to borrowers with a credit score below this level.[10] Although the rule targeted lenders, investors purchasing asset-backed securities also adhered to it. As a result, loans made to borrowers with a credit score just above this threshold had a higher unconditional likelihood of being securitized than loans made to borrowers just below the threshold.

The premise is that the discontinuity in the likelihood of securitization induces a discontinuity in banks' screening incentives. To test this hypothesis, Keys et al. (2010) use a two-step approach. First, they look for a discontinuity in the number of loans securitized above and below the threshold:

$$Y_i = \alpha + \beta T_i + \theta f(CreditScore_i) + \delta T_i f(CreditScore_i) + \epsilon_i \qquad (6)$$

where Y_i is the number of loans for each credit score i, T_i is an indicator that takes value 1 if the credit score is larger than the threshold and 0 otherwise, and ϵ_i is a zero-mean error term. $f(CreditScore)$ and $T f(CreditScore)$ are flexible polynomials, aimed to fit the empirical distribution of the data. β represents the size of the discontinuity and is estimated by the difference in these two smoothed functions, at the cut-off.

Second, the authors evaluate the performance of the loans by examining realized defaults, up to 15 months after origination. If lenders screened used the same intensity to screen loans around the threshold—which should be similar in terms of hard information—then the two groups of loans should have equal performance. They estimate a second specification, similar to Eq. (6), where the variable Y_i becomes the share of loans in default within 10 to 15 months of origination. Here, β measures the change in the default rate at the threshold.

The first set of estimations show that loans just above the threshold have more than double chances of being securitized than loans just below the

---

10. Government-sponsored enterprises, Fannie Mae and Freddie Mac, all were urged not to lend to borrowers with credit scores lower than 620.

threshold. And, second, doubling the securitization volume on otherwise similar loans is associated with a 10%-25% increase in defaults, which the authors link to weaker bank screening.

Purnanandam (2010) complements these findings by showing that the weaker screening was not confined to a narrow segment of borrower FICO scores, but that banks highly involved in securitization did not actively screen entire loan portfolios. The author combines banking characteristics from Call Reports with loan-level information from the HDMA database. For identification, he exploits the liquidity shock that affected the secondary mortgage market in 2007, forcing banks to keep on their balance sheets loans that previously were intended for sale. Purnanandam (2010) then compares observed defaults on mortgage loans granted by banks highly exposed to securitization versus lowly exposed banks, in a difference-in-differences setup:

$$default_{it} = \mu_i + \beta_1 after_t + \beta_2 after_t presec_i + \beta_3 after_t premortgage_i + X_{it} + \epsilon_{it} \tag{7}$$

where the dependent variable measures the default rate of the mortgage portfolio of bank i in quarter t, μ_i are bank fixed effects, and X_{it} are time-varying bank characteristics. The coefficient on the $after_t$ variable captures the change in the time trend of the default rate after the mortgage crisis. β_2 measures the change in default rate for banks that originated loans primarily to sell them to third parties, relative to the corresponding change for banks that originated loans primarily to retain them to maturity. The second interaction term controls for time-varying bank involvement in mortgage lending, to isolate the coefficient β_2 from changes in the overall lending portfolios of banks.

The regression is estimated on a matched sample of banks that differ in their securitization activities, but that have otherwise granted mortgages to observationally equivalent borrowers, in similar geographical areas, and at similar rates. A statistically and economically significant positive β_2 suggests that loans made by banks active in securitization were of inferior quality, with disproportionately higher borrower defaults. The matched sample of banks mitigates concerns that the effect might be because of observable differences in the quality of the loans, suggesting it is rather consistent with diluted screening incentives.

2.3.2 Corporate Lending

Although most loan-level empirical evidence points to weaker lending standards and excessive risk in subprime mortgage loans caused by bank securitization activities, corporate lending offers a different picture.

Benmelech et al. (2012) show that securitization was not associated with riskier lending in the US corporate loan market prior to the financial crisis. They assemble loan-level information about syndicated loans from Dealscan and Creditflux, matched with firm financials from Compustat, from 1997 to

2007. Because syndicated loans are large ($522 million, on average), only parts of them are typically securitized.

The authors identify partially securitized loans by looking at the identity of the lenders in the syndicate. In addition, they construct a control sample of unsecuritized loans. The research question is similar to Keys et al. (2010): Do banks expend less effort in screening for soft information loans that they securitize? Because soft information is unobservable, the authors use as a proxy the ex-post performance on the loans, controlling for observables at the time of origination. Several measures of performance are used.[11] The detail of the data allows estimation at the loan level, with fixed effects for the leader bank in the syndicate. This removes a possible source of sample selection bias, which could arise if unsecuritized loans were originated by banks with relatively weaker screening capabilities. A dummy on the securitized loans measures the marginal effect of securitization on loan performance, within the loans originated by a given bank.

Benmelech et al. (2012) find that securitized syndicated loans did not underperform syndicated, but unsecuritized loans. They offer a possible explanation specific to the syndicated loan market. Because there are several lenders in a syndicate, if the remaining lenders were able to compensate for weak screening and monitoring from the party engaged in securitization, then loan quality might remain high.

The better performance of securitized business loans, however, is not restricted to the syndicated credit market. Using different data and a new empirical approach, Albertazzi et al. (2016) find only a limited role of asymmetric information in the securitization of SME loans. Here, the authors separate adverse selection from moral hazard by adapting the methodology introduced by Chiappori and Salanie (2000), of testing for asymmetric information in insurance contracts. Applied to securitized loans, this implies jointly estimating a model for the probability of a loan being securitized and one for the probability that the loan quality deteriorates. The analysis uses loan-level data from the Bank of Italy Credit Register and Supervisory Records, covering all firms borrowing from Italian banks over 2002-07. The data include information about the performance of both securitized and nonsecuritized loans until 2011, as well as bank and firm financials.

Albertazzi et al. (2016) argue that securitization increases information asymmetries if, accounting for characteristics observable to investors, there is positive correlation between the securitization of loans and the probability that these loans deteriorate into nonperforming. Specifically, the probability of securitization and underperformance of a loan granted to firm f by bank b at time t can be assumed to depend on observable characteristics, θ, representing the information set of the investors in ABS:

---

11. These include secondary market loan prices, credit ratings, spreads on credit default swaps, implied probabilities of default based on accounting information, and violations of loan covenants.

$$Prob\left(Secnritization_{fbt} = 1 \mid \theta_{fbt}\right) = F_S\left(\eta\theta_{fbt} + \epsilon_{fbt}\right)$$
$$Prob\left(Deterioration_{fbt} = 1 \mid \theta_{fbt}\right) = F_D\left(\eta'\theta_{fbt} + \epsilon'_{fbt}\right)$$

where the functions F can be linear probability models, logit or probit, and ϵ_{fbt} and ϵ_{fbt}' are the error terms. The correlation between the error terms provides a test for the presence of information asymmetries.

$$H_0(1) : Corr\left(\epsilon_{fbt}, \epsilon'_{fbt}\right) > 0 \tag{8}$$

Firms with multiple bank relationships help distinguish between adverse selection and moral hazard. Under the premise that adverse selection affects all financiers alike, ex-ante, a weak firm is equally likely to default on all exposures, not only on the securitized exposure. The incidence of moral hazard because of lack of monitoring, however, should have a larger negative effect on the lender's own exposure. To disentangle the two effects, the authors decompose the error terms, ϵ_{fbt} and ϵ_{fbt}', into two components: firm-time fixed effects (α_{ft} and α'_{ft}) and the remaining errors, μ_{fbt} and μ'_{fbt}.

Testing for adverse selection comes down to assessing whether there is positive correlation between the coefficients of the firm-time fixed effects:

$$H_0(2) : Corr\left(\alpha_{ft}, \alpha'_{ft}\right) > 0 \tag{9}$$

And, the behavior of the remaining bank-firm residuals provides a test for moral hazard:

$$H_0(3) : Corr\left(\mu_{fbt}, \mu'_{fbt}\right) > 0 \tag{10}$$

The authors find supporting evidence for $H_0(1)$, consistent with the presence of information asymmetries. Decomposing this effect further, they confirm that $H_0(2)$ holds, while $H_0(3)$ is rejected, implying that these asymmetries of information result from adverse selection, and not from moral hazard. The negative effect of adverse selection, however, is dominated by positive selection of observables at the time of securitizing the loans. As a result, overall, securitized SME loans perform better than the unsecuritized ones.

2.4 Securitization and Financial Stability

Because securitized markets have developed in close connection to the banking system, another important question is whether these markets are susceptible to the main vulnerability of banks: the risk of an inefficient run (Diamond & Dybvig, 1983; Diamond & Rajan, 2005). Runs sometimes are caused by contagion from a bad to a good market. In fact, Gorton and Metrick (2012) document a run in the sale and repurchase (repo) market, in which banks exchange securitized assets for funding from outside investors.[12]

Financial distress starts in the securitized subprime mortgage market, the authors argue, and spreads to the less risky, nonsubprime securitized assets through the repo market. Up to 2007, some repo agreements are backed by subprime housing assets. The deterioration in this sector increases uncertainty about bank solvency and counterparty risk in the repo market. This leads to a generalized withdrawal of repo funding, affecting also nonsubprime assets.

To test this hypothesis, the authors assemble different datasets. The main dataset has information about 392 securitized bonds from dealer banks, covering nonsubprime credit products such as credit cards, student loans, auto loans, and commercial mortgage-based securities. It contains spreads on the bonds, as well as repo rates and haircuts. To proxy for fundamentals in subprime market, the authors use the ABX index, a synthetic tradable index that references 20 equally weighted subprime mortgage-backed securities. Finally, bank counterparty risk is captured by the three-month LIBOR-OIS, which is the spread between the rate charged for unsecured interbank borrowing (LIBOR) and the rate on an overnight interest swap (OIS), exchanging a floating Fed fund rate for a fixed rate, both with a maturity of three months.

Gorton and Metrick (2012) prove contagion to the nonsubprime sectorby showing that their measure of counterparty risk, the LIBOR-OIS spread, increases following subprime distress, subsequently leading the spreads of nonsubprime securitized assets, which also are used as collateral in the repo market. They run the following specification, separately on credit card, auto loans, student loans, and commercial mortgage-backed securities:

$$\Delta Y_{i,t} = a_1 + b_1 \Delta LibOis_t + b_2 \Delta ABX_t + b_3 \Delta X_t + \epsilon_{i,t} \qquad (11)$$

where the $Y_{i,t}$ is, in turn, the weekly spread, the repo rate, and the repo haircut on bond i at time t. $LibOis_t$ is a vector of the last four observations of the LIBOR-OIS spread, ABX_t is a vector of the last four observations of the ABX spread, and X_{it} is a vector of financial controls, including the 10-year Treasury rate, the returns on the SandP index, the VIX index, the slope of the yield curve, and the overnight swap spread.

The results from the main specification consistently show that the LIB-OIS variables are jointly significant when explaining spreads, repo rates, and haircuts across the four classes of nonsubprime bonds. This supports the hypothesis

---

12. In the repo market, agreements are established between banks looking for funds and institutional investors. The transactions frequently are backed by securitized bonds: The investors buy the asset as collateral from the bank and, at the same time, the bank agrees to repurchase the asset at some later time, for a set price. The difference between the sale price and the repurchase price is the repo rate. Typically, the value of the collateral contracted upon is lower than the value of the securitized assets, with the difference being the "haircut." If the bank defaults on the promise to repurchase the asset, then the investor has the right to terminate the agreement and keep the collateral.

of contagion, suggesting that runs remain a threat to the functioning of modern banking markets.

3 Global Banking

In addition to becoming wider in scope, banks have become wider in geography. The degree to which the global banking system is integrated has important consequences for the transmission of monetary policy and economic shocks between monetary areas. It also has implications for the stability of the global financial system, firms' access to finance, and, potentially, the real economy of countries other than the country where the shocks originate (host countries). It is important for policymakers to understand these effects, so that they are better able to design policy that has its desired impact. These policies can also spill over across borders, potentially implying a need for international coordination in local prudential policymaking.

The literature studying the link between foreign markets and bank lending is relatively new. Some of the earlier papers found evidence that shocks to the Japanese financial system were transmitted to the US bank lending market (Peek & Rosengren, 1997), and affected the US economy (Peek & Rosengren, 2000). The literature, however, truly developed only after the financial crisis. Its aim has been to understand the implications of global banking for cross-border economic shock transmission, including monetary policy (Bräuning & Ivashina, 2017) and other economic shocks (Cetorelli & Goldberg, 2012b). The concept of cross-border lending was not mentioned in regulatory guidelines until 2006 (Aiyar, Calomiris, & Wieladek, 2014).

Global banking models have evolved from relatively straightforward exporting of local impulses (Peek & Rosengren, 1997) to more complex models involving global loan portfolios and liquidity management (Cetorelli & Goldberg, 2012a; Giannetti & Laeven, 2012). They borrow heavily from the bank lending channel (BLC) literature (Kashyap & Stein, 2000), and have only recently begun to incorporate foreign exchange, through FX Swaps (Bräuning & Ivashina, 2017), or to study real effects (Ongena et al., 2015).

3.1 Methodology

In terms of econometric methodology, this literature uses a range of panel data econometric techniques to aid in uncovering the transmission channels. These techniques, along with what makes them useful in a global banking context, are discussed in this section.

As in the BLC literature, if researchers want to be able to say anything about a shock's transmission through banks, they need to disentangle loan demand from loan supply because we view an equilibrium outcome. Initial work on the BLC literature (Kashyap & Stein, 2000) relied on proxies for time-varying loan demand, such as GDP growth, and on the assumption that all banks face homogeneous loan demand. Recent literature about the BLC and global banking have employed more sophisticated approaches, such as using time-varying country/firm effects (Altunbas, Gambacorta, & Marques-Ibanez, 2010; Bräuning & Ivashina, 2017) or explicitly modeling firm heterogeneity (Ongena et al., 2015).

The interaction of time- and country-fixed effects (e.g. country-year fixed effects) is used to control for country level loan demand and other time varying country level effects (omitted variables). This fixed-effects specification absorbs factors such as the demand for bank debt in a particular country, at a particular time. By including these country-level effects, researchers are able to make statements about effects at bank level, i.e. how changes in the supply of bank loans vary by banks' characteristics. Put differently, the inclusion of these fixed effects allows researchers to analyze within-country variation.

Another fixed effect specification is the use of both bank-year fixed effects and firm-year fixed effects. The former controls for bank factors that vary with time, such as the shock to Japanese banks documented in Peek and Rosengren (1997), causing an overall contraction in lending by these banks at that particular time. The latter controls for loan demand factors at borrower level.[13] Bräuning and Ivashina (2017) are able to use this fixed-effect specification because they employ data from the syndicated loan market in which loans involve multiple banks and banks lend to multiple firms, i.e. bank-firm level data. As a result, the authors are able to make statements about bank-firm level factors (e.g., the probability of firm i obtaining a loan from bank j in time t), while controlling for time-varying bank and firm specific effects.

The use of fixed effects, however, does have its disadvantages, as Khwaja and Mian (2008) make clear. With loan-level (bank-firm-level) data, the use of firm-level fixed effects can effectively exclude parts of the sample and potentially diminish external validity. This occurs because many firms, especially SMEs, have a relationship with only one bank (Degryse, Kim, & Ongena, 2009). A solution is to control for observable key firm characteristics. Khwaja and Mian (2008) show that controlling for firm characteristics, including firm-level fixed effects, has little impact on the estimated coefficient. In Ongena et al. (2015), this problem is particularly relevant as their dataset contains mainly SMEs, and the inclusion of firm-level fixed effects would have excluded two-thirds of their sample. They resolve this issue by following the solution of Khwaja and Mian (2008), while employing higher-level fixed effects (country and industry).

In addition, the literature often makes use of lags of the dependent variable. The number of lags used varies and depends on the frequency of the data (4 lags for quarterly; 12 lags for monthly). Such dynamic panel data models are constructed to allow for dynamics in changes of the loan supply. They reflect the

---

13. The use of this fixed-effect specification, in the global banking literature, often includes the use of country-time effects or explicit controls for macro effects at country level, e.g. GDP growth rates.

fact that changes in monetary policy take time to percolate into the banking system. The inclusion of dynamics in what is often a fixed-effects regression, however, causes inconsistency in the parameter estimates (Nickell, 1981).

After demand and supply have been disentangled, the traditional BLC literature explains heterogeneous changes to banks' loan supply by differences in banks' characteristics, such as size (Kashyap & Stein, 2000). This raises a potential issue of simultaneity bias as a bank's loan growth affects its size. To resolve this issue, the traditional literature uses bank size in the previous period, because it is unlikely to be determined by its growth in loans in the current period. As a precaution, the literature tends to lag all bank characteristics, regardless of whether the potential for simultaneity bias is clear. The global banking literature has used the same approach (Cetorelli & Goldberg, 2012a).

The potential for independent variables to be endogenous and the problem of Nickell bias in these dynamic panel data models has led the BLC literature to adopt estimation techniques that specifically address these issues, such as the Generalized Method of Moments (GMM) estimators developed by Arellano and Bond (1991) and extended by Arellano and Bover (1995) and Blundell and Bond (1998).[14] The global banking literature has borrowed from the traditional BLC literature and has begun using these estimation techniques (Cerutti, 2015; Wu, Luca, & Jeon, 2011).

Although the majority of the literature does not explicitly model the degree of financial integration, Popov and Ongena (2011) do measure the degree of integration in the interbank market in a first-stage regression. Their measure is the co-integration (Engle & Granger, 1987) between the rates in the domestic interbank market and the rates in a benchmark market (Germany). By basing the relationship of interbank lending rates on an error-correction model, they are able to disentangle the long-run co-movement of the interbank rates from the short-run adjustment toward the equilibrium. They then use the coefficient estimates from this first-stage regression as an explanatory variable in later regressions measuring the impact of interbank integration on borrowing constraints and loan rates.

Popov and Ongena (2011) make use of a three-stage Tobit scheme, following Heckman (1979), in order to account for a double-selection bias. This bias arises from the fact that loan rates are observed conditional only on firms not being credit constrained, and firm credit constraints are observed only when they have a positive credit demand. The correction has been used for similar purposes in studies about consumer debt, where this method is used to differentiate between desired and actual debt (Cox & Jappelli, 1993; Hayashi, 1982).

In the section that follows, we review a handful papers in depth and highlight the methodologies, data, and their findings.

---

14. See Ehrmann, Gambacorta, Martínez-Pagés, Sevestre, and Worms (2001) for an early use of these estimators in the traditional bank lending channel literature.

3.2 Global Banking and Credit

The main concept in this literature is that global banks have global balance sheets that can be affected by monetary policy changes (Cetorelli & Goldberg, 2012a) or other economic shocks (Cetorelli & Goldberg, 2012b) in their home countries or the host countries of their branches or subsidiaries. We can distinguish outward transmission, i.e., transmission of a home country shock to the host country, and inward transmission, i.e., transmission of a shock in the host country toward the home country. These shocks, in turn, affect the allocation of capital between the head office and subsidiaries, affecting loan supply in both home and host countries.[15]

The altering of individual banks' home and host country loan portfolios affects the proportion of loans granted by global banks, as a whole, in the host country. Shocks in the home country have the potential to affect the credit cycle in host countries (Giannetti & Laeven, 2012). Lastly, the decision to re-adjust an international loan portfolio and liquidity management (central bank deposits) also considers the FX market and the cost of hedging (Bräuning & Ivashina, 2017).

In an alternative strand of the global banking literature, researchers have analyzed the effects of cross-border prudential policy[16] spillovers as an additional source of impulse to local banking systems. These shocks occur when a change in home country macroprudential policies affects banks' behavior in host countries (and vice versa). Buch and Goldberg (2017) conducted a meta-analysis of a multistudy initiative of the International Banking Research Network (IBRN). In the IBRN study, 15 central banks and two international organizations conducted country-level analyses about the international spillovers of prudential policy for bank lending. Buch and Goldberg (2017) find that, although these spillovers sometimes occur, they are not large on average. The effects also vary across prudential instruments, while bank-specific characteristics, such as business models or balance sheet conditions, affect the size and direction of the spillovers.

Cetorelli and Goldberg (2012a) conduct a two-step Kashyap and Stein (2000) style analysis to test for differences in the response of US banks to monetary policy, based on whether banks have foreign operations. This is done by first estimating:

$$\Delta \log\left(Y_{i,t}\right) = \sum_{j=1}^{4} \alpha_{tj} \cdot \Delta \log\left(Y_{i,t-j}\right) + \beta t \cdot X_{i,t-1} + Controls + \epsilon_{i,t} \qquad (12)$$

---

15. Ongena et al. (2015) depart from the concept of home/host but rather focuses on the transmission of international shocks to banks with more or less global balance sheets.
16. Examples of such policies include limits on loan-to-value ratios, debt-to-income ratios, credit growth, as well as reserve and capital requirements.

where $\Delta log(Y_{i,t})$ is the change in the total lending of bank i at time t. $X_{i,t-1}$ is the log of the bank's liquidity ratio. Control variables include banks' capitalization ratios, size, and nonperforming loans, included following the BLC literature. The first lag of X_i and the controls are used in order to avoid simultaneity bias.[17] State and metropolitan area fixed effects are included, to account for unobserved loan demand factors. Eq. (12) is estimated for each quarter, resulting in a time series of β_t estimates, which are used in the next step.

The second step of the analysis uses the estimated β_t's as dependent variables, to determine how the sensitivity of bank lending to bank balance sheet characteristics, in this case liquidity, varies with monetary policy changes. This is done as follows:

$$\hat{\beta}_t = \eta + \sum_{j=1}^{n} \phi_j \cdot MP_{t-j} + \delta \cdot Controls + u_t \tag{13}$$

where MP_{t-j} is an indicator of monetary policy, for which an increase corresponds to a tightening of monetary policy.[18] The authors select a lag, n, of 8 to capture a slow response of lending to monetary policy conditions. Controls include GDP growth and its lags to account for business cycle fluctuations. Time-fixed effects also are included. Eq. (13) is run for a sample of large domestic banks and for large global banks. The authors use Newey-West robust standard errors to account for autocorrelation in the standard errors (Newey & West, 1987).

The sign of the sum of the coefficients of MP_{t-j} is positive, because bank lending is expected to be more dependent on liquidity during tight monetary policy and less dependent during expansionary monetary policy. By splitting the sample into global banks and domestic banks, the authors are able to test if the ϕ_j's are significantly different from zero in each specification. Then they draw conclusions about the bank lending channel's flow through global or domestic banks. Cetorelli and Goldberg (2012a) find, contrary to the traditional BLC literature (Kashyap & Stein, 2000), that large banks are sensitive to monetary policy if they are not global. Similarly, the authors find that small banks affiliated with large global banks are less sensitive to monetary policy shocks than small banks affiliated with large domestic banks. They argue that this is because large global banks can use foreign liquidity to insulate the loan supplies of their affiliates.

Bräuning and Ivashina (2017) focus on the hedging costs arising from currency mismatches between global banks' funding and investment activities. The

---

17. For example, banks might be large because they have experienced high loan growth.
18. The choice of the monetary policy indicator is nontrivial, and it is not always simply the central bank's policy rate. The correct measure depends on the currency area. For example, the three-month Euro Interbank Offered Rate (3m EURIBOR) or the Eonia rate are common choices in studies of Euro Zone countries, while the Bernanke and Mihov (1998) measure if often used for U.S studies.

authors argue that if currency flows are large enough, the cost of hedging will increase, which will decrease the return on lending in the foreign currency. They show that an increase in the monetary policy interest rate differential, between two currency areas, decreases foreign lending, leading to a redeployment of capital through the global balance sheet and an increase in local lending.

At the aggregate macro level, they show that there is a positive relationship between foreign bank reserve holdings and the difference between the overnight rate on excess reserves ($IOER_{US-HQ}$). Specifically, they find that an increase in the $IOER_{US-HQ}$ of 0.25% leads to a 6% increase in deposits with the US Federal Reserve (with the funds transferred from their foreign offices) and a 2.5% decrease in lending to US firms. They also document an increase in banks' FX swapping activity into high yield currencies, as well as an increase in the cost of hedging in response to a decrease in the monetary policy rate in the home country.

At the bank level, they document a reallocation of loan volumes, because an increase in the $IOER_{US-HQ}$ leads to a 1% decrease in lending in the foreign currency. The effects are particularly strong for lowly capitalized banks.

Additionally, at firm level, Bräuning and Ivashina (2017) find that increasing the $IOER_{US-HQ}$ by 0.25% leads to a 1% lower probability of a particular bank lending to a particular firm in a given period (extensive margin), as well as an associated 3% decline in the lending volume (intensive margin). Lastly, they show that, at the aggregate domestic credit supply level, firms that had a larger share of foreign global banks in their syndicate, which subsequently experienced monetary easing in the country of their headquarters, faced a stronger contraction in credit. Specifically, a one standard deviation increase in the past share of foreign global banks in the syndicate leads to a 6.5% decrease in the probability of obtaining a loan and a 4% drop in volume of granted loans, after an expansionary monetary policy in the home of the foreign bank.

Giannetti and Laeven (2012) find that global banks redistribute their loan portfolios based on their funding conditions at home. During good times (low funding costs), global banks tend to redistribute their loan portfolio in favor of foreign markets (flight abroad), and when funding conditions are poor, they tend to favor their home country (flight home). Furthermore, the authors show that the globalization of banking activities affects the amplitude of credit cycles, and that banks export home-grown shocks to host markets.

Giannetti and Laeven (2012) test their first hypothesis that global banks redistribute their loan portfolio based on their funding conditions at home, by analyzing the behavior of the coefficient:

$$Loan\ Share_{ijt} = \alpha_0 + \alpha_1 Funding\ Conditions_{i,t-1} + \Gamma X_{ijt} + \varepsilon_{ijt} \qquad (14)$$

where $LoanShare_{ijt}$ is the ratio of syndicated loans originated to borrowers in country j, by bank i, in year-month t to total loan supply. $LoanShare_{ijt}$ cannot be affected by overall loan supply shocks, because it captures the geographic distribution of new loans.

Funding Conditions$_{i,t-1}$ is measured by either the median ratio of market equity to book equity, or by the average spread in the interbank market over the overnight spread, in country i, during month-year t. Firms have a lower cost of issuing equity when market valuations are higher, which is captured by a higher market-to-book equity ratio (Baker, Foley, & Wurgler, 2009; Pagano, Panetta, & Zingales, 1998). The interbank spread measures banks' short-term funding conditions. Because the study uses syndicated loan data, and multiple banks lend to multiple firms within the same country, identification relies on host country-year fixed effects, X_{ijt}. This controls for time-varying host-country variability, such as host country loan demand.

The authors find that one standard deviation increase in banks' market-to-book equity ratios increases the proportion of foreign loans by close to 5%; one standard deviation decrease in interbank spreads decreases the proportion of foreign loans by a similar amount. The authors stress that these findings are distinct from a flight to quality (a preference for lower risk assets in tighter funding conditions). They do so by including interactions between funding conditions and a variable measuring creditor rights in the host country. Then, they show that the flight abroad is stronger for countries with strong creditor rights (perceived as safe), ruling out the flight to quality argument.

Giannetti and Laeven (2012) proceed by testing their second hypothesis: The degree of globalization of banking activities in a host country affects the impact of home economic shocks on the credit cycles of the host country. Changes to bank funding conditions affect the degree of their home bias in issuing new loans, with an effect on the aggregate supply of credit in the host countries where they operate. The authors show that this home bias varies over time.

Adding the volatility of home bias to a host country's credit cycle should increase its overall volatility. This increase in volatility of the host country loan supply is determined by its exposure to foreign funded loans:

$$Vol(LoanSupply)_{jt} = \alpha_0 + \alpha_1 \frac{Loans from Foreign_{jt}}{Total Loans_{jt}}$$
$$+ \alpha_2 \frac{Loans to Foreign_{jt}}{Total Loans_{jt}} + \eta_{ijt} \tag{15}$$

where Vol(Loan Supply)$_{jt}$ is measured as the deviations of a country's real credit per capita from its trend. The use of real credit allows for a country's credit cycles to be disconnected from the dynamics of its GDP.

The authors find that the proportion of foreign loans in a host country explains between 20% and 40% of the volatility of credit, depending on the specification used. They conclude that countries dominated by foreign banks should have highly volatile business credit. They argue that banks are more inclined to adjust their foreign loans when funding conditions change. As a result, home countries of international banks should experience less variation in their supply of loans.

Cetorelli and Goldberg (2012b) take the perspective of the foreign branch by employing US Call Report data about the activity of foreign banks in the United States. The authors leverage a funding shock to the foreign parent bank to test for internal capital markets. This shock is measured as the degree to which the parent was exposed to Asset Back Commercial Paper conduits as a proportion of its equity capital, as of December 31, 2006. The authors find higher internal capital transfers for branches with parents subject to larger funding shocks, the largest effects being among the biggest branches. The median-sized bank (total assets of $1B), with a parent ABCP exposure ratio equal to 1, would have experienced an internal fund withdrawal (transfer to parent) of $343 million more than a parent bank without ABCP exposure. This is approximately 12% of the average level of internal balance at the branch, an economically significant effect.

The authors also document a positive and significant link between changes in net internal borrowing and branch credit supply. Specifically, they estimate that, for the median-sized branch, a $1 decrease in internal funding would result in a $0.40 to $0.50 decrease in total domestic lending. This is also an economically significant effect. Lastly, they show that the loan supply of larger branches is less sensitive to changes in internal funds. This might be because of increased access to alternative funding sources, which are not available to smaller branches.

Ongena et al. (2015) take a more traditional view of the bank as local entity, but they determine its global operations in terms of its funding sources. They use a unique combination of databases and exploit the Lehman failure to test for the existence of the international bank lending channel. Then, the authors measure real effects at both firm and country level. They find supporting evidence for the existence of the international bank lending channel, where, after the shock, foreign-owned, or internationally borrowing domestic banks contract their loan supply more than locally funded domestic banks.

When looking at firm-level effects, the authors find that credit-dependent firms, which borrow from foreign banks or internationally borrowing domestic banks, experience negative financial and real effects. These effects are especially pronounced when a firm has a relationship with only one bank, is small, or it has limited tangible assets. As previously mentioned, Ongena et al. (2015) do not include firm-fixed effects in their specification because that would have effectively excluded two-thirds of their sample. They resolve this issue by following the solution of Khwaja and Mian (2008) and include key firm characteristics as control variables, with higher-level fixed effects.

Lastly, at country-level, Ongena et al. (2015) found that firms more reliant on foreign funding, from countries with slow contract enforcement and a low level of financial development, were especially affected.

4 Conclusion

We reviewed the data, econometric techniques and estimates with respect to two recent and salient developments in the banking industry, i.e., securitization and globalization. Although our review established that access to ever-more granular micro data has enabled researchers to arrive at estimates that are better identified and more reliable than ever before, much work remains to be done. Saturation with fixed effects, for example, is a welcome development that might warrant more applied methodological scrutiny, however, whereby the eventually inevitable trade-off between internal and external validity might have to be made more explicit. Another area that might require more thought, at an almost science-philosophical level, is the optimal reliance on quasi-experimental regulatory and legal shocks to help identify banking phenomena of interest. To the extent that such shocks might be mostly present in times and places where reactive or erratic policymaking takes center stage, empirical work might itself gain internal validity but lose external validity. More research about making this trade-off more visible and manageable seems warranted.

Acknowledgments

Degryse acknowledges financial support from Fund for Scientific Research Flanders under FWO G.0857.16. Ongena acknowledges financial support from ERC ADG 2016—GA 740272 lending.

References

Acharya, V., Schnabl, P., Suarez, G., 2013. Securitization without risk transfer. Journal of Financial Economics 107, 515–536. https://doi.org/10.1016/j.jfineco.2012.09.004.

Adrian, T., Shin, H.S., 2010. Liquidity and leverage. Journal of Financial Intermediation 19, 418–437. http://www.sciencedirect.com/science/article/pii/S1042957308000764. https://doi.org/10.1016/J.JFI.2008.12.002.

Aiyar, S., Calomiris, C., Wieladek, T., 2014. Does macro-prudential regulation leak? Evidence from a UK policy experiment. Journal of Money, Credit and Banking 46, 181–214. https://doi.org/10.1111/jmcb.12086.

Albertazzi, U., Bottero, M., Ongena, S., 2016. Asymmetric information and the securitization of SME loans. http://www.ssrn.com/abstract=2934230. https://doi.org/10.2139/ssrn.2934230.

Allen, F., Gale, D., 2007. Understanding financial crises. Oxford University Press.

Altunbas, Y., Gambacorta, L., Marques-Ibanez, D., 2010. Bank risk and monetary policy. Journal of Financial Stability 6, 121–129. https://doi.org/10.1016/j.jfs.2009.07.001.

Arellano, M., Bond, S., 1991. Some tests of specification for panel data: Monte Carlo evidence and an application to employment equations. The Review of Economic Studies 58, 277–297.

Arellano, M., Bover, O., 1995. Another look at the instrumental variable estimation of error-components models. Journal of Econometrics 68, 29–51. https://doi.org/10.1016/0304-4076 (94)01642-D.

Baker, M., Foley, C.F., Wurgler, J., 2009. Multinationals as arbitrageurs: the effect of stock market valuations on foreign direct investment. The Review of Financial Studies 22, 337–369. http://www.jstor.org/stable/40056913.

Benmelech, E., Dlugosz, J., Ivashina, V., 2012. Securitization without adverse selection: the case of CLOs. Journal of Financial Economics 106, 91–113. https://doi.org/10.1016/j.jfineco.2012.05.006.

Bernanke, B., Mihov, I., 1998. Measuring monetary policy. The Quarterly Journal of Economics 113, 869–902.

Blundell, R., Bond, S., 1998. Initial conditions and moment restrictions in dynamic panel data models. Journal of Econometrics 87, 115–143. https://doi.org/10.1016/S0304-4076(98) 00009-8.

Bräuning, F., Ivashina, V., 2017. Monetary policy and global banking. http://www.nber.org/papers/w23316.pdfhttps://doi.org/10.3386/w23316.

Buch, C., Goldberg, L., 2017. Cross-border prudential policy spillovers: how much? How important? Evidence from the international banking research network. Discussion papers 02/2017, Deutsche Bundesbank.

Carbo-Valverde, S., Degryse, H., Rodríguez-Fernández, F., 2015. The impact of securitization on credit rationing: Empirical evidence. Journal of Financial Stability 20, 36–50. https://doi.org/10.1016/j.jfs.2015.06.004.

Cerutti, E., 2015. Drivers of cross-border banking exposures during the crisis. Journal of Banking & Finance 55, 340–357. https://ac-els-cdn-com.ezproxy.uzh.ch/S037842661400288X/1-s2.0-S037842661400288X-mahttps://doi.org/10.1016/j.jbankfin.2014.08.021.

Cetorelli, N., Goldberg, L., 2012a. Banking globalization and monetary transmission. The Journal of Finance 67, 1811–1843.

Cetorelli, N., Goldberg, L., 2012b. Follow the money: Quantifying domestic effects of foreign bank shocks in the great recession. The American Economic Review 102, 213–218.

Chiappori, P., Salanie, B., 2000. Testing for asymmetric information in insurance markets. Journal of Political Economy 108, 56–78. https://doi.org/10.1086/262111.

Claessens, S., van Horen, N., 2014. Foreign banks: Trends and impact. Journal of Money, Credit and Banking 46, 295–326. https://doi.org/10.1111/jmcb.12092.

Cox, D., Jappelli, T., 1993. The effect of borrowing constraints on consumer liabilities. Journal of Money, Credit and Banking 25, 197–213. http://www.jstor.org/stable/2077836http://about.jstor.org/terms.

Degryse, H., Kim, M., Ongena, S., 2009. Microeconometrics of banking: Methods, applications, and results. Oxford University Press. https://books.google.co.za/books?hl=enandlr=andid=BUikLmFvD4UCandoi=fndandpg=PR9andots=LizchV.

Demyanyk, Y., Hemert, O.V., 2009. Understanding the subprime mortgage crisis. In: The review of financial studies.24, pp. 1848–1880. https://doi.org/10.2307/20869292.

Diamond, D., Dybvig, P., 1983. Bank runs, deposit insurance, and liquidity. Journal of Political Economy 91, 401–419. https://doi.org/10.1086/261155.

Diamond, D., Rajan, R., 2005. Liquidity shortages and banking crises. The Journal of Finance 60, 615–647. https://doi.org/10.1111/j.1540-6261.2005.00741.x.

Djankov, S., McLiesh, C., Shleifer, A., 2007. Private credit in 129 countries. Journal of Financial Economics 84, 299–329. https://doi.org/10.1016/j.jfineco.2006.03.004. arXiv:arXiv:1011.1669v3.

Ehrmann, M., Gambacorta, L., Martínez-Pagés, J., Sevestre, P., Worms, A., 2001. Financial systems and the role of banks in monetary policy transmission in the Euro area. p. 33.

Engle, R., Granger, C., 1987. Co-integration and error correction: Representation, estimation, and testing. Econometrica 55, 251. https://doi.org/10.2307/1913236.

Giannetti, M., Laeven, L., 2012. Flight home, flight abroad, and international credit cycles. The American Economic Review 102, 219–224.

Goetzmann, W., Rouwenhorst, K.G., 2008. The history of financial innovation. In: Carbon finance, environmental market solutions to climate change. Yale School of Forestry and Environmental Studies, pp. 18–43. Chapter 1.

Gorton, G., Metrick, A., 2012. Securitized banking and the run on repo. Journal of Financial Economics 104, 425–451. https://doi.org/10.1016/j.jfineco.2011.03.016.

Gorton, G., Pennacchi, G., 1995. Banks and loan sales marketing nonmarketable assets. Journal of Monetary Economics 35, 389–411. http://www.sciencedirect.com/science/article/pii/0304393 29501199X. https://doi.org/10.1016/0304-3932(95)01199-X.

Hayashi, F., 1982. The permanent income hypothesis: Estimation and testing by instrumental variables. Journal of Political Economy 90, 895–916. http://www.jstor.org/stable/1837125.

Heckman, J., 1979. Sample selection bias as a specification error. Econometrica 47, 153. https://doi.org/10.2307/1912352.

Holmstrom, B., Tirole, J., 1997. Financial intermediation, loanable funds, and the real sector. The Quarterly Journal of Economics 112, 663–691. https://doi.org/10.1162/003355397555316.

Ioannidou, V., Ongena, S., Peydró, J.-L., 2015. Monetary policy, risk-taking, and pricing: Evidence from a quasi-natural experiment. Review of Finance 19, 95–144. https://doi.org/10.1093/rof/rfu035.

Jiménez, B.G., Ongena, S., Peydró, J.-l., Saurina, J., 2012. Credit supply and monetary policy: Identifying the bank balance-sheet channel with loan applications. American Economic Review 102, 2301–2326.

Jiménez, G., Ongena, S., Peydró, J.-L., Saurina, J., 2014. Hazardous times for monetary policy: What do twenty-three million bank loans say about the effects of monetary policy on credit risk-taking? Econometrica 82, 463–505. https://doi.org/10.3982/ECTA10104.

Kashyap, A., Stein, J., 2000. What do a million observations on banks say about the transmission of monetary policy? The American Economic Review 90, 407–428. http://www.jstor.org/stable/117336.

Keys, B., Mukherjee, T., Seru, A., Vig, V., 2010. Did securitization lead to lax screening? Evidence from subprime loans. The Quarterly Journal of Economics 125, 307–362. http://www.jstor.org/stable/40506283.

Khwaja, A.I., Mian, A., 2008. Tracing the impact of bank liquidity shocks: Evidence from an emerging market. The American Economic Review 98, 1413–1442. http://www.jstor.org/stable/29730128.

Loutskina, E., 2011. The role of securitization in bank liquidity and funding management. Journal of Financial Economics 100, 663–684. https://doi.org/10.1016/j.jfineco.2011.02.005.

Maddaloni, A., Peydró, J.-L., 2011. Bank risk-taking, securitization, supervision, and low interest rates: Evidence from the Euro-area and the U.S. lending standards. The Review of Financial Studies 24, 2121–2165. https://doi.org/10.2307/20869300.

Mian, A., Sufi, A., 2009. The consequences of mortgage credit expansion: Evidence from the U.S. mortgage default crisis. The Quarterly Journal of Economics 124, 1449–1496. https://doi.org/10.2307/40506264.

Morais, B., Peydró, J.-L., Ruiz, C., 2019. The international bank lending channel of monetary policy rates and quantitative easing. The Journal of Finance. .

Newey, W., West, K., 1987. A simple, positive semi-definite, heteroskedasticity and autocorrelation consistent covariance matrix. Econometrica 52, 345–380.

Nickell, S., 1981. Biases in dynamic models with fixed effects. Econometrica 49, 1417. https://doi.org/10.2307/1911408.

Ongena, S., Peydró, J.-L., van Horen, N., 2015. Shocks abroad, pain at home? Bank-firm-level evidence on the international transmission of financial shocks. IMF Economic Review 63, 698–750. https://doi.org/10.1057/imfer.2015.34.

Pagano, M., Panetta, F., Zingales, L., 1998. Why do companies go public? An empirical analysis. The Journal of Finance 53, 27–64. https://doi.org/10.1111/0022-1082.25448.

Parlour, C., Plantin, G., 2008. Loan sales and relationship banking. The Journal of Finance 63, 1291–1314. https://doi.org/10.1111/j.1540-6261.2008.01358.x.

Peek, J., Rosengren, E., 1997. The international transmission of financial shocks: the case of Japan. The American Economic Review 87, 495–505. http://www.jstor.org.ezproxy.uzh.ch/stable/pdf/2951360.pdf?refreqid=excelsior:a45b7.

Peek, J., Rosengren, E., 2000. Collateral damage: Effects of the japanese bank crisis on real activity in the United States. The American Economic Review 90, 30–45. http://www.jstor.org/stable/117280.

Pennacchi, G., 1988. Loan sales and the cost of bank capital. The Journal of Finance 43, 375–396.

Petersen, M., Rajan, R., 1994. The benefits of lending relationships: Evidence from small business data. The Journal of Finance 49, 3–37. https://doi.org/10.1111/j.1540-6261.1994.tb04418.x.

Popov, A., Ongena, S., 2011. Interbank market integration, loan rates, and firm leverage. Journal of Banking & Finance 35, 544–559. https://ac.els-cdn.com/S0378426610003122/1-s2.0-S0378426610003122-main.pdf?_tid=0e7.

Purnanandam, A., 2010. Originate-to-distribute model and the subprime mortgage crisis. The Review of Financial Studies 24, 1881–1915. https://doi.org/10.2307/20869293.

Rajan, R., 2006. Has finance made the world riskier? European Financial Management 12, 499–533. https://doi.org/10.1111/j.1468-036X.2006.00330.x.

Wu, J., Luca, A., Jeon, B.N., 2011. Foreign bank penetration and the lending channel in emerging economies: Evidence from bank-level panel data. Journal of International Money and Finance 30, 1128–1156. https://doi.org/10.1016/j.jimonfin.2011.05.011.

Chapter 24

Regional Innovation in the United States: A Poisson Stochastic Frontier Approach With Finite Mixture Structure

Kyriakos Drivas*, Claire Economidou† and Mike G. Tsionas‡

*Department of International & European Economic Studies, Athens University of Economics and Business, Athens, Greece, †Department of Economics, University of Piraeus, Piraeus, Greece, ‡Department of Economics, Lancaster University Management School, Lancaster, United Kingdom

Chapter Outline

1 Introduction

Estimation of productive efficiency is performed in the framework of frontier methodologies, which have been used extensively in economics. Rather than fitting functions that intersect data, frontier methodologies are concerned with the construction of frontiers that envelop the data and the benchmarking of performance of a decision-making unit (e.g. country, region, firm) to the best practice, the frontier.[1] Units perform better than others when they use their inputs more optimally than others to produce countable outcome. The most optimal units form the efficient frontier, while the worst performers are situated below the frontier; their distance from the frontier represents their productive inefficiency.

---

1. For comprehensive reviews of frontier methodologies, see, Kumbhakar and Lovell (2000) and Coelli, Rao, and Battese (2005).

Panel Data Econometrics. https://doi.org/10.1016/B978-0-12-815859-3.00024-X

The stochastic frontier (SF) methodology, in particular, constructs the efficient frontier by estimating the underlying production technology (represented either by production, cost, profit, revenue, or distance functions) across all units in the sample and specifies a two-part error term that accounts for both random error and the degree of technical inefficiency. Since its inception (Aigner, Lovell, & Schmidt, 1977; Meeusen & van den Broeck, 1977), the traditional SF model has been modified in many ways to confront various issues. Some recent developments have proposed modifications with respect to the distributional assumptions concerning inefficiency imposed by standard stochastic frontier models to account for perfectly efficient units (Kumbhakar, Parmeter, & Tsionas, 2013; Sickles & Qian, 2009).[2] Others have suggested augmentations of the traditional stochastic frontier model with a Markov-switching structure (Tsionas & Kumbhakar, 2004) or a finite mixture (latent class) structure (Bos, Economidou, & Koetter, 2010; Bos, Economidou, Koetter, & Kolari, 2010; Greene, 2002a, 2002b, 2005; Orea & Kumbhakar, 2004) to allow for various degrees of technological and inefficiency induced heterogeneity among units. In all basic or modified versions of the SF, the stochastic frontier is constructed by using continuous data analysis.

In the social science literature, however, there are plenty of cases where the dependent variable is a count, taking nonnegative integer values. For example, applications of count data models are widespread in economics in modeling the relationship between number of patents granted and R&D expenditures of firms (Hausman, Hall, & Griliches, 1984) and in finance in modeling, for example, bank failures (Davutyan, 1989), unpaid installments by creditors of a bank (Dionne, Artis, & Guillen, 1996), among other applications.

A few attempts in the literature have developed count data stochastic frontier techniques. The studies of Fè-Rodríguez (2007) are the first to estimate production frontiers and calculate efficiency for discrete conditional distributions when output is an economic bad, and the work of Hofler and Scrogin (2008) for economic goods. Both studies, however, lack generality, as neither of these works can analyze both types of commodities in a single model. A more flexible count data stochastic frontier model that overcomes the restrictions of the past studies is introduced by Fè-Rodríguez and Hofler (2013). The authors evaluate its applicability and estimate a knowledge production function, using maximum simulated likelihood, for the number of patents awarded to 70 pharmaceuticals in the United States in 1976 given their expenditures on R&D. The proposed model, however, does not address dynamics and heterogeneity in the data.

---

2. For example, to account for fully efficient units, Sickles and Qian (2009) suggest right (upper-bound) truncation, whereas Kumbhakar et al. (2013) censoring of the distribution of inefficiency to overcome the typical assumption of continuous distribution of inefficiency imposed by conventional stochastic frontier modeling, and consequently, perfectly efficient units could be deemed inefficient because their full-efficiency probability is zero.

This chapter purports to enrich the current menu of approaches within the SF paradigm. Specifically, our contribution lies in introducing stochastic frontier estimation techniques appropriate for count models, while accounting for potential endogeneity of regressors and technological and efficiency induced heterogeneity in the data. To allow for different technological regimes across units, a finite mixture structure is employed to allocate regime membership. To this end, we develop a Poisson stochastic frontier model for count data augmented with a finite mixture structure.

Our chapter relates and adds to the economics of innovation and growth literature. The standard approach in the economics literature has been the use of a knowledge (innovation) production function, in which the innovative output, the counts of patents, is produced analogously to the production of real output, employing existed knowledge and human capital allowing no waste in their use.[3] More recently, a cognate strand of research employs frontier analyses to the production of innovation (Cullmann, Schmidt-Ehmcke, & Zloczysti, 2012; Rousseau & Rousseau, 1997, 1998; Wang, 2007; Wang & Huang, 2007) and, therefore, consider the existence of (in)efficiency.[4] In estimating innovation efficiency, however, these studies have overlooked the appropriateness of technology, stressed by recent contributions in the economics literature (Acemoglu & Zilibotti, 2001; Basu & Weil, 1998; Jones, 2005), as economic units choose the best technology available to them, given their input mix. The latter implies the possible existence of multiple technology regimes and not just one, described by a single frontier as is the case with past innovation efficiency studies.

In this study, we estimate a stochastic frontier of innovation production in a panel of 50 US states from 1993 to 2006 applying novel stochastic frontier techniques for count data in a dynamic and heterogenous setup. To our knowledge, empirical evidence based at disaggregated level analysis of innovation efficiency in the United States has been extremely thin.[5] Because the states are in the same country and, therefore, share common institutions, among other things, an interesting issue that arises is whether small differences across

---

3. The empirical testing of growth models typically has examined the effect of R&D on productivity or output growth ignoring any waste in the use of innovation resources. See, for example, Jones (1995), Coe and Helpman (1995), Aghion and Howitt (1998), Griffith, Redding, and van Reenen (2004), Zachariadis (2003), Bottazzi and Peri (2003), Bottazzi and Peri (2007), and Mancusi (2008) among others.

4. See Cruz-Cázaresa, Bayona-Sáezb, and García-Marco (2013) for an updated review on innovation efficiency studies.

5. The study of Thomas, Sharma, and Jain (2011) is among the very few attempts that examines innovation efficiency of the United States at the state level for 2004–2008. The study, however, measures innovation efficiency based on the ratio of R&D outputs (e.g., patents granted or scientific publications) to R&D inputs (e.g., R&D expenditure), concluding that only 14 out of 51 states show modest improvements in innovation efficiency. A closer to ours study is that of Fè-Rodríguez and Hofler (2013), which proposes a stochastic frontier count model and performs a cross-section analysis to study innovation efficiency in a number of pharmaceutical firms in the United States.

regions, for instance, in fiscal or employment policies have different innovation implications. According to our findings, they do. Our results support the existence of two distinct innovation classes, a very efficient one, which contains the majority of the states and exhibits positive technical growth, and a smaller, less efficient class that experiences very modest technical growth.

The reminder of the chapter proceeds as follows. Section 2 introduces a Poisson stochastic frontier model with finite mixture structure appropriate for count data, allowing for technological and efficiency induced heterogeneity and endogenous regressors. Section 3 provides empirical evidence that demonstrates the applicability of the method proposed. Finally, Section 4 summarizes our findings and offers conclusions.

2 Methodology

In this section, we briefly sketch the basic idea of a standard stochastic frontier model with the use of a production function. Similar analysis could be performed, for example, with cost, profit, and revenue functions. We then modify the traditional stochastic frontier modeling to allow for discrete conditional distributions and, therefore, introduce a Poisson stochastic frontier model. To account for potential endogeneity in the regressors as well as technological and inefficiency induced heterogeneity, we enhance the Poisson stochastic frontier model with finite mixture structure.

2.1 A Brief Sketch of Stochastic Frontier Analysis

Assume a production function of a good or idea is described by the following equation:

$$Q_{it}^* = f(X_{it}, t; \beta) \exp\{v_{it}\} \tag{1}$$

where Q^* is the maximum (frontier) attainable output produced of unit i at time t given available vector of inputs, X, f, and parameter vector β characterize the production technology, t is a time trend variable that captures neutral technical change (Solow, 1957), and v_{it} is an i.i.d. error term distributed as $N(0, \sigma_v^2)$. Some units, however, might employ existing production resources less efficiently and, therefore, produce less than the frontier output. As Fig. 1 shows, for a given technology and set of inputs, there are units that produce at points ii and iii, in other words, their actual output is less than the frontier output.

To also allow for such cases, we model the performance of firms' production by means of stochastic frontier production model as follows:

$$Q_{it} = Q_{it}^* \exp\{-u_{it}\} \tag{2}$$

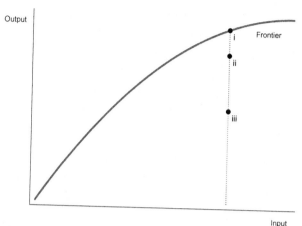

FIG. 1 A stochastic frontier model of production.

where $u_{it} \geq 0$ is assumed to be i.i.d., with a half-normal distribution truncated at zero $|N(0, \sigma_u^2)|$, and independent from the noise term, v_{it}.[6] Technical efficiency is measured as the ratio of actual over maximum output, $\frac{Q_{it}}{Q_{it}^*}$, such that $0 \leq \frac{Q_{it}}{Q_{it}^*} \leq 1$ and $\frac{Q_{it}}{Q_{it}^*} = 1$ implies full efficiency. The standard way to calculate technical efficiency is to define a functional form of the efficient frontier and then log-linearize Eq. (2).

In the presence of count data, however, one cannot apply the log-linear transformation to Eq. (2).[7] An additional problem in count data sets is the existence of zero output in the set. Because log of zero is not defined, a high proportion of the data could be discarded. To circumvent the discrete nature of the data, however, one can approximate the discrete random variable by a continuous one. In doing so, there is a possible loss of efficiency and even a source of model misspecification (Cameron & Trivedi, 2013).[8]

In this paper, we focus on count data frontier models and, therefore, we approach Eq. (1) as a Poisson process. This is the task of the next section.

---

6. The residual in Eq. (2) is decomposed as $\exp\{\varepsilon_{it}\} = \exp\{v_{it}\} \exp\{-u_{it}\}$ and one can identify its components, $\exp\{v_{it}\}$ and $\exp\{-u_{it}\}$ by reparameterizing λ_o in the maximum likelihood procedure, where $\lambda_o(= \sigma_u/\sigma_v)$, the ratio of the standard deviation of efficiency over the standard deviation of the noise term, and $\sigma(=(\sigma_u^2 + \sigma_v^2)^{1/2})$ is the composite standard deviation. The frontier is identified by the λ_o for which the log-likelihood is maximized (see Kumbhakar & Lovell, 2000).

7. For example, let $Q = 4$ and $Q^* = 11$, then there is no integer value of efficiency solving the equation.

8. Fè-Rodríguez and Hofler (2013) notes that discrete distributions often violate the third-moment restrictions imposed by a continuous data stochastic frontier model. In case that output is discrete, then the log-linear transformation of output can exhibit skewness of wrong sign. The latter would result to zero inefficiency in the model, even when there is substantial one.

2.1.1 A Poisson Stochastic Frontier

Suppose that actual output, Q_j, has a Poisson distribution, conditional on input vector X, with the conditional mean of the distribution $Q_j \mid \lambda_j \sim$ Poisson(λ_j), that is:

$$p(Q_j \mid \lambda_j) = \exp(-\lambda_j) \frac{\lambda_j^{Q_j}}{Q_j!} \tag{3}$$

where $Q_j \in 0, 1, 2, \ldots$ are nonnegative integers (counts), j is state-year observation, and λ_j is the mean of Poisson process and defined as[9]:

$$\log \lambda_j = x_j' \beta + v_j - u_j \tag{4}$$

where x is log of the inputs vector X, β a vector of parameters, $v_j \sim \text{iid} N(0, \sigma_v^2)$ and $u_j \sim \text{iid} N(0, \sigma_u^2)$ a half-normal distribution.

The distribution of Q_j has density given by:

$$p(Q_j \mid \theta) = \left(2\pi\sigma_v^2\right)^{-1/2} \left(\frac{\pi}{2}\sigma_u^2\right)^{-1/2} \int_0^{+\infty} \int_0^{+\infty}$$

$$\exp(-\lambda_j) \frac{\lambda_j^{Q_j} - 1}{Q_j!} \exp\left[-\frac{\left(\log \lambda_j - x_j'\beta + u_j\right)^2}{2\sigma_v^2} - \frac{u_j^2}{2\sigma^2}\right] d\lambda_j du_j \tag{5}$$

where $\theta = (\beta', \sigma_v, \sigma_u)' \in \Theta \subset \mathfrak{R}^{k+2}$.

The outer integral is available in closed form and one gets:

$$p(Q_j \mid \theta) = \frac{2}{\sigma} \int_0^{+\infty} \exp(-\lambda_j) \frac{\lambda_j^{Q_j} - 1}{Q_j!} \varphi\left(\frac{\log \lambda_j - x_j'\beta}{\sigma}\right) \Phi\left(-\lambda_o \frac{\log \lambda_j - x_j'\beta}{\sigma}\right) d\lambda_j \tag{6}$$

where $\sigma^2 = \sigma_v^2 + \sigma_u^2$, $\lambda_o = \frac{\sigma_u}{\sigma_v}$ and φ, Φ denote the density and the distribution function respectively of the standard normal variate.

2.1.2 Technical Efficiency

We now turn into calculating (in)efficiency. From Eq. (3) the distribution of u_j conditional on λ_j has the well-known Jondrow, Lovell, Materov, and Schmidt (1982) (JLMS) density:

$$p(u_j \mid \lambda_j, Q_j) = \left(2\pi\sigma_*^2\right) \exp\left(-\frac{\left(u - \mu_*\right)^2}{2\sigma_*^2}\right) \Phi\left(-\frac{\mu_*}{\sigma_*}\right)^{-1} \tag{7}$$

---

9. To ease notation throughout the whole section, we define j to be a vector of state-year $[i\ t]$ with $i = 1, \ldots, n$ and $t = 1, \ldots, T$ observations.

where $\mu_* = -\left(\log \lambda_j - x'\beta\right)\frac{\sigma_u^2}{\sigma^2}$ and $\sigma_*^2 = \frac{\sigma_u^2 \sigma_v^2}{\sigma^2}$.
The mean of distribution is:

$$E\left(u_j \mid \lambda_j, Q_j\right) = \sigma_* \left[\frac{\varphi\left(\epsilon_j\left(\log\lambda_j\right)\lambda_o/\sigma\right)}{\Phi\left(-\epsilon_j\left(\log\lambda_j\right)\lambda_o/\sigma\right)} - \epsilon_i\left(\log\lambda_j\right)\lambda_o/\sigma \right] \tag{8}$$

where $\epsilon_i(\log\lambda_j)$ is equal to $(\log\lambda_j - x'_j\beta)\lambda_o/\sigma$.[10]

As λ_j is unobserved, Eq. (6) cannot be used directly. Instead, we can use:

$$E\left(u_j \mid \lambda_j, Q_j\right) = \sigma_* \int_0^{+\infty} \left[\frac{\varphi\left(\epsilon_j\left(\log\lambda_j\right)\lambda_o/\sigma\right)}{\Phi\left(-\epsilon_j\left(\log\lambda_j\right)\lambda_o/\sigma\right)} - \epsilon_j\left(\log\lambda_j\right)\lambda_o/\sigma \right]\left(-\lambda_j\right)\exp\left(-\lambda_j\right)\frac{\lambda_j^{Q_j}}{Q_j!} d\lambda_j$$

$$\tag{9}$$

Using the change of variables $\log \lambda_i = \zeta_j$ the integral can be transformed as follows:

$$E\left(u_j \mid \lambda_j, Q_j\right) = \sigma_* \int_{-\infty}^{+\infty} \left[\frac{\varphi\left(\epsilon_j\left(\zeta_j\right)\lambda_o/\sigma\right)}{\Phi\left(-\epsilon_j\left(\zeta_j\right)\lambda_o/\sigma\right)} - \epsilon_j\left(\zeta_j\right)\lambda_o/\sigma \right]\frac{\exp\left(\zeta_j + 1 - \exp\left(\zeta_j\right)\right)}{Q_j!} d\zeta_j$$

$$\tag{10}$$

Eq. (10) is just a conditional distribution in the Gibbs sampler. The final measure of inefficiency is the average of u_j across all MCMC draws. Therefore, in effect, we integrate out parameter uncertainty and condition only on the data. The integral is evaluated numerically.[11] Eq. (10) is the analogue of the JLMS measure and provides the mean efficiency for count data frontier models.

2.2 Endogenous Regressors

The usual concern with estimating production functions is the endogeneity of regressors, i.e., regressors that can be correlated with the error term. In conjunction with Eqs. (3) and (4) we assume:

$$x_j = \Gamma z_j + v_{j1} \tag{11}$$

where z_j is an $m \times 1$ vector of covariates, $v_j = [v_{j0}, v'_{j1}]' \in N_{k+1}(0, \Sigma)$, and Γ is a $k \times m$ matrix of parameters.

---

10. See Kumbhakar and Lovell (2000, pp. 77–78).
11. We use adaptive 20-point Gaussian quadrature. Relative to a 10-point rule, the results are virtually the same. We truncate the infinite range of integration to an interval [a, b]. Because $\lambda_j \geq 1$ in our sample and artificial data that we examine later, we set $a = 0$ and the upper bound b is determined so that the integral changes by less than 10^{-6}. A value of $b = 10$ was found more than adequate. Bayesian identification is guaranteed whenever the likelihood is bounded, and the prior is proper. See Appendix for identification of our model parameters.

The distribution of Q_j has now density given by:

$$p(Q_j \mid \theta) = (2\pi)^{-(k+1)/2} |\Sigma|^{-1/2} \frac{1}{Q_j} \left(\frac{\pi}{2}\sigma_u^2\right)^{-1/2}$$

$$\int_0^\infty \int_0^\infty \exp\left(-\lambda_j\right) \lambda_j^{Q_j} \exp\left[-1/2\left(u_{\widetilde{j0}}x_j - \Gamma z_j\right)' \Sigma^{-1} \left(u_{\widetilde{j0}}x_j - \Gamma z_j\right) - \frac{u_j^2}{2\sigma_u^2}\right] du_j d\lambda_j$$

(12)

where $u_{\widetilde{j0}} = \log \lambda_j + u_j - x_j'\beta$ is a function of latent variables.

We can formulate the likelihood based on the density in Eq. (12) and maximize with respect to the parameters using standard conjugate-gradient algorithms (Terza, Basu, & Rathouz, 2008).

Having controlled for potential endogeneity in the regressors, we now turn to modeling different technology classes.

2.3 Technology Classes

Firms use the best available technology given their input mix. Accordingly, they belong in different technological regimes. As Fig. 2 shows, for a given technology and set of inputs, there are units that produce output at point *ii* and, therefore, are inefficient compared to their own frontier and class (*A*) as their actual output is less than the maximum (frontier) attainable output, while other states produce at *iii* and exhibit some inefficiency compared to their own frontier and class (*B*).

Regime membership, however, is unobserved. We account for the existence of different technology classes, in which technology class membership is a function of covariates, z_j, and therefore advocate for a stochastic frontier model

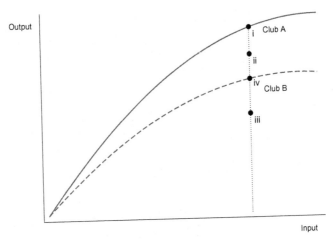

FIG. 2 Different stochastic frontier models of production.

augmented with mixture structure (Geweke, 2007). The focus is on technological and inefficiency induced heterogeneity. The finite mixture approach assumes that units have access to a finite number of technologies and the inefficiency of a unit is associated with a particular technology regime. The rationale behind the mixture approach is to probabilistically identify which unit is using what technology and then measure inefficiency as a probability weighted average computed using each of these technologies as the benchmark technology.

Consequently, given the Poisson stochastic frontier model, Eq. (4) is modified as follows:

$$\log \lambda_j = x'_j \beta_{|c} + v_{j|c} - u_{j|c} \tag{13}$$

where $c \in \{1, \dots, G\}$ and G is the number of distinct groups (classes), $v_{j|c} \sim$ i. i. d. $N(0, \sigma^2_{v|c})$, and $u_{j|c} \sim$ i. i. d. $N(0, \sigma^2_{u|c})$.

We assume:

$$P\left(c = g \mid z_j, \delta\right) = \frac{\exp\left(z'_j \delta_g\right)}{\sum_{g'=1}^{G} \exp\left(z'_j \delta_{g'}\right)} \quad g = 1, \dots, G \tag{14}$$

The covariates z_j determine directly the probability of classification in class g, and they are assumed to be the same with the covariates that we have used in Eq. (11). For normalization purposes, we assume: $\delta_G = 0_{(m \times 1)}$. In obvious notation, $\delta = [\delta'_j, \dots, \delta'_G]'$.

For the mixture model given by the Poisson model, and Eqs. (13), (14) to account for endogeneity of regressors we also use Eq. (11).

If we denote the density in Eq. (12) by $p(Q_j \mid \theta_g)$, the density of the mixture model is:

$$p\left(Q_j \mid \theta\right) = \sum_{g=1}^{G} p\left(Q_j \mid \theta_g\right) P\left(c = g \mid z_j, \delta\right) \tag{15}$$

The probability of classification of observation j into group g given the data can be computed from Eq. (14) using Bayes's theorem as follows:

$$P\left(c = g \mid Q_j, z_j, \delta\right) = \frac{p\left(Q_j \mid \theta_g\right) P\left(c = g \mid z_j, \delta\right)}{\sum_{g'=1}^{G} p\left(Q_j \mid \theta_{g'}\right) P\left(c = g' \mid z_j, \delta\right)}, \quad g = 1, \dots, G \tag{16}$$

where maximum likelihood parameter estimates are substituted for the unknowns.

The likelihood maximization in Eq. (13) depends not only on inputs and outputs per region, but also on efficiency (λ and σ). In contrast to a priori clustering on the basis of some individual proxy, both the parameters β and efficiency u can be determined endogenously through latent sorting into G classes.

3 Empirical Application

In this section, we provide an empirical application of our proposed methodology. The aim is to examine whether states in the United States, one of the most technologically advanced countries and an innovation leader in the world, belong in the same (or not) technology regime, and are (in)efficient in producing new knowledge (innovation).

Our empirical specification builds on knowledge (innovation) production function, which was introduced in the seminal work of Griliches (1979) and empirically implemented by many studies in the literature (Hall & Ziedonis, 2001; Jaffe, 1986; Pakes & Griliches, 1984). The production of knowledge, the innovative output or the creation of new designs in the R&D sector as in Romer (1990), is the product of knowledge generating inputs similar to the production of physical goods. Some observable measures of inputs, such as R&D expenditures and researchers, are invested in the knowledge production process and directed toward producing economically valuable knowledge, usually proxied by patents.[12] Therefore, the production of knowledge can be described as follows:

$$Q_{it} = f(A_{it}, H_{it}) \tag{17}$$

where Q is counts of patents, A the stock of knowledge proxied by R&D stock, and H is human capital devoted to development of knowledge proxied by the number of researchers. The units of each observation are state, i, and time, t.

In this chapter, we model the performance of states' knowledge production by means of stochastic frontier production to account for inefficient use of knowledge resources.[13] To further account for different technologies employed in the knowledge production, we augment the model with a finite mixture structure. Class membership is estimated conditional on a set of covariates, included in the vector z, and are state tax policies and labor mobility strictness.

More specifically, state tax policies and laws can affect the level of technology via their impact on R&D stock and human capital. Because the knowledge resources (e.g., R&D and researchers) are limited, a state can remain competitive in the innovation terrain by offering motives to stimulate existing knowledge resources or to attract more innovative firms from other states. One way to achieve that is to set low corporate and income tax rates and/or high R&D tax credits (Bloom, Griffith, & Reenen, 2002; Mamuneas & Nadiri, 1996;

---

12. The idea of using patents counts as a metric for innovation output to examine R&D productivity dates at least back to Hausman et al. (1984). For a more extensive review of early work of using patent counts, consult Hall, Jaffe, and Trajtenberg (2001). Since then, a number of papers have employed patent counts as innovation output to measure R&D (in)efficiency (e.g., Cullmann et al., 2012; Fu & Yang, 2009; Sharma & Thomas, 2008; Wang & Huang, 2007).

13. States also can be inefficient, if they use an input mix at which marginal returns to inputs do not equalize with true factor market prices. We do not consider this allocative efficiency because input prices are not available for the disaggregated (state level) data we use in our analysis. Therefore, in this study, the term efficiency refers purely to technical efficiency.

Palazzi, 2011; Wu, 2005). Labor laws also can influence innovation and techno-logical progress by restricting or enhancing scientific labor mobility. As techno-logical know-how acquired through research experience is embedded in the scientist's human capital, this knowledge becomes available to a competitor when the employee switches jobs. Noncompetition contracts—more commonly called noncompetes—is an employment agreement that limits employees' job options after leaving a company. Although the legitimate reason to enforce non-competes is to encourage employer investment in training and information that otherwise would never take place if employees are free to depart, the literature has documented that noncompetes could limit or even impede innovation (Belenzon & Schankerman, 2013; Marx, Strumsky, & Fleming, 2009; Saxenian, 1994).

We redefine the production frontier as a latent class frontier, which can be characterized by a system of equations: G stochastic production frontiers and a multinomial logit model with conditioning variables in the vector z (R&D tax credits, corporate tax rate, personal tax rate, and noncompetes) for the sorting (of states) into each of the G regimes. For a translog specification of the pro-duction function, in which the production output, Q_i, has a Poisson distribution with the conditional mean of the distribution $Q_i \mid \lambda_i \sim \text{Poisson}(\lambda_i)$ and with a general index of technical change specified by means of time dummies t and regimes $c(=1, \ldots, G)$, we can write a latent class stochastic frontier as:

$$\ln Q_{it} = \beta_{0|c} + \beta_{1|c} \ln A_{it} + \beta_{2|c} \ln H_{it} + \frac{1}{2}\beta_{11|c} \ln A_{it}^2 + \frac{1}{2}\beta_{22|c} \ln H_{it}^2 + \beta_{12|c} \ln A_{it} \ln H_{it}$$

$$+ \gamma_{At|c} \ln A_{it} * t + \gamma_{Ht|c} \ln H_{it} * t + \delta_{1t|c} * t + \frac{1}{2}\delta_{2t|c} * t^2 + v_{it|c} - u_{it|c} \tag{18}$$

Eq. (18), together with Eq. (16), can be estimated as a system. The param-eters of the system, β and efficiency u, are determined endogenously through latent sorting into G classes. Consequently, each class, c, is characterized by its own elasticities of capital and labor and level of efficiency.

An advantage of our modeling approach compared to previous latent class studies (Greene, 2002a, 2002b, 2005; Orea & Kumbhakar, 2004) is that we allow states to switch technology regimes over time. Within each period, observations of a single state are not independent because the state must fall within one of the regimes during that period, and the probability of being in a regime depends on the average of the variables used to estimate regime membership. Across periods, however, observations about a single state are treated as independent. For exam-ple, in moving from $t = t_1$ to $t = t_2$, a region is treated as a different i in the panel dimension it, and it can switch regimes. This flexibility adds an important dimen-sion to our analysis as one can study regime migrations.

3.1 Data

Our empirical analysis is based on a sample of 50 US states from 1993 to 2006. Data are retrieved from various sources.

The innovative output, the result of knowledge production, is hard to capture. As new designs are usually patented, we measure the innovative output as number of patents, which are materialized innovations of business value and are actively traded in intellectual property markets. We count patents by the location of the assignee (the patent owner) whether it is an individual, firm, or university. Data about patent counts by assignee at grant date, as well as information about the geographic location of the assignees, are extracted from the NBER Data Project.[14] We classify, during the years of our analysis, about 1 million (to be precise: 1,057,301) patents assigned to US-located entities. When patents have more than one patent assignees, we count these patents only once based on the first assignee.[15]

Information about the two inputs of knowledge production function, R&D expenditure (for constructing R&D capital stocks), and doctoral scientists and engineers devoted to research (for human capital) is extracted from the National Science Foundation Science and Engineering State Profiles. To calculate R&D (constant $2000 million US) stock, we use the perpetual inventory method as in Guellec and van Pottelsberghe (2004).[16]

Finally, information about states' tax variables and labor mobility strictness comes from a variety of sources. The state top income tax rate is obtained from the National Bureau of Economic Research (NBER),[17] the top corporate tax rate from the University Michigan Ross School of Business,[18] and statutory R&D tax credits from Wilson (2009) for 32 states that have enacted tax credits at some time. Data about noncompete scores are obtained from Garmaise (2009), who made use of Malsberger's (2004) 12-question scheme where, based on states' overall responses, a value was assigned for each state, ranging from 0 (low) to 9 (high), depending on the enforceability of noncompetes.

Annual data are used in our analysis, with the exception of variables extracted from the National Science Foundation database, which are provided biannually. We use STATA's interpolation methods to fill in the gaps. All monetary variables are expressed in constant $2000 million US.

Summary statistics of the variables considered in our analysis for each state and for the period under investigation are shown in Table A.1 in the Appendix. California (CA), New York state (NY), and Texas (TX) are among the top patent producers and have the highest accumulated technological knowledge (R&D stock) and human capital (scientists). At the opposite side of the spectrum are the states of Alaska (AK), Wyoming (WY), and South Dakota (SD). There is little variation across states, in terms of the policy variables.

---

14. https://sites.google.com/site/patentdataproject/Home.
15. A mere 1.5% of patents in our sample is co-assigned.
16. Following the literature, we have tried different depreciation percentages, e.g., 15% and 20%. The resulted R&D stocks are highly correlated.
17. http://users.nber.org/taxsim/.
18. http://www.bus.umich.edu/otpr/otpr/default.asp.

Corporate and income taxes both range between 0% and 11% across states, with California reporting the highest personal tax rate and one of the highest corporate tax rates. In terms of R&D tax credit, 32 states have some sort of R&D tax credit and the highest values, on average, for the years under consideration are observed in California (15%) and Rhode Island (RI) (15.7%). Finally, California, for example, has completely disregarded noncompete agreements during our sample period, whereas Florida (FL) has the most vigorous enforcement of noncompetes.

3.2 Results

Before embarking on exploring whether states in the United States belong in different (or same) innovation classes and whether states migrate across classes, we perform a small-scale Monte Carlo experiment to explore the consequences of using a log-normal distribution when the data have been generated from a Poisson distribution.

3.2.1 Monte Carlo Experiment

To investigate the consequences of using a log-normal distribution when the data have been generated from a Poisson distribution, we conduct a small-scale Monte Carlo experiment. The number of observations is $n = 700$ and the two regressors are generated as: $x_{i1} \sim$ i. i. d. $N(0, 1)$, and $x_{i2} = x_{i1} + 0.5\zeta_i$, where $\zeta_i \sim$ i.i.d. $N(0,1)$. The data generating process is: $\log \lambda_i = \beta_0 + 0.7x_{i1} + 0.3x_{i2} + v_i - u_i$ where $v_i \sim$ i. i. d. $N(0, \sigma_v^2)$ and $u_i \sim$ i. i. d. $N^+(0, \sigma_u^2)$. We fix $\sigma_v = 0.1$ and we examine various combinations of β_0 (whose true value was proved to be critical) with $\sigma_u = 0.1$ or $\sigma_u = 0.2$. We use 10,000 simulations in which the regressors x_{i1} and x_{i2} vary randomly according to the assumptions we have made. For each repetition, we compute estimated inefficiency from Eq. (10) and compare it to actual inefficiency using their correlation coefficient and their median deviation in the sample. Fig. 3 demonstrates the Monte Carlo results.

As the upper panel of Fig. 3 shows, the correlation between actual and estimated efficiency calculated from a log-normal distribution is rather small. Similar findings hold for the median deviation (lower panel) between actual and estimated efficiency. Consequently, the log-normal distribution is not always a good approximation to the Poisson distribution.

3.2.2 Do States Belong in Different Innovation Regimes?

We first investigate whether states can be described by a common innovation production function. In estimating the mixture model specified in Eq. (18), we first need to determine the number of classes, G. There is little guidance as to the appropriate number of groups based on economic growth theory. Multiple regime endogenous growth models, such as the ones developed in Azariadis and Drazen (1990), Easterly and Levine (2001), and Kejak (2003), corroborate

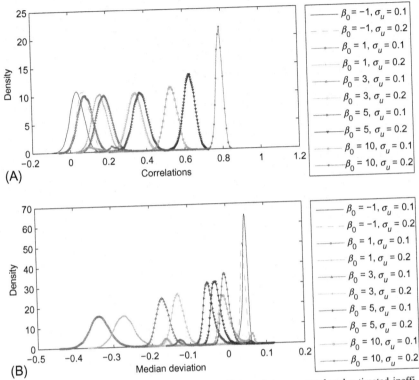

FIG. 3 Monte Carlo results. (A) Correlation coefficients between actual and estimated inefficiency and (B) median deviations between actual and estimated inefficiency.

the possibility of multiple steady states or growth regimes without, however, being explicit about the exact number of regimes.

We, therefore, rely upon statistical methods for determining the number of classes. The main computational problem is that a number of numerical integrations are needed with respect to λ_i and u_i. Empirically, the determination of the number of classes is specified here using the Bayesian Information Criterion (BIC) defined as $BIC = 2L - p \; log \; (n)/n$, where p is the total number of parameters and L the average log-likelihood, primarily because it provides consistent estimators of the model order, G. The preferred specification has the highest BIC value.

We find strong evidence in favor of two classes.[19] Accordingly, we classify states in our sample as belonging to classes A or B, respectively.

---

19. Classes (G): $G = 1$ with BIC equal to -575.12; $G = 2$ with BIC equal to -568.29; and $G = 3$ with BIC equal to -569.41. In the latter class, however, parameters are jointly not significantly different from zero, and the number of observations is very small.

Table 1 reports the estimated parameters for the translog production function with a time trend (top panel), efficiency parameters (middle panel), and membership probability parameters (bottom panel) for every regime, A and B. To examine whether parameter estimates differ significantly across regimes, we perform Wald tests for joint equality across regimes.[20]

The middle panel of Table 1 shows that inefficiency matters, too. This is confirmed by the parameters σ and λ, which measure the total variance and the relative magnitude of variance that is attributed to inefficiency, respectively. A positive and significant λ shows that much of this variance indeed consists of inefficiency. This result reflects an important advantage of our stochastic frontier approach to a comparable data envelopment analysis. If λ—the efficiency to noise ratio—is statistically insignificant, then almost all of the unexplained variance is indeed noise, while a statistically significant λ is an indication of inefficiency rather than noise.[21]

The bottom panel of Table 1 demonstrates the importance of the conditioning variables. The use of finite mixture specification implies an estimation of membership likelihood relative to the reference group, which is group A, here. For example, an increase in the R&D tax credit of 1% decreases the probability of belonging to regime A by 0.89%.[22]

The prior class probabilities (at the data means) at the bottom panel of Table 1 show that technology class A contains 23% of our sample, whereas technology class B contains 77%. The allocation of the states into the two innovation classes, A and B, is shown in Table A.1 in the Appendix. The same state can be classified as belonging to class A for some years, but also as belonging to class B for some others. The majority of states, however, fall into one class (B, in this case). The smaller class, A, contains eight states, namely Alaska (AK), Maine (ME), Mississippi (MS), Montana (MT), North Dakota (ND), South Dakota (SD), West Virginia (WV), and Wyoming (WY), which, on average, are not high innovation performers in terms of patents production, R&D, and scientists, according to the state summary statistics. A few states, namely Arkansas (AR), Hawaii (HI), Nebraska (NE), and Rhode Island (RI) move back and forth between the two classes, with Nebraska being the state with the most transitions between the two innovation groups.

The performance of the two classes when it comes to the sorting variables— the state policies—included in the vector z is the following: In class A, the mean R&D tax credit is, on average, 2.59%, whereas it is 4.01% in technology class B (P-value = 0.001). The corporate tax rate is 6.62% for class A and 6.56% for

---

20. Wald tests available upon request, demonstrate that parameters are jointly significantly different across the two regimes. We further test whether parameters of the mixture model variables are jointly significantly different across the two regimes and find evidence in favor.
21. This is clearly something that a DEA model would fail to capture.
22. We calculate probabilities by taking the exponent of the logit coefficients from the bottom panel of Table 1.

TABLE 1 Mixture Model Results

	A Class		B Class	
	Coeff.	St. Dev.	Coeff.	St. Dev.
Frontier				
lnR&D	0.330	0.023	0.117	0.015
lnHC	0.870	0.016	0.332	0.015
T	0.l00	0.007	0.028	0.007
$1/2\ ln\ R\&D^2$	0.084	0.003	−0.128	0.002
lnHC * lnR&D	−0.120	0.002	0.154	0.031
t * lnR&D	−0.043	0.003	0.027	0.002
$1/2lnHC^2$	0.073	0.002	0.002	0.001
t * lnHC	0.00l	0.001	−0.132	0.004
$1/2t^2$	−0.00l	0.001	−0.005	0.002
Constant	6.322	0.001	1.256	0.001
σ	0.303	0.017	0.335	0.025
λ_o	1.172	0.213	0.032	0.001
	Efficiency estimates			
	Mean	St. Dev.	Mean	St. Dev.
	0.887	0.210	0.914	0.150
	Finite mixture model coefficients			
R&D tax credit	Reference group		−0.112	0.022
Corporate tax rate	Reference group		−0.040	0.018
Personal tax rate	Reference group		−0.031	0.022
Noncompetes	Reference group		−0.662	0.034
Constant	Reference group		−0.019	0.007
	Prior class probabilities at data means			
	0.23		0.77	

Note: λ and σ are efficiency parameters, where $\lambda_o(=\sigma_u/\sigma_v)$, the ratio of the standard deviation of efficiency over the standard deviation of the noise term, and $\sigma(=(\sigma_u^2+\sigma_v^2)^{1/2})$, the composite standard deviation; BIC $= -568.29$.

class B (P-value $= 0.820$), personal income tax rate is 5.29% for class A and 5.23% for class B (P-value $= 0.83$) and, finally, noncompetes mean score in class A is 3.27 and 4.51 in class B (P-value $= 0.000$). Statistical differences between classes A and B, however, are significant at 1% only for the variables R&D tax credit and noncompetes. Although policy variables often are time invariant and do not differ between the two groups, group B is the class where states, on average, provide more innovation-friendly environments to firms.

The marginal product, at the data means, of capital (labor) is 0.34 (0.54) in class A, while in class B is about 0.48 (0.64).[23] It appears that states in class B benefit from the fact that the marginal productivity of a unit of their researchers and R&D capital stock is higher than that of class A. Marginal products are estimated conditional on four innovation policy variables. Although these variables do not greatly vary between the two classes, they can enhance the productivity of labor and capital in class B. Our capital and labor estimates are in line with existing empirical literature (Barro & Sala-i-Martin, 1995; Bos, Economidou, & Koetter, 2010; Koop, 2001; Wang, Cockburn, & Puterman, 1998). States in both classes produce at constant returns to scale, as is often reported in the literature (Barro & Sala-i-Martin, 1995; Mankiw, Romer, & Weil, 1992).

Including a time trend t for each class allows us to measure technical change. Interestingly, for the states that consider the frontier of technology class B their benchmark, we find that technical growth is 2.3% per year, whereas states in class A experience a modest technical growth of about 0.2%.

Not all states, in either class, however, grow with such growth rates, as the latter describe the growth of states which are on either frontier and consequently are fully efficient. Members of class A appear to be quite efficient (88.7%), when it comes to their own best practice, in producing innovation. The performance of states' innovation efficiency in class B, however, is even more remarkable because these states produce innovation with even less slack (91.4%). The latter group, therefore, produces more patents for every dollar spent.

Fig. 4 plots the evolution of mean efficiency (bold line) as well as its standard deviation (dashed line) in class A (left panel) and class B (right panel).

As Fig. 4 shows, the mean efficiency in class A has a rather volatile pattern because it exhibits a decrease until the middle of sample and then in increases. In contrast, the mean efficiency of states in class B has remained stable throughout the sample period. Members of class A show higher efficiency dispersion than members in class B as the pattern of the standard deviation of mean efficiency level indicates. In both groups, however, there is a clear increase in the dispersion of efficiency for the last 5 years of our sample period.

---

23. Our data are transformed, i.e., inputs are measured relative to their means, and therefore translog elasticities at means with respect to R&D stock and researchers are equal to the coefficients of R&D stock and researchers, respectively.

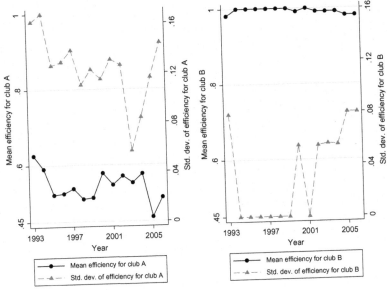

FIG. 4 Efficiency patterns.

The decomposition components, and, in particular, the technical and efficiency changes, can shed some light on leader/follower models of technical growth. In these models, all firms have access to the same technology, and the leader firm (the one with the highest TFP growth) develops a new technology and, via knowledge diffusion, the rest of the firms (followers) can imitate the technology (Cameron, Proudman, & Redding, 2005; Griffith et al., 2004; Kneller & Stevens, 2006; Scarpetta & Tressel, 2002).

In our set-up, leader states that operate on, or close to, the frontier, can try to push the frontier further outward through technical growth. Follower states might be left behind, unless they manage to increase efficiency by adopting existing advanced technologies and move closer to the frontier. Consequently, technical growth accompanied by improvements in efficiency could be an evidence of leader-follower behavior. Given the positive technical change in both classes and the evolution of efficiency in each class, our findings provide rather a nuanced evidence for some subperiods in our sample (mainly for states in class A) of the leader-follower behavior.

In sum, we find support of two innovation classes in the United States, with different implications for their members' innovation growth: a highly efficient large class that experiences significant technical growth and a less efficient smaller class with very mild technical growth. Nevertheless, there is no evidence of technological catch-up in either class.

3.2.3 Do States Change Innovation Class Membership?

In our finite mixture model, states are not restricted to one class. In principle, a state in class A can migrate to become a member of class B (and vice versa). One of the key assumptions in our modeling strategy is that classes in our mixture model are conditional on a set of innovation policy variables, i.e., taxes and enforcement of noncompetes. As mentioned earlier, only the R&D tax credit and noncompetes differences between the two classes are statistically significant and, therefore, in this section, we further explore only these policy variables.

Fig. 5 plots the conditional probability from Eq. (16) and R&D tax credit of states in groups A (left panel) and B (right panel).

The conditional probability of being a member of class A shows a volatile pattern, with some sharp changes in the middle (about 2001) and at the end (about 2005) of our sample. The mean of R&D tax credit exhibits, overall, an upward trend with some sudden changes about 2001, because some states at that time enacted favorable R&D tax credits. Overall, the link between the development of the mean of R&D tax credit and the conditional probability of belonging to class A is rather weak. Only some states in class A manage to capitalize on the high R&D tax credits they offer to their firms and eventually become a member of class B. The story appears to be slightly different for the states in class B. Ex-ante 2001, there seems to be no relation at all; ex-post 2001, a positive relationship emerges. In other words, post 2001, the higher the R&D tax credit of the states is, the higher the conditional probability of belonging in class B.

Next, Fig. 6 displays the conditional probability of being a member of class A and the development of the mean of noncompetes.

The enforcement of noncompetes does not vary much across states and over time, as Table A.1 in the Appendix indicates. Therefore, the mean of

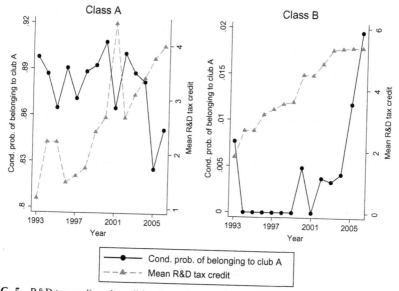

FIG. 5   R&D tax credit and conditional probability of belonging to class A.

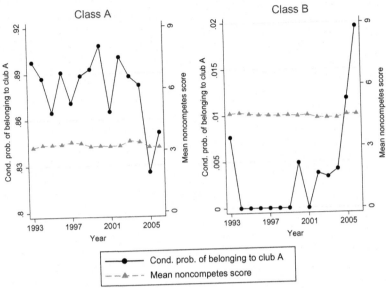

FIG. 6 Noncompetes and conditional probability of belonging to class *A*.

noncompetes score is stable. The conditional probability of being member of group *A* does not vary much, either. Overall, the link between the development of the mean of R&D tax credit and the conditional probability of belonging to class *A* is, on average, absent.

We now investigate the transition probabilities of states switching innovation classes. Table 2 reports these probabilities. As we saw, some states in class *B* and for some time in class *A* have been rather successful in increasing R&D tax credits (or lowering noncompetes). These states might try to make the shift from class *A* to class *B*. In Table 2, we observe that over the sample period (less than) 5% of the states in class *A* manage to shift to class *B*.[24] For instance, the states of New Mexico (NM) and Vermont (VT), former members of class *A*, now join class *B*, with Vermont showing an increase in R&D tax credit from 0% to 10%, and New Mexico showing a slight reduction in personal tax rate. We also find that 1.7% of the states in class *B*—Alabama (AL) and Louisiana (LA)—make the opposite move.

Given that the dispersion of efficiency levels is greater in class *A* than *B*, as is shown in Table 1 (middle panel), some states are better off being efficient in the more efficient class *B* than inefficient in class *A*, while enjoying technological progress in the former group.

---

24. As we allow states to move back and forth between classes *A* and *B*, 5% also includes these cases.

TABLE 2 Migrations Between Classes

From	To		Totals
	A	B	
A	95%	5%	160
B	1.7%	98.3%	540
Totals	161	539	700

4 Conclusions

Applications of count models have been ample in various disciples. In many contexts, the measuring of technical efficiency is of central importance. Only recently have there been some attempts in the stochastic frontier paradigm to model efficiency when the dependent variable has discrete conditional distribution.

This chapter develops a methodology appropriate for count data stochastic frontier models allowing for technological and inefficiency induced heterogeneity in the data and controlling for endogenous regressors. We, therefore, extend and generalize important aspects of past related studies in the field. The proposed model is a Poisson stochastic frontier model augmented with finite mixture structure. We derive the corresponding log-likelihood function and conditional mean of inefficiency to estimate technology regime-specific inefficiency. We believe that the methodology we propose could be useful for applied researchers conducting efficiency studies using count data in various scientific fields, in particular in economics and finance.

To demonstrate the applicability of the proposed model, we estimate a knowledge production function for the states of the United States, in which the dependent variable is counts of patents. In particular, we examine whether states belong in the same innovation regime, and whether they are efficient in producing innovation. Relevant past studies typically assume that knowledge resources are used efficiently, whereas the few, which account for the latter, consider the underlying knowledge production technology to be identical for all units.

Our empirical results show that the Poisson stochastic frontier model augmented with latent class structure can be implemented in studying the innovation performance of the states, offering useful insights. Our findings support the existence of two distinct innovation classes with different implications for their members' innovation growth.

Appendix

Model's Parameter Identification

Bayesian identification is guaranteed whenever the likelihood is bounded and the prior is proper. That is, if we have a proper prior $p(\beta,\sigma)$ then[25] the posterior is always finitely integrable, that is, it exists. Boundedness of the likelihood can be shown using the arguments at the end of the proof of Proposition 1. In what follows, we show that the posterior is always finitely integrable under more general conditions.

Proposition 1. *Suppose $\beta \in \mathfrak{D}$, any bounded subset of $\mathfrak{R}^k$ (no matter how large) and $p(\sigma) \propto \sigma^{-(v+1)} \exp\left\{-\frac{q}{2\sigma^2}\right\}$, where $v \geq 0$ and $q > 0$. Then the posterior is finitely integrable.*

Proof
Using Eqs. (3) and (4), after integrating with respect to $u = [u_1, \ldots, u_n]$, we can write the posterior as follows:

$$p\left(\beta,\sigma,\lambda_0,\lambda \mid Q\right) \propto \exp\left\{-\sum_{j=1}^{n}\lambda_j - \sum_{j=1}^{n}\left(Q_j - 1\right)\log\lambda_j\right\} \cdot$$

$$\sigma^{-(n+v+1)}\exp\left\{-\frac{1}{2\sigma^2}\left[q + \sum_{j=1}^{n}\left(\log\lambda_j - x_j'\beta\right)^2\right]\right\}\Pi_{j=1}^{n}\,\Phi\left(-\frac{\lambda_0}{\sigma}\left(\log\lambda_j - x_j'\beta\right)^2\right)\cdot p\left(\lambda_0 \mid \beta,\sigma\right),\quad \beta\in\mathfrak{D}$$

$$(19)$$

Because we do not make any particular assumptions about $p(\lambda_0 \mid \beta,\sigma)$, we have the bound[26]:

$$p(\beta,\sigma,\lambda \mid Q) \leq \exp\left\{-\sum_{j=1}^{n}\lambda_j - \sum_{j=1}^{n}\left(Q_j - 1\right)\log\lambda_j\right\}\cdot\sigma^{-(n+v+1)}$$

$$\times\exp\left\{-\frac{1}{2\sigma^2}\left[q + \sum_{j=1}^{n}\left(\log\lambda_j - x_j'\beta\right)^2\right]\right\},\quad \beta\in\mathfrak{D}\quad (20)$$

We can integrate the bound with respect to σ to obtain:

$$p(\beta,\lambda \mid Q) \leq \exp\left\{-\sum_{j=1}^{n}\lambda_j - \sum_{j=1}^{n}\left(Q_j - 1\right)\log\lambda_j\right\}\cdot\left[q + \sum_{j=1}^{n}\left(\log\lambda_j - x_j'\beta\right)^2\right]^{-(n+v)/2},\quad \beta\in\mathfrak{D}$$

$$(21)$$

Because $q > 0$, and $\mathfrak{D}$ is finite, we have, after integrating out β:

$$p(\lambda \mid Q) \leq \exp\left\{-\sum_{j=1}^{n}\lambda_j - \sum_{j=1}^{n}\left(Q_j - 1\right)\log\lambda_j\right\}\quad (22)$$

---

25. We do not need a proper prior on λ_0. The proof is trivial, and we omit it.
26. Constants are omitted from all upper bounds in the following.

It is easy to show that $\{-\sum_{j=1}^{n}(Q_j - 1)\log \lambda_j\} < \infty$, and therefore $\int p(\lambda \mid Q)$ $d\lambda < \int_{\mathfrak{R}_+^n} \exp \{-\sum_{j=1}^{n}\lambda_j\}d\lambda_j = 1$. Therefore, the posterior is finitely integrable. $\square$

Notice that with $v = 0$ the prior $p(\sigma) \propto \sigma^{-(v+1)}\exp\{-\frac{q}{2\sigma^2}\}$ is improper and parameter β_i can belong to $[-10^{12}, 10^2](i = 1, \ldots, k)$. In turn, we can take $\mathfrak{D} = [-10^{12}, 10^{12}]^k$. So, the assumptions are mild enough for our purposes. In a similar way, one can show that posterior moments if β exist up to order $n - k$, i.e., $\int_{\mathfrak{R}^k}\beta^p p(\beta \mid Q)d\beta < \infty$, $0 \leq p < n - k$.

In the next proposition, we remove the assumption that β belongs to a finite domain and that σ has a prior of the form stated in the assumptions of Proposition 1.

Proposition 2. *Suppose* $\hat{\beta}(\lambda) = (X'X)^{-1}X'\log \lambda, s^2(\lambda) = (\log \lambda - X\hat{\beta}(\lambda))'$ $(\log \lambda - X\hat{\beta}(\lambda))$ *for any* $\lambda \in \mathfrak{R}_+^n$, *and* $s^2(\lambda)$ *is bounded away from zero, i.e.,* $s^2(\lambda) > \epsilon > 0$. *Then the posterior is finitely integrable.*

Proof

From Eq. (21) in the proof of Proposition 1 we have:

$$p(\beta, \lambda \mid Q) \leq \exp\left\{-\sum_{j=1}^{n}\lambda_j - \sum_{j=1}^{n}\left(Q_j - 1\right)\log \lambda_j\right\} \cdot \left\{(\log \lambda - X\beta)'(\log \lambda - X\beta)\right\}^{-(n-k+1)/2}$$

(23)

which can be written as:

$$p(\beta, \lambda \mid Q) \leq \exp\left\{-\sum_{j=1}^{n}\lambda_j - \sum_{j=1}^{n}\left(Q_j - 1\right)\log \lambda_j\right\} \cdot \left\{s^2(\lambda) + [\beta - \hat{\beta}(\lambda)]'X'X[\beta - \hat{\beta}(\lambda)]\right\}^{-(k+p)/2}$$

(24)

where $p = n - k, \hat{\beta}(\lambda) = (X'X)^{-1}X'\log \lambda, s^2(\lambda) = (\log \lambda - X\hat{\beta}(\lambda))'(\log \lambda - X\hat{\beta}(\lambda))$. Because the second term is in the form of a multivariate Student-t distribution with p degrees of freedom, integrating with respect to β we obtain:

$$p(\beta, \lambda \mid Q) \leq \exp\left\{-\sum_{j=1}^{n}\lambda_j - \sum_{j=1}^{n}\left(Q_j - 1\right)\log \lambda_j\right\} \cdot \left|s^2(\lambda)(X'X)^{-1}\right|^{1/2}$$

$$\propto \exp\left\{-\sum_{j=1}^{n}\lambda_j - \sum_{j=1}^{n}\left(Q_j - 1\right)\log \lambda_j\right\} \cdot \left\{s^2(\lambda)\right\}^{-(p+k-1)/2}$$

(25)

Therefore,

$$p(\beta, \lambda \mid Q) \leq \exp\left\{-\sum_{j=1}^{n}\lambda_j - \sum_{j=1}^{n}\left(Q_j - 1\right)\log \lambda_j\right\} \cdot \epsilon^{-(p+k-1)/2}$$

By the reasoning about the finiteness of the exponential term in Proposition 1, the posterior, and posterior moments up to order $n - k$, exist. $\square$

TABLE A.1 Summary Statistics and States' Allocation per Innovation Classes

State	Patents		R&D stock		Scientists		R&D Tax Credit		Corporate Tax		Personal Tax		Noncompetes		Class A	Class B
	Mean	St. Dev.	Mean	St. Dev.	Mean	St. Dev.	Mean	St. Dev.	Mean	St. Dev.	Mean	St. Dev.	Mean	St. Dev.		
AK	35.64	13.65	827.91	190.43	1295.64	88.33	0.00	0.00	9.40	0.00	0.00	0.00	3.00	0.00	14	0
AL	251.50	63.21	10232.51	562.85	7105.21	1191.18	0.00	0.00	6.50	0.00	3.09	0.11	5.00	0.00	2	12
AR	139.00	43.65	1777.62	229.41	3128.36	431.41	0.00	0.00	6.50	0.00	7.24	0.08	5.00	0.00	9	5
AZ	650.21	158.10	12157.40	3984.27	7739.43	1199.92	10.21	2.94	6.90	0.00	5.26	0.64	3.00	0.00	0	14
CA	16174.07	4777.37	210655.50	33458.35	84556.93	10096.99	15.00	0.00	8.97	0.22	10.25	0.77	0.00	0.00	0	14
CO	987.29	214.68	17906.91	3067.81	13117.21	1664.53	0.00	0.00	4.80	0.20	4.94	0.19	2.00	0.00	0	14
CT	2294.64	268.80	19884.92	6064.61	10257.21	1146.03	6.00	0.00	8.61	1.21	4.64	0.23	3.00	0.00	0	14
DE	1994.71	245.34	7207.65	698.14	3917.57	435.27	5.00	5.19	8.70	0.00	6.77	0.76	6.00	0.00	0	14
FL	1917.64	515.61	21802.29	2361.26	17484.29	2119.59	0.00	0.00	5.50	0.00	0.00	0.00	8.43	0.94	0	14
GA	833.71	173.30	11361.72	3128.72	12178.50	1714.06	6.43	4.97	6.00	0.00	5.83	0.02	5.00	0.00	8	6
HI	60.64	18.23	1934.93	135.79	2794.07	275.21	10.00	10.38	6.40	0.00	8.57	0.73	3.00	0.00	0	14
IA	494.07	130.32	5437.08	644.61	4919.21	292.95	6.50	0.00	10.86	1.03	5.99	0.28	6.00	0.00	0	14
ID	1183.86	737.02	4208.47	1308.76	2499.86	359.05	2.14	2.57	7.86	0.20	8.10	0.20	6.00	0.00	0	14
IL	4358.00	579.03	42800.89	6765.41	23691.57	1448.58	6.50	0.00	5.34	1.06	3.00	0.00	5.00	0.00	0	14
IN	958.43	219.77	15489.39	2549.40	9662.21	853.13	5.00	0.00	4.49	2.17	3.40	0.00	5.00	0.00	0	14
KS	276.57	50.19	4968.84	2394.31	4306.29	366.55	6.50	0.00	4.28	0.90	6.49	0.01	6.00	0.00	0	14
KY	311.79	82.68	3199.03	973.58	4914.43	520.27	0.00	0.00	8.16	0.33	6.18	0.02	6.00	0.00	0	14

LA	322.21	106.29	2863.49	538.01	5943.57	231.35	2.29	3.75	8.00	0.00	3.70	0.15	2.57	1.99	2	12
MA	3043.21	572.64	57521.14	8130.20	29144.21	3809.21	10.00	0.00	8.66	0.55	5.69	0.31	6.00	0.00	0	14
MD	854.71	208.22	41447.00	4840.35	25256.86	3298.45	5.00	5.19	7.00	0.00	5.08	0.43	5.00	0.00	0	14
ME	101.50	26.10	1032.15	427.52	2458.71	131.69	3.93	2.13	8.93	0.00	8.74	0.02	4.00	0.00	14	0
MI	3567.36	583.01	69929.04	9629.45	17645.43	1536.94	0.00	0.00	2.13	0.18	4.24	0.23	5.00	0.00	0	14
MN	2267.00	376.67	18438.57	3819.77	11415.07	1363.55	2.50	0.00	9.80	0.00	8.38	0.34	5.00	0.00	0	14
MO	777.79	143.90	10705.79	1360.25	9797.79	534.37	6.04	1.74	6.27	0.07	5.90	0.62	7.00	0.00	0	14
MS	105.79	33.82	2160.86	760.69	3375.64	227.73	0.00	0.00	5.00	0.00	5.07	0.01	4.00	0.00	0	14
MT	98.71	20.60	691.84	251.87	1979.57	188.29	2.86	2.57	6.75	0.00	7.25	0.20	2.00	0.00	14	0
NC	1087.50	298.51	19402.82	5125.77	17308.93	2469.09	3.93	2.13	7.23	0.38	8.20	0.26	4.00	0.00	14	0
ND	45.50	14.48	716.71	357.47	1629.43	462.49	4.00	0.00	10.00	1.27	5.41	0.02	0.00	0.00	0	14
NE	161.36	31.47	1918.63	534.77	2969.93	113.23	0.21	0.80	7.81	0.00	6.98	0.13	4.00	0.00	14	0
NH	330.00	63.92	4000.73	1719.61	2658.14	364.82	0.00	0.00	7.95	0.89	0.00	0.00	2.00	0.00	8	6
NJ	4072.07	691.12	53508.25	4670.01	23378.36	1919.00	9.29	2.67	9.00	0.00	7.01	1.08	4.00	0.00	0	14
NM	219.93	66.86	16344.35	2429.10	8444.43	786.31	0.00	0.00	7.60	0.00	7.43	0.97	2.00	0.00	0	14
NV	391.43	160.98	1789.66	565.60	2106.57	325.07	0.00	0.00	0.00	0.00	0.00	0.00	5.00	0.00	4	10
NY	8081.14	1326.58	63772.80	2054.90	45883.79	2404.17	0.00	0.00	8.39	0.68	7.29	0.45	3.00	0.00	0	14
OH	3028.50	549.58	35754.15	1632.93	21681.64	1757.48	1.50	2.98	8.46	0.65	7.27	0.27	5.00	0.00	0	14
OK	428.57	83.24	3077.24	317.61	4956.64	242.98	0.00	0.00	6.00	0.00	5.99	0.19	1.00	0.00	0	14
OR	590.21	96.57	7514.46	3715.70	8121.00	1125.80	5.00	0.00	6.60	0.00	9.07	0.02	6.00	0.00	0	14
PA	2571.43	349.99	45865.43	2184.12	28078.14	2477.25	7.14	4.69	10.24	0.89	2.86	0.11	6.00	0.00	0	14
RI	185.71	25.86	5034.06	2133.85	2865.21	323.32	15.69	4.52	9.00	0.00	9.69	0.39	3.00	0.00	0	14

Continued

TABLE A.1 Summary Statistics and States' Allocation per Innovation Classes—cont'd

State	Patents		R&D stock		Scientists		R&D Tax Credit		Corporate Tax		Personal Tax		Noncompetes		Class A	Class B
	Mean	St. Dev.	Mean	St. Dev.	Mean	St. Dev.	Mean	St. Dev.	Mean	St. Dev.	Mean	St. Dev.	Mean	St. Dev.		
SC	387.57	75.42	4832.02	1306.03	5502.14	477.64	2.14	2.57	5.00	0.00	7.08	0.01	5.00	0.00	0	14
SD	51.79	25.14	357.06	107.10	1144.29	61.17	0.00	0.00	0.00	0.00	0.00	0.00	5.00	0.00	14	0
TN	568.71	130.03	8839.92	2402.95	9607.86	690.70	0.00	0.00	6.11	0.21	0.00	0.00	7.00	0.00	0	14
TX	4777.79	1386.10	47634.33	10747.15	34721.00	3513.42	2.14	2.57	0.32	1.20	0.00	0.00	3.29	0.73	0	14
UT	485.93	104.44	5536.01	1345.80	5325.14	451.99	3.43	3.08	5.00	0.00	6.07	0.08	6.00	0.00	0	14
VA	896.64	124.27	20974.31	6079.52	19467.71	2852.81	0.00	0.00	6.00	0.00	5.82	0.01	3.00	0.00	12	2
VT	75.57	15.46	1785.01	183.03	1913.00	203.29	2.86	4.69	9.32	0.70	9.10	0.99	5.00	0.00	0	14
WA	1546.50	516.79	36153.02	8424.19	15551.71	2205.27	0.00	0.00	0.00	0.00	0.00	0.00	5.00	0.00	0	14
WI	1377.14	238.50	11873.46	2208.67	9228.29	873.28	5.00	0.00	7.90	0.00	6.82	0.09	3.00	0.00	0	14
WV	57.86	18.77	1923.62	345.04	2279.29	188.73	10.00	0.00	9.00	0.00	6.50	0.00	2.00	0.00	14	0
WY	42.57	14.92	359.22	42.49	889.93	87.05	0.00	0.00	0.00	0.00	0.00	0.00	4.00	0.00	14	0

State's two-letter abbreviation reported in first column; R&D stock in millions of constant (2000) US dollars; Scientists (science, engineering, and health researchers) are in thousands; R&D tax credit, corporate tax, and personal tax are percentages (%); and noncompetes range from 0 (low enforceability) to 12 (high enforceability). Classes A and B are technological regimes (classes).

Acknowledgments

We thank Konstantinos Vasileiou for excellent research assistance. We also thank Jaap W.B. Bos for useful insights and suggestions. Kyriakos Drivas gratefully acknowledges financial support from the *National Strategic Reference Framework* No: SH1_4083. The usual disclaimer applies.

References

Acemoglu, D., Zilibotti, F., 2001. Productivity differences. Quarterly Journal of Economics 116 (2), 563–606.

Aghion, P., Howitt, P., 1998. Endogenous growth theory. MIT Press, Cambridge, MA.

Aigner, D.J., Lovell, K.C., Schmidt, P., 1977. Formulation and estimation of stochastic frontier production function models. Journal of Econometrics 6 (1), 21–37.

Azariadis, C., Drazen, A., 1990. Threshold externalities in economic development. The Quarterly Journal of Economics 105 (2), 501–526.

Barro, R.J., Sala-i-Martin, X.X., 1995. Economic growth. McGraw-Hill, New York.

Basu, S., Weil, D., 1998. Appropriate technology and growth. Quarterly Journal of Economics 113 (4), 1025–1054.

Belenzon, S., Schankerman, M., 2013. Spreading the word: geography, policy and knowledge spillovers. Review of Economics and Statistics 95 (3), 884–903.

Bloom, N., Griffith, R., Reenen, J.V., 2002. Do R&D tax credits work? Evidence from a panel of OECD countries 1979–1997. Journal of Public Economics 85 (1), 1–31.

Bos, J., Economidou, C., Koetter, M., 2010. Technology clubs, R&D and growth patterns: evidence from EU manufacturing. European Economic Review 54 (1), 60–79.

Bos, J., Economidou, C., Koetter, M., Kolari, J., 2010. Do all countries grow alike? Journal of Development Economics 91 (1), 113–127.

Bottazzi, L., Peri, G., 2003. Innovation and spillovers in regions: evidence from European patent data. European Economic Review 47 (4), 687–717.

Bottazzi, L., Peri, G., 2007. The international dynamics of R&D and innovation in the long run and in the short run. Economic Journal 117 (518), 486–511.

Cameron, G., Proudman, J., Redding, S., 2005. Technological convergence, R&D, trade and productivity growth. European Economic Review 49 (3), 775–807.

Cameron, C.A., Trivedi, P.K., 2013. Regression analysis of count data, second ed. Econometric society monograph no. 53, Cambridge University Press, p. 1998.

Coe, D., Helpman, E., 1995. International R&D spillovers. European Economic Review 39 (5), 859–887.

Coelli, T., Rao, D.P., Battese, G.E., 2005. An introduction to efficiency analysis, second ed. Springer, New York.

Cruz-Cázaresa, C., Bayona-Sáezb, C., García-Marco, T., 2013. You can't manage right what you can't measure well: technological innovation efficiency. Research Policy 42 (6–7), 1239–1250.

Cullmann, A., Schmidt-Ehmcke, J., Zloczysti, P., 2012. Innovation, R&D efficiency and the impact of the regulatory environment: a two-stage semi-parametric DEA approach. Oxford Economic Papers 64 (1), 176–196.

Davutyan, N., 1989. Bank failures as Poisson variates. Economics Letters 29 (4), 333–338.

Dionne, G., Artis, M., Guillen, M., 1996. Count data models for a credit scoring system. Journal of Empirical Finance 3 (3), 303–325.

Easterly, W., Levine, R., 2001. It's not factor accumulation: stylized facts and growth models. The World Bank Economic Review 15 (2), 177–219.

Fè-Rodríguez, E., 2007. Exploring a stochastic frontier model when the dependent variable is a count. University of Manchester. School of Economics discussion paper series no. 0725.

Fè-Rodríguez, E., Hofler, R., 2013. Count data stochastic frontier models, with an application to the patents-R&D relationship. Journal of Productivity Analysis 39 (3), 271–284.

Fu, X., Yang, Q., 2009. Exploring the cross-country gap in patenting: a stochastic frontier approach. Research Policy 38 (7), 1203–1213.

Garmaise, M.J., 2009. Ties that truly bind: non-competition agreements, executive compensation and firm investment. Journal of Law, Economics, and Organization 27 (2), 376–425.

Geweke, J., 2007. Interpretation and inference in mixture models: simple MCMC works. Computational Statistics & Data Analysis 51 (7), 3529–3550.

Greene, W.H., 2002a. Alternative panel data estimators for stochastic frontier models. Mimeo. Retrieved from: http://pages.stern.nyu.edu/wgreene/.

Greene, W.H., 2002b. Econometric modeling guide. Econometric Software, Inc., New York

Greene, W.H., 2005. Reconsidering heterogeneity in panel data estimators of the stochastic frontier model. Journal of Econometrics 126 (2), 269–303.

Griffith, R., Redding, S., van Reenen, J., 2004. Mapping the two faces of R&D: productivity growth in a panel of OECD industries. Review of Economics and Statistics 86 (4), 883–895.

Griliches, Z., 1979. Issues in assessing the contribution of R&D to productivity growth. Bell Journal of Economics 10 (1), 92–116.

Guellec, D., van Pottelsberghe, B., 2004. From R&D to productivity growth: do the institutional settings and the source of funds of R&D matter? Oxford Bulletin of Economics and Statistics 66 (3), 353–378.

Hall, B., Jaffe, A., Trajtenberg, M., 2001. The NBER patent citation data file: lessons, insights and methodological tools. NBER working paper no. 8498.

Hall, B.H., Ziedonis, R.H., 2001. The patent paradox revisited: an empirical study of patenting in the U.S. semiconductor industry, 1979–1995. RAND Journal of Economics 32 (1), 101–128.

Hausman, J.A., Hall, B., Griliches, Z., 1984. Econometric models for count data with an application to the patents-R&D relationship. NBER working paper no. 0017.

Hofler, R., Scrogin, D., 2008. A count data stochastic frontier. Discussion paper, University of Central Florida.

Jaffe, A.B., 1986. Technology opportunity and spillovers of R&D: evidence from firms' patents, profits, and market value. American Economic Review 76 (5), 984–1001.

Jondrow, J., Lovell, C.K., Materov, I., Schmidt, P., 1982. On the estimation of technical inefficiency in the stochastic frontier production function models. Journal of Econometrics 19 (2–3), 233–238.

Jones, C.I., 1995. Time series test of endogenous growth models. Quarterly Journal of Economics 110 (2), 495–525.

Jones, C.I., 2005. The shape of production functions and the direction of technical change. Quarterly Journal of Economics 120 (2), 517–549.

Kejak, M., 2003. Stages of growth in economic development. Journal of Economic Dynamics and Control 27 (5), 771–800.

Kneller, R., Stevens, P., 2006. Frontier technology and absorptive capacity: evidence from OECD manufacturing industries. Oxford Bulletin of Economics and Statistics 68 (1), 1–21.

Koop, G., 2001. Cross-sectoral patterns of efficiency and technical change in manufacturing. International Economic Review 42 (1), 73–103.

Kumbhakar, S.C., Lovell, K.C., 2000. Stochastic frontier analysis. Cambridge University Press, Cambridge.

Kumbhakar, S.C., Parmeter, C., Tsionas, E., 2013. A zero inefficiency stochastic frontier model. Journal of Econometrics 172 (1), 66–76.

Malsberger, B., 2004. Covenants not to compete: A state-by-state survey. A Bloomberg BNA Publication, Washington, DC.

Mamuneas, T., Nadiri, M., 1996. Public R&D policies and cost of behavior of the US manufacturing industries. Journal of Public Economics 63 (1), 57–81.

Mancusi, M.L., 2008. International spillovers and absorptive capacity: a cross-country cross-sector analysis based on patents and citations. Journal of International Economics 76, 155–165.

Mankiw, G.N., Romer, D., Weil, D.N., 1992. A contribution to the empirics of economic growth. Quarterly Journal of Economics 107 (2), 407–437.

Marx, M., Strumsky, D., Fleming, L., 2009. Mobility, skills, and the Michigan non-compete experiment. Management Science 55 (6), 875–889.

Meeusen, W., van den Broeck, J., 1977. Efficiency estimation from Cobb-Douglas production functions with composed error. International Economic Review 18 (2), 435–444.

Orea, L., Kumbhakar, S.C., 2004. Efficiency measurement using a latent class stochastic frontier model. Empirical Economics 29 (1), 169–183.

Pakes, A., Griliches, Z., 1984. Patents and R&D at the firm level: a first look. In: Griliches, Z. (Ed.), R&D, patents and productivity. University of Chicago Press, Chicago and London.

Palazzi, P., 2011. Taxation and innovation. OECD taxation working papers, no. 9, OECD, Paris. https://doi.org/10.1787/5kg3h0sf1336-en.

Romer, P.M., 1990. Endogenous technological change. Journal of Political Economy 98 (5), 71–102.

Rousseau, S., Rousseau, R., 1997. Data envelopment analysis as a tool for constructing scientometric indicators. Scientometrics 40 (1), 45–56.

Rousseau, S., Rousseau, R., 1998. The scientific wealth of European nations: taking effectiveness into account. Scientometrics 42 (1), 75–87.

Saxenian, A., 1994. Regional advantage: Culture and competition in Silicon Valley and route 128. Harvard University Press, Cambridge, MA.

Scarpetta, S., Tressel, T., 2002. Productivity and convergence in a panel of OECD industries: Do regulations and institutions matter? Working paper 342, OECD.

Sharma, S., Thomas, V., 2008. Inter-country R&D efficiency analysis: an application of data envelopment analysis. Scientometrics 76 (3), 483–501.

Sickles, R., Qian, J., 2009. Stochastic frontiers with bounded inefficiency. Mimeo, Rice University.

Solow, R.M., 1957. Technical change and the aggregate production function. Review of Economics and Statistics 39 (3), 312–320.

Terza, J., Basu, A., Rathouz, P., 2008. Two-stage residual inclusion estimation: addressing endogeneity in health econometric modeling. Journal of Health Economics 27 (3), 531–543.

Thomas, V., Sharma, S., Jain, S., 2011. Using patents and publications to assess R&D efficiency in the states of the USA. World Patent Information 33 (1), 4–10.

Tsionas, E., Kumbhakar, S., 2004. Markov switching stochastic frontier model. The Econometrics Journal 7 (2), 398–425.

Wang, E.C., 2007. R&D efficiency and economic performance: a cross-country analysis using the stochastic frontier approach. Journal of Policy Modeling 29 (2), 345–360.

Wang, P., Cockburn, I., Puterman, M., 1998. Analysis of patent data: a mixed-Poisson-regression-model approach. Journal of Business & Economic Statistics 16, 27–41.

Wang, E.C., Huang, W., 2007. Relative efficiency of R&D activities: a cross-country study accounting for environmental factors in the DEA approach. Research Policy 36 (2), 260–273.

Wilson, D.J., 2009. Beggar thy neighbor? The in-state, out-of-state, and aggregate effects of R&D tax credits. Review of Economics and Statistics 91 (2), 431–436.

Wu, Y., 2005. The effects of state R&D tax credits in stimulating private R&D expenditure: a cross-state empirical analysis. Journal of Policy Analysis and Management 24 (4), 785–802.

Zachariadis, M., 2003. R&D, innovation, and technological progress: a test of the Schumpeterian framework without scale effects. Canadian Journal of Economics 36 (3), 566–586.

Chapter 25

Making Inference of Bank Managerial Preferences About Performance: A Panel Analysis

E.C. Mamatzakis*, C. Staikouras† and Mike G. Tsionas‡

*University of Sussex Business School, University of Sussex, Brighton, United Kingdom, †School of Business Administration, Athens University of Economics and Business, Athens, Greece, ‡Department of Economics, Lancaster University Management School, Lancaster, United Kingdom

Chapter Outline

1 Introduction

The impediments associated with agency costs, whether for financial or nonfinancial industries, have been documented in early studies of management (Wiseman & Gomez-Mejia, 1998). Because of the separation of ownership and control in big firms, agency costs can arise in the case of absence of complete information whereby shareholders could be unable to monitor management, leading to managerial discretion that might induce nonoptimal behavior. For example, managers might resort to practices away from maximizing profits or minimizing costs. As long as the interests of managers and shareholders are not perfectly aligned and shareholders cannot insure themselves against possible suboptimal behavior, managers might show expense-preference behavior or if they are highly risk averse, any other strategy that

Panel Data Econometrics. https://doi.org/10.1016/B978-0-12-815859-3.00025-1

might reduce profits (Carpenter & Sanders, 2004; D'Amato & Gallo, 2017; Delgado-García, de Quevedo-Puente, & Díez-Esteban, 2013).

To this day, the ability to provide a way of revealing managerial preferences over firm performance has been rather elusive. We are aware, however, that management behavior matters a great deal for firm performance (see for example, D'Amato & Gallo, 2017; Delgado-García et al., 2013; Delgado-García, de la Fuente-Sabaté, & de Quevedo-Puente, 2010; Jensen & Meckling, 1976). Indeed, the effect of management behavior on firm performance has been the central focus of an extended literature (see Dalton & Dalton, 2011; Delgado-García et al., 2010; Jensen, 1986, 1993; Shleifer & Vishny, 1986, 1997). The empirical evidence suggests that financial decisions and investment decisions, and thereby firm's value, are affected significantly by the presence of conflicts of interest between managers and shareholders as well as between debt holders and shareholders (see for example Chen, Delmas, & Lieberman, 2015; Miller & Parkhe, 2001). The link between firm performance, risk, and management behavior also has been proposed in management research as closely related to agency costs (Brush, Bromiley, & Hendrickx, 2000; Jensen & Meckling, 1976; Mingfang & Simerly, 1998; Wiseman & Gomez-Mejia, 1998), while some research looks at the public policy aspects of risk (Marquis & Huang, 2009).

Building on this literature, this study aims to shed light onto the underlying managerial behavior with respect to bank performance. Classical economic theory postulates that in a perfectly competitive market, firms maximize expected profits, and profit maximization is equivalent to cost minimization. In an environment of perfect competition, persistent departures from profit, maximizing behavior, and persistent inefficient operation (on the cost and/or on the revenue side) inevitably would threaten the survival of firms. When the conditions of perfect competition are relaxed, however, inefficient operation can persist and managerial incentives can diverge from profit maximization (Williamson, 1963). Kaysen (1960) has argued that in large industries with barriers to entry, managers have the option of pursuing any of a number of non-profit objectives, as long as they earn an acceptable return. In addition, he found that managers' discretion associated with size has a negative impact on firms' economic efficiency. Tirole (1988), moreover, argues that because of shareholders' incomplete information, managers might be allowed to inflate the need for personnel, or similarly, firm's growth might be pursued by the managers not for profit-maximization reasons but because it might allow them to enjoy greater opportunities for promotion. Thus, maximization of profits and/or minimization of costs are not necessarily observed in practice because of both exogenous factors (i.e., regulation, competition, economic shocks) and endogenous factors (i.e., manager's incentive structure) that can lead to suboptimal performance. Furthermore, Leibenstein's (1966) study on the X-inefficiency concept, in which he showed how different principal-agent goals, inadequate incentives, and imperfect contracts could create sources of inefficiency, further supports the cornerstone behind our analysis, that is, to reveal managerial preferences between cost and revenue efficiency.

The incentives underpinning managerial preferences with respect to performance raise interesting research questions, particularly regarding the banking industry. This industry plays a central role in providing sufficient credit to the economy, in the transmission of monetary policy, and in enhancing the overall stability of financial markets (Miller & Parkhe, 2001). Dewatripont and Tirole (1994), moreover, note that principal-agent problems are of particular importance in banking, in which debt is highly dispersed among bank depositors, which are too small to ensure sufficient pressure on bank management to avoid excessive risk-taking and stimulate high efficiency. In light of the current difficult economic environment with slow credit growth, high funding costs, and increasing nonperforming loans, as a result of the financial and the sovereign debt crisis, the examination of managers' preferences with respect to performance has become even more appealing and is of particular interest for both supervisors and policymakers.

This chapter focuses on bank managers' preferences with respect to performance and, in particular, evaluates whether managers assign equal weight to cost and revenue optimization strategies or whether they exhibit some degree of asymmetry in their strategies. It follows previous literature on modeling risk in banking in relation to bank managers' preferences (see Delgado-García et al., 2010, 2013). We measure performance using both accounting measures, such as the relative revenue and cost ratios, and more comprehensive measures of performance, such as revenue and cost efficiency scores in line with Miller and Parkhe (2001) and Chen et al. (2015).[1] According to the ECB (2010), cost and revenue efficiencies provide an assessment of banks' performance and are important drivers of banks' profitability, making cost and revenue efficiencies components of profit efficiency.[2] If bank managers' incentive is profit maximization and they have no personal preferences, we would expect them to be equally interested in improving cost and revenue efficiency. This might not be proven in practice, however, though as Gordon (1961) argue "almost certainly, the personal and group goals of executives are a part of the total value system— the desires for security, power, prestige, advancement within the organization, and so on. Profits are viewed as the basic constraint subject to which other goals can be followed." Williamson (1963) suggested that, according to the expense

---

1. The analysis of bank efficiency has attracted a lot of research attention (see Berger & Mester, 1997), not only because efficiency scores provide an accurate evaluation of the performance of individual banks and of the industry as a whole, but also because of the information that they entail regarding the cost of financial intermediation. Over the years, a large number of topics have been investigated, including the comparison of efficiency scores across countries, the effects of bank regulation on efficiency (e.g., Kumbhakar, Lozano-Vivas, Lovell, & Iftekhar, 2001), the relationship between efficiency and ownership characteristics, the effects of market power on efficiency (e.g., Berger & Mester, 1997; George, Wiklund, & Zahra, 2005), the relationship of efficiency with risk and many other research questions.

2. Empirical studies about cost and profit efficiency in banking provide evidence that profit inefficiency could be more important quantitatively than cost inefficiency (Berger & Mester, 1997), which could imply some persistency in inefficiencies on the revenue side.

preference theory, certain classes of expenditure, such as staff expense, expenditures for emoluments, and funds available for discretionary investment, might have an additional positive benefit for managers. This could indicate that bank managers are willing to sacrifice part of cost efficiency in return for these additional benefits. Alternatively, market conditions might force bank managers to focus their efforts on cost reduction instead of revenue maximization, especially in an environment of increasing competition (Helmalin, 1992).

Given the existence of some degree of managerial discretion and the plethora of theories regarding managerial behavior, we aim to address the following questions: Are bank managers equally interested in pursuing cost and revenue performance enhancing strategies or is there some degree of asymmetry in their preferences? Does this (a) symmetry differ across countries, over time, or across various types of financial institutions? And finally, what factors have an impact upon managers' behavior?

In attempting to respond to these questions, we draw from the literature about corporate governance and competition to form three alternative hypotheses that could influence managerial behavior: the "symmetric preference" hypothesis, the "revenue emphasis" hypothesis, and the "cost emphasis" hypothesis. We use two alternative definitions of performance: classical accounting ratios and efficiency scores estimated using the Stochastic Frontier Approach; and we employ the framework of a generalized behavioral function similar to Elliott, Komunjer, and Timmermann (2005) in order to reveal managerial preferences. We consider that bank managers operate based on a generalized management behavior function with unknown shape parameter, which provides information regarding their underlying preferences with respect to cost and revenue performance. We employ GMM estimation as in Elliott et al. (2005) to empirically estimate the parameter "alpha," which provides information regarding the shape of this behavior function that is tested using a X^2-test. In our framework, asymmetries would reveal managerial preferences over cost or revenue performance. The empirical concerns the EU-15 banking market over the period 2008–15, while we also examine managerial preferences across banks with different organizational type.

The rest of the chapter follows: Section 2 presents the main hypotheses we test in our study and the related literature. Section 3 analyzes the methodological specification of the models employed; Section 4 describes the data. Section 5 provides the empirical estimations and discusses the main results. Section 6 offers some concluding remarks and policy implications.

2 Hypotheses to be Tested and Related Literature

In order to explain the primary motives that influence managerial behavior we draw from the literature on corporate governance and competition and form three hypotheses.

Hypothesis 1 (the "symmetric preference" hypothesis): Bank managers exhibit symmetric preferences and assign equal weight to both cost-minimization and revenue-maximization.

According to the neoclassical theory of profit maximization, a firm's goal is to maximize expected profits, whether by maximizing revenue or by minimizing costs. Under this hypothesis, we expect managers to have symmetric preferences with respect to accounting performance ratios. Because cost and revenue efficiencies are important drivers of banks' profitability, managers that seek to maximize profits also have an incentive to maximize both cost and revenue efficiency. Under this hypothesis, one would expect managers to exhibit symmetric preferences with respect to cost and revenue efficiency.

Hypothesis 2 (the "revenue emphasis" hypothesis): Bank managers exhibit higher preference for being efficient on the revenue side than being efficient on the cost side. In other words, managers have more slack for being cost inefficient than being revenue inefficient.

Williamson (1963) argued against the neoclassical theory that firm management primarily is driven by the goal of profit maximization, especially in an environment characterized by a separation of ownership and control of firms, a less competitive environment, and a highly regulated industry. Instead, he suggested that managers might pursue a strategy of maximizing their personal utility by supporting excessive allocation of resources in salaries, larger staff, and extra bonuses and privileges. According to the expense preference behavior hypothesis, which has been tested empirically in banking with inconclusive results,[3] management might not have a neutral attitude toward costs. Firm managers might aim to maximize their utility, and their underlying individual preferences might not be consistent with profit maximization. Under the expense preference theory, firm managers might opt to overspend, for example, in hiring staff, on office furnishings and equipment, or on other perquisites and might perceive certain expense items as a source of security, power, status, prestige, and professional achievement. According to Williamson (1963), "...the utility-maximizing theory is based on the proposition that opportunities for discretion and managerial tastes will have a decided impact on the expenditures of the firm." This would imply that bank managers might be willing to sacrifice cost-efficient operation and incur a higher relative cost ratio in favor of

---

3. For example, Edwards (1977), Hannan (1979), Hannan and Mavinga (1980) found evidence of expense preference behavior in the US depository industries, while it also reported a decrease in expense preference behavior after deregulation in the banking industry. On the other hand, Rhoades (1980), Smirlock and Marshall (1983), Blair and Placone (1988), and Mester (1989) provided evidence inconsistent with expense-preference behavior among the US banks and saving and loans.

additional expenses that will maximize their utility function. In this, case bank managers will have a lower preference for being efficient on the cost side compared to the revenue side.

In addition, Baumol (1982) argues "that the typical large corporation in the United States seeks to maximize not its profits but its total revenues...subject to a minimum profit constraint." According to the revenue-maximizing hypothesis, which could apply to large oligopolistic firms or firms with a separation of ownership and control, management is motivated by managers' efforts to maximize their own income and prestige, which has been shown to depend at times on firms' sales rather than profit. The separation of ownership and control might result in business decisions that will be geared more toward revenue maximization, subject to a minimum profit constraint, which will satisfy owners (George et al., 2005; Knott & Posen, 2005). According to this theory, one would expect bank managers to prefer to maximize their revenues (and their revenue efficiency respectively) and dedicate less effort to achieve operation at minimum cost.

A third strand of the literature that supports Hypothesis 2 is related to the "quiet life hypothesis" developed by Hicks (1935). As Hicks (1935) noted: "The best of all monopoly profits is the quiet life." In particular, he suggested that the reduction in competitive pressure in concentrated markets might result in lessened effort by managers to maximize operating efficiency. In addition to the traditionally recognized higher prices and reduced output from market power, there also might be a higher cost per unit of output in concentrated markets because of slack management and thus higher cost inefficiency.

Hypothesis 3 (the "cost emphasis" hypothesis): Bank managers exhibit higher preferences for being efficient on the cost side than on the revenue side. In other words, managers have more slack for being revenue inefficient over being cost inefficient.

According to Williamson (1963) managerial discretion depends on, among other things, the condition of the environment. As conditions improve, bank managers might have more room for discretionary spending, whereas a deterioration of the environment can lead to a reversal of this trend. As a result, one could expect that in a distressed economic environment with limited good investment opportunities, bank managers would focus more on reducing their costs and enhancing their cost efficiency in order to enhance performance. Helmalin (1992), who investigated the relationship between competition and executive behavior, argued that, among other things, competition would alter the relative value of different managerial actions. Helmalin (1992) argues that, in particular, "tightening the price cap lowers the executive's income and it enhances the value of trying to lower costs (choosing a harder action), and both effects lead the executive to lower costs." A similar argument for why tightening the price cap can lead a firm to increase its efforts to reduce costs, is offered by Cabral and Riordan (1989), who state that: "As the cap tightens, demand increases, so the value of a reduction in unit cost also increases."

This could be supported further by the concept of "discretionary profit" proposed by Williamson (1963). He argues that managers desire to earn profits that exceed a minimum acceptable level, which is determined based on the performance of competitors, historical performance of the firm, and special circumstances. He defines discretionary profit as the amount by which earnings exceed this minimum performance constraint. This could indicate that if owners are satisfied by an amount of profit that is below maximum profit, managers have fewer incentives to maximize revenues.

3   Methodology

3.1   A managerial Preference Function

We assume that bank managers have a specific preference function with respect to performance that takes a flexible functional form with an unknown shape. The shape of the preference function can be revealed by a parameter, which defines whether it is symmetric with respect to cost versus revenue performance. If managerial preferences are symmetric, then the manager is indifferent between revenue and cost efficiency. If managerial preferences are asymmetric, however, a positive or negative difference between revenue and cost efficiency could matter to bank managers' preferences. In order to provide a functional form that could consider managerial preferences with respect to performance, we opt for a function similar to the one of Elliott et al. (2005).[4] As the main input in the managerial behavioral function, we use two alternative definitions: the difference between the relative revenue and cost ratios, and the difference between revenue and cost efficiency. The shape of the managerial behavior function is measured by a single parameter, which captures whether the preference function is symmetric and effectively reveals managerial preferences.

Following Elliott et al. (2005), we opt for a generalized bank managerial behavioral function based on the underlying managers' incentives to maximize profits. To this end, we assume that the behavior of bank managers (MB) follows the function:

$$MB(p, \alpha) = [\alpha + (1 - 2\alpha)1(R - C < 0)]|R - C|^p \tag{1}$$

where $p = 1, 2$, $\alpha \in (0,1)$ captures asymmetry if exists, 1 is an indicator, and $R - C$ is the difference between revenue and cost efficiency or, alternatively,

---

4. The norm has been that rational forecasts are based on an underlying symmetric and quadratic loss function. This symmetry in the loss function has been crucial in rational expectations theory. Elliott et al. (2005) show that if the underlying loss function were asymmetric, we would observe deviation from rational behavior. Rationality could be restored, however, in the case that all interest parties share exactly the same loss function or information about the observed asymmetry is revealed.

the difference between the relative revenue and cost accounting ratios, that is, revenue (cost) to assets or revenue (cost) to equity.

Eq. (1) indicates that in the case where the shape parameter alpha equals 0.5 ($\alpha = 0.5$), bank managers' preferences are symmetric and, therefore, give equal weight for both $R - C > 0$ and $R - C < 0$. This would suggest that managers are equally interested in being cost and revenue efficient (or in minimizing costs and maximizing revenues in order to increase profits), which is in line with the neoclassical symmetric preferences hypothesis. In the case in which $\alpha < 0.5$, managers' behavior function is asymmetric toward attaching higher preference for $R - C < 0$ compared to $R - C > 0$. That is, bank managers place more emphasis on the cost side, preferring to be more cost efficient than revenue efficient. In case of accounting ratios, bank managers would give preference to having a lower relative cost ratio instead of a higher relative revenue ratio. The opposite holds for $\alpha > 0.5$, in which case bank managers have asymmetric preferences toward higher revenue efficiency (for $R - C > 0$) and focus their management efforts on the revenue side, in line with the "revenue emphasis" hypothesis.

For robustness, in the empirical analysis, we consider two general forms for the behavioral function, the lin-lin case for $p = 1$, and the quad-quad case for $p = 2$. Fig. 1 presents the nonlinear managerial behavior function for three different shape parameters (only the quadratic case is depicted). α takes the value

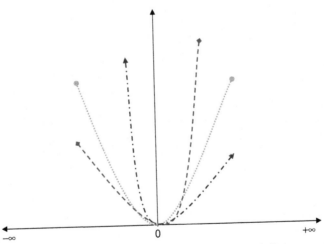

FIG. 1 Different shapes of the managerial behavior functions. *Note*: This figure presents the quadratic managerial behavior function (for $p = 2$ in Eq. (1)) for three different shape parameters of estimated α. The horizontal axis shows the difference between revenue and cost efficiency (or alternatively, the difference between the relative revenue and the relative cost ratios); the vertical axis is the quadratic managerial behavior function (Eq. 1). α takes the value of 0.5 for a symmetric function (symmetric preference hypothesis—the green line) and the values 0.2 and 0.8 for an asymmetric behavior function (the blue and red line, respectively).

of 0.5 for a symmetric function and the values 0.2 and 0.8 for an asymmetric behavior function.

To recover managerial behavior from Eq. (1), we need to estimate the value of the single parameter α. To do so, we follow Hansen and Singleton (1982), who were the first to suggest the idea of recovering a parameter from the data that is most consistent with optimizing behavior and assessing the extent to which optimality restrictions are satisfied. By observing the sequence of revenue efficiency (or the relative revenue ratio) $\{R\}$ for $\tau \leq t < T + \tau$, the estimate of α is given using a linear GMM instrumental variable estimator $\hat{a}_T$, as follows:

$$\hat{a}_T = \frac{\left[\dfrac{1}{T}\displaystyle\sum_{t=\tau}^{T+\tau-1} v_t |R-C|^{p-1}\right]\hat{S}^{-1}\left[\dfrac{1}{T}\displaystyle\sum_{t=\tau}^{T+\tau-1} v_t\mathbf{1}(R-C<0)|R-C|^{p-1}\right]}{\left[\dfrac{1}{T}\displaystyle\sum_{t=\tau}^{T+\tau-1} V_t|R-C|^{p-1}\right]\hat{S}^{-1}\left[\dfrac{1}{T}\displaystyle\sum_{t=\tau}^{T+\tau-1} |R-C|^{p-1}\right]} \tag{2}$$

where v_t is a $d \times \mathbf{1}$ vector of instruments, which is a subset of the information set regarding bank performance as measured by revenue/cost efficiency (or the relative revenue/relative cost ratios), while $\hat{S}$ is given by:

$$\hat{S} = \frac{1}{T}\sum_{t=\tau}^{T+\tau-1} v_t v_t' (\mathbf{1}(R-C<0) - \hat{a}_\tau)^2 |R-C|^{2p-2} \tag{3}$$

Since $\hat{S}$ depends on $\hat{a}_T$, estimation is performed iteratively, assuming $S = I$ in the first iteration to estimate $\hat{a}_{T,1}$, until convergence.

Elliott et al. (2005) show that the estimator of $\hat{a}_T$ is asymptotically normal, and they construct a J-statistic, which is distributed as a $X^2(d-1)$ variable for $d > 1$ and takes the form:

$$J = \frac{1}{T}\left[\left(\sum_{t=\tau}^{T+\tau-1} vt[\mathbf{1}(R-C<0)]|R-C|^{p-1'}\right)S^{\wedge}-1 \right. \\ \left. \times \left(\sum_{t=\tau}^{T+\tau-1} vt[\mathbf{1}(R-C<0) - \hat{a}T)]|R-C|^{p-1}\right)\right] \sim X_{d-1}^2 \tag{4}$$

In the empirical analysis, we use three instruments: a constant, the lagged difference in efficiency scores (or in relative revenue and cost ratios), and the lagged cost efficiency (or the lagged relative cost ratio, respectively). We performed robustness checks by using subsets of our three instruments, which yielded close estimates for the parameters but with inferior standard errors, while impairing the speed of algorithm convergence. Elliott et al. (2005) argue: "Outside this situation, one could attempt to use data-based methods for selection of moment conditions using criteria such as those proposed by Donald and Newey (2001), replacing their MSE loss with our loss L in Eq. (1) evaluated at $(p, \hat{a})$ where $\hat{a}$ is a consistent estimate of a."

3.2 Cost and Revenue Efficiency

For the estimation of bank efficiency, we employ the Stochastic Frontier Approach (SFA) developed by Aigner, Lovell, and Schmidt (1977) and Meeusen and van den Broeck (1977). We focus on both cost and revenue efficiencies as they reflect two different managerial skills, that is, bank managers' ability to minimize costs and to maximize revenues, respectively.

Cost efficiency is derived from a cost frontier, which captures the minimum level of cost at which it is possible to produce a given vector of output at given input prices. In particular, we assume the following specification for the cost frontier:

$$C_{it} = f(P_{it}, Y_{it}, N_{it}) + v_{it} + u_{it} \qquad (5)$$

where C_{it} is the total cost for bank i at year t, P is a vector of input prices, Y is a vector of outputs, and N is a vector of fixed netputs.[5] The Stochastic Frontier Approach assumes a composite error term, ε_{it}, which is disentangled in two components: v_{it}, which corresponds to the random fluctuations and is assumed to follow a symmetric normal distribution around the frontier, and u_{it}, which accounts for the firm's inefficiency that might raise costs above the best-practice level and is assumed to follow a half-normal distribution. Cost efficiency is then given by the ratio of minimum cost to observed cost:

$$CostEFF_i = \frac{\hat{C}^{min}}{\hat{C}_i} \qquad (6)$$

For the measurement of revenue efficiency, we follow Berger and Mester (1997) and estimate an alternative revenue function. Berger and Mester (1997) argue that alternative revenue efficiency might be more suitable than standard revenue efficiency if any of the following conditions hold: there are significant unmeasured differences in the quality of banking services; outputs are not completely variable, so that a bank cannot achieve every output scale and product mix; banks have some market power in the output market; and output prices are not accurately measured.

In detail, alternative revenue efficiency measures by how close a bank comes to earning maximum revenues given its output levels (rather than its output prices as in the case of standard revenue efficiency). Thus, the revenue function employs the same exogenous variables as the cost function and can be expressed as:

$$R_{it} = f(P_{it}, Y_{it}, N_{it}) + v_{it} - u_{it} \qquad (7)$$

where R_{it} is total revenue for bank i at year t. In the case of the revenue function, the composite error term becomes $\varepsilon_{it} = v_{it} - u_{it}$, where u_{it} is assumed to follow a half-normal distribution. Revenue efficiency then is given by the ratio of

---

5. Fixed netputs are quasi-fixed quantities of either inputs or outputs that affect variable costs.

predicted actual revenues to the predicted maximum revenues earned by the best-practice bank:

$$RevEFF_i = \frac{R_i}{\hat{R}^{max}} \qquad (8)$$

For the empirical estimation of the cost (and alternative revenue) function, we opt for the translog[6] specification[7]:

$$
\begin{aligned}
\ln C_i(R_i) = {} & \alpha_0 + \sum_i \alpha_i \ln P_i + \sum_i \beta_i \ln Y_i + \frac{1}{2}\sum_i\sum_j \alpha_{ij} \ln P_i \ln P_j + \frac{1}{2}\sum_i\sum_j \beta_{ij} \ln Y_i \ln Y_j \\
& + \sum_i\sum_j \delta_{ij} \ln P_i \ln Y_j + \sum_i \zeta_i \ln N_i + \frac{1}{2}\sum_i\sum_j \zeta_{ij} \ln N_i \ln N_j + \frac{1}{2}\sum_i\sum_j \theta_{ij} \ln P_i \ln N_j \\
& + \sum_i\sum_j \kappa_{ij} \ln Y_i \ln N_j + \mu_1 t + \frac{1}{2}\mu_2 t^2 + \sum_i \nu_i t \ln P_i + \sum_i \xi_i t \ln Y_i + \sum_i \rho_i t \ln N_i \\
& + \sum_i \varphi_i D_i + u_i \pm v_i
\end{aligned}
\qquad (9)
$$

where C is total cost, R is total revenues, P is a vector of input prices, Y is the outputs vector, N is a vector of fixed netputs, t is a time trend, and D_i is a vector of country dummies, used to capture country-level heterogeneity both in terms of the general macroeconomic environment and in terms of the banking industry of each country. Standard linear homogeneity and symmetry restrictions are imposed in all quadratic terms in line with economic theory. Eq. (9) is estimated via a maximum likelihood procedure parameterized in terms of the variance parameters $\sigma_\varepsilon^2 = \sigma_u^2 + \sigma_v^2$ and $\gamma = \sigma_u^2/\sigma_\varepsilon^2$. Bank-specific inefficiency estimates are calculated using the distribution of the inefficiency term conditional to the estimate of the composite error term following Jondrow, Lovell, Materov, and Schmidt (1982).

4 Data Description

Our dataset includes commercial, cooperative, and savings banks in EU-15 countries (namely, Austria, Belgium, Denmark, Finland, France, Germany, Greece, Ireland, Italy, Luxembourg, Netherlands, Portugal, Spain, Sweden, and the United Kingdom) that are listed in the IBCA—Bankscope database over the period 2008–15.[8] We restrict our analysis to credit institutions that report positive equity capital. After reviewing the data for reporting errors and other

---

6. The translog function has been widely applied in the literature because of its flexibility. Berger and Mester (1997) found that both the translog and the Fourier flexible form specifications yielded essentially the same average level and dispersion of measured efficiency, and both ranked the individual banks in almost the same order.

7. For simplification, we omit the subscripts for time (t).

8. The Bankscope database reports published financial statements from banks worldwide, homogenized into a global format, which are comparable across countries and therefore suitable for a cross-country study. Nevertheless, we should note that all countries suffer from the same survival bias.

inconsistencies,[9] we obtain an unbalanced panel dataset of 18,813 observations, including 2861 different banks.[10]

In the first part of our analysis, we examine bank performance using accounting ratios of performance. Accounting-based studies of bank performance use comprehensive information from financial statements to measure performance, as measured by return on assets (ROA) or return on equity (ROE). To this end, we decompose these two commonly used accounting ratios of performance into a revenue ratio and a cost ratio component in order to explore managerial preferences. In particular, we calculate the relative revenue ratio for bank i as the ratio of total revenue of bank i to total assets of bank i divided by the average revenue ratio in the sample. Similarly, the relative cost ratio of bank i is defined as the ratio of total cost of bank i to total assets of bank i divided by the average cost ratio in the sample. We alternatively also define relative revenue and cost ratios in terms of equity instead of total assets. Total cost is the sum of overheads (personnel and administrative expenses), interest, fees, and commission expenses, while total revenue is defined as the sum of interest revenue, fees, and commission and net trading income.

For the estimation of cost and revenue efficiency, we employ the intermediation approach for the definition of bank inputs and outputs, proposed by Sealey and Lindley (1977), which assumes that the bank collects funds, using labor and physical capital, to transform them into loans and other earning assets.[11] In particular, we specify three inputs—labor, physical capital, and financial capital—and two outputs—loans and other earning assets (government securities, bonds, equity investments, CDs, T-bills, equity investment etc.).[12] For the estimation of cost and alternative revenue efficiency, input prices are required. The price of financial capital totals interest expenses divided by total interest-bearing borrowed funds, while the price of labor is defined as the ratio of personnel expenses to total assets. The price of physical capital is the ratio of other administrative expenses to fixed assets. We include

---

9. We eliminate all observations in which inputs and outputs are outside the ± 3 standard deviation interval.
10. The number of banks by year included in our sample is: 2008: 1542; 2009: 2430; 2010: 2504; 2011: 2521; 2012: 2530; 2013: 2655; 2014: 2597, and 2015: 2034. Exits from the sample primarily happened because of either bank failures or mergers with other banks (except for 2011). It should be noted that for the first and the last year of our sample, 2004 and 2011 respectively, the coverage of the Bankscope database is much more limited because of the inherent features of this database. Our sample covers the largest credit institutions in each country, as defined by their balance sheet aggregates. Note that German banking accounts for large number of relatively small banks.
11. For a review of the various approaches that have been proposed in the literature for the definition of bank inputs and outputs, see Berger and Mester (1997).
12. Although off-balance sheet activities are part of banks' business, we cannot include them in our analysis because our sample also includes small banks that do not have OBS items or data are not available in the Bankscope database. By including off-balance sheet items in the output vector, the sample size would have been substantially reduced and would no longer be representative of the banking sector in each country.

equity as a fixed netput following Färe, Grosskopf, and Weber (2004), who argue that using bank equity as a quasi-fixed input in the analysis of bank profit efficiency is sufficient to account for both the risk-based capital requirements and the risk-return tradeoff that bank owners face.[13]

Table 1 provides descriptive statistics of the variables used in this study for the overall sample and by country over the period 2004–11. We observe considerable variations across countries in relation to costs, revenues, bank outputs and inputs. In particular, Spain and Sweden have the lowest average cost to assets ratio (at 3.5%), while Denmark stands at the other end of the spectrum (at 5%). In addition, Denmark has the highest revenue to assets ratio (at 6.6%), while Finland and Ireland have the lowest. In the vast majority of EU-15 countries, loans comprise the largest part of banks' balance sheet, except from Luxembourg, Belgium, and the UK. With respect to input prices, no significant variation is observed in the price of labor across countries, which ranges from 0.6% in Ireland to 1.8% in Denmark. There is, however, some variation with respect to the price of physical capital, which ranges from 48.7% in Spain to 286.8% in Luxembourg, while the price of deposits ranges from 1.6% in Sweden to 4.3% in the Netherlands. In addition, banks' average equity to assets ratio ranges from 6.5% in Germany and Ireland to 14.2% in Sweden.

Table 1 also presents the average cost and revenue efficiency scores for the overall sample and by country over the period 2008–15, as estimated using the Stochastic Frontier Approach (see Section 3.1). The average cost efficiency for EU-15 countries is at 0.86, ranging from 0.71 in the Netherlands to 0.89 in Germany, which has the most cost-efficient banking system. The average revenue efficiency is at 0.79 for the whole sample, with Sweden and Ireland being the most efficient (at 0.82) and the UK being at the other end of the spectrum, with average inefficiency at 0.69. Overall, inefficiencies appear to be larger on the revenue side compared to the cost side both for EU-15 as a whole and for the majority of countries in our sample. Only in Greece, Ireland, and the Netherlands, banks appear to be on average more efficient in minimizing their costs than maximizing their revenues. Looking at the average cost and revenue efficiency scores by type of bank (not shown in the table), we observe that cooperative banks exhibit on average higher cost efficiency (at 0.87), followed by savings banks (at 0.85), and commercial banks (at 0.79). Savings and cooperative banks, however, exhibit similar average levels of revenue efficiency (about 0.80), while commercial banks present an average revenue efficiency score of 0.75. Our results are in line with the vast majority of the literature that has found average cost inefficiency scores for EU countries in the range of 0.15–0.20 (see for example Cavallo & Rossi, 2001; Chen et al., 2015; Miller & Parkhe, 2001).[14]

---

13. In addition, Berger and Mester (1997) argue that a bank's capital further affects costs by providing an alternative to deposits as a funding source for loans.

14. To the best of our knowledge, no study has examined alternative revenue efficiency in European banking.

TABLE 1 Descriptive Statistics

	C-EFF	R-EFF	C/A	R/A	y_1/A	y_2/A	n_1/A	w_1	w_2	w_3	Obs
Austria	0.80	0.78	4.0	5.0	56.9	39.0	7.6	1.2	2.4	88.0	1278
	(0.09)	(0.11)	(0.9)	(1.2)	(15.3)	(15.1)	(3.0)	(0.4)	(1.2)	(114.4)	
Belgium	0.79	0.79	4.5	5.2	47.5	48.1	7.0	1.0	3.5	196.2	87
	(0.11)	(0.14)	(1.5)	(1.8)	(19.7)	(19.1)	(5.7)	(0.7)	(2.0)	(222.3)	
Denmark	0.86	0.74	5.0	6.6	61.8	31.3	13.1	1.8	2.3	154.4	464
	(0.08)	(0.14)	(1.0)	(1.2)	(11.1)	(11.8)	(4.8)	(0.6)	(1.1)	(162.7)	
Finland	0.87	0.70	3.8	4.6	63.6	30.7	7.7	0.8	3.5	243.0	39
	(0.09)	(0.19)	(1.5)	(1.6)	(21.4)	(18.6)	(2.4)	(0.6)	(2.3)	(208.9)	
France	0.80	0.78	4.5	5.6	64.2	30.7	8.9	1.2	3.0	164.4	931
	(0.10)	(0.13)	(1.1)	(1.3)	(18.6)	(18.4)	(4.5)	(0.6)	(1.4)	(138.1)	
Germany	0.89	0.81	4.5	5.5	57.9	37.5	6.5	1.4	2.5	86.4	10,693
	(0.07)	(0.08)	(0.7)	(0.7)	(12.8)	(12.8)	(2.0)	(0.4)	(0.6)	(85.0)	
Greece	0.74	0.76	4.9	6.2	68.9	23.1	7.9	1.3	3.2	109.9	96
	(0.11)	(0.17)	(1.2)	(1.3)	(10.6)	(10.5)	(4.5)	(0.5)	(1.4)	(90.0)	
Ireland	0.77	0.82	3.7	4.6	67.3	29.5	6.5	0.6	3.7	208.9	37
	(0.10)	(0.10)	(1.1)	(1.4)	(8.9)	(8.5)	(5.5)	(0.3)	(1.5)	(183.1)	
Italy	0.81	0.76	4.1	5.3	68.4	26.7	11.3	1.4	3.0	105.2	3390
	(0.11)	(0.12)	(0.8)	(1.1)	(13.3)	(13.0)	(4.0)	(0.3)	(1.6)	(115.3)	

	C-EFF	R-EFF	C/A	R/A	y₁/A	y₂/A	n₁/A	w₁	w₂	w₃	Obs
Luxembourg	0.80	0.78	4.1	5.3	33.8	61.7	6.7	0.9	3.0	286.8	167
	(0.11)	(0.11)	(1.7)	(2.3)	(18.4)	(18.2)	(5.3)	(0.7)	(1.7)	(255.6)	
Netherlands	0.71	0.74	4.7	5.7	57.6	34.2	7.5	0.9	4.3	157.8	87
	(0.14)	(0.19)	(1.7)	(2.1)	(21.0)	(18.5)	(3.7)	(0.5)	(2.1)	(163.3)	
Portugal	0.77	0.74	4.6	5.4	60.0	33.1	8.8	1.1	3.7	193.5	105
	(0.11)	(0.19)	(1.3)	(1.4)	(20.3)	(20.7)	(6.8)	(0.6)	(1.9)	(207.7)	
Spain	0.87	0.79	3.5	4.6	71.7	23.1	8.9	0.9	2.5	48.7	709
	(0.08)	(0.12)	(0.9)	(1.0)	(12.2)	(12.0)	(3.8)	(0.4)	(1.2)	(63.7)	
Sweden	0.87	0.82	3.5	5.1	74.9	22.4	14.2	1.2	1.6	200.2	439
	(0.06)	(0.11)	(0.8)	(0.9)	(11.1)	(10.9)	(4.9)	(0.3)	(1.0)	(156.5)	
UK	0.77	0.69	4.0	5.2	47.2	47.0	9.4	0.9	3.1	247.4	291
	(0.15)	(0.18)	(1.6)	(2.1)	(18.5)	(19.7)	(6.5)	(0.5)	(1.8)	(209.8)	
EU-15	0.86	0.79	4.3	5.4	60.7	34.6	8.0	1.3	2.6	103.1	18,831
	(0.09)	(0.11)	(0.9)	(1.0)	(14.9)	(14.8)	(3.9)	(0.4)	(1.1)	(115.2)	

Note: The table presents descriptive statistics of the main variable used in our analysis for the full sample over the examined period. Figures are country means over the period 2008–15 (standard deviations are presented in parentheses). *C-EFF* = cost efficiency estimated using the Stochastic Frontier Approach; *R-EFF* = revenue efficiency estimated using the Stochastic Frontier Approach; *C/A* = total cost to total assets (in %); *R/A* = total revenue to total assets (in %); y_1/A = net loans to total assets (in %); y_2/A = other earning assets to total assets (in %); n_1/A = equity to total assets (in %); w_1 = price of labor (in %); w_2 = price of deposits (in %); w_3 = price of physical capital (in %); *Obs* = number of observations.

Sources: Bankscope database and own estimations.

To shed more light onto our analysis, we compare the main characteristics of the most efficient banks, which rank high in terms of both cost and revenue efficiency, with the least efficient ones.[15] Overall, the most efficient banks exhibit a higher net interest margin, return on average assets and return on average equity ratios, lower cost to income ratio, higher capitalization ratio, and lower loan loss provisions to loans ratio compared with the least efficient banks in our sample. All of these performance measures, therefore, suggest that the most efficient and the least efficient banks have significant differences in their ability to use resources and generate earnings.

5 Empirical Results

5.1 Managerial Preferences Across Countries and Over Time Using Accounting Ratios

We first estimate managerial preferences using accounting ratios as measures of bank performance. Accounting ratios are widely used by bank managers and financial analysts as performance benchmarks, mainly because of their simple calculation method. We estimate Eqs. (2), (3) with GMM for both the lin-lin ($p = 1$) and the quad-quad case ($p = 2$) for the entire sample over the period 2008–15 using the difference between the relative revenue and cost ratios.

Table 2 presents the results for the shape parameter, alpha (α), of the underlying managerial behavior function for the difference between the relative revenue to assets and cost to assets ratios (panel A) and for the difference between the relative revenue to equity and cost to equity ratios (panel B). Our estimated alphas are all statistically different from zero and take values about 0.5, indicating that bank management preferences are symmetric for both the relative revenue and cost to assets ratios and the relative revenue and cost to equity ratios. The symmetry in managerial preferences, however, is more evident in the case of the relative revenue and cost to assets ratio and particularly under the quadratic specification of the managerial preference function.

Looking at the evolution of managerial preferences over time (Table 3), the estimated alphas in the case of the relative revenue and cost to assets ratio exhibit a broadly symmetric picture over the examined period. After the financial crisis in 2009, we observe increasing asymmetry in managerial preferences, consistent with the revenue emphasis hypothesis. The evolution of estimated alphas in the case of the relative revenue and cost to equity ratio show increased variability over time. In particular, managerial preferences in 2009 are asymmetric and consistent with the cost emphasis hypothesis, whereas in 2011 we observe asymmetry in the opposite direction, consistent with the revenue

---

15. Banks that make up the most efficient bank category rank at the top 25% of the sample in terms of both cost and revenue efficiency; banks in the least efficient bank category rank at the bottom 25% in terms of both efficiency scores.

TABLE 2 Managerial Preferences for the Whole Sample Using Accounting Ratios

	(a) Lin-Lin Case			(b) Quad-Quad Case		
	$\hat{a}$	SE	$J_{\hat{a}}$	$\hat{a}$	SE	$J_{\hat{a}}$
A. Difference between relative revenue to assets and cost to assets ratios						
$D=1$	0.472	0.004	1.95E−26	0.500	0.005	9.01E−25
$D=2$	0.468	0.004	1.18E+03	0.507	0.005	646.611
$D=3$	0.458	0.004	3.27E+03	0.507	0.005	646.611
B. Difference between relative revenue to equity and cost to equity ratios						
$D=1$	0.537	0.004	1.56E−25	0.500	0.005	1.52E−27
$D=2$	0.545	0.004	1.60E+03	0.538	0.005	548.173
$D=3$	0.554	0.004	2.87E+03	0.540	0.005	817.290

Note: This table presents estimates of the shape parameter, α, of the managerial behavior function for the whole sample over the period 2008–15. The estimate of α is given using the linear GMM instrumental variable estimator of Eq. (2). D is number of GMM instruments (a constant, the lagged difference in relative revenue and cost ratios and the lagged relative cost ratio). We report results for two different forms of the behavioral function, the lin-lin case for $p=1$, and the quad-quad case for $p=2$. $J_{\alpha}=J$-test under ith null hypothesis distributed as a $X^2(d-1)$ variable for $d>1$.

TABLE 3 Managerial Preferences by Year Using Accounting Ratios

	A. Difference Between Relative Revenue to Assets and Cost to Assets Ratios			B. Difference Between Relative Revenue to Equity and Cost to Equity Ratios		
	$\hat{a}$	SE	$J_{\hat{a}}$	$\hat{a}$	SE	$J_{\hat{a}}$
2008	0.558	0.016	4.916	0.466	0.025	2.176
2009	0.561	0.013	0.281	0.453	0.020	0.173
2010	0.421	0.012	4.017	0.297	0.015	4.206
2011	0.569	0.012	1.367	0.490	0.017	1.946
2012	0.678	0.012	3.910	0.629	0.017	1.061
2013	0.615	0.009	3.697	0.578	0.014	1.235
2014	0.576	0.010	1.924	0.577	0.014	1.290
2015	0.555	0.011	8.759	0.549	0.016	4.194

Note: This table presents estimates of the shape parameter, α, of the managerial behavior function by year for the whole sample. The estimate of α is given using the linear GMM instrumental variable estimator of Eq. (2). We report only the estimates of α using three instruments (a constant, the lagged difference in relative revenue and cost ratios, and the lagged relative cost ratio) and results for the linear form of the behavioral function, the lin-lin case for $p=1$. Results for the quad-quad case (for $p=2$) are identical and presented in the Appendix. $J_{\alpha}=J$-test under ith null hypothesis distributed as a $X^2(d-1)$ variable for $d>1$.

emphasis hypothesis. Overall, the higher variability of managerial preferences over time in the case of the relative revenue and cost to equity ratio compared to the relative revenue and cost to assets ratio might be affected by the evolution of the denominator, that is, the declining bank equity during the financial crisis.

To shed more light onto our analysis, Table 4 presents managerial preferences by country. Estimated alphas for both the relative revenue to assets and cost to assets ratios (panel A) and for the relative revenue to equity and cost to equity ratios (panel B) reveal significant cross-country variability. For the majority of countries (Austria, Belgium, Germany, Spain, Finland, Ireland,

TABLE 4 Managerial Preferences by country using accounting ratios

	A. Difference Between Relative Revenue to Assets and Cost to Assets Ratios			B. Difference Between Relative Revenue to Equity and Cost to Equity Ratios		
	$\hat{a}$	SE	$J_{\hat{a}}$	$\hat{a}$	SE	$J_{\hat{a}}$
Austria	0.653	0.013	189.371	0.600	0.024	21.079
Belgium	0.805	0.043	8.589	0.776	0.059	5.803
Germany	0.653	0.005	1.17E+03	0.681	0.006	391.799
Denmark	0.256	0.020	58.578	0.123	0.016	27.265
Spain	0.582	0.022	93.504	0.601	0.031	53.630
Finland	0.633	0.078	0.215	0.774	0.083	0.753
France	0.500	0.016	377.868	0.441	0.021	198.205
Greece	0.368	0.050	30.497	0.195	0.047	18.144
Ireland	0.762	0.071	6.554	0.903	0.055	5.864
Italy	0.283	0.020	88.689	0.215	0.023	25.941
Luxembourg	0.745	0.046	11.838	0.631	0.075	10.590
Netherlands	0.748	0.047	18.841	0.681	0.061	9.226
Portugal	0.666	0.052	3.802	0.799	0.050	4.621
Sweden	0.189	0.029	24.478	0.070	0.015	14.424
UK	0.556	0.032	29.058	0.544	0.049	25.792

Note: This table presents estimates of the shape parameter, α, of the managerial behavior function by country over the period 2008–15. The estimate of α is given using the linear GMM instrumental variable estimator of Eq. (2). We report only the estimates of α using three instruments (a constant, the lagged difference in relative revenue and cost ratios, and the lagged relative cost ratio) and results for the linear form of the behavioral function, the lin-lin case for $p = 1$. Results for the quad-quad case (for $p = 2$) are identical and presented in the Appendix. $J_a = J$-test under ith null hypothesis distributed as a $X^2(d - 1)$ variable for $d > 1$.

Luxembourg, Netherlands, and Portugal) estimated alphas are higher than 0.5, suggesting asymmetry in managerial preferences. More specifically, our results appear to be consistent with Hypothesis 2, the revenue emphasis hypothesis, which suggests that managers might support excessive allocation of resources in salaries, larger staff, and extra bonuses in line with the expense preference behavior theory. Managerial preferences in Denmark, Italy, Sweden, and Greece, however, appear to be consistent with Hypothesis 3, the cost emphasis hypothesis, which argues that management puts more weight on the cost side because of the competitive conditions in the market or because of the concept of discretionary profit. Finally, results for France and the UK indicate the existence of symmetry in managerial preferences in these countries, in line with Hypothesis 1.

5.2 Managerial Preferences Across Countries and Over Time Using Efficiency Scores

Table 5 presents the results for the shape of managerial preferences using revenue and cost efficiency. Efficiency scores are more comprehensive measures for bank performance because they are based on the concept of economic efficiency and are estimated using an optimization process (revenue maximization and cost minimization). We first estimate Eqs. (2), (3) with GMM for both the lin-lin ($p = 1$) and the quad-quad case ($p = 2$) for the entire sample over the period 2008–15. In this case, we observe a different picture as estimated alphas take values significantly lower than 0.5, indicating asymmetric preferences, consistent with the cost emphasis hypothesis. In particular, alpha is at 0.3 and 0.28 in the linear and nonlinear cases, respectively.

TABLE 5 Managerial Preferences for the Whole Sample Using Efficiency Scores

	(a) Lin-Lin Case			(b) Quad-Quad Case		
	$\hat{a}$	SE	$J_{\hat{a}}$	$\hat{a}$	SE	$J_{\hat{a}}$
$D = 1$	0.309	0.003	3.32E−25	0.282	0.004	7.47E−26
$D = 2$	0.308	0.003	27.815	0.281	0.004	16.923
$D = 3$	0.303	0.003	270.626	0.271	0.004	140.676

Note: This table presents estimates of the shape parameter, α, of the managerial behavior function for the whole sample over the period 2008–15. The estimate of α is given using the linear GMM instrumental variable estimator of Eq. (2). D is number of GMM instruments (a constant, the lagged difference in revenue and cost efficiency, and the lagged cost efficiency). We report results for two different forms of the behavioral function, the lin-lin case for $p = 1$, and the quad-quad case for $p = 2$. $J_{\alpha} = J$-test under ith null hypothesis distributed as a $X^2(d − 1)$ variable for $d > 1$.

This finding suggests that bank managers attach greater importance to being efficient on the cost side than to being revenue efficient and confirms the general perception in the literature that there are significant revenue inefficiencies. Moreover, this result would imply that if bank managers face a tradeoff between cost and revenue efficiency, they prefer to have a higher level of cost than revenue efficiency. This could be because of the change-in-the-relative-value-of-actions effect that competition has on executive behavior suggested by Helmalin (1992). Another possible explanation for the fact that managers have more control on their costs than their revenues, which are affected to a larger extent by exogenous factors. Therefore, they put more emphasis on the cost side than the revenue side.

Looking at the evolution of estimated alphas over time, Table 6 shows some variation over the examined period. Under the linear specification, asymmetry in bank managers' preferences decreases until 2010, and increases thereafter. A similar picture emerges in the case of the quadratic specification, with alphas increasing until 2009, and decreasing thereafter. The evolution of alphas over time is consistent with Hypothesis 3, verifying our previous findings.

Next, we focus on cross-country analysis. Table 7 presents results for the shape parameter of the underlying managerial behavior function estimated at the country level. The reported alphas for the majority of countries take values lower than 0.5, suggesting the existence of asymmetric preferences, consistent

TABLE 6 Managerial Preferences by Year Using Efficiency Scores

	(a) Lin-Lin Case			(b) Quad-Quad Case		
	$\hat{a}$	SE	$J_{\hat{a}}$	$\hat{a}$	SE	$J_{\hat{a}}$
2008	0.286	0.012	1.42E−27	0.252	0.015	5.48E−29
2009	0.313	0.009	6.87E−27	0.291	0.012	1.19E−27
2010	0.316	0.009	3.04E−28	0.293	0.012	1.05E−27
2011	0.316	0.009	1.40E−29	0.291	0.012	4.47E−27
2012	0.314	0.009	4.98E−27	0.291	0.012	6.26E−27
2013	0.313	0.009	6.07E−29	0.283	0.011	6.84E−27
2014	0.310	0.009	1.54E−27	0.281	0.011	7.86E−28
2015	0.289	0.010	8.63E−28	0.259	0.012	5.53E−29

Note: This table presents estimates of the shape parameter, α, of the managerial behavior function by year for the whole sample. The estimate of α is given using the linear GMM instrumental variable estimator of Eq. (2). We report only the estimates of α using three instruments (a constant, the lagged difference in efficiency scores, and the lagged cost efficiency) and results for two different forms of the behavioral function, the lin-lin case for $p = 1$, and the quad-quad case for $p = 2$. $J_{\hat{a}} = J$-test under ith null hypothesis distributed as a $X^2(d − 1)$ variable for $d > 1$.

TABLE 7 Managerial Preferences by Country Using Efficiency Scores

	(a) Lin-Lin Case			(b) Quad-Quad Case		
	$\hat{a}$	SE	$J_{\hat{a}}$	$\hat{a}$	SE	$J_{\hat{a}}$
Austria	0.407	0.014	9.84E−29	0.398	0.019	3.05E−29
Belgium	0.535	0.054	3.60E−31	0.513	0.063	4.78E−30
Germany	0.236	0.004	3.54E−26	0.205	0.005	6.91E−26
Denmark	0.220	0.019	2.62E−28	0.177	0.021	9.69E−30
Spain	0.326	0.018	7.18E−29	0.238	0.018	1.46E−28
Finland	0.342	0.077	1.44E−31	0.178	0.059	8.35E−32
France	0.566	0.016	6.88E−28	0.412	0.024	2.75E−28
Greece	0.484	0.051	5.09E−30	0.533	0.057	5.04E−30
Ireland	0.500	0.083	0.000	0.680	0.101	4.42E−30
Italy	0.387	0.008	1.78E−27	0.367	0.010	3.83E−28
Luxembourg	0.482	0.039	4.14E−30	0.460	0.050	2.28E−29
Netherlands	0.616	0.052	1.55E−31	0.532	0.065	1.23E−29
Portugal	0.615	0.048	2.88E−31	0.423	0.062	2.36E−29
Sweden	0.354	0.023	1.26E−31	0.288	0.027	1.68E−29
UK	0.397	0.029	1.39E−31	0.331	0.035	1.67E−31

Note: This table presents estimates of the shape parameter, α, of the managerial behavior function by country over the period 2008–15. The estimate of α is given using the linear GMM instrumental variable estimator of Eq. (2). We report only the estimates of α using three instruments (a constant, the lagged difference in efficiency scores, and the lagged cost efficiency) and results for two different forms of the behavioral function, the lin-lin case for $p = 1$, and the quad-quad case for $p = 2$. $J_a = J$-test under *i*th null hypothesis distributed as a $\chi^2(d − 1)$ variable for $d > 1$.

with Hypothesis 3. Some variability in alphas across countries also is reported. For example, in Belgium we observe symmetric preferences between revenue and cost efficiency compatible with Hypothesis 1, whereas in the linear case Netherlands and Portugal exhibit asymmetry toward the direction of putting emphasis on revenue efficiency compared to cost efficiency in line with Hypothesis 2 (the revenue emphasis hypothesis). Results for France, Greece, Ireland, and Portugal are ambiguous, because the shape of the estimated alphas for these countries changes between the linear and the quadratic specifications. We observe that for most countries with alphas taking values higher than 0.5 or close to 0.5 there is variability in the quadratic specification compared to the linear specification.

Table 8 presents estimated alphas by country and by year, for those countries in our sample with an adequate number of bank-year observations, using efficiency scores.[16] This analysis provides further evidence in favor of the existence of asymmetry in bank managers' preferences, consistent with Hypothesis 3. Nevertheless, we observe diverging trends with respect to the evolution of alphas over time: Austria, France, Germany, and Italy exhibit relatively stable alphas over time; Denmark, Greece, and Spain alphas follow an upward trend toward symmetry; in Portugal, managerial preferences become more asymmetric over time. For Luxembourg, Sweden, and the UK, alphas steadily decline over the examined period, deviating from symmetry.

Overall, we appear to get conflicting results when comparing results from the relative accounting ratio analysis and the efficiency analysis. This can be explained, however, by the fact that several studies find that efficiency and accounting measures of performance are not always highly correlated (Miller & Parkhe, 2001). This is because frontier efficiency is superior to the standard accounting ratios, because it is estimated using statistical techniques that remove the effects of differences in input prices and other exogenous market factors affecting the standard performance ratios in order to obtain better estimates of the underlying performance of the managers (Miller & Parkhe, 2001). Because management usually does not change often (and even when it does change), it is difficult to implement new policies and procedures quickly, making it more likely that managerial preferences would not fluctuate markedly over short periods of time. This is consistent with our results from the efficiency analysis, but it is not confirmed by the accounting ratio analysis. As a result, we consider that managerial preferences in terms of revenue and cost efficiency are superior to the accounting ratio analysis.

5.3 Managerial Preferences by Organizational Type Using Efficiency Scores

To understand what drives the shape of managerial preferences with respect to cost and revenue efficiency, we also examine whether organizational form affects managers' behavior. The diversity of ownership structure is a pervasive characteristic of the European banking industry. Alongside commercial banks, most European countries host a significant sector of cooperative banks and savings banks (either privately owned or publicly owned). Therefore, we estimate the shape parameter of the underlying managerial behavior function for commercial, savings, and cooperative banks separately.

Looking at the estimated alphas across different organizational types (see Table 9), we observe that bank managers in all types of banks (commercial,

---

16. Belgium, Finland, and Ireland are excluded from the analysis because of lack of a sufficient number of yearly observations.

TABLE 8 Managerial Preferences by Country Over Time Using Efficiency Scores

		$\hat{a}$	SE	$J_{\hat{a}}$
Austria	2008	0.393	0.040	0.608
	2009	0.394	0.039	0.736
	2010	0.400	0.038	0.366
	2011	0.409	0.037	10.203
	2012	0.409	0.039	0.920
	2013	0.413	0.036	5.775
	2014	0.405	0.037	0.044
	2015	0.393	0.049	1.298
Denmark	2008	0.116	0.049	3.930
	2009	0.155	0.054	2.936
	2010	0.174	0.055	0.981
	2011	0.154	0.052	2.111
	2012	0.187	0.056	1.608
	2013	0.254	0.048	0.948
	2014	0.172	0.043	5.780
	2015	0.243	0.053	0.384
France	2008	0.582	0.060	0.086
	2009	0.571	0.048	4.818
	2010	0.571	0.046	1.574
	2011	0.579	0.046	3.375
	2012	0.590	0.044	1.988
	2013	0.576	0.043	5.471
	2014	0.554	0.042	5.425
	2015	0.540	0.045	4.629
Germany	2008	0.240	0.013	2.857
	2009	0.240	0.012	0.056
	2010	0.243	0.011	1.035
	2011	0.237	0.011	8.771
	2012	0.239	0.011	1.707

Continued

TABLE 8 Managerial Preferences by Country Over Time Using Efficiency Scores—cont'd

		$\hat{a}$	SE	$J_{\hat{a}}$
	2013	0.234	0.011	0.900
	2014	0.233	0.011	1.242
	2015	0.210	0.012	0.131
Greece	2008	0.325	0.166	1.137
	2009	0.500	0.158	0.888
	2010	0.500	0.144	5.777
	2011	0.565	0.150	1.677
	2012	0.500	0.144	0.614
	2013	0.629	0.129	3.125
	2014	0.457	0.138	0.721
	2015	0.500	0.177	0.541
Italy	2009	0.390	0.022	1.503
	2010	0.391	0.022	3.341
	2011	0.397	0.022	1.975
	2012	0.390	0.022	2.916
	2013	0.388	0.021	1.519
	2014	0.374	0.022	4.428
	2015	0.357	0.025	2.656
Luxembourg	2008	0.552	0.111	0.339
	2009	0.544	0.102	0.597
	2010	0.500	0.118	5.378
	2011	0.500	0.118	0.433
	2012	0.500	0.102	0.485
	2013	0.395	0.100	2.484
	2014	0.436	0.117	1.135
	2015	0.396	0.136	4.090
Netherlands	2012	0.635	0.170	0.296
	2013	0.552	0.150	0.669
	2014	0.466	0.129	0.233
	2015	0.610	0.130	2.441

TABLE 8 Managerial Preferences by Country Over Time Using Efficiency Scores—cont'd

		$\hat{a}$	SE	$J_{\hat{a}}$
Portugal	2010	0.500	0.144	1.139
	2011	0.500	0.134	0.883
	2012	0.677	0.141	1.271
	2013	0.693	0.119	1.024
	2014	0.594	0.119	0.501
	2015	0.617	0.115	0.435
Spain	2008	0.201	0.071	0.951
	2009	0.287	0.047	0.128
	2010	0.302	0.048	2.384
	2011	0.298	0.047	4.161
	2012	0.320	0.046	1.043
	2013	0.321	0.046	0.888
	2014	0.351	0.049	2.201
	2015	0.384	0.053	0.640
Sweden	2008	0.445	0.071	1.643
	2009	0.401	0.067	1.690
	2010	0.367	0.064	0.417
	2011	0.348	0.062	3.689
	2012	0.322	0.067	1.540
	2013	0.247	0.059	9.228
	2014	0.322	0.066	2.597
	2015	0.265	0.057	2.931
UK	2008	0.397	0.104	1.338
	2009	0.455	0.080	2.825
	2010	0.290	0.078	2.717
	2011	0.298	0.075	4.892
	2012	0.281	0.073	0.768

Continued

TABLE 8 Managerial Preferences by Country Over Time Using Efficiency Scores—cont'd

	$\hat{a}$	SE	$J_{\hat{a}}$
2013	0.191	0.064	7.686
2014	0.247	0.067	1.255
2015	0.296	0.080	0.563

Note: This table presents estimates of the shape parameter, α, of the managerial behavior function by country over time. The estimate of α is given using the linear GMM instrumental variable estimator of Eq. (2). We report only the estimates of α using three instruments (a constant, the lagged difference in relative revenue and cost ratios, and the lagged relative cost ratio) and results for the linear form of the behavioral function, the lin-lin case for $p = 1$. Results for the quad-quad case (for $p = 2$) are identical and presented in the Appendix. $J_\alpha = J$-test under ith null hypothesis distributed as a $X^2(d - 1)$ variable for $d > 1$.

TABLE 9 Managerial Preferences by Type of Bank Using Efficiency Scores

	(a) Lin-Lin Case			(b) Quad-Quad Case		
	$\hat{a}$	SE	$J_{\hat{a}}$	$\hat{a}$	SE	$J_{\hat{a}}$
I. Commercial banks						
$D = 1$	0.446	0.010	1.57E−28	0.400	0.012	5.82E−28
$D = 2$	0.446	0.010	0.006	0.400	0.012	0.024
$D = 3$	0.446	0.010	0.214	0.400	0.012	0.305
II. Savings banks						
$D = 1$	0.312	0.007	1.58E−28	0.282	0.008	1.42E−26
$D = 2$	0.312	0.007	0.243	0.282	0.008	0.448
$D = 3$	0.312	0.007	0.529	0.282	0.008	0.566
III. Cooperative banks						
$D = 1$	0.275	0.004	8.84E−26	0.242	0.005	3.11E−27
$D = 2$	0.275	0.004	0.896	0.242	0.005	0.475
$D = 3$	0.275	0.004	8.344	0.242	0.005	4.371

Note: This table presents estimates of the shape parameter, α, of the managerial behavior function by type of bank for the whole sample. The estimate of α is given using the linear GMM instrumental variable estimator of Eq. (2). We report only the estimates of α using three instruments (a constant, the lagged difference in relative revenue and cost ratios, and the lagged relative cost ratio) and results for the linear form of the behavioral function, the lin-lin case for $p = 1$. Results for the quad-quad case (for $p = 2$) are identical and presented in the Appendix. $J_\alpha = J$-test under ith null hypothesis distributed as a $X^2(d - 1)$ variable for $d > 1$.

savings, and cooperative banks) exhibit asymmetric preferences with respect to cost and revenue efficiency, which is consistent with Hypothesis 3.

Overall, our results confirm the findings for the whole sample, although we do find that the asymmetry in bank managers' preferences varies across banks with different organizational types. Asymmetry is higher in cooperative banks, followed by savings banks, while commercial banks present more symmetric preferences. In particular, alpha is estimated at 0.45 for commercial banks (0.4 in the quadratic case), at 0.31 for savings banks (0.28 in the quadratic case), and at 0.28 for cooperative banks (0.24 in the quadratic case). This result is of interest because it indicates that differences in the organizational structure also are reflected in bank managerial behavior. We show that different types of banks provide different services because of historical reasons, manage different types of risks, and exhibit different efficiency scores. Reasons for different organizational forms leading to different efficiency levels have been explored in the literature (see Chen et al., 2015; Hull & Rothenberg, 2008; Jiang, Tao, & Santoro, 2010; Miller & Parkhe, 2001), highlighting the importance of management being constrained by capital market discipline. For example, bank managers in cooperative banks might pay particular attention to expenses, and this kind of preferences is picked up by the reported alphas. This is because the main objective of cooperative banks could be to maximize customer-owner benefits by offering favorable interest rates on loans and deposits and lower transaction costs rather than maximizing profits (Miller & Parkhe, 2001). It generally is thought, however, that savings banks are inclined to support regional projects rather than maximizing shareholder wealth (Gardener, Molyneux, Williams, & Carbo, 1997) and that traditional savings banks are obliged to finance any growth strategies from retained earnings, which could have a restraining impact on the distribution of profits to beneficiaries (Bergendahl & Lindblom, 2008). Cooperative and savings banks usually operate in concentrated markets, where according to Berger and Mester (1997) bank managers might prefer to operate on a minimum required effort mode rather than enhance their efforts to raise revenues.

Overall, our analysis by country, by organizational type, and by year reveals strong evidence of the existence of asymmetry in bank managers' preferences, because they appear to value more cost efficiency than revenue efficiency, consistent with Hypothesis 3.

5.4 Second Stage Regression: Factors Affecting Alphas

The last part of our analysis relates bank managers' preferences in the EU-15 countries to various characteristics of EU banking markets and the regulatory environment. To this end, we opt for a regression analysis using estimated alphas across countries and over time as the dependent variable (from Table 8). On the right side of the regression model, we include variables such as the Herfindahl Index, which measures bank concentration; the interest rate spread, which is a proxy of the degree of competition; a measure of risk (the z-score)[17]; the domestic credit to the private sector as a percent of GDP ratio to capture the size of the banking system; the Fraser Index on regulation; the Fraser Index on legal system and property rights; an index capturing supervisory disciplinary power[18]; and a sovereign lending rate.

Table 10 presents the regression results. Overall, looking at the coefficient of the Herfindahl Index in all specifications, we observe a positive relationship between concentration and estimated alphas. This suggests that the lack of competition and market discipline increases the asymmetry in bank managers' preferences with respect to cost and revenue efficiency. The interest spread also enters the regression with a negative sign, suggesting that a higher degree of competition is associated with a higher alpha. The z-score that captures default risk also has a negative relationship with alpha, suggesting that an increase in risk (a reduction in z-score) would cause an increase in alpha. A negative relationship also is observed between alpha and the size of the banking sector, as measured by the domestic credit to the private sector ratio. Concerning the variables capturing various aspects of regulation and supervision, we find no statistically significant relationship with alpha. The same holds for the sovereign lending rate variable.

5.4.1 Panel Vector Autoregression (VAR) Analysis

As a robustness test and in order to deal with potential issues of endogeneity bias, we also employ a panel-VAR model to examine the relationship between bank management preferences and various banking sector characteristics.[19] The main advantage of this methodology is that all variables enter as endogenous within a system of equations, which enables us to reveal the underlying

---

17. The z-score is defined as (average return on assets + equity/assets)/(standard deviation of the return on assets) and can be interpreted as the number of standard deviations by which returns would have to fall from the mean to wipe out all equity in the bank.
18. This variable is constructed by adding 1 if the answer is yes and 0 otherwise, for each one of the following questions: (1) Can the supervisory authorities force a bank to change its internal organizational structure? (2) Are there any mechanisms of cease-desist type orders whose infraction leads to automatic imposition of civil and penal sanctions on banks' directors and managers? (3) Can the supervisory agency order the bank's directors or management to constitute provisions to cover actual or potential losses? (4) Can the supervisory agency suspend director's decision to distribute dividends? (5) Can the supervisory agency suspend director's decision to distribute bonuses? (6) Can the supervisory agency suspend director's decision to distribute management fees? (7) Can the supervisory agency supersede bank shareholder rights and declare bank insolvent? (8) Does banking law allow supervisory agency to suspend some or all ownership rights of a problem bank? (9) Regarding bank restructuring and reorganization, can supervisory agency remove and replace management? (10) Regarding bank restructuring and reorganization, can supervisory agency remove and replace directors?
19. For a brief presentation of the panel-VAR methodology, see Appendix A.

TABLE 10 Second Stage Regressions: The Impact of Bank-Specific and Institutional Variables on Bank Managerial Preference

	Model 1	Model 2	Model 3	Model 4	Model 5
HHI	0.0842*	0.0842**	0.0834*	0.0918*	0.0848**
	0.056	0.050	0.059	0.054	0.050
IntSpread	−0.1039***	−0.0976***	−0.1006***	−0.1074***	−0.1053***
	0.000	0.000	0.000	0.001	0.000
z-Score	−0.0087**	−0.0079*	−0.0078*	−0.0069*	−0.0092**
	0.019	0.055	0.058	0.099	0.020
DCPC	−0.1919***	−0.1588*	−0.1717**	−0.2021***	−0.1965***
	0.003	0.063	0.035	0.002	0.003
FR-regul.		−0.0285			
		0.410			
FR-legal			−0.0146		
			0.573		
Supervision				0.0095	
				0.461	
SovLendR					−0.0052
					0.362
Constant	1.1044**	1.123***	1.1047**	1.0377**	1.1537**
	0.017	0.009	0.013	0.032	0.019
R^2	0.5219	0.5408	0.5305	0.5357	0.5246
	$F_{(4,11)} =$ 22.75 (0.000)	$F_{(5,11)} =$ 12.77 (0.000)	$F_{(5,11)} =$ 18.43 (0.000)	$F_{(5,11)} =$ 17.60 (0.000)	$F_{(5,11)} =$ 20.51 (0.000)
Obs.	89	89	89	89	89

Note: The table presents regression results using estimated alphas across countries and over time as the dependent variable (from Table 8). HHI = logarithm of Herfindahl Index; IntSpread = lending rate minus deposit rate; z-score = defined as (average return on assets + equity/assets)/(standard deviation of the return on assets); DCPC = logarithm of the domestic credit to the private sector as a percent of GDP; FR-regulation = Fraser Index on market regulation; FR-legal = Fraser index on Legal System and Property Rights; Supervision = index measuring official disciplinary power; SovLendR = sovereign lending rate. ***, **, * indicate significance at 1%, 5%, and 10% significance level, respectively.
Sources: ECB, World Development Indicators; Bankscope; Fraser Institute, own calculations.

causality among them.[20] We specify a panel-VAR model where the key variable is alpha, the shape parameter of the managerial behavior function; we also include the main right side variables of the previous section. We present both impulse response functions (IRFs),[21] which present the response of each variable to its own innovation and to the innovations of the other variables, as well as variance decompositions (VDCs), which show the percentage of the forecast error variance of one variable that is explained by the same and other variables within the panel-VAR.

Fig. 2 presents the IRFs diagrams for the case that the panel-VAR includes; alpha, the Fraser Index on regulation, an index capturing supervisory disciplinary power, and the risk variable (z-score). Looking at the first row of Fig. 2, we observe that the effect of a one standard deviation shock of the supervision index on alpha is positive. The effect of a one standard deviation shock of the Fraser regulation index on alpha is negative; the same applies for the z-score variable.[22] Table 11 presents VDCs and reports the total effect accumulated over 10 and 20 years. Our results indicate that about 15% of alpha's forecast error variance after 20 years is explained by disturbances in the supervisory index, while 3.6% and 2.7% of the variation is explained by disturbances in the Fraser regulation index and the z-score variable, respectively.

Fig. 3 presents the IRFs diagrams for the second set of variables under examination: alpha, the Herfindahl Index, the ratio of domestic credit to the private sector, and the sovereign risk variable. Looking at the first row of Fig. 3, the effect of a one standard deviation shock of the domestic credit to the private sector ratio on alpha is negative, as is the sovereign risk variable. A much smaller negative effect is observed in the case of the Herfindahl Index. Turning to the VDCs results (Table 12), we observe that 1.4% of alpha's forecast error variance after 20 years is explained by Herfindahl Index's disturbances and another 1.4% by disturbances of the domestic credit ratio. Moreover, 2.7% of alpha's forecast error variance after 20 years is explained by sovereign risk.

---

20. Prior to the estimation of the panel VAR, we have to decide the optimal lag order j of the right-hand variables in the system of equations. To do so, we opt for the Arellano-Bover GMM estimator for the lags of $j = 1$, 2 and 3. We use the Akaike Information Criterion (AIC) to choose the optimal lag order. The AIC suggests that the optimum lag order is one, which is confirmed by the Arellano-Bond AR tests. To test for evidence of autocorrelation, more lags were added. The Sargan tests provide evidence of lag order one. We also perform the Sahpiro-Francia W0 normality test and find evidence of no violation. Results are available upon request.

21. To analyze the impulse response functions, we need an estimate of their confidence intervals. We calculate standard errors of the impulse response functions with Monte Carlo simulations and generate confidence intervals. Monte Carlo simulations method randomly generates a draw of coefficients of the VAR using the estimated coefficients and their variance covariance matrix to recalculate the impulse responses. We repeat the procedure 500 times ensure that results are similar. Then, the 5th and 95th percentiles of this distribution are generated and used as a confidence interval for the impulse responses.

22. Where confidence interval of IRFs is wide, results should be treated with caution.

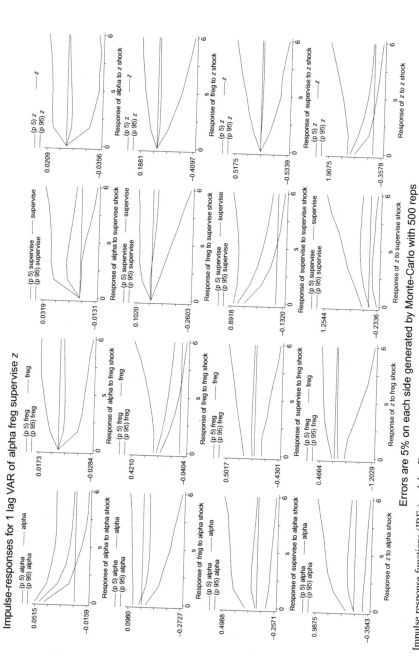

FIG. 2 Impulse response functions (IRFs)—alpha, Fraser regulation, supervision index, z-score. *Note:* Figure presents impulse response functions (IRFs), which show the responses of a variable of interest to a shock of one plus/minus standard deviation of the same variable or another variable within the panel-VAR. Variables within the panel-VAR are estimated alphas by country and by year (from Table 8); z-score = (average return on assets + equity/assets)/(standard deviation of the return on assets); FR-regulation = Fraser Index on market regulation; Supervision = an index measuring official disciplinary power.

TABLE 11 Variance Decomposition Estimations for Alpha, Fraser Regulation, Supervision Index, z-Score

	s	Alpha	Freg	Supervise	z
Alpha	10	0.7895	0.0341	0.1493	0.027
Freg	10	0.1034	0.8239	0.0438	0.0289
Supervise	10	0.0196	0.014	0.9613	0.0052
z	10	0.0772	0.0177	0.1835	0.7216
Alpha	20	0.7857	0.0362	0.1512	0.0269
Freg	20	0.1132	0.792	0.0673	0.0275
Supervise	20	0.0197	0.015	0.9598	0.0056
z	20	0.0785	0.018	0.1921	0.7114

Note: Table presents the variance decompositions (VDC), which show the components of the forecasts error variance of all variables within the panel-VAR. Variables within the panel-VAR are estimated alphas by country and by year (from Table 8); z-score = (average return on assets + equity/assets)/ (standard deviation of the return on assets); FR-regulation = Fraser Index on market regulation; Supervision = index measuring official disciplinary power.

6 Conclusion

Although the idea that different principal-agent goals, inadequate incentives and imperfect contracts can create sources of inefficiency and thus X-efficiency crucially depends on the underlying behavioral objectives pursued by managers is not new (Kumbhakar & Lovell, 2000), no studies in the literature explicitly investigate the incentives underpinning managerial preferences with respect to cost and revenue efficiency. The large body of the literature examining banks' cost and profit efficiency, however, appear to conclude that there is some persistency in inefficiencies both on the cost and on the revenue sides. This study attempts to investigate the underlying managerial behavior with respect to performance, which is measured using both accounting measures, such as the relative revenue and cost ratios, and more comprehensive measures of performance, such as revenue and cost efficiency scores. In particular, we examine whether managers are equally interested in pursuing cost and revenue efficiency-enhancing strategies or whether there is some degree of asymmetry in their preferences. We consider that banks' operation crucially depends on a generalized management behavior function with unknown shape parameter that provides information regarding the underlying preferences of their management.

Results based on accounting ratios for the overall sample indicate that managerial preferences are broadly symmetric, though this picture changes when we

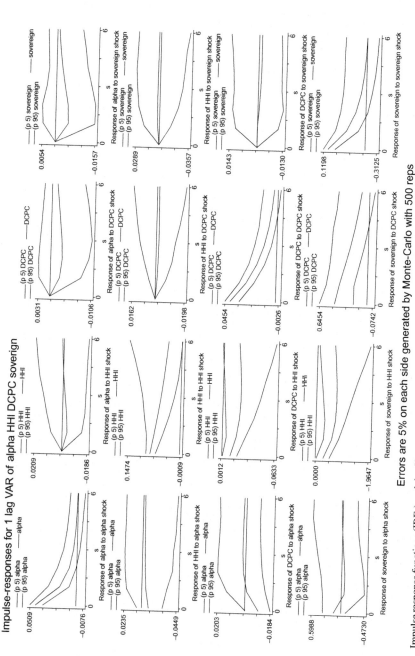

FIG. 3 Impulse response functions (IRFs)—alpha, Herfindahl Index, domestic credit to the private sector and sovereign risk. *Note:* Figure presents impulse response functions (IRFs), which show the response of a variable of interest to a shock of one plus/minus standard deviation of the same variable or another variable within the panel-VAR. Variables within the panel-VAR are estimated alphas by country and by year (from Table 5); HHI = logarithm of Herfindahl Index; DCPC = logarithm of the domestic credit to the private sector as a percent of GDP; sovereign = sovereign lending rate.

TABLE 12 Variance Decomposition Estimations for Alpha, Herfindahl Index, Domestic Credit to the Private Sector and Sovereign Risk

	s	Alpha	HHI	DCPC	Sovereign
Alpha	10	0.946	0.014	0.014	0.027
HHI	10	0.006	0.992	0.001	0.002
DCPC	10	0.019	0.510	0.469	0.002
Sovereign	10	0.006	0.662	0.099	0.232
Alpha	20	0.941	0.019	0.014	0.027
HHI	20	0.006	0.992	0.001	0.002
DCPC	20	0.018	0.549	0.431	0.002
Sovereign	20	0.006	0.699	0.089	0.206

Note: Table presents the variance decompositions (VDC), which show the components of the forecasts error variance of all variables within the panel-VAR. Variables within the panel-VAR are estimated alphas by country and by year (from Tables 5 and 6). HHI = logarithm of Herfindahl Index; DCPC = logarithm of the domestic credit to the private sector as a percent of GDP; sovereign = sovereign lending rate.

look at country-level results, which are consistent with the revenue emphasis hypothesis. Our analysis based on efficiency scores, however, provides evidence that bank managers' underlying preference function is asymmetric and consistent with the cost emphasis hypothesis. Thus, if banks' managers face a tradeoff between cost and revenue efficiency, they would show preference for having a higher level of revenue compared to cost inefficiency. This result is broadly confirmed by our cross-country analysis; this asymmetry also holds for banks with different organizational types.

This study offers insights to a wide audience that includes practitioners, shareholders, policymakers, and market participants because it reveals that bank managers have asymmetric preferences, which would lean toward revenue optimization in most cases, suggesting that they would favor more leeway toward discretionary spending.

By becoming common knowledge, this information provides an opportunity of adjustment in preferences if needed.

A Appendix

TABLE A1 Managerial Preferences by Country Using Accounting Ratios (Additional Results)

	A. Difference Between Relative Revenue to Assets and Cost to Assets Ratios			B. Difference Between Relative Revenue to Equity and Cost to Equity Ratios		
	$\hat{a}$	SE	$J_{\hat{a}}$	$\hat{a}$	SE	$J_{\hat{a}}$
Austria	0.653	0.013	189.371	0.600	0.024	21.079
Belgium	0.805	0.043	8.589	0.776	0.059	5.803
Germany	0.653	0.005	1.17E+03	0.681	0.006	391.801
Denmark	0.256	0.020	58.578	0.123	0.016	27.266
Spain	0.582	0.022	93.506	0.601	0.031	53.631
Finland	0.633	0.078	0.215	0.774	0.083	0.7525
France	0.500	0.016	377.98	0.440	0.021	198.817
Greece	0.368	0.050	30.496	0.195	0.047	18.144
Ireland	0.762	0.071	6.554	0.903	0.055	5.864
Italy	0.283	0.020	88.690	0.215	0.023	25.94
Luxembourg	0.745	0.046	11.837	0.631	0.075	10.590
Netherlands	0.748	0.047	18.841	0.681	0.061	9.226
Portugal	0.666	0.052	3.802	0.799	0.050	4.621
Sweden	0.189	0.029	24.478	0.070	0.015	14.424
UK	0.556	0.032	29.057	0.544	0.049	25.792

Note: This table presents estimates of the shape parameter, α, of the managerial behavior function by country over the period 2008–15. The estimate of α is given using the linear GMM instrumental variable estimator of Eq. (2). We report estimates for the quad-quad case (for $p = 2$) using three instruments (a constant, the lagged difference in relative revenue and cost ratios, and the lagged relative cost ratio). $J_{\alpha} = J$-test under ith null hypothesis distributed as a $X^2(d - 1)$ variable for $d > 1$.

TABLE A2 Managerial Preferences by Year Using Accounting Ratios (Additional Results)

	A. Difference Between Relative Revenue to Assets and Cost to Assets Ratios			B. Difference Between Relative Revenue to Equity and Cost to Equity Ratios		
	$\hat{a}$	SE	$J_{\hat{a}}$	$\hat{a}$	SE	$J_{\hat{a}}$
2008	0.558	0.015	4.917	0.466	0.025	2.177
2009	0.561	0.013	0.281	0.453	0.020	0.173
2010	0.421	0.012	4.017	0.297	0.015	4.206
2011	0.569	0.012	1.367	0.490	0.017	1.945
2012	0.678	0.012	3.910	0.629	0.017	1.061
2013	0.615	0.009	3.697	0.578	0.014	1.234
2014	0.576	0.010	1.924	0.577	0.014	1.290
2015	0.555	0.011	8.759	0.549	0.016	4.194

Note: This table presents estimates of the shape parameter, α, of the managerial behavior function by year for the whole sample. The estimate of α is given using the linear GMM instrumental variable estimator of Eq. (2). We report estimates for the quad-quad case (for $p = 2$) using three instruments (a constant, the lagged difference in relative revenue and cost ratios, and the lagged relative cost ratio). J_α = J-test under ith null hypothesis distributed as a $X^2(d-1)$ variable for $d > 1$.

References

Aigner, D.J., Lovell, C.A.K., Schmidt, P., 1977. Formulation and estimation of stochastic frontier production function models. Journal of Econometrics 6 (1), 21–37.

Baumol, W.J., 1982. Contestable markets: an uprising in the theory of industry structure. American Economic Review 72, 1–15.

Bergendahl, G., Lindblom, T., 2008. Evaluating the performance of Swedish savings banks according to service efficiency. European Journal of Operational Research 185, 1663–1673.

Berger, A., Mester, L., 1997. Inside the black box: what explains differences in the efficiencies of financial institutions. Journal of Banking and Finance 21, 895–947.

Blair, D.W., Placone, D.L., 1988. Expense-preference behavior, agency costs, and firm organization. Journal of Economics and Business 40, 1–15.

Brush, T.H., Bromiley, P., Hendrickx, M., 2000. The free cash flow hypothesis for sales growth and firm performance. Strategic Management Journal 21, 455–472.

Cabral, L., Riordan, M.H., 1989. Incentives for cost reduction under price cap regulation. Journal of Regulatory Economics 1, 93–102.

Carpenter, M.A., Sanders, W.M.G., 2004. The effects of top management team pay and firm internationalization MNC performance. Journal of Management 30, 509–528.

Cavallo, L., Rossi, S.P., 2001. Scale and scope economies in the European banking systems. Journal of Multinational Financial Management 11, 515–531.

Chen, C.-M., Delmas, M.A., Lieberman, M.B., 2015. Production frontier methodologies and efficiency as a performance measure in strategic management research. Strategic Management Journal 36 (1), 19–36.

Dalton, D.R., Dalton, C.M., 2011. Integration of micro and macro studies in governance research: CEO duality, board composition, and financial performance. Journal of Management 37, 404–411.

D'Amato, A., Gallo, A., 2017. Does bank institutional setting affect board effectiveness? Evidence from cooperative and joint-stock banks. Corporate Governance: An International Review 25, 78–99.

Delgado-García, J.B., de la Fuente-Sabaté, J.M., de Quevedo-Puente, E., 2010. Too negative to take risks? The effect of the CEO's emotional traits on firm risk. British Journal of Management 21, 313–326.

Delgado-García, J.B., de Quevedo-Puente, E., Díez-Esteban, J.M., 2013. The impact of corporate reputation on firm risk: a panel data analysis of Spanish quoted firms. British Journal of Management 24, 1–20.

Dewatripont, M., Tirole, J., 1994. The prudential regulation of banks. MIT Press, Cambridge, Massachusetts, London, England.

Donald, S.G., Newey, W.K., 2001. Choosing the number of instruments. Econometrica 69, 1161–1192.

Edwards, F.R., 1977. Managerial objectives in regulated industries: expense preference behavior in banking. Journal of Political Economy 85, 147–162.

Elliott, G., Komunjer, I., Timmermann, A., 2005. Estimation and testing of forecast rationality under flexible loss. Review of Economic Studies 72, 1107–1125.

European Central Bank (2010). Beyond ROE—How to measure bank performance. Appendix to the report on EU banking structures, ECB (September 2010).

Färe, R., Grosskopf, S., Weber, W., 2004. The effect of risk-based capital requirements on profit efficiency in banking. Applied Economics 36, 1731–1743.

Gardener, E., Molyneux, P., Williams, J., Carbo, S., 1997. European savings banks: facing up to the new environment. International Journal of Bank Marketing 15 (7), 243–254.

George, G., Wiklund, J., Zahra, S.A., 2005. Ownership and the internationalization of small firms. Journal of Management 31, 210–233.

Gordon, R.A., 1961. Business leadership in the large corporation. University of California Press, Berkeley.

Hull, C., Rothenberg, S., 2008. Firm performance: the interactions of corporate social performance with innovation and industry differentiation. Strategic Management Journal 29 (7), 781–789.

Hannan, T.H., 1979. Expense-preference behavior in banking: a reexamination. Journal of Political Economy October, 891–895.

Hannan, T.H., Mavinga, F., 1980. Expense preference and managerial control: the case of the banking firm. The Bell Journal of Economics 87, 671–682.

Hansen, L., Singleton, L., 1982. Generalised instrumental variables estimation of nonlinear rational expectations models. Econometrica 50, 714–735.

Helmalin, B.E., 1992. The effects of competition on executive behavior. The RAND Journal of Economics 23 (3), 350–365.

Hicks, J.R., 1935. Annual survey of economic theory: the theory of monopoly. Econometrica. .

Jensen, M., Meckling, W., 1976. Theory of firm: managerial behaviour, agency costs and capital structure. Journal of Financial Economics 3, 305–360.

Jensen, M., 1986. Agency costs of free cash flow, corporate finance, and takeovers. American Economic Review 76 (1986), 323–329.

Jiang, R.J., Tao, Q.T., Santoro, M.D., 2010. Alliance portfolio diversity and firm performance. Strategic Management Journal 31 (10), 1136–1144.

Jondrow, J., Lovell, C.A.K., Materov, I., Schmidt, P., 1982. On the estimation of technical inefficiency in the stochastic frontier production model. Journal of Econometrics 19 (2/3), 233–238.

Kaysen, C., 1960. The corporation: How much power? What scope? In: Mason, E.S. (Ed.), The corporation in modern society. Harvard University Press, Cambridge.

Knott, A., Posen, H., 2005. Is failure good? Strategic Management Journal 26 (7), 617–641.

Kumbhakar, S.C., Lovell, C.A.K., 2000. Stochastic frontier analysis. Cambridge University Press, New York.

Kumbhakar, S.C., Lozano-Vivas, A., Lovell, C.A.K., Iftekhar, H., 2001. The effects of deregulation on the performance of financial institutions: the case of Spanish savings banks. Journal of Money, Credit and Banking 33 (1), 101–120.

Leibenstein, H., 1966. Allocative efficiency vs. 'X-efficiency'. American Economic Review 56 (3), 392–415.

Marquis, C., Huang, Z., 2009. The contingent nature of public policy and the growth of U.S. commercial banking. Academy of Management Journal 52, 1222–1256.

Meeusen, W., van den Broeck, J., 1977. Efficiency estimation from Cobb-Douglas production functions with composed error. International Economic Review 18 (2), 435–444.

Mester, L.J., 1989. Testing for expense preference behavior: mutual versus stock savings and loans. The Rand Journal of Economics 40, 483–495.

Miller, S., Parkhe, A., 2001. Is there a liability of foreignness in global banking? An empirical test of banks' X-efficiency. Strategic Management Journal 23 (1), 55–75.

Mingfang, L., Simerly, R.L., 1998. The moderating effect of environmental dynamism on the ownership and performance relationship. Strategic Management Journal 19, 169–180.

Rhoades, S.A., 1980. Monopoly and expense preference behavior: an empirical investigation of a behavioralist hypothesis. Southern Journal of Economics October, 419–432.

Sealey, C., Lindley, J., 1977. Inputs, outputs and a theory of production and cost of depository financial institutions. Journal of Finance 32, 1251–1266.

Shleifer, A., Vishny, R.W., 1986. Large shareholders and corporate control. Journal of Political Economy 94 (1986), 461–488.

Shleifer, A., Vishny, R.W., 1997. A survey of corporate governance. Journal of Finance 52 (2), 737–783.

Smirlock, M., Marshall, W., 1983. Monopoly power and expense-preference behavior: theory and evidence to the contrary. The Bell Journal of Economics 14, 166–178.

Tirole, J., 1988. The theory of industrial organization. MIT Press, Cambridge, Massachusetts, London, England.

Williamson, O.E., 1963. Managerial discretion and business behavior. The American Economic Review 53 (5), 1032–1057.

Wiseman, R.M., Gomez-Mejia, L.R., 1998. A behavioral agency model of managerial risk taking. Academy of Management Review 23, 133–153.

Further Reading

Williams, J., 2004. Determining management behavior in European banking. Journal of Banking and Finance 28, 2427–2460.

Chapter 26

The Impact of Explicit Deposit Insurance on Market Discipline ☆

Vasso Ioannidou* and Jan de Dreu†

*Accounting and Finance Department, Lancaster University Management School, Lancaster, United Kingdom, †BBVA, Global Debt Advisory, Ciudad BBVa, Madrid, Spain

Chapter Outline

1 Introduction

The provision and design of deposit insurance systems presents governments with an unprecedented set of challenges. Deposit insurance systems typically are motivated by a desire to decrease the risk of systemic bank runs (see, for example, Diamond & Dybvig, 1983) and to protect small, uninformed depositors (see Dewatripont & Tirole, 1994). Often, however, they are blamed for increasing the incentives of banks to take excessive risk by reducing, or even eliminating, the incentives of depositors to monitor and discipline their banks (see, among others, Kane, 1989; Calomiris, 1999).

☆ We would like to thank the Bank Supervisory Authority in Bolivia, and in particular Enrique Hurtado, Juan Carlos Ibieta, Guillermo Romano, and Sergio Selaya, for providing the means and support to construct our dataset. We also like to thank the Netherlands Organization for Scientific Research (NWO) for a travel grant. For valuable suggestions and comments, we would like to thank Adam Ashcraft, Fabio Braggion, Hans Degryse, Sonia Falconieri, Harry Huizinga, Ed Kane, Steven Ongena, Jan van Ours, Joe Peek, Fabiana Penas, Bas Werker, Maurizio Zanardi, as well as seminar participants at the 2005 Bank Structure Conference, the University of Bologna, the K.U. of Leuven, the Ente Luigi Einaudi, and the Dutch Central Bank. Any remaining errors are our own.

Panel Data Econometrics. https://doi.org/10.1016/B978-0-12-815859-3.00026-3

Depositor discipline is commonly understood as a situation in which depositors penalize banks for extra risk-taking by requiring higher interest rates or by withdrawing their deposits from riskier banks, which, in turn, reduces banks' incentives to take risk in the first place. The main challenge facing policymakers is how to design deposit insurance schemes that protect financial systems from systemic bank runs, while maintaining sufficient incentives for depositors to monitor and discipline their banks as to avoid excessive risk taking.

This research contributes to this challenge by studying how the introduction of a deposit insurance scheme affected depositors' discipline. The analysis takes advantages of the introduction of an explicit deposit insurance scheme in Bolivia in 2001 and compares the behavior of small and large depositors before and after the introduction of the scheme. The comparison is between implicit, blanket guarantees that preceded the introduction of the scheme and explicit, but partial deposit insurance. Variation in the insurance coverage across banks allows us to further study the role of insurance coverage within each class of depositors.

The country-specific circumstances during the sample period and the characteristics of the scheme provide for an interesting setting. First, the sample period, 1998–2003, is characterized by a recession that weakened the banking sector, giving depositors reasons to worry about their deposits—a natural prerequisite for market discipline (Flannery & Sorescu, 1996). Second, apart from the introduction of a deposit insurance scheme in December 2001, no other major regulatory reforms occurred during the sample period, which makes it possible to compare the behavior of depositors before and after the regime-change.

The presence of depositor discipline predicts that bank risk is positively correlated with deposit interest rates and negatively correlated with the volume of deposits. (Riskier banks have to pay for their deposits, and they are able to attract fewer deposits.) The presence of both effects on price and quantities is important in order to eliminate alternative, demand-driven, hypotheses (Park, 1995). Previous studies tend to provide evidence either on interest rates or on deposits, but not both at the same time because of data limitations (see Demirgüç-Kunt & Huizinga, 2004; Martinez Peria & Schmukler, 2001).

We find that an increase in bank risk is associated with higher interest rates and lower deposits. This is consistent with the hypothesis that depositors discipline their banks by requiring higher interest and withdrawing deposits from riskier banks. Our findings indicate that most depositor discipline is exercised by large depositors. The introduction of explicit deposit insurance caused a significant reduction in market discipline (i.e., the sensitivity of interest rates and deposits to bank risk indicators decreased by 50%–90%). All other things being equal, as the decrease in market discipline grows larger, the insurance coverage also grows larger. Almost complete elimination of deposit discipline observed when insurance coverage is higher than 60%.

The chapter relates to the empirical literature about depositor discipline and deposits insurance.[1] Using data from more than 30 developed and developing countries, Demirgüç-Kunt and Huizinga (2004) find that bank interest rates are lower and less sensitive to indicators of bank risk in counties with explicit deposit insurance. They also find that these effects are more pronounced for countries with more generous deposit insurance systems (e.g., systems without co-insurance, high coverage rates). Using data from Argentina, Chile, and Mexico during the 1980s and 1990s, Martinez Peria and Schmukler (2001) find no statistically significant difference in the behavior of small and large depositors and conclude that deposit insurance was not credible during their sample period. Our results highlight that absent credibility concerns about the insurer, explicit deposit insurance schemes can have devastating effects on depositors' incentives to monitor and discipline their banks. Their dampening effect operates mainly though large depositors—the class of depositors who are sensitive to their banks' risk in the first place. These results provide support to deposit insurance schemes with deposit insurance limits per depositor. Such systems provide support to small, unsophisticated depositors, while maintaining large depositors' sensitivity toward the bank's risk-taking.

The remainder of the chapter proceeds as follows. Section 2 describes the deposit insurance system in Bolivia and contrasts it to deposit insurance systems elsewhere. Section 3 discusses our empirical strategy, and Section 4 describes the data. Section 5 reports and discusses the paper's key findings, and Section 6 offers conclusions.

2 The Bolivian Deposit Insurance Scheme

Bolivia introduced an explicit deposit insurance system on December 20, 2001 (Law 2297). Before that, there were implicit blanket guarantees. For example, when Banco Sur and Banco de Cochabamba failed in 1994, the Bolivian Central Bank (BCB) covered 100% of its private-sector deposits. Similarly, when Banco International de Desarrollo failed in 1997, the BCB put a coverage limit up to $200,000 per account, which covered more than 98% of its private-sector deposits. With the passage of Law 2297 in 2001, the "Fund for Financial Restructuring" (thereafter the Fund) was created to protect the deposits of failing financial institutions in Bolivia. All licensed depository institutions operating in the country were required to contribute to the Fund, with insurance premiums proportional to the institution's deposits to the private sector. At full capitalization, the Fund would constitute 5% of banking sector deposits. Until full capitalization was reached, the BCB was the responsible party. After full

---

1. See, among others, Baer and Brewer (1986), Barajas and Steiner (2000), Billet, Garfinkel, and O'Neal (1998), Calomiris and Powell (2000), Cook and Spellman (1991), Demirgüç-Kunt and Huizinga (2004), Ellis and Flannery (1992), Flannery (1982), Furfine (2001), Hannan and Hanweck (1988).

capitalization, the BCB was required by law to supply any lacking resources by debiting against future contributions of financial institutions to the Fund.[2] The BCB's backstop support aimed at strengthening the credibility of the newly established system.

The deposit insurance coverage was limited and varied across banks and time depending on the institution's liability composition. In particular, the Fund covered up to 50% of the financial institution's qualifying liabilities referred to as "total preferred obligations" (TPOs). TPOs are divided into two classes: first-order obligations and second-order obligations. First-order obligations consist primarily of private-sector deposits.[3] Second-order obligations are subordinated to first-order obligations and includes obligations to the public sector, the Bolivian central bank, and foreign financial entities. Interbank deposits were not insured. The deposit insurance coverage rate (CR) of private-sector deposits varied across banks and time depending on their composition of TPOs as follows:

$$CoverageRate = \begin{cases} 100\% & \text{if } First/TPOs \leq 50\% \\ 50\%*(First/TPOs)^{-1} & \text{if } First/TPOs > 50\% \end{cases} \quad (1)$$

Fig. 1 provides graphical illustration of the coverage rate as a function of the financial institution's ratio of first-order obligations to TPOs.

Table 1 provides descriptive statistics about banks' liability composition and coverage rate (CR). Two patterns are worth pointing out. First, both before and after deposit insurance was introduced, first-order obligations were almost always more than 50% of TPOs (84.4% on average), which implies that deposits to the private sector were only partially insured. The average CR was 60%, with a standard deviation of 10%, and a minimum and maximum coverage rate of 50% and 100%, respectively. Full coverage was extremely rare because first-order obligations were less than 50% of TPOs for only 1.9% of our bank-month observations. Therefore, our comparison is between implicit blanket guarantees and explicit partial-deposit insurance. Second, the ratio of first-order obligations to TPOs increased after 2001. This is consistent with deposits perceived as safer and thus more attractive after explicit insurance was introduced.

Table 2 compares the Bolivian deposit insurance scheme to deposit insurance schemes in other countries using information from Demirgüç-Kunt et al. (2005). As can be observed in Table 1, many of the characteristics of the Bolivian scheme are shared by the majority of deposit insurance schemes in the rest of the world; except that 90% of the schemes in the rest of the world provide full insurance up

---

2. Third paragraph of Article 127, Law 2297.
3. No distinction is made between domestic and foreign currency denominated deposits. More than 90% of deposits and credits in the Bolivian banking sector are in US dollars. This high degree of dollarization is a long-lasting effect of hyperinflation in the 1980s. Because the economy is highly dollarized, the exchange rate policy follows a crawling peg with the US dollar. During the sample period, the exchange rate has been depreciating at a roughly constant rate of 6.5% per annum, with a peak of 9.7% in 2002.

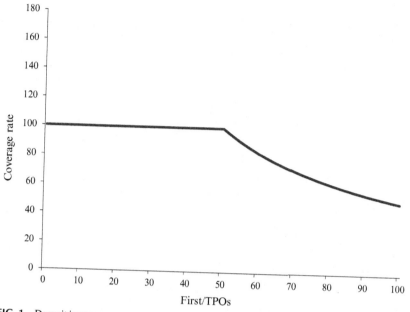

FIG. 1 Deposit insurance coverage rate. This figure provides a graphical illustration of the deposit insurance coverage rate in Bolivia (Eq. 2).

to a certain amount per depositor (or per account). Depositors that are above this limit are covered only partially with the degree of coverage decreasing as the value of their deposits increases above the insurance limit. In Bolivia, the coverage rate within the same bank does not vary with the size of the account (i.e., it is the same for both large and small depositors), but it varies across banks and time depending on the bank's liability composition of TPOs.

This unusual feature of the Bolivian scheme is an example of the role of private-interest groups in influencing regulation and deposit insurance design in particular.[4] The absence of an explicit coverage limit per account or per depositor was the result of pressure from financial institutions against the first draft of the deposit insurance law that included a coverage limit of $10,000 per account. This first draft was submitted to Congress in 1999 but failed to pass, given the strong opposition from the country's "business elite." The approved scheme in 2001 was more generous to large depositors than the original proposal.

---

4. Other such examples are plentiful in the literature. For example, Kroszner and Strahan (2001) find that the voting behavior in the US House of Representatives on the limitation of deposit insurance to a single account per bank is consistent with private interest theories of regulation. Similarly, Laeven (2004) finds that cross-country differences in deposit insurance coverage also can be explained by private-interest theories.

TABLE 1 Preferred Obligations and Deposit Insurance Coverage Rate

	Before	After	Difference
First/TPOs			
Mean	79.2	85.28	6.08***
Standard deviation	10.84	11.55	
Median	82.12	88.46	
Min	38.27	34.22	
Max	99.24	98.79	
Obs	610	312	
Coverage rate			
Mean		59.7	
Standard deviation		9.9	
Median		56.5	
Min		50.6	
Max		100.0	
Obs		312	

This table reports the average ratio of first-order obligations to total preferred obligations (First/TPOs) of all banks in our sample before and after the introduction of explicit deposit insurance in December 2001 as well as summary statistics for the effective deposit insurance coverage rate, calculated using Eq. (1). *** indicates that the difference between the average First/TPOs before and after the introduction of deposit insurance is statistically significantly different from zero at the 1% level.

3 Methodology

To examine whether depositors respond to increases in bank risk by reducing their supply of deposits, we study the sensitivity of deposit interest rates and deposit volumes to bank risk and how these changes after the introduction of explicit deposit insurance. Market discipline implies that an increase in bank risk leads to a decrease in the supply of deposits. Therefore, higher bank risk should be associated with higher interest rates and lower deposits. To examine whether there is evidence of market discipline in our sample we estimate:

$$InterestRate_{i,t} = \alpha_1 + \beta_1 BankRisk_{i,t-k} + \gamma_1 X_{i,t-k} + \varepsilon_{i,t} \tag{2}$$

$$\Delta Deposits_{i,t} = \alpha_2 + \beta_2 BankRisk_{i,t-k} + \gamma_2 X_{i,t-k} + \eta_{i,t}, \tag{3}$$

where $i = 1, ..., N$ and $t = 1, ..., T$, and N is the number of banks and T is the number of observations per bank. The panel is unbalanced, which implies that T

TABLE 2 Characteristics of the Deposit Insurance Scheme in Bolivia and Other Countries

Characteristics of Deposit Insurance Scheme	Bolivia	All Countries	High and Upper Middle Income	Lower Middle and Low Income
Compulsory participation	Yes	91.5	95.7	86.1
Permanent fund	Yes	83.1	73.9	94.6
Risk-adjusted premiums	No	24.4	19.6	30.6
Interbank deposits insured	No	17.3	6.7	30.6
Foreign currency deposits insured	Yes	76.5	75.6	77.8
Insurance limit per account/depositor	No	90.9	97.9	82.9
Fraction of banking sector deposits covered	60	52.4	54.8	49.7

This table compares the Bolivian deposit insurance scheme to deposit insurance schemes in other countries. Information about the characteristics of deposit insurance systems in other countries is taken from Demirgüç-Kunt, Karacaovali, and Laeven (2005). As of 2003, there are 88 countries with an explicit deposit insurance scheme, 47 of which are classified as High and Upper Middle Income countries. The column, "All Countries," reports the percentage of explicit deposit insurance schemes with a certain characteristic among countries with an explicit deposit insurance scheme. The columns "High and Upper Middle Income" and "Lower Middle and Low Income" report corresponding characteristics for these two groups.

varies across banks. $InterestRate_{i,t}$ is the interest rate on deposits in bank i at time t, while $\Delta Deposits_{i,t}$ is the growth rate of deposits in bank i at time t.[5] $BankRisk_{i,t-k}$ is a vector of publicly observable indicators of bank risk, and $X_{i,t-k}$ is a vector of control variables such as indicators of macroeconomic

---

5. Following the literature, the growth rate of deposits is used instead of the level because the latter depends more on bank characteristics (e.g., bank size and business orientation) than on supply and demand conditions in a given month. However, using growth rates, instead of levels, makes it more difficult to find statistically significant coefficients for the bank risk indicators. Even if bank risk affects the level of deposits, it might not affect its growth rate. Moreover, the growth rate series has a lot more noise than the level series. To reduce this, we use quarterly average growth rates instead of monthly growth rates. To ensure that our independent variables are predetermined, in the quantity equation we use $k=3$ (i.e., the explanatory variables are determined one period before the last period used to calculate the growth rate of deposits).

and political conditions. All explanatory variables are included with a lag because bank risk indicators are available publicly from the supervisory authority with a lag of about 20–30 days, and it can take some time before changes in bank risk and economic conditions lead to changes in deposit interest rates and volumes. The specific variables used in these vectors are standard in the literature and are discussed in the data section that follows. A positive β_1 and a negative β_2 are consistent with the presence of market discipline.

If explicit deposit insurance reduced depositors' incentives to monitor and discipline their banks, the sensitivity of deposit interest rates and volumes to bank risk should be weaker in the post-2001 period, when explicit deposit insurance was introduced. To test this hypothesis, we augment Eqs. (2), (3) as follows:

$$InterestRate_{i,t} = \alpha_1 + \beta_1 BankRisk_{i,t-k} + \theta_1 BankRisk_{i,t-k}DI_{t-k} + \delta_1 DI_{t-k} + \gamma_1 X_{i,t-k} + \varepsilon_{i,t}$$

$$(4)$$

$$\Delta Deposits_{i,t} = \alpha_2 + \beta_2 BankRisk_{i,t-k} + \theta_2 BankRisk_{i,t-k}DI_{t-k} + \delta_2 DI_{t-k} + + \gamma_2 X_{i,t-k} + \eta_{i,t},$$

$$(5)$$

where DI_{t-k} is a dummy variable that equals one when there is explicit deposit insurance, and equals zero otherwise. A decrease in market discipline following the introduction of explicit deposit insurance is consistent with $\beta_1 > 0$, $\theta_1 < 0$, $\beta_2 < 0$, and $\theta_2 > 0$.

Finally, we also examine whether the effect of deposit insurance on market discipline depends on the deposit insurance coverage rate, CR, by allowing for triple interactions with the coverage rate in equations Eqs. (4), (5).

4 Data

The study makes use of a detailed monthly bank-level dataset about the Bolivian banking sector from 1998:1 to 2003:12. The data and information necessary to create consistent time series (e.g., definitions of variables and changes in laws and regulations) were provided by the Bolivian Superintendence of Banks and Financial Entities (SBEF). To ensure comparability of the financial institutions in our sample, we focus our analysis on commercial banks. This does not involve any significant loss because commercial banks are a dominant part of the market, accounting for more than 80% of the total banking sector deposits and loans.

Table 3 provides an overview of all banks active in Bolivia during the sample period. There are 16 banks at the beginning of the sample period and 12 at the end. (One bank failed, another bank was taken over, one foreign bank left the Bolivian market, and one troubled bank was sold after intervention by the SBEF.) The five largest banks in Bolivia, two of which are foreign, have a market share of 70% of total assets. There are no government-owned or de novo banks during the sample period.[6] Six out of 12 banks that are present until

---

6. The last government-owned bank, Banco del Estado, was liquidated in 1994.

TABLE 3 Overview of Commercial Banks Operating in Bolivia During the Sample Period

Bank Name	Market Share		Ownership	Country of Parent Bank	Explicit Deposit Insurance From the Home Country
	January, 1998	December, 2003			
Banco Santa Cruz	22.23	11.21	Foreign Subsidiary (07-17-98)	Spain	No
Banco Nacional de Bolivia	12.94	16.24	Domestic		
Banco Industrial	11.22	15.95	Domestic		
Banco Mercantil	11.21	15.06	Domestic		
Banco de la Unión	9.55	8.35	Domestic		
Banco de Crédito de Bolivia	7.73	11.69	Foreign Subsidiary (12-30-92)	Peru	No
Banco Boliviano Americano	5.82		Domestic		
Banco Económico	5.50	6.31	Domestic		
BHN Multibanco	4.27		Domestic		
Banco de La Paz	3.75		Domestic		
Banco Ganadero	1.97	4.86	Domestic		
Banco Solidario	1.49	2.99	Foreign Owned (03-15-99)	Mixed	No

Continued

TABLE 3 Overview of Commercial Banks Operating in Bolivia During the Sample Period—cont'd

| Bank Name | Market Share | | Ownership | Country of Parent Bank | Explicit Deposit Insurance From the Home Country |
	January, 1998	December, 2003			
Citibank	1.30	5.77	Foreign Branch (10-10-66)	United States	No
Banco de la Nación Argentina	0.79	0.40	Foreign Branch (04-28-58)	Argentina	No
Banco Real/ABN Amro	0.37		Foreign Branch	Brazil/ Netherlands	No
Banco do Brasil	0.23	1.18	Foreign Branch (07-01-61)	Brazil	No

This table provides an overview of all commercial banks operating in Bolivia during the sample period, 1998:1 to 2003:12. "Market Share" is determined with respect to total assets. "Ownership" indicates whether a bank is domestic or foreign. Foreign banks are distinguished into subsidiaries or branches of foreign banks and foreign-owned banks. The latter refers to banks in which 50% of their shares or more are owned by foreign investors. The dates in parentheses indicate when a bank changed from domestic to foreign owned or the date a foreign branch started its operations in Bolivia. "Country of Parent Bank" indicates the country where the bank's parent company is headquartered. "Explicit Deposit Insurance from Home Country" indicates whether deposits of foreign-owned banks in Bolivia are insured by the home country.

the end of the sample period are foreign-owned, accounting for 33% of the total assets. Since 1993, foreign and domestic banks have been subject to the same regulations and, as of December 2001, both foreign and domestic banks are covered by the newly introduced deposit insurance scheme. None of the foreign banks in the sample is subject to explicit deposit insurance from its home country.

For the analysis, we study the interest rates and volumes of savings deposits denominated in US dollars, which represent more than 90% of the total banking sector deposits. Savings deposits allow us to better capture the sensitivity of both deposit rates and volumes to bank fundamentals. Interest rates and volumes on savings deposits can adjust at any point in time reflecting current economic conditions. By contrast, interest rates on time deposits are fixed for a set period and banks can freeze the withdrawal of time deposits until contractual maturity, while demand deposits pay little (to no) interest.

To capture bank characteristics and risk, we use a number of accounting ratios that are available publicly and have been used previously in the extant empirical literature. This includes equity to total assets, nonperforming loans to total assets, loan loss reserves to total assets, overhead expenses to total assets, returns to total assets, liquid assets to total assets, bank size measured as the log of total assets, and an indicator of foreign ownership (a dummy variable that equals one if more than 50% of a bank's equity is foreign owned).[7]

To control for macroeconomic conditions, we include the Bolivian growth rate of real GDP and the US inflation rate.[8] We also constructed a dummy variable to control for episodes of political instability. We control for two such events: violent confrontations between the police and the public because of the coca eradication policy introduced after pressure from the United States and international organizations, and the severe uncertainty in the financial markets during the elections of July 2002, when Evo Morales became a viable candidate.[9]

---

7. Bank size could be capturing a bank's market power and reputation, but it also could be capturing a lower probability of failure because of too-big-to-fail policies, better access to funds, better diversification of risk, etc. The foreign bank dummy could control for possible fixed-effect differences between domestic and foreign banks. In sensitivity analysis, it also interacts with bank-risk indicators to examine whether foreign banks are subject to more or less market discipline than domestic banks.

8. Including the inflation rate in the equation, instead of using real interest rates, allows for the estimated coefficient on the inflation rate to be different from one, indicating the degree to which banks compensate depositors for the inflation tax.

9. Before the elections of July 2002, there was severe uncertainty in the financial markets because Evo Morales—the leader of the coca growers, a congressman, and a presidential candidate—was gaining popularity. If Morales had won (he lost by a small margin), it would have meant a major change in the political and economic system toward socialism.

5 Results

Results in Table 4 provide strong evidence that depositors discipline banks by requiring higher interest rates and decreasing their deposits from riskier banks. Results in columns 1 and 2 indicate that banks with higher leverage capital ratio (equity-to-total assets) pay lower interest rates on their deposits and have a higher growth of deposits. Banks with higher nonperforming loans to total assets ratios pay higher interest rates on their deposits and have lower growth rate of deposits. The opposite instead holds for banks with higher loan loss reserves. Banks with higher overhead expenses to total assets—a proxy used for managerial inefficiency—pay higher interest rates on their deposits and have a lower growth rate of deposits. Bank profitability as captured by return on assets is found not to matter. Overall, these results are consistent with the hypothesis that depositors discipline their banks by decreasing their deposits and requiring higher premiums from riskier banks.

The estimated coefficients for liquidity, bank size, and foreign ownership suggest that banks with higher liquidity, larger banks, and foreign-owned banks have a lower demand for deposits because they all are associated with lower interest rates and lower deposit growth—though the foreign bank coefficient is not always statistically significant.

Interest rates on deposits are higher when the inflation rate and the growth rate of real GDP are higher. Both are found not to matter with respect to the growth rate of deposits.[10] Political instability instead is associated with both higher interest rates and a lower growth rate of deposits, suggesting that when systematic risk increases, depositors decrease their supply of deposits across the board.[11] As pointed out by Levy-Yeyati, Martinez Peria, and Schmukler (2004) such factors are particularly important for developing countries.

To evaluate the economic significance of our results, in columns 3 and 4 of Table 4 we also report marginal effects based on our estimates from columns 1 and 2. For continuous variables, we estimate the change in the dependent variable for a one-standard deviation increase in the explanatory variable. For discrete variables, we report the change in the dependent variable if the explanatory variable increases from zero to one. Results indicate that a one-standard deviation increase in each of the first four bank risk indicators is associated with 31–88 basis points increase in interest rates. This is quite large, considering that the average interest rate during the sample period is 3.7%. Marginal effects for growth of deposits are also quite large, ranging between 5.26% and 11.52%.

---

10. Results with respect to bank risk are similar if the macroeconomic controls and the political instability dummy variable are replaced with time dummies. Results are available on request.
11. We used robustness tests by experimenting with separate dummies for each event. This analysis indicated that the most important event of political instability was the uncertainty before and during the elections of 2002.

TABLE 4 Do Depositors Penalize Their Banks for Higher Risk-Taking?

	Coefficient Estimates		Marginal Effects	
	InterestRates	ΔDeposits	InterestRates	ΔDeposits
	(1)	(2)	(3)	(4)
Leverage capital ratio	−0.04***	1.30**	−0.34***	11.52**
	(0.01)	(0.66)	(0.09)	(5.85)
Nonperforming loans to total assets	0.05***	−1.78***	0.31***	−11.18***
	(0.01)	(0.40)	(0.07)	(2.51)
Loan loss reserves to total assets	−0.024***	1.55***	−0.88***	5.26***
	(0.03)	(0.54)	(0.10)	(1.83)
Overhead expenses to total assets	1.77***	−24.84***	0.42***	−5.91***
	(0.31)	(5.96)	(0.08)	(1.42)
Return on total assets	−0.002	0.17	−0.01	1.13
	(0.01)	(0.13)	(0.05)	(0.91)
Liquid assets to total assets	−0.02***	−0.49	−0.12***	−2.40
	(0.01)	(0.51)	(0.05)	(2.51)
Log of total assets	−0.46***	−6.25***	−0.59***	−7.88***
	(0.07)	(2.21)	(0.10)	(2.79)
Foreign bank	−0.47***	−1.38	−0.47***	−1.38
	(0.09)	(2.31)	(0.09)	(2.31)
US inflation rate	0.66***	0.22	0.49***	0.16
	(0.06)	(1.19)	(0.05)	(0.89)
Growth rate of real GDP in Bolivia	0.18***	−0.04	0.23***	−0.06
	(0.02)	(1.01)	(0.03)	(1.55)
Political instability	0.34**	−5.97**	0.34**	−5.97**
	(0.16)	(2.82)	(0.16)	(2.82)
Observations	842	863	842	863
R-square	0.74	0.14	0.74	0.14

Columns 1 and 2 report coefficient estimates for the interest rate and deposit growth equations. Columns 3 and 4 report marginal effects. For continuous (discrete) variables, the marginal effects indicate the estimated change in the dependent variable for a one-standard deviation increase (for an increase from zero to one) in the explanatory variable. Standard errors are reported in parentheses. ***, **, * denote statistical significance at the 1%, 5%, and 10% levels, respectively.

Next, we evaluate the introduction of explicit deposit insurance on depositors' incentives to discipline their banks by estimating Eqs. (4), (5). If explicit deposit insurance reduces depositor discipline, the sensitivity of deposits interest rates and the growth rate of deposits to bank risk should be weaker in the post-2001 period. Our findings, reported in Table 5, confirm this prediction. The four bank risk indicators previously found to capture market discipline—leverage ratio, nonperforming loans, loan loss reserves, and overhead expenses—have again signs consistent with market discipline ($\hat{\beta}_1 > 0$ and $\hat{\beta}_2 < 0$), while their interaction terms with DI_{t-k} have opposite signs ($\hat{\theta}_1 < 0$ and $\hat{\theta}_2 > 0$), resulting in sizable reductions to the original coefficients. The combined coefficients, $\hat{\beta}_1 + \hat{\theta}_1$ and $\hat{\beta}_2 + \hat{\theta}_2$, are 50%–90% smaller. Some of the combined coefficients are statistically significant with the expected signs, suggesting that the introduction of deposit insurance did not completely eliminate market discipline. In particular, the leverage capital ratio and the ratio of nonperforming loans to total assets are statistically significant in both equations, while the ratio of overhead expenses to total assets is significant only in the interest rate equation.

Next, we distinguish between small and large depositors. In particular, the data about the volume of deposits are available by size of account: accounts up to $500, accounts between $501 and $1000, accounts between $1001 and $5,000, etc., accounts with more than $2,000,000. The 14 size categories allow us to estimate Eqs. (3), (5) separately for accounts of different sizes and examine whether small and large depositors behave differently both before and after the introduction of explicit deposit insurance. This is of interest because deposit insurance systems often are motivated or designed to protect small depositors that might be unable or find it too expensive to monitor their banks.

Table 6 reports estimation results for Eq. (3) using alternative thresholds for small and large depositors. For small depositors, we report results for accounts with at most $1000, at most $5000, at most $10,000. For large depositors, we report results with a least $10,000, $20,000, or $30,000. Results indicate that sensitivity to bank risk emerges between $1000 and $5000. In particular, depositors with $1000 at most are not found to respond to risk. When the threshold is increased to $5000, small depositors start to respond in a fashion consistent with market discipline. These effects become stronger, in terms of size and significance, when the threshold is increased to $10,000. Stronger sensitivity is observed when we consider larger depositors with accounts of at least $10,000, $20,000, or $30,000. To put these figures in perspective, one should consider that the annual per capita Bolivia GDP around that time is about $1000. Consistent with earlier results, our findings in Table 7 indicate that deposit insurance reduced the sensitivity of large depositors to bank risk, but did not affect the behavior of small depositors, unless accounts greater than $10,000 are included in the definition of small. (We report results using two alternative thresholds, $10,000 and $20,000.) Overall, these results are consistent with the hypothesis that most of the market discipline comes from larger depositors and

TABLE 5 Did the Introduction of Explicit Deposit Insurance Decrease Depositor Discipline?

	InterestRates	DI interaction	ΔDeposits	DI interaction
	(1)	(2)	(3)	(4)
Leverage capital ratio	−0.07***	0.05***	1.50*	−0.74
	(0.01)	(0.01)	(0.84)	(0.73)
Nonperforming loans to total assets	0.03	−0.06***	−2.69***	1.61***
	(0.02)	(0.02)	(0.76)	(0.66)
Loan loss reserves to total assets	−0.36***	0.33***	4.60**	−4.22**
	(0.04)	(0.05)	(1.99)	(1.84)
Overhead expenses to total assets	2.44***	−1.36***	−35.77***	27.96*
	(0.34)	(0.50)	(11.60)	(15.69)
Return on total assets	0.03**	−0.04***	0.56	−0.49
	(0.01)	(0.01)	(0.45)	(0.46)
Liquid assets to total assets	−0.05***	0.05***	−0.11	−0.17
	(0.01)	(0.01)	(0.51)	(0.67)
Log of total assets	−0.42***		−6.50***	
	(0.09)		(2.31)	
Foreign bank	−0.43***		−2.79	

Continued

TABLE 5 Did the Introduction of Explicit Deposit Insurance Decrease Depositor Discipline?—cont'd

	InterestRates		ΔDeposits	
		DI interaction		DI interaction
	(1)	(2)	(3)	(4)
	(0.09)		(3.55)	
US Inflation rate	0.28***		−2.39	
	(0.05)		(2.18)	
Growth rate of real GDP in Bolivia	−0.01		−1.06	
	(0.03)		(1.22)	
Political instability	0.45**		−6.79***	
	(0.15)		(2.69)	
Observations	842		863	
R-square	0.81		0.15	

The table reports estimation results for the interest rate and deposits growth equations allowing for interactions between indicators of bank risk and the deposit insurance dummy, DI. The interaction terms are reported under the columns "DI interaction." DI equals one from December 2001 until December 2013 and equals zero otherwise. Standard errors are reported in parentheses. ***, **, * denote statistical significance at the 1%, 5%, and 10% levels, respectively.

TABLE 6 Do Small and Large Depositors Behave Differently?

	Small Depositors				Large Depositors	
	≤$1000	≤$5000	≤$10,000	>$10,000	>$20,000	>$30,000
Leverage capital ratio	0.26	0.27***	0.27***	1.29**	1.62**	1.63**
	(0.21)	(0.09)	(0.09)	(0.68)	(0.83)	(0.82)
Nonperforming loans to total assets	-0.32	-0.19*	-0.15**	-2.11***	-2.34***	-2.38***
	(0.22)	(0.10)	(0.07)	(0.50)	(0.57)	(0.57)
Loan loss reserves to total assets	-0.25	-0.08	0.03	2.14***	2.36***	2.41***
	(0.28)	(0.13)	(0.12)	(0.69)	(0.80)	(0.80)
Overhead expenses to total assets	-7.22***	-1.69	-2.08**	-27.14***	-29.55***	-29.25***
	(2.84)	(1.29)	(0.99)	(7.07)	(8.24)	(8.29)
Return to total assets	-0.07	-0.05	-0.01	0.23	0.28	0.29
	(0.09)	(0.07)	(0.04)	(0.15)	(0.18)	(0.19)
Liquid assets to total assets	-0.27	-0.12	-0.02	-0.68	-0.89	-0.93
	(0.20)	(0.09)	(0.08)	(0.55)	(0.65)	(0.64)
Log of total assets	-2.88**	-0.09	0.18	-7.39***	-7.88***	-8.00***
	(1.47)	(0.60)	(0.43)	(2.40)	(2.65)	(2.64)
Foreign bank dummy	1.11	-0.43	-0.78**	-1.64	-2.50	-2.36
	(0.99)	(0.44)	(0.39)	(2.47)	(2.95)	(2.94)

Continued

TABLE 6 Do Small and Large Depositors Behave Differently?—cont'd

	Small Depositors				Large Depositors	
	≤$1000	≤$5000	≤$10,000	>$10,000	>$20,000	>$30,000
US inflation rate	−1.79***	−1.04**	0.23	−0.56	−0.71	−0.81
	(0.63)	(0.44)	(0.31)	(1.22)	(1.36)	(1.38)
Growth rate of real GDP in Bolivia	0.48	0.23	0.18	−1.45	−1.79	−1.83
	(0.47)	(0.23)	(0.20)	(1.36)	(1.60)	(1.60)
Political instability dummy	−0.48	0.95	−1.09	−7.63***	−8.90***	−8.42**
	(1.50)	(1.21)	(0.76)	(3.09)	(3.58)	(3.57)
Observations	834	839	839	844	844	844
R-square	0.10	0.09	0.10	0.13	0.13	0.13

*The table reports estimation results for the deposits growth equations by size of account. The columns under Small Depositors report specifications for the growth of deposits for accounts with at most, $1000, $5000, or $10,000, respectively. The columns under Large Depositors report specifications for the growth of deposits for accounts with at least $10,000, $20,000, or $30,000. Standard errors are reported in parentheses. ***, **, * denote statistical significance at the 1%, 5%, and 10% levels, respectively.*

TABLE 7 Did the Introduction of Explicit Deposit Insurance Affect Small and Large Depositors Differently?

	Small Depositors				Large Depositors			
	≤$10,000	DI	≤$20,000	DI	>$10,000	DI	>$20,000	DI
Leverage capital ratio	0.30*** (0.11)	−0.08 (0.11)	0.43*** (0.11)	2.06* (1.12)	1.61* (0.92)	−0.83 (0.81)	2.07* (1.11)	−1.15 (0.96)
Nonperforming loans to total assets	−0.25** (0.13)	0.22* (0.12)	−0.36*** (0.14)	−3.54*** (1.01)	−3.17*** (0.88)	2.00*** (0.78)	−3.49*** (1.01)	2.18*** (0.90)
Loan loss reserves to total assets	−0.08 (0.29)	−0.28 (0.30)	0.60* (0.33)	6.90*** (2.73)	5.94*** (2.28)	−5.53*** (2.10)	6.80*** (2.70)	−6.35*** (2.50)
Overhead expenses to total assets	−2.41* (1.38)	4.70** (2.03)	−5.39*** (1.80)	−45.39*** (15.95)	−39.80*** (13.34)	32.12* (17.32)	−44.64*** (15.77)	40.48** (20.71)
Return to total assets	−0.04 (0.08)	0.04 (0.09)	0.11 (0.10)	0.86 (0.59)	0.70 (0.49)	−0.64 (0.50)	0.94* (0.57)	−0.89 (0.59)
Liquid assets to total assets	−0.04 (0.10)	0.05 (0.13)	0.10 (0.12)	−0.54 (0.67)	−0.38 (0.58)	−0.01 (0.73)	−0.59 (0.67)	0.18 (0.83)
Log of total assets	0.37 (0.46)		0.25 (0.42)	−7.41*** (2.86)	−7.02*** (2.57)		−7.43*** (2.84)	
Foreign bank dummy	−0.45 (0.46)		−1.33*** (0.52)	−4.27 (4.31)	−2.99 (3.62)		−4.16 (4.26)	

Continued

TABLE 7 Did the Introduction of Explicit Deposit Insurance Affect Small and Large Depositors Differently?—cont'd

| | Small Depositors | | | | Large Depositors | |
| | ≤$10,000 | ≤$20,000 | >$10,000 | | >$20,000 | |
	DI	DI	DI		DI	
US inflation rate	-0.59*	-0.12	-3.61	-2.75	-3.52	
	(0.35)	(0.37)	(2.83)	(2.39)	(2.81)	
Growth rate of real GDP in Bolivia	-0.25	-0.07	-1.67	-1.35	-1.68	
	(0.20)	(0.19)	(1.60)	(1.37)	(1.60)	
Political instability dummy	-1.39*	-1.41*	-9.48***	-8.38***	-9.05***	
	(0.76)	(0.78)	(3.34)	(2.92)	(3.35)	
Observations	839	839	844	844	844	
R-square	0.11	0.18	0.14	0.14	0.14	

The table reports estimation results for the deposits growth equations by size of account allowing for interactions between indicators of bank risk and the deposit insurance dummy, DI. The interaction terms are reported under the columns "DI," which equals one from December 2001 until December 2013 and equals zero otherwise. The columns under Large Depositors report specifications for the growth of deposits for accounts with, at most, $1000, $5000, or $10,000, respectively. The columns under Large Depositors report specifications for the growth of deposits for accounts with at least $10,000, $20,000, or $30,000. Standard errors are reported in parentheses. ***, **, * Depositors report specifications for the growth of deposits for accounts with at least $10,000, $20,000, or $30,000. Standard errors are reported in parentheses. ***, **, * denote statistical significance at the 1%, 5%, and 10% levels, respectively.

that the introduction of the explicit deposit insurance scheme affected mainly those who were active in the first place. These findings support a deposit insurance scheme with limited coverage per depositor.

Next, to examine whether the effect of deposit insurance depends on the coverage rate, we also estimate Eqs. (4), (5), exploiting the variation in the coverage rates across banks. The results, presented in the first panel of Table 8, show that the reduction in market discipline depends positively on the coverage rate (i.e., the higher the coverage rate, the larger the reduction in market discipline). In Fig. 2, we report the values and the statistical significance of the combined coefficients, $\hat{\beta}_1 + \hat{\lambda}_1 C_{i,t-k}$ and $\hat{\beta}_2 + \hat{\lambda}_2 C_{i,t-k}$, for different values of $C_{i,t-k}$. Fig. 2 shows clearly that as the coverage rate increases to more than 60%, many of the coefficients start to become insignificant. More importantly, when the coverage rate is 100%, none of the coefficients remains statistically significant.

6 Conclusions

This paper examines the effect of explicit deposit insurance on market discipline using the experiences of Bolivia between 1998 and 2003. The sample period is characterized by a severe recession that significantly weakened the health of the banking sector. Therefore, depositors have reasons to worry about the safety of their deposits. More importantly, during the sample period, only one major regulatory reform was adopted—the introduction of a deposit insurance system in December 2001. This makes it possible to investigate the effect of explicit deposit insurance on market discipline by comparing the behavior of depositors before and after the introduction of this system. Moreover, the characteristics of the Bolivian system allow us to examine whether the effect of deposit insurance depends on the coverage rate, without having to compare the behavior of small and large depositors.

In contrast to other studies about developing countries, we find a strong link between bank fundamentals and the supply of deposits, consistent with the hypothesis that market discipline was at work prior to the introduction of explicit deposit insurance. In particular, we find that an increase in bank risk leads to higher interest rates and lower deposits. Our results also suggest that most of the market discipline comes from large depositors.

More importantly, we find that the introduction of explicit deposit insurance caused a significant reduction in market discipline (i.e., market discipline is 50%–90% smaller after the introduction of deposit insurance). Exploiting the variation in the coverage rate across banks and time, we show that the effect of deposit insurance on market discipline depends on the coverage rate: the higher the coverage rate, the lower the decrease in market discipline. As the coverage rate increases to more than 60%, market discipline is reduced significantly, and it is completely eliminated when the coverage rate reaches 100%.

These results indicate that, absent credibility issues, explicit deposit insurance systems can substantially undermine depositors' sensitivity to bank risk.

TABLE 8 Does the Effect of Deposit Insurance Depends on the Deposit Insurance Coverage Rate?

	Panel 1				Panel 2			
	Interest Rates		Deposits		Interest Rates		Deposits	
	Coverage		Coverage		Coverage		Coverage	
Leverage capital ratio	−0.07***	0.07***	1.47*	−1.39	−0.06***	0.06***	1.47*	−1.53
	(0.01)	(0.02)	(0.80)	(1.27)	(0.01)	(0.02)	(0.82)	(1.29)
Nonperforming loans to total assets	0.01	−0.02	−2.32***	1.99*	0.01	−0.02	−2.47***	2.32**
	(0.02)	(0.03)	(0.69)	(1.08)	(0.02)	(0.03)	(0.69)	(1.08)
Loan loss reserves to total assets	−0.30***	0.33***	4.06**	−5.57**	−0.28***	0.34***	4.43**	−6.44**
	(0.04)	(0.06)	(1.71)	(2.56)	(0.04)	(0.07)	(1.82)	(2.90)
Overhead expenses to total assets	2.26***	−1.40*	−34.35***	38.80*	2.19***	−1.79**	−35.50***	41.35*
	(0.32)	(0.79)	(10.54)	(21.13)	(0.32)	(0.84)	(11.05)	(24.22)
Return to total assets	0.02	−0.03*	0.53	−0.63	0.02	−0.02	0.53	−0.66
	(0.01)	(0.02)	(0.42)	(0.51)	(0.01)	(0.02)	(0.45)	(0.56)
Liquid assets to total assets	−0.04***	0.06***	−0.14	0.09	−0.04***	0.06**	−0.15	0.29
	(0.01)	(0.02)	(0.51)	(0.96)	(0.01)	(0.02)	(0.50)	(1.02)
Log of total assets	−0.45***		−6.93***		−0.44***		−7.09***	
	(0.09)		(2.28)		(0.09)		(2.29)	
Foreign bank dummy	−0.45***		−3.78		−0.50***		−3.88	
	(0.09)		(3.42)		(0.10)		(3.70)	

TABLE 8 Does the Effect of Deposit Insurance Depends on the Deposit Insurance Coverage Rate?—cont'd

| | Panel 1 | | | | Panel 2 | | | |
| | Interest Rates | | Deposits | | Interest Rates | | Deposits | |
	Coverage		Coverage		Coverage		Coverage	
US inflation rate	0.32***		−2.14		0.38***		−2.27	
	(0.06)		(1.88)		(0.06)		(1.99)	
Growth rate of real GDP in Bolivia	0.03		−1.00		0.02		−0.99	
	(0.03)		(1.20)		(0.03)		(1.19)	
Political instability dummy	0.22		−8.16**		0.22		−8.39**	
	(0.18)		(3.67)		(0.18)		(3.83)	
Observations	842		863		863		863	
R-square	0.78		0.15		0.78		0.15	

For the interest rates columns, the dependent variable is the interest rate on savings deposits, and for the deposits columns, the dependent variable is the average growth rate of savings deposits. Panel 1 investigates whether the effect of deposit insurance depends on the deposit insurance coverage rate. Panel 2 estimates the specification reported in panel 1 using instrumental variables estimation. To determine the instrument for the coverage rate, we use banks' liabilities structure one year before the introduction of deposit insurance. The "Coverage" columns show the coefficients of the interaction terms between the coverage rate and indicators of bank risk. Standard errors are reported in parentheses. ***, **, * denote statistical significance at the 1%, 5%, and 10% levels, respectively.

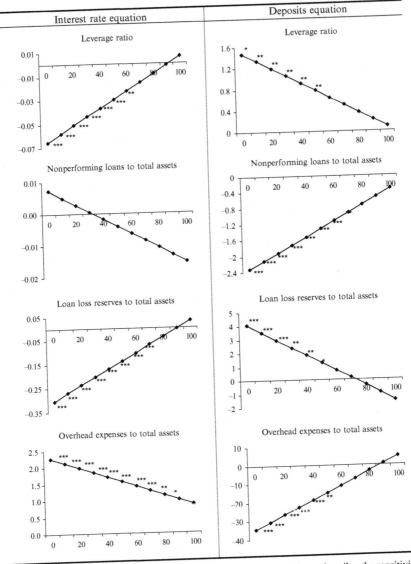

FIG. 2 Market discipline and deposit insurance coverage rate. This figure describes the sensitivity of interest rates and deposits on bank risk for different values of deposit insurance coverage (CR). These estimates are calculated using estimates from Table 8, Panel 2. The vertical axis measures the combined coefficients and horizontal axes deposit insurance coverage rate.

These findings also emphasize the need for high degrees of co-insurance and "tailor-made" systems that preserve the incentives of a critical mass of depositors, willing and able to monitor and discipline their banks. In this case, the deposit insurance system covered a significant part of the deposits of those who were active in first place (i.e., the large depositors), and thus caused an almost complete elimination of market discipline. These results provide support to schemes with deposit insurance limits per depositor. Such systems provide support to small, unsophisticated depositors, while maintaining large depositors' sensitivity toward the bank's risk-taking.

References

Baer, H., Brewer, E., 1986. Uninsured deposits as a source of market discipline: some new evidence. In: Economic Perspectives. Federal Reserve Bank of Chicago, pp. 23–31.

Barajas, A., Steiner, R., 2000. Depositor behavior and market discipline in Colombia. (IMF Working Paper 00/214). International Monetary Fund, Washington, DC.

Billet, M.T., Garfinkel, J.A., O'Neal, E.S., 1998. The cost of market versus regulatory discipline in banking. Journal of Financial Economics 48, 333–358.

Calomiris, C.W., 1999. Building an incentive-compatible safety net. Journal of Banking and Finance 23 (10), 1499–1519.

Calomiris, C.W., Powell, A., 2000. Can emerging market bank regulators establish credible discipline? The case of Argentina, mimeo. Banco Central de la Republica Argentina.

Cook, D.O., Spellman, L.J., 1991. Federal financial guarantees and the occasional market pricing of default risk: evidence from insured deposits. Journal of Banking & Finance 15 (6), 1113–1130.

Demirgüç-Kunt, A., Huizinga, H., 2004. Market discipline and deposit insurance. Journal of Monetary Economics 51 (2), 375–399.

Demirgüç-Kunt, A., Karacaovali, B., Laeven, L., 2005. Deposit insurance around the World: a comprehensive database. (Working Paper 3628). World Bank, Washington, DC.

Dewatripont, M., Tirole, J., 1994. The prudential regulation of banks. MIT Press, Cambridge, MA.

Diamond, D.W., Dybvig, P.H., 1983. Bank runs, deposit insurance, and liquidity. Journal of Political Economy 91 (3), 401–419.

Ellis, D.M., Flannery, M.J., 1992. Does the debt market assess large banks' risk? Time series evidence from money center CDS. Journal of Monetary Economics 30 (3), 481–502.

Flannery, M.J., 1982. Retail bank deposits as quasi-fixed factors of production. American Economic Review 72 (3), 527–536.

Flannery, M.J., Sorescu, S.M., 1996. Evidence of market discipline in subordinated debenture yields: 1983-1991. Journal of Finance 51 (4), 1347–1377.

Furfine, C., 2001. Banks as Monitors of Other Banks: evidence from the overnight federal funds market. Journal of Business 74 (1), 33–57.

Hannan, T.H., Hanweck, G.A., 1988. Bank insolvency risk and the market for large certificates of deposit. Journal of Money, Credit, and Banking 20 (2), 203–211.

Kane, E.J., 1989. The S&L insurance mess: how did it happen? Urban Institute Press, Washington, DC.

Kroszner, R.S., Strahan, P.E., 2001. Obstacles to optimal policy: the interplay of politics and economics in shaping bank supervision and regulation reforms. In: Mishkin, F.S. (Ed.), Prudential supervision: What works and what doesn't. University of Chicago Press, Chicago, pp. 233–273.

Laeven, L., 2004. The political economy of deposit insurance. Journal of Financial Services Research 26 (3), 201–224.

Levy-Yeyati, E., Martínez Pería, M.S., Schmukler, S., 2004. Market discipline in emerging economies: beyond bank fundamentals. In: Hunter, W., Kaufman, G., Tsatsaronis, K. (Eds.), C. Borio. MIT Press, Market Discipline Across Countries and Industries, pp. 135–146.

Martinez Peria, M.S., Schmukler, S.L., 2001. Do depositors punish banks for bad behavior? Market discipline, deposit insurance, and banking crises. Journal of Finance 56 (3), 1029–1051.

Park, S., 1995. Market discipline by depositors: evidence from reduced form equations. Quarterly Review of Economics and Finance 35 (3), 497–514.

Further Reading

Cook, D.O., Spellman, L.J., 1994. Repudiation risk and restitution costs: toward understanding premiums on insured deposits. Journal of Money, Credit, and Banking 26 (3), 439–459.

D'Amato, L., Grubisic, E., Powel, A., 1997. Contagion, bank fundamentals or macroeconomic shock? An empirical analysis of the Argentine 1995 banking problems, mimeo. Banco Central de la Republica Argentina.

Kane, E.J., 1987. Who should learn what from the failure and delayed bailout of the ODGF? In: Proceedings of a conference on bank structure and competition. Federal Reserve Bank of Chicago, pp. 306–326.

Klein, M.A., 1971. A theory of the banking firm. Journal of Money, Credit, and Banking 3 (2), 205–218.

Park, S., Peristiani, S., 1998. Market discipline by thrift depositors. Journal of Money, Credit, and Banking 30 (3), 347–364.

Chapter 27

Export Pricing at the Firm Level With Panel Data ☆

Sofia Anyfantaki*,†, Sarantis Kalyvitis*, Margarita Katsimi*,‡ and Eirini Thomaidou*

*Athens University of Economics and Business, Athens, Greece, †Bank of Greece, Athens, Greece, ‡CESifo, Munich, Germany

Chapter Outline

1 Introduction

Given the importance of exports for sustainable growth and long-run welfare, extensive theoretical and empirical literature that attempts to explore and explain the behavior of exporting firms has emerged. This literature, prompted by the availability of large datasets at the micro level, has documented a number of robust facts about the substantial and systematic variation in export performance across firms. These include the higher probability of exporting by more productive firms, which have greater size and higher export revenues, enter more markets, pay higher wages, and are skill and capital intensive. Initiated by the work of Melitz (2003) and Bernard, Eaton, Jensen, and Kortum (2003), the literature has emphasized the gains from intra-industry trade in markets with heterogeneous companies. Not surprisingly, empirical research with

---

☆ Disclaimer: The views expressed in this article are those of the authors and do not necessarily reflect those of the Bank of Greece or the Eurosystem.

Panel Data Econometrics. https://doi.org/10.1016/B978-0-12-815859-3.00027-5

firm-level data, to a large extent, has replaced traditional approaches with standard trade statistics at the product level.[1]

Stylized facts also show that exporters have a different pricing behavior compared to companies that serve only the domestic market. Export prices, defined as the ratio of export value over quantity for a given firm-product-destination category (also referred to as unit values), are differentiated depending on the characteristics of the destination country and firm attributes. Notably, the empirical regressions about export pricing face the challenge of embedding mechanisms closely related to prices, such as quality, markups, and financial frictions, which are largely unobservable or hard to quantify.

In this chapter, we review the growing empirical literature dealing with the determinants of export prices, a topic that, up to now, has received relatively less attention than other strands that have examined exporting decisions at the company level (for instance, the entry/exit choice into/from the export market, or the determinants of total value and volume of exports). The study discusses how export pricing has been tackled in related empirical papers and how the main results identify theoretical channels, although in many cases ambiguities remain. A newly compiled panel dataset from Greek exporting firms that covers the period 2003–15 then is used to present a number of estimated regressions with export price as the dependent variable. These specifications link export prices to main destination features, such as distance, remoteness, size, and income (gravity-type regressions) and company attributes, and it is shown how they nest the main economic hypotheses introduced in theoretical models.

The rest of the chapter is structured as follows. Section 2 reviews the empirical literature about export pricing with emphasis placed on microeconomic studies that link firm-level data with destination characteristics. Section 3 reports evidence from studies about export quality and prices, and Section 4 reviews the literature about frictions in export pricing. Section 5 describes the dataset of Greek exporters and presents results from empirical specifications that are comparable with the rest of the literature. Section 6 offers conclusions.

2 Export Pricing With Micro Data: Gravity-Type Models

The main motivation for studying export pricing comes from the frequent documentation of systematic heterogeneity in the prices charged for the same traded products. Starting with Schott (2004), it has been established that, even within narrowly defined product categories, average prices differ systematically with the characteristics of exporting countries, such as skill and capital intensity. In an extensive study using trade data about export pricing,

---

1. Bernard, Jensen, Redding, and Schott (2007, 2012), Redding (2011), Melitz and Trefler (2012), and Melitz and Redding (2014) provide extensive surveys of related theoretical and empirical literature.

Baldwin and Harrigan (2011) establish that disaggregated export unit values are related positively to distance—a result also found by Hummels and Skiba (2004)—and negatively related to market size.

Because many companies set different prices across destinations, even within narrowly defined product categories, explaining product-level findings about export price variations requires firm-level data. The main empirical studies about the determinants of export pricing with firm-level data are, in chronological order: Bastos and Silva (2010) for Portugal, Martin (2012) for France, Manova and Zhang (2012) for China, Harrigan, Ma, and Shlychkov (2015) for the United States, de Lucio, Mínguez, Minondo, and Requena (2016) for Spain, and Görg, Halpern, and Muraközy (2017) for Hungary. These papers use gravity-type regressions that relate export prices with destination characteristics, such as size (captured by gross domestic product), income (captured by gross domestic product per capita), and market toughness (proxied by distance and remoteness). Some of these papers also control for firm attributes, such as size and productivity. In this subsection, this strand of empirical literature is reviewed and the main implications are presented.

Bastos and Silva (2010), using a cross-section dataset of Portuguese exporters for 2005, provide evidence that firms set higher prices in richer and more distant countries, whereas they find no effect of market size on prices. These relationships reflect not only the typical sorting of heterogeneous firms across markets, but also the within-firm variation of prices across destinations. Within product categories, higher-productivity firms tend to set higher prices to a given destination and also serve more distant markets, which are interpreted as evidence of quality differentiation.

Martin (2012) uses shipments of French exporters for 2003 and finds that companies charge higher free-on-board unit values on exports to more distant countries. His results indicate that, as distance doubles, the price charged by an exporter increases by 3.5%, whereas the estimated elasticity is 0.05, which is remarkably close to the one obtained by Bastos and Silva (2010) for Portugal (0.052). Income has also a positive impact on prices as expected, whereas the size of the country does not turn out significant. Notably, prices within more differentiated industries are more responsive to changes in distance, which indicates that in these sectors, firms have more room to adjust their markups or their quality across destinations. Overall, the estimates imply that prices in more distant destinations are higher not only because distance increases transport costs, but also because companies charge higher prices net of transportation costs.

The most detailed study about the behavior of export prices is the one by Manova and Zhang (2012), who focus on Chinese exporters for 2005 and establish some stylized facts about export pricing at the firm level. Among other researchers, they show that, within narrowly defined product categories, firms charge higher prices in richer, larger, bilaterally more distant and less remote economies (with the elasticity with respect to distance amounting to 0.01). Notably, companies earn more revenues from a specific good in markets where they set higher prices, a pattern that is more prominent in richer countries and for goods with bigger potential for quality upgrading. The authors also find that, within each product, firms serving more destinations offer a wider range of export prices, especially for products with greater scope for quality differentiation.

Harrigan et al. (2015) use data from US firms for 2002 and establish that, within narrow product categories, exporters charge higher prices in more distant countries. The effect of distance on prices is the largest one compared to those reported in other studies (yielding an elasticity in the vicinity of 0.19). The authors also report that more productive firms set higher prices, whereas skill-intensity and capital-intensity firms have a positive and a negative effect on prices, respectively. In contrast, they find no significant effect of company size on export pricing. Their overall assessment is that these effects are indicative of quality, rather than cost, competition.

In a study with data from Spanish manufacturing exporters for 2014, de Lucio et al. (2016) add the transaction dimension to the analysis of export pricing. They confirm that more productive exporters set higher prices and that export prices are higher in more distant and richer destinations. In particular, they demonstrate that doubling the distance leads to a 3.1% increase in prices. In addition, they show that differences in company prices at the product-destination level are associated with the number of varieties covered by each product category, the volume of transactions, and the vertical differentiation of products within firms. Their findings point toward quality competition as a major driving force of pricing within Spanish exporters.

Görg et al. (2017) explore the relationship between export unit values and destination characteristics using panel data from Hungarian firms for 1998–2003 and show that export unit values increase with distance. Similarly to Martin (2012) and de Lucio et al. (2016), they find that a doubling of distance is associated with a 7.5% increase in average product prices. Prices also are positively correlated with destination income and negatively with destination size. These patterns of price discrimination across markets are consistent with firms shipping higher-quality varieties to higher-income and more distant markets, but also with companies charging variable markups across markets (pricing-to-market).

In summary, the common finding across the aforementioned papers is that exporters set higher prices in more distant and richer destinations. In contrast to the prediction of Melitz-type theoretical models with heterogeneous firms that more productive firms self-select into exporting setting lower prices because of lower marginal costs, there is ample evidence that higher-productivity exporters set higher prices. These findings can be justified by several not-mutually-exclusive mechanisms: exporting firms might sell a range of varieties within product categories with different levels of quality across markets, charge variable markups across markets, or be subject to other frictions that affect their pricing decisions. In the following sections, these channels and their implications for export prices at the firm level are explored in the context of related empirical studies.

3   Quality and Firm Export Pricing

A strand of the literature about exports has explored the role of product-quality differentiation for export pricing and has found that consumers are willing to pay a premium for high-quality, high-cost varieties, pointing out the importance of the quality of goods produced and exported for economic outcomes (see, among others, Hallak, 2006; Hallak & Schott, 2011; Hallak & Sivadasan, 2013; Hausmann, Hwang, & Rodrik, 2007; Hummels & Klenow, 2005; Sutton & Trefler, 2016; Verhoogen, 2008). In this vein, Schott (2008) has documented a large difference in product prices within the most disaggregated level of product classification: US consumers pay less for goods that are "Made in China" than for similar goods "Made in OECD" (Organization for Economic Co-operation and Development countries). Fontagné, Gaulier, and Zignago (2008) report that, on average, Japanese export prices are 2.9 times higher than Chinese, for the same products shipped to the same markets within the same year. Their empirical analysis indicates that the products of developed countries are not directly competing with those of developing countries. These stylized facts broadly support models where consumers value quality, but quality is expensive to produce. Consumers choose goods on the basis of quality-adjusted prices and are willing to pay a higher price for an expensive, high-quality good (Harrigan et al., 2015).

As heterogeneous companies compete on both prices and quality, high-quality firms might therefore become (growing) exporters in spite of charging higher prices: The most profitable firms use higher-quality inputs to produce upgraded versions of their products and sell them, in possibly the toughest markets, at higher prices. Johnson (2012) estimates a multicountry trade model with heterogeneous firms using sectoral level data to examine within-exporter variation in prices across destinations. In accordance with the evidence reported by the papers surveyed in the previous section, Johnson finds that prices in the majority of sectors are increasing in the difficulty of entering the destination market, proxied by distance. The overall picture is in line with the Alchian and Allen (1964) conjecture, which states that the demand for higher-quality (and more expensive) products should increase with transport costs, an effect known as "shipping the good apples out." Moreover, several studies have found that demand for high-quality goods increases with income per capita (Linder, 1961). The main implication is that, in addition to the efficiency sorting of heterogeneous exporters, a quality sorting of heterogeneous firms across markets arises, i.e., within product categories, higher-productivity companies tend to ship greater quantities at higher prices to a given destination, consistent with higher quality. Eckel, Iacovone, Javorcik, and Neary (2015) examine the implications of cost-based versus quality-based competence for multiproduct Mexican exporting (and nonexporting) firms and find that firms in (non) differentiated sectors exhibit (cost) quality competence.

Can export quality be linked to export pricing? The main challenge here is that product quality is unobserved. Empirical literature has attempted to exploit the availability of trade data at a highly disaggregated level, and readily observable prices (unit values), calculated as values over quantities, have been used as a proxy for export quality. This assumption, however, suffers from several shortcomings generated by differences in the composition of goods, production costs, and pricing strategies within a given product category across exporters. If, for example, exporters that use lower-cost inputs are systematically less productive than their competitors and sell more expensive varieties, then by measuring relative quality with relative prices, a positive effect on output quality can be detected spuriously. Moreover, standard supply or demand shocks will affect equilibrium prices, without necessarily affecting product quality. In a seminal contribution about assessing quality with trade data, Khandelwal (2010) exploits price and quantity information to estimate the quality of US imports, based on a straightforward intuition extensively used in the industrial organization literature: "conditional on price, [...] higher market shares are assigned higher quality" (Khandelwal, p. 1451).

The main empirical evidence about export pricing and quality comes from studies with trade data. Hummels and Klenow (2005) infer quality, by adopting the premise that if large exporters systematically sell high quantities at high prices, then they also will produce higher-quality goods. The authors show that richer countries export higher quantities of each good at modestly higher prices, consistent with higher quality. Hallak and Schott (2011) rely on trade balances to identify quality: When observed export prices are constant, countries with trade surpluses seemingly offer higher quality than countries running trade deficits. Consumers are assumed to care about price relative to quality in choosing among products and, therefore, two countries with the same export prices but different global trade balances must have products with different levels of quality. Vandenbussche (2014) develops an export quality indicator based on Di Comité, Thisse, and Vandenbussche (2014), which disentangles quality (vertical differentiation) from cost and taste effects (horizontal differentiation), to generate quality ranks of EU manufacturing products over the period 2007–11. The rankings confirm that quality upgrading results in higher willingness to pay by consumers and, therefore, quality offers a way to escape cost competition. Feenstra and Romalis (2014) add a supply-side dimension by arguing that, as foreign demand rises, less efficient exporters enter with lower quality, thus generating a negative relation between trade and quality. They decompose available unit values of internationally traded goods into quality and quality-adjusted price components using an endogenous quality decision, in order to aggregate individual products to industry-level indexes of export quality and prices. Henn, Papageorgiou, Romero, and Spatafora (2017) use reduced-form quality-augmented gravity-type equations based on Hallak (2006), to estimate aggregate and product export quality indices and find that quality upgrading is particularly rapid during the early stages of development.

At the firm level, Crozet, Head, and Mayer (2012) obtain direct assessments of quality for one exported product (French champagne) and show that higher quality firms export more quantities at higher prices, with quality explaining roughly one-third of export prices. Gervais (2015) shows that product demand might play an important role in explaining plant outcomes in addition to plant efficiency and obtains plant-level measures of product quality. The author uses US Census firm-level data and confirms that prices increase in quality after controlling for productivity (which affects prices negatively). Moreover, price variations understate variation in product quality across plants: a one standard deviation increase in estimated quality is associated with a half-standard deviation increase in price.

4 Frictions in Firm Export Pricing

4.1 Markups and Exchange Rate Pass-Throughs

Markups are an integrated component of export pricing in trade models, which typically adopt the assumption of monopolistic competition. In the Melitz (2003) model with CES preferences and iceberg trade costs, however, heterogeneous exporters charge a constant markup above marginal cost across countries and price discrimination is absent (see, for example, Arkolakis, Costinot, & Rodríguez-Clare, 2012). Melitz and Ottaviano (2008) extend the Melitz (2003) setup and use linear demand to introduce endogenous variations in markups across destinations, which respond to the toughness of competition in a market. They show that larger markets exhibit tougher competition in the form of hosting more, and larger, competing firms, leading to lower markups and prices. Gopinath, Gourinchas, Hsieh, and Li (2011) offer ample evidence in favor of market segmentation and show that markup gaps contribute to the variability in price gaps, suggesting that pricing-to-market takes place at the wholesale level.

De Loecker and Warzynski (2012) introduce a methodology to estimate firm-level markups and use data from Slovenian manufacturing exporting firms to establish that they charge higher markups on-average, after controlling for productivity, and that company markups increase upon export entry. De Loecker, Goldberg, Khandelwal, and Pavcnik (2016) extend this framework to obtain markups for large multiproduct Indian exporting firms and show that the decline in marginal costs because of trade liberalization does not translate to equal price declines, because markups increase. Gullstrand, Olofsdotter, and Thede (2014) analyze the relationship between price variations in products across export destinations for firms in the Swedish food supply chain and find that exporters that have greater ability to discriminate between markets are associated with a higher markup.

On top of the evidence that exporters adjust, at least partially, their markups as part of their pricing strategies, there is also evidence that export prices do not change proportionately in response to changes in exchange rates. In an extensive study about the effects of exchange rate movements on export pricing, Berman, Martin, and Mayer (2012) show that high-performance French exporting firms largely absorb exchange rate movements in their markups (pricing-to-market). Chatterjee, Dix-Carneiro, and Vichyanond (2013) and Li, Ma, and Xu (2015) observe similar patterns for Brazilian and Chinese exporting firms, respectively. Caselli, Chatterjee, and Woodland (2017) show that Mexican exporters increase their markups following a real depreciation and that the increase of markups is significantly higher for higher-performance products, which in turn translates into heterogeneity in producer price responses. Kalyvitis, Katsimi, Pappa, and Restrepo (2017) find that initially high-productivity Greek exporters raised their prices and markups following euro adoption, a finding that is interpreted as evidence of a positive demand shift for these firms. Chen and Juvenal (2016) use a sample of Argentinean wine exporters and confirm that pricing-to-market increases with firm productivity. Moreover, they link export prices, exchange rate pass-through and quality by showing that pricing-to-market rises with quality: Prices rise higher in response to real exchange rate shifts as the quality of the wines exported rises.

4.2 Financial Constraints

The cost needs of exporters are inherently different compared to firms that serve the domestic market. Specifically, fixed and variable costs tend to be higher for exporters and need to be paid up front because of long time lags between production and sales, for example, because of the need to build advertising and distributional networks, acquire specific legislative and regulatory information and requirements, and customize products. Also, the realization of revenues is uncertain and typically involves more complex, riskier, and less enforceable contracts between the lender and the borrower. As a result, potential exporters must have enough liquidity at hand and, not surprisingly, there is empirical evidence that financial constraints affect exporting decisions (Bellone, Musso, Nesta, & Schiavo, 2010; Berman & Héricourt, 2010; Feenstra, Li, & Yu, 2014; Greenaway, Guariglia, & Kneller, 2007; Manova, Wei, & Zhang, 2015; Minetti & Zhu, 2011; Muûls, 2015). When financial constraints affect variable and especially marginal costs, export prices are affected as well, as more credit-constrained exporters face higher marginal costs (Feenstra et al., 2014; Manova, 2013).

Financial constraints, therefore, can play a central role in export pricing decisions. Secchi, Tamagni, and Tomasi (2016) report that Italian firms facing tighter credit conditions charge higher prices than unconstrained firms exporting the same product to the same destination. More recent studies attempt to link export pricing with endogenous quality and financial constraints. Fan, Lai, and Li (2015) introduce credit constraints and endogenous quality in a Melitz-type model and test the empirical relationship between credit constraints, quality, and prices using Chinese firm-level panel data. They find that lower credit constraints increase both the price and the quality of products, which confirms the quality sorting hypothesis, as also implied by the positive estimated association between prices and productivity. In a similar vein, Dinopoulos, Kalyvitis, and Katsimi (2017) document that less financially constrained Greek exporters charge higher prices and have higher export revenues. They propose a model with endogenous product quality and credit constraints, a model that features variable price elasticity of demand, and they find that less credit-constrained exporters face less elastic demand and export higher-quality products.

5 Inspecting the Evidence: An Application With Panel Data From Greek Exporters

5.1 The Dataset for Greek Exporting Firms

This section presents an empirical application on export pricing using a new dataset that combines data from two sources: International trade flows of Greek firms are identified at the firm-level and are matched through the ICAP database to firms' characteristics. More specifically, firm-level data on nonoil products for Greek manufacturing exporters from 2003 to 2015 are obtained from the Eurostat's Extra-EU and Intra-EU trade statistics.[2] When goods are declared to the EU statistics, they are classified according to the eight-digit Combined Nomenclature or CN8, which is the most detailed product classification system for keeping foreign trade statistics in the EU. Free-on-board export values are collected at a monthly frequency and are aggregated to annual values and quantities traded by a company to obtain export prices (unit values) as the ratio of these two variables. Defining products at a highly disaggregated level minimizes the scope for factors such as product quality differences, which are likely to determine price variations within firms.

Following the main studies surveyed in the previous section, the behavior of aggregate export prices is examined by running gravity-type regressions of export prices on main features of the destination country, namely bilateral distance to Greece, overall economic remoteness, income, and size. Following related empirical literature, data about GDP and GDP per capita are obtained

---

2. Extrastat is the system that produces statistics on trade in goods of EU member states with non-EU member states and Intrastat produces statistics about trade in goods between countries of the EU.

from the World Bank's World Development Indicators. Bilateral distances from Greece are obtained from CEPII. Remoteness, which proxies geographical isolation from most other nations or closeness to small countries but far away from big economies, is measured as a weighted average of a country's bilateral distance to all other countries in the world using countries' GDP as weights. The degree of financial constraints for each company is proxied by the credit rating score from the ICAP database, which is a 10-scale indicator controlling for insolvency, excessive and/or bad debts, overdue accounts, and other typical commercial risks, and is used routinely by Greek banks to make decisions about whether to supply credit to firms. It also is used by firms in assessing the credibility of their clients and thus provides a form of extra liquidity through short-term financing from suppliers.

To address noise or error, data are trimmed using the following rules. First, quantities equal to one or two on a monthly basis are excluded to deal with rounding errors and misreporting. To avoid product classification inconsistencies, product codes that do not match through years are excluded. Also, the data are cleaned by dropping observations with large price variations across destinations. Large variations refer to prices that differ from a factor of five or more from the mean across all destinations. Finally, the remaining price-based outliers are identified and excluded from the sample by censoring the extreme quantiles of each firm's price distribution, below the 1st and above the 99th percentile.

After dropping these outliers, the matched sample from 2003 to 2015 contains 161,045 firm-product-destination matched observations. In Table 1, the summary statistics are shown. For the period 2003–15, there is an average of 898.3 firms employing 110.4 workers with an export volume of 5.85 million euros per year, exporting 1908.3 CN8 products to 129.3 destinations. On average, for the same period, each company exports 5.8 CN8 products to 6.5

TABLE 1 Summary Statistics for Greek Exporters, 2003–15

Average number of firms per year	898.3
Average employment	110.4
Average value of exports (in million euros)	5.851
Number of destinations per year	129.9
Number of destinations per firm	6.5
Number of products (CN8 classification) per year	1908.3
Number of products (CN8 classification) per firm	5.8

destination markets. These figures are not far from those reported in other datasets and ensure that the dataset is comparable to those used in other empirical studies.[3]

5.2 Panel Data Evidence From Greek Exporters

This subsection presents some empirical results about export pricing from Greek firms and compares them with those in the prior literature. Table 2 follows Manova and Zhang (2012) and considers, in a gravity-type regression, the correlation between average export prices across firms and features of the destination market. Average export prices are product-level prices obtained after

TABLE 2 Export Pricing With Average Product-Level (Trade) Data

	Dependent Variable: Average Price Across Firms		
	All	Rich	Poor
	(1)	(2)	(3)
Distance	−0.015**	0.006	−0.026**
	(−2.08)	(0.78)	(−2.18)
Remoteness	0.231***	0.068**	0.418***
	(8.20)	(2.20)	(10.43)
GDP per capita	0.088***	0.079***	0.084***
	(12.46)	(8.66)	(8.01)
GDP	0.029***	0.002	0.046***
	(5.62)	(0.43)	(4.82)
Product FE	Yes	Yes	Yes
# of observations	158,792	78,381	77,131
R^2	0.751	0.779	0.758
Cluster	CN8	CN8	CN8
# of clusters	3746	2732	3119

Notes: t statistics in parentheses. *P < 0.10, **P < 0.05, ***P < 0.01. All variables are in logs. A constant term and year fixed effects are included in all regressions. The dataset spans the years 2003–2015. The dependent variable is the average (across firms) log price, defined as revenue over quantity, of a product–destination in a year.

---

3. For example, Bastos and Silva (2010) report that Portuguese firms exported on average 9.9 CN8-classified products to 3.4 countries in 2005.

aggregating the revenues and quantities of a certain product exported to a certain destination, such that they equal the values that product-level (trade) data would report. Year dummies are included to control for symmetric developments common to all destinations; for instance, the world trade crisis or the overall evolution of Greek aggregates, such as the wage rate (Berman et al., 2012). Product fixed effects, which capture systematic differences in prices because of the inherent characteristics of products across categories, such as differences in consumer appeal, comparative advantage, transportation and distribution costs, different units used across goods, and other product characteristics that affect all exporters equally, also are included (Manova & Zhang, 2012).

Column 1 of Table 2 reports the estimates from the regression of product-level prices in the sample and shows that the average export price is higher in less distant, less central, richer, and bigger markets. The sample also is split in destinations above and below median income level. The negative association of product-level prices with distance and the positive association with market size are driven by poor destinations, whereas there are no associations for rich destinations. The rest of the coefficients retain their signs in both specifications, with the positive correlation between prices and market remoteness being more than five times stronger in poor destinations.

As discussed in detail in the survey of the literature about export pricing at the firm level in the previous sections, product-level prices do not distinguish in the different patterns between productivity, quality, or other heterogeneous characteristics across firms. The richness of the dataset therefore is exploited to present regressions on the determinants of firm-level export prices. These regressions always control for the following firm characteristics. First, the number of destinations as a proxy for the firm's productivity is included (Berman et al., 2012). Second, a standard feature of models with heterogeneous firms is that higher productivity translates into a larger company. A standard measure of firm size is total (export) sales, which represent quantities times prices; therefore, any measurement error in prices might appear on both sides in regressions with prices as the dependent variable. To address this concern, Kugler and Verhoogen (2012) proxy plant size by employment, which has the advantage that measurement error is likely to be less severe and, importantly, uncorrelated with measurement error in output values and quantities.

Following Manova and Zhang (2012), firm-product fixed effects are included that, in addition to subsuming the role of product characteristics common to all firms, such as those included in Table 2 with product-level prices, are invariant across export markets and control for firm attributes, such as overall production efficiency, managerial talent, labor force composition, and general input quality, that affect the firm's export performance equally across products. They also help address the concern that consumers get different utilities from the products of different companies. To account for the potential correlation in the error term across firms and destinations within a product, errors are clustered by product (or by destination-product when the destination-specific variables do not enter in the specification).[4]

Table 3 presents the results from the panel dataset with firm-level data. Columns 1–4 include sequentially the four destination variables as dependent variables along with the set of controls, whereas column 5 includes jointly the four destination characteristics. Turning first to the controls, employment systematically enters with a positive and statistically significant sign. The coefficient on the (log) number of employees suggests that the price elasticity with respect to firm size is economically significant: a firm with double employment charges higher prices by approximately 16% ($\exp(0.15) - 1$). This value is somewhat higher than that obtained by Kugler and Verhoogen (2012) for Colombian plants (2.6%), but close to that of Secchi et al. (2016) for Italian firms (23.9%).

Regarding the destination characteristics, the firm-product fixed effects imply that the coefficients of interest are identified purely from the variation in prices across destinations for a given exporter-product pair. As shown in columns 1 and 5, the estimates of the destination coefficient are now different compared to the product-level data in Table 2. Specifically, the distance coefficient is insignificant, but remoteness remains positive and significant, although its magnitude is less pronounced. Destination income also is positive and significant, whereas the size of the country is not associated with prices.

Motivated by the findings of various studies on the differential impact of firm productivity on export pricing, an exercise based on interaction terms is performed in column 6. Specifically, interaction terms of the number of destinations with country features are included in the empirical specification. These terms aim at capturing whether firms with different productivity (proxied by the number of destinations served) charge different prices depending on market characteristics. Notably, the interaction of the number of destinations with remoteness is positive, whereas the coefficient on remoteness is insignificant. This finding implies that firms serving a larger number of destinations charge higher prices in less tough (more remote) destinations within the same product category. Income enters again with a positive sign, but the interaction term with the number of destinations is negative, indicating that this comovement is less prominent for companies that supply more countries.

Next, the relationship between firm export prices and financial constraints is examined. The last three columns of Table 3 introduce the credit score of the firm as a measure of its financial constraints. Given that there are no destination-specific variables, the simple product fixed effects are replaced by product-destination pair fixed effects, which implicitly control for product

---

4. Robustness checks have been made, controlling for firm-specific variables, such as age, and time dummies for the world trade crisis in 2008 and 2009. All the results are qualitatively similar to those presented here. Also, the results are similar when different sources of heteroskedasticity are allowed in the error term, or heteroskedasticity-robust standard errors are used.

TABLE 3 Export Pricing at the Firm Level

				Dependent Variable: Export Price (Firm-Product-Destination)					
	1	2	3	4)	5	6	7	8	9
Distance	−0.000				0.004	0.014		0.004	0.014
	(−0.07)				(0.86)	(0.80)		(0.87)	(0.82)
Remoteness		0.038**			0.077***	−0.040		0.077***	−0.042
		(2.39)			(4.97)	(−0.68)		(4.97)	(−0.72)
GDP per capita			0.042***		0.045***	0.102***		0.045***	0.102***
			(13.26)		(11.03)	(6.51)		(11.03)	(6.51)
GDP				0.010***	−0.001	0.003		−0.001	0.002
				(6.95)	(−0.32)	(0.25)		(−0.33)	(0.24)
Rating							0.014**	0.017*	0.017*
							(2.24)	(1.78)	(1.83)
Employment	0.155***	0.154***	0.156***	0.163***	0.150***	0.151***	0.019	0.147***	0.148***
	(20.72)	(19.87)	(19.05)	(21.83)	(16.52)	(14.60)	(0.78)	(15.56)	(14.01)
# of destinations	−0.010	−0.009	−0.007	−0.009	−0.007	−1.007*	−0.023***	−0.009	−1.038*
	(−1.07)	(−1.00)	(−0.80)	(−0.98)	(−0.84)	(−1.77)	(−3.46)	(−1.01)	(−1.82)
# of destinations × distance						−0.003			−0.003
						(−0.64)			(−0.66)

# of destinations × remoteness						0.029**			0.030**
						(2.09)			(2.14)
# of destinations × GDP per capita						−0.015***			−0.015***
						(−4.12)			(−4.12)
# of destinations × GDP						−0.001			−0.001
						(−0.43)			(−0.41)
Destination-product FE	No	No	No	No	No	No	Yes	No	No
Firm-product FE	Yes	Yes	Yes	Yes	Yes	Yes	Yes	Yes	Yes
# of observations	140,788	139,896	140,096	140,096	139,563	139,563	128,450	139,563	139,563
R^2	0.888	0.889	0.889	0.889	0.890	0.890	0.916	0.890	0.890
Cluster	CN8	CN8	CN8	CN8	CN8	CN8	CN8 & dest	CN8	CN8
# of clusters	3191	3181	3187	3187	3181	3181	19,120	3181	3181

Notes: t statistics in parentheses *P < 0.10, **P < 0.05, ***P < 0.01. All variables are in logs. A constant term and year fixed effects are included in all regressions. The dataset spans the years 2003–15. The dependent variable is the firm log price, defined as revenue over quantity, of a product to a destination in a year.

characteristics that are invariant across manufacturers and trade partners. They also consider features of the importing country that affect all products and firms selling there, such as consumer income, regulatory restrictions, legal institutions, inflation, and exchange rates. These fixed effects take account of transportation costs, bilateral tariffs, demand conditions, market toughness, and other economic factors that influence exporters in any given destination-product market. Finally, destination-product fixed effects account for measurement error given the possibility that all firms have more incentives to be truthful about exports of some products to certain markets, or that customs officials are more conscientious about given goods in some countries (Manova & Zhang, 2012).

In column 7, the credit score is introduced as an independent variable and destination-related controls are suppressed. The rating enters with a positive and statistically significant sign, which indicates that a less financially constrained exporter sets a higher price compared to that set by a constrained firm exporting the same CN8 product to the same destination market. The coefficient on the number of destinations now has a negative and statistically significant sign, whereas the firm size is insignificant; both are identified by the variation within a destination-product and a firm-product market. The robustness of the finding on the coefficient of the credit score is further explored in column 8, in which a similar specification to that of column 5 is adopted, one that controls for the destination characteristics. The coefficient on the rating remains positive, but is now only marginally significant. The rest of the coefficients are virtually identical to those obtained in column 5. Finally, in column 9, the four interaction terms are included. The broad picture, when compared to that without the credit score of the corresponding column 6, remains virtually unaffected with the credit score turning out again positive and marginally significant.

The main findings are that Greek exporting firms set higher prices in richer and less central destinations. The association with centrality is more prominent for more efficient firms, whereas the association with income is less pronounced for these firms. These stylized facts about export pricing are identified from the variation across destinations within firm-product pairs. Given that trade models with heterogeneous firms predict either a constant markup (CES demand), or lower markups in markets where competition is tougher (linear demand), i.e., big, distant, and less remote destinations, the positive association of prices with destination remoteness and the lack of association with destination size indicate that variable markups within firm-product pairs could, at least partly, rationalize export pricing by Greek exporters. The quality differentiation channel, however, also can be consistent with the positive association between prices and remoteness, which is stronger for more efficient firms—as anticipated by the Alchian-Allen hypothesis that the demand for higher-quality goods increases with transport costs. Yet the finding that the positive association of prices with destination income is driven by less efficient firms, which have higher marginal costs and are more likely to face tighter financial constraints, merits further examination.

6 Conclusions

Given the ever-increasing availability of micro data about exporting firms and their characteristics, the empirical literature about export pricing at the firm level is constantly maturing to the point where one can now sketch out a handful of empirical paradigms and use them to organize related empirical specifications. Our review of this evidence indicates that empirical papers about export pricing offer a useful complement to theoretical studies. They deliver intuitive and sometimes quite compelling explanations for important patterns, including some that are difficult to quantify, such as the choice of quality or variable markups.

It should be stressed that sprinkled throughout the survey are some discussions about research that are hard to categorize into a single canonical framework. For example, the association of pricing with quality might co-exist with financial constraints at the company level, which in turn affect both outcomes. Complications like these suggest why observable outcomes, such as prices, are associated with nonobservable outcomes in industrial organization, such as quality or frictions, in ways that are hard to quantify, although casual empiricism suggests that they are plausibly interrelated. The contrast between the implications of different results obtained in empirical papers about export pricing is a key reason why this research agenda area presents novel opportunities that could lead to important insights in international economics and beyond.

Acknowledgments

Part of the research project was conducted at the Lab of International Economic Relations, Athens University of Economics and Business.

References

Alchian, A., Allen, W., 1964. University economics, 3rd ed. Wadsworth, Belmont, CA.

Arkolakis, C., Costinot, A., Rodríguez-Clare, A., 2012. New trade models, same old gains? American Economic Review 102 (1), 94–130.

Baldwin, R., Harrigan, J., 2011. Zeros, quality, and space: trade theory and trade evidence. American Economic Journal: Microeconomics 3 (2), 60–88.

Bastos, P., Silva, J., 2010. The quality of a firm's exports: where you export to matters. Journal of International Economics 82 (2), 99–111.

Bellone, F., Musso, P., Nesta, L., Schiavo, S., 2010. Financial constraints and firm export behaviour. World Economy 33 (3), 347–373.

Berman, N., Héricourt, J., 2010. Financial factors and the margins of trade: evidence from cross-country firm-level data. Journal of Development Economics 93 (2), 206–217.

Berman, N., Martin, P., Mayer, T., 2012. How do different exporters react to exchange rate changes? Quarterly Journal of Economics 127 (1), 437–492.

Bernard, A.B., Eaton, J., Jensen, J.B., Kortum, S., 2003. Plants and productivity in international trade. American Economic Review 93 (4), 1268–1290.

Bernard, A.B., Jensen, J.B., Redding, S.J., Schott, P.K., 2007. Firms in international trade. Journal of Economic Perspectives 21 (3), 105–130.

Bernard, A.B., Jensen, J.B., Redding, S.J., Schott, P.K., 2012. The empirics of firm heterogeneity and international trade. Annual Review of Economics 4 (1), 283–313.

Caselli, M., Chatterjee, A., Woodland, A., 2017. Multi-product exporters, variable markups and exchange rate fluctuations. Canadian Journal of Economics 50 (4), 1130–1160.

Chatterjee, A., Dix-Carneiro, R., Vichyanond, J., 2013. Multi-product firms and exchange rate fluctuations. American Economic Journal: Economic Policy 5 (2), 77–110.

Chen, N., Juvenal, L., 2016. Quality, trade, and exchange rate pass-through. Journal of International Economics 100, 61–80.

Crozet, M., Head, K., Mayer, T., 2012. Quality sorting and trade: firm-level evidence for French wine. Review of Economic Studies 79 (2), 609–644.

De Loecker, J., Goldberg, P.K., Khandelwal, A.K., Pavcnik, N., 2016. Prices, markups, and trade reform. Econometrica 84 (2), 445–510.

De Loecker, J., Warzynski, F., 2012. Markups and firm-level export status. American Economic Review 102 (6), 2437–2471.

Di Comité, F., Thisse, J., Vandenbussche, H., 2014. Verti-zontal differentiation in export markets. Journal of International Economics 93 (1), 50–66.

Dinopoulos, E., Kalyvitis, S., Katsimi, M., 2017. Variable export price elasticities and credit constraints: Theory and evidence from Greek firms. AUEB working paper.

Eckel, C., Iacovone, L., Javorcik, B., Neary, J.P., 2015. Multi-product firms at home and away: Cost versus quality-based competence. Journal of International Economics 95 (2), 216–232.

Fan, H., Lai, E., Li, Y.A., 2015. Credit constraints, quality, and export prices: theory and evidence from China. Journal of Comparative Economics 43 (2), 390–416.

Feenstra, R.C., Li, Z., Yu, M., 2014. Exports and credit constraints under incomplete information: theory and evidence from China. Review of Economics and Statistics 96 (4), 729–744.

Feenstra, R., Romalis, J., 2014. International prices and endogenous quality. Quarterly Journal of Economics 129 (2), 477–527.

Fontagné, L., Gaulier, G., Zignago, S., 2008. Specialization across varieties and north-south competition. Economic Policy 23, 51–91.

Gervais, A., 2015. Product quality and firm heterogeneity in international trade. Canadian Journal of Economics 48 (3), 1152–1174.

Gopinath, G., Gourinchas, P.-O., Hsieh, C.-T., Li, N., 2011. International prices, costs, and markup differences. American Economic Review 101 (6), 2450–2486.

Görg, H., Halpern, L., Muraközy, B., 2017. Why do within-firm-product export prices differ across markets? Evidence from Hungary. The World Economy 40 (6), 1233–1246.

Greenaway, D., Guariglia, A., Kneller, R., 2007. Financial factors and exporting decisions. Journal of International Economics 73 (2), 377–395.

Gullstrand, J., Olofsdotter, K., Thede, S., 2014. Markups and export-pricing strategies. Review of World Economics 150 (2), 221–239.

Hallak, J.C., 2006. Product quality and the direction of trade. Journal of International Economics 68 (1), 238–265.

Hallak, J.C., Schott, P.K., 2011. Estimating cross-country differences in product quality. Quarterly Journal of Economics 126 (1), 417–474.

Hallak, J.C., Sivadasan, J., 2013. Product and process productivity: implications for quality choice and conditional exporter premia. Journal of International Economics 91 (1), 53–67.

Harrigan, J., Ma, X., Shlychkov, V., 2015. Export prices of U.S. firms. Journal of International Economics 97 (1), 100–111.

Hausmann, R., Hwang, J., Rodrik, D., 2007. What you export matters. Journal of Economic Growth 12, 1–25.

Henn, C., Papageorgiou, C., Romero, J.M., Spatafora, N., 2017. Export quality in advanced and developing economies: evidence from a new data set. World Bank Policy Research working paper 8196.

Hummels, D., Klenow, P.J., 2005. The variety and quality of a nation's exports. American Economic Review 95 (3), 704–723.

Hummels, D., Skiba, A., 2004. Shipping the good apples out? An empirical confirmation of the Alchian-Allen conjecture. Journal of Political Economy 112 (6), 1384–1402.

Johnson, R.C., 2012. Trade and prices with heterogeneous firms. Journal of International Economics 86 (1), 43–56.

Kalyvitis, S., Katsimi, M., Pappa, E., Restrepo, B.J., 2017. The single currency effect on exports: Firm heterogeneity, markups, and the euro. AUEB working paper.

Khandelwal, A., 2010. The long and short (of) quality ladders. Review of Economic Studies 77 (4), 1450–1476.

Kugler, M., Verhoogen, E., 2012. Prices, plant size, and product quality. Review of Economic Studies 79 (1), 307–339.

Li, H., Ma, H., Xu, Y., 2015. How do exchange rate movements affect Chinese exports? A firm-level investigation. Journal of International Economics 97 (1), 148–161.

Linder, S.B., 1961. An essay on trade and transformation. Almqvist & Wiksell, Stockholm.

de Lucio, J., Mínguez, R., Minondo, A., Requena, F., 2016. The variation of export prices across and within firms. Bank of Spain working paper 1634.

Manova, K., 2013. Credit constraints, heterogeneous firms and international trade. Review of Economic Studies 80 (2), 711–744.

Manova, K., Wei, S., Zhang, Z., 2015. Firm exports and multinational activity under credit constraints. Review of Economics and Statistics 97 (3), 574–588.

Manova, K., Zhang, Z., 2012. Export prices across firms and destinations. Quarterly Journal of Economics 127 (1), 379–436.

Martin, J., 2012. Markups, quality, and transport costs. European Economic Review 56 (4), 777–791.

Melitz, M.J., 2003. The impact of trade on intra-industry reallocations and aggregate industry productivity. Econometrica 71 (6), 1695–1725.

Melitz, M.J., Ottaviano, G.I.P., 2008. Market size, trade, and productivity. Review of Economic Studies 75 (1), 295–316.

Melitz, M.J., Redding, S.J., 2014. Heterogeneous firms and trade. In: Helpman, E., Gopinath, G., Rogoff, K. (Eds.), Handbook of international economics. 4th ed. Elsevier, Amsterdam, pp. 1–54.

Melitz, M.J., Trefler, D., 2012. Gains from trade when firms matter. Journal of Economic Perspectives 26 (2), 91–118.

Minetti, R., Zhu, S.C., 2011. Credit constraints and firm export: microeconomic evidence from Italy. Journal of International Economics 83 (2), 109–125.

Muûls, M., 2015. Exporters, importers and credit constraints. Journal of International Economics 95 (2), 333–343.

Redding, S.J., 2011. Theories of heterogeneous firms and trade. Annual Review of Economics 3 (1), 77–105.

Schott, P.K., 2004. Across-product versus within-product specialization in international trade. Quarterly Journal of Economics 119 (2), 647–678.

Schott, P.K., 2008. The relative sophistication of Chinese exports. Economic Policy 53, 5–49.

Secchi, A., Tamagni, F., Tomasi, C., 2016. Export price adjustments under financial constraints. Canadian Journal of Economics 49 (3), 1057–1085.

Sutton, J., Trefler, D., 2016. Deductions from the export basket: capabilities, wealth and trade. Journal of Political Economy 124 (3), 826–878.

Vandenbussche, H., 2014. Quality in exports. European economy. Economic papers 528, Brussels.

Verhoogen, E.A., 2008. Trade, quality upgrading, and wage inequality in the Mexican manufacturing sector. Quarterly Journal of Economics 123 (2), 489–530.

Chapter 28

The Relationship Between Economic Growth and Democracy: Alternative Representations of Technological Change

Nam Seok Kim* and Almas Heshmati[†]

*Department of Economics, Maxwell School of Citizenship and Public Affairs, Syracuse University, Syracuse, NY, United States, [†]Department of Economics, Sogang University, Seoul, South Korea

Chapter Outline

1 Introduction

It is widely known that institutions matter to long-run economic growth. But how do they matter? Of late, the belief that democracy has positive impacts on gross domestic product (GDP) growth has been gaining momentum through some empirical and theoretical studies. Acemoglu, Naidu, Restrepo, and Robinson (forthcoming) suggest that democracy has a significant and robust positive effect on GDP. They add that democratization increases GDP per capita by about 20% in the long run. Persson and Tabellini (2007) suggest that abandoning democracy can cause negative growth effects. According to the developmental state theory, however, the quality of an institution that leads

Panel Data Econometrics. https://doi.org/10.1016/B978-0-12-815859-3.00028-7

to economic growth is not consistent with democratic quality.[1] In some East Asian countries, including South Korea and Taiwan, strategies for economic growth are aimed at controlling institutions efficiently in order to allocate capital and resources according to the government's objectives.[2] Democracy and human rights are mobilized in implementing these strategies with the goal of achieving economic growth. By persuading residents to focus primarily on economic growth, developmental states create an atmosphere in which sacrificing personal freedom could be justified. Although their strategies do not guarantee democratic values and transparency in institutions, the countries experienced tremendous economic growth during the 1970s and 1980s.

Literature about the relationship between democracy and economic growth is growing. In spite of several empirical researches, however, the nature of this relationship and its determinants are yet to be established. Therefore, one can ask the basic question: Is East Asia's experience an exception in the relationship between economic growth and democracy? We need to analyze a large sample of global economic data observed over a long period to clarify the direction and magnitude of the relationship between economic growth and democracy.

This study suggests some robust patterns between economic growth and democracy by estimating nations' production functions using panel data. It also generalizes the settings of the used production function for formulating static and dynamic models. As a variable of democracy, it uses the dichotomous democracy dummy variable constructed by Acemoglu et al. (forthcoming). Controlling time-specific effects is one of the most important issues in estimating a production function. Therefore, our study implemented the single time trend (STT), multiple time trends (MTT), and general index (GI) representations of technological changes. The STT used in this chapter is similar to the STT used by Solow (1957). The derivation in terms of this trend indicate the magnitude of unobservable technical changes. This STT can be generalized to MTT and GI formulations. Baltagi and Griffin (1988) used year dummy variables to generalize the measure of unobservable technical changes, but it is still a function of time.

By considering technology indices containing technology shifters (TS), this study found some possible channels between economic growth and democracy. TS are a more generalized concept than the GI because TS can measure changes in which the technology is specified in a known form. Heshmati and Kumbhakar (2013) applied this TS model to the Organization for Economic Cooperation and Development (OECD) countries. Credit guarantee, trade openness, foreign direct investment (FDI) net inflows, electricity consumption, number of firms, and governmental consumption are included as TS in this chapter.[3] The results

---

1. For the developmental state theory, see Wade (1990) and Haggard (1990).
2. For additional information about East Asia, see Johnson (1982), Amsden (1989) and Woo (1991).
3. Pellegrini and Gerlagh (2004) also considered investment and trade openness as linkages between corruption and economic growth.

also suggest some differences in the effects of economic policies and economic shocks between democratic and nondemocratic countries.

A generalization of the static model for formulating a dynamic model enables this chapter to reassure the positive and significant impacts of democracy on economic growth. The concepts of the optimal target level of GDP and adjustment speed are used actively to construct a flexible adjustment dynamic model. Empirical studies that have attempted to specify target levels and adjustment speeds have been severely tried by the capital structure theory. Modigliani and Miller (1958) suggested a fundamental model related to the capital structure theory. According to them, a firm's target debt ratio is determined based on the costs and benefits of debt and equity. Marsh (1982) suggests the famous empirical method to prove the capital structure theory by inserting the target debt ratio in a key regression analysis. In their empirical studies, Banerjee, Heshmati, and Wihlborg (2000), Heshmati (2001), and Lööf (2004) have constructed systems of equations that include an equation for the main regression model, an equation for the target level of the debt ratio, and an equation for the adjustment speed of the debt ratio. Instead of a target level of debt ratio and adjustment speed of debt ratio, in the context of economic growth, we implement the target level of GDP and flexible adjustment speed of GDP toward the target level. The functional forms for the target level and adjustment speed are also different from previous studies about the capital structure theory. Based on the likelihood ratio test, the proper functional form and flexible speed of adjustment is chosen for our analysis.

Regardless of which model is used to estimate the production function, there are positive and significant impacts of democracy on economic growth. In this study, credit guarantee (percent of GDP of domestic credit to the private sector by banks) is the most significant positive possible channel among different observable TS. FDI inflows is also a positive and significant possible channel, but this technology shifter is significant in only two models among three TS' models. In addition, the marginal effects of an increase in credit guarantee and FDI inflows are stronger in democratic countries. On the other hand, the marginal effects of an increase in trade openness, electricity consumption, the number of firms, and in government consumption are stronger in nondemocratic countries. Estimation results of the dynamic model also suggest that, ceteris paribus, democracy has positive and significant impacts on economic growth.

In the dynamic model, the adjustment speed is accelerated by an increase in trade openness and FDI inflows; the adjustment speed is delayed by an increase in government consumption and by improvements in infrastructure related to electricity.

The rest of this study is organized as follows. In Section 2, the study shows the static model approach using the production function. After explaining econometric specifications, this section also gives the estimation results. Section 3 carries forward the discussion about the dynamic model approach.

The concept of a dynamic model and methods for estimating a dynamic model also are detailed in this section. After interpreting the estimation results of the dynamic model, the chapter gives a conclusion in Section 4 by synthesizing results from the static model and dynamic models.

2 A Static Model

2.1 Motivation

Static model is a basic and fundamental way to estimate the impact of democracy on economic growth. We can test the role of democracy and democratization through estimating each nation's production function. Several important facts have to be considered when choosing a proper econometric model for estimating the production function through panel data. This study applies STT, MTT, the GI, and TS' representations of technology to the translog production function.

First, this research uses panel data arranged by each country and year to clarify the existence of institutional elements in the production function. Therefore, we have to properly control the effects caused by time variation. Time effects can be captured by implementing STT, MTT, and GI models. These three approaches allow for a stepwise generalization of technology representation in the production function.

Second, to estimate the production function, deciding the specifications and deriving other information, including technical changes and total factor productivity (TFP), are also important. In this respect, the translog production functional form is a convenient and useful functional form. The translog production function has been used widely in empirical studies because of its general and simple characteristics. Because the translog production function does not impose any priori restrictions on the return to scale and elasticities of substitution, it allows the flexible nature of production activities to be considered.[4] Moreover, the translog production function has richer specifications of the relationships between output and inputs than other linear specifications, including the Cobb-Douglas approach (Evans, Green, & Murinde, 2002).

After Berndt and Christensen (1973) and Christensen, Jorgenson, and Lau (1973) suggested the standard form of the translog production function, many papers implemented the translog production function for productivity analyses and production function estimations. Through a flexible functional form for the production function, we can decompose technical change into a neutral part and a nonneutral part affecting production through inputs. The neutral part is affected only by time variation. The nonneutral part is the remaining part of

---

4. Kim (1992) and Lyu, White, and Lu (1984) give details about the strengths and weaknesses of estimating the translog production function.

the technical change. Overall TFP and its variations are influenced by two technical change components and the scale effect.

Third, if we can find possible important channels between economic growth and democracy, we can derive policy implications about the economy and society. The STT, MTT, and GI models are nonobservable time trend and time dummy representations of technology. TS is an alternative representation of technology that is applied in our study to find the kind of observable possible channels discussed earlier.

2.2 Econometric Specifications

2.2.1 The Single Time Trend Model

As its name implies, a STT means that there is a unique time trend in the production function. In other words, the output in production increases or decreases linearly as time passes. We can assume that a STT is valid historically because we can observe that humankind's production has increased consistently.[5] We can check this validity through the value of the neutral part of technical changes or coefficients related to the STT. After the STT method is implemented, the translog production function can be expressed as:

Model 1 (M1): The STT model:

$$GDP_{it} = \beta_0 + \sum_j \beta_j x_{jit} + \beta_d D_{it} + \beta_t t$$

$$+ \left(\frac{1}{2}\right) \left\{ \sum_j \sum_k \beta_{jk} x_{jit} x_{kit} + \beta_u t^2 \right\} + \sum_j \beta_{jt} x_{jit} t + C_i + \varepsilon_{it} \quad (1)$$

where x_{jit} is the log of inputs j (capital stock K_{it}, labor force L_{it}) for country i in time period t, D_{it} is the democracy dummy variable and GDP_{it} is the log of GDP level (more explanations about each variable are provided in the Data section). C_i indicates the full set of country-specific fixed effects.

By the definition of the translog production function, inputs and time trend have squared and interacted terms. Through these squared and interacted terms, nonlinearity between inputs and output and substitution/complementarity between inputs and input-biased technological changes can be captured. D_{it} is a dummy variable and as such is not squared or interacted because D_{it} is the controlled part from the error term ε_{it}. D_{it} is not interpreted as inputs in an analysis of this production function but rather as a shifter of the production function.

We can derive information from M1 including elasticities, returns to scale (RTS), rate of technical change, and TFP growth. The rate of technical change can be decomposed into neutral and nonneutral parts as:

---

5. Solow (1957) also supposed a single time trend in his growth model.

E1: Input elasticities (E_j), technical chance (TC), and RTS in a STT model:

$$E_{jit}^{STT} = \frac{\partial GDP_{it}}{\partial x_{jit}} = \beta_j + \sum_{k=1} x_{kit} + \beta_{jt}t, \quad RTS_{it}^{STT} = \sum_{j=1}^{J} E_{jit}^{STT} \tag{2}$$

As indicated in E1, elasticities can be derived easily by the first-order derivative. RTS are the sum of elasticities of inputs.

E2: The rate of technical change in a STT model:

$$TC_{it}^{STT} = \frac{\partial GDP_{it}}{\partial t} = \beta_t + \beta_u t + \sum_j \beta_{jt} x_{jit} \tag{3}$$

Technical change, in fact, is the elasticity of the time trend in a mathematical sense. The first part, $\beta_t + \beta_u t$, is the neutral rate of technical change, which is affected only by the time effect. The second part, $\sum_j \beta_{jt} x_{jit}$, is the nonneutral technical change, which is not related to the time-specific effect but is related to changes in inputs affecting economies of scale.

E3: TFP growth in a STT model:

$$TFP_{it} = (RTS_{it}^{STT}) - 1 \left(E_{K_{it}}^{STT} \Delta \log K_{it} + E_{L_{it}}^{STT} \Delta \log L_{it} \right) + TC_{L_{it}}^{STT} \tag{4}$$

TFP can be calculated as shown in E3. Because the elasticities, RTS, technical changes, and TFP growth can be calculated for each observation, an interesting analysis is possible by comparing sample means between specific groups. These input elasticities, rate of technical change, RTS, and TFP components vary by observation. They provide detailed information about countries' response heterogeneity to changes in inputs. For example, we can generate the sample mean of this information according to country characteristics, such as continent location and income group. Moreover, we can compare the sample mean between groups of democratic countries and groups of nondemocratic countries.

2.2.2 The Multiple Time Trends Model

The STT model has an important shortcoming related to controlling time variations. When there are some obvious global shocks that affect all identities in the panel data, assuming a unique time trend can be unconvincing. The slopes and intercepts of the time trend likely will change after encountering global shocks that are strong enough. The first oil shock, the second oil shock, and the 2008 global economic crisis are typical examples of strong global shocks. In this case, when there are γ shocks, there are $\gamma + 1$ time trends. The econometric model for applying MTT can be expressed as:

Model 2 (M2): The MTT model:

$$GDP_{it} = \beta_0 + \sum_j \beta_j x_{jit} + \beta_d D_{it} + \sum_s \beta_s t_s + \left(\frac{1}{2}\right) \left\{ \sum_j \sum_k \beta_{jk} x_{jit} x_{kit} + \sum_s \beta_{ss} t_s^2 \right\}$$

$$+ \sum_j \beta_{jt} x_{jit} t_s + C_i + \varepsilon_{it} \tag{5}$$

Time trend t_s indicates MTT by $t_s = d_s t$ where d_s is a time dummy representing the time interval s of unspecified length. Like M1, inputs and time trends are squared and interacted with each other. In this study, the threshold of MTT is 2008; therefore, we have two time trends. Extending a STT to a multiple one allows for heterogeneity in trend effects, namely changes in both the intercept and the slopes.

Elasticities, rate of technical change, and RTS are derived by the same principle (described as E1). Getting the technical change is different from E2:

E4: The rate of technical change in a MTT model:

$$TC_{it}^{MTT} = \sum_s (w_s \beta_s + \beta_{ss} t_s) + \sum_j \beta_{jt} x_{jit} \qquad (6)$$

Here, w_s represents the weights of each time interval in aggregation of the time effect. Accordingly, the neutral technical change is $\sum_s (w_s \beta_s + \beta_{ss} t_s)$ and the nonneutral technical change is $\sum_j \beta_{jt} x_{jit}$ (Heshmati, 1996). TFP also can be obtained through a MTT model using methods similar to E3 through aggregation of the TFP components.

2.2.3 The General Index Model

A researcher determines the thresholds separating MTT. If unspecified, the thresholds can be identified by switching regression models. Researchers can decide the borders of MTT based on their intuition or based on scientific evidence. Regardless of their decision's accuracy, MTT cannot be independent of a researcher's observations and perspectives. In order to include all possible potential shocks that are not observed by researchers, year dummies are used widely for estimating production and cost functions. This method was devised by Baltagi and Griffin (1988). In the translog production function case, time dummies are added for every year instead of time trends. Time dummies are not squared because they have values of only 0 and 1. The econometric model for the GI can be indicated as:

Model 3 (M3): The GI model:

$$GDP_{it} = \beta_0 + \sum_j \beta_j x_{jit} + \beta_d D_{it} + A(t) + \left(\frac{1}{2}\right) \left\{ \sum_j \sum_k \beta_{jk} x_{jit} x_{kit} \right\}$$
$$+ \sum_j \beta_{jt} x_{jit} A(t) + C_i + \varepsilon_{it} \qquad (7)$$

where $A(t) = \sum_t z_t d_t$; d_t is time dummy for the year t and z_t is the corresponding coefficient. Because coefficients are included in $A(t)$, M3 has interacted coefficients and is nonlinear in parameters. This is a big difference compared to M1 or M2, which are log-linear models in terms of coefficients. There are interacted and squared terms of inputs and time trends allowing for nonlinearity in explanatory variables, but there is no interaction between coefficients. Therefore, M1 and M2 can be estimated using the linear method. M3, however, is nonlinear in terms of coefficients because of the interaction between them. We have to apply nonlinear estimation methods to conduct a proper analysis of M3, which is regarded as an equation system.

Elasticities and RTS are derived through procedures indicated in E1. Technical change is derived through methods different from E2 and E4. TFP also can be derived by a method similar to E3.

E5: The rate of technical change in a GI model:

- Neutral technical change: $A(t) - A(t-1)$
- Nonneutral technical change: $(A(t) - A(t-1))\,(\beta_{Kt}\,\log K_{it} + \beta_{Lt}\,\log L_{it})$
- TC_{it}^{GI} = Neutral technical change + nonneutral technical change.

2.2.4 The Technology Shifters Model

It is well known that in estimating the production function, a researcher's observations do not identify the level of technology very well. In order to enhance the estimation's accuracy, we can add some variables that capture the level of technology in the production function. Many variables can act as indicators of the technology level. For example, nations with advanced technologies are inclined to have higher average educational attainments, more FDI inflows, and a more active movement of loans in the private sector. In order to have a more advanced level of technology, a nation also should increase the availability of electricity and guarantee a proper-sized domestic market. These factors can capture a nation's technology level because they have a high correlation with its technology level.

By grouping these variables according to their functions and categories, we can build some indices consisting of several variables. Each variable, which constructs an index related to the level of technology of all the nations, is called a technology shifter. Consequently, the variables mentioned earlier, including the size of the domestic market, FDI inflows, and electricity consumption also are classified as TS. By inserting these indices constructed by TS, we can implement the TS model. First, let us assume a STT for this model:

Model 4 (M4): TS combined with a STT model:

$$
\begin{aligned}
GDP_{it} = {}& \beta_0 + \sum_j \beta_j x_{jit} + \beta_d D_{it} + \beta_t t + \sum_m \sum_p \delta_m T_m\left(Z_{it}^{mp}\right) \\
& + \left(\frac{1}{2}\right)\left\{\sum_j \sum_k \beta_{jk} x_{jit} x_{kit} + \beta_u t^2 + \sum_m \sum_p \delta_{mm}\left(T_m\left(Z_{it}^{mp}\right)\right)^2\right\} \\
& + \sum_j \beta_{jt} x_{jit} t + \sum_m \sum_p \delta_{mt} T_m\left(Z_{it}^{mp}\right) t + \sum_j \sum_m \sum_p \gamma_{jm} x_{jit} T_m\left(Z_{it}^{mp}\right) \\
& + \sum_m \sum_p \theta_{tm} D_{it} T_m\left(Z_{it}^{mp}\right) + C_i + \varepsilon_{it}
\end{aligned}
\tag{8}
$$

$T_m(Z_{it}^{mp})$ are technology indices and Z_{it}^{mp} are observable technology factors (TS). In other words, $T_m(Z_{it}^{mp}) = \ln\left(\sum_{p=1}^{P_m} \gamma^{mp} Z_{it}^{mp}\right)$; $\sum_{p=1}^{P_m} \gamma^{mp} = 1 \ \forall \ m$ (Heshmati & Kumbhakar, 2013). Inputs, time trend, and indices are squared and interacted with each other. Technology is specified by using a time trend to capture its unspecified long term and by using specific observable factors. Moreover, democracy dummy variables are interacted with technological indices to find a medium between economic growth and democracy. As in the GI model M3, TS model M4 also has nonlinearity in terms of coefficients because M4 is a system of equations. Because of its nonlinear relationship, we have to apply the nonlinear estimation method.

TS are not just highly related to the level of technology but also are deeply related to democracy. For example, in a developmental state, credit guarantee mainly is determined by government officers or politicians. Naturally, artificial adjustments in credit guarantee provoke inefficiencies in the economy. Improper and less productive funding cannot maximize its effect, and the total amount of credit guarantee in the economy is affected. On the other hand, democratization entails transparency in credit guarantee decisions both in the private and public sectors. Transparent decisions regarding credit guarantee result in capital being allocated to the best places to maximize its effects. This transparent and efficient cycle reproduces new capital, and, therefore, the total amount of credit guarantee consistently increases if the other conditions are constant.

Many studies give positive relationships between democracy and trade or between democracy and FDI inflows. It has been proven empirically that openness has some causal effects on democratization.[6] It also is widely known that there is a positive relationship between globalization and democracy in both directions.[7] Yu (2010) suggests that democracy fosters trade, and Busse (2003) discusses how multinational firms invest more in democratic countries.

By concentrating on the interacted term, we can determine which TS form significant possible channels between democracy and economic growth. If θ_{tm} and γ^{mp} are both significant, that technology shifter acts as a link between democracy and economic growth.

MTT and the GI models also can be applied to a TS model:

Model 5 (M5): TS combined with a MTT model:

$$
\begin{aligned}
GDP_{it} = {} & \beta_0 + \sum_j \beta_j x_{jit} + \beta_d D_{it} + \sum_s \beta_s t_s + \sum_m \sum_p \delta_m T_m \left(Z_{it}^{mp} \right) \\
& + \left(\frac{1}{2} \right) \left\{ \sum_j \sum_k \beta_{jk} x_{jit} x_{kit} + \sum_s \beta_{ss} t_s^2 + \sum_m \sum_p \delta_{mm} \left(T_m \left(Z_{it}^{mp} \right) \right)^2 \right\} \\
& + \sum_s \sum_j \beta_{jt} x_{jit} t_s + \sum_s \sum_m \sum_p \delta_{mt} T_m \left(Z_{it}^{mp} \right) t_s \\
& + \sum_j \sum_m \sum_p \gamma_{jm} x_{jit} T_m \left(Z_{it}^{mp} \right) + \sum_m \sum_p \theta_{tm} D_{it} T_m \left(Z_{it}^{mp} \right) + C_i + \varepsilon_{it}
\end{aligned}
$$

$$(9)$$

---

6. For additional reading, see López-Córdova and Meissner (2005).
7. See also Eichengreen and Leblang (2006).

Model 6 (M6): TS combined with a GI model:

$$GDP_{it} = \beta_0 + \sum_j \beta_j x_{jit} + \beta_d D_{it} + A(t) + \sum_m \sum_p \delta_m T_m\left(Z_{it}^{mp}\right)$$

$$+ \left(\frac{1}{2}\right)\left\{\sum_j \sum_k \beta_{jk} x_{jit} x_{kit} + \sum_m \sum_p \delta_{mm}\left(T_m\left(Z_{it}^{mp}\right)\right)^2\right\}$$

$$+ \sum_j \beta_{jt} x_{jit} A(t) + \sum_m \sum_p \delta_{mt} T_m\left(Z_{it}^{mp}\right) A(t)$$

$$+ \sum_j \sum_m \sum_p \gamma_{jm} x_{jit} T_m\left(Z_{it}^{mp}\right) + \sum_m \sum_p \theta_{tm} D_{it} T_m\left(Z_{it}^{mp}\right) + C_i + \varepsilon_{it}$$

$$(10)$$

Elasticities, RTS, rate of technical change, and TFP and its decomposition can be derived through a simple use of E1, E2, E3, E4, and E5.

2.3 Data

This study uses panel data. To estimate a production function using panel data through pooling each nation's time series, we need access to output, inputs, and other country characteristics and control variables. The data need to include real GDP as a dependent variable (GDP_{it}), the number of employees, and capital stock for inputs (x_{jit}), the democracy dummy variable for the key control variable (D_{it}), and TS (Z_{it}^{mp}) for analyzing the effects of possible channels between economic growth and democracy. These shifters are used to represent technology or the sources of a shift in the production function over time. The vector of inputs includes the labor force variable as L_{it} and the capital stock variable as L_{it}. The coverage period for all the variables is from 1980 to 2014.

2.3.1 Variables' Definitions

Real GDP is more appropriate than nominal GDP for our analysis because of differences in inflation rates across countries. If inputs and output are measured in terms of quantity, a transformation to fixed values is not required. Monetary values of output and inputs allow us to account for quality differences, which are reflected in prices, revenues, and costs. Therefore, nominal GDP as a monetary aggregate value includes information not only about output variations by inputs, but also about output variations by economic cycles. Using nominal GDP is not consistent with our goal of concentrating on inputs and output by analyzing the production function. Data about population are used widely for the labor force variable. To be more precise in an analysis of the production function, however, we insert data about the number of employees that is adjusted for the unemployment rate. For the capital variable, we use capital stock data accounting for new investments and depreciation of capital.

Data for these variables are obtained from the Penn World Table 9.0 (PWT).[8] Although PWT is a long and wide panel data, it still has many missing unit observations, mainly in the beginning years for developing countries. Therefore, replacing missing observations with observations from other datasets is required to obtain a larger sample and a more robust estimation. Missing observations of real GDP and labor force in PWT are replaced by data from the World Bank's World Development Indicators (WDI).[9] The base year of real GDP in WDI and units of labor force in WDI are adjusted to be consistent with PWT. GDP_{it}, L_{it}, and K_{it} are a log of real GDP, labor force, and capital stock, respectively. A logarithmic transformation of the variables in the simple Cobb Douglas production function allows for a direct interpretation of the relationship as a percentage of elasticities of output with respect to the percentage of changes in inputs.

The democracy dummy variable D_{it} is the key control variable in this production function estimation. We use the democracy dummy variable constructed in Acemoglu et al. (forthcoming). The variable represents changes in democracy in each nation over time. The constructed democracy dummy variable had a value of 1 if the nation was democratic in a specific year or a value of 0 if the nation was not democratic in that specific year. This variable captures and clarifies the relationship between democracy and economic growth. A positive relationship is expected. In our paper, whether each observation has a value of 1 or 0 depends on the following criteria:

The first criterion is based on the Freedom House and Polity IV datasets. If a nation in a specific year has a free or partially free rating in the Freedom House dataset and has a positive Polity IV score, then the nation is regarded as democratic in that year and therefore has a value of 1. If a nation does not satisfy these requirements, then it is regarded as nondemocratic and therefore has a value of 0.

Following this criterion, we can identify missing observations of the democracy dummy variable that are caused by missing observations for a specific year for that nation in the Freedom House dataset or the Polity IV dataset. In this case, we can replace that missing observation by using Cheibub, Gandhi, and Vreeland (2010) and Boix, Miller, and Rosato (2012) datasets. The missing observation has a value of 1 if the nation in that specific year is democratic in more than one dataset among these two datasets made by Cheibub et al. (2010) and Boix et al. (2012). If the observation is nondemocratic in both Cheibub et al. (2010) and Boix et al. (2012) datasets, then the democracy dummy variable had a value of 0 in our dataset.

---

8. Real GDP is indicated in PWT as Real GDP at constant 2011 national prices (in million US$). Number of employees is indicated in PWT as Number of persons engaged (in millions). Finally, capital stock is given in PWT as Capital stock at constant 2011 national prices (in million US$).
9. Real GDP is indicated in WDI as GDP (constant 2010 US$), and labor force as Labor force, total.

Some shortcomings can result from the fact that the democracy dummy variable ignores the intensity of democracy by including only a value of 0 or 1. Using a dummy variable, however, also has many advantages. To be specific, by expressing the democratic situation using only 0 and 1, we can minimize the damage from measurement errors. Many people prefer expressing each nation's degree of democracy in several categories, but we can find disadvantages in using categorical indices of democracy. Let us consider an index of democracy represented by 10 integers from 1 to 10. The differentials between 2 and 3 and 7 and 8 both are equal to 1, but the two differentials cannot be interpreted equally in terms of effect even though their magnitudes are both 1. In other words, a categorical expression of democracy is not appropriate for a regression analysis because an ambiguity in its quantitative interpretation. Moreover, coefficients derived from this categorical index of democracy are not convincing, yet they provide evidence of heterogeneity in effects. Even though a categorical index of democracy can be constructed by a scientific measure and objective criteria, we have to avoid its shortcomings because the meaning of differentials between categories is not globally consistent over all the categories. These shortcomings and trade-offs between the measurement effect and the homogeneity effect can be overcome more easily using a dichotomous democracy dummy variable. The appendix gives two tables describing variable. Table A1 shows all cases of democracy transitions within a nation. The transitions occurred 128 times in 66 nations. Table A2 gives a list of countries with no transitions in democracy; 49 nations are always democratic in this dataset; 29 nations are always nondemocratic in the dataset.

2.3.2 Observable Technology Shifters

The first thing to mention about data on TS Z_{it}^{mp} are the variables chosen for the TS. Briefly, TS are variables that construct an index of the level of technology in the production function. This technology index is indicated as $T_m(Z_{it}^{mp})$ in our regression analysis. Technology usually is assumed to be exogenous and, in the absence of past information, is represented by a time trend representing the unknown state of technology that is progressing at the same speed and with the same effects across countries and over time. Unlike time dummies or time trends, TS are observable and allow for heterogeneity in effects across countries and over time. Therefore, TS should be related deeply to the level of technology in a nation. In our study, each index of the level of technology contains three TS.

In addition, TS also can have a potential relationship with democracy. In other words, TS in our model not only capture the direct level effects of technology in each nation, but they also act as an efficient indirect medium between economic growth and democracy. Because this chapter deals with various countries, including developing ones, there are many missing observations in TS. Consequently, constructing three indices is almost impossible because many

TS are required for the three indices, and that generated a lot of missing unit observations. Therefore, this model contains two indices of the level of technology in each nation. All the datasets for TS are obtained from the World Bank WDI database.

The first index deals with the openness of each nation and its financial fundamentals. TS in this index are credit guarantee, trade, and FDI inflows. For credit guarantee, we use WDI's data about "domestic credit to private sector by banks (defined as percent of GDP)." WDI's "trade openness (defined as import and export share of GDP)" data are used for our trade variable. WDI's "foreign direct investment, net inflows (percent of GDP)" is used for our FDI inflows variable. FDI is a source of transfer of finance, technology, management, and skills.

The second index implies a nation's infrastructure and the magnitude of its domestic market. The TS in this index are electricity consumption, governmental consumption expenditure, and the number of firms. WDI's data about "electric power consumption (KWh per capita)" is used for the electricity consumption variable. For governmental consumption expenditure, we use WDI's "general government final consumption expenditure (defined as per cent of GDP)." Data about "listed domestic companies, total" from WDI is used for the number of firms. Listed companies in general are large and are involved in innovation activities.

In our regression model, credit guarantee, trade, and FDI inflows are indicated as Z_{it}^{11}, Z_{it}^{12}, and Z_{it}^{13}, respectively. Likewise, electricity consumption, the number of firms, and governmental consumption expenditure are indicated as Z_{it}^{21}, Z_{it}^{22}, and Z_{it}^{23}, respectively.[10]

2.3.3 Managing the Missing Units' Data

Applying proper methods for handling missing observations are important mainly because of the many missing observations in technology shifter Z_{it}^{mp}. First, if an observation has a missing value at GDP_{it} or D_{it}, that observation is deleted from our dataset because GDP_{it} is our dependent variable and D_{it} is our key control variable, and, as such, no imputation should be applied. Even after inserting missing observations about the labor force using WDI, there are some missing observations at L_{it}. In this case, the remaining missing observations are covered by each nation's sample mean by decade. There could still be some remaining missing observations because an entire decade might have no observations. In this case, the observations are dropped from the dataset. The variable capital stock K_{it} follows the same procedure for handling missing observations as L_{it}. This procedure helps us avoid dropping entire observations because of missing unit observations.

---

10. Z_{it}^{11}, Z_{it}^{12}, and Z_{it}^{13} are expressed as CG_{it}, TO_{it}, and FDI_{it} in the dynamic model. Z_{it}^{21}, Z_{it}^{22}, and Z_{it}^{23} are expressed as EC_{it}, NL_{it}, and GC_{it} in the dynamic model. In this static model, we use Z_{it}^{mp} because this shortens the expression of our translog regression model.

In the case of technology shifter Z_{it}^{mp}, we insert each nation's sample mean by decade for the missing observations. The next step for handling missing observations varies according to each technology shifter. First, the remaining missing observations of credit guarantee Z_{it}^{11} are deleted (203 observations from 4825 observations). In case of FDI inflows Z_{it}^{13}, the remaining missing observations are replaced by their minimum values of 0 (93 observations). This method can be used as a reasonable and rational remedy for missing observations in Z_{it}^{13}. Most of the missing observations in Z_{it}^{13} come from developing countries' datasets. Therefore, these missing observations will have significantly lower values than the sample mean. Inserting 0 does not mean an extreme case of a closed economy because Z_{it}^{13} originally was defined as a share of GDP.

The remaining missing observations of trade Z_{it}^{12} are replaced by a total sample mean of 79.9 (104 observations). Governmental consumption expenditure Z_{it}^{23} follows the same procedure as trade. A total sample mean of 15.8 is inserted for missing observations (159 observations).

Relative to these missing observations, electricity consumption Z_{it}^{21} and the number of firms, Z_{it}^{22} has many more missing observations even after inserting each nation's sample mean by decade. For two TS, we insert their minimum values at those missing observations (Z_{it}^{21} – 884 observations and Z_{it}^{22} – 1964 observations). This procedure is the same as that employed in the case of FDI inflows Z_{it}^{13}. Table 1 provides summary statistics of the data variables. It indicates the values of the variables before taking a logarithmic form. After handling missing observations, we have 4622 observations for 144 nations observed unbalanced for the period 1980–2014.

TABLE 1 Summary Statistics of the Data, $N = 4622$

Variable	Mean	Median	Std Dev	Minimum	Maximum
GDP	437,005.40	56,982.26	1,358,618.00	336.10	1,7150,538.00
Capital	1,458,643.00	184,047.30	4,459,800.00	475.42	67,590,072.00
Labor	17.48	3.44	69.31	0.05	798.36
Democracy	0.59	1.00	0.49	0.00	1.00
Credit guarantee	39.22	26.98	35.88	0.15	253.44
Trade	79.73	69.52	49.96	6.32	531.73
FDI	3.73	1.69	8.17	0.00	255.42
Electricity	2831.04	1000.17	4176.37	12.49	25,590.69
No of firms	252.19	20.00	755.37	0.00	8090.00
Gov. consumption	15.84	15.68	6.33	0.00	84.51

2.4   Estimation Method

Before estimating the production model, we look at the correlation between the variables. The correlation matrix (Table 2) provides correlation coefficients between different pairs of variables. With the exception of trade and FDI, the remaining variables are positively correlated, with GDP suggesting explanatory variations in GDP. The capital and labor correlation is 0.57, suggesting no serious multicollinearity and confounded effects. Democracy is correlated positively with GDP and capital, but negatively with labor. TS, except for two cases, are positively correlated with each other.

The 144 nations that constituted the data used in this study were not chosen randomly because the WDI dataset has many missing unit observations, especially in technology shifter variables in developing countries. Therefore, the 144 selected countries tended to be more developed than those countries that were omitted. As the results from the Hausman test indicate, the fixed effects model is preferred to the random effects model.

In M1 and M2, although the independent variables are interacted or squared, their coefficients remain linear. Consequently, M1 and M2 require the linear regression method. On the other hand, M3, M4, M5, and M6 are all regarded as systems of equations. The coefficients' interactions result in nonlinearity, which we had to overcome. A full information maximum likelihood estimation enables us to estimate nonlinear systems of equations. In the SAS program, the "proc model FIML" can be implemented with a little arrangement of parameters and variables.

2.5   Estimation Results

2.5.1   An Analysis of Coefficients

Results of the estimates for M1 to M6 are aggregated in Table 3. Table 4 gives the elasticities derived from M1, M2, and M3, while Table 5 gives the elasticities from M4, M5, and M6.[11] In Tables 4 and 5, we can see that the elasticities of capital stock and labor force ($E_{K_{it}}$ and $E_{L_{it}}$) are always positive and reasonable. This means this econometric specification of the translog production function is consistent with our intuition in terms of inputs.[12] Moreover, we can check that inserting technology indices $T_m(Z_{it}^{mp})$ successfully captured the level of technology because the elasticities of $T_m(Z_{it}^{mp})$ always had positive mean values (e_T_1 and e_T_2). In Table 3, the coefficients of the first time trend and the second time trend in Model 2 and Model 5 are all significant. Based on the fact that

---

11. The label N_America means North America and S_America means South America. The labels Income_L, Income_M, and Income_H mean the low-income country group, middle-income group, and high-income group. Income is defined as GDP divided by the labor force (GDP_{it}/L_{it}). Demo means democratic country groups and Nondemo means nondemocratic country groups.
12. Note that β_j is just one part of the impacts of inputs on GDP_{it}. Whole impacts that capital and labor have are made up of β_{jk}, β_{jt}, and γ_{jm}.

TABLE 2 The Correlation Matrix, $N = 4622$

	GDP	Capital	Labor	Demo	Credit	Trade	FDI	Elec	No Firm	Gov. Cons
GDP	1.00									
Capital	0.98	1.00								
Labor	0.60	0.57	1.00							
Demo	0.11	0.13	−0.02	1.00						
Credit	0.26	0.29	0.16	0.30	1.00					
Trade	−0.19	−0.18	−0.17	−0.06	0.19	1.00				
FDI	−0.06	−0.05	−0.04	0.01	0.10	0.41	1.00			
Electricity	0.24	0.25	−0.02	0.21	0.49	0.17	0.06	1.00		
No of firms	0.75	0.73	0.44	0.20	0.31	−0.17	−0.05	0.28	1.00	
Gov. consumption	0.00	0.02	−0.08	0.06	0.17	0.18	0.04	0.26	0.00	1.00

TABLE 3 Estimation Results for M1, M2, M3, M4, M5, and M6

	M1_STT		M2_MTT		M3_GI	
	Coeff	Std Err	Coeff	Std Err	Coeff	Std Err
K_{it}	0.85***	0.03	0.81***	0.03	0.82***	0.03
L_{it}	−0.47***	0.07	−0.15***	0.06	−0.37***	0.06
D_{it}	0.02***	0.007	0.03***	0.01	0.02***	0.007
t	0.009***	0.002	−	−	−	−
t_1	−	−	−0.01***	0.00	−	−
t_2	−	−	0.08***	0.01	−	−
$K_{it}K_{it}$	−0.03***	0.007	−0.01**	0.01	−0.03***	0.006
$L_{it}L_{it}$	0.05***	0.01	0.05***	0.01	0.04***	0.01
tt	0.0005***	0.00	−	−	−	−
t_1t_1	−	−	0.001***	0.00	−	−
t_2t_2	−	−	−0.01***	0.00	−	−

	M4_TS_STT		M5_TS_MTT		M6_TS_GI	
	Coeff	Std Err	Coeff	Std Err	Coeff	Std Err
K_{it}	0.98***	0.05	0.90***	0.05	0.91***	0.05
L_{it}	−0.38***	0.08	−0.17**	0.07	−0.26***	0.07
D_{it}	0.07***	0.02	0.06**	0.02	0.11***	0.02
t	0.005*	0.003	−	−	−	−
t_1	−	−	−0.01***	0.00	−	−
t_2	−	−	0.09***	0.01	−	−
$K_{it}K_{it}$	−0.02***	0.009	−0.01	0.01	−0.01	0.01
$L_{it}L_{it}$	0.05***	0.01	0.06***	0.01	0.06***	0.01
tt	0.0005***	0	−	−	−	−
t_1t_1	−	−	0.001***	0.00	−	−
t_2t_2	−	−	−0.008***	0.00	−	−
$T_1(Z^{1P}_{it})$	−0.004	0.02	0.04	0.03	−0.03	0.02
$T_2(Z^{2P}_{it})$	−0.11**	0.05	−0.06	0.05	−0.09*	0.05
Z^{11}_{it}	0.10***	0.02	0.20***	0.03	0.01***	0.00
Z^{12}_{it}	−0.001**	0	−0.002**	0.00	−0.0001	0.00

Continued

TABLE 3 Estimation Results for M1, M2, M3, M4, M5, and M6—cont'd

	M4_TS_STT		M5_TS_MTT		M6_TS_GI	
	Coeff	Std Err	Coeff	Std Err	Coeff	Std Err
Z_{it}^{21}	0.17***	0.04	0.17***	0.05	0.16***	0.04
Z_{it}^{22}	0.11***	0.04	0.19***	0.07	0.12**	0.05
$D_{it}T_1(Z_{it}^{1P})$	0.04***	0.006	0.04***	0.01	0.02***	0.00
$D_{it}T_2(Z_{it}^{2P})$	−0.02***	0.005	−0.02***	0.01	−0.02***	0.01

Note: ***P-value <0.01; **P-value <0.05; *P-value <0.10; 4622 observations.

TABLE 4 Elasticities Calculated Based on Estimation Results From M1, M2, and M3

	$E_{K_{it}}$	$E_{L_{it}}$	TC	Neutral	n_neutral	RTS	TFP
A. Elasticities, technical change, RTS, TFP_M1_Single time trend (Mean)							
Asia	0.583	0.295	0.008	0.019	−0.011	0.878	0.004
Africa	0.645	0.179	0.009	0.019	−0.010	0.823	0.004
N_America	0.520	0.476	0.005	0.018	−0.013	0.995	0.005
S_America	0.595	0.232	0.009	0.019	−0.010	0.826	0.005
Europe	0.553	0.278	0.010	0.020	−0.010	0.831	0.007
Income_L	0.651	0.224	0.008	0.019	−0.011	0.875	0.005
Income_M	0.595	0.232	0.010	0.019	−0.010	0.827	0.004
Income_H	0.544	0.278	0.009	0.019	−0.009	0.823	0.005
Demo	0.582	0.264	0.010	0.020	−0.010	0.847	0.006
Nondemo	0.619	0.215	0.008	0.018	−0.010	0.834	0.003
Mean	0.597	0.245	0.009	0.019	−0.010	0.842	0.005
B. Elasticities, technical change, RTS, TFP_M2_Multiple time trends (Mean)							
Asia	0.613	0.322	−0.022	0.011	−0.033	0.935	−0.024
Africa	0.651	0.260	−0.018	0.012	−0.030	0.910	−0.021
N_America	0.566	0.434	−0.026	0.015	−0.040	0.999	−0.026
S_America	0.626	0.276	−0.018	0.011	−0.029	0.902	−0.021
Europe	0.605	0.293	−0.019	0.011	−0.029	0.898	−0.02

TABLE 4 Elasticities Calculated Based on Estimation Results From M1, M2, and M3—cont'd

	$E_{K_{it}}$	$E_{L_{it}}$	TC	Neutral	n_neutral	RTS	TFP
Income_L	0.646	0.299	−0.022	0.012	−0.034	0.946	−0.023
Income_M	0.626	0.277	−0.019	0.011	−0.030	0.904	−0.022
Income_H	0.602	0.288	−0.017	0.011	−0.028	0.890	−0.020
Demo	0.617	0.297	−0.021	0.010	−0.031	0.914	−0.023
Nondemo	0.637	0.275	−0.017	0.013	−0.030	0.912	−0.020
Mean	0.625	0.288	−0.019	0.011	−0.031	0.913	−0.022
C. Elasticities, technical change, RTS, TFP_M3_General index (Mean)							
Asia	0.588	0.274	0.006	0.015	−0.009	0.861	0.002
Africa	0.642	0.174	0.007	0.014	−0.007	0.816	0.002
N_America	0.534	0.423	0.004	0.014	−0.010	0.957	0.003
S_America	0.597	0.222	0.007	0.014	−0.008	0.819	0.002
Europe	0.559	0.265	0.007	0.016	−0.009	0.824	0.005
Income_L	0.649	0.209	0.007	0.015	−0.008	0.858	0.003
Income_M	0.597	0.223	0.007	0.015	−0.008	0.820	0.002
Income_H	0.551	0.266	0.007	0.015	−0.008	0.817	0.002
Demo	0.586	0.251	0.007	0.016	−0.009	0.836	0.004
Nondemo	0.620	0.206	0.006	0.013	−0.007	0.825	0.001
Mean	0.599	0.232	0.007	0.015	−0.008	0.832	0.002

even squared terms of MTT have significant coefficients, we can see that the specification of MTT by choosing 2008 as the threshold was efficient.

The first order coefficient β_d is positive and significant in all the six models. Just based on Model 1, Model 2, and Model 3, we can say that democracy has positive impacts on economic growth independent of the methods used to capture time effects. In Model 4, Model 5, and Model 6, because the sum of β_d and θ_{tm} is always positive and significant, we can say that democracy has positive impacts on economic growth. The existence and direction of institutional elements, however, is not sufficient for us to evaluate democracy's contribution to economic growth in detail. Concentrating on the interacted term $\sum_m \sum_p \theta_{tm} D_{it} T_m(Z_{it}^{mp})$ is required in the TS model to satisfy these goals.

TABLE 5 Elasticities Calculated Based on Estimation Results From M4, M5, and M6

	$E_{K_{it}}$	$E_{L_{it}}$	e_D$_{it}$	TC	Neutral	n_neutral	RTS	TFP	e_T$_1$	e_T$_2$
A. Elasticities, technical change, RTS, TFP_M4_Technology shifters_Single time trend (Mean)										
Asia	0.454	0.294	0.009	0.009	0.016	-0.008	0.747	0.001	0.022	0.158
Africa	0.584	0.162	0.040	0.009	0.016	-0.007	0.746	0.002	0.016	0.045
N_America	0.327	0.457	-0.020	0.006	0.015	-0.010	0.784	0.002	0.048	0.233
S_America	0.492	0.232	0.018	0.008	0.016	-0.008	0.724	0.002	0.043	0.107
Europe	0.397	0.309	0.000	0.010	0.017	-0.007	0.706	0.006	0.042	0.208
Income_L	0.577	0.200	0.036	0.009	0.016	-0.007	0.777	0.003	0.017	0.057
Income_M	0.491	0.233	0.023	0.009	0.017	-0.007	0.724	0.002	0.029	0.117
Income_H	0.393	0.305	-0.000	0.008	0.016	-0.008	0.698	0.003	0.039	0.204
Demo	0.454	0.275	0.013	0.010	0.017	-0.008	0.729	0.004	0.044	0.147
Nondemo	0.537	0.204	0.025	0.008	0.015	-0.007	0.740	0.000	0.006	0.094
Mean	0.487	0.246	0.018	0.009	0.016	-0.008	0.733	0.003	0.029	0.126
B. Elasticities, technical change, RTS, TFP_M5_Technology shifters_Multiple time trends (Mean)										
Asia	0.507	0.321	0.017	-0.02	0.014	-0.042	0.828	-0.03	0.023	0.145
Africa	0.607	0.235	0.044	-0.02	0.015	-0.04	0.842	-0.03	0.016	0.042
N_America	0.405	0.444	-0.01	-0.03	0.017	-0.048	0.850	-0.03	0.054	0.203
S_America	0.542	0.268	0.026	-0.02	0.014	-0.042	0.810	-0.03	0.048	0.099

Europe	0.475	0.308	0.012	−0.02	0.014	−0.042	0.783	−0.03	0.049	0.190
Income_L	0.594	0.277	0.039	−0.02	0.015	−0.039	0.871	−0.02	0.016	0.050
Income_M	0.541	0.270	0.030	−0.02	0.014	−0.042	0.811	−0.03	0.034	0.109
Income_H	0.473	0.301	0.009	−0.02	0.014	−0.043	0.774	−0.03	0.046	0.188
Demo	0.513	0.298	0.023	−0.02	0.014	−0.042	0.811	−0.03	0.048	0.134
Nondemo	0.571	0.259	0.031	−0.02	0.015	−0.040	0.830	−0.03	0.008	0.087
Mean	0.536	0.282	0.026	−0.02	0.015	−0.041	0.819	−0.03	0.032	0.115

C. Elasticities, technical change, RTS, TFP_M6_Technology shifters_General index (Mean)

Asia	0.476	0.877	0.004	0.007	0.013	−0.006	1.353	0.025	0.016	0.159
Africa	0.588	0.846	0.045	0.007	0.012	−0.005	1.433	0.027	0.007	0.046
N_America	0.371	0.877	−0.02	0.005	0.012	−0.007	1.249	0.012	0.023	0.233
S_America	0.513	0.876	0.018	0.007	0.012	−0.006	1.389	0.022	0.017	0.110
Europe	0.430	0.916	−0.01	0.008	0.014	−0.006	1.346	0.013	0.018	0.213
Income_L	0.578	0.836	0.042	0.007	0.013	−0.005	1.414	0.025	0.012	0.055
Income_M	0.511	0.876	0.021	0.007	0.013	−0.006	1.387	0.023	0.010	0.119
Income_H	0.429	0.917	−0.01	0.007	0.013	−0.006	1.346	0.018	0.020	0.210
Demo	0.477	0.887	0.008	0.008	0.014	−0.006	1.364	0.020	0.022	0.151
Nondemo	0.549	0.860	0.028	0.006	0.011	−0.005	1.409	0.026	0.002	0.094
Mean	0.506	0.876	0.016	0.007	0.013	−0.006	1.382	0.022	0.014	0.128

In Model 4, Model 5, and Model 6, we can consider the elasticity of democracy (D_{it}), e_D_{it} as:

E6: Elasticity of D_{it} in the TS model:

$$e_{D_{it}} = \beta_d + \sum_m \sum_p \theta_{tm} T_m \left(Z_{it}^{mp} \right) \tag{11}$$

Because we divide technical change into a neutral part and a nonneutral part, we also can divide e_D_{it} into a neutral part (β_d) and a nonneutral part $\sum_m \sum_p \theta_{tm} T_m(Z_{it}^{mp})$. There are two ways to interpret the coefficient θ_{tm} of the interaction term $\sum_m \sum_p \theta_{tm} D_{it} T_m(Z_{it}^{mp})$. First, θ_{tm} determines the direction and magnitude of the nonneutral part. That is, when democracy is interacted with TS, it will affect GDP with an amount of θ_{tm}. In this interpretation, technology shifter Z_{it}^{mp} acts as a possible channel between democracy and economic growth. Second, note that θ_{tm} can be observed in the regression equations only when D_{it} has a value of 1. Therefore, we can interpret θ_{tm} as the differences in the effect of each technology shifter between democratic and nondemocratic countries.

Let us concentrate on the first way to interpret θ_{tm}. The interacted terms $\sum_m \sum_p \theta_{tm} D_{it} T_m(Z_{it}^{mp})$ always have significant coefficients, however, the direction of these coefficients varies depending on $T_m(Z_{it}^{mp})$. When $T_1(Z_{it}^{1p})$ is interacted, the coefficients are positive. When $T_2(Z_{it}^{2p})$ is interacted, the coefficients are negative. Let us check each technology shifter to interpret specific implications. The coefficients of the third technology shifter Z_{it}^{13} and Z_{it}^{23} can be derived by subtracting the sum of another two shifters' coefficients from 1 because of the constraints we have imposed $\sum_{p=1}^{P_m} \gamma^{mp} = 1 \; \forall \; m$.

Z_{it}^{11} stands for credit guarantee. Z_{it}^{11}'s coefficients are always positive and significant. Because $D_{it} T_1(Z_{it}^{1p})$'s coefficients are also positive, we can suggest that credit guarantee acts as a positive linkage between democracy and economic growth. Because Z_{it}^{12}'s coefficients are not significant in M6, we cannot determine the role of Z_{it}^{12} and Z_{it}^{13} in M6. When we look at M4 and M5, the TS STT model and the TS MTT model, however, we also can clarify the roles of Z_{it}^{12} and Z_{it}^{13}. According to M4 and M5, trade openness can be interpreted as a negative medium between democracy and economic growth. FDI inflows, however, turn out to be a positive medium between democracy and economic growth.

Because the coefficients of $D_{it} T_2(Z_{it}^{2p})$ are all significantly negative and because the coefficients of Z_{it}^{21} and Z_{it}^{22} are all significantly positive, we can draw some inferences from all TS in $T_2(Z_{it}^{2p})$. When electricity consumption per capita and the number of listed firms are interacted with the democracy dummy variable, they have negative effects on production output. This means that these two variables can have negative linkages between democracy and economic growth. Moreover, as the sum of coefficients of Z_{it}^{21} and Z_{it}^{22} does not exceed 1 in all three models, governmental consumption also can be interpreted as a negative link between democracy and economic growth.

The roles of credit guarantee, FDI inflows, and government consumption between democracy and economic growth are consistent with our expectation. More democratic countries guarantee transparency in credit guarantee decisions both in the private and public sectors. This transparency leads capital to be allocated to productive candidates. Therefore, the allocative efficiency of capital improves.[13] Transparency derived from democratization plays a key role in reducing capital distortions that exist in industry level and firm level allocations. In addition, because multinational firms invest more in democratic countries,[14] democratization attracts more FDI inflows. Because productive foreign firms begin to compete with domestic firms, innovation activities of firms and spillover effects from already productive firms become more vibrant.[15] Technological changes were the fundamental reason for economic growth in the 19th and 20th centuries. Because the contributions of both credit guarantee and FDI inflows to technological changes increase as the quality of democracy improves, it is natural for us to interpret them as positive linkages between economic growth and democracy.

We also can give reasons why government consumption and trade openness turn out to be negative linkages between economic growth and democracy by considering technological changes. As the quality of democracy improves, the government's consumption share of GDP can increase or decrease. It is relatively certain, however, that the structure of government consumption will change as the quality of democracy improves. Tabellini and Alesina (1990) show that most of the voters prefer a budget deficit; they also suggest that a balanced budget amendment is not durable under majority voting rule. Plumper and Martin (2003) added that in semidemocratic countries, as political participation increases, governments are inclined to overinvest in the provision of public goods. We also have seen many populist regimes and their governments' spending. When democratization takes place, elected governments provide policies or public goods in order to react to median voters' requests. It is natural for us to expect an increase in welfare policies, which will make the relative size of technological investments of governments (which lead to technological changes) to become smaller because the magnitude of the government's total budget is limited. Because technological changes are the main factor causing economic growth in a production function analysis, changes in the structure of government consumption that resulted from democratization will affect economic growth negatively. Alesina and Rodrik (1994) suggest that policies that maximize economic growth are optimal for a government that cares only about capitalists. It is evident that it is difficult for median voters to prefer such political parties.

---

13. The importance of allocative efficiency is presented in much research, including some seminal papers such as Olley and Pakes (1996) and Foster, Haltiwanger, and Krizan (2001).
14. For additional reading, see Busse (2003).
15. Borensztein, Gregorio, and Lee (1998) and Alfaro, Chanda, Ozcan, and Sayek's (2004) papers clarify the positive impacts of FDI on economic growth.

As Yu's (2010) findings support, democracy fosters trade openness. In contrast to FDI inflows, however, this static model suggests that trade openness is a negative medium between economic growth and democracy. It is well known that trade's impact on economic growth has been significantly positive. Recent papers suggest that trade causes more innovation activities in domestic firms.[16] Therefore, it is difficult for us to describe trade openness' role as a negative linkage between economic growth and democracy based on existing literature. Yanikkaya (2003) provides one possible way to interpret the results of this static model by suggesting unconventional implications. Yanikkaya's paper suggests that in developing countries, trade restrictions have strong positive impacts on economic growth under certain conditions. If this fact is generalized, we can imagine that a mechanism that lowered trade restrictions caused by democratization can lower economic growth.

The results of electricity consumption and number of listed firms are not identical to our general intuition. Why do electricity consumption and the number of firms act as negative linkages between democracy and economic growth? First, electricity consumption consists of household usage, public usage, and industrial usage. GDP growth will be highly correlated to industrial usage. As our data about electricity consumption per capita include information about household usage, the linkage's direction can be negative. It can be accepted that waste and inefficiencies in household consumption can be fostered in a free atmosphere. Therefore, when interacted with democracy, electricity consumption can be a negative link between economic growth and democracy. Second, for a number of listed firms global outsourcing can be the reason for this negative link. As an economy grows, the number of firms increases. As globalization deepens, however, global outsourcing also increases as an economy grows. The firms whose production procedures are centered mainly in foreign countries will contribute less to GDP than those firms whose production procedures are rooted mainly in home countries. These effects of global outsourcing could change the direction of Z_{it}^{22}'s (number of listed firms) role in being a link between economic growth and democracy.

Let us now consider a second way of interpreting the meaning of θ_{tm}. Table 6 gives a list of TS that have significant coefficients at the interacted term $\sum_m \sum_p \theta_{tm} D_{it} T_m(Z_{it}^{mp})$.

TS that are underlined in Table 6 are significant in all the three models and their directions are consistent through the three models. TS with a plus (+) sign are positive links between democracy and economic growth as dealt with earlier. Likewise, TS with a minus (−) sign are negative links between democracy and economic growth.

---

16. Bloom, Draca, and Reenen (2016) showed that imports from China increased European firms' innovation activities and productivity. Acharya and Keller (2009) suggested that goods trade is one of the main channels of technology transfer.

TABLE 6 Technology Shifters and Their Directions Which Have Significant Coefficients in the Interacted term $\sum_m \sum_p \theta_{tm} D_{it} T_m(Z_{it}^{mp})$

Model 4:

Credit guarantee, $Z_{it}^{11}(+)$/Trade, $Z_{it}^{12}(-)$/FDI, $Z_{it}^{13}(+)$/Electricity consumption, $Z_{it}^{21}(-)$/Number of firms, $Z_{it}^{22}(-)$/Government consumption, $Z_{it}^{23}(-)$

Model 5:

Credit guarantee, $Z_{it}^{11}(+)$/Trade, $Z_{it}^{12}(-)$/FDI, $Z_{it}^{13}(+)$/Electricity consumption, $Z_{it}^{21}(-)$/Number of firms, $Z_{it}^{22}(-)$/Government consumption, $Z_{it}^{23}(-)$

Model 6:

Credit guarantee, $Z_{it}^{11}(+)$/Electricity consumption, $Z_{it}^{21}(-)$/Number of firms, $Z_{it}^{22}(-)$/Government consumption, $Z_{it}^{23}(-)$

As θ_{tm} appears in the regression equations only when $D_{it} = 1$, TS with a (+) sign have more marginal effects in democratic countries. On the other hand, TS with a (−) sign have smaller marginal effects in democratic countries. This means that TS with a (−) sign have bigger marginal effects in nondemocratic countries. In other words, credit guarantee and FDI inflows have more marginal effects in democratic countries. Trade openness, electricity consumption, number of listed firms, and government consumption have much higher marginal effects in the case of nondemocratic countries.

2.5.2 An Analysis of Elasticities

In Tables 4 and 5, elasticities derived from the six models are arranged according to criteria: continent, income level, and the democracy dummy variable D_{it}. Income means GDP divided by the labor force. There are some tendencies in these tables. First, as income increases, $E_{K_{it}}$ and RTS decrease. Second, democratic countries have lower $E_{K_{it}}$ as compared to nondemocratic countries. Third, most of negative parts of the technical changes are derived from the nonneutral part, whereas most of the positive parts of the technical change are derived from the neutral part. Finally, elasticities of democracy are sometimes negative in high-income countries and high-income continents. We also can find several other tendencies in these tables. But these four tendencies are the most remarkable ones that we could catch.[17]

---

17. The separate estimation of this static model also is implemented according to each income group (low, middle, and high as in Tables 4 and 5). The direction and magnitude of coefficients for the democracy dummy variable vary according to income groups and models. Because this paper concentrates on the global impacts of democracy on economic growth, those results for each income group are excluded even though they require intense analysis. It is natural for us to make a detailed analysis about democracy's impacts in high-income countries, middle-income countries, and low-income countries.

3 A Dynamic Model

3.1 Motivation

The empirical production models are discussed in the previous section of this paper with different generalizations related to representations of technology. Models M1–M6 are static models. Through these six models, we explain GDP output levels using the production function. To be specific, the GDP output level is explained by inputs (capital stock and labor force), technology indices constructed by six TS and a dichotomous democracy dummy variable. The functional forms of the production function are translog production function forms. This econometric specification turned out to be appropriate for our analysis. According to the estimation results of these static models, the role of inputs is consistent with the theoretical prediction. Moreover, the technology indices represent the level of technology successfully. The existence and direction of institutional elements in the production function are robustly consistent through all the six models. The implications derived by TS are also consistent for four TS (credit guarantee, electricity consumption, number of listed firms, and government consumption) through all the TS models.

In spite of these advantages of the static models' specifications, we have to consider alternative generalized empirical models for two main reasons. First, the GDP level cannot be explained enough by the production side of a nation's economy because a considerable part of the observed GDP output is explained by the demand side of a country's economy. Therefore, an omitted variable bias can be troublesome when we try to explain the GDP output level using production side variables only. Second, the static models assume that all changes and effects take place immediately. In practice, however, changes take place gradually and are a part of a process that requires a dynamic adjustment process toward a target level of GDP.

By using a dynamic model, we can solve these two problems. Inserting a lagged GDP variable as an independent variable can help avoid the first problem caused by the demand side of an economy being included in the GDP. Acemoglu et al. (forthcoming) use a lagged GDP variable and the dichotomous democracy dummy variable as explanatory variables. The results of their analysis are similar to the results of this paper's static model because both studies provide evidence that democracy has a significant and robust positive effect on GDP. In addition, a dynamic model's specifications provide information about the path of adjustment toward the target level of GDP and the speed of the adjustment process.

There are many ways to construct a dynamic model using lagged GDP as an independent variable. In choosing a specific form of a dynamic model, we have to consider that we are concentrating on the role of institutions. Devising a dynamic model that reflects the institutional element successfully will be a key criterion when we evaluate whether this dynamic model is appropriate for our research question. By using the concept of the target GDP level and the concept of adjustment speed, we can make a dynamic model for exploring the relationship between democracy and GDP growth.

3.1.1 Target Level of GDP and Adjustment Speed

Target level of the GDP of a specific country in a specific year GDP_{it}^*, also can be interpreted as a predicted or an expected optimal level of GDP for each country and year. The public sector, the private sector, or producers including government officers, politicians, researchers, reporters, and businessmen have their expectations. The information set used for the prediction might not only contain all observable macroeconomic indices, but also unobserved country-specific characteristics or time-specific characteristics as well as exogenous shocks. This target level of GDP is used widely when government officers or politicians make economic policies such as investments in infrastructure, education, and developing technology. In addition, GDP_{it}^* also can act as a criterion when we evaluate the results of an economic policy or when we analyze economic cycles. Accordingly, the target level of GDP, GDP_{it}^*, also can be considered as the GDP level in a steady state.

Adjustment parameter δ_{it} explains the differences between GDP_{it}^* and the realized GDP level GDP_{it}. The word "adjustment" is used to mean the actual or observed GDP_{it}'s adjustment toward GDP_{it}^*. In other words, δ_{it} represents the magnitude of the expected proper adjustment between two subsequent years or the rate of convergence of GDP_{it} to GDP_{it}^*. Economic policies usually encounter unexpected impacts. Moreover, proper policies for attaining GDP_{it}^* might not be executed because the implementation of certain policies can present obstacles. Therefore, even though government officers do their best to attain the target level GDP_{it}^* every year, we observe that the realized GDP_{it} tends to be different from GDP_{it}^*. Some variables that form the differences between GDP_{it} and GDP_{it}^* construct the adjustment parameter δ_{it}. The parameter differs from 1 because it is costly and also because of limited resources. In other words, it is not feasible to adjust to the target level in one single period. Therefore, the speed of adjustment that is constructed by the functions of some variables differs among countries and over time because every country has different levels of costs and resources that may change over time. For example, the economic situation of a small open economy is highly dependent on global economic trends. Therefore, the government's policy to attain GDP_{it}^* can be interfered with easily. When we embrace GDP_{it}^* and δ_{it}, we can consider a system of equations for a dynamic GDP model.

3.2 Econometric Specifications

3.2.1 Model

The main idea for this dynamic model is that the realized GDP level always tends to be different from the GDP target level, a difference that is explained by adjustment speed. Based on these facts, we can consider the equation:

E7:

$$\text{GDP}_{it} - \text{GDP}_{i\,t-1} = \delta_{it}\left(\text{GDP}_{it}^* - \text{GDP}_{i\,t-1}\right) \tag{12}$$

As indicated in equation E7, δ_{it} quantifies the difference between $\text{GDP}_{it} - \text{GDP}_{i\,t-1}$ and $\text{GDP}_{it}^* - \text{GDP}_{i\,t-1}$. If $\delta_{it} = 1$, it takes just one period for the entire adjustment to be completed. This means that the country in time t is at the nation's target level of GDP. $\delta_{it} < 1$ implies that the adjustment that occurred from year $t - 1$ to t was smaller than the required magnitude of adjustment for GDP_{it}^*. We can check that $\text{GDP}_{it} \rightarrow \text{GDP}_{it}^*$ as $t \rightarrow \infty$ when $|\delta_{it}| < 1$. If $\delta_{it} > 1$, the nation's GDP is adjusted more than the required magnitude.

GDP_{it}^* is affected by some variables, and we can consider a function $F(\cdot)$ that represents a detailed relationship between key variables differing in countries and time dimensions:

E8:

$$\text{GDP}_{it}^* = F(X_{it}, X_i, X_t) \tag{13}$$

X_{it} is a vector of variables affecting the target GDP level, GDP_{it}^*. (We discuss the variables included in X_{it} in the next section). X_i are country-specific variables but also can be represented by country dummy variables. X_t are a set of time-specific variables but also can be represented by time dummy variables or a time trend. Because X_{it} can vary across countries and over time, it also is possible that GDP_{it}^* varies across countries and over time. This means a country's target level of GDP might change over time. Therefore, GDP's dynamic nature can be captured through these settings. The ratio between GDP's target level and realized GDP ($\text{GDP}_{it}^* / \text{GDP}_{it}$) can measure the degree of optimality of a specific nation's GDP in a specific year.

Likewise, δ_{it} is affected by several variables and we can express δ_{it} by a function $G(\cdot)$:

E9:

$$\delta_{it} = G(Z_{it}, Z_i, Z_t) \tag{14}$$

where Z_{it} is a vector of variables determining the adjustment speed δ_{it}. (Detailed information about the variables included in Z_{it} is given in the next section.) Z_i and Z_t are country-specific and time-specific effects represented by country or time dummy variables (or time trend). By construction, we also can consider the dynamic nature of the adjustment speed, δ_{it}. This is attributed to the fact that countries' adjustment speeds might differ from each other and change over time.

Although we acknowledge that countries might not have optimal target levels of GDP at any point in time, one of the powerful advantages of this model is that it can show the optimal behavior of a country. This is possible because adjustment speed δ_{it} includes information about the adjustment costs that governments are required to pay to attain GDP_{it}^*. Realized GDP, GDP_{it} can be interpreted as a result of a government's decision that is always vulnerable to adjustment costs. If realized GDP is simply regressed on X_{it} or Z_{it} alone, then the inferred relationship suffers from specification errors. The aggregation of effects can be the reason for these specification errors. In addition, the absence of adjustment costs and the employment of nondynamic adjustments also can contribute to these specification errors. E7 can be arranged again as Model 7 (M7) in order to avoid misspecification errors:

Model 7 (M7): Dynamic model with adjustment speed and target level of GDP:

$$GDP_{it} = (1 - \delta_{it})GDP_{it-1} + \delta_{it}GDP_{it}^* + \beta_d D_{it} + e_{it} \qquad (15)$$

where e_{it} is the statistical error term. This chapter assumes that e_{it} has mean 0 and constant variance. The exact form of functions $F(\cdot)$ and $G(\cdot)$ will be decided based on the results of the likelihood ratio functional form test. D_{it} is a dichotomous democracy dummy variable. D_{it} also is used in the static model in this chapter. By implementing this democracy dummy variable D_{it}, we can extract the impact of democracy on economic growth from the error term. The main focus of this dynamic model is checking the existence of democracy's positive impacts on economic growth, which already has been proven by the static model. It should be noted that this functional form is nonlinear for both parameters and explanatory variables.

3.2.2 Variables and Functional Forms for GDP_{it}^* and δ_{it}

As shown in the analysis of static models, the GDP output level is highly related to production inputs such as capital stock and labor force. Economists have been trying to explain the production output of economic agents such as firms and nations using capital stock and labor force for a long time. Therefore, considering capital stock and labor force in expecting or estimating target GDP_{it}^* are essential. Although population is also a useful criterion for the size of the domestic market, we exclude the population variable because of a potential multicollinearity problem with the labor force variable. In sum, for X_{it}, let us use capital stock (K_{it}) and labor force (L_{it}). Considering K_{it} and L_{it} for X_{it} also is consistent with the static model because those two variables are considered as inputs in the translog production function of the static models.

For Z_{it}, we consider six variables. First, if a nation's economy is largely dependent on global trends, adjustments to target level GDP will encounter many obstacles. To be specific, as the trade's share of GDP or foreign FDI inflows' share of GDP increases, the adjustment speed becomes more vulnerable to trade openness and FDI inflows. This is mainly because the effect of the government's policies for attaining GDP_{it}^* will not have a significant impact on the realized GDP level without proper changes in trade or FDI inflows. Therefore, we have to include trade's share of GDP and FDI's share of GDP in Z_{it}. In addition, most of the government's policies for achieving GDP_{it}^* contain fiscal policy measures such as changes in government consumption. A larger share of the government's consumption as a part of GDP can imply that the impact of the policies made by government consumption becomes stronger. Consequently, the government consumption's share of GDP should be considered in order to capture adjustment speed effectively.

Another fact that we have to consider is that the impact of external shocks, including the government's policies, will vary according to private economic agents' abilities to actively react to the shocks. For example, economic agents' ability to react to government policies is determined mainly by their budget constraints. Large-scale domestic credit to the private sector by banks can guarantee flexible budget constraints for economic agents. This is attributed to the fact that most of the economic agents, including households and firms, supply their required capital by taking loans from banks when they have to execute important consumption or investment decisions such as buying a house or building a factory. Therefore, in Z_{it}, banks' domestic credit to the private sector (defined as percent of GDP) is included in this study.

Another way in which firms finance their budgets is through financial markets. An active financial market guarantees companies have more chances of getting funding for their costs. Therefore, the number of listed firms should be used for explaining adjustment speed by considering firms' financing processes. The quality of infrastructure of each nation also should be considered when we construct adjustment speed. Countries with poor infrastructure usually have a hard time maximizing the positive impacts of economic shocks. Electricity consumption per capita can effectively represent the level of infrastructure because electricity is a key input for industrial production. In sum, there are six variables: trade openness (TO_{it}), FDI inflows (FDI_{it}), government consumption (GC_{it}), credit guarantee (CG_{it}), number of listed firms (NL_{it}), and electricity consumption (EC_{it}) in Z_{it}.[18] All these six variables are in logarithmic form here.

Functions F and G that explain GDP^*_{it} and δ_{it} have country-specific and time-specific variables. First, for Z_i, which indicates country-specific variables for δ_{it}, we use individual country dummy variables. Also, as time-specific variables Z_t for δ_{it}, we use year dummy variables. Therefore, the heterogeneity in δ_{it} is controlled by two-way fixed effects. It is difficult for us to assume the existence of group characteristics or the existence of global time trends in adjustment speed δ_{it}. Consequently, controlling all individual effects can make better estimators.

For GDP^*_{it}, we use income level group fixed effects as country-specific variables X_i. Income level means GDP_{it}/L_{it}, which already has been used in the analysis of elasticities in the static model. We also can interpret it as the GDP level per labor force. All nations can be divided by five or ten income level groups, and we tested this model by implementing both groups. We also can divide all

---

18. These six variables are the same as the technology shifters variables' Z^{11}_{it}, Z^{12}_{it}, Z^{13}_{it} Z^{21}_{it}, Z^{22}_{it}, and Z^{23}_{it} used in the static models. However, new notations CG_{it}, TO_{it}, FDI_{it}, EC_{it}, NL_{it}, and GC_{it} are used in the dynamic model for convenience.

countries just by the GDP level. Dividing nations by income level groups, however, is the better option because the heterogeneity between developed and developing countries cannot be properly considered by the GDP level. The STT was implemented for X_t, time-specific variables explaining GDP_{it}^*. Because GDP_{it}^* is the target level of GDP explained by capital stock and labor force, using a STT for controlling time effects is a natural method.

In sum, this chapter specifies country-specific variables and time-specific variables differently for GDP_{it}^* and δ_{it}, mainly because we have an interaction term made up of GDP_{it}^* and δ_{it} in our main estimation model. We use a dataset of 144 nations covering 35 years. If we control GDP_{it}^* also by two-way fixed effects, many dummy variables are created in the interaction term $\delta_{it}GDP_{it}^*$. When we estimate the equation Model 7 (M7) with both GDP_{it}^* and δ_{it} controlled by two-way fixed effects, MLE estimation hardly converges. Sometimes, we can get some convergent results by implementing various starting points of the MLE estimation, but all the convergent results have unrealistic implications about capital share and labor share. Implementing income level group fixed effects and STT for GDP_{it}^* is the best way to improve the possibility of convergence and reduce specification errors.

Functions F and G are both linear functions in this dynamic setting. We can assume functions F and G as translog functions as in the static model, but the lagged variable of GDP_{it}, $GDP_{i\,t-1}$, already is included in this dynamic model. Therefore, the demand of controlling by the translog function is lower than it is in the static model. Moreover, because there is an interaction term $\delta_{it}GDP_{it}^*$ in the estimation model, setting F and G as translog functions can create many parameters. This might make the interpretation more difficult and complex. Based on this discussion, functions F and G are:

E10:

$$GDP_{it}^* = F(X_{it}, X_i, X_t) = \beta_0 + \beta_K K_{it} + \beta_L L_{it} + \beta_t t + Income_g \qquad (16)$$

and E11:

$$\delta_{it} = G(Z_{it}, Z_i, Z_t)$$
$$= \propto_0 + \propto_{CG} CG_{it} + \propto_{TO} TO_{it} + \propto_{FDI} FDI_{it} + \propto_{EC} EC_{it} + \propto_{NL} NL_{it}$$
$$+ \propto_{GC} GC_{it} + Country_i + Year_t \qquad 17)$$

$Income_g$ means the full set of income level fixed effects. I implemented both five and ten income groups for robustness. $Country_i$ is the full set of country fixed effects. $Year_t$ indicates the full set of year fixed effects.

3.3 Data

All these variables already have been used in the static models, and the dataset for this dynamic model is the same as that used for the static models. Penn World Table 9.0 (PWT) and the WDI are the main sources of the variables.

For GDP_{it} and $GDP_{i\ t-1}$, PWT's "real GDP at constant 2011 national prices (in million US$)" is used. PWT gives capital stock as "capital stock at constant 2011 national prices (in million US$)." The number of employees is appropriate for the labor force variable. The number of employees is indicated in PWT as "number of persons engaged (in millions)."

For the number of listed firms (NL_{it}), WDI's "listed domestic companies, total" is used. WDI's "electric power consumption (KWh per capita)" is used for the electricity consumption variable (EC_{it}). For trade openness (TO_{it}), WDI data for "trade openness (defined as import and export share of GDP)" is used. WDI's "foreign direct investment, net inflows (percent of GDP)" is used for the FDI inflows variable (FDI_{it}). For government consumption (GC_{it}) and credit guarantee (CG_{it}), WDI's "general government final consumption expenditure (defined as percent of GDP)" and "domestic credit to private sector by banks (defined as percent of GDP)" are used, respectively. D_{it} is also the same as the democracy dummy variable used in the static models. The methods of handling the missing observations are also the same as those used in the static models. After handling missing unit data, this study has 4622 observations for 144 nations observed unbalanced for 1980–2014. Because this dynamic model requires a lagged GDP variable $GDP_{i\ t-1}$, the total number of observations is 4478.

3.4 Estimation Method

The 144 nations that constitute the data in this study were not chosen randomly because the WDI dataset has many missing unit observations especially in the Z_{it} (TS' variables) in developing countries. Therefore, the 144 selected countries tend to be more developed than those that were omitted, which means that the fixed effects model is preferred to the random effects model. At the function $G(Z_{it}, Z_i, Z_t)$ that is explaining the adjustment speed δ_{it}, individual country fixed effects and year fixed effects are implemented.

The coefficients' interaction at $\delta_{it}GDP_{it}^*$ results in nonlinearity that has to be overcome. A full information maximum likelihood estimation enables us to estimate a nonlinear system of equations made by actual GDP, target GDP and speed of adjustment. In the SAS program, "proc model FIML" can be implemented with a little arrangement of parameters and variables. The correlation matrix (Table 2), indicates that the problems caused by multicollinearity are not expected.

3.5 Estimation Results

Table 7 shows the estimation results of M7. Because there are two ways to specify $Income_g$, the third column of the table shows the results derived using five income groups for $Income_g$ and the fourth column uses ten income groups for

TABLE 7 Estimation Results for M7.

Target level of GDP (GDP_{it}^*): Single time trend & Income level groups

Adjustment speed (δ_{it}): Two way fixed effects(By nations and years)

		5 Income Level Groups	10 Income Level Groups
	L likelihood	6588	6587
GDP_{it}^*	D_{it}	0.01267***	0.014189***
	K_{it}	0.663267***	0.582054***
	L_{it}	0.325295***	0.374526***
δ_{it}	GC_{it}	−0.01757***	−0.03143***
	FDI_{it}	0.002652***	0.004489***
	TO_{it}	0.011469***	0.025836***
	CG_{it}	−0.00136	−0.00253
	EC_{it}	−0.01178***	−0.01981***
	NL_{it}	0.001272	0.001079

Note: ***P-value < 0.01; **P-value < 0.05; *P-value < 0.10; 4478 observations.

$Income_g$. Table 8 is a summary of some statistics that are estimated through M7. Variables in Table 8 are classified according to continent, three income levels, and democracy as in the analysis of static models (Tables 4 and 5). This analysis is possible because GDP_{it}^* and δ_{it} have different values for each identity and each year.

According to Table 7, the two likelihood ratios made by the two methods of specifying $Income_g$ are almost the same. The direction of coefficients and their statistical significance are also very similar. Only the magnitude of these coefficients differs according to method by which $Income_g$ is specified. First, we can check that the determinants of GDP_{it}^*, K_{it}, and L_{it} have positive and significant impacts on GDP_{it}^*. Moreover, the magnitude of the coefficients of both K_{it} and L_{it} is reasonable and close to the traditional share of capital and labor. This shows that GDP_{it}^* successfully explains the target level of GDP of each nation.

Among the determinants of δ_{it}, two variables are positively significant toward δ_{it} and two variables that are negatively significant toward δ_{it}. Two variables related to the openness of one nation, TO_{it} and FDI_{it}, have positive coefficients that are statistically significant. TO_{it} has a bigger magnitude of positive impact on δ_{it} than does FDI_{it}. On the other hand, GC_{it} and EC_{it} have negative effects of δ_{it}. Credit guarantee (CG_{it}) and the number of listed firms (NL_{it})

TABLE 8 Statistics Calculated Based on Estimation Results From Dynamic Models

	GDP^*_{it}	GDP_{it}	δ_{it}	GDP_{it} $-GDP_{i\,t-1}$	GDP^*_{it} $-GDP_{i\,t-1}$	$\delta_{it}(GDP^*_{it}$ $-GDP_{i\,t-1})$
A. Model 7. Five income level groups for fixed effects of GDP^*_{it} (Mean)						
Asia	12.895	11.946	0.088	0.045	0.994	0.040
Africa	10.672	9.553	0.042	0.037	1.155	0.033
N_America	15.312	14.752	0.024	0.025	0.585	0.012
S_America	12.524	10.998	0.019	0.029	1.555	0.018
Europe	13.210	12.170	0.012	0.021	1.061	0.009
Income_L	10.874	9.844	0.040	0.037	1.067	0.032
Income_M	12.730	11.088	0.028	0.035	1.676	0.027
Income_H	13.041	12.390	0.058	0.028	0.679	0.019
Demo	12.717	11.535	0.023	0.032	1.214	0.019
Nondemo	11.452	10.451	0.071	0.035	1.036	0.036
Mean	12.211	11.102	0.042	0.033	1.142	0.026
B. Model 7. Ten income level groups for fixed effects of GDP^*_{it} (Mean)						
Asia	12.413	11.946	0.131	0.045	0.512	0.039
Africa	10.204	9.553	0.058	0.037	0.687	0.031
N_America	15.084	14.752	0.033	0.025	0.356	0.011
S_America	11.823	10.998	0.030	0.029	0.854	0.017
Europe	12.813	12.170	0.013	0.021	0.663	0.008
Income_L	10.338	9.844	0.084	0.037	0.531	0.030
Income_M	12.024	11.088	0.032	0.035	0.971	0.026
Income_H	12.833	12.390	0.064	0.028	0.471	0.018
Demo	12.204	11.535	0.032	0.032	0.700	0.018
Nondemo	11.011	10.451	0.102	0.035	0.595	0.035
Mean	11.727	11.102	0.060	0.033	0.658	0.025

have insignificant coefficients in Model 7 (M7). One of the most important things that we consider is that the adjustment speed δ_{it} can have positive or negative values. The optimal value of GDP change, $GDP^*_{it} - GDP_{i\,t-1}$, and the realized value of GDP change, $GDP_{it} - GDP_{i\,t-1}$, which is adjusted by δ_{it}, also can have both positive and negative values. We have to interpret the coefficients of determinants of δ_{it} based on these facts.

In literature about capital structure, some restrictions about the adjustment speed and target level are imposed. The actual realized debt ratio finally depends on firms' decisions. Therefore, the possibilities of overshooting adjustment and negative adjustment are relatively low. Imposing some restrictions on δ_{it} and GDP^*_{it}, however, can be misleading because this study is about the nature of national GDP. This is mainly because GDP_{it}, which means the realized GDP level, is impossible to be determined by each nation's government. It is also difficult to have an expectation about GDP_{it} because the exact mechanism determining GDP_{it} has not been clarified yet and there are always a lot of unexpected shocks. Consequently, it is always possible that δ_{it} has an overshooting effect ($\delta_{it} > 1$) or that a negative adjustment occurs ($\delta_{it} < 0$).

Table 9 shows the actual distribution of adjustment speed δ_{it}, $GDP_{it} - GDP_{i\,t-1}$, and $GDP^*_{it} - GDP_{i\,t-1}$. Based on the first estimation results, which use five income level groups for controlling GDP^*_{it}, 12.6% of the adjustment speed δ_{it} among 4478 observations have negative values. Just 0.3% of δ_{it} are larger than 1,[19] 14.5% of $GDP_{it} - GDP_{i\,t-1}$, which means the realized GDP change is negative. On the

TABLE 9 Minimum, Maximum and Number of Negative Observations

	Mean	Std Dev	Minimum	Maximum	Number of Negative Observations (%)
A. Model 7. Five income level groups for fixed effects of GDP^*_{it}					
δ_{it}	0.042	0.086	−0.107	1.122	565(12.6%)
$GDP_{it} - GDP_{i\,t-1}$	0.033	0.063	−0.714	0.724	697(15.5%)
$GDP^*_{it} - GDP_{i\,t-1}$	1.142	0.721	−0.451	3.288	89(1.9%)
B. Model 7. Ten income level groups for fixed effects of GDP^*_{it}					
δ_{it}	0.060	0.113	−0.249	1.126	694(15.4%)
$GDP_{it} - GDP_{i\,t-1}$	0.033	0.063	−0.714	0.724	697(15.5%)
$GDP^*_{it} - GDP_{i\,t-1}$	0.658	0.429	−0.466	2.620	183(4%)

19. Similarly, based on the second estimation results which use ten income level groups for controlling GDP^*_{it}, just 0.3% of δ_{it} are bigger than 1.

other hand, just 1.9% of $\text{GDP}_{it}^* - \text{GDP}_{i\,t-1}$ have negative values. Considering these facts about data distribution, we interpret the coefficients of determinants of adjustment speed δ_{it} after following two exclusion standards. Because only a few observations show that $\delta_{it} > 1(0.3\%)$, this study excludes the cases that satisfy $\delta_{it} > 1$. In addition, only a few observations show that $\text{GDP}_{it}^* - \text{GDP}_{i\,t-1}$ is negative (at the most 4%). Therefore, it is natural to make a conclusion while assuming that $\text{GDP}_{it}^* - \text{GDP}_{i\,t-1}$ has positive values.

First, we have to analyze the determinants of adjustment speed when $0 < \delta_{it} < 1$. Because $\text{GDP}_{it}^* - \text{GDP}_{i\,t-1}$ is assumed to be positive, $\text{GDP}_{it} - \text{GDP}_{i\,t-1}$ also is positive in this case, meaning that economic growth occurs between the two periods. As the trade's share of GDP and FDI inflows' shares of GDP increase, the adjustment speed δ_{it} gets closer to 1. In other words, the realized GDP change $\text{GDP}_{it} - \text{GDP}_{i\,t-1}$ adjusts faster to an optimal GDP change $\text{GDP}_{it}^* - \text{GDP}_{i\,t-1}$ as trade openness and FDI inflows increase. Realized GDP becomes closer to the optimal target level of GDP GDP_{it}^*. On the other hand, as the government consumption's share of GDP increases, the adjustment speed δ_{it} gets closer to 0. Electricity consumption per capita (EC_{it}) has the same effects as government consumption. As the government consumption's share of GDP increases and as the quality of infrastructure related to electricity improves, it will take longer for GDP_{it} to reach GDP_{it}^*.

Next, we can interpret these coefficients when $\delta_{it} < 0$. In this case, $\text{GDP}_{it} - \text{GDP}_{i\,t-1}$ becomes negative, which means that GDP declines between the two periods. Note that δ_{it} is not smaller than -1. First, as the proportion of trade openness and FDI among GDP increases, the adjustment speed gets closer to 0. This also means that the realized GDP change $\text{GDP}_{it} - \text{GDP}_{i\,t-1}$ adjusts to the optimal GDP change $\text{GDP}_{it}^* - \text{GDP}_{i\,t-1}$ faster if a nation's economy, including trade and FDI, has a higher degree of openness. When the government consumption's share of GDP and electricity consumption per capita increase, adjustment speed δ_{it} becomes closer to -1. Similar to the previous case, the GDP_{it}'s adjustment toward GDP_{it}^* becomes slower.

Whether the economy is growing or declining, TO_{it}, FDI_{it}, GC_{it}, and EC_{it} have consistent impacts on adjustment speed δ_{it}. TO_{it} and FDI_{it} stimulate the adjustment of GDP_{it} toward GDP_{it}^*, but GC_{it} and EC_{it} deter its adjustment. These findings about trade openness and FDI inflows were not expected. When we constructed the function explaining δ_{it}, we expected that higher openness and bigger FDI inflows will delay the adjustment of GDP_{it}. Also, we expected that, as the government consumption's share of GDP increases, vulnerability toward external shocks resulting from many factors, including openness, will decrease. This lowered vulnerability was expected to stimulate the adjustment speed. These expectations, however, were incorrect according to M7's estimation. One fact that is consistent with expectations, however, is that the impact of trade and FDI inflows on adjustment speed can be offset by government consumption. Because investments in infrastructure related to electricity are made mainly by the government, the coefficient of EC_{it} has the same direction as that of GC_{it}. Based on these facts, governments can control the adjustment process against the power of openness.

The dynamic model shows us that the impact of democracy on GDP levels is positive and highly significant according to Table 7. The demand side of the economy and the dynamic aspects of economic growth are omitted in the static models (M1–M6), but M7 considers these two aspects. Both the static model and the dynamic model support the contention that democracy can be regarded as one of the most important factors for analyzing economic growth. In addition, at least during 1980–2014, the impact of democracy on economic growth was positive.

4 Conclusion

This study obtains consistent, yet variable and informative results, from a panel data of 144 nations through the use of static and dynamic models' GDP specifications. This dataset covers the period 1980–2014. The GDP models—M1, M2, M3, M4, M5, and M6—point out the existence of positive institutional elements in the production function. Models M4, M5, and M6 show various results related to TS' specifications and found some possible channels between economic growth and democracy. To control for time-specific effects, a STT, MTT, and GI representations of technological changes are used. Dynamic settings constructed by optimal target level of GDP and flexible adjustment speed toward the target level are implemented in Model M7, which also shows democracy's positive and significant impacts on economic growth. Many interpretations about determinants of adjustment speed also are possible in Model M7.

The results of the static models study show that, as Acemoglu et al. (forthcoming) pointed out, there is a robust and positive relationship between democracy and economic growth. Positive impacts of democracy on economic growth are seen by estimating the production function by different methods. However, we also found some interesting linkages between democracy and economic growth. Credit guarantee and FDI inflows turned out to be positive linkages between democracy and economic growth. And they had bigger marginal effects in democratic countries than in nondemocratic countries. Trade, electricity infrastructure, the number of listed firms, and government consumption acted as negative factors between democracy and economic growth. These four variables had bigger marginal effects in nondemocratic countries than in democratic countries. Model M7, the dynamic model, also supported the positive impacts of democracy on GDP levels. TS' variables in the static models are used as determinants of adjustment speed in the dynamic model (M7). The effects to adjustment speed derived from trade openness and FDI inflows were the opposite of the effects caused by government consumption and electricity infrastructure.

Even though this study clarified robust impacts of democracy and identified some possible channels between democracy and economic growth, it would have been better if the dynamic model also had found and tested possible channels between democracy and economic growth. When we implement the dichotomous democracy dummy variable as the explanatory variable for the target level of GDP, we can analyze some possible channels between economic growth and democracy. It was impossible, however, to discover meaningful factors between the two concepts using the dynamic model because the role of democracy in the target level of GDP was not consistent with the findings of the static models. If one can find significant possible channels between democracy and economic growth that also are consistent with the nature of the optimal target level of GDP and adjustment speed, it will be a great contribution to this field.

A Appendix

TABLE A1 Cases of Transitions in Democracy Within a Nation (128 Times in 66 Nations)

Country	Year	Transition
Albania	1990–1991	Nondemocratic-democratic
	1995–1996	Democratic-nondemocratic
	1996–1997	Nondemocratic-democratic
Azerbaijan	1991–1992	Nondemocratic-democratic
	1992–1993	Democratic-nondemocratic
Argentina	1982–1983	Nondemocratic-democratic
Bangladesh	1990–1991	Nondemocratic-democratic
	2006–2007	Democratic-nondemocratic
	2008–2009	Nondemocratic-democratic
Armenia	1995–1996	Democratic-nondemocratic
	1997–1998	Nondemocratic-democratic
Bhutan	2007–2008	Nondemocratic-democratic
Bolivia	1981–1982	Nondemocratic-democratic
Brazil	1984–1985	Nondemocratic-democratic
Burundi	2004–2005	Nondemocratic-democratic
	2013–2014	Democratic-nondemocratic
Belarus	1994–1995	Democratic-nondemocratic
Cambodia	1992–1993	Nondemocratic-democratic
	1994–1995	Democratic-nondemocratic

TABLE A1 Cases of Transitions in Democracy Within a Nation
(128 Times in 66 Nations)—cont'd

Country	Year	Transition
Cabo Verde	1990–1991	Nondemocratic-democratic
Central African Republic	1992–1993	Nondemocratic-democratic
	2002–2003	Democratic-nondemocratic
Chile	1988–1989	Nondemocratic-democratic
Comoros	1989–1990	Nondemocratic-democratic
	1994–1995	Democratic-nondemocratic
	1995–1996	Nondemocratic-democratic
	1998–1999	Democratic-nondemocratic
	2001–2002	Nondemocratic-democratic
Congo	1991–1992	Nondemocratic-democratic
	1996–1997	Democratic-nondemocratic
Croatia	1999–2000	Nondemocratic-democratic
Benin	1990–1991	Nondemocratic-democratic
El Salvador	1983–1984	Nondemocratic-democratic
Ethiopia	1994–1995	Nondemocratic-democratic
	2004–2005	Democratic-nondemocratic
Fiji	1986–1987	Democratic-nondemocratic
	1989–1990	Nondemocratic-democratic
	1999–2000	Democratic-nondemocratic
	2000–2001	Nondemocratic-democratic
	2005–2006	Democratic-nondemocratic
	2013–2014	Nondemocratic-democratic
Djibouti	1998–1999	Nondemocratic-democratic
	2009–2010	Democratic-nondemocratic
Georgia	1991–1992	Nondemocratic-democratic
Gambia	1993–1994	Democratic-nondemocratic
Ghana	1995–1996	Nondemocratic-democratic
Guatemala	1985–1986	Nondemocratic-democratic
Guinea	2009–2010	Nondemocratic-democratic

Continued

TABLE A1 Cases of Transitions in Democracy Within a Nation (128 Times in 66 Nations)—cont'd

Country	Year	Transition
Haiti	1990–1991	Democratic-nondemocratic
	1993–1994	Nondemocratic-democratic
	1998–1999	Democratic-nondemocratic
	2005–2006	Nondemocratic-democratic
	2009–2010	Democratic-nondemocratic
Honduras	1981–1982	Nondemocratic-democratic
Indonesia	1998–1999	Nondemocratic-democratic
Kenya	2001–2002	Nondemocratic-democratic
Korea, Republic of	1987–1988	Nondemocratic-democratic
Kyrgyzstan	2004–2005	Nondemocratic-democratic
	2008–2009	Democratic-nondemocratic
	2010–2011	Nondemocratic-democratic
Lebanon	2004–2005	Nondemocratic-democratic
Lesotho	1992–1993	Nondemocratic-democratic
	1997–1998	Democratic-nondemocratic
	2001–2002	Nondemocratic-democratic
Liberia	2005–2006	Nondemocratic-democratic
Madagascar	1991–1992	Nondemocratic-democratic
	2008–2009	Democratic-nondemocratic
	2010–2011	Nondemocratic-democratic
Malawi	1993–1994	Nondemocratic-democratic
Mali	1991–1992	Nondemocratic-democratic
	2011–2012	Democratic-nondemocratic
	2012–2013	Nondemocratic-democratic
Mauritania	2006–2007	Nondemocratic-democratic
	2007–2008	Democratic-nondemocratic
Mexico	1993–1994	Nondemocratic-democratic
Mozambique	1993–1994	Nondemocratic-democratic
Nepal	1989–1990	Nondemocratic-democratic

TABLE A1 Cases of Transitions in Democracy Within a Nation (128 Times in 66 Nations)—cont'd

Country	Year	Transition
	2001–2002	Democratic-nondemocratic
	2005–2006	Nondemocratic-democratic
Nicaragua	1989–1990	Nondemocratic-democratic
Niger	1991–1992	Nondemocratic-democratic
	1995–1996	Democratic-nondemocratic
	1998–1999	Nondemocratic-democratic
	2008–2009	Democratic-nondemocratic
	2009–2010	Nondemocratic-democratic
Nigeria	1983–1984	Democratic-nondemocratic
	1998–1999	Nondemocratic-democratic
Pakistan	1987–1988	Nondemocratic-democratic
	1998–1999	Democratic-nondemocratic
	2007–2008	Nondemocratic-democratic
Panama	1989–1990	Nondemocratic-democratic
Paraguay	1988–1989	Nondemocratic-democratic
Peru	1991–1992	Democratic-nondemocratic
	1992–1993	Nondemocratic-democratic
	1999–2000	Democratic-nondemocratic
	2000–2001	Nondemocratic-democratic
Philippines	1986–1987	Nondemocratic-democratic
Guinea–Bissau	1993–1994	Nondemocratic-democratic
	1997–1998	Democratic-nondemocratic
	1999–2000	Nondemocratic-democratic
	2002–2003	Democratic-nondemocratic
	2004–2005	Nondemocratic-democratic
	2011–2012	Democratic-nondemocratic
	2013–2014	Nondemocratic-democratic
Romania	1990–1991	Nondemocratic-democratic
Russian Federation	2003–2004	Democratic-nondemocratic

Continued

TABLE A1 Cases of Transitions in Democracy Within a Nation (128 Times in 66 Nations)—cont'd

Country	Year	Transition
Senegal	1999–2000	Nondemocratic-democratic
Sierra Leone	1995–1996	Nondemocratic-democratic
	1996–1997	Democratic-nondemocratic
	2001–2002	Nondemocratic-democratic
South Africa	1980–1981	Democratic-nondemocratic
	1982–1983	Nondemocratic-democratic
	1991–1992	Democratic-nondemocratic
	1993–1994	Nondemocratic-democratic
Zimbabwe	1986–1987	Democratic-nondemocratic
Suriname	1989–1990	Nondemocratic-democratic
Thailand	1990–1991	Democratic-nondemocratic
	1991–1992	Nondemocratic-democratic
	2005–2006	Democratic-nondemocratic
	2007–2008	Nondemocratic-democratic
	2013–2014	Democratic-nondemocratic
Tunisia	2013–2014	Nondemocratic-democratic
Turkey	1982–1983	Nondemocratic-democratic
Uganda	1984–1985	Democratic-nondemocratic
Uruguay	1984–1985	Nondemocratic-democratic
Venezuela	2008–2009	Democratic-nondemocratic
	2012–2013	Nondemocratic-democratic
Zambia	1990–1991	Nondemocratic-democratic

TABLE A2 Countries With No Transitions

Nations that are always democratic (49 nations)

Australia, Austria, Belgium, Botswana, Bulgaria, Canada, Sri Lanka, Colombia, Costa Rica, Cyprus, Czech, Denmark, Dominican Republic, Ecuador, Estonia, Finland, France, Germany, Greece, Hungary, India, Ireland, Israel, Italy, Jamaica, Japan, Latvia, Lithuania, Luxembourg, Malaysia, Mauritius, Mongolia, Montenegro, Namibia, Netherlands, New Zealand, Norway, Poland, Portugal, Serbia, Slovakia, Slovenia, Spain, Sweden, Switzerland, Trinidad and Tobago, Ukraine, United Kingdom of Great Britain and Northern Ireland, United States

Nations that are always nondemocratic (29 nations)

Algeria, Angola, Bahrain, Cameroon, Chad, China, Congo, Equatorial Guinea, Gabon, Iran, Iraq, Kazakhstan, Jordan, Kuwait, Lao People's Democratic Republic, Morocco, Oman, Qatar, Rwanda, Saudi Arabia, Singapore, Viet Nam, Swaziland, Tajikistan, Togo, United Arab Emirates, Egypt, Burkina Faso, Yemen

References

Acemoglu D., Naidu S., Restrepo P. and Robinson J.A., Democracy does cause growth, Journal of Political Economy, forthcoming.

Acharya, R.C., Keller, W., 2009. Transfer through imports. The Canadian Journal of Economics 42 (4), 1411–1448.

Alesina, A., Rodrik, D., 1994. Distributive politics and economic growth. Quarterly Journal of Economics 109 (2), 465–490.

Alfaro, L., Chanda, A., Ozcan, S.K., Sayek, S., 2004. FDI and economic growth: the role of local financial markets. Journal of International Economics 64 (1), 89–112.

Amsden, A.H., 1989. Asia's next giant: South Korea and late industrialization. Oxford University Press, New York.

Baltagi, B., Griffin, J., 1988. A general index of technical change. Journal of Political Economy 96 (1), 20–41.

Banerjee, S., Heshmati, A., Wihlborg, C., 2000. The dynamics of capital structure. In: SSE/EFI Working Paper Series. No. 333.

Berndt, E.R., Christensen, L.R., 1973. The translog function and the substitution of equipment, structures, and labor in US manufacturing 1929–68. Journal of Econometrics 1 (1), 81–113.

Bloom, N., Draca, M., Reenen, J.V., 2016. Trade induced technical change? The impact of chinese imports on innovation, IT and productivity. Review of Economic Studies 83, 87–117.

Boix, C., Miller, M., Rosato, S., 2012. A complete data set of political regimes, 1800–2007. Comparative Political Studies 46 (12), 1523–1554.

Borensztein, E., Gregorio, J.D., Lee, J.W., 1998. How does foreign direct investment affect economic growth? Journal of International Economics 45 (1), 115–135.

Busse, B., 2003. Democracy and FDI. HWWA Discussion Paper 220.

Cheibub, J.A., Gandhi, J., Vreeland, J.R., 2010. Democracy and dictatorship revisited. Public Choice 143 (1-2), 67–101.

Christensen, L.R., Jorgenson, D.W., Lau, L.J., 1973. Transcendental logarithmic production frontiers. The Review of Economics and Statistics 55 (1), 28–45.

Eichengreen, B., Leblang, D., 2006. Democracy and globalization. NBER Working Paper No. 12450.

Evans, A.D., Green, C.J., Murinde, V., 2002. Human capital and financial development in economic growth: new evidence using the translog production function. International Journal of Finance and Economics 7, 123–140.

Foster, L., Haltiwanger, J.C., Krizan, C.J., 2001. Aggregate productivity growth, lessons from microeconomic evidence. In: New developments in productivity analysis. NBER, pp. 303–372.

Haggard, S., 1990. Pathways from the periphery: The politics of growth in the newly industrializing countries. Cornell University Press, Ithaca.

Heshmati, A., 1996. On the single and multiple time trends representation of technical change. Applied Economics Letters 3, 495–499.

Heshmati, A., 2001. The dynamics of capital structure: evidence from Swedish micro and small firms. Research in Banking and Finance 2, 199–241.

Heshmati, A., Kumbhakar, S., 2013. A general model of technical change with an application to the OECD countries. Economics of Innovation and New Technology 23, 25–48.

Johnson, C., 1982. MITI and the Japanese miracle: The growth of industrial policy: 1925–1975. Stanford University Press.

Kim, H.Y., 1992. The translog production function and variable returns to scale. The Review of Economics and Statistics 74 (3), 546–552.

Lööf, H., 2004. Dynamic optimal capital structure and technical change. Structural Change and Economic Dynamics 15, 449–468.

López-Córdova, E.J., Meissner, C.M., 2005. The globalization of trade and democracy, 1870–2000. In: NBER working paper series. NBER working paper No. 11117.

Lyu, S.L., White, F.C., Lu, Y., 1984. Estimating effects of agricultural research and extension expenditures on productivity: a translog production function approach. Southern Journal of Agricultural Economics 16 (2), 1–8.

Marsh, P., 1982. The choice between equity and debt: an empirical study. Journal of Finance 37 (1), 121–144.

Modigliani, F., Miller, M.H., 1958. The cost of capital, corporation finance and the theory of investment. The American Economic Review 48 (3), 261–297.

Olley, G.S., Pakes, A., 1996. The dynamics of productivity in the telecommunication equipment industry. Econometrica 64 (6), 1263–1297.

Pellegrini, L., Gerlagh, R., 2004. Corruption's effect on growth and its transmission channels. Kykos International Review of Social Sciences 57 (3), 429–456.

Persson, P., Tabellini, G., 2007. The growth effect of democracy: is it heterogeneous and how can it be estimated? In: NBER working paper series. NBER working paper No. 13150.

Plumper, T., Martin, C.W., 2003. Democracy, government spending, and economic growth: a political-economic explanation of the barro-effect. Public Choice 117, 27–50.

Solow, R.M., 1957. Technical change and the aggregate production function. The Review of Economics and Statistics 39 (3), 312–320.

Tabellini, G., Alesina, A., 1990. Voting on the budget deficit. American Economic Review 80 (1), 37–49.

Wade, R., 1990. Governing the market: Economic theory and the role of government in east asian industrialization. Princeton University Press, Princeton.

Woo, J.E., 1991. Race to the swift: State and finance in Korean industrialization. Columbia University Press, New York.

Yanikkaya, H., 2003. Trade openness and economic growth: a cross-country empirical investigation. Journal of Development Economics 72, 57–89.

Yu, M., 2010. Trade, democracy, and the gravity equation. Journal of Development Economics 91 (2), 289–300.

Further Reading

Chalmers, J., 1982. MITI and the Japanese Miracle: The growth of industrial policy, 1925–1975. Stanford University Press, Stanford.

Chapter 29

Analysis of Stochastic Dominance Ranking of Chinese Income Distributions by Household Attributes

Esfandiar Maasoumi*, Almas Heshmati[†] and Biwei Su[†]
*Department of Economics, Emory University, Atlanta, GA, United States, †Department of Economics, Sogang University, Seoul, South Korea

Chapter Outline

1 Introduction

Improvement of general social welfare ideally is assessed "uniformly" and robust to the choice of welfare functions. The prevalent approach, however, is based on "complete" ranking of income profiles based on specific preference functions. For example, income inequality traditionally is captured by Gini or Theil coefficients, which are specific functions of the Lorenz curves. The latter plots the cumulative share of total income against the cumulative proportion of income receiving units. Its divergence from a line of perfect equality can be measured by many indices of inequality, such as Gini coefficient or Theil's (Heshmati, 2006). Complete ranking of well-being distributions is useful for "quantification" and monitoring. However, it lacks broad acceptance of their underlying value judgments; conclusions based on these approaches often vary with the choice of indices and the parameters used to compute those indices. This ambiguity is problematic for policy analysis and decision making.

Panel Data Econometrics. https://doi.org/10.1016/B978-0-12-815859-3.00029-9

Indices also are summary measures and, therefore, often fail to different degrees to reveal important heterogeneity and aspects of the evolution of the whole income distribution, at different quantiles, and for different subgroups (see Maasoumi & Heshmati, 2000).

Based on the expected utility paradigm, uniform dominance rankings can shed further light and expose the degree of robustness of index-based assessments.

Stochastic dominance relations are defined over relatively large classes of utility functions and have the potential to offer powerful majority inferences in regard to welfare rankings of different distributions. Recently developed non-parametric tests enable one to assess such relations to a degree of statistical certainty. If dominance relations are implied, one can distinguish the better-off groups unambiguously, and then monitor quantitatively with any preferred index and its declared weighting of different groups and attributes. The inability to imply a dominance relation, however, is equally valuable and informative, indicating that any welfare ordering based on a particular index is highly subjective and might be reversed or changed by other induces.

There is growing adoption of uniform rankings of income and well-being states within or between different regions and subgroups. For example, Maasoumi and Heshmati (2000) analyze changes in the Swedish income distribution over time and across different population subgroups. Similarly, dominance ranking of US household income by various household attributes from 1968 to 1997 was examined in Maasoumi & Heshmati, 2008. Lean and Valenzuela (2012) employ stochastic dominance analysis on Australian income and expenditure distributions for the population to study inequality and relative welfare in Australia from 1983 to 2004. Sarkar (2012) examines the performance of rural India, urban India, female-headed household, and backward-caste household in terms of poverty, inequality, and welfare for 2009–2010 and 2004–2005.

Surprisingly, stochastic dominance seldom has been applied to data in China. Existing studies examine income inequality between urban and rural regions, by gender and province. Examples include statistical analysis of the range and variance of income (e.g., Sicular, Yue, Gustafasson, & Li, 2007), regression-based methods and Blinder-Oaxaca decomposition (e.g., Shi, Sicular, & Zhao, 2002), and Gini and Theil's inequality indices (e.g., Bonnefond & Clement, 2012; Kanbur & Zhang, 2005; Tong & Zhang, 2006; Wu & Perloff, 2005). Several studies use stochastic dominance technique for analysis of inequality or welfare in China. One is from Millimet and Wang (2006), who test for stochastic dominance to assess and decompose the distribution of gender earning differentials in urban China in the mid-1990s. They find large earning differentials in the lower tail of the distribution using both annual earnings and hourly wages, but no differential in the upper tail. Similarly, Anderson and Ge (2009) find evidence of strong welfare (robust) gains from 1990 to 1999 in all regions together, with significant and persistent welfare disparities among cities, Eastern coastal area, and the interior. Cai, Chen, and Zhou (2010) consider changes in income and consumption inequality in China's urban population from 1992 to 2003.

We examine more recent dominance relations, from 2000 to 2009, and for several household attributes that have not been studied before. We also examine an aggregation method for estimating "permanent" or longer-run incomes/ expenditures over several years. This is made possible by the availability of the panel data employed here and is essential in the study of "mobility," and evolution of states that is not merely temporal or transitory. Relatedly, partial effect of characteristics, such as education and region, can vary widely over time and is subject to fluctuations in income. We determine these partial effects on a stable measure of income/expenditure.

The longitudinal (panel) covariance structure of the data is not the focus of this study and is not exploited in this paper. This is an issue of efficiency of estimates of partial effects. In our analysis of partial effect of an attribute, such as education, in dominance rankings, we "purge" the outcome variable from the projection effects of all other factors, including observed and unobserved individual and time effects. Consequently, this is a case of longitudinal inference in which individual-specific heterogeneity is eliminated by transformations that are different from the better known within and between transformations and by differencing. Time aggregation that estimates "permanent incomes," and unrestricted partial residual analysis of expenditures/incomes, removes both the other observed and unobserved effects. We allow for group (cluster) heterogeneity, which is not estimated or identified separately as is common in standard panel data methods.

We consider statistical tests for first- and second-order stochastic dominance. The tests studied here are multivariate generalizations of the Kolmogorov-Smirnov statistics when weak dependence is permitted in the processes. Four waves of household survey data have been used for analysis in two parts. Part one is "unconditional" tests for stochastic dominance between years for the entire distribution of the annual average incomes. Part two contains "conditional" tests for stochastic dominance between population subgroups that are categorized by household attributes, such as household registration type, household size, age, gender, education, and marital and child-rearing status. Here, "conditional" implies before stochastic dominance tests for subgroups of one certain household attribute, such as household registration type, we control for influences from all other household attributes previously mentioned through regression analysis and data transformation.

This chapter proceeds as follows. Section 2 introduces the data that we used in this research. Section 3 provides theory, methods, and the test statistics. Section 4 gives results analysis. Section 5 contains the summary of the major findings and conclusion.

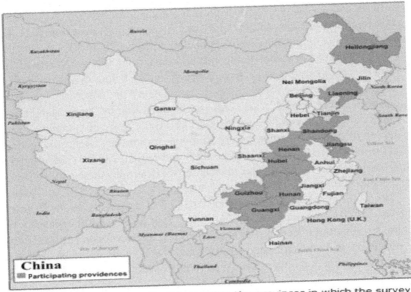

The darker shaded regions in this map are the provinces in which the survey

FIG. 1 Map of CHNS survey regions.

2 Data and Data Transformation

In this study, we use China Health and Nutrition Survey (CHNS) household data, which is collected by the Carolina Population Center at the University of North Carolina at Chapel Hill, the Institute of Nutrition and Food Hygiene, and the Chinese Academy of Preventive Medicine.[1] This ongoing longitudinal survey has eight waves: 1989, 1991, 1993, 1997, 2000, 2004, 2006, and 2009. The sample households randomly are drawn from nine provinces: Heilongjiang, Liaoning, Shandong, Jiangsu, Henan, Hubei, Hunan, Guangxi, and Guizhou (Fig. 1 shows the map of the regions). Each wave covers about 3800 households with a total of 14,000 individuals. While we trace the surveyed households over time, the sample size drops rapidly. Finally, we form a panel data set of 1225 households from four waves of the survey: 2000, 2004, 2006, and 2009, covering information of household per capita income and social or demographic characteristics for each household. The darker shaded regions in this map are the provinces in which the survey been conducted.

Household per capita income accounts for all forms of cash and in-kind income, including the value of farm products produced by rural households and retained for self-consumption, in-kind subsidies, transfers, and earnings from assets such as rental revenues from real estate. In order to avoid biases from inflation, all the income values are transformed to fixed 2009 prices using the consumer price indices provided by CHNS.

---

1. A detailed description of the data and quality control procedures can be obtained from http://www.cpc.unc.edu/projects/china.

The household characteristics that we control for are household registration type, household size, educational level, age, gender, and marital and child-rearing status of head of the household. Because several of the household characteristics change over time, we choose to use those records of head of the household in 2009 as a reference.

Definition of income and subgroups of household are given in Table 1. Household registration types are either urban or rural, in accordance with the

TABLE 1 Description of Income and Subgroups of Households

Variables	Definition
Income	Household per capita income for each year/average household per capita income for 4 years
Household registration type	Urban/rural
Education	
Edu0	Received no education
Edu1	Received 6 years of education (Primary school)
Edu2	Received 9 years of education (Junior middle school)
Edu3	Received 12 years of education (Senior middle school)
Edu4	Received 14 or 14+ years of education (Technical school and above)
Age cohort	
Agecohort1	15–40
Agecohort2	40–65
Agecohort3	66 and above
Gender of household head	Male/female
Marital status	Single, divorced and widowed/married
Rearing child	Yes/No
Household size	
HHsize1	Live alone
HHsize2	2 Family members in a household
HHsize3	3 Family members in a household
HHsize4	4 Family members in a household
HHsize5	5 or more family members in a household

birthplace of the household head. The sample of the household size group is divided into five groups: live alone, two family members, three family members, four family members, and five or more family members. Four educational levels are included: no education, primary education, junior middle school, senior middle school, and technical school education and higher. The productivity sample is divided into three age cohorts: from 15 to 40, 41 to 65, and older than 65. Gender groups stand for female-headed households and male-headed households. Marital status contains two groups: (1) those who are single, divorced, or widowed and (2) those who are married. Child-rearing divides the sample into two subgroups: households with a child who requires daily care and those without.

Our analysis consists of two parts: First, stochastic dominance tests are conducted between pairwise groups with respect to their marginal income distributions at each point in time. We reference these rankings as "unconditional". Secondly, we conduct rankings tests by controlling for household attributes (conditional).

We compare household per capita income in the years 2000, 2004, 2006, and 2009. For the "conditional" rankings between subgroups, we obtain the average household per capita income from 2000 to 2009 as an estimate of long-run (permanent) income. We estimate the "Mincer"-type earnings relations (Mincer, 1974) for these per capita aggregates:

$$\ln (\text{Income}) = f (\text{Province, household registration, household size,}$$
$$\textit{gender}, \text{education, age cohort, marital and child} - \text{rearing status})$$

where "income" is the average household per capita income from 2000 to 2009, and with attributes of the household head as recorded in 2009. Dummies for provinces are added for regional heterogeneity.

We subtract the joint fitted effects of controlled characteristics from the income variable, except for any specific characteristic of interest. The distribution of the "residual" we obtained then is ranked by SD tests. For example, to isolate the impact of "registration type," the residual is defined as follows:

$$\text{Residual} = \ln (\text{income}) - [\text{Estimated effects} (X_i * \beta_i)]$$

where X_i excludes "registration type." This is a Frisch-Waugh procedure in this linear-in-parameters setting. In "big data" settings and/or in more complex models, similar techniques have been developed to accommodate treatment effect analysis with many variables. See Heshmati and Rudolf (2014) and Chernozhulov et al. (webpage, http://www.mit.edu/~vchern/).

3 Theory, Methods, and the Test Statistics

As in Maasoumi and Heshmati's (2008) work about ranking PSID incomes by various household attributes, we use parametric bootstrap procedures to estimate the probability of rejection of the SD hypothesis. The SD test is explained and developed for dependent data in Linton, Maasoumi, and Whang (2005) based on an extended Kolmogorov-Smirnov test for first- and second-order dominance.

3.1 Theory and Methods

Let X and Y be income variables at two different points in time, or for different regions, or individual or household characteristics. Let $X_1, X_2, \ldots, X_n$, be n not necessarily independent and identically distributed (i.i.d.) on X, and $Y_1, Y_2, \ldots, Y_n$, be n not necessarily i.i.d. on Y income variables. Let U_1 denote the class of all von-Neumann-Morgenstern-type utility functions (Von-Neumann & Morgenstern, 1953), u, such that $u' \geq 0$, (increasing). Also, let U_2 denote the class of all utility functions in U_1 for which $u'' \leq 0$ (strict concavity), and U_3 denote a subset of U_2 for which $u''' \geq 0$. Let $F(x)$ and $G(x)$ denote the cumulative distribution functions for the two comparison groups, respectively. Quantiles $q_x(p)$ and $q_y(p)$ are implicitly defined by, for example, $F[X \leq q_x(p)] = p$.

Definition 1 X First Order Stochastic Dominates Y, denoted X FSD Y, if and only if any one of the following equivalent conditions holds:

(1) $E[u(X)] \geq E[u(Y)]$ for all $u \in U_1$, with strict inequality for some u.
(2) $F(x) \leq G(x)$ for all x in the support of X, with strict inequality for some x.
(3) $q_x(p) \geq q_y(p)$ for all $0 \leq p \leq 1$, with strict inequality for some p.

Definition 2 X Second Order Stochastic Dominates Y, denoted X SSD, if and only if any one of the following equivalent conditions holds:

(1) $E[u(X)] \geq E[u(Y)]$ for all $u \in U_2$, with strict inequality for some u.
(2) $\int_{-\infty}^{x} F(t)dt \leq \int_{-\infty}^{x} G(t)dt$, for all x in the support of X and Y, with strict inequality for some x.
(3) $\int_{0}^{p} q_x(t)dt \leq \int_{0}^{p} q_y(t)dt$, for all $0 \leq p \leq 1$, with strict inequality for some p.

The tests of FSD and SSD are based on empirical evaluations of conditions 2 or 3 in the previous definitions. Mounting test on condition 2 requires empirical cumulative distribution function (CDF) and comparisons at a finite number of observed ordinates. This approach fixes the critical value (zero) at the boundary of our null hypothesis and estimates the associated "significance level" by boot-strapping the sample or its blocks. This renders our tests "asymptotically similar" and unbiased on the boundary, which is similar to inference based on P-values.

3.2 The Test Statistics

Suppose that there are two prospects X_1 and X_2 and let $A = \{X_k: k = 1, 2\}$. Let $\{X_{ki}: i = 1, 2 \ldots N\}$ be realizations of X_k for $k = 1, 2$. We group the data into subgroups, of household registration type or household heads' gender, for example, and then make comparisons across homogenous populations. For $k = 1, 2$ define:

$$F_k(x, \theta) = P(X_{ki}(\theta) \leq x)$$

and

$$\overline{F}_{kN}(x, 0) = \frac{1}{N} \sum_{i=0}^{N} 1(X_{ki}(0) \leq x)$$

We denote $F_k(x) = F_k(x, 0_{k0})$ and $\overline{F}_{kN}(x, 0_{k0})$ and let $F(x_1, x_2)$ be the joint c.d. f. of $(X_1, X_2)'$. Now we define the functional forms of the joint distribution:

$$d = \min_{k \neq l} \sup_{x \in \chi} [F_k(x) - F_l(x)]$$

$$s = \min_{k \neq l} \sup_{x \in \chi} \int_{-\infty}^{x} [F_k(x) - F_l(x)] dt$$

where χ denotes a given set contained in the union of the supports of X_{ki} for $k = 1, 2$. Without loss of generality, we assume that the supports are bounded. The hypotheses of interest are:

$$H_0^d : d \leq 0 \text{ vs. } H_1^d : d > 0$$

$$H_0^s : s \leq 0 \text{ vs. } H_1^s : s > 0$$

The null hypothesis H_0^d implies that the prospects in A are not first-degree stochastically maxima, i.e., there exists at least one first-degree prospect in A that dominates the others. For the second-order case, the test statistics are:

$$DN = \min_{k \neq l} \sup_{x \in \chi} \sqrt{N} [\overline{F}_{kN}(x, \dot{0}_k) - \overline{F}_{lN}(x, \dot{0}_l)]$$

$$SN = \min_{k \neq l} \sup_{x \in \chi} \sqrt{N} \int_{-\infty}^{x} [\overline{F}_{kN}(x, \dot{\theta}_k) - \overline{F}_{lN}(x, \dot{\theta}_l)]$$

In our algorithm, we compute approximation to the suprema in D_N, S_N based on taking maxima over some smaller grid of points $X_J = \{x_1, \dots, x_j\}$ where $J < n$. We obtain simple bootstrap estimates of the probability $\{D_N \leq 0\}$ and probability $\{S_N \leq 0\}$. If the probability is high (0.90 or higher), we can infer dominance to a desirable degree of confidents. If it is a low probability (0.10 or smaller), we can infer the presence of significant crossing of the empirical CDFs, implying an inability to rank the outcomes (Maasoumi & Heshmati, 2008).

4 Analysis of the Results

4.1 Unconditional Analysis

The first part of Table 1 shows the summary of the data by years of observation. The balance number of households observed all four waves is 1225. The mean income continuously increases from 5606 yuan[2] in 2000 to 13,410 yuan in 2009, that is, even after adjusting for inflation, the income has doubled in 10 years. Similarly, the dispersion in income increases from 5651 yuan in 2000 to 13,388 yuan in 2009.

In the second part of Table 2, our SD test statistics are summarized by their mean and standard errors, as well as the probability of the test statistic. Subgroups are compared pairs: one group is denoted as "X" and the other by "Y." Thus, "FSDxoy" denotes first-order stochastic dominance of X over Y and "SSDxoy" denotes second-order dominance. "FOmax" and "SOmax" denote first- and second-order maximality.

We infer that there is no FSD between any two years. The probability for first order of stochastic dominance varies from 0.0000 to 0.3170, suggesting that the null hypothesis—first-order stochastic dominance—is unlikely to be

TABLE 2 Kolmogorov-Smirnov Test for Stochastic Dominance Over Years Conditional on Other Attributes

Characteristics			Obs		Mean		Std Dev	
2000			1225		5606		5651	
2004			1225		7618		6992	
2006			1225		8675		8586	
2009			1225		13,410		13,388	

Test	Mean	Std Err	Prob		Mean	Std Err	Prob
2000 (x) vs. 2004 (y)				2000 (x) vs. 2006 (y)			
FSDxoy	0.1594	0.0171	0.0000	FSDxoy	0.0969	0.0172	0.0000
FSDyox	0.0009	0.0012	0.0680	FSDyox	0.0176	0.0091	0.0000
FOmax	0.0009	0.0012	0.0680	FOmax	0.0176	0.0091	0.0000
SSDxoy	0.5013	0.0580	0.0000	SSDxoy	0.2831	0.0528	0.0000
SSDyox	−0.1150	0.0202	1.0000	SSDyox	0.0173	0.0097	0.0360
SOmax	−0.1150	0.0202	1.0000	SOmax	0.0173	0.0097	0.0360

Continued

2. Chinese currency $1 = 6.86$ yuan on October 2, 2018.

TABLE 2 Kolmogorov-Smirnov Test for Stochastic Dominance Over Years Conditional on Other Attributes—cont'd

Test	Mean	Std Err	Prob		Mean	Std Err	Prob
2000 (x) vs. 2009 (y)				2004 (x) vs. 2006 (y)			
FSDxoy	0.3722	0.0159	0.0000	FSDxoy	0.0557	0.0153	0.0000
FSDyox	0.0000	0.0001	0.3080	FSDyox	0.0014	0.0034	0.2570
FOmax	0.0000	0.0001	0.3080	FOmax	0.0013	0.0031	0.2570
SSDxoy	0.6053	0.0335	0.0000	SSDxoy	0.2448	0.0725	0.0010
SSDyox	−0.3722	0.0159	1.0000	SSDyox	−0.0278	0.0194	0.9330
SOmax	−0.3722	0.0159	1.0000	SOmax	−0.0279	0.0193	0.9340
2004 (x) vs. 2009 (y)				2006 (x) vs. 2009 (y)			
FSDxoy	0.2552	0.0183	0.0000	FSDxoy	0.2130	0.0188	0.0000
FSDyox	0.0000	0.0000	0.3070	FSDyox	0.0000	0.0002	0.3170
FOmax	0.0000	0.0000	0.3070	FOmax	0.0000	0.0002	0.3170
SSDxoy	0.4572	0.0353	0.0000	SSDxoy	0.3792	0.0372	0.0000
SSDyox	−0.2552	0.0183	1.0000	SSDyox	−0.2130	0.0188	1.0000
SOmax	−0.2552	0.0183	1.0000	SOmax	−0.2130	0.0188	1.0000

FSDxoy, first-order stochastic dominance of x over y; FSDyox, first-order stochastic dominance of y over x; FOmax, first-order maximal; SSDxoy, second-order stochastic dominance of x over y; SSDyox, second-order stochastic dominance of y over x; SOmax, second-order maximal; Prob, reject the null hypothesis of no dominance when the statistics are negative.

accepted. Second-order dominance, however, is inferred in all comparisons and, without exception, to a high degree of statistical confidence. The latter years SSD the prior years, which implies a uniform improvement in incomes in China during the 10 years, regardless of which social welfare function or index is employed. These rankings cannot be attributed to any single factor or group of factors in this marginal distribution exercise.

4.2 Conditional Analysis

As mentioned previously, the households are distinguished by the 2009 characteristics of household heads, but mean income is defined as period average of household per capita income. The characteristics that we use are household registration type, gender, age, household size, education, and marital and child-rearing status. The conditional analysis of the data for each characteristic is discussed below.

The generic Mincer-type income equation is specified linearly as function of household type, household heads, and household characteristics as:

$$Income_{it} = \alpha_i + \beta_{urban}urban_{it} + \beta_{male}male + \sum_{j=1}^{3}\beta_n agecohort_{nit} + \sum_{j=1}^{5}\beta_j HHsize_{jit}$$
$$+ \sum_{1}^{5}\beta_m Educ_{mit} + \beta_{married}married_{it} + \beta_{child}child_{it} + \varepsilon_{it}$$

where income is per capita average income over time. Explanatory variables include household (registration type, household size, and child rearing) and head of household characteristics (gender, age, education, and marital status). We examine conditional income distributions, controlling for household attributes. We investigate income distribution from different registration types, years, gender, age cohorts, household sizes, education levels, marital status and child-rearing, by comparing distribution of residuals of the least squares regression of income on all attributes (including provincial location heterogeneity). This approach has the advantages and shortcomings of linear projections. In its favor, we would argue that some nonlinearities that flow from strong constant coefficient assumptions are accounted for by our unrestricted estimation approach. We are not focused on unbiased estimation of partial effects and parameters.

4.2.1 Test Results for Household Registration Type

The mean values for household registration type reported in Table 3 gives a higher average income for the urban group (10,771 yuan) than for rural group

TABLE 3 Kolmogorov-Smirnov Test for Stochastic Dominance Relations for Household Registration Type, Gender of Household Head, and Marital and Child Rearing Status Conditional on Other Attributes

Characteristics	Obs	Mean	Std Dev	Characteristics	Obs	Mean	Std Dev
Rural	911	8878	4689	Female headed	133	8964	5398
Urban	314	10,771	6808	Male headed	1092	8035	5302

Test	Mean	Std Err	Prob	Test	Mean	Std Err	Prob
Rural (x) vs. Urban (y)				Female (x) vs. Male (y)			
FSDxoy	0.1679	0.0304	0.0000	FSDxoy	0.0198	0.0175	0.0000
FSDyox	0.0013	0.0080	0.5300	FSDyox	0.1125	0.0413	0.0000
FOmax	0.0013	0.0080	0.5300	FOmax	0.0191	0.0164	0.0000
SSDxoy	0.6551	0.1333	0.0000	SSDxoy	0.0075	0.0362	0.4600
SSDyox	−0.0074	0.0156	0.6800	SSDyox	0.2780	0.1460	0.0220
SOmax	−0.0074	0.0156	0.6800	SOmax	0.0029	0.0300	0.4820

Continued

TABLE 3 Kolmogorov-Smirnov Test for Stochastic Dominance Relations for Household Registration Type, Gender of Household Head, and Marital and Child Rearing Status Conditional on Other Attributes—cont'd

Characteristics	Obs	Mean	Std Dev	Characteristics	Obs	Mean	Std Dev
Not rearing child	1114	10,545	5365	Single/divorced	130	9137	5028
Rearing child	111	8814	4730	Married	1095	10,006	5344

Test	Mean	Std Err	Prob	Test	Mean	Std Err	Prob
No (x) vs. Yes (y)				Single (x) vs. Married (y)			
FSDxoy	0.2634	0.0493	0.0000	FSDxoy	0.0979	0.0359	0.0000
FSDyox	0.0136	0.0085	0.0000	FSDyox	0.0127	0.0154	0.2240
FOmax	0.0136	0.0085	0.0000	FOmax	0.0122	0.0142	0.2240
SSDxoy	−0.0409	0.0219	0.9610	SSDxoy	0.3129	0.1400	0.0020
SSDyox	0.6203	0.1491	0.0000	SSDyox	−0.0463	0.0389	0.9080
SOmax	−0.0409	0.0219	0.9610	SOmax	−0.0478	0.0342	0.9100

FSDxoy, first-order stochastic dominance of x over y; FSDyox, first-order stochastic dominance of y over x; FOmax, first-order maximal; SSDxoy, second-order stochastic dominance of x over y; SSDyox, second-order stochastic dominance of y over x; SOmax, second-order maximal; Prob, reject the null hypothesis of no dominance when the statistics are negative.

(8878 yuan). Surprisingly, the results from the SD test reveal that there is neither first- nor second-order dominance of urban households over rural households. Because the probability for urban households to FSD rural households is 0.53 and for SSD is 0.68, both suggest weak evidence of stochastic dominance. This provides a contrast with previous studies (Benjamin, Brandt, & Giles, 2005; Gustafsson, Li, & Sato, 2014; Heshmati, 2007; Jin, Qian, Wang, & Choi, 2014; Khan & Riskin, 1998; Wang & Wan, 2015, among others), which indicate significant rural-urban inequality in China. One reason is that "inequality" can account for dispersion, possibly beyond SSD utility functions that are merely concave. Secondly, we control for the projection effect of other attributes, such as education and other distinctions between urban and rural households that contribute to inequality. After eliminating those effects, the inequality between urban and rural residents is not significantly because of "registration status."

4.2.2 Test Results for Gender of Household Head

From Table 3 we can see that there are nearly 10 times as many male-headed households (MHH) as female-headed households (FHH). On average, FHH have higher per capita incomes than MHH, but there is no statistically strong evidence of MHH first- or second-order dominating FHH. This basically implies that if other factors were equal, FHH and MHH would enjoy the same level of well-being. At first glance, one might think that this finding runs contrary to the finding of gender inequality in China in earlier studies (Heshmati & Su, 2017; Hughes & Maurer-Fazio, 2002; Macpherson & Hirsch, 1995; Su & Heshmati, 2013; Wang & Cai, 2006; among others). A careful comparison would suggest, however, that previous studies do not control for individual attributes as we do, and ranking by specific inequality measures might be because of the corresponding welfare function being more restrictive than allowed in merely increasing and concave classes. Certain preference functions will exist with specific weights to certain subgroups, which will rank two outcome distributions. Such rankings will not be "uniform" and are more than usually subjective.

4.2.3 Test Results for Marital and Child Rearing Status

In Table 3, it is found that one-tenth of household heads are single or divorced; the mean value of single/divorced group income is lower than that for the married ones, 9137 yuan vs. 10,006 yuan. This difference is consistent with SD rankings, suggesting that married group second-order dominates the single/divorced group at 91% level of significance.

About 90% of the households indicate that they do not spend time on child-rearing child during the survey year. The mean and the dispersion of income for that group are higher than those for households that spend time for child rearing. In the SD test, the former group second-order dominates the latter one at 96% level, showing that taking care of dependent children has a negative impact on per capita income and on the household's welfare level.

4.2.4 Test Results for Age Cohorts

Table 4 summarizes the results for age groups: 15–40, 41–65, and 65+. The mean values and the dispersion of incomes for the three age cohorts are

TABLE 4 Kolmogorov-Smirnov Test for Stochastic Dominance Relations Among Age Cohorts Conditional on Other Attributes

Characteristics	Obs	Mean	Std Dev
Age1 (15–40)	368	9189	5481
Age2 (40–65)	591	9311	5147
Age3 (65+)	266	9289	5420

Continued

TABLE 4 Kolmogorov-Smirnov Test for Stochastic Dominance Relations Among Age Cohorts Conditional on Other Attributes—cont'd

Test	Mean	Std Err	Prob		Mean	Std Err	Prob
Age1(x) vs. Age2 (y)				Age1 (x) vs. Age3 (y)			
FSDxoy	0.0298	0.0165	0.0090	FSDxoy	0.0465	0.0234	0.0020
FSDyox	0.0276	0.0205	0.0070	FSDyox	0.0487	0.0268	0.0000
FOmax	0.0157	0.0094	0.0160	FOmax	0.0312	0.0162	0.0020
SSDxoy	0.0707	0.0756	0.1660	SSDxoy	0.0715	0.1036	0.3270
SSDyox	0.0458	0.0666	0.3180	SSDyox	0.0958	0.0725	0.0490
SOmax	0.0038	0.0215	0.4840	SOmax	0.0159	0.0433	0.3760
Age2 (x) vs. Age3 (y)							
FSDxoy	0.0554	0.0300	0.0090				
FSDyox	0.0516	0.0284	0.0000				
FOmax	0.0326	0.0169	0.0090				
SSDxoy	0.1009	0.1332	0.3060				
SSDyox	0.1304	0.1049	0.0600				
SOmax	0.0257	0.0446	0.3660				

FSDxoy, first-order stochastic dominance of x over y; FSDyox, first-order stochastic dominance of y over x; FOmax, first-order maximal; SSDxoy, second-order stochastic dominance of x over y; SSDyox, second-order stochastic dominance of y over x; SOmax, second-order maximal; Prob, reject the null hypothesis of no dominance when the statistics are negative.

different. Household heads between 40 and 65 years old have the highest mean income, but the lowest dispersion. Looking at the SD test results, there are no strong instances of FSD or SSD by age. The per capita disposable incomes of age cohorts are second-order maximal, implying that they might be ranked only at higher levels than SSD. The results reveal that though age is considered highly related to one's productivity and therefore one's income level, this is not uniformly so for per capita "long-run" incomes.

4.2.5 Test Results for Educational Levels

It is generally held that education has a positive effect on earnings and bargaining power. From Table 5, we can see that mean incomes are increasing functions of the years of schooling. Educational returns reach the highest level for people who have finished technical school or tertiary education. We find that the group with technical/tertiary education SSD the groups with no education, primary,

TABLE 5 Kolmogorov-Smirnov Test for Stochastic Dominance Among Educational Levels Conditional on Other Attributes

Characteristics	Obs	Mean	Std Dev
Edu0 (No education)	224	6177	4259
Edu1 (Primary)	257	7050	5201
Edu2 (Junior High)	405	8478	5329
Edu3 (Senior High)	147	9588	6109
Edu4 (Technical/Tertiary)	192	14,454	8118

	Mean	Std Err	Prob	Test	Mean	Std Err	Prob
Edu1 (x) vs. Edu2 (y)				Edu1 (x) vs. Edu3 (y)			
FSDxoy	0.1537	0.0353	0.0000	FSDxoy	0.2346	0.0461	0.0000
FSDyox	0.0088	0.0083	0.1310	FSDyox	0.0061	0.0107	0.2530
FOmax	0.0088	0.0083	0.1310	FOmax	0.0061	0.0107	0.2530
SSDxoy	0.7005	0.1812	0.0000	SSDxoy	1.1563	0.2511	0.0000
SSDyox	−0.0145	0.0117	0.9010	SSDyox	−0.0234	0.0130	0.9570
SOmax	−0.0145	0.0117	0.9010	SOmax	−0.0234	0.0130	0.9570
Edu1 (x) vs. Edu4 (y)				Edu1 (x) vs. Edu0 (y)			
FSDxoy	0.4153	0.0426	0.0000	FSDxoy	0.0095	0.0127	0.1500
FSDyox	−0.0040	0.0059	0.6400	FSDyox	0.1155	0.0358	0.0000
FOmax	−0.0040	0.0059	0.6400	FOmax	0.0093	0.0121	0.1500
SSDxoy	1.6467	0.1904	0.0000	SSDxoy	−0.0192	0.0253	0.8900
SSDyox	−0.0532	0.0161	0.9990	SSDyox	0.5415	0.1945	0.0020
SOmax	−0.0532	0.0161	0.9990	SOmax	−0.0201	0.0207	0.8920
Edu2 (x) vs. Edu3 (y)				Edu2 (x) vs. Edu4 (y)			
FSDxoy	0.1188	0.0407	0.0000	FSDxoy	0.2935	0.0371	0.0000
FSDyox	0.0149	0.0150	0.1300	FSDyox	−0.0046	0.0053	0.7220
FOmax	0.0147	0.0147	0.1300	FOmax	−0.0046	0.0053	0.7220
SSDxoy	0.5280	0.2303	0.0030	SSDxoy	1.2661	0.1829	0.0000
SSDyox	0.0006	0.0262	0.7050	SSDyox	−0.0217	0.0098	0.9830
SOmax	−0.0007	0.0198	0.7080	SOmax	−0.0217	0.0098	0.9830
Edu2 (x) vs. Edu0 (y)				Edu3 (x) vs. Edu4 (y)			
FSDxoy	0.0010	0.0032	0.1880	FSDxoy	0.2260	0.0488	0.0000
FSDyox	0.2912	0.0393	0.0000	FSDyox	0.0067	0.0071	0.0600

Continued

TABLE 5 Kolmogorov-Smirnov Test for Stochastic Dominance Among Educational Levels Conditional on Other Attributes—cont'd

	Mean	Std Err	Prob	Test	Mean	Std Err	Prob
FOmax	0.0010	0.0032	0.1880	FOmax	0.0067	0.0071	0.0600
SSDxoy	−0.0346	0.0149	0.9970	SSDxoy	0.9276	0.2015	0.0000
SSDyox	1.1739	0.1762	0.0000	SSDyox	−0.0009	0.0090	0.5070
SOmax	−0.0346	0.0149	0.9970	SOmax	−0.0009	0.0090	0.5070
Edu3 (x) vs. Edu0 (y)				Edu4 (x) vs. Edu0 (y)			
FSDxoy	0.0014	0.0036	0.0850	FSDxoy	−0.0054	0.0054	0.7330
FSDyox	0.3472	0.0479	0.0000	FSDyox	0.4977	0.0440	0.0000
FOmax	0.0014	0.0036	0.0850	FOmax	−0.0054	0.0054	0.7330
SSDxoy	−0.0424	0.0156	0.9970	SSDxoy	−0.1027	0.0213	1.0000
SSDyox	1.6042	0.2386	0.0000	SSDyox	1.8755	0.1933	0.0000
SOmax	−0.0424	0.0156	0.9970	SOmax	−0.1027	0.0213	1.0000

FSDxoy, first-order stochastic dominance of x over y; FSDyox, first-order stochastic dominance of y over x; FOmax, first-order maximal; SSDxoy, second-order stochastic dominance of x over y; SSDyox, second-order stochastic dominance of y over x; SOmax, second-order maximal; Prob, reject the null hypothesis of no dominance when the statistics are negative.

and junior high school education. Nevertheless, the group for technical/tertiary education shows no dominance relationship over the group for senior high school education, even if the mean income difference between those two groups is as large as 4866 yuan. The group with senior high school education SSD the groups with no education and primary education, but no ranking order can be established compared with the group with junior high school education. The group with junior high school education SSD the group with no education. It seems that the comparisons between two adjacent educational levels is weak. SSD relationships, however, are implied between educational levels separated by at least one interval. It would seem that there is too much variance in outcomes within each educational group to allow uniform rankings between groups with close educational attainment.

4.2.6 Test Results for Household Sizes

Examination of the mean incomes in Table 6 reflects negative effects of household size on per capita household income level. It drops from 9461 yuan for households with only one person (HH1) to 4632 yuan for households with five or more people (HH5). The largest two groups are households with two or three family members—the combined observations for those two groups represents

TABLE 6 Kolmogorov-Smirnov Test for Stochastic Dominance for Household Size Conditional on Other Attributes

Characteristics	Obs	Mean	Std Dev
HH1 (live alone)	50	9461	6021
HH2 (2 family members)	373	7460	6443
HH3 (3 family members)	319	6091	5367
HH4 (4 family members)	220	5160	3955
HH5 (4+ family members)	263	4632	3744

Test	Mean	Std Err	Prob				
HH1 (x) vs.HH2 (y)				HH1 (x) vs. HH3 (y)			
FSDxoy	0.0241	0.0170	0.0010	FSDxoy	0.0139	0.0115	0.0040
FSDyox	0.2664	0.0637	0.0000	FSDyox	0.3487	0.0645	0.0000
FOmax	0.0241	0.0170	0.0010	FOmax	0.0139	0.0115	0.0040
SSDxoy	−0.0647	0.0494	0.8960	SSDxoy	−0.0612	0.0448	0.9090
SSDyox	0.7957	0.2641	0.0000	SSDyox	1.7952	0.4402	0.0000
SOmax	−0.0647	0.0494	0.8960	SOmax	−0.0612	0.0448	0.9090
HH1 (x) vs. HH4 (y)				HH1 (x) vs. HH5 (y)			
FSDxoy	0.0139	0.0246	0.0290	FSDxoy	0.0016	0.0067	0.1120
FSDyox	0.4357	0.0691	0.0000	FSDyox	0.4804	0.0697	0.0000
FOmax	0.0139	0.0246	0.0290	FOmax	0.0016	0.0067	0.1120
SSDxoy	−0.0136	0.0474	0.6240	SSDxoy	−0.0747	0.0474	0.9410
SSDyox	2.7932	0.5951	0.0000	SSDyox	2.7185	0.5164	0.0000
SOmax	−0.0136	0.0474	0.6240	SOmax	−0.0747	0.0474	0.9410
HH2 (x) vs. HH3 (y)				HH2 (x) vs. HH4 (y)			
FSDxoy	0.0040	0.0063	0.0560	FSDxoy	−0.0028	0.0027	0.6890
FSDyox	0.1088	0.0326	0.0000	FSDyox	0.2060	0.0399	0.0000
FOmax	0.0040	0.0062	0.0560	FOmax	−0.0028	0.0027	0.6890
SSDxoy	−0.0753	0.0312	0.9920	SSDxoy	−0.1246	0.0355	1.0000
SSDyox	0.3937	0.1288	0.0000	SSDyox	0.7570	0.1382	0.0000
SOmax	−0.0754	0.0306	0.9920	SOmax	−0.1246	0.0355	1.0000
HH2 (x) vs. HH5 (y)				HH3 (x) vs. HH4 (y)			
FSDxoy	0.0000	0.0001	0.0420	FSDxoy	0.0097	0.0152	0.0420
FSDyox	0.2529	0.0352	0.0000	FSDyox	0.1139	0.0383	0.0000

Continued

TABLE 6 Kolmogorov-Smirnov Test for Stochastic Dominance for Household Size Conditional on Other Attributes—cont'd

Test	Mean	Std Err	Prob				
FOmax	0.0000	0.0001	0.0420	FOmax	0.0094	0.0143	0.0420
SSDxoy	−0.1470	0.0349	1.0000	SSDxoy	−0.0085	0.0346	0.6200
SSDyox	0.8186	0.1208	0.0000	SSDyox	0.5275	0.1973	0.0040
SOmax	−0.1470	0.0349	1.0000	SOmax	−0.0095	0.0325	0.6240
HH3 (x) vs. HH5 (y)				**HH4 (x) vs. HH5 (y)**			
FSDxoy	0.0019	0.0064	0.1450	FSDxoy	0.0162	0.0198	0.1550
FSDyox	0.1421	0.0344	0.0000	FSDyox	0.0821	0.0309	0.0000
FOmax	0.0019	0.0064	0.1450	FOmax	0.0141	0.0158	0.1550
SSDxoy	−0.0351	0.0310	0.8720	SSDxoy	−0.0275	0.0634	0.8010
SSDyox	0.7267	0.1748	0.0000	SSDyox	0.3513	0.2029	0.0150
SOmax	−0.0351	0.0310	0.8720	SOmax	−0.0358	0.0429	0.8160

FSDxoy, first-order stochastic dominance of x over y; FSDyox, first-order stochastic dominance of y over x; FOmax, first-order maximal; SSDxoy, second-order stochastic dominance of x over y; SSDyox, second-order stochastic dominance of y over x; SOmax, second-order maximal; Prob, reject the null hypothesis of no dominance when the statistics are negative.

more than half of the total number of households. The two most common family sizes in the Chinese society have per capita mean incomes below those for HH1. In terms of the SD, those who live alone (HH1) SSD the groups of households with three (HH3) or more than four (HH5) family members. HH1 also second-order dominates the group for households with two family members (HH2) but with lesser probability of 0.8960. Nevertheless, it is interesting to find that there is no dominance relation between HH1 and HH4. HH2 shows a strong second stochastic dominance over HH3, HH4, and HH5. But for the comparisons between HH3, HH4, and HH5, the probability is too low to support a strong inference of dominance.

5 Summary and Conclusion

Income inequality and welfare in China has been a focus of many empirical studies based mostly on strong cardinal rankings by indices, such as the Gini coefficient or the Atkinson Index. These types of approaches are known to suffer from the lack of universal acceptance of the value judgments of the underlying welfare functions, sometimes resulting in contradicting conclusions. Such analyses also face the problem of cross-section distribution fluctuations. Instantaneous income inequality measures, although useful for monitoring smooth trends, can produce a chaotic and inconsistent view of well-being and its evolution. The purpose of this study is to avoid those shortcomings and draw a more robust conclusion about income distribution in China, and factors that contribute to its differences between groups and over time. To achieve this, we consider Kolmogorov-Smirnov test procedures for first- and second-order stochastic dominance relations, controlling for income fluctuations, and household characteristics that stand out as difference makers in long-term outcomes. We find that education of household head and family size clearly matter, and the observed differences/rankings are uniform, robust to choice of preference functions and indices.

The SD tests results show a steadily rising per capita household welfare from 2000 to 2009. This is both expected and a desirable outcome because the rapid economic growth in contemporary China undeniably has raised the quality of life. Our subgroup-specific findings suggest a number of important items for policy concern. Even though first-order dominance is rare, second-order dominance holds in most of cases. First, we find that after controlling for other attributes, there is no stochastic dominance relation between urban and rural residents, female-headed and male-headed household, and age cohorts, meaning those attributes might have limited contributions to increased income inequality. Second, our results show that the group of married household heads SSD the group of single/divorced ones, and the group of nonchild-rearing SSD the group of child-rearing, noting that the former group has a higher level of welfare than the latter one. Third, groups with higher levels of education second-order dominates groups with lower levels of education, suggesting that the latter groups have higher inequality when compared to the former groups. And fourth, large-size families have higher income inequality and lower welfare level than small-size families.

Based on our findings, we conclude that ceteris paribus influence of household registration type, gender of the household head, and age cohort contribute less to income well-being than other household attributes. Household heads who are single/divorced or have a low level of education and households with a child who needs daily caring or with a large family size tend to have a lower welfare level. Thus, policies that are favorable to those population subgroups are recommended to reduce or eliminate inequality in China.

We caution that our samples cover only 9 of 31 provinces. There is a risk of oversimplification in attempting to summarize our key findings and apply it to China as a whole. Given data is available, further research could be conducted using national household-level data sets.

References

Anderson, G., Ge, Y., 2009. Intercity income inequality growth and convergence in China. Journal of Income Distribution 18 (1), 1–41.

Benjamin, D., Brandt, L., Giles, J., 2005. The evolution of income inequality in rural China. Economic Development and Cultural Change 53 (4), 769–824.

Bonnefond, C., Clement, M., 2012. An analysis of income polarisation in rural and urban China. Post-Communist Economies 24 (1), 15–37.

Cai, H.B., Chen, Y.Y., Zhou, L.A., 2010. Income and consumption inequality in Urban China. Economic Development and Cultural Change 58 (3), 385–413.

Gustafsson, B., Li, S., Sato, H., 2014. Data for studying earnings, the distribution of household income and poverty in China. China Economic Review 30, 419–431.

Heshmati, A., 2006. The world distribution of income and income inequality: a review of the economic literature. Journal of World Systems Research 12 (1), 60–107.

Heshmati, A., 2007. Income inequality in China. In: Heshmati, (Ed.), Recent developments in the Chinese economy. Nova Science Publishers, NY.

Heshmati, A., Rudolf, R., 2014. Income versus consumption inequality in Korea: evaluating stochastic dominance rankings by various household attributes. Asian Economic Journal 28 (4), 413–436.

Heshmati, A., Su, B., 2017. Analysis of gender wage differential in China's urban labor market. Singapore Economic Review 60 (2), 423–445.

Hughes, J., Maurer-Fazio, M., 2002. Effects of marriage, education, and occupation on the female/male wage gap in China. Pacific Economic Review 7 (1), 137–156.

Jin, H., Qian, H., Wang, T., Choi, E.K., 2014. Income distribution in urban China: an overlooked data inconsistency issue. China Economic Review 30, 383–396.

Kanbur, R., Zhang, X.B., 2005. Fifty years of regional inequality in China: a journey through central planning, reform, and openness. Review of Development Economics 9 (1), 87–106.

Khan, A.R., Riskin, C., 1998. Income and inequality in China: composition, distribution and growth of household income, 1988 to 1995. The China Quarterly 154, 221–253.

Lean, H.H., Valenzuela, M.R., 2012. Inequality in Australia 1983-2004: a stochastic dominance approach. Department of Economics. ISSN1441-5429 (Discussion Paper).

Linton, O., Maasoumi, E., Whang, Y.J., 2005. Consistent testing for stochastic dominance: a sub-sampling approach. Review of Economic Studies 72, 735–765.

Maasoumi, E., Heshmati, A., 2000. Stochastic dominance amongst Swedish income distributions. Econometric Reviews 19 (3), 287–320.

Maasoumi, E., Heshmati, A., 2008. Evaluating dominance ranking of PSID incomes by various household attributes. In: Advances in income inequality and concentration measures. Routledge, London.

Macpherson, D., Hirsch, B., 1995. Wages and gender composition: why do women's jobs pay less? Journal of Labor Economics 133 (3), 84–89.

Millimet, D.L., Wang, L., 2006. A distributional analysis of the gender earnings gap in urban China. Contributions to Economic Analysis and Policy 5 (1), 1–50.

Mincer, J., 1974. Schooling, experience, and earnings. Human Behavior and Social Institutions No. 2, National Bureau of Economic Research, NY.

Sarkar, S., 2012. Application of stochastic dominance: a study in India. Procedia Economics and Finance 1, 337–345.

Shi, X.Z., Sicular, T., Zhao, Y.H., 2002. Analyzing urban-rural income inequality in China. In: International symposium on equity and social justice. Discussion Paper.

Sicular, T., Yue, X.M., Gustafasson, B., Li, S., 2007. The urban-rural income gap and inequality in China. Review of Income and Wealth 53 (1), 93–126.

Su, B., Heshmati, A., 2013. Analysis of the determinants of income and income gap between urban and rural China. China Economic Policy Review 2 (1), 1–29.

Tong, G.R., Zhang, J.B., 2006. Study on the trend of chinese peasant income distributions. The Journal of Quantitative and Technical Economics 8, 3–10.

Von-Neumann, J., Morgenstern, 1953. Theory of games and economic behavior. Princeton University Press, Princeton, NJ.

Wang, C., Wan, G., 2015. Income polarization in China: trends and changes. China Economic Review 36, 58–72.

Wang, M.Y., Cai, F., 2006. Gender wage differentials in China's urban labor marker. UNU-WIDER, Research Paper No. 146.

Wu, X.M., Perloff, J.M., 2005. China's income distribution, 1985-2001. The Review of Economics and Statistics 87 (4), 763–775.

Chapter 30

The Neural Network Production Function: Panel Evidence for the United States

Mike G. Tsionas*, Konstantinos N. Konstantakis[†] and Panayotis G. Michaelides[†]

*Department of Economics, Lancaster University Management School, Lancaster, United Kingdom, [†]National Technical University of Athens, Athens, Greece

Chapter Outline

1 Introduction

In economics and engineering, the success of a proposed theoretical approach often depends critically on model building, and the economist or engineer needs to make many crucial decisions (Griffin, Montgomery, & Rister, 1987). For example, the typical pattern followed in applied business models begins with a production function, and the producers operate with their production functions maximizing outputs obtainable from the given set of inputs they use (see among others Hagspiel, Huisman, and Kortb (2016)). The next step is introduction of first-order conditions for cost minimization and profit maximization, and so on, in which producers are assumed to satisfy these conditions (Kumbhakar & Lovell, 2000). In this context, the economist or engineer often needs to adopt a functional form to model one or more relationships. Given that the researcher is not in a position to know the true functional form behind the data, the model builder's task becomes complicated by the growing number of functional forms (Griffin et al., 1987).

Panel Data Econometrics. https://doi.org/10.1016/B978-0-12-815859-3.00030-5

In this framework, several efforts to construct flexible forms have emerged. For the formalization of the notion of flexibility, see Diewert (1971); however, different definitions of flexibility exist as a result of the immanent character of the concept, which is rather complex and difficult to define. For instance, local flexibility (or, simply, flexibility) usually implies that an approximating functional form has zero error (i.e., perfect approximation) at a particular point (McFadden, 1963). For example, second-order Taylor expansions have been popular in this context, but such forms often introduce large errors in the approximating function (see, e.g., Despotakis, 1986). From an empirical point of view, an estimated Taylor series expansion is still an approximation. In other words, it fits the data from the true form, but does not expand it. Therefore, there actually might be no point where the true function (or its gradients) is perfectly approximated. White (1980) found that OLS estimators of Taylor series expansions are not reliable indicators of the parameters for the true expansion of a function (Griffin et al., 1987; Loyer, Henriques, Fontulb, & Wiseall, 2016). Therefore, in econometrics studies, the local information needs to become available to the full domain of the data, the so-called calibration (Shoven & Whalley, 1992).

As a result, such a (locally) flexible estimate cannot be considered as being reliable and, therefore, global flexibility (or Sobolev flexibility) usually is preferred to simple or local flexibility in the sense that second-order restrictions are everywhere absent (Gallant, 1981, 1982). In this context, global flexibility of Sobolev space is intractable for obtaining parameter estimates, so estimation of globally flexible forms uses traditional distance measures and techniques such as ordinary least squares (OLS). The globally flexible character of the approximation, however, is shown by Elbadawi, Gallant, and Souza (1983) to produce quite satisfactory results and is consistent with the argument by Rice (1964) about the importance of a suitable globally flexible functional form (Griffin et al., 1987).

The choice of an appropriate functional form for the production function has been a crucial issue for production studies (Kumbhakar & Tsionas, 2010) since the work of Cobb and Douglas (1928). The econometric limitations of the Cobb-Douglas function (e.g., Hoch, 1958), led to the development of the constant elasticity of substitution (CES), the translog, and other functional forms. Therefore, the researcher has available a number of flexible functional forms, which have gained some popularity because of the available computational method (Thompson Gary, 1988).

The idea of imposing the necessary conditions of economic theory in production functions is not new. One of the first attempts was by Gallant (1982) and Gallant and Golub (1984), who used numerical techniques. The importance of estimating functional forms that satisfy the conditions of economic theory is researched in Diewert and Wales (1987) and stressed by Terrell (1996). Thus far, only a small number of studies report the degree to which the estimated functions satisfy these conditions (Reinhard & Thijssen, 1998; O'Donnell & Coelli, 2005).

To sum up, it is of paramount importance to be able to find a suitable globally flexible functional form for the production function, which finds countless applications. In this vein, this chapter introduces the corresponding production function, which often is needed by practitioners. Of course, the proposed functional form satisfies the typical assumptions made by economic production models, such as monotonicity, curvature, homogeneity, homotheticity, and continuity. Therefore, the proposed approach exhibits satisfactory global properties highly desirable to model production and consumption choices in general equilibrium models (Hudson & Jorgenson, 1974; Jorgenson & Slesnick, 1987; Reister & Edmonds, 1981).

To do so, we exploit the semiparametric nature of artificial neural networks (ANNs), which are rich in parameters, in order to impose all the properties that mathematical production theory dictates regarding the production function. In this work, we propose and estimate a new production function based on AANs, which we call the neural network production function (NPF). This specification is a global approximation to any arbitrary production function: It satisfies all the properties dictated by economic theory globally; it provides good fit to real-world data because it is data driven; it allows for arbitrary returns to scale; and it is relatively simple to estimate.

Our proposed method is partly consistent with other researchers, such as Du, Christopher, and Racine (2013), in the sense that it is able to handle multiple general shape constraints for multivariate functions, or Kuosmanen and Kortelainen (2012) and Kuosmanen and Johnson (2010), who employ nonparametric least squares methods in order to ensure convexity. Despite the fact that a small fraction of these desirable properties also might be possessed by one or other of the already known production function specifications. However, neither possesses all of them simultaneously.

The chapter is structured as follows: Section 2 provides a brief overview of the related literature about neural networks in economics; Section 3 introduces the NPF and its properties; Section 4 presents the measures of interest; Section 5 sets out the quantitative methods of this paper; Section 6 presents the empirical results; and Section 7 offers conclusions.

2 Neural Networks in Business and Economics

In spite of the semiparametric nature of artificial neural networks (ANNs), which are rich in parameters, researchers in economics seem to have failed, so far, to fully exploit the highly attractive features of neural networks.

The use of ANNs in economics per se is rather limited; nevertheless, a plethora of econometric and computational models exists in literature that explores the capabilities of ANNs. One of the first attempts was made by Kuan and White (1994), who introduced the perspective of ANNs to assess the linearity or non-linearity of a time series. Hutchinson, Lo, and Poggio (1994) created an ANN model for option pricing based on the asymmetry properties that the time series data exhibit. Vishwakarma (1994) created an ANN model to examine the business cycles turning points. Brockett et al. (1994) developed a neural network model as an early warning system for predicting insurer insolvency. Serrano-Cinca (1997) used a feed-forward neural network model in an attempt to classify companies on the basis of information provided by their financial statements. Gruca and Klemz (1998) showed that neural networks (NNs) offer superior estimates of asymmetric cross-elasticities. Faraway and Chatfield (1998) investigated the predicting capabilities of a variety of neural networks models with those obtained from Box-Jenkins and Holt-Winters methods. Adya and Collopy (1998) investigated the forecasting capabilities of NNs based on the effectiveness of validation and the effectiveness of implementation. Swanson and White (1995, 1997a, 1997b) compared the predictive power of nonlinear, linear, and ANN models in economic and financial time series data. Their results provided evidence in favor of the predictive power of ANNs, implying that time series exhibit nonlinear properties. Luxhøj, Riis, and Stensballe (1996) created a hybrid econometric-neural network model for forecasting total monthly business sales, with excellent forecasting performance. Jain and Nag (1998) used a data-driven, nonparametric, neural network-based approach to predict the long-run operating performance of new ventures, comparing at the same time the classification accuracy of the neural network model with that of a logit model. Their results suggested that the neural networks generally outperformed logit models. Indro, Jiang, Patuwo, and Zhang (1999) used ANNs to predict the performance of equity mutual funds that follow value, blend, and growth investment styles. Results showed that ANNs generated better forecasting results than linear models for funds of all styles.

Gencay (1999) and Qi and Maddala (1999) tested the use of both ANN and linear models to determine the predictive power on both economic and financial time series data. Their results provided strong evidence in favor of ANNs. Charalabous et al. (2000) compared the predictive performance of three neural network methods—the learning vector quantization, the radial basis function, and the feedforward network—with the performance of the logistic regression and the backpropagation algorithm. According to their findings, contemporary neural network methods provide superior results compared to those obtained from the logistic regression method and the backpropagation algorithm. Furthermore, Yao, Li, and Tan (2000) forecasted the option prices of Nikkei 225 index futures using neural networks. The results suggested that, for volatile markets, a neural network option pricing model outperforms the traditional Black and Scholes model. Malhotra and Malhotra (2003) compared the performance of multiple discriminant analysis (MDA) and neural networks in identifying potential problematic loans and found that the neural network models consistently perform better. Chang, Choy, Cooper, and Ruefli (2009) showed that productive efficiency of US accounting firms has increased after 2002.

In the following section, based on ANNs, we propose a novel production function specification, the NPF, and prove that it constitutes a global approximation to any arbitrary production function.

3 Semiparametric NPF

In general, production function gives the maximum amount of output that can be produced with a given amount of input, based on the use of a given production technology. More formally, the production function is defined as: $f(x) = max_y\{y \in \mathbb{R}_+^M : y \in T(x,y)\}$, where $y \in \mathbb{R}_+^M$ denotes all the output vectors, $x \in \mathbb{R}_+^N$ denotes all the input vectors, and $T(x,y)$ is the technology set defined as $T(x,y) = \{(x,y) : x \in \mathbb{R}_+^N$ can produce $y \in \mathbb{R}_+^M\}$.

In this work, we use ANNs, which are collections of functions that relate an output variable Y to certain input variables $X' = [X_1, \dots, X_n]$. The input variables are combined linearly to form k intermediate variables $Z_1, \dots, Z_K$: $Z_K = X'\beta_k(k = 1, \dots, K)$, where $\beta_k \in \mathbb{R}^K$ are parameter vectors. The intermediate variables are combined nonlinearly to produce Y:

$$Y = \sum_{k=1}^{K} \alpha_k \varphi(Z_k)$$

where φ is an activation function, the α_k's are parameters, and K is the number of intermediate nodes (Kuan & White, 1994).

The mechanism behind ANNs is that they combine simple units with intermediate nodes, so they can approximate any smooth nonlinearity (Chan & Genovese, 2001).

In Theorem 1 (Appendix), we state a fundamental result regarding the approximating capabilities of ANNs, which shows that they are universal approximators of functions. In order to apply Theorem 1, we have to formally define the set of production functions and then prove that this set is a compact subset of $\mathbb{R}$.

If a production function is defined as: $f(x) = max\{y \in \mathbb{R}_+^M : y \in T(x,y)\}$ then, we define the set of all production functions to be $\bigcup_{i \in I} max_y\{y_i \in \mathbb{R}_+^M : y_i \in T(x,y_i)\}$. Now, we have to prove that this set is a compact subset of $\mathbb{R}$, so as to make use of Theorem 1.

Theorem 2 If the set $T(x,y) = \{(x,y) : x \in \mathbb{R}_+^N$ can produce $y \in \mathbb{R}_+^M\}$ is closed and bounded, then the set of production functions, defined as $\bigcup_{i \in I} max_{y_i}\{y_i \in \mathbb{R}_+^M : y_i \in T(x,y_i)\}$, is a compact set.
Proof
See Appendix. □

The proposed functional form satisfies the typical assumptions made by economic production models, such as monotonicity, curvature, homogeneity, homotheticity, and continuity.

Next, we proceed by stating two theorems, which prove that the NPF is a global approximator to any arbitrary production function.
Theorem 3 If $\bigcup_{i \in I} max_{y_i}\{y_i \in \mathbb{R}_+^M : y_i \in T(x,y_i)$ is a compact subset of $\mathbb{R}$ and $\varphi : \mathbb{R}_+^{M \times N} \to \mathbb{R}$ is a nonconstant, bounded, and continuous function, then all the functions of the form $f(x) = x^a \prod_{k=1}^{K} \varphi^{\alpha_k}(x^{\beta_k})$, where: $x^a = \prod_{i=1}^{N} x_i^{a_i}$, $\alpha \in \mathbb{R}^N$

and $x^{\beta_\kappa} = \prod_{i=1}^{N} x_i^{\beta_i}$ also are continuous, bounded, and nonconstant, where, in general: $x^\xi = \prod_{i=1}^{N} x_i^\xi, \xi \epsilon \mathbb{R}$ and, $a \in \mathbb{R}^N$ denote vector parameters, and α_κ, $\beta_\kappa \in \mathbb{R}^K$ denote the neural parameters.

Proof
See Appendix. □

Theorem 4 If the set $\bigcup_{i \in I} max_{y_i} \{ y_i \in \mathbb{R}_+^M : y_i \in T(x, y_i) \}$ is a compact subset of $\mathbb{R}$, then the family of functions defined as $\mathcal{F} = \{ f(x) \in \mathbb{C}(\mathbb{R}^M) : f(x) = x^a \prod_{\kappa=1}^{K} \varphi^{\alpha_\kappa}(x^{\beta_\kappa}), a \in \mathbb{R}^N, a_\kappa, \beta_\kappa \in \mathbb{R}^K \}$ is dense in the set of production functions.

Proof
See Appendix. □

The result of Theorem 4 implies that NPF is a global approximator to any arbitrary production function.

Next, according to mathematical production theory, a well-defined production function should satisfy a number of properties (see Appendix). Based on these desirable properties, Theorem 5 imposes all the necessary conditions on the NPF specification.

Theorem 5 If the activation function φ, $\varphi : X \to C^m[0, 1]$, $m = 1, \dots, N$ is: nonconstant, bounded, increasing monotonic, and concave, then the production function of the form: $f(x) = x^a \prod_{\kappa=1}^{K} \varphi^{\alpha_\kappa}(x^{\beta_\kappa})$ is well-defined under the following conditions:

(i) $a_i \geq 0 \; \forall \, i \in \{1, \dots, N\}$
(ii) $a_\kappa, \beta_\kappa \geq 0 \; \forall \, \kappa \in \{1, \dots, K\}$

Proof
See Appendix. □

4 Measures of Interest

Following the related literature of production theory, in this section, we summarize the derivation of key measures of interest derived from the proposed NPF specification. We begin by providing an alternative form of the NPF specification based on logarithmic transformation that facilitates the estimation. Therefore, every NPF of the form: $f(x) = x^a \prod_{\kappa=1}^{K} \varphi^{\alpha_\kappa}(x^{\beta_\kappa})$, where a, α_κ, β_κ denote vector parameters and x denotes a 1xN vector of inputs, has a representation of the form: $F(x) = aX + A_\kappa \Phi((\beta_\kappa X))$, where $a \in \mathbb{R}^N$, $A_\kappa = [a_1, \dots, a_K]$, $\beta_\kappa \in \mathbb{R}^\kappa$, $X \equiv \ln x$, $F(x) = \ln f(x)$ and $\Phi(.) \equiv \ln \varphi(.)$.

Because x is an input vector, our proposed NPF has the following estimable form representation:

$$F(x_i) = \sum_{i=1}^{N} a_i X_{i,t} + \sum_{\kappa=1}^{K} a_\kappa \Phi(\beta_{\kappa,i} X_{i,t}) + u_t$$

where the error term u_t has the usual properties and $t = 1, \dots, T$ is the length of the series.

In this work, we use the popular logistic activation function, that is,

$$\varphi(z) = \left(\frac{1}{1 - e^{-z}}\right), z \in \mathbb{R}$$

For other activation functions, see Bishop (1995). The empirical results are robust, however, regardless of the activation function used (Haykin, 1999).

The following lemmas summarize how the RTS and the elasticities of substitution are derived using the NPF specification.

Lemma 1 For every production function of the form:

$$F(X_t) = \sum_{i=1}^{N} a_i X_{i,t} + \sum_{\kappa=1}^{K} a_\kappa \Phi\left(\beta_{\kappa,i} X_{i,t}\right) + u_t$$

where $a \in \mathbb{R}^N$, $A_\kappa = [a_1, \ldots, a_K]$, $\beta_\kappa \in \mathbb{R}^\kappa$, $X \equiv \ln x$, $F(x) = \ln f(x)$, and $\Phi(.) \equiv \ln \varphi(.)$: the returns to scale are computed using the following formula:

$$\text{RTS} = \sum_{i=1}^{N} a_i + \sum_{\kappa=1}^{K} \left(\sum_{i=1}^{N} a_\kappa \beta_{\kappa,i}\right) \frac{\partial \Phi\left(\beta_{\kappa,i} X_{i,t}\right)}{\partial X_{i,t}}$$

Proof

The proof is a straightforward application of the definition of RTS. □

Lemma 2 For every production function of the form: $F(X_t) = \sum_{i=1}^{N} a_i X_{i,t} + \sum_{\kappa=1}^{K} a_\kappa \Phi\left(\beta_{\kappa,i} X_{i,t}\right) + u_t$ the elasticity of substitution between the nth and the zth is computed using the following formula:

$\sigma_{x_n x_z}$

$$= -\frac{A(x_n)A(x_z)[\ln x_n A(x_n) + \ln x_z A(x_z)]}{\ln x_n \ln x_z \left\{ \sum_{\kappa=1}^{K} a_\kappa \beta_\kappa^2 \left[\frac{\partial^2 \ln \varphi}{\partial \ln x_n^2} A(x_z)^2 \right] + \sum_{\kappa=1}^{K} a_\kappa \beta_\kappa^2 \left[\frac{\partial^2 \ln \varphi}{\partial \ln x_z^2} A(x_n)^2 \right] - 2 \frac{\partial^2 \ln \varphi}{\partial \ln x_n \partial \ln x_z} A(x_n)A(x_z) \right\}}$$

where: $A(x_n) = a_n + \sum_{\kappa=1}^{K} a_\kappa \beta_\kappa \frac{\partial \ln \varphi\left(\beta_\kappa \sum_{i=1}^{N} \ln x_i\right)}{\partial \ln x_i}$, $\forall n \in \{1, \ldots, N\}$.

Proof

The proof is a straightforward application of the definition of elasticity of substitution. □

Next, we extend the estimable form of the proposed specification with the term δt, where t denotes time. Lemma 3 summarizes the derivation of TFP using the NPF specification.

Lemma 3 For every production function of the form:

$$F(X_t) = \sum_{i=1}^{N} a_i X_{i,t} + \sum_{\kappa=1}^{K} a_\kappa \Phi\left(\beta_{\kappa,i} X_{i,t}\right) + \delta t + u_t$$

where: $a_i, a_\kappa, \beta_{\kappa,i}, \delta \in \mathbb{R}$.

The total fact productivity (TFP) is equal to:

$$TFP = \frac{\partial \ln f(X)}{\partial t} = \delta$$

Proof
The proof is a straightforward application of the definition of TFP. □

We continue by making a fairly standard assumption that will lead us to the estimation of technical efficiency. Following Kumbhakar and Lovell (2000), we assume that the error term of the NPF, u_t, is decomposed to two new error terms, namely ε_t and v_t. The following assumption summarizes the new estimable form of our NPF.

Without loss of generality, let the estimable form for our proposed NPF function be the following:

$$F(X_{j,t}) = \sum_{i=1}^{N} a_i X_{ij,t} + \sum_{\kappa=1}^{K} a_{\kappa j} \Phi(\beta_{\kappa,i} X_{ij,t}) + \delta t + u_{j,t}$$

$$u_{j,t} = v_{j,t} + \varepsilon_{j,t}$$

$j = 1, \ldots, J$ is the panel dimension; the error term, $\varepsilon_{j,t}$, is assumed to be $I.I.D.$ $(0, \sigma^2)$ and uncorrelated with the regressors, while $v_{j,t} \geq 0$.

Notice that no distributional assumptions need to made for either $u_{i,t}$ or $v_{i,t}$, (Kumbhakar & Lovell, 2000). The following lemma (Lemma 4) summarizes how technical efficiency is derived using our NPF specification.

Lemma 4 For every production function of the form:

$$F(X_{j,t}) = \sum_{i=1}^{N} a_i X_{ij,t} + \sum_{\kappa=1}^{K} a_{\kappa} \Phi(\beta_{\kappa,i} X_{ij,t}) + \delta t + u_{j,t}$$

$$u_{j,t} = v_{j,t} + \varepsilon_{j,t}$$

where $a_i, a_\kappa, \beta_{\kappa,i}, \delta \in \mathbb{R}$ with $\varepsilon_{j,t} \sim iid(0, \sigma^2)$ and $v_{j,t}$ the point measure of technical efficiency is defined by the following expression:

$$TE_j = \exp\left(-\widehat{v_j^*}\right)$$

where the residuals are corrected so that $-\widehat{v_j^*} = \widehat{v_j} - \max_j\{\widehat{v_j}\}$.

Proof
The proof is a straightforward application of the definition of Technical Efficiency. See Kumbhakar and Lovell (2000). □

5 Econometric Estimation

For the estimation of the proposed NPF specification, which is nonlinear with respect to $\beta_\kappa \in \mathbb{R}^\kappa$, we will use the following algorithm:

Estimation Algorithm

Step 1: For $k = 1$, where k is the number of nodes, choose randomly the parameters $\overline{\beta_{\kappa,i}}, \kappa = 1, \ldots, K$.

Step 2: For these parameter values of $\overline{\beta_{\kappa,i}}, \kappa = 1, \ldots, K$ estimate $\alpha_i, a_\kappa, \kappa = 1, \ldots, K$ and $i = 1, \ldots, N$ using OLS in the following equation:

$$F(X_{j,t}) = \delta t + \sum_{i=1}^{N} a_i X_{ij,t} + \sum_{\kappa=1}^{K} a_\kappa \Phi(\beta_{\kappa,i} X_{ij,t}) + u_{j,t}$$
$$u_{j,t} = v_{j,t} + \varepsilon_{j,t}$$

where $t = 1, \dots, T$ is the length of the series, $\varepsilon_{j,t}$, is assumed to be $I.I.D.(0, \sigma^2)$ and uncorrelated with the regressors, while $v_{j,t} \geq 0$, where: $u_{j,t} = v_{j,t} + \varepsilon_{j,t}$.

Step 3: For the estimated values of the parameters α_i, a_κ, $\kappa = 1, \dots, K$ and $i = 1, \dots, N$, which can be regarded as known, consider $\beta_{\kappa,i}$, $k = 1, \dots, K$ as a parameter and find its value routinely using numerical analysis techniques for nonlinear equations, e.g. some Newton-like method.

Step 4: For these values of $\beta_{\kappa,i}^* k = 1, \dots, K$ re-estimate the set of parameters, α_i, a_κ, $\kappa = 1, \dots, K$ and $i = 1, \dots, N$, using OLS.

Step 5: For the whole set of parameters $a_i, a_\kappa, \beta_{\kappa,i}^*, \kappa = 1, \dots, K$, compute a relevant criterion, such as the final prediction error (FPE) or the Hannan Quinn Information Criterion (HQIC).

Step 6: Repeat steps 1–5 for $k = 2, 3, 4, \dots$ and keep the value of k that optimizes the aforementioned criterion. For $k^* \in \{1, \dots, N\}$ that optimizes the criterion selected, keep the calculated values of $\overline{\beta_{\kappa,i}}^*$, and the estimated values $\overline{\alpha_i}, \overline{a_\kappa}, \kappa = 1, \dots, K, i = 1, \dots, N$.

In this chapter, in order to compute the parameters $\beta_{\kappa,i}$, $k = 1, \dots, K$ as described, we use the so-called Broyden-Fletcher-Goldfarb-Shannon (BFGS) method, which belongs to the family of Quasi-Newton, second derivative line search methods (see Appendix).

For the model selection, described in Step 5, we employed the FPE and the HQIC.

The full model is described by the following equation:

$$F(X_t) = \sum_{i=1}^{N} a_i X_{i,t} + \sum_{\kappa=1}^{K} a_\kappa \Phi\left(\sum_{i=1}^{N} \beta_{\kappa,i} X_i\right) + u_t$$

where: $t = 1, \dots, T$ is the time dimension that corresponds to the number of observations and K denotes the number of nodes, of the previous equation. Then, for each variable excluded by the model, $K = K - 1, K - 2, \dots$ the FPE criterion is calculated by the following formula (Lutkepohl, 2005):

$$FPE^o = L_T(K)\left(\frac{T+K}{T-K}\right)$$

while the HQIC is calculated by the formula:

$$HQIC^o = -2\frac{L_T(K)}{T} + \frac{2\ln\{\ln(T)\}}{T}K$$

The optimum model parameters, i.e. number of nodes, are those for which the information criterion of the respective model attains its minimum value, i.e. $FPE^* = argmin_{k \in K}\{FPE^o, K = K - 1, K - 2, \dots\}, HQIC^* = argmin_{k \in K}\{HQIC^o, K = K - 1, K - 2, \dots\}$.

The aforementioned strategy could be followed using other criteria (e.g. AIC, BIC).

6 Empirical Analysis

We illustrate the estimation of the proposed NPF function using data for the US sectoral economy. In this context, we use panel data for the US economy for the period 1957–2006 (just before the first signs of the US and global economic recession). Our investigation stops in 2006 because after that time, the dynamics of the traditional economic structures changed dramatically, both in the United States and globally. Therefore, any examination beyond this period would produce skewed and biased results.

There are two main strands in the literature of efficiency measurement. The first is based on the DEA approach and its variations. See among others, Doumpos and Cohen (2014), Wang et al. (2014), and Ghrahraman and Prior (2016). The second strand is based on the Stochastic Frontier Approach (SFA). See, among others, Liadaki and Gaganis (2010).

Our proposed estimation method follows the latter approach. It is well-known that there are serious problems in dealing with aggregate measures of productivity and efficiency in the sense that the simplistic analysis focusing only on aggregate measures might be misleading (e.g., Bartelsman & Dhrymes, 1998). This is the reason why this chapter analyzes the measured patterns in the US sectoral economy by addressing the measurement issues in the subsectors, considered to be the decision-making unit.

In terms of the variables employed: (R) is the total R&D expenses, (Y) is the gross domestic product, (L) expresses the full-time equivalent employees, and (K) expresses the net stock of physical capital. All observations are in billions of dollars in 1957 prices and cover the 14 main sectors of the US economy. The data about R&D come from the National Scientific Foundation of United States, data about Y and K come from the National Bureau of Economic Activity, and data about L come from the Bureau of Labor Statistics. Table 1 summarizes the data used.

The stationarity characteristics of the time series variables were investigated using the Levin, Lin, and James Chu (2002) panel unit root test, while the possible existence of cointegration was examined by means of Pedroni's (1999, 2001) test. Having investigated the stationarity properties of the time series employed, we induced stationarity by means of first differences because the cointegration results did not support any long-run relationship among the variables at hand (the results are available upon request). See, among others, Chirinko and Mallick (2011). Therefore, we employed the following NPF specification for the US economy.

$$Y_t = aX_t + A_\kappa \Phi(\beta_\kappa X_t) + \delta t$$

TABLE 1 Data and Sources

Sectors	Description	NACE Classification	Variables Available	Source
1	Agriculture, forestry, and fishing	A01, A02, A03	Output (Y)	Bureau of Economic Activity
2	Mining, petroleum and coal products	B, C10-C12, C13-C15, C16, C17, C18, C19, C20, C21, C22, C23, C24, C25, C26, C27, C28, C29, C30, C31-C32, C33		
3	Electricity, gas and water	D, E36, E37-E39		
4	Construction	F		
5	Food & beverages, wood products and furniture, metal products	I	Capital (K)	Bureau of Economic Activity
6	Wholesale trade	G45, G46		
7	Retailtrade	G47		
8	Transport and storage	H49, H50, H51, H52, H53		
9	Information& technology industry	J58, J59-J60, J61, J62-J63, S95	R&D expenses	National Scientific Foundation of the United States
10	Real estate and business services, finance and insurance	K64, K65, K66, L, L68A, M71, M72, N77		
11	Communication social and personal services	M73, M74-M75, N79, N80-N82, O, Q87-Q88, R90-R92, R93, S94, S96, T, U		

Continued

TABLE 1 Data and Sources—cont'd

Sectors	Description	NACE Classification	Variables Available	Source
12	Business management services	M69-M70, N78	Labor (L)	Bureau of Labor Statistics
13	Educational organizations	P		
14	Health services	Q86		

where Y_t is the total product of the US economy, $X_t = (K_t, R_t, L_t)$ is 3×1 vector of aggregate inputs representing the net stock of physical capital, R&D expenditures, and labor, respectively.

The full-blown model is as follows:

$$\ln y_{j,t} = a_{0,j} + a_1 \ln K_{j,t} + a_2 \ln R_{j,t} + a_3 \ln L_{j,t} + \gamma_1 \varphi \left(\beta_{11} \ln K_{j,t} \right.$$

$$\left. + \beta_{12} \ln R_{j,t} + \beta_{13} \ln L_{j,t} \right) + \delta t + u_{j,t}$$

$$s.t \left\{ \begin{array}{l} a_i \geq 0 \forall i = 0, 1, \ldots, N \\ \gamma_\kappa, \beta_{\kappa i} \geq 0, \forall \kappa = 1, \ldots, K \end{array} \right\}$$

$$u_{j,t} = v_{j,t} + \varepsilon_{j,t}$$

$$\varepsilon_{j,t} \sim iid \left(0, \sigma^2 \right)$$

$$v_{j,t} \geq 0$$

In applied research, it is common to estimate complete production models, obtain measures of scale economies and total factor productivity growth (Jelinek, 1987; Tsionas & Loizides, 2001; Remer & Mattos, 2003; Kumbhakar & Tsionas, 2010). The results are presented in Tables 2–3. We begin by investigating the NPF specification, i.e. the optimum number of nodes that should be included in the proposed NPF. Based on the results, one node outperforms the two and three nodes specification (see Table 2).

Based on the results of Table 3, all computed betas are statistically significant. The same is in force regarding the alpha, gamma, and delta parameters (Table 4). The delta parameter is the TFP of the US sectoral economy, which is estimated to be approximately 0.2%, a consistent estimate with the related literature, which suggests that the US economy exhibits small changes in the productivity levels. See among others, Stern (2001), Cardarelli and Lusinyan (2015).

TABLE 2 Estimated Model Criteria

	1 Node	2 Nodes	3 Nodes
HQIC	−254.95	−201.32	−177.65
FPE	−245.34	−200.55	−173.92

TABLE 3 Computed Parameters

	β_{11}	β_{12}	β_{13}
Computed value (t-stat)	0.012 (2.156)	0.025 (3.213)	0.121 (5.004)
Initial value	Random normal deviates		
Iterations to convergence	64		

TABLE 4 Estimated Parameters

	a_0	a_1	a_2	a_3	γ_1	δ
Estimate	0.060	0.321	0.294	0.290	5.280	0.002
Std deviation	2.35	0.064	0.051	0.071	3.856	0.001
z-value	7.07	13.551	5.210	4.350	6.720	2.99
p-value	0.000	0.000	0.000	0.000	0.000	0.000

Next, turning to the results in Table 5 and Fig. 1, we can see that the US economy is characterized by almost constant returns to scale for the period investigated, which is consistent with the relevant literature. See Basu (1996) and Basu and Fernald (1997), Dimelis (2001). Meanwhile, all the elasticities of substitution among the various inputs, i.e., labor and capital (Fig. 2), exhibit an inelastic behavior, i.e., the substitution becomes gradually more difficult over time. The elasticity of substitution between capital and R&D, however, exhibits an elastic behavior in the sense that substitution becomes gradually easier. See Revankar (1971), Zellner and Ryu (1998), Duffy and Papageorgiou (2000), and Duffy, Papageorgiou, and Perez-Sebastian (2004).

TABLE 5 RTS, TFP and Elasticities of Substitution

Measures of Interest	Average Value	St. Dev.	Overall Assessment
σ_{KL}	0.752	0.012	Inelastic
σ_{KR}	1.634	0.125	Elastic
σ_{LR}	0.951	0.114	Inelastic
RTS	0.987	0.052	Constant (approx.)
TFP	0.002	0.001	Technical progress

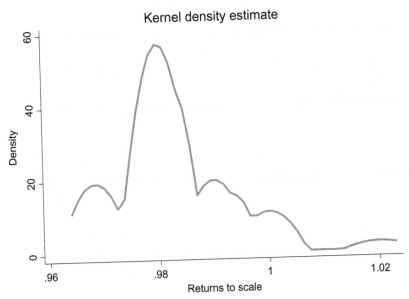

FIG. 1 Kernel density estimate of returns to scale.

Finally, Table 6 and Fig. 3 summarize the technical efficiency estimates for all 14 sectors of the US economy. Based on our findings, the variation of technical efficiency ratings is considerable (the standard deviation is 17%). Specifically, sectoral technical efficiency ranges between 47% and 98%. Only 4 of the 14 sectors achieved technical efficiency levels below 80%. For these sectors, considerable gains can be attained in their overall competitiveness by improving their resource use.

Among the sectors with the highest technical efficiency levels are owner-occupied health services (96%), wholesale trade (98%), retail trade (96%), and construction (95%). Contrarily, the sectors with the lowest technical

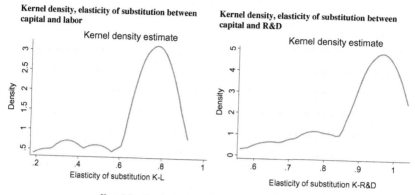

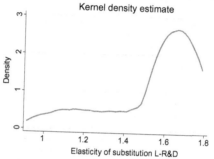

FIG. 2 Kernel density estimates elasticities of substitution.

TABLE 6 Technical Efficiency of US Sectors

Sectors	Description	TE	Variance
1	Agriculture, forestry, and fishing	0.49	0.02
2	Mining, petroleum and coal products	0.47	0.04
3	Electricity, gas, and water	0.48	0.03
4	Construction	0.95	0.05
5	Food & beverages, wood products and furniture, metal products	0.85	0.04
6	Wholesale trade	0.98	0.05
7	Retailtrade	0.96	0.07
8	Transport and storage	0.85	0.03
9	Information & technology industry	0.91	0.02
10	Real estate and business services, finance and insurance	0.93	0.06

Continued

TABLE 6 Technical Efficiency of US Sectors—cont'd

Sectors	Description	TE	Variance
11	Communication social and personal services	0.91	0.07
12	Business management services	0.94	0.03
13	Educational organizations	0.61	0.06
14	Health services	0.96	0.04
	Overall		
Mean TE		0.81	
S.D TE		0.17	

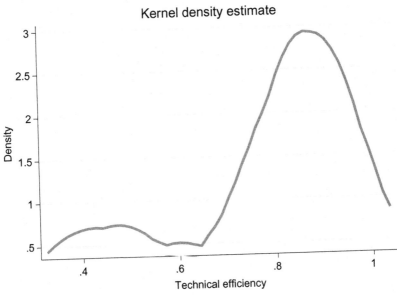

FIG. 3 Kernel density estimate of technical efficiency.

efficiency levels are agriculture, forestry and fishing (49%), electricity, gas and water (48%), and mining, petroleum and oil products (47%).

The estimated mean technical efficiency was found to be 81%, which, because this is an input-oriented technical efficiency, it has a direct cost interpretation. On average, the US sectoral economy could achieve a 19% decrease in total cost of production, without changing the input mix, production technology and input usage. In other words, it is possible for the US economy to

TABLE 7 Annual (Mean) Technical Efficiency

Year	Mean TE
1999	0.821
2000	0.823
2001	0.821
2002	0.820
2003	0.820
2004	0.817
2005	0.815
2006	0.811

become more technically efficient and to maintain the same level of sectoral output by reducing by almost 19% labor, capital, physical capital, and R&D expenses.

Table 7 depicts the average technical efficiency of the whole US economy for each year of the period 1999–2006, just before the US subprime crisis. During the period 2000–2006, the efficiency scores are gradually deteriorating, exhibiting a slight decrease. This, in turn, could be associated to the upcoming subprime crisis that took global dimensions.

The aim of the empirical analysis is not to provide a deep and sophisticated analysis of the US economy, but rather to offer an illustration of the methodology proposed and a brief discussion of its main results. Future research about the implications of our findings for the US economy would be of great interest.

7 Conclusion

The need of an appropriate functional form, capable of perfectly expressing the various properties of production theory has been a pressing issue for production studies since the pioneering work of Cobb and Douglas (1928) because the main target of each producer/firm, which is represented by a production function, is the maximization of the firm's outputs obtainable at the given set of inputs it uses. In order to achieve this maximum, the maximization process involves the use of first-order and second-order conditions, in which producers are assumed to satisfy these conditions (Kumbhakar & Lovell, 2000). Thus far, the various limitations of the Cobb-Douglas function have led to the development of different functional forms such as the CES, the translog, etc. In this framework, efforts to construct flexible forms have emerged (see Diewert, 1971); however, different definitions of flexibility have arisen as a result of the immanent character of the concept, which is rather complex and difficult to define.

In this chapter, we exploited the semiparametric nature of artificial neural networks (ANNs), which are rich in parameters, to impose all the properties that mathematical economic theory dictates regarding the production function. In this work, we proposed and estimated a new production function based on AANs, which we called the NPF. This specification is a global approximation to any arbitrary production function; it satisfies all the properties dictated by economic theory globally; it provides good fit to real-world data because it is data driven; it allows for arbitrary returns to scale; and it is relatively simple to estimate. Despite the fact that a small fraction of these desirable properties also might be possessed by one or other of the already known production function specifications, neither possesses all of them simultaneously.

We illustrated our proposed specification using aggregate data for the US economy for the time period 1957–2006, just before the first signs of the US subprime crisis made their appearance, which would have skewed the results. When estimated empirically, the model has a statistically significant behavior and the US economy is operating with approximately constant returns to scale (CRTS), a finding that is consistent with the relevant literature. Future and more extended research about the topic would be of great interest, focusing on modeling complex production networks, where the distribution of the (multiple) outputs could be modeled as a random Markov field process on a directed network with edge weights.

Appendix

Theorem 1 Consider $X \subseteq \mathbb{R}^N$ a compact subset of $\mathbb{R}^N$ for some $N \in \mathbb{N}$, and $C(X)$ the space of all real valued functions defined on X. Let $\varphi : X \to \mathbb{R}$ be a nonconstant, bounded, and continuous function. Then, the family:
$$\mathcal{F} = \{F(x) \equiv \textstyle\sum_{i=1}^{N} a_i \varphi\left(w_i^T x + b_i\right), a_i, b_i \in \mathbb{R}, \ w_i \in \mathbb{R}^N\} \ \text{is dense on } C(X).$$

Proof
The proof is a straightforward application of Hornik's (1991) Theorem. □

Proof (Theorem 2)
Let $T(x,y) = \{(x,y) : x \in \mathbb{R}_+^N$ can produce $y \in \mathbb{R}_+^M\}$ be closed and bounded, then $\bigcup_{i \in J} max_{y_i}\{y_i \in \mathbb{R}_+^M : y_i \in T(x,y_i)\} \subseteq Y \subseteq \mathbb{R}_+^M$ is also closed and bounded. Because every closed and bounded subset of $\mathbb{R}^N$ is compact (Rudin, 1976), then the union is also compact. □

Proof (Theorem 3)

(i) Let $x_j \in X \subseteq \mathbb{R}_+^N$, then by the definition of production functions, for every x_j there exists a $y_J \in Y \subseteq \mathbb{R}_+^M$ such that $f(x_j) = y_J, \forall j \in J$. Therefore, we can infer that $f\left(x_j\right) = x_j^a \prod_{\kappa=1}^{K} \varphi^{\alpha_\kappa}\left(x_j^{\beta_\kappa}\right)$ is continuous because φ is a continuous activation function.

(ii) In order to prove that the production function, f, is nonconstant, it suffices to prove that $\forall x_1, x_2 \in \mathbb{R}_+^N$, $x_1 \neq x_2$, $f(x_1) \neq f(x_2)$.

Let x_1, $x_2 \in \mathbb{R}_+^N$, that correspond to y_1, $y_2 \in Y \subseteq \mathbb{R}_+^M$. By definition, the activation function, φ, is nonconstant. Thus, it holds that $\prod_{\kappa=1}^{K} \varphi^{\alpha_\kappa} \left(x_1^{\beta_\kappa} \right) \neq \prod_{\kappa=1}^{K} \varphi^{\alpha_\kappa} \left(x_2^{\beta_\kappa} \right)$, which, in turn, implies that $f(x_1) \neq f(x_2)$.

(iii) Because the set $T(x,y) = \{(x,y) : x \in \mathbb{R}_+^N$ can produce $y \in \mathbb{R}_+^M\}$ is closed and bounded, then the production set $Y \subseteq \mathbb{R}_+^M$ is closed and bounded. Therefore, from continuity of the production function, it is immediate that $f(x) = max \{y \in \mathbb{R}_+^M : y \in T(x,y)\}$ also is bounded, regardless of the form of the production function. $\square$

Proof (Theorem 4)

From Theorem 2, the set of all production functions is compact. From Theorem 3 any function of the form $f(x) = x^a \prod_{\kappa=1}^{K} \varphi^{\alpha_\kappa} \left(x^{\beta_\kappa} \right), a \in \mathbb{R}^N, \alpha_\kappa, \beta_\kappa \in \mathbb{R}^\kappa\}$ is continuous, bounded, and nonconstant. Then, from Theorem 1, the family $\mathcal{F} = \left\{ f(x) \in \mathbb{C}\left(\mathbb{R}^M\right) : f(x) = x^a \prod_{\kappa=1}^{K} \varphi^{\alpha_\kappa} \left(x^{\beta_\kappa} \right), a \in \mathbb{R}^N, a_\kappa, \beta_\kappa \in \mathbb{R}^K \right\}$ is dense in $C(X)$ for every compact subset $X \subseteq \bigcup_{i \in I} max_{y_i} \{ y_i \in \mathbb{R}_+^M : y_i \in T(x,y_i)\} \subseteq Y \subseteq \mathbb{R}_+^M$. $\square$

Proof (Theorem 5)

(i) We need to prove that $f(0) = 0$. Because the activation function, φ, is bounded, then it is immediate that $f(0) = 0$ since $f(0) = \prod_{i=1}^{N} 0^{a_i} \prod_{\kappa=1}^{K} \varphi^{\alpha_\kappa} \left(0^{\beta_\kappa}\right) = 0$.

(ii) Because the set $T(x,y) = \{(x.\ y) : x \in \mathbb{R}_+^N$ can produce $y \in \mathbb{R}_+^M\}$ is compact, then by definition, $f(x) = max \{y \in \mathbb{R}_+^M : y \in T(x,y)\}$ and it is immediate that every production function is bounded, regardless of its functional form.

(iii) Let x', $x \in X \subseteq \mathbb{R}_+^N$ such that $x' \geq x$ i.e. $x_i' \geq x_i \forall i \in \{1, \dots, N\}$. If $\alpha_i \geq 0 \forall i \in \{1, \dots, N\}$ then $\prod_{i=1}^{N} x_i'^{a_i} \geq \prod_{i=1}^{N} x_i^{a_i}$. Using the fact that by definition φ is increasing and $\alpha_\kappa, \beta_\kappa \geq 0 \forall \kappa \in \{1, \dots, K\}$, then it is immediate that the NPF specification is also increasing.

(iv) Let $x \geq 0$ and $f(\lambda x) > 0$. Then:

$$\lim_{\lambda \to \infty} f(\lambda x) = \lim_{\lambda \to \infty} \prod_{i=1}^{N} \lambda^{a_i} x_i^{a_i} \prod_{\kappa=1}^{K} \varphi^{\alpha_\kappa} \left(\lambda x^{\beta_\kappa} \right) = \lim_{\lambda \to \infty} \prod_{i=1}^{N} \lambda^{a_i} x_i^{a_i} M^K = M^K \lim_{\lambda \to \infty} \prod_{i=1}^{N} \lambda^{a_i} x_i^{a_i}$$

$$= M^K \lim_{\lambda \to \infty} \prod_{i=1}^{N} \lambda^{a_i} \prod_{i=1}^{N} x_i^{a_i}$$

$$= M^K \prod_{i=1}^{N} x_i^{a_i} \lim_{\lambda \to \infty} \prod_{i=1}^{N} \lambda^{a_i} = \infty$$

Because φ is bounded, there exists some $M \in \mathbb{R}$, such that $\varphi \leq M$.

(v) It is immediate from Theorem 3.

(vi) It suffices to prove that $f((1-\theta)x+\theta z) \geq \min\{f(x),f(y)\}$.

Because φ is convex for every $x \in \mathbb{R}^N$, it holds true that:

$$\prod_{\kappa=1}^{K} \varphi^{\alpha_\kappa}\left(((1-\theta)x+\theta z)^{\beta_\kappa}\right) \geq \min\left\{\prod_{\kappa=1}^{K} \varphi^{\alpha_\kappa}\left(x^{\beta_\kappa}\right), \prod_{\kappa=1}^{K} \varphi^{\alpha_\kappa}\left(z^{\beta_\kappa}\right)\right\}$$

Therefore,

$$f((1-\theta)x+\theta z) = \prod_{i=1}^{N}((1-\theta)x+\theta z)^{\alpha_i} \prod_{\kappa=1}^{K} \varphi^{\alpha_\kappa}\left(((1-\theta)x+\theta z)^{\beta_\kappa}\right)$$

$$\geq \min\left\{x^a \prod_{\kappa=1}^{K} \varphi^{\alpha_\kappa}\left(x^{\beta_\kappa}\right), z^a \prod_{\kappa=1}^{K} \varphi^{\alpha_\kappa}\left(z^{\beta_\kappa}\right)\right\} = \min\{f(x),f(z)\}.$$

Let $u = \max\{f(x),f(y)\}$, $u \in \mathbb{R}_+^M$, $x, y \in \mathbb{R}_+^N$.

Because f is homogenous, we have that $f\left(\frac{u}{f(x)}x\right) \geq u, f\left(\frac{u}{f(y)}y\right) \geq u$.

Because f is concave, by setting $\theta = \frac{f(y)}{f(x)+f(y)}$, we have that
$f\left((1-\theta)\frac{u}{f(x)}x + \frac{u}{f(y)}y\right) \geq \min\left\{f\left(\frac{u}{f(x)}x\right), f\left(\frac{u}{f(y)}y\right)\right\} = u \Rightarrow f\left(\frac{(x+y)}{f(x)+f(y)}\right) \geq u\,(1)$

Using the homogeneity of f, the following holds:

$$f\left(\frac{(x+y)}{f(x)+f(y)}\right) \leq \frac{u}{f(x)+f(y)} f(x+y)\,(2)$$

From Eqs. (1), (2), we get: $u \leq \frac{f(x+y)u}{f(x)+f(y)} \Rightarrow f(x+y) \geq f(x)+f(y)$. $\square$

Definition of a Well-Defined Production Function

If the production function satisfies the following conditions (see, among others, Varian, 1992, Mas-Colell, Whinston, & Green, 1995), then it is well defined:

(i) $f(0_n) = 0_m$.

(ii) The production function f has a finite domain if the input domain $x \in \mathbb{R}_+^N$ is also finite.

(iii) $f(x) \geq f(x')$ for every $x \geq x'$.

(iv) If $x \geq 0$ or $x > 0$ and $f(\lambda^*x) > 0$ for some $\lambda^* > 0$, then $\lim_{\lambda \to \infty} f(\lambda x) = \infty$.

(v) The production function f is right continuous for every $x \in \mathbb{R}_+^N$.

(vi) $f((1-\theta)x+\theta y) \geq \min\{f(x),f(y)\}$ for every $x, y \in \mathbb{R}_+^N$ and $0 \leq \theta \leq 1$.

(vii) $f(x+z) \geq f(x)+f(z)$ for every $x, z \in \mathbb{R}_+^N$.

Broyden-Fletcher-Goldfarb-Shannon Method

BFGS is a Newton-like method that uses a quadratic Taylor specification of the objective function $f(x)$, in a d-vicinity of $x \in \mathbb{R}$.

$$f(x+d) \approx q(d) = f(x) + d^T g(x) + \tfrac{1}{2} d^T H(x) d$$

where $g(x)$ is the gradient vector and $H(x)$ is the Hessian matrix.

The necessary condition for a local minimum of $q(d)$ with respect to d results in the linear system:

$$g(x) + H(x) d = 0$$

which, in turn, gives the Newton direction d for line search:

$$d = -H(x)^{-1} g(x)$$

Where $\det H(x) \neq 0$ and the exponent -1 denotes matrix inversion.

The exact Newton direction is reliable when: The Hessian matrix exists and is positive definite; and the difference between the true objective function and its quadratic approximation is not large.

The main idea behind the BFGS method is to use matrices that approximate the Hessian matrix and/or its inverse, instead of computing the Hessian matrix (as in typical Newton-type methods). Using standard notation, the matrices are: $B \approx H$ and $D \approx H^{-1}$. These matrices are adjusted on each iteration and the BFGS updating formula, which converges to $H(x^*)$, is the following:

$$B_{k+1} = B_k - \frac{B_k s_k s_k^T B_k}{s_k^T B_k s_k} + \frac{y_k y_k^T}{y_k^T s_k}$$

where: x^* denotes the solution, $s_k = x_{k+1} - x_k$, and $y_k = g_{k+1} - g_k$, and T denotes transposition.

As a starting point, the initial B_0 can be set to some symmetric positive definite matrix.

The BFGS method exposes superlinear convergence; resource-intensity is estimated as $O(n^2)$ per iteration for n-component argument vector. See, for example, Nocedal (1980).

References

Adya, M., Collopy, F., 1998. How effective are neural networks at forecasting and prediction? A review and evaluation. Journal of Forecasting 17, 481–495.

Bartelsman, E.J., Dhrymes, J.P., 1998. Productivity dynamics: U.S. manufacturing plants, 1972–1986. Journal of Productivity Analysis 9, 5–34.

Basu, S., 1996. Procyclical productivity: increasing returns or cyclical utilization? Quarterly Journal of Economics 111 (3), 719–751.

Basu, S., Fernald, J., 1997. Returns to scale in U.S. production: estimates and implication. Journal of Political Economy 105, 249–283.

Bishop, C.M., 1995. Neural networks for pattern recognition. Clarendon Press, Oxford.

Cardarelli, R., Lusinyan, L., 2015. US total factor productivity slowdown: evidence from the U.S. states. IMF working paper series, WP/15/116.

Brockett, P.L., Cooper, W.W., Golden, L.L., Pitaktong, U., 1994. A neural network method for obtaining early warning of insurer insolvency. Journal of Risk and Insurance 61 (3), 402–424.

Chan, N.H., Genovese, R.C., 2001. A comparison of linear and nonlinear statistical techniques in performance attribution. IEEE Transactions on Neural Networks 12 (4), 922–928.

Chang, H., Choy, H.L., Cooper, W.W., Ruefli, W.T., 2009. Using Malmquist indexes to measure changes in the productivity and efficiency of US accounting firms before and after the Sarbanes–Oxley act. Omega 37, 951–960.

Charalabous, C., Charitou, A., Kaourou, F., 2000. Comparative analysis of artificial neural network models: application in bankruptcy prediction. Annals of Operations Research 99 (1–4), 403–425.

Chirinko, S.R., Mallick, D., 2011. Cointegration, factor shares, and production function parameters. *Economic Letter*s 112 (2), 205–206.

Cobb, C.W., Douglas, P.H., 1928. A theory of production. American Economic Review 18 (1), 139–165(Supplement).

Despotakis, K.A., 1986. Economic performance of flexible functional forms. European Economic Review 30 (6), 1107–1143.

Diewert, W.E., 1971. An application of the shephard duality theorem: a generalized leontief production function. Journal of Political Economy 79, 461–507.

Diewert, W., Wales, T.J., 1987. Flexible functional forms and global curvature conditions. Econometrica 55 (1), 43–68.

Dimelis, P.S., 2001. Inventory investment over the business cycle in the EU and the US. International Journal of Production Economics 71 (1-3), 1–8.

Doumpos, M., Cohen, S., 2014. Applying data envelopment analysis on accounting data to assess and optimize the efficiency of Greek local governments. Omega 46, 74–85.

Du, P., Christopher, F.P., Racine, J.S., 2013. Nonparametric kernel regression with multiple predictors and multiple shape constraints. Statistica Sinica 23 (3), 1347–1371.

Duffy, J., Papageorgiou, C., 2000. A cross-country empirical investigation of the aggregate production function specification. Journal of Economic Growth 5, 83–116.

Duffy, J., Papageorgiou, C., Perez-Sebastian, F., 2004. Capital-skill complementarity? Evidence from a panel of countries. Review of Economics and Statistics 86, 327–344.

Elbadawi, I., Gallant, A.R., Souza, G., 1983. An elasticity can be estimated consistently without a priori knowledge of functional form. Econometrica 51, 1731–1752.

Faraway, J., Chatfield, C., 1998. Time series forecasting with neural networks: a comparative study using the airline data. Applied Statistics 47 (2), 231–250.

Gallant, A.R., 1981. On the bias in flexible functional forms and an essentially unbiased form. Journal of Econometrics 15, 211–245.

Gallant, A.R., 1982. Unbiased determination of production technologies. Journal of Econometrics 20, 285–323.

Gallant, A.R., Golub, G.H., 1984. Imposing curvature restrictions on flexible functional forms. Journal of Econometrics 26, 295–321.

Gencay, R., 1999. Linear, non-linear and essential foreign exchange rate prediction with simple technical trading rules. Journal of International Economics 47 (1), 91–107.

Ghrahraman, A., Prior, D., 2016. A learning ladder toward efficiency: proposing network-based stepwise benchmark selection. Omega 63, 83–93.

Griffin, R.C., Montgomery, J.M., Rister, M.E., 1987. Selecting functional form in production analysis. Western Journal of Agricultural Economics 12, 216–227.

Gruca, T.S., Klemz, B.R., 1998. Using neural networks to identify competitive market structures from aggregate market response data. Omega 26 (1), 49–62.

Hagspiel, V., Huisman, K.J.M., Kortb, P.M., 2016. Volume flexibility and capacity investment under demand uncertainty. International Journal of Production Economics 178, 95–108.

Haykin, S., 1999. Neural networks. Prentice-Hall, New Jersey.

Hoch, I., 1958. Simultaneous equation bias in the context of the cobb-douglas production function. Econometrica 26, 566–578.

Hornik, K., 1991. Approximation capabilities of multilayer feedforward networks. Neural Networks 4, 251–257.

Hudson, E.A., Jorgenson, D., 1974. U.S. Energy Policy and Economic Growth, 1975–2000. Bell Journal of Economics 5 (2), 461–514.

Hutchinson, J.M., Lo, A.W., Poggio, T., 1994. A nonparametric approach to pricing and hedging derivative securities via learning networks. Journal of Finance 49, 851–889.

Indro, D.C., Jiang, C.X., Patuwo, B.E., Zhang, G.P., 1999. Predicting mutual fund performance using artificial neural networks. Omega 27 (3), 373–380.

Jain, B.A., Nag, B.N., 1998. A neural network model to predict long-run operating performance of new ventures. Annals of Operations Research 78 (0), 83–110.

Jelinek, M., 1987. Engineering costs and production economics. International Journal of Production Economics 12 (1-4), 315–326.

Jorgenson, D.W., Slesnick, D.T., 1987. Aggregate consumer behavior and household equivalence scales. Journal of Business & Economic Statistics 5 (2), 219–232.

Kuan, C.M., White, H., 1994. Artificial neural networks: an econometric perspective. Econometric Reviews 13, 1–91.

Kumbhakar, S.C., Lovell, K.C.A., 2000. Stochastic frontier analysis. Cambridge University Press, Cambridge.

Kumbhakar, S.C., Tsionas, E.G., 2010. Estimation of production risk and risk preference function: a nonparametric approach. Annals of Operations Research 176 (1), 369–378.

Kuosmanen, T., Johnson, A., 2010. Data envelopment analysis as nonparametric least squares regression. Operations Research 58 (1), 149–160.

Kuosmanen, T., Kortelainen, M., 2012. Stochastic non-smooth envelopment of data: semi-parametric Frontier estimation subject to shape constraints. Journal of Productivity Analysis 38 (1), 11–28.

Levin, A., Lin, C.-F., James Chu, C.-S., 2002. Unit root tests in panel data: asymptotic and finite-sample properties. Journal of Econometrics 108 (1), 1–24.

Liadaki, A., Gaganis, C., 2010. Efficiency and stock performance of EU banks: is there a relationship? Omega 38 (5), 254–259.

Loyer, J.-L., Henriques, E., Fontulb, M., Wiseall, S., 2016. Comparison of machine learning methods applied to the estimation of manufacturing cost of jet engine components. International Journal of Production Economics 178, 109–119.

Lutkepohl, H., 2005. New introduction to multiple time series analysis. Springer-Verlag, Berlin, Heidelberg.

Luxhøj, J.T., Riis, J.O., Stensballe, B., 1996. A hybrid econometric–neural network modeling approach for sales forecasting. International Journal of Production Economics 43 (2–3), 175–192.

Malhotra, R., Malhotra, D.K., 2003. Evaluating consumer loans using neural networks. Omega 31, 83–96.

Mas-Colell, A., Whinston, M.D., Green, J., 1995. Microeconomic theory. Oxford University Press.

McFadden, D., 1963. Constant elasticity of substitution production functions. Review of Economic Studies 30 (2), 73–83.

Nocedal, J., 1980. Updating quasi-newton matrices with limited storage. Mathematics of Computation 35 (151), 773–782.

O'Donnell, C.J., Coelli, T.J., 2005. A Bayesian approach to imposing curvature on distance functions. Journal of Econometrics 126, 493–523.

Pedroni, P., 1999. Critical values for cointegration tests in heterogeneous panels with multiple regressors. Oxford Bulletin of Economics and Statistics 61, 653–670.

Pedroni, P., 2001. Purchasing power parity tests in cointegrated panels. Review of Economics and Statistics 83, 727–731.

Qi, M., Maddala, C.S., 1999. Economic factors and the stock market: a new perspective. Journal of Forecasting 18, 151–166.

Reinhard, S., Thijssen, G., 1998. Resource use efficiency of Dutch dairy farms; a parametric distance function approach. In: 1998 Annual meeting, No. 21022, August 2–5. American Agricultural Economics Association (New Name 2008: Agricultural and Applied Economics Association), Salt Lake City, UT.

Reister, D.B., Edmonds, J.A., 1981. Energy demand models based on the translog and CES functions. Energy 6, 917–926.

Remer, D.A., Mattos, F.B., 2003. Cost and scale-up factors, international inflation indexes and location factors. International Journal of Production Economics 84 (1), 1–16.

Revankar, N.S., 1971. A class of variable elasticity of substitution production functions. Econometrica 39, 61–71.

Rice, J.R., 1964. The approximation of functions. Vol. 1. Addison-Wesley Publishing Co, Reading, MA.

Rudin, W., 1976. Principles of mathematical analysis, 3rd ed. McGraw and Hill, United States.

Serrano-Cinca, C., 1997. Feedforward neural networks in the classification of financial information. The European Journal of Finance 3, 183–202.

Shoven, J.B., Whalley, J., 1992. Applying general equilibrium. Cambridge University Press, New York.

Stern, A., 2001. Multiple regimes in the US inventory time-series: a disaggregate analysis. International Journal of Production Economics 71 (1–3), 45–53.

Swanson, N.R., White, H., 1995. Model-selection approach to assessing the information in the term structure using linear models and artificial neural networks. Journal of Business & Economic Statistics 13 (3), 265–275.

Swanson, N.R., White, H., 1997a. A model selection approach to real-time macroeconomic forecasting using linear models and artificial neural networks. The Review of Economics and Statistics 79 (4), 540–550.

Swanson, N.R., White, H., 1997b. Forecasting economic time series using flexible versus fixed specification and linear versus nonlinear econometric models. International Journal of Forecasting 13 (4), 439–461.

Terrell, D., 1996. Incorporating monotonicity and concavity conditions in flexible functional forms. Journal of Applied Econometrics 11 (2), 179–194.

Thompson Gary, D., 1988. Choice of flexible functional forms: review and appraisal. Western Journal of Agricultural Economics 13 (2), 169–183.

Tsionas, E.G., Loizides, J., 2001. A note on joint estimation of scale economies and productivity growth parameters. International Journal of Production Economics 70 (1), 37–43.

Varian, R.H., 1992. Microeconomic analysis, 3rd ed. W.W Norton & Company Inc.

Vishwakarma, K.P., 1994. Recognizing business cycles turning points by means of neural networks. Computational Economics 7, 175–185.

Wang, K., Huang, W., Wu, J., Liu, Y.-N., 2014. Efficiency measures of the Chinese commercial banking system using an additive two-stage DEA. Omega 44, 5–20.

White, H., 1980. Using least squares to approximate unknown regression functions. International Economic Review 21, 149–170.

Yao, J., Li, Y., Tan, C.L., 2000. Option price forecasting using neural networks. Omega 28, 455–466.

Zellner, A., Ryu, H., 1998. Alternative functional forms for production, cost and returns to scale functions. Journal of Applied Econometrics 13, 101–127.

Further Reading

Akaike, H., 1974. A new look at the statistical model identification. IEEE Transactions on Automatic Control 19 (6), 716–723.

Arrow, K.J., Chenery, H.B., Minhas, B., Solow, R.M., 1961. Capital-labor substitution and economic efficiency. The Review of Economics and Statistics 43 (5), 225–254.

Baily, M.N., Gordon, R.J., Nordhaus, W.D., Romer, D., 1988. The productivity slowdown, measurement issues, and the explosion of computer power. Brookings Papers on Economic Activity 1988 (2), 347–431.

Berndt, R.E., Christensen, R.L., 1973. The translog function and the substitution of equipment, structures and labor in U.S. manufacturing 1929–68. *Journal of Econometrics* 1 (1), 81–113.

Binner, J.M., Bissoondeeal, R.K., Elger, T., Gazely, A.M., Mullineux, A.W., 2005. A comparison of linear forecasting models and neural networks: an application to Euro inflation and Euro Divisia. Applied Economics 37 (6), 665–680.

Dickey, D.A., Fuller, W.A., 1979. Distribution of the estimators for autoregressive time series with a unit root. Journal of the American Statistical Association 74, 427–431.

Diewert, W.E., 1987. Flexible forms and global curvature conditions. Econometrica 55 (1), 43–68.

Golmohammadi, D., 2011. Neural network application for fuzzy multi-criteria decision making problems. International Journal of Production Economics 131 (2), 490–504.

Henderson, D.J., Parmeter, C.F., 2009. Imposing economic constraints on nonparametric regression: survey, implementation and extensions. In: Li, Q., Racine, J.S. (Eds.), Advances in econometrics: Nonparametric methods. In: Vol. 25. Elsevier Science, pp. 433–469.

Jin, Y., Zeng, Z., 2016. Risk, risk aversion, and a finance-augmented neoclassical economic model of production. International Journal of Production Economics 176, 82–91.

Johansen, S., 1988. Statistical analysis of cointegration vectors. Journal of Economic Dynamics and Control 12 (2–3), 231–254.

Johansen, S., 1995. Likelihood-based inference in cointegrated vector autoregressive models. Oxford University Press, New York.

Johansen, S., Juselius, K., 1990. Maximum likelihood estimation and inference on cointegration with applications to the demand for money. Oxford Bulletin of Economics and Statistics 52 (2), 169–210.

Jorgenson, D.W., Fraumeni, B.M., 1981. Relative prices and technical change. In: Berndt, E.R., Field, B.C. (Eds.), Modeling and measuring natural resource substitution. MIT Press, Cambridge, MA.

Kauermann, G., Teuber, T., Flaschel, P., 2012. Exploring US business cycles with bivariate loops using penalized spline regression. Journal of Computational Economics 39 (4), 409–427.

Kiani, K.M., 2005. Detecting business cycle asymmetries using artificial neural networks and time series models. Computational Economics 26 (1), 65–85.

Kiani, K.M., 2007. Asymmetric business cycle fluctuations and contagion effects in G7 countries. International Journal of Business and Economics 6 (3), 237–253.

Kiani, K.M., 2009. Asymmetries in macroeconomic time series in eleven Asian economies. *International Journal of Business and Economics* 8 (1), 37–54.

Kiani, M.K., 2011. Fluctuations in economic and activity and stabilization policies in the CIS. Computational Economics 37 (2), 193–220.

Kiani, K.M., Bidarkota, P.V., 2004. On business cycle asymmetries in G7 countries. Oxford Bulletin of Economics and Statistics 66 (3), 333–351.

Kiani, K.M., Bidarkota, P.V., Kastens, T.L., 2005. Forecast performance of neural networks and business cycle asymmetries. Applied Financial Economics Letters 1 (4), 205–210.

Kiani, K.M., Kastens, T.L., 2006. Using macro-financial variables to forecast recessions: an analysis of Canada, 1957–2002. Applied Econometrics and International Development 6 (3), 97–106.

Konishi, S., Kitagawa, G., 1996. Generalized information criteria for model selection. Biometrika 83 (4), 875–890.

Kourentzes, N., 2013. Intermittent demand forecasts with neural networks. International Journal of Production Economics 143 (1), 198–206.

Leon-Ledesma, A.M., McAdam, P., Willman, A., 2010. Identifying the elasticity of substitution with biased technical change. American Economic Review 100 (4), 1330–1357.

Newey, W.K., West, K.D., 1994. Automatic lag selection in covariance matrix estimation. Review of Economic Studies 61 (4), 631–654.

Phillips, P.C.B., Perron, P., 1988. Testing for a unit root in time series regression. Biometrika 75 (2), 335–346.

Schwarz, G.E., 1978. Estimating the dimension of a model. Annals of Statistics 6 (2), 461–464.

Sheela, G.K., Deepa, S.N., 2013. Review on methods to fix number of hidden neurons in neural networks. Mathematical Problems in Engineering 2013, 11. https://doi.org/10.1155/2013/425740. Article ID 425740.

Index

Note: Page numbers followed by *f* indicate figures *t* indicate tables *b* indicate boxes, and *np* indicate footnotes.